Essentials of Dance Psychology

Sanna Nordin-Bates, PhD
The Swedish School of Sport and Health Sciences

Library of Congress Cataloging-in-Publication Data

Names: Nordin-Bates, Sanna, 1980- author.
Title: Essentials of dance psychology / Sanna Nordin-Bates.
Description: Champaign, IL : Human Kinetics, Inc., 2023. | Includes bibliographical references and index.
Identifiers: LCCN 2022006805 (print) | LCCN 2022006806 (ebook) | ISBN 9781718207554 (paperback) | ISBN 9781718207561 (epub) | ISBN 9781718207578 (pdf)
Subjects: LCSH: Dance—Psychological aspects. | Dancers—Psychology.
Classification: LCC GV1588.5 .N67 2023 (print) | LCC GV1588.5 (ebook) | DDC 792.8—dc23/eng/20220321
LC record available at https://lccn.loc.gov/2022006805
LC ebook record available at https://lccn.loc.gov/2022006806

ISBN: 978-1-7182-0755-4 (print)

Copyright © 2023 by Human Kinetics

Human Kinetics supports copyright. Copyright fuels scientific and artistic endeavor, encourages authors to create new works, and promotes free speech. Thank you for buying an authorized edition of this work and for complying with copyright laws by not reproducing, scanning, or distributing any part of it in any form without written permission from the publisher. You are supporting authors and allowing Human Kinetics to continue to publish works that increase the knowledge, enhance the performance, and improve the lives of people all over the world.

Notwithstanding the above notice, permission to reproduce the following material is granted to persons and agencies who have purchased this work: Forms 0.1–14.1

The online learning content that accompanies this product is delivered on HK*Propel*, HKPropel.HumanKinetics.com. You agree that you will not use HK*Propel* if you do not accept the site's Privacy Policy and Terms and Conditions, which detail approved uses of the online content.

To report suspected copyright infringement of content published by Human Kinetics, contact us at **permissions@hkusa.com**. To request permission to legally reuse content published by Human Kinetics, please refer to the information at **https://US.HumanKinetics.com/pages/permissions-information**.

The web addresses cited in this text were current as of March 2022, unless otherwise noted.

Acquisitions Editor: Bethany J. Bentley; **Managing Editor:** Anne E. Mrozek; **Indexer:** Katy Balcer; **Permissions Manager:** Dalene Reeder; **Graphic Designer:** Denise Lowry; **Cover Designer:** Keri Evans; **Cover Design Specialist:** Susan Rothermel Allen; **Photograph (cover):** Photographer: Johannes Hjorth. Dancer: Ahtayaw Ea.; Clothes: Linn Kristina Design. **Photographs (interior):** Johannes Hjorth; **Photo Production Manager:** Jason Allen; **Senior Art Manager:** Kelly Hendren; **Illustrations:** © Human Kinetics, unless otherwise noted; **Production:** Westchester Publishing Services; **Printer:** Versa Press; **Other credits:** We thank Jan Åström and the Ballet Academy in Stockholm, Sweden, for assistance in providing the location for the photo shoot for this book.

Printed in the United States of America   10 9 8 7 6 5 4 3 2 1

The paper in this book is certified under a sustainable forestry program.

Human Kinetics
1607 N. Market Street
Champaign, IL 61820
USA

United States and International
Website: **US.HumanKinetics.com**
Email: info@hkusa.com
Phone: 1-800-747-4457

Canada
Website: **Canada.HumanKinetics.com**
Email: info@hkcanada.com

E8365

Tell us what you think!
Human Kinetics would love to hear what we can do to improve the customer experience.
Use this QR code to take our brief survey.

I dedicate this book to my mother, Elisabet, who first introduced me to the magic of dance, and to my daughters, Alicia and Adeline, who remind me daily of what dance is really about: joy.

Contents

Preface vii
Acknowledgments xi

Introduction to Dance Psychology — 1
What Is Dance Psychology? 2
Cognitive Behavioral Therapy in Dance Psychology 4

Part I Individual Differences

1 Personality — 19
What Is Personality? 20
Structure of Personality 20
Origins of Personality 25
Consequences of Personality 27
Narrow Identity: Are Dancers at Risk? 28

2 Perfectionism — 37
What Is Perfectionism? 38
Origins of Perfectionism in Dance 40
Consequences of Perfectionism 42
How Can Perfectionism Be Managed? 46

3 Self-Esteem and Self-Confidence — 51
What Are Self-Esteem and Self-Confidence? 52
Origins of Self-Esteem 53
Consequences of Self-Esteem 54
Origins of Self-Confidence 55
Consequences of Self-Confidence 60
How Can Self-Esteem and Self-Confidence Be Strengthened? 62

4 Anxiety — 69
What Is Anxiety? 70
Sources of Anxiety 72
Consequences of Anxiety 75
How Can Anxiety Be Managed? 79

Part II Dance-Specific Characteristics and Dispositions

5 Motivation — 89
What is Motivation? 90
Achievement Goal Theory Perspective on Motivation 90

Self-Determination Theory Perspective on Motivation 96
How Can Healthy Motivation Be Nurtured? An Intrapersonal Perspective 102

6 Attentional Focus   109
What Is Attentional Focus? 110
Performance-Related Consequences of Different Attentional Foci 116
Attentional Focus Research in Dance 117
Why Attentional Focus Has an Impact 119
How Can Optimal Attentional Focus Be Nurtured? 121

7 Creativity   127
What Is Creativity? 128
Sources of Creativity 132
Correlates of Creativity 138
How Can Creativity Be Nurtured? 140

Part III Psychological Skills

8 Mindfulness   149
What Is Mindfulness? 150
Origins of Mindfulness 154
Consequences of Mindfulness 154
Mindfulness Research in Dance 156
Why Mindfulness Has an Impact 158
How Can Mindfulness Be Nurtured? 159

9 Goal Setting and Self-Regulation   165
What Is Goal Setting? 166
Sources of Goals: Assigned Goals Versus Personal Values 170
Consequences of Goal Setting 171
Why Goal Setting Has an Impact 172
What Is Self-Regulation? 174
How Can Goal Setting and Self-Regulation Be Optimized? 176

10 Imagery   183
What Is Imagery? 184
Revised Applied Model of Deliberate Imagery Use 184
Sources of Imagery 190
Consequences of Imagery 194
Why Imagery Has an Impact 195
How Can Imagery Be Optimized? 197

Part IV Dance Environments and Challenges

11 Motivational Climates — 203
What Is a Motivational Climate? 204
Achievement Goal Theory Perspective: Task- and Ego-Involving Climates 204
Self-Determination Theory Perspective: Need-Supportive Versus Controlling Leadership 206
Origins of Motivational Climates: What Makes Teachers Support or Thwart Healthy Motivation? 207
Consequences of Motivational Climates 208
How Are Healthy Motivational Climates Created? 214

12 Talent — 221
What Is Talent? 222
Sources of Talent 229
Consequences of Talent Beliefs and Talent Identification 236
How Can Talent Identification and Development Be Optimized? 239

13 Injury — 243
What Are the Key Psychological Aspects of Injury in Dance? 244
Psychological Risk Factors for Acute Injury: Stress-Injury Model 245
Beyond the Stress-Injury Model: Other Psychological Risk Factors for Dance Injury 249
Dancers' Injury Experiences 251
Psychological Aspects of Injury Rehabilitation 252
Using Psychology to Reduce Injury Risk and Optimize Rehabilitation 255

14 Body Image and Disordered Eating — 261
What Is Body Image? 262
Eating Disorders Versus Disordered Eating 264
Origins of Negative Body Image and Disordered Eating in Dance 271
Consequences of Body Image and Disordered Eating 278
How Can Healthy Body Image Be Nurtured? 281
How Can Disordered Eating Be Prevented, Identified, and Managed? 281

Glossary 287
References 297
Index 329
About the Author 339

Preface

For all of us involved in the training and development of dancers, what could be more important and exciting than understanding why dancers think and behave as they do? Or how can we create healthy creative dance environments and optimize dance performance? This book will help you on your way to becoming a better informed, well-balanced, and high-performing dancer; a better educated teacher able to inspire and sustain high levels of both performance and psychological health; a more evidence-based physiotherapist, manager, or other professional working with dancers; or (why not?) a dance psychologist. It will not only help you understand the fundamental theoretical underpinnings of this exciting field but also how to apply them in dance practice.

The book is built on a foundation of evidence from dance and sport psychology research, with applied experiences worked in and used as examples throughout. Where appropriate, evidence from other areas of psychology (e.g., clinical, educational) is used. A thorough coverage of topics relevant to dancers, teachers, and others working to support dancers is included, making the book suitable for one slightly longer or two short courses in introductory dance psychology.

Because dance and sports have numerous similarities, many of the topics in this book are those typically covered in sport psychology textbooks (e.g., motivation, goal setting). However, the specific topics presented in this book have been selected based on many years of experience teaching dancers, dance teachers, and dance science students. These topics form a collection of what is both highly relevant and of particular interest to students in dance science, health, and education—and to students of dance itself, of course. Some topics often covered by sport psychology books (e.g., aggression) are not featured here, but the topic of creativity (which typically does not feature in sport psychology books) has a full chapter devoted to it. Topics for which more dance-specific research has been conducted (e.g., injury, disordered eating) are given a little more space. And, of course, dance-specific language and examples are used throughout!

This book has 15 chapters, starting with "Introduction to Dance Psychology." After that, chapters are divided into four parts:

I. Individual Differences,
II. Dance-Specific Characteristics and Dispositions,
III. Psychological Skills, and
IV. Dance Environments and Challenges.

Depending on your interests (and perhaps your course leader's plans) you can read the chapters in any order; they do not rely on you having read the previous chapters in order to understand them. Instead, each chapter contains clear links to other chapters, as appropriate. That way you can easily find out more about something that catches your eye—and hopefully also learn about links between topics that you did not know existed. The one exception is the Introduction, which serves as a foundation for all other chapters. It is therefore recommended that you read the Introduction first, regardless of where else you wish to continue. In so doing, you will learn about the field of dance psychology, including its relationship to sister disciplines such as sport psychology, and about influences from clinical psychology. You will also learn the fundamental principles from cognitive behavioral therapy (CBT) such as functional analysis, which will be used in examples throughout the book.

In Part I, we will delve into dancers' individual differences, an area of personality psychology primarily concerned with traits that are mostly stable across time and situations. As such, we will consider personality, perfectionism, self-esteem, self-confidence, and performance anxiety. This will help you address some intriguing questions, such as:

› What is personality, and what does it have to do with dance? (chapter 1)

- Is perfectionism a help or a hindrance to dancers? (chapter 2)
- How can a dancer's self-confidence be supported? (chapter 3)
- Should we try to reduce symptoms of performance anxiety or accept them as they are? (chapter 4)

Part II is a logical continuation of the individual differences introduced in Part I, but topics related to dance-specific characteristics and dispositions are commonly considered more variable over time and situations than personality traits. These include, for example, motivation, attentional focus, and creativity and will help inform your thinking on key questions such as:

- How can we support healthy, long-lasting motivation for dance? (chapter 5)
- What is meant by optimal attentional focus? (chapter 6)
- Is creativity relevant just for choreographers, or for every dancer? (chapter 7)

In Part III, a range of psychological skills is introduced, including mindfulness, goal setting, self-regulation, and imagery. For example,

- How can mindfulness be useful to dancers? (chapter 8)
- What are meaningful effective goals in an inherently subjective domain like dance? (chapter 9)
- How can imagery be used for best effect? (chapter 10)

Finally, Part IV introduces a series of topics related to dance environments and challenges, that is, the social aspects of teaching and learning dance (the motivational climate), the challenges of talent identification and development, injury, body image, and disordered eating. They will equip you to better answer questions such as:

- How do dance teachers influence a dancer's motivation, learning, and well-being? (chapter 11)
- Should the talent development of dancers begin as early as possible? (chapter 12)
- How can psychological factors increase injury risk? (chapter 13)
- What measures can be put in place to prevent the development of disordered eating in dance? (chapter 14)

To support your learning, each chapter contains recurring features, including a recognizable chapter structure, relevant definitions, case studies, practical exercises (typically with downloadable worksheets and sometimes with sound files), a section identifying critical aspects of research into each topic, and key points and recommendations.

In addition to the book itself, *Essentials of Dance Psychology* comes with a host of accompanying resources to support teaching and learning. For students, these include the online Student Resources section with downloadable worksheets, three audio files with guided exercises, vocabulary study aids, two goal-setting templates, and lettering art. The latter comprise five custom-made pieces that summarize key messages from the text in a beautiful way, ready for you to print out and use as you see fit. For example, you might use them as posters on your wall, send them as postcards to a friend, or put them into your training diary for inspiration. For instructors, the extra resources include an Instructor Guide with chapter summaries, a sample course outline, teaching tips, test bank, and a PowerPoint presentation package. Both the Student Resources and the Instructor Guide are available through HK*Propel*.

This book is unique in several ways. It is the first textbook to be published in the area of dance psychology. Although numerous textbooks can introduce you to sport and exercise psychology, none approach the topic from a dance perspective. A few books are focused on applied dance and performance psychology; however, these are aimed at dancers and are not theoretical in nature. Therefore, they do not meet the needs for academic study in the area.

Another unique feature of this book is its integration of topics and evidence from different areas of psychology. As noted above, the topics chosen and the evidence base introduced at the start of each chapter are in many ways informed by sport psychology, and many references are made to scientific studies done with athletes. However, these are integrated with dance-specific content wherever possible, including in the language used and in the research examples presented (where there has been dance-specific research conducted in that area). Each chapter also contains a composite case study of a dancer, which provides a flavor of how the topics can be expressed or experienced in practice. The case studies have been written on the basis of interviews with experts in dance and psychology to ensure that they are interesting and relevant to you as a dance psychology student.

Beyond integrating sport and dance psychology, aspects of CBT are also interwoven throughout the book, because tools from CBT (such as functional analysis) are immensely helpful in understanding human behavior and cognition. Functional analysis is therefore introduced in the Introduction and used in all subsequent chapters. Several of the exercises and worksheets integrated throughout the book also build on CBT principles and practices. So-called third-wave CBT also includes mindfulness—a topic that is highly relevant to dancers and their teachers. Mindfulness has received a huge rise in attention (both research attention and applied work) in sports, and it is time for this to be reflected also in academic writings for dance. Indeed, as you will see in chapter 8, the practice and skill of mindfulness can offer something that is easily integrated into dance practice with large potential benefits.

This book is for you whether you are mostly interested in furthering your dance understanding, teaching, or clinical practice on the basis of scientific evidence; looking to improve your work–life balance as a dancer; or simply want to understand yourself and other dancers better. By delving into the topics presented here, you will gain a thorough, evidence-based understanding of factors that shape dance environments and the dancers within them. You will also learn ways to help dancers both feel and perform well. And if you are anything like me, there are few things more intriguing. Let's get started!

Acknowledgments

In writing this work, I am deeply indebted to a whole host of inspiring and generous people.

I thank Professor **Jennifer Cumming** at the University of Birmingham, who 20 years ago invited me to focus my PhD on dance within a sports science department. *Where would I have been without you?*

Many inspiring and generous **collaborators, colleagues, students, research participants, dancers and dance teachers** have shared their enthusiasm and knowledge with me over the years—and, hopefully, for many more years to come. *You are the essence of it all!*

The members of my **Dance Psychology Network**, who always remind me that relatedness nurtures enjoyment.

Many others freely gave their time and expertise to this book. I thank Caroline-Olivia Elgan, Charlotte Downing, Janet Karin, and Lucie Clements for reading and commenting on chapter drafts. *Invaluable!*

My gratitude to Felicia Andersson, Ahtayaw Ea, Karolina Holmqvist, William Lundberg, Daphne Mørk-Jensen, Lea Sjövall, and my own Alicia Nordin-Bates, whose dancing and modeling are shown in the photos. *You really lifted this book to the next level.*

Britt Tajet-Foxell, Carolyn Carattini, Clare Guss-West, Erin Sanchez, Gene Moyle, Heidi Haraldsen, Henrik Gustafsson, Imogen Aujla, Janet Karin, Kit Holder, Leigh Skvarla, Lucie Clements, Peta Blevins, and Tama Barry contributed to composite case studies. *What a dream team!*

And I thank **Johannes Hjorth** for going waaay above and beyond in producing the custom photography for this book. *Simply stunning.*

Introduction to Dance Psychology

"Whatever you can do or dream you can, begin it. Boldness has genius, power and magic in it. Begin it now."

William Hutchison Murray, mountaineer and writer

CHAPTER OBJECTIVES

After reading this chapter, you will be able to

1. describe what dance psychology is;
2. outline what well-being is, including hedonic and eudaimonic perspectives;
3. understand basic principles about learning and behavior from cognitive behavioral therapy (CBT), including the nature of classical and instrumental conditioning;
4. use basic functional analysis to understand the consequences and maintenance of dancer behaviors; and
5. think critically about the nature and potential uses for dance psychology in your own practice.

Key Terms

classical conditioning	functional analysis	positive reinforcement
cognitive behavioral therapy	hedonic well-being	punishment
eudaimonic well-being	instrumental conditioning	respondent behaviors
exposure	intermittent reinforcement	safety behaviors
extinction	modeling	self-reinforcing
	negative reinforcement	

The term *psychology* derives from the Latin *psychologia* and means the study of the soul. This makes sense because the soul was, at that time, seen as the seat of human feelings and desires. The meaning of the term *psychology* then shifted as thinking and reasoning became seen more as faculties of the mind. Today we typically describe psychology as the science of mind and behavior. Dance psychology, therefore, concerns the scientific study of mind and behavior as they pertain to dancers, teachers, and dance practice.

What Is Dance Psychology?

Dance psychology may be considered a sister discipline to sport psychology. Far more extensively researched and practically applied around the world, sport psychology has often provided a foundation for dance psychology research and practice. In line with this tradition, sport psychology provides an important foundation for this book. For example, summaries of study results are often sourced from sports but illustrated and contrasted with dance psychology research wherever possible. Both dance and sport psychology may be considered to sit under the broader umbrella of performance psychology, which also includes the psychology of other performance domains such as music and theater; at times, domains such as business and the military are also incorporated (see e.g., Hays & Brown, 2004; Nordin-Bates, 2012; Portenga et al., 2017). Division 47 of the American Psychological Association, also known as the Society for Sport, Exercise, and Performance Psychology, defined this broader area of performance psychology as "the study and application of psychological principles of human performance to help people consistently perform in the upper range of their capabilities and more thoroughly enjoy the performance process" (Portenga et al., 2017, p. 52).

Dance psychology, the scientific study of mind and behavior as they pertain to dancers, teachers, and dance practice, can be conceptualized in several other ways. For instance, some researchers study dance through the lenses of cognitive psychology and neuroscience, thereby investigating topics such as aesthetic appreciation, how humans perceive and memorize dance, and how dance is represented in the brain (Bläsing et al., 2018). Others explore dance psychology by questions such as whether humans are born to dance and whether dancing makes people healthier and happier (Lovatt, 2019). There is also a growing research interest in the use of dance to improve health, including physical (e.g., Yan et al., 2018) and psychosocial health (e.g., Chappell et al., 2021). Although clearly valuable, areas such as these fall outside the scope of this book.

There is far more research into some topics than others. For example, chapter 13 has 37 dance-specific references relating to psychological aspects of injury, and chapter 14 has 69 dance-specific resources relating to body image and disordered eating. In contrast, chapter 9 has just three references relating to goal setting and/or self-regulation in dance, and none of those are empirical investigations directly targeting these topics. A similar dearth of evidence is true for mindfulness (chapter 8). Overall, we might conclude that dance psychology research has thus far taken more of a problem focus than a strength focus (Draugelis et al., 2014; Stark & Newton, 2014).

Is Dance Psychology Merely a Smaller Version of Sport Psychology?

Although sport psychology is larger and more established, dance psychology is not quite a smaller version of the same thing. In particular, it is important to focus education and research in dance psychology on the topics that are most relevant to the dance community rather than uncritically adopting sport psychology curricula and research topics. As such, the present book includes a chapter on creativity (chapter 7), a highly valued aspect of dance practice yet a topic rarely studied in sports (although it does appear to be on the rise; see Richard & Runco, 2020). The chapter on imagery (chapter 10) deals not only with imagery as a form of mental practice (as is typical of sport psychology) but also with imagery as an artistic tool to enhance outcomes such as aesthetic experience, meaning making, and audience communication. In a series of two investigations with performing artists, Nathalie Lacaille and her coauthors (2005, 2007) went beyond the achievement goals traditionally studied in sports to include *intrinsic goals*. They argued that such goals might be most appropriate for artists because of their focus on artistic aspects.

Despite the noted differences, most chapters in this book resemble those found in sport psychology books, and most dance psychology research studies resemble those in sports. This reflects the many similarities between domains; indeed, both dancers and athletes practice motor skills in attempts to learn, improve, and perform well; in so doing they are affected by intrapersonal traits and characteristics such as personality (chapter 1), perfectionism (chapter 2), self-confidence (chapter 3), anxiety (chapter 4), motivation (chapter 5) and attentional focus (chapter 6). They are also affected by interpersonal relationships via motivational climates (chapter 11). Athletes and dancers alike need to cope with challenges around talent (chapter 12), injury (chapter 13), and at times suffer from problems with body image and disordered eating (chapter 14). To understand such challenges, tools from **cognitive behavioral therapy** (CBT) can be useful (introduction) and psychological skills, including mindfulness (chapter 8), goal setting (chapter 9) and imagery (chapter 10), may be utilized.

In sum, there is every reason to believe that dance and sport psychology can learn from each other. Further support for this idea comes from the fact that theoretical frameworks and measurement tools borrowed from sports typically do hold up well when used in dance investigations. Indeed, many theories are not specific to movement domains like sports to begin with but are about humans in general (e.g., the Big Five theory of personality outlined in chapter 1, or the achievement goal theory of motivation described in chapter 5). Taking inspiration from a well-cited quote from personality psychology (Kluckhohn et al., 1953), we might say that:

EVERY DANCER is in certain respects
 a) like all other people,
 b) like some other people (athletes, musicians . . .),
 c) like no other person

and that

EVERY SCIENCE is in certain respects
 a) like all other sciences,
 b) like some other sciences (sport science, music science . . .),
 c) like no other science.

What Can Dance Psychology Do?

The overall aim of dance psychology education and research can be said to be enhancement of a range of performance-related and well-being-related outcomes. For instance, an appropriate attentional focus will help dancers perform better, creating a healthy motivational climate should facilitate enjoyment and creativity, and working with psychological skills such as mindfulness and imagery can help dancers return faster and stronger from injury. In this book, correlates and consequences of different issues and topics are therefore grouped under these two broad headings: well-being related, and performance related. This is a recurrent feature of nearly all chapters. Performance-related correlates and consequences naturally comprise performance itself (e.g., dancing better after a mindfulness intervention) but also creativity and behavioral aspects that directly affect performance, such as training intensity, adherence, and dropout.

Well-being-related outcomes are more complex and therefore require a little more introduction. First, well-being can be viewed as both hedonic and eudaimonic (Ryan & Deci, 2001; for a review, see Lundqvist, 2011). **Hedonic well-being** is about feeling well and living the good life; as such, happiness, pleasure, and satisfaction are sources of hedonic well-being. Studies that capture positive and negative affect are typical examples.

Eudaimonic well-being is about meaning, purpose, and development. When we strive for personally meaningful goals, therefore, we may obtain eudaimonic well-being—even if hedonic well-being is relatively low at the same time, such as when goal striving is challenging and unpleasant (e.g., very tiring). Studies into basic psychological need satisfaction (chapter 5), such as dancers experiencing a sense of autonomy, competence, and relatedness, are good examples of research into eudaimonic well-being. Other aspects of eudaimonic well-being include self-acceptance, having a sense of purpose, personal growth, and various aspects of functioning well in social situations (see Lundqvist, 2011).

In this book, a broad range of correlates and consequences are listed under the broad heading of "well-being-related outcomes," including becoming more confident, feeling more intrinsically motivated, and experiencing more positive and less negative emotions. To avoid adding new or varied headings in different chapters, some psychological variables that are not strictly indicators of either hedonic or eudaimonic well-being are also included (e.g., self-esteem, which some argue is more of a facilitator of other outcomes; Lundqvist, 2011). Variables representing ill-being (e.g., burnout, disordered eating) are also listed in the sections about well-being-related consequences. This is partly logical, because outcomes like these sometimes represent the conceptual opposites of positively oriented outcomes such as those previously listed (e.g., if we feel bad, we do not feel good). However, it is possible to experience aspects of well-being and ill-being simultaneously, such as when a dancer experiences a positive sense of skill mastery but also poor social functioning.

Overall, then, the heading "well-being-related consequences" is used somewhat liberally. Those conducting their own empirical investigations into well-being would do well to consider very precisely what they wish to capture and use a relevant theoretical framework to understand whether it is an indicator of well-being or perhaps of something else (e.g., a well-being facilitator or an aspect of ill-being; see Lundqvist, 2011; Ryan & Deci, 2001; for good examples in dance, see Draugelis et al., 2014; Stark & Newton, 2014).

Cognitive Behavioral Therapy in Dance Psychology

Performance psychology, clinical psychology, and psychotherapy share a focus on understanding and changing behavior. As such, theories and tools from one of these areas may often be fruitfully applied to another. In this book, I have chosen to highlight the promising overlap between dance psychology and cognitive behavioral therapy. CBT is a large umbrella of theories and techniques that focus variously on cognitive aspects (the C in CBT, e.g., thought patterns, anxiety) and behavioral aspects (the B in CBT, e.g., goal setting, avoidance; e.g., Gustafsson & Lundqvist, 2020). CBT also concerns how cognitions, behaviors, and emotions interact. Although the T in CBT denotes *therapy*, the use of CBT with nonclinical populations can be considered cognitive behavioral *training* (Gustafsson & Lundqvist, 2016, 2020). In other words, CBT can be helpful both for problem-solving (e.g., managing debilitating performance anxiety) and for proactive skill building (e.g., identifying patterns of thought and behavior in different situations to optimize self-awareness, performance, and well-being).

CBT boasts a vast evidence base for promoting all manner of behavior change (e.g., David et al., 2018; Gustafsson & Lundqvist, 2020; Kaczkurkin & Foa, 2015). As such, it is well-suited for work with active people such as dancers; after all, we not only want to understand or change dancers' and teachers' internal thoughts and emotions but also their actual behaviors (Wadström & Ekvall, 2013). For instance, we may want to help someone do more of a behavior (e.g., stand more at the front during classes) or less of a behavior (e.g., stop avoiding challenging situations). In CBT terms, the word *behavior* is used more broadly than in everyday language; for example, self-confidence and motivation are also considered behaviors. While this may seem strange, it makes sense to look at the enhancement of such cognitive aspects in behavioral terms. For instance, how does a self-confident dancer behave, and how can we help someone to behave more like a confident dancer? What do intrinsically motivated dancers do that helps them sustain their love of dance across time?

In this book, both cognitive and behavioral aspects are considered. For example, identifying cognitive distortions typical of perfectionists (chapter 2) or using an imagery program (chapter 10) are very much cognitive psychology activities, whereas the creation and use of an exposure hierarchy (chapter 4) is a typical behavioral psychology activity. Sport psychology has often used more of the former perspective however (Gustafsson et al., 2017; Gustafsson & Lundqvist, 2020), and that is inevitably reflected also in this book, because it uses sport psychology as its main foundation.

CBT, and behavior therapy in particular, is founded on learning theory (Gustafsson et al., 2017; Wadström & Ekvall, 2013), according to which humans learn via three main avenues:

1. **Modeling** (also known as vicarious or observational learning). When we learn by this route, we observe others do something and thereby gain knowledge of how it should be done. This form of learning is further outlined in chapter 3, because it is a key source of self-efficacy (Bandura, 1986).
2. **Instrumental conditioning** (also known as operant conditioning). When we learn

through instrumental conditioning, our behaviors are guided by the consequences of our actions. This form of learning will be outlined in more depth later, with an introduction to **functional analysis** and its potential uses in dance.

3. **Classical conditioning** (also known as respondent conditioning). When we learn by classical conditioning, we create associations between previously unrelated things. This form of learning will also be outlined in more depth later, including its links to anxiety and avoidant dance behaviors.

Instrumental Conditioning: Learning and Behaving in Line With Consequences

Have you ever wondered why a dancer seems to be focused and serious in one class but chatty and giggly in another? Or why some teachers (and parents) constantly seem to nag their dancers without much effect? The answer might lie in instrumental conditioning, or how consequences steer behavior.

A particularly powerful way in which human beings adapt and adjust to their circumstances is by changing behaviors in light of the consequences that they yield. For instance, a child who gets praised by her teacher for doing an exercise correctly is likely to continue doing the exercise in that way. A dancer who feels that a particular conditioning exercise is not giving any results is likely to give that exercise up in favor of another one that seems more promising. In general, we tend to do things that bring us some kind of benefit or act in ways that help us avoid some kind of problem, discomfort, or disadvantage. We also tend to do fewer things (or stop doing things) that lead to problems, discomfort, or disadvantages, and we tend to avoid acting in ways that do not bring any benefit or reward. This is the essence of instrumental conditioning (Reinebo et al., 2020; Wadström & Ekvall, 2013).

Although it can be a challenge to identify the causes of certain behaviors, it is worthwhile if we truly want to understand behaviors in context and perhaps begin to change them. To do so, functional analysis is a valuable tool and will be described next. Functional analysis is evidence-based but also inherently practical in nature—a good combination for dancers, teachers, parents, and support staff alike! Besides being useful to you in its own right, the introduction that follows will also prepare you for the rest of this book because each chapter contains example functional analyses.

Functional Analysis

A dance coach might wonder why one of his dancers seems to practice so much outside of scheduled sessions; a parent might wonder why her house rules never seem to be followed; and a dancer might be confused about why she is performing better during stage performances than in rehearsals. Situations and issues like these can often be understood through functional analysis (figure 0.1).

As shown in figure 0.1, functional analysis includes three main components (Gustafsson & Lundqvist, 2020; Reinebo et al., 2020; Wadström & Ekvall, 2013):

› *Antecedents* are the situations, stimuli, demands, or cues in our environment that make a person do something—that is, antecedents lead to behaviors.
› *Behaviors* are the things we do when encountering a particular antecedent and may be overt and observable (e.g., moving in a particular way, saying something) as well as covert (e.g., thinking particular thoughts). Behaviors lead to consequences or are repeated over time due to the consequences they yield (or that a person hopes they will yield).
› *Consequences* result from a particular behavior. For instance, we may avoid difficult or boring tasks like the dancer in the preceding example; we may also feel proud, competent, or ashamed, or be rewarded or punished in some other way.

In considering these examples of basic functional analyses, you may wish to draw them out, perhaps adding other potential behaviors and consequences to make them more realistic. Indeed, the examples provided here mostly comprise single antecedents (A), behaviors (B), and consequences (C); in reality, several of each can exist and interrelate.

› Being given food at lunchtime (A) and eating (B) leads to feeling comfortably full and reenergized (C). These consequences are likely to mean the person will eat again the next time she is given food at lunchtime (behavior maintenance).
› Buying new dance shoes (A) and using them in class (B) leads to pain in one's feet (C). This consequence likely means the person will not use these shoes again, at least not in the same way.
› A dancer sits next to someone much more flexible than he, and he does not want to look incompetent in front of others (A). He therefore avoids stretching (B) and consequently avoids looking incompetent (C). This is a short-term outcome; if the avoidance behavior is maintained he might also become less flexible over time (C).

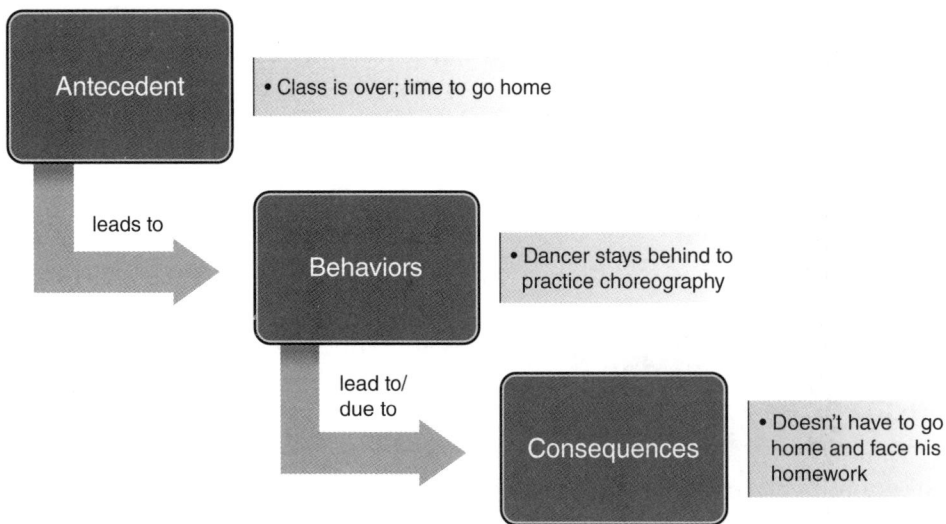

Figure 0.1 Functional analysis example of a dancer who stays behind after classes to practice choreography, because this way he does not have to go home and do his homework.

› A teacher observes her students performing less well than expected (A), shouts at them to get a grip or else (B), and notices an immediate improvement in their focus and performances (C). This, too, is a short-term outcome; in the long term, another consequence might be a dwindling number of students in the class.

A slightly more complex functional analysis is illustrated in figure 0.2. In this example, a teacher overprepares her lessons because she is worried of what might happen if she does not have a full foolproof plan for anything that might happen in class. As a result, she spends many hours preparing each class and is simply exhausted. Although she realizes that her preparations are excessive, the relief inherent in having another class go without incidents helps to ensure that her overpreparation behaviors are maintained over time. Put differently, the short-term benefit (relief: "it went okay!") outweighs the long-term cost (exhaustion). In fact, we humans are surprisingly strongly motivated to avoid discomfort in the short term, even at the risk of highly undesirable long-term consequences. Therefore, short-term reinforcements such as praise, pleasure, or avoiding negative outcomes serve to maintain a wide range of otherwise counterproductive and even damaging behaviors (Gustafsson & Lundqvist, 2020; Reinebo et al., 2020).

The kinds of behaviors that may be understood via functional analysis are endless; to practice making basic such analyses, you can use form 0.1.

Types of Reinforcement

As you already know by now, learning theory states that behaviors are maintained or modified as a result of the reinforcement (consequences) experienced (Gustafsson & Lundqvist, 2020; Reinebo et al., 2020; Wadström & Ekvall, 2013). For instance, a smile and a nod from a teacher may act as **positive reinforcement**, which increases the likelihood of a behavior being performed again. Being positively reinforced also makes a behavior more likely to be maintained over time, because we want to experience the positive reinforcement again. For example, if I have a choice of dance styles (A) and choose jazz (B), which turns out to be really enjoyable (C), then I am likely to pick jazz again in the future so that I can experience that enjoyment again.

In general, it is desirable if dance involvement includes a variety of positive reinforcements that originate in the dance activity itself—that is, when dance is **self-reinforcing**. In motivation theory this is referred to as an activity being intrinsically motivating (chapter 5). Self-reinforcing dance activity is under greater personal control, is more enjoyable, and is sustainable across time. Relying on extrinsic reinforcements such as receiving praise or being superior to others is less sustainable, which means

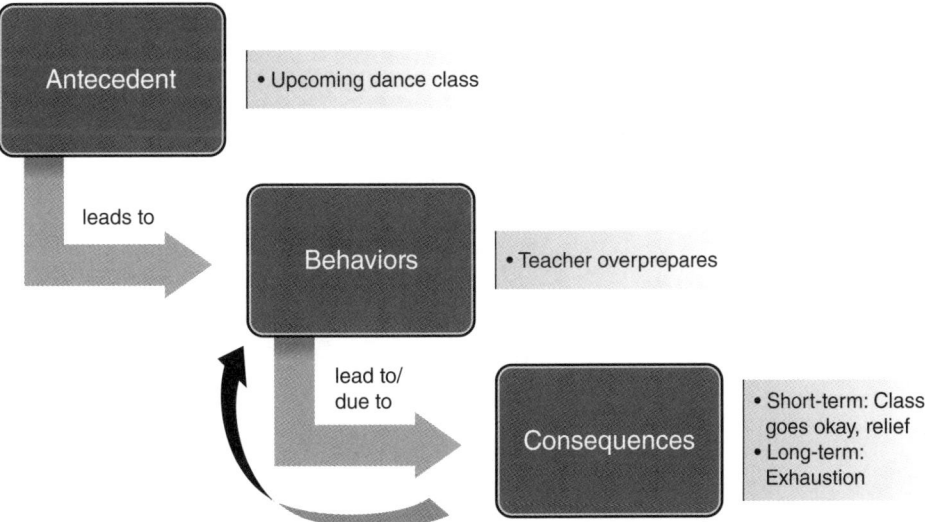

Figure 0.2 Functional analysis example of how overpreparation may result in different short-term and long-term consequences. The recursive arrow indicates that the short-term consequence (in this case, relief) makes the behavior more likely to reoccur in similar situations in the future (behavior maintenance).

Form 0.1 GET PRACTICAL: FUNCTIONAL ANALYSIS

In this exercise, you can practice making functional analyses by analyzing three case studies.

1. A trainee teacher is trying out different teaching methods. One day, she tries to point out what each student is doing wrong to see if this helps them understand. She notices that some students translate her feedback and are able to do better; this feels good. Other students visibly slump and seem to lose energy, which is very disappointing. Another day, the trainee tries to point out what each student is doing right. She notices that many students perk up and do the subsequent exercise with more energy, which helps the teacher feel that she is doing something right.
   a. What antecedents (A), behaviors (B), and consequences (C) can you identify? You may want to draw or write several analyses.
   b. What kinds of behavior(s) is the trainee teacher likely to use in the future?

2. A dancer believes that she must get everything right and should never make mistakes. When mistakes do happen, she scowls and, if possible, goes for a water break. If she has a challenging event coming up, she will practice alone for hours and sometimes days before the event. This gives her some relief: "At least I have done everything I can." Once, she pretended that she was ill just so that she didn't have to attend an event where she didn't know if she would look good enough.
   a. What antecedents (A), behaviors (B), and consequences (C; both short- and long-term) can you identify? You may want to draw or write several analyses.
   b. What potential problems can you identify or foresee?

3. A dance student grew up being the best in his local school. He was often praised and typically had some sort of solo in the end-of-year shows. He later moves on to a high-level school in a bigger city, where he is no longer the best. He practices some things near the teacher and with great energy (e.g., jumps, which he excels at). Other things, such as turns, he prefers not to do at all if he can help it, but when he cannot avoid doing them, he stands at the back and plays it safe.
   a. What antecedents (A), behaviors (B), and consequences (C; both short- and long-term) can you identify? You may want to draw or write several analyses.
   b. What potential problems can you identify or foresee?

Go to *HKPropel* to download this form.

From S. Nordin-Bates, *Essentials of Dance Psychology* (Champaign, IL: Human Kinetics, 2023).

that dropout is likely when such reinforcements are not forthcoming (e.g., when moving to a higher level and praise and a sense of superiority become increasingly rare).

Another kind of reinforcement that increases the likelihood of a behavior being repeated and maintained is known as **negative reinforcement**. Being negatively reinforced makes a behavior more likely to be repeated and maintained because we want to keep avoiding the unpleasant or undesirable. For example, if I have a headache (A) and take a painkiller (B), which reduces my headache (C), then I am likely to take painkillers again the next time I feel a headache coming on so that I do not have to experience that pain. When dancers undertake specific preperformance rituals, fake injury, or repeatedly seek reassurance, they typically seek negative reinforcement. For example, a dancer avoids feeling anxious (C) by repeatedly asking his friends what they think (B), because he knows that they will talk positively about him and his capabilities. Because the anxiety reduction is desirable to him, he is likely to seek this reassurance again the next time he is anxious (behavior maintenance). Indeed, negative reinforcement underpins anxiety problems in general, from mild performance anxiety to debilitating stage fright and generalized anxiety disorder (Gustafsson & Lundqvist, 2020; Wadström & Ekvall, 2013; see also chapter 4).

Teachers who shout or threaten their dancers are trying to limit behaviors in the belief that the shouts or threats will be a consequence that their dancers do not want to experience again. **Punishment**, then, represents a type of reinforcement that aims to reduce the occurrence of a behavior. To work (i.e., reduce or eliminate a particular behavior), punishment must normally occur directly, be strongly aversive to the recipient, and happen every time the behavior occurs (Wadström & Ekvall, 2013). Typically, it also requires people to feel capable of avoiding the behavior in question and for the punishment to have relevance to the target behavior. As such, burning oneself on a candle is an effective form of punishment; few people make that mistake repeatedly. In contrast, punishments such as occasionally making dancers run laps to show one's displeasure are ineffective.

Unfortunately, punishment is not uncommon, especially in hierarchical and authoritarian settings, because leaders are often strongly reinforced by punishing their performers. For example, a teacher who shouts that the dancers will have to rehearse all night if they do not soon start to perform up to her standards may be "rewarded" with immediate reductions in chatting and giggling, and improvements in both task-related focus and effort as the dancers do everything they can to please their leader (i.e., short-term consequences, C). Yet such punishment typically has several negative side-effects:

› Punishment typically only yields short-term effects because people muster all their resources to avoid the punishment reoccurring. If and when the punishment does not come (e.g., when the person issuing the punishment is not present), the behavior tends to reoccur. After all, its original reinforcers are unlikely to have disappeared.

› If punishment is perceived as unjust or irrelevant to the target behavior (e.g., harsh critique of the way someone performs a step), people often do not stop the behavior itself; instead, they simply stop doing the behavior in front of the person issuing the punishment. For example, dancers might keep doing the step in their preferred way but away from the critical choreographer's eyes.

› Punishment is a key component in both physical abuse (e.g., hitting, excessive training loads) and psychological abuse (e.g., screaming, belittling). Although a discussion of abuse is outside the scope of this chapter, it is a breach of human rights and may constitute a criminal offense (Mountjoy et al., 2016).

› Punishment impairs the potential for learning and development. It conveys no information about what should be done (focused on, expressed, tried) and typically leads to several consequences that, in turn, impair learning and performing. These include suboptimal thoughts and emotions (fear, anger, less focus on the task at hand), behaviors (e.g., stop trying, playing it safe), a generally negative atmosphere, and nontrusting relationships.

Overall, then, punishment can be inefficient, counterproductive, and abusive. When there is a need to reduce or eliminate particular behaviors, a more effective strategy is typically to couple clear instructions and positive reinforcement of desired behaviors with **extinction** of the undesired behavior.

Behaviors that are not positively or negatively reinforced will be extinguished and cease to exist (in motivation theory this is known as amotivation; see chapter 5). Returning to the example of the enjoyable jazz class, it is possible that the enjoyment is decreased because of changes in teachers, peers, or class demands. If I continued for mostly or only for reasons of enjoyment (C) but cease to experience that enjoyment over time, I am likely to stop taking jazz classes. In general terms, anyone involved in dance is there due to one or more reinforcements; if these reinforcements stop, they leave (i.e., the lack of reinforcement has extinguished the behavior). A person who is involved in dance over a long period of time often has a large set of reinforcers at play, however; this means they are unlikely to drop out suddenly, as might be the case when a person tries something new for the first time. In table 0.1, different types of reinforcement are further detailed and exemplified.

There is much variation in what individuals experience as positive or negative reinforcement and as punishment. This means that when a teacher or parent gives positive feedback (e.g., praise, a smile or nod) it may or may not be perceived as positively reinforcing. For example, a mother may praise her son after a successful show; the son, however, drops out of dance because he finds the classes boring. His mother's praise is not enough of a positive reinforcement to boost his behavior (pursue dance), and no other reinforcements are strong enough to keep him in dance. Generally, the behavior with the strongest or most numerous reinforcers will win out over behaviors with weaker or fewer reinforcers, although people can also seek different reinforcements at different times (e.g., depending on their needs and moods at the time). The high degree of variation also means that what may look like the same behavior to others (e.g., pursuing choreography) can be driven by quite different reinforcements: from a single positive reinforcement for one person (e.g., seek out flow experiences), to several negative reinforcements for another (e.g., avoid disappointing others, not performing as much oneself), and, for yet another person, a combination of both (e.g., satisfy one's curiosity, not have to leave dance when retiring from performing).

Finally, reinforcements do not need to be constant, or even frequent, in order to maintain (drive) behavior. For instance, dancers typically do not stop rehearsing a skill straight away if they do not get praised for it, even if praise is the key driver of their behavior. Similarly, coffee drinkers do not stop drinking coffee as a result of a single bad-tasting cup. In fact, **intermittent reinforcement** is the most advantageous for long-term behavior maintenance, although frequent positive reinforcement is best when initially learning (Wadström & Ekvall, 2013). Thus, beginners learning skills for the first time should be amply praised and gen-

Table 0.1 **Different Types and Examples of Reinforcement**

Type of reinforcement	Nature of reinforcement	Examples

Positive reinforcement	Something pleasant or desirable is added	• Sensory pleasure (e.g., a movement that just feels nice; something tasting good)
		• Praise and other tangible and nontangible rewards
		• A sense of doing the right thing (e.g., acting in line with values)
		• Basic psychological needs fulfillment (see chapter 5), including
		  ◦ feeling autonomous (this is really me!)
		  ◦ feeling competent, feeling in control, and figuring things out (I can do this!)
		  ◦ feeling relatedness (I fit in; people are nice to me)

Negative reinforcement	Something unpleasant or undesirable is taken away	• Not failing (e.g., not falling over or being replaced) • No longer feeling pain or discomfort • Not disappointing other people • Not looking silly or incompetent • Not feeling awkward or guilty
Punishment	Something unpleasant or undesirable is added	• Feeling awkward or out of place • Harsh critical feedback • Pain, anxiety, and other forms of discomfort • Bullying, being excluded

These examples are intended to be illustrative but not exhaustive.

erally helped to experience success. Once a skill begins to be mastered, the reinforcements can be thinned out.

While intermittent reinforcement is very practical for everyday teaching and learning, it does mean that inefficient behaviors are sometimes maintained for longer than might be desirable. Consider, for example, the teacher who sticks to a rigid set of ideas about how to teach. Even if she does not get frequent positive reinforcement for these behaviors (e.g., the students do not all progress quickly), her teaching methods may not be extinguished because they appeared to be effective in the past and still seem to work some of the time (intermittent reinforcement). Of course, her behaviors may also be maintained for other reasons (e.g., because her behavioral repertoire is narrow, in which case further education is probably the best option).

In this book, examples of functional analyses are provided in every chapter; feel free to browse some of them before doing the Thinking Critically exercise.

THINKING CRITICALLY

- What kinds of situations, skills, or people do you actively seek out and find rewarding?
- What kinds of situations, skills, or people do you avoid?
- Can you make basic functional analyses for two of the examples that you just thought of, showing the reasons for your maintenance of these behaviors over time by outlining one or several antecedents, behaviors, and consequences?

Making functional analyses is not always easy; however, in wanting to understand and perhaps modify behaviors, they are worth spending some time on. Remember that if a behavior is repeated over time, there is something that maintains it. Sometimes the reinforcer is obvious (e.g., a dancer makes her friends laugh, and she beams with delight) and sometimes less so (e.g., a dancer dances despite pain because doing so makes him feel mentally tough, like he has what it takes to be a real dancer). In sum, it sometimes takes work to uncover the true reasons behind why dancers behave the way they do.

Classical Conditioning: Learning and Behaving by Association

Have you ever wondered why a particular smell or song can trigger vivid memories of a situation or choreography that you learned several years ago? Or why some people will not even go near a particular school or theater? The answer might well lie in classical conditioning, or association learning.

Through classical conditioning, an initially neutral stimulus becomes able to evoke an emotional reaction. For instance, a piece of music (an originally neutral stimulus) can become a powerful emotional trigger if it is frequently listened to during a particularly happy or sad period of one's life (e.g., Juslin, 2013). When listened to weeks, months, and even years later, the song evokes the same emotion in the listener as was experienced when the association was made. Classical conditioning is intimately linked to the notion of **respondent behaviors**, which are reactions that are largely outside of our control, such as sweating in response to exercise, sexual arousal, and anxiety (Wadström & Ekvall, 2013). Respondent behaviors are inborn rather than learned; indeed, humans generally have similar reactions to threats or frightening stimuli such as unexpected loud noises, losing our balance near a height, or wild carnivorous animals running in our direction (see chapter 4). In our modern times, threats may take the shape of performing difficult skills in front of critical juries or speaking in front of a crowd.

Through classical conditioning, our inborn reactions to threat can become associated with almost any other previously neutral stimuli, such as seeing a particular building ("Eek! I got injured there once.") or hearing a particular piece of music ("That song we danced to still gives me the creeps."). This kind of association learning only occurs if the person tries to avoid or reduce the natural reaction to threat (i.e., anxiety), however, rather than experiencing it in full and allowing it to run its course (Gustafsson & Lundqvist, 2016, 2020; Gustafsson et al., 2017). The concept of avoidance is further outlined next and expanded on in chapter 4 as regards anxiety specifically.

The Common Use of Avoidance: Desiring to Feel Good

A key principle of behavior change, as it is conceptualized in behavior therapy, is really quite straightforward: expose yourself to your fears and they will subside (Gustafsson & Lundqvist, 2016, 2020; Gustafsson et al., 2017). Yet this deceptively simple principle is often underutilized. We can go to ourselves and our loved ones for examples: chances are good that at least one of you is scared of something (e.g., spiders, heights, a particular choreography, or a person). Now ask yourself what you (or they) do when you experience this fear or discomfort. If you are like most people, you probably do your best to avoid the feeling by staying away from the things that makes you uncomfortable. In other words, we seek negative reinforcement.

Why do we behave this way? The simple answer is that humans are strongly motivated to avoid discomfort. If we hate public speaking, we do not volunteer to give speeches; if we feel uncomfortable with a particular dance style, we give it up in favor of another style; and if there is a person that we really dislike, we may walk a slightly different way so that we do not have to bump into them. In other words, we normally and instinctively help ourselves feel better by escaping situations and thereby the associated unpleasant feelings. We can escape in two ways:

1. *Actual escaping.* To get a clear image of escape, think of young children: when in a situation they dislike, it is fairly common for them to actually run away, hide, and refuse to go back. For instance, a young child in his first dance class may run to the side to sit with his parent if he finds an exercise intimidating. Teenagers and adults also practice escape tactics regularly, albeit in slightly more obscure ways. For instance, the teenager who quits her modern dance course because she does not like the way she looks in the mirror is escaping the unpleasant sensations she feels in classes. Other examples include avoiding asking a stern and imposing teacher for advice or leaving directly after a performance to avoid having to discuss how it went.

2. *Using tricks (safety behaviors).* When actual escape is not an option, many of us use little tricks to help us cope with the unpleasant sensations that we experience. This might include distracting oneself with music or joking around prior to a performance to avoid the gnawing feelings of anxiety. Other safety behaviors include adding extra training to reduce fears of being inadequate, always facing a particular way in the studio so as to hide one's worst side, hiding at the back of the studio to avoid teacher comments, or wearing baggy clothing to avoid seeing one's shape in the mirror.

Escapes and **safety behaviors** reduce unpleasant sensations and help us feel better in the moment. Put differently, they are strong negative reinforcers. Unfortunately, this is precisely what keeps problems such as anxiety, perfectionism, depression, and many others going over time (Gustafsson & Lundqvist, 2016, 2020; Gustafsson et al., 2017; Wadström & Ekvall, 2013). For instance, a dancer with low self-confidence (see chapter 3) avoids situations that might expose her perceived inadequacies (e.g., auditions, volunteering to choreograph for the school show; behaviors, B, in functional analysis). By avoiding such situations, she avoids unpleasant sensations in the short term ("Phew, I got out of it, now nobody will laugh at my stupid attempts"; a consequence, short-term C, in functional analysis) yet maintains her low self-confidence in the long run ("I am so terrible, I do not even put myself forward to help with the choreography"; long-term C).

As another example, consider a teacher with disordered eating (see chapter 14) who avoids situations that might trigger overeating (e.g., birthday celebrations; B). By not showing up or perhaps using tricks if he has to go ("I do not need anything; I have already eaten at home"; B), the anxiety associated with potential overeating is avoided (short-term C). At the same time, avoidance of normal eating situations maintains a part of the eating disorder (long-term C). Just like in these examples, we humans are often surprisingly shortsighted, which means that unhelpful behaviors are maintained due to the short-term reinforcements that they provide, even when long-term consequences are very problematic.

The Power of Exposure: Meeting Challenges and Facing Discomfort

By avoiding discomfort and escaping from challenging situations, thoughts, or emotions, we never truly experience that our discomfort will, in fact, reduce if only we stay in the uncomfortable situation. Stress reactions do not continue indefinitely; instead, they typically rise to a quick peak before reaching a plateau, and then they decrease. Therefore, we can reduce our discomfort by considering what maintains it over time (e.g., by functional analysis) and then meeting it head on. Note that it is subjectively perceived discomfort that is referred to here, not actual danger. Indeed, it can be powerful just to learn that the natural reaction to threats (i.e., the stress or anxiety reaction; see chapter 4) is in itself harmless (Gustafsson & Lundqvist, 2020). By staying in the situation, however uncomfortable, we make it possible for new learning to take place. Put differently, the association between an originally neutral stimulus and the inborn stress response can become uncoupled, such that the stimulus is again neutral and nonthreatening (Gustafsson & Lundqvist, 2020; Wadström & Ekvall, 2013).

Exposure refers to the systematic approach of facing and staying with one's discomfort in situations that are otherwise typically avoided (e.g., Gustafsson & Lundqvist, 2020). For obvious reasons, exposure often seems frightening or even unnecessary to the person concerned. Yet in some activities, including horseback riding and swimming, the exposure principle is well-known and common practice; "Get back on the horse" is the normal recommendation for someone who has fallen off while riding. Similarly, swimming teachers (and many parents) know not to take a child out of the water if they have had a scare (e.g., had their head under water for the first time and swallowed some water). Instead, the principle is to calm them down while remaining in the water. Either through experience or the customs in these activities, it is understood that avoidance can cause long-term problems.

The principles of exposure are well established and have been successfully used to treat a range of problems: from animal phobias to social phobia, from health anxiety to disordered eating and performance anxiety (e.g., Kaczkurkin & Foa, 2015). In some cases (e.g., simpler phobias), exposure therapy is the only strategy required to deal with a problem; for complex problems (e.g., anorexia nervosa), it can be part of a package of different interventions or therapeutic tools. A key to practical interventions is to use exposure in combination with strategies to prevent avoidance—that is, not using safety behaviors to soften or avoid feelings of distress during exposure but rather being there fully with all senses (Gustafsson & Lundqvist, 2020; Wadström & Ekvall, 2013).

Taking fear of failure as an example, it stands to reason that people who are fearful of failing typically avoid situations where they think they might fail. They usually also engage in safety behaviors such as overpreparation and repeatedly seeking reassurance. Therefore, they never experience what would happen if they really did fail, and so their fear is maintained. As a result, exposure for people with fear of failure centers on making mistakes. Of course, the strength of the fear will help determine the different steps in the exposure process (e.g., Gustafsson et al., 2017), and few people will want to go straight into facing their worst fear. Instead, the first steps might be talking about failure or imagining failing. Thereafter, they may move on to making small mistakes in the studio, and so on until the worst-case scenario (e.g., making a mistake in a competition) has been encountered, experienced, and normalized. These steps are typically planned out in advance, creating an exposure hierarchy.

Key principles for facilitating safe systematic exposure are outlined in table 0.2 (e.g., Gustafsson & Lundqvist, 2020; Gustafsson et al., 2017; Wadström & Ekvall, 2013). These principles are provided here to promote general understanding and as a self-help tool for relatively mild challenges. For instance, if you tend to overprepare before dance performances and think it would be interesting—if a little scary—to see what happens if you drop these overcautious strategies, then self-help could work well. Several other suggestions of potential situations in which to try exposure are provided in the Get Practical exercise in chapter 4. Importantly, the CBT principles outlined in table 0.2 and elsewhere in this chapter are far from complete step-by-step guides; to competently and safely guide another person through exposure takes both education and supervised practice. For moderate to severe anxiety and avoidance problems, therefore, consult an appropriately qualified specialist such as a CBT psychologist or psychotherapist.

Moving up an exposure hierarchy is certainly not always smooth sailing (e.g., Gustafsson et al., 2017). Indeed, it is commonplace to go back to a previous step several times or to run away from a situation that you were intending to meet. If this happens, do not lose heart. Go back and evaluate what happened. Were there some safety behaviors that you had been unaware of and that also need to be dropped? Perhaps the hierarchy needs to be redesigned, because some situations were more or less uncomfortable than first anticipated.

Table 0.2 **Step-By-Step Considerations in Dealing With Avoidance by Systematic Exposure**

Step	Description
1. Clarify the discomfort	Specify what it is, specifically, that causes feelings of discomfort. What would happen if you stopped avoiding this situation?
2. Clarify the avoidance	What do you do to avoid your discomfort?
3. Identify safety behaviors	Do you overprepare? Depend on wearing particular clothing? Are there things that you do that you would not want to be without (e.g., "If I didn't do that, I would surely not make it"). Safety behaviors can be hard to spot, so be prepared for some detective work. It may help to imagine what you do in the challenging situation by going through it systematically in your mind.
4. Make an exposure hierarchy	Write a list of situations that represent a hierarchy, from most to least uncomfortable. Rate each step from 0 (no discomfort) to 100 (maximum discomfort). For more information, see chapter 4.
5. Take one thing at a time	Make a commitment to try out the lowest step in the hierarchy. Enter the situation and refrain from using any safety behaviors.
6. Stay in the moment, observe	Discomfort is likely to appear; in fact, it must, or the exposure will not work! When it does, simply observe the sensations without trying to reduce them with any tricks or avoidance. Be brave and simply stay in the moment. Note what happens.
7. Move up the hierarchy	When symptoms have subsided (or when you are confident that you have learned to act in a functional way despite symptoms), it is time to move to the next step. For some challenges it may be possible to take one step directly after another; for others there might be a need to wait a while (hours, or even days) between steps.
8. Evaluate and plan for maintenance	Make notes about what was done and how it felt. What do the results suggest? Once satisfied, make a plan for how the benefits can be maintained in the future (e.g., by regularly exposing yourself to the previously avoided situation).

CRITICAL ASPECTS OF RESEARCH IN DANCE PSYCHOLOGY AND LIMITATIONS OF THIS BOOK

1. Dance psychology is a relatively young research area, and there is a real need for further investigation into many, if not most, of the topics in this book. In considering the applicability of theories, models, and research findings from other domains, we must distinguish between research into *relationships between variables* (e.g., are dancers in ego-involving motivational climates more likely to be anxious? Is goal setting associated with improvements in self-confidence?) and *levels of a construct* (e.g., How anxious are dancers? Are dancers often perfectionistic?). Thus far, research suggests that relationships between variables are very similar across domains. This means that if a study in sports indicates that athletes in ego-involving motivational climates are more likely to be anxious, then this is likely also true for dancers. As for levels of a construct, research in other domains naturally cannot help us draw conclusions about dance-specific contexts, making dance-specific research crucial.

2. Most studies in our field (and many in sports) use cross-sectional designs, which means that the authors can discuss correlates (i.e., things that co-occur or are related), but not really effects or consequences. Naturally, this limits the conclusions that may be drawn. More generally, any given research study can be considered just one small puzzle piece in our quest for more knowledge. For this reason, it is

wise to avoid describing the results of a single study as facts or that we have proof of something. Many studies (ideally with a range of research designs, in varied populations, and conducted by several separate research groups) are required before we can be certain that a finding is close to the truth. Many qualitative researchers strongly question the idea that research studies can ever uncover an underlying objective truth, instead emphasizing that many truths exist that are, at least in part, created in social interaction.

3. Research in dance psychology, and consequently the studies and examples represented in this book, mostly represents Western English-language populations. It is also heavily skewed in favor of dancers at relatively high levels in theatrical/stage dance styles such as classical ballet, modern, and contemporary dance. My own experience is biased in similar directions, with my research, teaching, and applied practice having been conducted in Europe, with high-level performers in those same styles. Psychologists sometimes call such participants WEIRD—that is, mostly representative of Western, educated, industrialized, rich, and democratic populations—and caution us to be careful in making generalizations (Henrich et al., 2010). My (arguably limited) experience with other styles such as ballroom, street dance, and Indian dance certainly suggests that the topics in this book could be relevant to them also; indeed, the research from sports should apply at least as well to other dance styles as it has been shown to for ballet, modern, and contemporary dance. I have also used some other styles in my examples (e.g., jazz) and endeavored to include mention of studies with different populations (e.g., classical Indian dance; Anoop & Malshe, 2011), but unfortunately such studies are few. Overall, the field would benefit immensely from more research with other dance populations.

KEY POINTS AND RECOMMENDATIONS REGARDING DANCE PSYCHOLOGY AND COGNITIVE BEHAVIORAL THERAPY

1. Dance psychology is an area of research, education, and practice that aims to enhance a wide range of aspects relating to performance and well-being for dancers, teachers, and other people involved in dance practice. Although it can be conceptualized and researched in several ways, the present book considers dance psychology a subdiscipline of performance psychology alongside sister disciplines such as sport and music psychology.

2. Basic principles from cognitive behavioral therapy can support dance psychology, for example, by enhancing our understanding of behavior:
   - Positive reinforcement is preferable to negative reinforcement, which in turn is preferable to punishment. Therefore, we should seek or provide regular positive reinforcement, primarily of the kind that makes dance self-reinforcing such as a sense of competence, artistry, pleasure, and meaningful social interactions.
   - When behaviors seem counterproductive, irrelevant, or otherwise problematic, start by identifying possible reasons why they are maintained over time. There are always one or more reinforcers underpinning a behavior that does not cease by itself. Functional analysis is a helpful tool to further an understanding of behavior, including how it is changed or maintained over time.

Part I
Individual Differences

1

Personality

*"Learning to dance gives you the greatest freedom of all:
to express your whole self, the person you are."*

Melissa Hayden, dancer

CHAPTER OBJECTIVES

After reading this chapter, you will be able to

1. describe what personality is;
2. discuss the structure of personality in terms of its deep-seated and stable aspects (traits) and its more situation-specific flexible expressions (states);
3. outline a range of consequences on performance and well-being of possessing low versus high levels of the Big Five personality traits;
4. understand the consequences of having a narrowly defined dancer identity and give suggestions for what may be done to broaden it;
5. identify different parts of your identity and their prominence in your life; and
6. think critically about the nature and impact of personality in dance settings.

Key Terms

agreeableness	heritability	neuroticism
athletic identity	interactionist perspective	normal distribution
Big Five		openness to experience
conscientiousness	interpersonal	personality
emotional stability	intrapersonal	role-related behaviors
	introversion	states
extroversion	narrow identity	traits

The term *personality* derives from the Latin *persona*, with which many dancers and others familiar with the arts are familiar—that is, the role or character played on stage. Specifically, persona used to mean the mask worn by actors. This suggests that personality is something that we can infer from how a person behaves. But even if this is partly true, personality is mostly about how we are inside. Some aspects of our personality we may not even be fully familiar with ourselves!

What Is Personality?

Personality as an area of interest to people is probably as old as dance itself. Indeed, many of us are intrigued by questions such as these:

› Are dancers the way they are because particular kinds of people choose dance, or does the dance environment shape them that way?
› To what extent does personality determine the kind of dance style you pick?
› Can personality be changed, and if so, how?

Before we delve further into the intriguing area of personality, however, we must clarify what it is. One useful definition is that personality concerns "psychological qualities that contribute to an individual's enduring and distinctive patterns of feeling, thinking and behaving" (Pervin & Cervone, 2010, p. 8). Thus, personality includes aspects *internal* to a person (e.g., how they feel) and aspects that are visible *externally* (e.g., how they behave). Moreover, personality consists of individual differences that are relatively stable over both situations (e.g., in dance class, in the workplace, and with friends) and over time (e.g., several months, years, or even a lifetime; Caspi et al., 2003; Orth & Robins, 2014; Pervin & Cervone, 2010). In fact, personality is related to numerous aspects of our everyday lives, including

› *cognitions* (what we are likely to think about, such as "How exciting to get cast for that new role!" or "Oh no. I can't believe I was cast for that role!"),
› *emotions* (what we feel, such as excited and upbeat, or worried and downcast), and
› *behaviors* (what we do, such as choosing a spot in the studio that is in direct view of the teacher or hiding in the back corner).

Despite personality affecting all these important aspects, we are not always aware of how our personalities—or indeed those of others—affect our lives. Delving into the scientific literature can help us understand more, thereby increasing awareness of both ourselves and others.

Structure of Personality

That personality is largely stable helps give us a sense of predictability and certainty. If we have a good sense of who we are and what important people around us are like, we can make educated guesses about such things as how we will react in certain situations. For instance, it is reassuring when a parent is consistently warm and caring, but it feels disconcerting if a person who we thought we were beginning to know suddenly behaves completely differently in two otherwise similar situations. In extreme cases, such as when a parent has a personality disorder, this increases the risk of mental illness in their children (e.g., Kuperman et al., 1999; Petfield et al., 2015).

Traits and States

An important distinction when studying personality is that between **traits** and **states**. Their differences are illustrated in table 1.1.

Most research studies are not well-funded, longitudinal, and complex in their designs, and the researchers who design studies have different interests and beliefs. Therefore, individual studies often focus only on traits or only on states. Some focus exclusively on the role of personal character-

Table 1.1 **Key Distinguishing Features of Personality Traits and States**

	Traits	States
Nature	Deep-seated	More superficial
Stability across time and situations	Generally stable	More variable
Captured by asking people . . .	. . . what they typically believe, feel, and do	. . . what they believe, feel, and do at a specific time
Visibility to others and self-awareness	Less obvious	More obvious
Susceptibility to outside influences (e.g., teacher behavior)	Less susceptible	More susceptible
Dance example	A dancer being conscientious in many situations, dance styles, and across teachers	A dancer being conscientious in one situation as a result of it being especially important to him or her

istics, while others focus exclusively on the role of the environment (e.g., how dancers perceive that their teachers behave). It is important to keep in mind that different perspectives and methods—and therefore also their findings—are *complementary* rather than right versus wrong. That is, we need to embrace an **interactionist perspective** if we want to truly understand the dancer in context, because both nature (personality, including genetics) and nurture (environment, including teachers, peers, and parents) are important. Both traits (how I typically feel and behave) and states (how I feel and behave in a particular moment) are valid representations of the human experience.

Major Personality Traits and the Big Five

Researchers interested in personality traits have used a variety of methods and perspectives to get at the central question of how many personality traits there are. One early attempt, in which Allport and Odbert (1936) painstakingly went through *Webster's New International Dictionary of the English Language*, resulted in a list of nearly 18,000 words that in some way described what people are like! The list was reduced to around 4,000 when more temporary states were removed—still not exactly workable. Further work by Cattell and colleagues refined this work into a well-known model known as the *16PF*, a list of 16 key personality factors (Cattell & Mead, 2008).

Cattell's 16 personality factors form a hierarchical structure, where the 16 more specific factors (known as primary traits) are subsumed under five more general factors (known as global traits). While these global traits have been important, it is a slightly different set of five personality traits that have become best known over time. Known as the **Big Five**, they encompass **openness to experience**, **conscientiousness**, **extroversion**, **agreeableness**, and **emotional stability** (Costa & McCrae, 1992). Emotional stability has often been studied as its opposite and then called **neuroticism**, but since it is convenient to consider all five traits in terms of their positive pole, many researchers have argued that *emotional stability* is a more appropriate term (Hills & Argyle, 2001).

The Costa and McCrae (1992) factors are hierarchical in nature, just like the personality factors outlined by Cattell many years prior. That is, numerous different personality traits are subsumed, or encompassed, under five broader headings. Researchers focus either on the broad set of five or on more specific subfactors or facets. Note also that while the Big Five factors are an internationally well-known way to understand and measure personality and there is much to commend this approach, it is not without its critics. For instance, some researchers have argued for the existence of a sixth factor (e.g., honesty-humility), and some argue that the five-factor structure is not fully consistent across languages and cultures (e.g., De Raad et al., 2010).

In table 1.2, the Big Five are described using examples pertinent to dance. Remember that the Big Five traits are not specific to dance, sports, or performance but together form a general theory of personality. Also keep in mind that personality traits follow a **normal distribution**; that is, all people tend to exhibit all traits to a lower or higher extent, with the majority of us falling somewhere in the middle. Therefore, it is usually not accurate to speak of people as being either introverts or extroverts (a more type-based idea that is often simplistic and less supported by research evidence; see Allen et al.,

Dancers high in the personality trait known as agreeableness typically enjoy cooperation.

Photographer: Johannes Hjorth. Dancers: Ahtayaw Ea, Felicia Andersson.

2013). Instead, it would be more accurate to say that a person has a *low level* or *high level* of extroversion.

> ### THINKING CRITICALLY
>
> - Are certain personality traits more valued in certain dance settings? Does this vary by dance style?
> - In your experience, are dancers with certain personality traits likely to be drawn to particular dance styles?
> - Does training in a particular dance style, or with particular teachers, strengthen certain personality traits do you think?

Personality Stability and Change

Although we need a sense of stability to feel safe, humans also need and value change. It would certainly be depressing if "personality were destiny" and we could never change and adapt! Fortunately, our personalities are malleable (Allen et al., 2013; Coulter et al., 2016; Specht et al., 2011):

1. *Our personalities naturally develop over time.* Change is most pronounced in childhood and during the teenage years, but we also adjust as we mature throughout adulthood and into old age (Specht et al., 2011).
2. *We can change our personalities.* Three main sources of change can be identified:

Table 1.2 **Big Five Personality Traits and How They May Be Manifested in Dance**

Component	DANCE EXAMPLES		
	Low scores might mean that a dancer is . . .		High scores might mean that a dancer is . . .
Openness to experience	• Traditional • Rigid • Most comfortable with familiar styles and exercises		• Open to new ideas (e.g., in improvisation and choreography) • Curious, imaginative • Keen on variety • Nonconformist, original
Conscientiousness	• Relaxed, casual • Flexible • Distractible • Disorganized		• Well-organized, focused • Disciplined, hard-working • Careful, reliable
Extroversion	• More quiet • Less action-oriented • Needs time for themselves • More focused on their inner life than outer events	Most people fall somewhere in the middle ⟷	• Sociable, happy to talk to anyone • Assertive, enthusiastic • More action-oriented • Happy being the center of attention
Agreeableness	• Reserved, shy, or even hostile • Skeptical • More likely to challenge others' ideas • Less likely to get involved		• Friendly, easygoing • Cooperative, considerate • Trusting • Generous, helpful • Likely to seek social harmony
Emotional stability	• Prone to strong emotional reactions • More likely to struggle with challenges • Self-conscious • More prone to anxiety and depression		• Even-tempered across situations • Less sensitive to stress • Calm • Resilient

a. *Major life events* that help shape our lives, such as moving away from home, can affect personality development (Specht et al., 2011). Beyond such normative and expected life events, unexpected and traumatic incidents can lead to a reevaluation of who one is and wants to be. For instance, persons going through a distressing event such as a major injury may reevaluate their values and priorities in life (Crawford et al., 2014; see also chapter 13).

b. *Deliberate systematic work* over a period of time. This may be in professional therapy, such as when a dancer works to reduce his levels of worry and perfectionism through therapeutic exercises in acceptance and self-compassion (see Roberts et al., 2017). We can also do work like this ourselves, such as via self-help books (e.g., Donachie & Hill, 2020; Fennell, 2016).

c. *Participation in activities such as sports and dance*. Outside of dance, it has been shown that having an active lifestyle appears to help children develop desirable personality traits (e.g., persistence, conscientiousness) and limit the development of less desirable traits (e.g., high emotional reactivity; Allen et al., 2015; Stephan et al., 2014). While no research has examined the development of the Big Five traits in relation to dance participation, an ethnographic account of identity development in ballet is of related interest (Pickard, 2015).

Models of Personality Structure

While the structure of personality has been illustrated in many and varied ways, two popular approaches are those of Hollander (1967) and McAdams (2013). Both conceive of personality as a layered structure, with a combination of more deep-seated traits and more variable statelike expressions of those traits (also known as **role-related behaviors**). There are also similarities with models used in cognitive behavioral therapy (CBT) of how our thinking about ourselves and the world is structured into different layers, including *core beliefs* in the center, *intermediate beliefs* (e.g., rules for living) in the middle, and *automatic thoughts* farthest out. Figure 1.1 is an illustration of personality structure that combines aspects of these models and uses dance-specific language to illustrate.

We can illustrate figure 1.1 with the following example. Jana is a modern dancer with a core personality that includes high levels of openness to experience and extroversion. That is, she has developed a personality that is curious and open-minded, and she is sociable and friendly in school, dance, and other contexts. If a teacher she had five years ago met her again tomorrow, she would recognize these traits as being typical for Jana. Her traits are expressed in typical dispositions such as

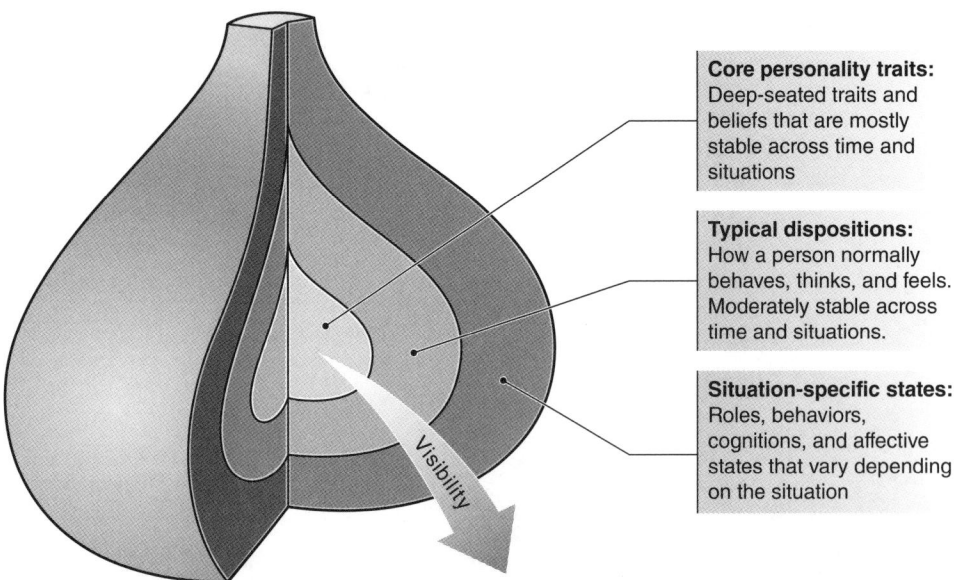

Figure 1.1 Personality structure may be considered as layered; core personality traits are the most deep-seated and stable aspect, and situation-specific states are the most visible and flexible.

liking being the center of attention in class, enjoying improvisation tasks, and being comfortable talking to people she does not know. Her traits and dispositions are not constant in every dance class, with every teacher, every day, however. For instance, if Jana takes class with a new teacher who expresses overt dislike of Jana's style in an improvisation task, she might withdraw from the task and not offer suggestions for how to approach a movement task later. She might be more sociable and talkative in a group she perceives as similarly extroverted and less so in a group she feels is dissimilar to her—that is, more introverted. In this way, Jana expresses situation-specific states that vary even if her core personality is largely constant. Depending on her goals and how much choice she has over where she spends her time, she might opt out of classes and contexts where her bubbly, chatty, and original personality is not valued, in favor of classes where she feels that it is welcomed. If so, her personality would remain unchanged by less comfortable encounters, such as those outlined. If she instead continues to take classes with teachers and peers who dissuade conversation and curious exploration of dance movements repeatedly over many months or years, her typical dispositions may start to change—and perhaps even her core personality. The latter is most likely if such interactions are experienced during childhood and early adolescence, when personality and identity are still being formed and social influences matter greatly.

Some aspects of personality may be inferred from a dancer's behavior. For instance, a teacher who has taught a group of dancers for a term or more is likely to have a reasonable idea of who is most extroverted versus most introverted. But beware—observation is not necessarily a reliable method for capturing personality. Given that there are different "layers to the onion," what you are observing might be role-related behaviors, or states, rather than deep-seated traits. Even when our personalities are mostly formed and stable, such as in a group of adult dancers, we learn to use role-related behaviors that we perceive to be effective and rewarding in specific contexts. For an example, see the functional analyses in figure 1.2. This example involves a dancer who is both a pupil in an academic school and in a dance school. In the first analysis, we can see that if he is positively reinforced for being quiet in dance class, he is more likely to be quiet again in future dance classes. In the second analysis, he encounters schoolteachers who encourage him to talk and praise him when he does. He learns that talking is desirable and becomes more likely to talk again during future such classes. In this way, his role-related behaviors may not represent his true personality, making him appear more introverted in dance but more extroverted in school.

Is Functional Analysis a State Approach?

As outlined in the introduction, functional analysis is built on the premise that we adapt our behaviors in relation to reinforcements obtained—or the lack thereof. For instance, a child who learns that she will only be praised by her parents when she performs exceptionally well is more likely to strive for perfection in her efforts to feel seen and valued. If this is pronounced and prolonged, she is likely to develop the personality trait of perfectionism. As another example, consider the dancer who gets praised when dancing with his own personal style in class. He is also taken to a variety of cultural experiences by his relatives and finds that he enjoys (positive reinforcement) these gatherings, where a wide range of art forms, styles, and personalities seem to be welcomed. To get these positive experiences again and again, the dancer starts to experiment more and more with personal expression and artistry. If our dancer has many experiences like this and continues to get intermittent positive reinforcement when doing so, he might develop the personality trait of openness to experience over time.

So-called *establishing conditions* affect the strength of the relationships in a functional analysis. For instance, persons with low emotional stability are more likely to interpret criticism from a teacher as punishment and therefore become more likely to avoid the behavior that led to the criticism. A person who is more emotionally stable may instead perceive the critique as useful information and is therefore less likely to avoid the behavior in the future. In this way, personality traits can act as establishing operations. In sum, functional analysis is not a fully state or situational approach, despite its emphasis on how behaviors adjust flexibly to reinforcement and punishment from one's environment; depending on how it is used, therefore, functional analysis can represent an interactionist perspective.

Origins of Personality

Just like leg length and hair color, personality is affected by genetic factors. Unlike physical traits, however, genetics explains a lower amount of variance in personality traits. Put differently, the **heritability**

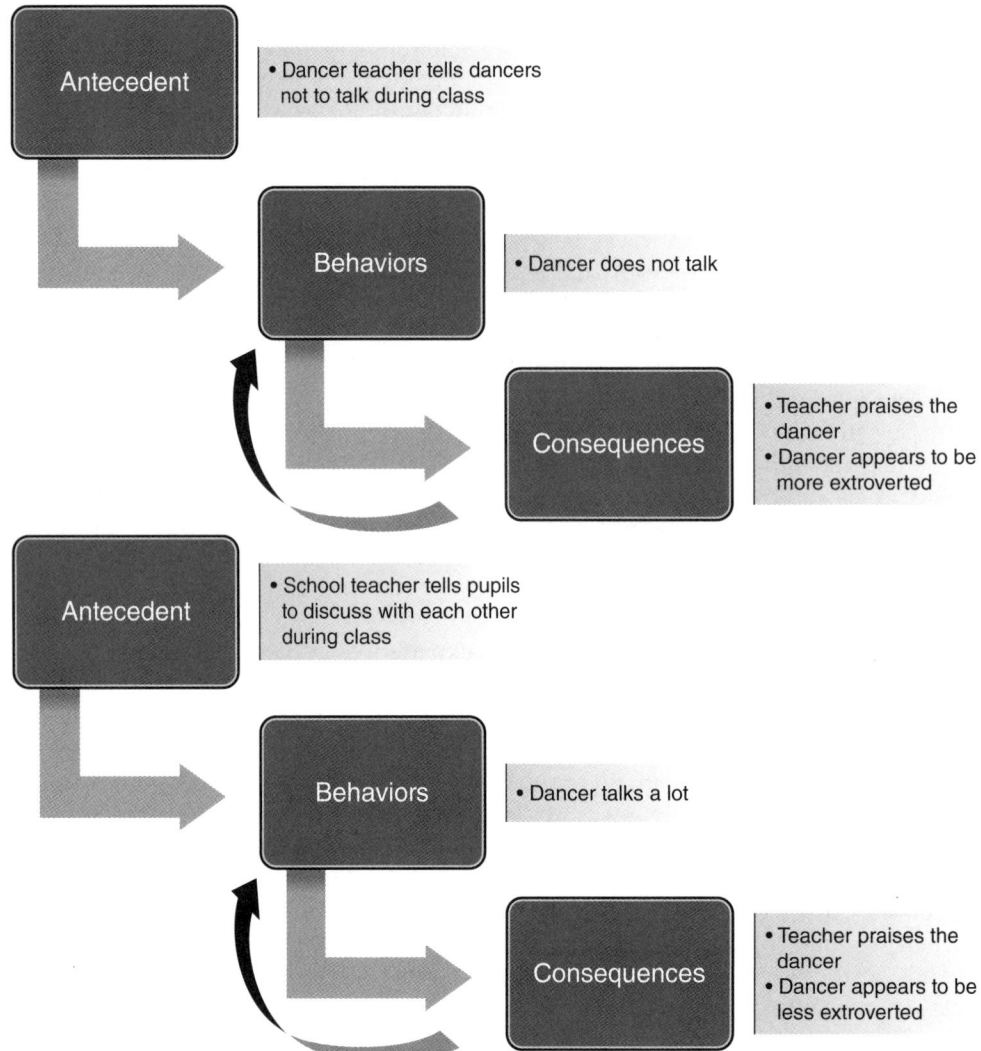

Figure 1.2 Functional analysis examples of how role-related behaviors may manifest in dance. The recursive arrows indicate that the consequences make the behavior more likely to reoccur in similar situations in the future (behavior maintenance).

is lower for psychological factors. Specifically, studies have found that genetic factors explain around 40 percent of the variance in personality traits at the population level, although the percentage does vary across different traits. Although this percentage may seem large, it does leave a large proportion to be explained by environmental and developmental factors. The latter includes upbringing (parental behaviors, sibling interactions, and surrounding milieu) and the social influences that we are exposed to as we grow up, such as school environments. Although no dance-specific research has been conducted into this particular issue, it seems logical to assume that dancers' personalities can be shaped by the dance environment or by individual teachers, if they spend a lot of time with them during childhood and teenage years (Allen & Laborde, 2014; Allen et al., 2015; Marchant-Haycox & Wilson, 1992). So it is likely that dancers are the way they are partly because particular kinds of people choose dance *and* because the dance environment helped shape them that way. We can also keep in mind that many dance styles are strongly female dominated and that women tend to have higher levels of conscientiousness and agreeableness and lower levels of emotional stability (Allen et al., 2011, 2013).

To further complicate matters, these factors interact via so-called gene-environment interactions (see Allen et al., 2013). While such research has not been performed in relation to dance, we may speculate that a dancer with a particular kind of genetic endowment is likely to experience slightly different kinds of interactions in her environment than another dancer with another kind of genetic endowment. As an example, a girl with a strong, muscular build who is also extroverted may be encouraged to try jazz dance. Her friend who has long turned-out legs, has a slim build, and is more introverted may instead be told that she is a good fit for ballet. To the extent that people act in line with such stereotypes and preconceived notions, they can live on over time. Similarly, dancers who mature at different times may be exposed to differences in their dance environment: Because late maturation has historically been associated with success in classical ballet, those who mature early may not succeed at audition to highly selective schools (Mitchell et al., 2016; see also chapter 12).

As you can see, personality is a complex soup of interacting factors, many of which cannot be observed directly (e.g., genetics). For a simplified visual illustration of the different factors contributing to dancers' personalities, see figure 1.3. The constructive take-home message in this regard is that there is much we can do to optimize dance environments so that as many dancers as possible can feel at home and be supported in their personality development when participating in dance, whatever their level. We may also need to become more aware of our own biases and traditions regarding what is seen as a desirable personality type for a particular style, class, or role. Is **introversion** praised ahead of extroversion when students are discouraged from speaking in dance class? Is openness to experience nurtured enough, so that we do not hamper creativity and choreography among students? Is emotional stability undermined when young people are placed in hierarchical, critical dance environments? Much research remains to be conducted into intriguing questions like these. In the meantime, we must use critical thinking and do our best to embrace individual differences.

Consequences of Personality

Research has established that personality affects a range of outcomes for both performance and well-being. While many of the studies and reviews cited here are from domains other than dance (typically sports), the small number of studies that do exist in dance appear to give similar results.

Performance-Related Consequences

Research into personality in sports and exercise has highlighted a range of performance-related correlates and consequences (for reviews, see Allen et al., 2013; Allen & Laborde, 2014; Steca et al., 2018).

› Performers with higher levels of conscientiousness seem to do better in sports. For instance, they are more likely to perform well in competitions and to compete at higher levels, likely because conscientious performers use behaviors such as good preparation strategies and have a strong work ethic.

› Performers with higher levels of extroversion and emotional stability are more prevalent at higher competitive levels.

› For those training and competing in groups or teams, agreeableness is beneficial to performance in a way it is not for individual performers.

› Performers with lower levels of emotional stability seem to do worse in sports. For instance, they are less likely to perform well

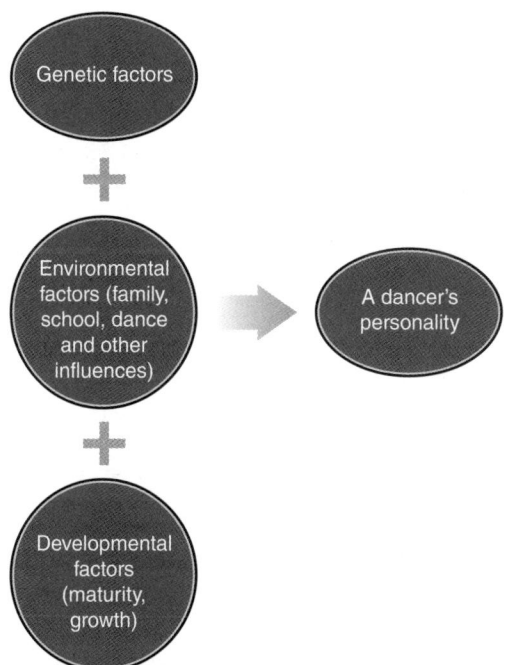

Figure 1.3 Genetic, environmental, and developmental factors all combine to create a dancer's personality.

under pressure and do not respond so well when unsuccessful.
- Persons with higher levels of conscientiousness are more likely to be physically active in life generally and to work harder when they exercise.

Against this backdrop, it would seem logical that conscientiousness is a personality trait that predicts performance (effort and success) also in dance. At the same time, we should be mindful of how success is defined. If success to you is winning dance competitions or mastering difficult technical feats, then conscientiousness is likely to be very valuable, because it is associated with being organized and diligent (table 1.2). Yet if your definition of success is more about emotional expression, artistry, and creativity, then openness to experience might be the more advantageous trait because it is associated with curiosity, imagination, and originality. Interestingly, a recent large-scale study found that a combination of openness to experience and intelligence were the best predictors of creative success in the arts (de Manzano & Ullén, 2018). A smaller study with students found that conscientiousness and intelligence (specifically spatial ability) were the best predictors of success in ballet (Jankovic & Bogaerts, 2021). Finally, it is important to keep in mind that personality is typically not systematically related to short-term success; instead, its effects seem to emerge over the longer term (up to several years; Allen et al., 2013).

Well-Being-Related Consequences

Just as personality can affect performance, it can have an impact on health and well-being. Some of these consequences are **intrapersonal**, while others are **interpersonal** (e.g., relationship satisfaction). Some key findings from research in this area are outlined next (for a review, see Allen et al., 2013; also see Allen et al., 2011). Most are derived from sports, but others come from domains such as work and the general population.

- People enjoy better self-esteem development as they go through life if they are emotionally stable, conscientious, and extroverted (Orth & Robins, 2014).
- Performers and leaders seem to be more committed to one another and experience better relatedness when levels of personality traits are high—that is, when they are highly agreeable, conscientious, extroverted, open to experiences, and emotionally stable.
- When performers and leaders perceive that they are dissimilar to one another (e.g., one is more extroverted than another), they instead experience lower commitment, relatedness, and satisfaction.
- Performers with higher levels of extroversion, openness to experience, and emotional stability use more adaptive coping skills (e.g., problem-solving), whereas those with low levels of emotional stability and openness to experience seem to use less adaptive coping skills (e.g., avoiding the problem).

In a rare study examining the Big Five among young dancers, it was found that neuroticism (i.e., low emotional stability) was associated with poorer self-regulation of eating attitudes (the ability to manage dietary intake in a healthy way; Scoffier-Mériaux et al., 2015). Their results also suggested that dancers who were less emotionally stable (e.g., more often feeling depressed) were, in part, less able to self-regulate their eating because they internalized thinness norms to a greater extent. Clinical psychology research similarly indicates that disordered eating can be predicted by lower emotional stability, lower levels of agreeableness and conscientiousness, and higher levels of openness to experience (Ghaderi & Scott, 2000). Similarly, persons with lower levels of emotional stability, agreeableness, and conscientiousness tend to report a more negative body image (Allen & Walter, 2016). An early study of personality with ballet students suggested that they were rather introverted, emotional, self-critical, and strongly motivated to achieve (Bakker, 1991). Although several aspects of this study (including its relatively small sample and outdated measurement tools) suggest we should not make too much of its conclusions, it is intriguing to speculate as to whether similar patterns would be found today.

In summary, research from several domains suggests that personality traits can both help and hinder people, in life generally and in specific activities such as dance. The most adaptive pattern appears to be high in all traits captured by the Big Five model.

Narrow Identity: Are Dancers at Risk?

Dance can take up more or less of our identities, and you have probably met many people who define themselves primarily, or perhaps exclusively, as dancers. Indeed, Turner and Wainwright (2003) wrote as follows about identity in classical ballet: "Professional ballet is not just something that you do—it is something that you are, and hence being a dancer is an embodiment of identity" (p. 284-285).

When a persons' identity (or *self-definition*) is primarily, or even exclusively, taken up by dance, this is known as having a **narrow identity**. Other related terms for this phenomenon include having a *unidimensional*, *foreclosed*, or *foreshortened* identity. In sports, **athletic identity** has been defined as "the degree to which an individual identifies with the athlete role" (Brewer et al., 1993, p. 237).

While all is going well, having a strong yet narrow identity (e.g., "I am a dancer") can be positive, because it is a source of positive identification with a group that nurtures commitment and gives a sense of meaning (Brewer et al., 1993; Pickard, 2015; Sabiston et al., 2018). Unfortunately, there are also several problems associated with having a narrowly defined dancer identity, especially when things do not go so well. These include difficulties in getting over mistakes, problems feeling at home in groups of non-dancers, struggles to see career possibilities in anything other than dance, and times of transition or injury being especially problematic (Ronkainen et al., 2016; Sabiston et al., 2018; Willard & Lavallee, 2016). Studies into the retirement experiences of elite gymnasts (Kerr & Dacyshyn, 2000) and ballet dancers (Willard & Lavallee, 2016) suggest that intensive early engagement in these activities had led to an early, intense, and singular focus and to lower role experimentation; as a result, the authors described the performers' identities as foreshortened or exclusive, and retirement became a very difficult process. If they were no longer performers—who were they?

Along similar lines, the authors of an ethnographic study with ballet dancers noted that injury and retirement can be deeply problematic for these dancers' identities because of the preoccupation with youthfulness, fitness, and ability in this art form (Turner & Wainwright, 2003; Wainwright & Turner, 2004; see also chapter 13). At the same time, some dancers reportedly dance better than ever after taking time off to have children, because this diversification of their identity makes them feel more free or broad-minded (Wainwright & Turner, 2004).

In another study, modern dancers with stronger dancer identities reported being less positive about their own bodies (Langdon & Petracca, 2010). An investigation with figure skaters took this one step further, finding that athletic identity strength was correlated with disordered eating symptoms (although other factors seemed to be more strongly predictive; Voelker et al., 2014). The authors reasoned that when an activity (sports, dance) is everything to a person, it becomes important to adapt oneself to fit in with the demands of that activity. For some, this adaptation goes as far as disordered eating, as they try to demonstrate their commitment or affirm their performer identities.

Notably, the potential problems outlined here may only result if the dancer identity is performance oriented. In other words, a strong affinity to dance may not be problematic unless this identity is also about needing to be competitive, successful, and socially recognized (Ronkainen et al., 2016; Voelker et al., 2014). These issues bear some similarity to the concept known as performance-based (or contingent) self-esteem, about which you can read more in chapter 3. Indeed, someone who identifies strongly as a dancer but sees dance mostly in terms of personal expression, social interaction, and helping others would likely not struggle as much when injured or transitioning as someone who sees dance as an arena in which to prove themselves as competent. The nature of the training climate is also likely to matter. Indeed, problems such as disordered eating are typically the result of complex interactions between personality and environments. For more about disordered eating, see chapter 14.

Dancers come in many forms. We should not assume that all dancers are at risk of a narrow identity, but when several of the following are true, there is likely to be an increased risk:

› The dancer has taken part in dance for many years, perhaps since early childhood.
› Dance is their number one interest.
› They spend many hours on most days of the week on dance.
› They come from a family of dancers.
› Most (or all) of their friends are dancers.
› Their romantic relationships are with dancers.
› Their career ambitions are strong and exclusively focused on dance.
› They are presently (or have been) enrolled in a school that integrates dance training with academic tuition, such that all their classmates (and perhaps all the students at their school) are also focused on dance.

As perhaps became clear when reading the preceding list, it is neither unusual nor surprising that dancers aspiring to become, or who already are, professionals can be at risk of a narrow identity (Daniels et al., 2005; Langdon & Petracca, 2010; Pickard, 2015; Willard & Lavallee, 2016). To avoid the associated risks, it is imperative to educate dancers about these matters and encourage them to diversify their interests and identities. A potential side benefit of this is wider and richer life experiences, which are highly valuable in choreography and boost expressivity on stage (see also chapter 7). In a recent study, ex-professional dancers strongly recommended diversification and "living as a whole person" to nurture confidence, life balance, and perspective; to cope with stress; and to help prepare for a second career (Kim et al., 2020). Contrast this with the following quote from a dancer in an international dance career transitions investigation:

> My feeling is it is unfair for parents and/or dance educators to allow a young dancer to stop exploring other interests and talents, seriously, all through their dance career. I was faced with having no clue about alternatives. I was a dancer, period. (Levine, 2004, p. 17)

For dancers seeking to expand their identities, it is important to avoid overload. Simply adding more activities to an already packed schedule is unlikely to be helpful. Therefore, use common sense and proceed with care when trying out the suggestions in table 1.3.

Table 1.3 **Steps Dancers May Take to Broaden Their Identities**

Small steps These may be suitable for the dedicated dancer who perceives no problems with their identity now and who does not have much time to explore things outside dance	Moderate steps These may be suitable for the dancer who is beginning to feel stifled by their narrow identity or who wants to ensure that there is more to their life than just dance	Big steps These may be suitable for the dancer who is experiencing problems related to their narrow identity (e.g., one who struggles to think of anything other than dance and fears retirement)
Take dance classes in several styles and with several teachers	Spend time regularly on other art forms or sports	Take up a hobby that has nothing to do with dance
Develop an evening habit of doing a non-dance activity such as reading fiction, chatting with non-dance friends online, or speaking to family members about non-dance matters	Make a habit of having one day per week spent entirely outside the dance world: exploring the city or nature, going to museums, or hanging out with friends	Create a plan to gradually reduce the percentage of waking time spent on dance-related activities (e.g., from 100% to 90% over three months, to 80% over the next three months, and so on) until balance is felt to have a positive impact
Take an interest in related art forms, such as music or theater	Deliberately spend more time with non-dance friends or relatives	Visit the workplaces or try out the hobbies of non-dance friends or relatives
Make an effort to watch films, read books, or play games that are non-dance-related	Take different kinds of dance classes in different dance schools or replace some dance time with gym or outdoor exercise	Gradually replace the number of hours spent in dance with hours spent on other forms of movement until balance is felt to have a positive impact
Subscribe to some non-dance-related social media	Subscribe to more social media that is non-dance-related than dance-related	Consider radically decreasing, or entirely removing, social media flows about dance

PERSON first DANCER second

Lettering art by Ink & Lise. Used with permission.

Go to HK*Propel* to download a full-sized version of this and other lettering art.

Paula: Case Study of Personality

Paula is a 37-year-old retired dancer. She left home early to pursue full-time training, which meant living with and taking both dance and academic classes with the same peer group. Because her family lived far away, she could only get home on the holidays. During her teens, Paula's dancer identity grew stronger and stronger; she was not simply a person who did dance—she was a dancer! In many ways, this was positive: she was highly committed, did not mind giving up other activities or missing parties in favor of extra rehearsals, and really enjoyed the company of other like-minded dancers. Moving into adulthood, Paula's strong dancer identity kept facilitating commitment, hard work, and success. Not even being pushed around by choreographers who suddenly wanted to rehearse late into the night felt problematic. Given that life was dance, where else would she be? Ultimately, this loyalty made her a favorite with teachers and management—they could always rely on Paula to go the extra mile.

The strong enmeshed dancer identity eventually began to take its toll. Paula saw how friends began to cultivate outside interests in preparation for post-dance careers; others planned to have children. At first dismissed as a lack of commitment on their part, Paula eventually saw that what they were doing was smart—unlike her, they were not putting all their eggs into one basket. Despite this growing realization, Paula's own retirement process was a messy affair. While changes in company management coinciding with recurrent injuries to her back made her feel that it was time, she never truly wanted to leave. The connections she had in dance were simply not the same in normal workplaces, and she missed the closeness and performances of her dance career so much. As she puts it, "if you take away half a person, how do you expect them to cope well?" Although Paula gradually made peace with her post-dance career in retail, she still wonders what might have been done differently.

Composite case study created on the basis of a conversation with Tama Barry, former professional ballet dancer and PhD candidate in social psychology at the University of Queensland, Australia.

| Form 1.1 | GET PRACTICAL: IDENTIFYING DIFFERENT PARTS OF YOUR IDENTITY |

Just like personality has aspects of both stability and flexibility, identity can be conceived of as both relatively stable and as something in gradual change across the life span. One way to consider identity is via the metaphor of a tree. Some trees are stable structures, anchored both deeply and widely in their surroundings with strong roots. Other trees are wispier, with few and perhaps shallow roots in the surrounding earth. For our purposes, the tree is the person, and the roots are their various identities. Now imagine a storm. *Which tree is likely to wave its branches in the wind around its stable structure, and which is likely to snap a branch or two—or even be uprooted?* Of course, the tree with more and deeper roots is likely to be more resilient to "storms," whether these are unwarranted criticisms from an important teacher, unfulfilled dreams of being cast for a particular role, or career-changing injuries. Now ask yourself: *How is my root system (i.e., my identity)?* To delve into this issue in a bit more depth, do the following exercise.

INSTRUCTIONS

1. Start by labeling the roots with your various identities. For instance, you may write "son/daughter," "student," or "barista" on some, and "dancer" or "teacher" on another.

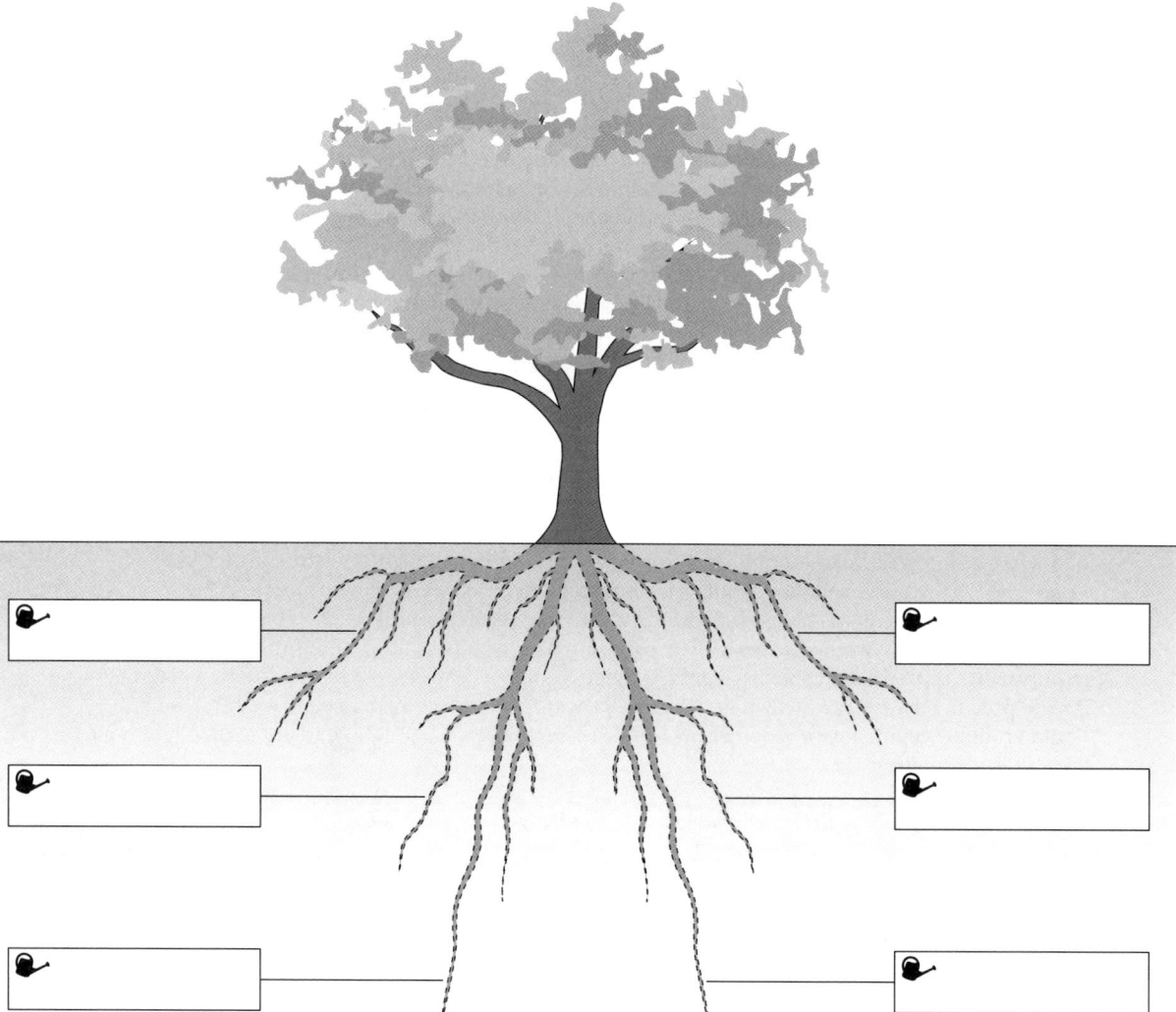

Form 1.1 *(continued)*

2. Fill in (strengthen, emphasize) the dotted lines of the roots to varying degrees corresponding with how strong you see each identity as being. For example, your student identity may be stronger or weaker (less central to you) than your dancer identity.
3. Consider which roots you are nurturing and how. Write this down in the adjacent text boxes.
4. Consider your different identities.
    › *How many are there? Are they similarly strong?*
    › *When it storms, which roots do I rely on? Will they be strong enough to hold me upright?*
    › *Are there any roots that I have been ignoring?*
    › *Are there any new identities that I would like to experiment with and grow?*

Go to HK*Propel* to download this form.

From S. Nordin-Bates, *Essentials of Dance Psychology* (Champaign, IL: Human Kinetics, 2023).

CRITICAL ASPECTS OF RESEARCH INTO PERSONALITY

1. Up-to-date research about personality in dance is very sparse. While there is some research in the area, much of it was published several decades ago (Bakker, 1988, 1991; Hamilton et al., 1989; Marchant-Haycox & Wilson, 1992; Taylor, 1997). All except one (Bakker, 1991) comprised very small samples (22-59 dancers) in cross-sectional designs and conceptualized personality differently from how it is described in this chapter. Some considered personality facets such as self-esteem and body image and are therefore cited in other chapters in this book.

2. Researchers have often conducted their studies using some aspect of personality as the independent variable and some performance-related or well-being-related outcome as the dependent variable (Allen & Laborde, 2014). Research of this kind can explore questions such as "Do particular personality traits predict particular outcomes?" However, performance and well-being may also affect personality over time. For instance, a dancer who has great success and is often put in the spotlight both on stage and in the media over a period of many years may well have his personality shaped in a different way from a peer who is less successful and often met by rejection. To get to the heart of questions such as these, longitudinal and bidirectional as well as qualitative studies would be required.

3. Conscientiousness appears to be a valuable personality trait across domains and for many different outcomes (e.g., performance, relationship satisfaction). The diligence and hard work typical of conscientious individuals are similar to the aspect of perfectionism known as *perfectionistic strivings*. In chapter 2 you will see that such traits and associated behaviors may be adaptive to a point, beyond which they become counterproductive (e.g., working too hard).

4. Future dance-specific research is especially warranted in some specific areas:
   - *The Big Five model of personality.* For instance, to what extent are conscientiousness and openness to experience predictive of success in different dance genres?
   - *How personality may be shaped by dance.* For instance, does dance training contribute to increases in conscientiousness and in general personality stability?
   - *The welcoming of different personality traits in dance.* For instance, how can teachers work with dancers with different personalities, making as many as possible feel welcomed and supported?

KEY POINTS AND RECOMMENDATIONS REGARDING PERSONALITY IN DANCE

1. Personality is likely to have a significant impact on the engagement with, experience in, and success in dance. Most likely, scoring high in the personality traits outlined in the Big Five model is beneficial in dance, just as in other domains. That is, dancers are more likely to flourish when they are *open to experiences*, *conscientious*, *extroverted*, *agreeable*, and *emotionally stable*.

2. Identifying oneself primarily as a dancer is a double-edged sword. When all is going well, it can be a source of belonging and pride; when encountering chal-

lenges such as injury and retirement, it can lead to an identity crisis. Dancers and teachers alike would do well to broaden their identities such that they can feel a sense of stability and meaning even when dance is not going well.

3. While personality is partly determined genetically and influenced by early experiences (in particular, the family), there is reason to believe that dance training can also affect personality development. It is a responsibility and an honor, therefore, for dance educators to try to support the development of dancers so they become *open-minded*, *conscientious*, *extroverted*, *agreeable*, and *emotionally stable* individuals—not just for dance, but for life.

2

Perfectionism

"Striving for excellence motivates you; striving for perfection is demoralizing."

Harriet Braiker, psychologist

CHAPTER OBJECTIVES

After reading this chapter, you will be able to

1. describe what perfectionism is, including its two dimensions: perfectionistic strivings and perfectionistic concerns;
2. discuss the nature of perfectionism in terms of its stability (traitlikeness), potential to change (malleability), and domain generality versus domain specificity;
3. outline a range of maladaptive and adaptive consequences of perfectionism and how these differ for perfectionistic strivings and perfectionistic concerns;
4. understand basic principles regarding the management of perfectionism (including what individual dancers and teachers may do) and when to seek clinical help;
5. identify cognitive distortions that are typical of perfectionists; and
6. think critically about the nature and impact of perfectionism in dance settings.

Key Terms

- 2 × 2 model of perfectionism
- black-and-white thinking
- cognitive distortions
- conditional regard
- interactionist perspective
- mixed perfectionism
- multidimensional
- non-perfectionism
- perfectionism
- perfectionistic cognitions
- perfectionistic concerns (PC)
- perfectionistic strivings (PS)
- person–environment fit
- pure evaluative concerns perfectionism (pure ECP)
- pure personal strivings perfectionism (pure PSP)
- social desirability
- traitlikeness

The term *perfection* derives from the Latin *perfectiō* and concerns the ideas of being ideal, faultless, flawless, the best possible, and unsurpassed. It is also related to being infallible or saintly. A perfectionist then is unwilling to settle for anything less than perfection. This provides important hints of perfectionism's *motivational qualities* (i.e., perfectionism drives a person to strive) as well as some of its affective *consequences* (e.g., perfectionists are typically unsettled).

What Is Perfectionism?

Perfectionism is an aspect of personality that has been given particular attention in the performance psychology literature, including in both sports and dance. In the Big Five model of personality (chapter 1), it is most closely related to conscientiousness, although aspects of perfectionism known as perfectionistic concerns are also related to low emotional stability (also known as *neuroticism*).

Although dance genres and contexts vary widely, perfectionism is sometimes considered an attractive attribute in many dance settings. Some dancers may even brag about being perfectionistic as a socially acceptable way of saying "I work hard," "I am diligent," or "I don't give up easily," attributes that many dancers are proud to display and that many teachers look for. A certain logic exists in the way perfection is deemed as worth striving for; specifically, if striving for and working toward something (e.g., performing a solo well) is good, then surely striving and working toward the utmost (perfection, flawlessness, idealistic ideals) is even more impressive and worthwhile. Many dance styles are also performed to audiences who, in part, pay to see something that they cannot do themselves. Other dancers compete against one another in festivals and competitions where only the best get noticed. Little wonder then that dance can become a perfectionistic climate in which only the best is seen as good enough and striving more is better. Modern dance legend Martha Graham famously said, "Practice is a means of inviting the perfection desired."

While perfectionism may be considered desirable, we can also readily find examples of perfectionism leading to undesirable consequences, ranging from mild (low mood, irritability) to moderate (low self-confidence, high performance anxiety) and severe (burnout, eating disorders). In this chapter, we will delve more deeply into the intriguing topic of perfectionism. What is it practically? What does research say about its nature and consequences? How can we work with it so that it hampers neither happiness nor progress?

Is Perfectionism a Trait?

Perfectionism is often denoted as a trait, and longitudinal investigations typically find that it is largely stable over time (e.g., Nordin-Bates et al., 2016). Occasionally, however, **perfectionistic cognitions** have been studied as a statelike expression of perfectionism (e.g., Hill & Appleton, 2011). In a small intervention study with young ballet students, a series of workshops focused on imagery and implicit learning seemed to reduce the frequency of perfectionistic cognitions of the students during ballet class (Karin & Nordin-Bates, 2020).

Another angle on the issue of the **traitlikeness** of perfectionism is to consider whether people are generally perfectionistic in all areas of life (domain general) or only in some, such as dance (domain-specific). Large positive correlations between perfectionism scores of athletes in sports and in general life suggest that it is domain general (Hill, 2016). Other researchers have found that sport-specific measures of perfectionism are better able to predict sport-related outcomes and argue that perfectionism is best considered domain-specific (e.g., Gotwals et al., 2010). Bridging these two positions, one informative study found that while *some* people are perfectionistic generally (across domains), *most* are perfectionistic only in selected domains (Stoeber & Stoeber, 2009). Indeed, athletes in another study were more likely to be perfectionistic in sports than in their studies and more perfectionistic in their studies than in life generally (Dunn et al., 2005).

Most likely, perfectionism is highest in the domain in which a person is most highly invested: where they spend the most time and energy, and where the most is at stake. This reasoning could also be applied to the issue of whether perfectionism is more prevalent at higher levels of expertise. Although no investigation into differences in perfectionism between dancers at different levels exist, researchers have shown that athletes at higher competitive levels are more perfectionistic (Rasquinha et al., 2014). Again, this is likely because they are more invested in sports than their lower-level counterparts. In sum, perfectionism is not something that comes and goes from one day to another as a truly statelike thing (e.g., emotions) might, but neither is it completely unchangeable. It may affect a dancer mainly in dance or in several life domains.

Structure of Perfectionism: Strivings and Concerns

Historically, perfectionism has been described in many and varied ways, but common to many of these has been the idea that perfectionism has two sides or comes in two versions. For instance, researchers have used terms such as *healthy* versus *unhealthy* or *adaptive* versus *maladaptive* perfectionism. Today such terms are often frowned upon because they mix up the nature of something (what perfectionism is) and its consequences (i.e., whether perfectionism leads to adaptive vs. maladaptive outcomes; Hill, 2016). Moreover, the debate around what perfectionism really is has subsided somewhat in recent years with many agreeing that perfectionism can be said to comprise two dimensions known as **perfectionistic strivings (PS)** and **perfectionistic concerns (PC**; Stoeber & Otto, 2006; also, Hill, 2016). These neutral and now more generally agreed upon terms are outlined in table 2.1 and will be used for the remainder of this chapter. It is the existence of these two dimensions (and their subdimensions, i.e., "ingredients") that underpins the often-stated notion that perfectionism is **multidimensional**. In other words, perfectionism is not one thing but a combination of several. Before moving forward, it is important to emphasize that PS is not simply about striving *high*; rather, it is about striving for *perfection*. As such, it is by its very nature a relatively extreme characteristic.

Perfectionistic concerns include self-criticism, worries, and a sense of never being good enough.

Table 2.1 **Key Features of Perfectionistic Strivings and Perfectionistic Concerns**

Dimension	A dancer with high levels of this dimension is . . .
PS	• always in pursuit of high (even unrealistic) goals • constantly seeking flawlessness • diligent and focused • hard working • holding themselves to high standards • sometimes organized, neat, and tidy*
PC	• very self-critical • feeling as though they are never good enough, never doing enough • worried about mistakes • fearful of failure • very concerned about and attentive to what others think of them (e.g., parents, teachers, peers, judges)

*Research findings differ as to whether organization, neatness, and tidiness are considered integral parts of PS. They are perhaps best viewed as relatively often, but not always, present when a person has high levels of PS.

Origins of Perfectionism in Dance

Many believe that perfectionism is common in dance or at least in styles such as classical ballet. Indeed, autobiographies such as that by Karen Kain et al. (1994) and the case study of Daria Klimentová (Nordin-Bates & Abrahamsen, 2016) show strong lived examples of perfectionism in ballet. Based on her own experiences and those of the young ballet dancers she studied over several years, Pickard (2015) wrote about perfectionism as endemic in the ballet world. Questionnaire-based studies have to some extent borne this out, indicating that perfectionistic tendencies seem to be somewhat common in vocational schools (Atienza et al., 2020; Cumming & Duda, 2012; Nordin-Bates et al., 2011) and among elite dancers (Eusanio et al., 2014) who focus on ballet and/or contemporary dance as well as among young competitive dancers (Molnar et al., 2021). Still, we should be cautious with terms such as *common* or *high level* because there are no cutoff scores for the questionnaires typically used to study perfectionism. This means we cannot count proportions of dancers scoring above versus below a cutoff and draw conclusions about perfectionism prevalence. Instead, we study tendencies and interpret the mean scores of the samples studied (e.g., whether or not the mean is close to the top of the rating scale). In fact, this is true for almost every topic in performance psychology and in this book; an exception is disordered eating, a clinical topic for which distinct cutoff scores and criteria exist (chapter 14).

Because perfectionistic tendencies appear to be at least somewhat common in dance, it becomes important to consider why. Are perfectionistic individuals likely to turn to dance, or is perfectionism nurtured by the dance environment? Although no studies in either dance or related domains have explored this intriguing question, both are likely to be somewhat true. First, it is known that social influences can nurture perfectionism. Most research in this area has focused on the impact of parents and the influence that they have on their children (e.g., Appleton & Curran, 2016; Flett et al., 2002; Speirs Neumeister et al., 2009). In such works, researchers have typically explored one or several of four potential explanations proposed by Flett et al. (2002). They argued that parents may nurture perfectionism through the following pathways:

› *Social expectations*. Perfectionism is more likely to develop in a child when caregivers hold high expectations and provide **conditional** (rather than unconditional) **regard**. In other words, conditional self-worth and perfectionism are likely outcomes if parents show their approval only in response to good (or even exceptional) behavior and performance.

› *Social reactions*. Children are more likely to develop perfectionism when parents are harsh, very critical, or chaotic. This involves children trying to be perfect to escape punishment, shame, and humiliation, or to feel in control in a chaotic environment.

› *Social modeling*. Perfectionism may develop through imitation—that is, children observ-

ing and modeling the perfectionistic behaviors of their parents.
> *Anxious rearing.* Perfectionism may also develop in response to anxious parenting; specifically, having parents who are overly worried about mistakes and imperfections might result in children becoming perfectionistic.

Research has supported the first three pathways, whereas less evidence currently exists for the fourth (Appleton & Curran, 2016; Flett et al., 2002; Speirs Neumeister et al., 2009). Overall, it is clear that parents can make their children become more (or indeed less) perfectionistic. But what about social influences from persons other than parents? A handful of studies suggest that social agents such as sport coaches can affect an athlete's perfectionism. For instance, athletes who perceive their coaches to be more controlling also report higher levels of perfectionism—and higher symptoms of burnout (Barcza-Renner et al., 2016; for more on the topic of controlling coaching, see chapter 11). In a recent longitudinal study, athletes who perceived pressure to be perfect, from either parents or coaches, were more likely to report elevated levels of both PS and PC (Madigan et al., 2019). Interestingly, only perceptions of coach pressure predicted increases in perfectionism over time.

To date, there are no studies specifically focused on how dance teachers may nurture or thwart the perfectionism of their dancers; however, dancers and teachers interviewed for a study on perfectionism and creativity gave several accounts of how teachers can indeed do both (Nordin-Bates, 2020). Another study indicated that more perfectionistic dance teachers and aesthetic sport coaches reported supporting the autonomy of their performers to a lesser extent (Nordin-Bates & Jowett, 2022). Other studies have shown that low levels of either autonomy or autonomy support are associated with higher levels of perfectionism (e.g., Haraldsen et al., 2019; Jowett et al., 2021; Nordin-Bates, 2020). Thus, it is possible that more perfectionistic dance teachers nurture perfectionism among their dancers partly because they support their autonomy to a lesser extent (or actively thwart their need for autonomy; chapter 5).

A case study of a retired ballerina, Daria Klimentová, further suggests that teachers and dance partners can affect perfectionism in dancers through the motivational climate they create (Nordin-Bates & Abrahamsen, 2016). Klimentová gave vivid examples of how a particularly positive, supportive partnership toward the end of her career was associated with lower levels of both PS and PC. Before that, she endured harsh criticism from a director while also having to train and perform with a partner with whom she was barely on speaking terms. It is perhaps unsurprising that this critical, blame-filled atmosphere coincided with a time in her career when she was particularly perfectionistic, anxious, and unhappy. Other scholars have similarly argued for the importance of taking an **interactionist perspective**, with consideration for the characteristics of both people and their environments (e.g., Haraldsen et al., 2019; Penniment & Egan, 2012). For example, the increased susceptibility of female ballet dancers to disordered eating is likely to result partly from an interaction between heightened perfectionism and exposure to thinness-related learning (i.e., being in an environment with strong cues that being thin is good; Penniment & Egan, 2012).

Clearly the behaviors of teachers, and perhaps also other aspects of the dance environment, are important in shaping perfectionism in dancers. Consider the other possibility: Do people with perfectionistic tendencies self-select into dance? Here too we lack evidence to say much about the extent to which this occurs. However, researchers in other areas have explored a concept known as **person–environment fit** based on the premise that persons feel and perform better in environments that fit their personalities (Amiot et al., 2006). Perfectionistic persons (e.g., those who seek flawlessness, set high goals, work diligently, seek to avoid failure, and tend toward **black-and-white thinking**) might be more likely to feel that they fit into the rigorous and hierarchical training structure that is typical of classical ballet (when taught in a traditional manner). Persons who are non-perfectionistic and enjoy uncertainty and open-ended exploration might avoid ballet in favor of, for example, contemporary dance. If so, it is perhaps both a blessing (that there are different dance styles to suit different people) and a curse (e.g., if dance preserves the status quo and inadvertently promotes perfectionism).

THINKING CRITICALLY

In your experience,
- Is perfection valued in your dance settings and style(s)?
- Does perfectionism seem to be common in dance?
- Does training in a particular style or with particular teachers affect perfectionism?

Consequences of Perfectionism

Now that we have clarified what perfectionism is, we can consider what it might lead to. Because its consequences are more clear-cut, we begin with PC and then move on to the mixed consequences of PS.

Maladaptive Consequences of Perfectionistic Concerns

The research literature clearly shows that PC leads to negative outcomes (Hill et al., 2018, 2020). If a dancer only has mild concerns, the negative outcomes are likely also relatively mild and infrequent; for instance, a dancer who is a little worried that she has not practiced enough before a competition is likely to have somewhat elevated anxiety. Her anxiety is probably specific to that competition rather than generalized to many situations. However, dancers with high levels of PC are likely to experience strongly debilitating outcomes and experience them more often. For instance, a dancer who thinks he is not good enough and worries greatly over what his teachers and parents will think of him when he performs is likely to experience intense anxiety. He might struggle to sleep or focus on anything other than the upcoming performance. He might withdraw socially, not even thinking about encouraging his friends who will also perform. If this continues over time, he is also at risk of problems such as depression, burnout, injury, and disordered eating.

In line with these examples, large-scale meta-analyses have confirmed that PC is associated with a wide range of problems (Hill et al., 2018, 2020):

> *Performance-related consequences.* Performers with elevated PC are more likely to hold ego-oriented and avoidance-oriented achievement goals and are more often motivated by extrinsic factors such as pressure. As outlined in chapter 5, such motivation is related to performance-related problems such as avoiding practicing things that one does not feel competent at, burning out, and dropping out. Higher levels of PC can also put performers at risk of injury (Madigan et al., 2018).

> *Well-being-related consequences.* Performers with higher levels of PC are more likely to report symptoms of ill-being, including anxiety, anger, burnout, depression, and disordered eating.

If perfectionistic concerns are so bad, why do people have them? One explanation is that PC can feed PS, which leads to partly positive outcomes. For instance, a dancer who worries about not having practiced enough (mild PC) will practice more if doing well is very important to her (mild PS; figure 2.1). This extra practice may lead to improved performance, thus alleviating worry. When it functions this way, worries are a self-regulatory mechanism whereby we align behavior (in this case, dance practice) with our goals (doing well).

This dance example is in line with a more fundamental explanation, which is that humans evolved

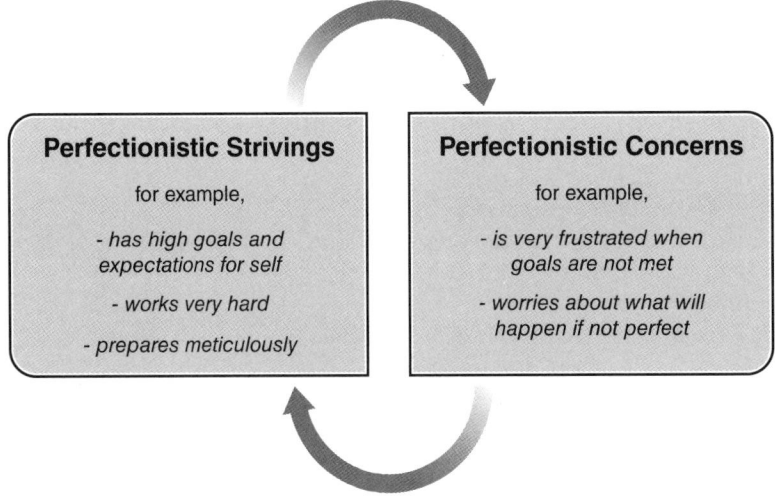

Figure 2.1 Perfectionistic strivings and concerns typically feed one another, which helps explain why they are typically positively and strongly correlated.

to maximize chances of survival (chapters 1 and 4). Worry and avoidance have survival value if they lead to vigilance against threats and make us take preventive action. In much the same way, dancers who avoid competing because they are afraid to fail will avoid failing and avoid the unpleasant anxiety. Dancers who stand at the back of the studio may not be commented on; thus, they avoid feeling evaluated. In fact, we all regularly do things to seek out rewards (e.g., sense of competence, praise) and avoid unpleasantness (e.g., looking silly, critical comments; see introduction). While this can be helpful, it is problematic if we start to avoid the very things we like to do or could learn from. For instance, a dancer who always stands at the back and never looks at the teacher (or himself in the mirror) may not learn as much. A dancer who is so afraid to fail that she never improvises or cocreates may not develop skills essential to the professional career she would like to have.

In short, avoidance may have short-term benefits (e.g., relief, lower anxiety) but long-term problems (e.g., lesser development). A tendency to focus on short-term benefits can also help keep perfectionism going over time (figure 2.2). In this functional analysis example, the prospect of performing a solo on stage is highly stressful to a perfectionistic dancer, who never wants to be seen doing anything wrong. To cope with her anxiety, she trains exceptionally hard and prepares everything in minute detail (i.e., overpreparation, a safety behavior). When the performance goes okay, the short-term effects include relief and lowered anxiety; often this is enough to maintain a behavior over time. Yet because her overpreparation is reinforced, long-term effects include not learning what would have happened if she had not overprepared and risking overtraining and injury.

Mixed Consequences of Perfectionistic Strivings

Although the evidence regarding PC is consistent, evidence regarding PS is inconsistent (Hill et al., 2018, 2020). On the positive side, some studies indicate that PS can enhance performance in sports (Stoeber et al., 2009) and music (Stoeber & Eismann, 2007). Similarly, interview studies have given examples of how PS can enhance performance by strengthening motivation, focus, and adherence (Hill et al., 2015; Nordin-Bates & Abrahamsen, 2016; Nordin-Bates & Kuylser, 2020). One dance student explained it as follows: "I mean you get further, I think, if you are perfectionistic . . . I have always been this way, striving for perfection. I think 99% of dancers are very much like that. You can't get anywhere if you're not" (interviewed in Nordin-Bates & Kuylser, 2020, p. 6).

Of course, there should be more to life than dance, and the performance benefits of PS may mean that dancers drive themselves rigorously in the pursuit of perfection with little balance between dance and

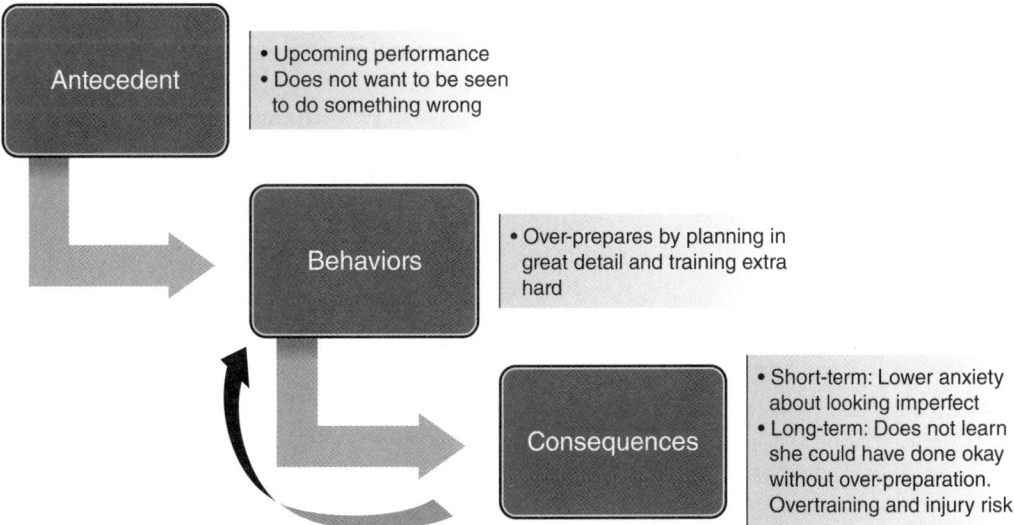

Figure 2.2 Functional analysis example of how perfectionism may manifest in dance. The recursive arrow indicates that the short-term consequences make the behavior more likely to reoccur in similar situations in the future (behavior maintenance).

other aspects of life. In a study that included musicians alongside dancers and athletes, a composer explained it succinctly: "I think as a [performer] I've benefitted from being a perfectionist. As a person I probably haven't" (Hill et al., 2015, p. 246).

So PS can boost performance, but it can also lead to less desirable outcomes. Indeed, when performers are given feedback that they are failing on a task, those higher in PS are more likely to withdraw their effort (Hill et al., 2011) and go on to perform worse than their less perfectionistic peers (Anshel & Mansouri, 2005). In one study, high levels of not only PC but also PS predicted disordered eating development among young female dancers over time (Nordin-Bates et al., 2016).

Why are the correlates and outcomes of PS so wide-ranging? Several points are worth keeping in mind. In particular, all quantitative studies in this area report strong positive correlations between PS and PC. This tells us something important: Dancers with PS are rarely completely free from PC (figure 2.1). Instead, the very nature of striving for perfection means that doubts and concerns are likely to grow, and dancers with high levels of PS are likely to experience at least some of the negative outcomes from PC. This is especially likely over time because nobody succeeds all the time, least of all perfectionists who set their goals so high. Dancers will also meet challenges such as injury, deselection, and disappointment. When dancers who strive for perfection meet these bumps in the road, the ground is fertile for doubts and concerns to grow. Why wasn't I selected? Should I have worked even harder? Why don't they like my style?

Even in the absence of PC, high levels of PS may be seen as a vulnerability (for examples, see Hill et al., 2015; Nordin-Bates & Kuylser, 2020). For instance, high levels of PS can lead to excessively hard, even obsessive, work that increases injury risk. It can also lead to rigidity and a narrow belief that improving one's technique, or perhaps even just one particular variation, is all that matters. Such rigidity can negatively affect creativity, for instance (Nordin-Bates, 2020). As a final example, a person with very high levels of PS is more likely to have their identity exclusively based in dance and consider all non-dance-related activities as unworthy distractions from their goal pursuit. Such a strong focus on oneself and one's development can boost short-term performance but is unlikely to nurture healthy relationships or a sense of balance, especially in the face of challenges such as injury, deselection, or retirement (for more about narrow identity, see chapter 1).

Understanding the Consequences of PS and PC

Several different approaches have been taken to study the correlates and effects of perfectionism. Historically, many focused on relationships between different dimensions (or subdimensions) of perfectionism and one or several outcome measures. For instance, researchers asked whether holding oneself to high standards (a subdimension of PS) had different correlates to concern over mistakes (a subdimension of PC); the answer is yes. For example, in one of the earliest studies into multidimensional perfectionism in dance, Carr and Wyon (2003) found that concern over mistakes and doubts about actions (two subdimensions of PC) were associated with dancers perceiving the motivational climate in their dance studio to be more ego-involving (e.g., punishment for mistakes; chapter 11). A recent study showed that physical and emotional exhaustion were negatively predicted by PS and positively predicted by PC; the reverse was true for levels of vigor (Jowett et al., 2021).

In sports, investigations of this type (known as taking an independent effects approach; Jowett et al., 2016) are plentiful and have yielded important information about the different—and sometimes similar—correlates of PS and PC. As you already know, however, PS and PC are typically strongly and positively correlated. In practice, this means dancers who have high levels of PS are likely to also have high levels of PC and vice versa. Making conclusions about the independent effects of PS and PC then becomes difficult because most people display some level of both.

Some researchers have investigated correlates of perfectionism by considering PS and PC in combination, for instance, by using cluster analysis to identify groups of performers with different combinations of PS and PC. One such study identified one group of dancers with perfectionistic tendencies (41% of the sample), one with moderate perfectionistic tendencies (44%), and one with no perfectionistic tendencies (15%; Nordin-Bates et al., 2011). Comparing these groups showed that the more perfectionistic dancers experienced more debilitative cognitions. For instance, the group with elevated perfectionistic tendencies reported higher levels of both cognitive and somatic anxiety, lower self-confidence, and more frequent debilitative imagery (e.g., imagining themselves making mistakes) than the other groups.

A more recent approach to understanding the interactive effects of PS and PC is to use the **2 × 2 model of perfectionism** (Gaudreau & Thompson, 2010). In this model, it is posited that persons may

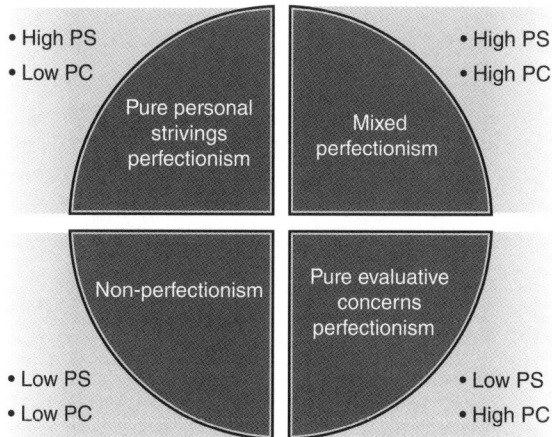

Figure 2.3 The 2 × 2 model of perfectionism.
Adapted from Gaudreau and Thompson (2010).

display perfectionism in three different guises in addition to non-perfectionism (figure 2.3).

As illustrated, the 2 × 2 model suggests that persons with high levels of PS and low levels of PC are displaying **pure personal strivings perfectionism** (pure PSP). Persons with low levels of PS yet high levels of PC are said to display **pure evaluative concerns perfectionism** (pure ECP; although whether persons who do not strive for perfection should be described using the epithet *perfectionism* can be disputed; Nordin-Bates & Kuylser, 2020). Persons with high levels of both constructs are said to display **mixed perfectionism**, and those with low levels of both would be said to display **non-perfectionism**. Researchers in both sports and dance eagerly adopted the 2 × 2 model to study perfectionism, and many valuable findings have emerged. While they are not all in line with the original hypotheses of the 2 × 2 model authors, the following findings from research using the model are informative (for a comprehensive review, see Hill et al., 2020):

› Depending on the outcome studied, pure PSP can be either more or less advantageous than non-perfectionism. For instance, performers with pure PSP seem to have higher intrinsic motivation and performance than their non-perfectionistic peers, but they also report higher extrinsic motivation, dietary restraint, and depressive symptoms in some studies. In dance, pure PSP has been associated with higher levels of engagement and lower levels of burnout than non-perfectionism (Jowett et al., 2021). In other studies, pure PSP dancers did not differ from their non-perfectionistic peers in terms of self-esteem, body dissatisfaction, and fear of failure (Cumming & Duda, 2012; Quested et al., 2014). In a recent investigation, dancers with high scores for pure PSP were more likely to endorse the goal of dancing for skill improvement and less likely to endorse the goal of dancing to meet expectations of others than were dancers with high scores for non-perfectionism (Molnar et al., 2021). However, there were no differences between pure PSP and non-perfectionism for goals such as enjoyment, appearance, or health.

› Pure ECP is highly problematic. For example, literature indicates that persons with pure ECP report higher amotivation, anxiety, and depressive symptoms than non-perfectionists. In dance, a recent investigation revealed that pure ECP was associated with higher levels of burnout and lower levels of engagement than any other type of perfectionism (Jowett et al., 2021). Similarly, Molnar et al. (2021) found that pure ECP was characterized by the least adaptive motivational profile.

› Mixed perfectionism seems to have (no pun intended!) mixed effects—although those with mixed perfectionism sometimes fare better than their pure ECP peers, this is not always the case. For instance, several dance studies suggest that both groups report similar levels of ill-being (e.g., body dissatisfaction, burnout symptoms, endorsement of extrinsic goals; Cumming & Duda, 2012; Molnar et al., 2021; Nordin-Bates et al., 2017; Quested et al., 2014). In one recent study, mixed perfectionism was associated with significantly *worse* scores for anxiety, exhaustion, and controlled forms of motivation than was pure ECP (Haraldsen et al., 2021). Dancers with mixed perfectionism also experience more problems than peers with pure PSP in terms of their feelings, cognitions, and performances. For example, they are more likely to work toward extrinsic goals such as improving appearance (e.g., Molnar et al., 2021).

Generally, the presence or absence of PC is a critical determinant of which group (model quadrant) seems to yield the best versus worst outcomes. In dance, several studies have been informed by the 2 × 2 model (Cumming & Duda, 2012; Haraldsen et al., 2021; Jowett et al., 2021; Molnar et al., 2021; Nordin-Bates, 2020; Nordin-Bates & Kuylser, 2020; Nordin-Bates et al., 2017; Quested et al., 2014). These authors typically caution educators to be mindful of dancers with elevated levels of PC—that is, dancers with mixed perfectionism or pure ECP. For instance, these dancers might need help to see that mistakes are an important part of any learning process. Such dancers are clearly at risk of a range of problems related to their dance involvement. They also seem to be numerous (13.19% to 30.92%), at least in the samples studied to date (young dance students primarily focused on ballet).

Qualitative investigations can help deepen our understanding of what the different intrapersonal combinations of PS and PC really mean in practice. For instance, a dancer characterized as having pure PSP reported having very high yet task-oriented goals, keeping a strict work ethic, but not worrying about mistakes or especially about others' opinions of her (Nordin-Bates & Kuylser, 2020). Her peers with mixed perfectionism placed a similarly high value on goals and hard work, although some of their goals seemed to be avoidance oriented (chapter 5). They also held a more mixed view of mistakes (i.e., as varyingly more and less acceptable), and they cared deeply about what important others, such as teachers, thought of them. The latter was true also of a dancer characterized as having pure ECP. He did not set high goals for himself, yet he worried about the expectations and opinions of others. When his strivings were elevated, such as around performance time, they also seemed to become rigid.

Finally, dancers characterized as non-perfectionists were considered (Nordin-Bates & Kuylser, 2020). Their concerns were indeed low because they worried little about the opinions of others or over mistakes. Yet their strivings were highly varied, likely a consequence of the different ages of the dancers in this group. Specifically, two younger dancers reported vague or nonexistent goals, but an older dancer reported both high and specific goals alongside a diligent work ethic. What is going on here? Why is such a dancer characterized as a non-perfectionist? To understand this question, it is important to keep in mind that it is *perfectionistic* strivings that were in focus, not high strivings or striving for excellence. To set high goals, work hard, and persevere is typically adaptive, and dancers who do these things should not be labeled as perfectionists!

How Can Perfectionism Be Managed?

When perfectionism is clearly problematic, clinical support is strongly recommended. In sport and clinical psychology, decreases in perfectionism have been noted not only following cognitive behavioral therapy (CBT) undertaken in person with a therapist (e.g., Gustafsson & Lundqvist, 2016) but also after using a self-help book (Donachie & Hill, 2020) or via the internet (e.g., Shafran et al., 2017). Growing evidence shows third-wave CBT strategies such as mindfulness and self-compassion help alleviate the pressures associated with perfectionism (e.g., Gustafsson & Lundqvist, 2016; Lee-Baggley et al., 2016; Mosewich et al., 2013).

Aside from clinical interventions, what can dancers do to manage subclinical perfectionism in their daily lives and prevent it from becoming problematic? Can teachers help? Answers to these questions must be tentative because we do not have a solid evidence base to suggest how perfectionism can be effectively managed in dance specifically. However, the experiences and recommendations of performance psychology consultants (Gustafsson & Lundqvist, 2016; Lee-Baggley et al., 2016; Nordin-Bates & Abrahamsen, 2016) are a useful source of guidance. Research into the antecedents of perfectionism in several domains can also form a starting point in formulating some cautious advice. Table 2.2 illustrates potential perfectionism management techniques for use by dancers and teachers and provides help in determining when it might be time to seek professional help from a qualified therapist.

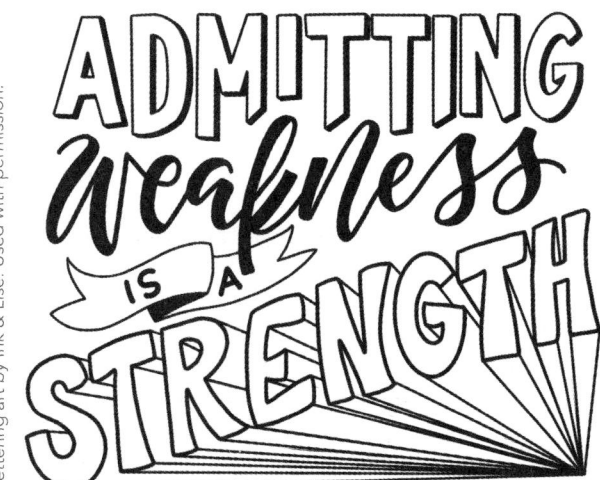

Go to *HKPropel* to download a full-sized version of this and other lettering art.

Lettering art by Ink & Lise. Used with permission.

Table 2.2 **Perfectionism Management Techniques and Advice About When to Seek Qualified Professional Help**

	What dancers can do	What teachers can do	When to seek professional help
High levels of PS	• Keep in mind why you dance in the first place • Set goals focused on artistry and self-improvement • Avoid comparing yourself to other dancers • Keep a training diary to identify potential overwork or rigidity • Plan for rest, recovery, and fun • Ensure there are other activities and roles in your life • Practice mindfulness • Try self-help books for perfectionism*	• Help set realistic and meaningful goals focused on self-improvement • Nurture intrinsic motivation by focusing on joy and meaning-making • Be aware of goals and practice habits becoming rigid • Point out the importance of rest, recovery, and fun • Encourage a dance–life balance	• When strivings become unrealistic and the dancer feels unable to take any joy in effort or progress (because "it is never enough") • When strivings become clearly obsessive or inflexible (e.g., the dancer allows himself/herself no slack despite tiredness or illness) • When striving for perfection in dance takes up so much of identity, time, or energy that there is no room for anything else
High levels of PC	• Deliberately make some mistakes to see what happens • Turn up to practices and performances without feeling 100% prepared (i.e., not overprepared) • Seek out teachers and classes where the focus is constructive and failure is seen as normal and good for learning • Trust yourself and how an exercise feels, rather than always looking to the teacher first • Focus on positive, constructive things related to music, artistry, and audience communication • Be open about struggles and imperfections (e.g., share imperfect pictures on social media)	• Role model a positive view of mistakes • Focus class structure and feedback on self-improvement • Encourage dancers to give themselves feedback and not always rely on teachers • Help dancers focus on the present moment (e.g., artistry) • Include creative exploration • Meet avoidance with personalized tasks • Share your own struggles and imperfections	• When levels of worry and doubt start to interfere with progress and well-being (e.g., difficulty sleeping or taking time off from dance) • When the dancer feels unable to make mistakes • When the dancer starts to avoid situations that feel threatening, when the pursuit of these would actually be of use to them and their goals (e.g., auditions) • When there seems to be risk of ill-health such as depression or disordered eating

*For example, Antony & Swinson (2009).

Peter: Case Study of Perfectionism

Peter is a dance student in full-time vocational training who prides himself on his work ethic. He is organized, focused, and goal oriented. In fact, these qualities have made him a favorite with teachers, who praise him for his dedication and attention to detail. One teacher even praised Peter's qualities in front of the other students, suggesting they were the kinds of habits that it takes to become a professional dancer. At this point, Peter beamed with pride. In everyday life, however, he is rarely proud of his accomplishments; instead, his extremely high goals and the rigorous standards he sets for himself ensure that there is almost constant dissatisfaction. Around performance time, such feelings are intensified because of the increased pressure to perform well—or indeed, perfectly. For example, Peter has strong anxiety reactions which include stomach upsets, catastrophic thinking, and sleep difficulties.

After two years of intense training, pressure, and stress, a new dancer joins Peter's class in the school, and they could not be more different. Where Peter is perfectionistic and structured, John is laid-back and disorganized. One day, John simply laughs after making a mistake on stage and Peter is amazed; he begins to watch John more closely. How can he be so relaxed about things? Surely that can never work. And how can he just stand there, at the front of the class, seemingly without a worry in the world when he doesn't even know the exercise properly? Yet over time, it becomes clear that making mistakes isn't so bad—at least John carries on regardless! When Peter inadvertently falls over in front of the teacher one day, the world does not collapse; instead, the teacher simply gives him some advice about how to move forward. Slowly but surely, Peter begins to experiment with how he plans, behaves, and evaluates himself. After some time, he even dares to show up to rehearsal without feeling 100 percent prepared. Although stressful at first, the extra time in bed that his reduced warm-up time allowed him was quite beneficial, only in a different way.

Composite case study created on the basis of the author's own consulting and research experiences in dance.

GET PRACTICAL: IDENTIFYING THE COGNITIVE DISTORTIONS TYPICAL OF PERFECTIONISTS

From time to time, we all fall into mental potholes known as **cognitive distortions** (irrational thought patterns) in our everyday lives. However, perfectionistic individuals do so more often, and they suffer the consequences in terms of lowered mood, well-being, and performance. In this exercise, you can practice identifying some of the cognitive distortions that are typical of perfectionists and how they can be dealt with. To do this task thoroughly, try to keep track of distortions as and when they emerge rather than having to remember them afterward (e.g., via a training diary or app). Choose whether to do the exercise for yourself or for someone you know well (e.g., a dancer that you teach). Of course, you cannot know all that goes on inside another person's mind, but you may notice such things as their reactions and explanations when things go wrong. The accompanying worksheet (form 2.1) can then support you in asking constructive questions.

Form 2.1 GET PRACTICAL: IDENTIFY THE COGNITIVE DISTORTIONS TYPICAL OF PERFECTIONISTS

COGNITIVE DISTORTION	ASK ONE OR MORE OF THE FOLLOWING:	MY EXAMPLE (SHORT DESCRIPTION, WITH DATE AND SETTING)	WHAT I ASKED	WHAT I NOTICED (FELT, LEARNED)
Black-and-white thinking results in • Seeing things as good or bad, success or failure, with no in-betweens • Feeling a roller coaster of emotions	1. Can the situation be viewed in a different way? 2. Is it possible that the truth is more complex? 3. What evidence is there that it is really like this? Is there evidence that it could be different? 4. If a friend felt like this, what would I/you say to them? 5. How is this thought helpful or hurtful? 6. Does this way of thinking help with attaining goals?			
Mental filtering is characterized by • Focusing on the negative, filtering out positive aspects • Often feeling down				
Catastrophizing causes a person to • Focus on what can go wrong and expect the worst • Exaggerate the importance of small mishaps, such as a mistake in class • Often feel anxious				
Tyranny of "should" makes a person • Often feel like they should do more and do better • Punish themself when not behaving "as one should" • Often feel guilty				
Emotional reasoning results in • Interpreting feelings and thoughts as truth (e.g., I know I am incompetent, because I can feel it) • Feeling that emotions control them, rather than the other way around				
Overgeneralizing causes a person to • Generalize one or a few qualities into a negative judgment about one's whole self • Mix up performance (e.g., failing a dance exam) with person (I am a failure) • Use strong, emotionally laden language (e.g., loser, always, never, worst) • Often experience strong negative emotions				

EXAMPLE: Thursday, May 1, in the studio. Catastrophized the fact I fell over and felt like I will never make it. Tried question 4 above and realized I would tell a friend it was really no big deal, everybody falls over, and the teacher says we should fall over sometimes to know we have really pushed our limits. Felt a bit better after trying that thought a few times.

From S. Nordin-Bates, *Essentials of Dance Psychology* (Champaign, IL: Human Kinetics, 2023).

Go to HKPropel to download this worksheet.

CRITICAL ASPECTS OF RESEARCH INTO PERFECTIONISM

1. Compared to many other topics in performance psychology, perfectionism might appear relatively well researched in dance. However, the number of studies is still very low compared to those from sport and clinical settings. Like for many topics in dance psychology, most studies have used cross-sectional designs, thus limiting the conclusions that may be drawn about consequences or effects.

2. There may be aspects of **social desirability** affecting results of studies in this area. *Social desirability* (or "faking good") occurs when a person tries to portray themselves in a socially desirable way that may or may not be deliberate. Regarding perfectionism, social desirability might be an issue if dancers see perfectionism as desirable, even as the way a proper dancer should be.

3. Future dance-specific research is warranted in certain areas such as:
   - *The origins of perfectionism.* For instance, to what extent do perfectionists self-select into dance training, and to what extent does the dance environment nurture perfectionism?
   - *The long-term consequences of perfectionism in dance.* For instance, what happens to dancers with high PS when they encounter challenges such as injury or not being selected at audition?
   - *The management of perfectionism in dance.* For instance, how can schools work with dancers to help them strive for excellence rather than be hampered by perfectionistic ideals?

KEY POINTS AND RECOMMENDATIONS FOR PERFECTIONISM IN DANCE

1. Striving for perfection can lead to some positive outcomes but also an increased risk of negative outcomes. This is especially likely over time because perfectionists typically do not handle challenges and failures well. Perfectionism should therefore be considered a vulnerability. Dancers need care both from themselves and others to avoid the associated risks.

2. Striving high or striving for excellence are not the same as striving for perfection.
   - The negative consequences that may come from PS likely do so because of the unrealistic nature of striving for something that is fundamentally unachievable. It is the perceived need or obligation to continuously push for unrealistic goals that feed rigidity, obsessiveness, and an excessively narrow focus on oneself and one's own goals.
   - Striving for excellence allows flexibility, individuality, and openness to exist alongside high goals and hard work. As such, it is far more likely to lead to success as well as a better quality of life.

Self-Esteem and Self-Confidence

"Every day there must be something I can't do, otherwise, it's boring."

Dominique Monet Robier, dancer

CHAPTER OBJECTIVES

After reading this chapter, you will be able to

1. describe self-esteem, self-confidence, and self-efficacy, including their similarities, differences, and influences on each other;
2. discuss the nature of and problems inherent to contingent self-esteem;
3. outline a range of sources and consequences of both self-esteem and self-confidence;
4. critically discuss the notion of overconfidence;
5. understand basic principles regarding enhancement of self-esteem, including what individual dancers and teachers may do and when to seek clinical help;

6. explain the six sources of self-efficacy and apply basic recommendations to nurture self-efficacy/self-confidence in dance;
7. identify the reasons why you are more or less confident; and
8. think critically about the nature and impact of self-esteem and self-confidence in dance settings.

Key Terms

contingent self-esteem	mastery model	self-constructs
coping model	observational learning	self-efficacy
emotional states	persuasion	self-esteem
imaginal experiences	physiological states	vicarious experiences
mastery experiences	self-confidence	

The term *esteem* is from the Latin *aestimare*, which means to value or appraise something. A person with high **self-esteem**, therefore, is someone who holds themselves in high regard and sees themselves as inherently valuable. The term *confidence* derives from the Latin term *confidentia*, meaning to have full trust in something. A person with high **self-confidence**, then, trusts their ability to accomplish tasks. These inherent differences in etymology are often lost in modern everyday language, where the two terms are often used interchangeably. After reading this chapter, you will better understand the important differences and partial overlaps between the constructs.

What Are Self-Esteem and Self-Confidence?

Self-esteem is how we value ourselves as people and is related to the terms *self-worth* and *self-regard*. Therefore, there is nothing "dancey" about self-esteem, although persons with high versus low self-esteem are likely to view their experiences in dance differently. More specifically, people with high (good, stable) levels of self-esteem believe they are worth as much as others and are generally positive toward themselves. They have a solid foundation on which they can build such things as learning and mental health. They do not become depressed when they perform poorly, struggle to learn something, or get deselected because they have a sense that they are worthwhile regardless of their achievements. In other words, they are more resilient. In contrast, persons with low (poor, transient) self-esteem are negative, are self-critical, and see themselves as less worthy than others. Such an unstable foundation means that learning experiences, mental health, and many other important parts of life become more difficult to achieve and maintain.

Self-esteem is an important foundation for **self-confidence**, which relates to how we evaluate our abilities to perform different tasks. For instance, a self-confident dancer might say things like "I am good at jazz dance" or "Yes, I should be able to manage that solo within the next three weeks." A person with low self-esteem will struggle to build self-confidence because they are typically critical of themselves. At the same time, it is important to be clear about the conceptual distinctions between self-esteem and self-confidence. To help you, key distinctions between the constructs are outlined in table 3.1.

Although self-esteem and self-confidence are different, they do affect each other. In particular, your level of self-esteem will affect how confident you feel in any given situation, such that dancers with high self-esteem are more likely to also be confident and vice versa. Additionally, the relationship is somewhat reciprocal; that is, a person with low self-esteem who is placed in healthy environments where self-confidence is allowed to grow can also build self-esteem over time. This is because managing tasks and doing things well is a part of our sense of self. In so doing, however, we must be aware of the perils of so-called **contingent self-esteem** (also known as *contingent self-worth* or *performance-based self-esteem*; e.g., Crocker & Knight, 2005).

With contingent self-esteem, a person hinges their own worth on their performances such that they feel worthwhile only when they perform well. If their performance level goes down, so does their self-esteem. It is easy to see how this is detrimental

Table 3.1 **Conceptual Distinctions Between Self-Confidence and Self-Esteem**

	Self-confidence	Self-esteem
Mostly concerned with . . .	Doing ("I can dance well")	Being ("I am a good person")
Level	More specific; we can have different levels of self-confidence for different activities (e.g., dance vs. schoolwork)	General; affects all areas of life
Ease of affecting	Easier to affect (e.g., by a teacher structuring classes so that students can experience success)	Harder to affect; typically requires systematic work or strong life experiences
After progress or success	Typically increases ("I am getting better at this!")	Should be undisturbed ("Dancing well does not mean I am a better person")
After a mistake or failure	Typically decreases ("I wasn't able to do it as I wanted")	Should be undisturbed ("Underperforming does not mean I am a bad person")

to a person and how it can lead to perfectionistic behaviors such as overpreparation and overwork (Curran, 2018). People with contingent self-esteem may struggle to say no to requests and demands, and often they do not let themselves rest and recover properly. They behave this way because only by performing well can they feel a modicum of worth, positivity, and relief. But, as all dancers know, the quality of this year's performance cannot rely on last year's training. We need to train regularly and repeatedly. For the person with contingent self-esteem, training and performing becomes a never-ending hamster wheel of striving, working, performing, and evaluating: Was I good enough this time? No wonder that contingent self-esteem is a known risk factor for burnout (Gustafsson et al., 2018).

Origins of Self-Esteem

Because self-esteem is the basic sense of our own worth and how much we like ourselves, it will come as no surprise that it is often shaped early on in life and is relatively stable over time (Orth & Robins, 2014). In other words, self-esteem is a trait (for more information about traits vs. states, see chapter 1). Some early scholars in this field found that dancers often suffer from low self-esteem, high levels of self-critique, and similar problems (e.g., Bakker, 1988; 1991; Bettle et al., 2001; Marchant-Haycox & Wilson, 1992). However, more recent and sometimes larger investigations refute this view by demonstrating moderate to high levels of self-esteem (Cerny Minton, 2001; Nordin-Bates et al., 2011b; Quested & Duda, 2011; Walker et al., 2011). For example, Cerny Minton (2001) found no differences in self-esteem between dance and non-dance students, and Nordin-Bates et al. (2011b) found no differences in self-esteem between injured and uninjured dancers. In a comparison of young talented dancers of different ages, the younger students (in the 10-12 and 13-15 age groups) reported greater self-esteem than their older peers (16-18 years; Walker et al., 2011).

To understand self-esteem among dancers, then, we must take a more fine-tuned view than simply considering dancers as a homogeneous group. For example, factors such as gender and the types of motivational climates that dancers are exposed to over long periods of time are likely to matter. We should also keep in mind that dance is far from the only thing affecting a dancer's self-esteem; indeed, genetics (e.g., Neiss et al., 2002), family environments, and learning experiences are typically considered to be the strongest influences on personality (chapter 1).

Early life experiences that help build self-esteem include unconditional love, warmth, and understanding. Conversely, children are more likely to develop low or unstable self-esteem when they do not feel loved, feel misunderstood, or are not given the attention they need. When love and attention are contingent on the child behaving in a particular way, contingent self-esteem may develop (Curran, 2018). For instance, a boy whose mother is a real dance fan might perceive that she is only fully focused on him when he performs well in his dance classes. Because children naturally desire parental love and attention, the boy might pursue dance and try to perform well because this seems the best way to get his mother's undivided attention and positive regard. If this continues over time and is not counteracted by other strong influences (e.g., influences from another parent), the boy may develop a self-esteem that is contingent on performing well, reflected in thoughts such as "I have to dance well or I am useless," and "Nothing I do is really worth it if it is not recognized by others."

Another source of low self-esteem can be feeling like the odd one out (Fennell, 2016). This is interesting in relation to dance because dance is not always considered worthwhile. For instance, if you are from a very academic family in which everyone else gets a traditional university education, you may feel like the odd one out if you want to become a dancer. Your family may not openly criticize your choices, but if you perceive that they never really understand you and do not see the value in what you do, this could undermine self-esteem. ("My talents are not as useful as those of others in my family.") Another example relates to boys in dance. Because many dance forms are strongly female dominated, it can be challenging for boys to take up dance and keep it up during adolescence and into adulthood. Some end up feeling like the odd one out both in dance (as the only boy in his class, for instance) and at school (as the only one who does not spend his free time on more traditionally masculine pursuits, such as team sports). Unless these boys are given unconditional love and acceptance from other sources (e.g., family members, teachers), they are at risk of low self-esteem. ("Nobody understands me; I don't really fit in anywhere.")

Can dance influence self-esteem? Although we lack reliable evidence regarding the development of self-esteem in dancers specifically, there is every reason to believe that dance training, including teacher behaviors, will help shape self-esteem. This is because

> many dancers train early in their lives while identity is still under development,
> many find dance personally important and are strongly passionate about it,
> many see their teachers as idols and role models and naturally want to please them, and
> some see their teachers more than they see their parents.

Dance is more likely to shape low self-esteem if dance is a major part of your identity (chapter 1); if you train a lot with the same teacher; if it is very important to you to do as they say; and if your training climate is critical, fault-finding, and person-oriented (i.e., commenting on what you are rather than what you do). Indeed, those who grow up with harsh, critical feedback risk having their self-esteem undermined. One reason is because harsh criticism nurtures self-criticism—the critical voice of the teacher becomes your own internal critical voice. This is particularly dangerous if there is a sense that one must always be on the lookout for mistakes and problems. In such environments, dancers are more likely to develop low self-esteem because their focus is honed to be critical.

Thankfully, dance also has every possibility of raising the self-esteem of its participants (e.g., Cerny Minton, 2001). (Specific suggestions on this topic are presented toward the end of this chapter.) Dance interventions for non-dancers (e.g., schoolchildren) also seem capable of positively affecting self-esteem and related constructs (e.g., body image, physical self-perceptions). A recent review concluded that the available evidence seems promising, but not all studies find positive effects and studies in the area would benefit from larger samples and more reliable designs (Schwender et al., 2018).

Consequences of Self-Esteem

As noted, self-esteem is concerned with the value that a person places on themselves, whereas self-confidence is concerned with the strength of a person's belief that they can master tasks. Therefore, it is unsurprising that performance-related outcomes have primarily been studied in relation to self-confidence, while well-being-related outcomes have been investigated extensively in relation to both constructs. The associated sections of this chapter reflect this fact.

Given the nature of self-esteem, it is obvious that people with better self-esteem feel more secure, are happier, and take the initiative more often (Baumeister et al., 2003). Research strongly indicates that people with higher self-esteem fare better in life (Orth & Robins, 2014). For instance, they enjoy better physical and mental health and are more satisfied in their relationships. They also perform better at work (Orth & Robins, 2014).

People with low levels of self-esteem are more insecure and self-critical. They think: "I'm no good, I will never make it. I just don't have what it takes." They also tend to discount good experiences with statements or thoughts such as "I was just lucky," "It only worked because I rehearsed like crazy," or "I couldn't have done it without my teacher." Dancers with low self-esteem are more likely to believe that minor mishaps are really problematic or even that their mistakes say something about them *as people*. For these dancers, falling out of a complicated pirouette series is not just a bit annoying, but a sign that they are a useless dancer and a useless person. Unsurprisingly, this conveys an increased risk of mental ill-being; as such, low self-esteem is part of the problems underpinning common diagnoses such as depression and disordered eating. Indeed, several studies demonstrate that low self-esteem predicts disordered eating among athletes (Petrie et al., 2009) and dancers (Nordin-Bates et al., 2016; see also chapter 14). Studies like these often note a strong negative correlation between self-esteem and perfectionism; it is logical, therefore, that many of the cognitive errors typical of perfectionists (e.g., black-and-white thinking; chapter 2) are typical also of people with low self-esteem.

As illustrated in figure 3.1, low self-esteem is often maintained over time because of the behaviors and cognitions involved. The core belief underpinning low self-esteem is a sense of not being good enough. To protect oneself from the possible (or imagined) consequences of this belief, a dancer with low self-esteem who is faced with the situation of a challenging audition may use strategies such as practicing a huge amount. She may also avoid the situation altogether. In the latter case, the core belief is typically reinforced directly: "I am clearly not good enough, I couldn't even face doing the audition." If she does audition, she will either perform well or perform poorly. In the former scenario, she is likely to attribute the success to her strategy—that she only made it because she practiced like crazy, because her teacher helped her, or perhaps because the jury was blind. In the latter scenario, the attribution becomes a direct confirmation of the core belief—"I didn't think I was good enough and here is the proof: I failed despite all my hard work!" As you can see, the core belief is reinforced regardless, making for a vicious circle. For more about what keeps low self-esteem going over time, see Fennell (2016).

Low self-esteem can be problematic, but high self-esteem is no magic cure-all (Baumeister et al., 2003). Indeed, you may know someone with an inflated sense of their own importance. Such narcissists are typically not pleasant and experience numerous problems despite their high self-esteem. Therefore, it is important to promote a healthy sense of self-esteem that is based on feeling secure, feeling worthwhile, and being a good person rather than on being infallible, superior, or entitled.

Origins of Self-Confidence

There are several ways to understand self-confidence and its origins. In sports, the most commonly studied models have been Vealey's (1986, 2001) model of sport confidence and Bandura's (1977) model of **self-efficacy**. There is overlap between the two, but here we focus on the latter because of its demonstrated applicability in several domains and because it translates well to dance.

According to Bandura (1977), self-efficacy is a situation-specific form of self-confidence. So, although you may have good confidence for tap dance generally, your confidence in performing

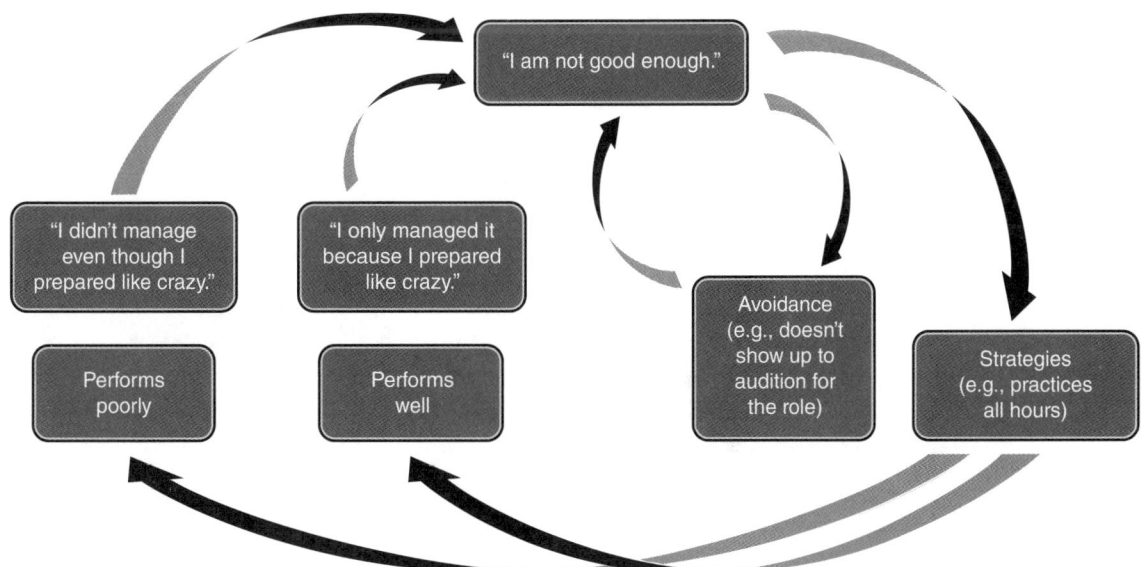

Figure 3.1 The vicious circle of how low self-esteem can be maintained over time.

one tap sequence well can be high while your confidence in another sequence is low. Figure 3.2 further illustrates the nature of self-efficacy. Self-efficacy is the specific expression of self-confidence, so it is appropriate to say, "I feel confident about that step," rather than the more cumbersome "I feel efficacious about that step." Also illustrated is the hierarchical structure of the self (Sabiston et al., 2018; Shavelson et al., 1976), which links all of the **self-constructs** considered in this chapter: self-esteem, self-confidence, and self-efficacy.

The reciprocal (bidirectional) relationships between self-constructs are also shown in figure 3.2. Thus, you can see how the effects of self-esteem permeate self-confidence and efficacy, so that a person with high levels of self-esteem is more likely to also be confident, both generally and in specific situations (a top-down approach; Sabiston et al., 2018). Although it is harder and takes longer, repeated exposure to positive experiences that help strengthen a dancer's self-efficacy can also grow into self-confidence for dance. If dance is an important part of that dancer's identity, and especially if they have similarly positive experiences in other domains, their self-esteem can also blossom over time (a bottom-up approach; Sabiston et al., 2018). Finally, if a dancer can be confident about a multitude of tasks (self-efficacy) and areas of dance (e.g., different styles and situations), then their confidence can be said to be more *robust* (Hays et al., 2007; Thomas et al., 2011). Robust confidence is advantageous because it helps a person to tackle challenges and bounce back after failure (i.e., be more resilient).

Bandura's Self-Efficacy Theory

Bandura developed self-efficacy theory as part of a broader social-cognitive theory (1986, 1997; also Maddux, 1995). Self-efficacy theory proposes that people are likely to engage with and put effort into tasks that they believe they can successfully perform—that is, that they have greater self-efficacy for. On the contrary, people tend to avoid doing tasks when they do not think they will be successful.

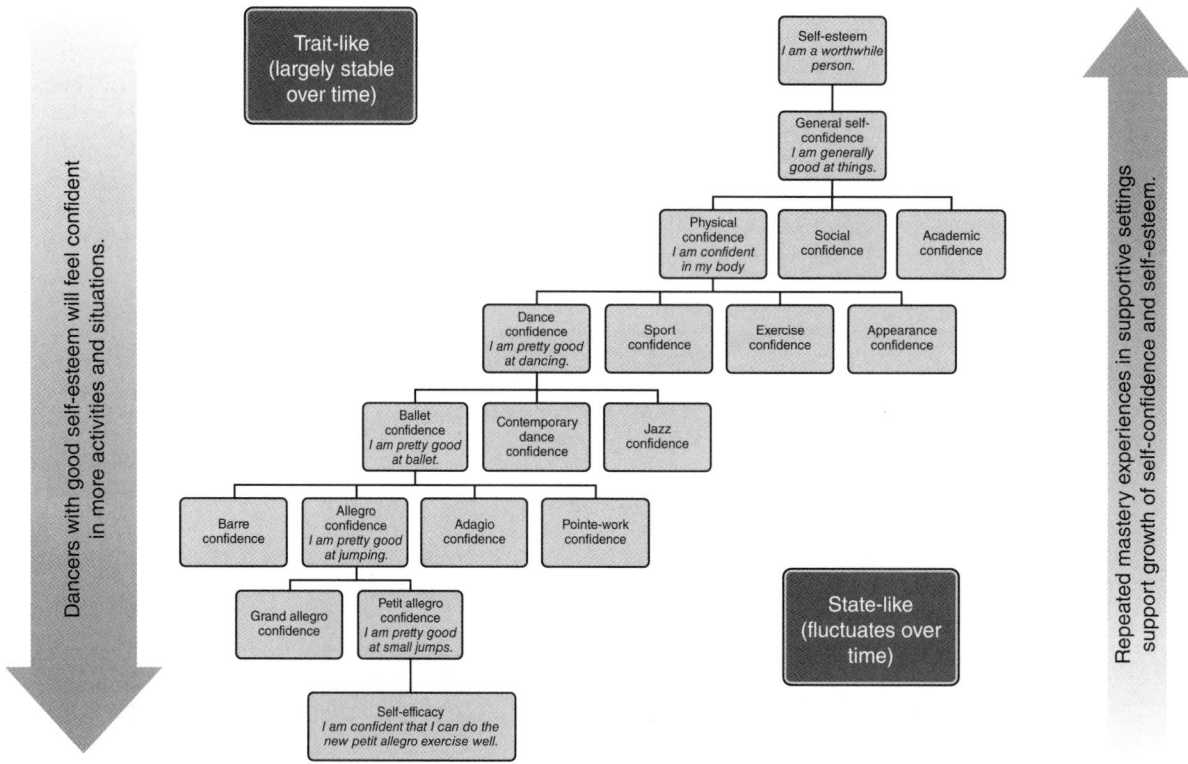

Figure 3.2 A simplified version of a hierarchy of self-constructs ranging from self-esteem to self-efficacy via various subtypes of self-confidence. All subtypes of self-confidence are examples only and are intended to be illustrative but not exhaustive. Only one subtype of self-confidence is expanded upon per line for the figure not to become unreasonably large. The specific hierarchy of self-constructs will be unique to each individual.

Freely after Shavelson et al. (1976, p. 408) and Hagger and Chatzisarantis (2005, p.75).

The six sources of self-efficacy detailed next give a comprehensive yet straightforward way of understanding how confidence can develop, thereby also providing a foundation for understanding how it can be strengthened.

Mastery Experiences (Performance Accomplishments)

The principle of **mastery experiences** reflects the old adage that "I've done it before, so I can do it again," and is the strongest source of self-efficacy (Bandura, 1997). For instance, if you have done a complicated bit of partner work repeatedly in practice, your confidence for doing it on the stage will be higher than if you had never managed it before. As such, success typically raises confidence, and failure typically lowers it. Mastery experiences may also be considered more broadly to include various forms of preparation (e.g., technical, physical, psychological) and states of health (e.g., injury, illness, fitness). Indeed, most of us will feel more confident when we are well-prepared and in good health compared with when we have just sustained an injury or have not managed to prepare as we prefer.

For this source of confidence to be stable, it is important that it is based on aspects that are largely within the dancer's control. This might include effort and preparation. ("I feel confident because I know I have prepared myself well and done everything I can.") If the dancer is very ego oriented (chapter 5), their sense of mastery and success is inherently fragile because it is derived from being superior to others—an uncontrollable source. Therefore, it is wise to base evaluations, feedback, and self-talk on reminders of more controllable aspects (e.g., having managed a skill before, being well prepared) rather than less controllable aspects (e.g., being the best, having been praised last time). Behind these basic principles are also at least two important considerations:

1. *The relationship is bidirectional.* While success usually leads to better confidence, better confidence also contributes to success (e.g., Feltz, 2007; Moritz et al., 2000; Samson & Solmon, 2011). The opposite is also true. So, with a combination of hard work and luck, dancers can end up in a positive spiral in which growing confidence and success spur one another on. Conversely, poor preparation, bad luck, or avoidance can leave a dancer in a negative spiral in which dwindling confidence and failure feed off one another. Importantly, any effects depend on an actual change of behavior because of confidence levels. For an example, consider the functional analyses presented in figure 3.3. In the first, the dancer is successful in her attempt to perform a particular pirouette. As a result, she feels happy and proud, which is reflected in good posture and an approach to the remainder of the class that is full of zest. Because of these behaviors, she learns well and her confidence starts to grow; therefore, she becomes more likely to succeed again with her pirouette.

   In the second example, the dancer does not succeed at first; in fact, she falls over in front of the class. Because she feels both annoyed and ashamed, her posture becomes droopy and she plays it safe for the rest of the class (i.e., puts in less effort and energy). Unsurprisingly, her learning becomes suboptimal, and her confidence is impaired; therefore, she is less likely to succeed with her pirouette next time too.

2. *People interpret events differently.* Confidence tends to be fairly stable, and one reason is because people who are already confident are more likely to look for positive experiences and to interpret ambiguous information in a positive way. For instance, consider Emma, a confident contemporary dance student who fell in class recently, and the teacher asked, "What was that, Emma?" But Emma can barely remember that it happened. She could laugh at the teacher's question because she herself saw it as a silly mistake that was quite funny. Conversely, people who are already low in confidence are more likely to look out for negative experiences and to interpret ambiguous information in a negative way. So, if the same thing happens to Carolyn, whose confidence is far lower than Emma's, she vividly remembers, even weeks later, the mistake that she was so embarrassed by. She also interprets the teacher's question, "What was that, Carolyn?" as evidence that the teacher sees her as not good enough. The latter is more likely for perfectionistic dancers. Consider, for instance, the words of a highly perfectionistic dancer: "I'm not a confident person whatsoever. I achieve amazing things, but it doesn't help with the confidence whatsoever" (previously unpublished quote from a dancer interviewed in Walker & Nordin-Bates, 2010).

   For this dancer, confidence was continuously fragile because, however well she performed

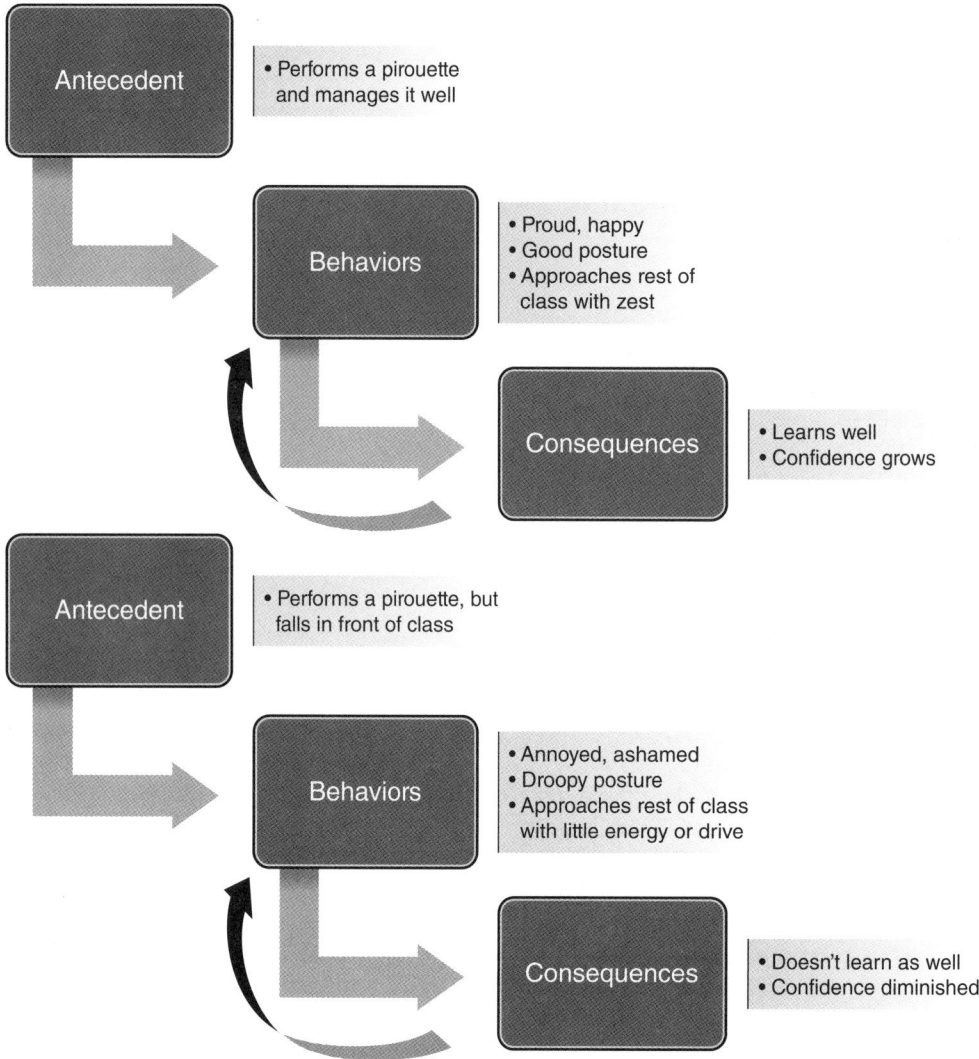

Figure 3.3 Functional analysis examples illustrating how self-confidence may manifest in dance. The recursive arrows indicate that the consequences make the behavior more likely to reoccur in similar situations in the future (behavior maintenance).

in the eyes of others, she was always finding fault and never felt good enough. She also attributed her success to factors largely outside (e.g., talent) rather than within (e.g., effort) her own control.

Vicarious Experiences (Modeling)

Vicarious experience as a source of confidence is about seeing something done; in essence, "If she or he can do it, so can I." By observing others we gain understanding about how tasks can be accomplished, and our certainty grows that we too can do them. The following quote from a contemporary dancer explains it nicely:

I do remember when I was younger seeing a piece performed . . . And I just felt that I could do that piece with them. And I did. In the end, I did that piece with that company. So it was like something I felt I could do . . . and all my teachers at that point were going "tss; you started too late; you'll be a really good teacher because you've done anatomy at university." . . . So I felt I really needed some self-confidence. And I would go and see other companies and watch them working, I would take workshops and, you know, get in there and do the stuff. But particularly watching performances made me think I could do it.

(Previously unpublished quote from a dancer interviewed in Nordin & Cumming, 2005)

In dance, it is typical for teachers to demonstrate exercises in class. While perhaps not primarily considered to be a confidence-raising tool, demonstrations enhance confidence because they help dancers understand. A full treatment of this topic is outside the scope of this book, but if you are interested in how to optimize this source of confidence and how teacher (and peer) demonstrations of skills affect learners, continue reading in the area known as **observational learning** (e.g., McCullagh & Weiss, 2002). Indeed, the increased availability of images and videos online surely means that dancers (and teachers) are engaging in observational learning more often than ever before. Whether this has led to dancers who are more confident is an open question, but the following aspects are important to keep in mind when considering how vicarious experiences (observations) affect self-efficacy:

> *Model competence.* Generally, we watch competent persons perform the skill we want to learn, and we are often reluctant to demonstrate anything we do not feel competent doing. This agrees with evidence suggesting that self-efficacy (and indeed learning) is better served when observing more competent models (Bandura, 1997; Usher & Pajares, 2008).

> *Model similarity.* Despite the logic of competent persons demonstrating skills to less competent learners, there is a major caveat: if the observer does not see themselves as similar to the model, they identify less with them and their confidence is not enhanced as much as when observing a model that is perceived to be more similar (Bandura, 1977; Usher & Pajares, 2008). This is a critical consideration in dance, where learners often watch models (in particular, teachers) who are far more competent than they. In such cases, observers may even reject the situation completely because "the fact that this ex-professional dancer can do the variation doesn't mean that I can." Indeed, research shows that self-efficacy is enhanced more by watching a so-called **coping model** (i.e., someone who gradually progresses through the challenges of learning a task) than a **mastery model** (someone who demonstrates correctly right away; see Bandura, 1977; Kitsantas et al., 2000).

THINKING CRITICALLY

- In your experience, what makes for a good demonstration?
- For teachers: When you demonstrate a skill, do you help dancers understand what to look for? What do you emphasize?
- For dancers: When your teacher demonstrates a skill, how do you observe them, from one angle or from several angles? Do you know what to focus on?
- When watching accomplished dancers, do you feel inspired or threatened?

Persuasion and Social Influences

This source of self-efficacy was labeled *verbal persuasion* by Bandura (1977), but in line with later evidence from sports (e.g., Hays et al., 2007, 2009; Thomas et al., 2021) and Vealey's model of sport confidence (1986, 2001) we may consider **persuasion** in broader terms—that is, as any form of input that convinces a dancer that they can or cannot do something. Positive persuasion includes people telling the dancer that they can do something, either directly ("You can do this!") or indirectly ("I believe in you. Remember all those times you did it in class?"). Beyond verbal input, teachers, parents, and peers can persuade a dancer through means such as body language (e.g., clapping or nodding encouragingly, looking dejected or shaking their heads, high fives). Critics and judges may persuade (influence confidence) via evaluations, assessments, and written reviews; and friends and family may not only give a traditional pep talk but also send encouraging messages by digital means. Explanations and instructions about how something can be achieved, sometimes known as *informational support*, would also fit into this category (e.g., Thomas et al., 2021).

As you might guess, positive sources of persuasion boost self-confidence while negative sources reduce it. For instance, a recent study with young athletes identified a lack of trust, negative feedback, various forms of pressure, and overly high expectations as sources of low confidence (Thomas et al., 2021). Thomas et al. (2021) also point out that pressure, high expectations, and negative persuasion can come from inside performers themselves (for more about the topic known as *self-talk*, see chapter 6). Overall, the following considerations are important to keep in mind:

> *The competence and prestige of the persuader.* While encouragement from family and friends is both nice and important, we tend to attribute greater weight to statements made by authorities in an area. Therefore, the words of a teacher or jury member have greater impact on a dancer's confidence—for better or worse.

> *Persuasion is a weaker source of efficacy information than mastery experiences.* This helps explain why some people go largely unaffected by praise and compliments. While persuasion and social support do matter, dancers with very low levels of confidence should be guided toward a multitude of sources of self-efficacy, ideally including mastery experiences (the strongest source).

Imaginal Experiences

The principle underlying **imaginal experiences** as a source of self-efficacy might be described by the question: "Can you imagine yourself doing it?" Although not everyone is aware of the impact of imagery on confidence and learning, most of us would feel lost indeed if asked to perform a skill that we were unable to imagine in our heads. Imagery is introduced comprehensively in chapter 10.

Physiological States

The basic principle underpinning this source of self-efficacy is that when we interpret our physical states as positive, we feel more confident. Conversely, negative interpretations make us feel less confident. Consider Mary, who is feeling nervous about a dance exam. She has butterflies in her stomach, which she really does not like; she thinks she needs to be calm to perform well and has thoughts such as "Why am I so nervous? I won't be able to dance well if my stomach is in an uproar!" By interpreting her symptoms negatively, her confidence is undermined. Beyond anxiety symptoms, this source of confidence also comprises such things as interpretations of fitness levels, energy and fatigue, health, appearance, and pain. For instance, if we think we are not fit enough to complete a challenging variation, our confidence will be lowered. If our bodies feel similar to how they felt when we last did very well, our confidence is likely to get a boost. A dancer who has poor body image is unlikely to yield self-efficacy from the source known as **physiological states**.

Emotional States

As for physiological states, the basic principle underpinning this source of self-efficacy is that when we interpret our **emotional states** positively, we feel more confident, while negative interpretations make us feel less confident. Consider Andrew, a teacher who will teach two new groups this coming semester. On the first day he meets one of these groups, he is in a great mood because he is well-rested and has had a very nice morning. His good mood buoys his self-efficacy for teaching the new group, and he feels confident about meeting them. The subsequent week, he is due to meet a second new group, but he is in a foul mood after sleeping poorly and receiving bad personal news. The bad mood puts a lid on his self-efficacy for teaching, and he mutters to himself that he will not do a good job.

Consequences of Self-Confidence

Many dancers and teachers know intuitively that self-confidence is important, and they are right. For instance, an interview study with freelance dancers reported on self-confidence as an important skill to possess because it helped with commitment and openness (Aujla & Farrer, 2015). Sport researchers in particular have demonstrated a wide range of performance-related and well-being-related consequences of having high versus low levels of confidence, and those of key relevance to dance will be discussed next.

Well-Being-Related Consequences of Self-Confidence

Feeling able to do things that matter to us (i.e., having self-efficacy) is an important part of psychological health (Maddux, 2002). Indeed, feeling out of control or unable to affect important parts of one's life is part of several psychiatric problems and disorders including depression, anxiety, and eating disorders (e.g., Eklund & Bäckström, 2006; Maddux, 1995). Conversely, having strong self-efficacy improves treatment outcomes for such disorders and for many everyday problems. Maddux (2002) writes: "Researchers have shown that enhancing self-efficacy beliefs is crucial to successful change and maintenance of virtually every behavior crucial to health."

In sports, research has shown that a lack of confidence is associated with a range of negative outcomes ranging from dissatisfaction to depression (for reviews, see Vealey, 1986, 2009). In particular, it has been established that confidence has an inverse relationship to performance anxiety, such that confident performers are less likely to be anxious, worried, or doubtful. A fascinating interview study with world class athletes provided in-depth examples of the (perceived) effects of high versus low self-confidence (Hays et al., 2009). The highlighted benefits of high confidence included affective (e.g., better mood, enjoyment, calm), behavioral (e.g., confident body language, greater effort), and cognitive impacts (e.g., being better able to focus on oneself and the task at hand rather than being distracted). These findings are logical also for dancers, but there is still a surprising lack of research into self-confidence in dance.

Performance-Related Consequences of Self-Confidence

Although no studies have examined directly whether more confident dancers actually dance better than their less confident peers, there is every reason to believe that this is so. Indeed, research in sports consistently indicates that athletes performing at higher levels are characterized by high levels of self-confidence (e.g., Feltz, 2007; Gould & Maynard, 2009; Hays et al., 2007, 2009; Vealey, 1986, 2001). More experienced dancers may be more confident (Nordin & Cumming, 2008), although this is less likely if the dancer is also perfectionistic (Nordin-Bates et al., 2011a). Of course, self-confidence cannot take the place of actual skill; indeed, an underlying premise of Bandura's (1977) theory is that self-efficacy is a major determinant of performance only when a person also has the skill and the motivation to perform. As such, two dancers who are equivalent in terms of technical and artistic competence may perform very differently at a given point in time, with the more confident dancer being likely to perform the best.

Another key point from Bandura's (1977) theory is that self-efficacy affects performance because of the behaviors and cognitions that it stimulates. This includes the kinds of activities that people pursue, the goals that they set, their hopes and expectations of success, and their effort and persistence. Indeed, Bandura (1977) wrote that "The strength of people's convictions in their own effectiveness is likely to affect whether they will even try to cope with given situations" (p. 193). In other words, dancers with low self-confidence are more likely to display avoidance behaviors such as not taking class with people they perceive to dance better than themselves or hiding at the back of the studio (figure 3.1). Those with particularly low self-confidence may drop out altogether if they feel unable to take on the challenges associated with training, performing, or competing. For more information about avoidance behaviors, see the introduction.

Is More Self-Confidence Better?

In conversations with dancers, it is common to experience perceptions and concerns that being confident is beneficial up to a certain point, beyond which it becomes counterproductive (e.g., Hanrahan, 1996). Stated differently, dancers may be worried about the negative effects of overconfidence. Interestingly, having boundless confidence seems to be lauded in many sport contexts—for example, how Weinberg and Gould (2018) introduce self-confidence in their bestselling textbook, *Foundations of Sport and Exercise Psychology*. At the same time, overconfidence does exist and can be detrimental (Ede et al., 2017; Woodman et al., 2010). For instance, overconfidence may lead to less effort being put in. A dancer who is unsure may prepare more carefully or take additional action such as asking for advice. Overconfident performers are less likely to do such things, and this may account for any performance decrements resulting from overconfidence. As a result, some have suggested that the relationship between confidence and performance is perhaps curvilinear (i.e., in the shape of an inverted U (Ede et al., 2017).

Note that it is only a *little* doubt that is proposed to be helpful; if self-doubt takes over and self-confidence is simply too low, the performer is not likely to even try. Put differently, self-awareness regarding one's weaknesses can be an advantage, and being unsure can lead to greater effort, at least if the outcome is highly valued (e.g., wanting to do well to be selected by a jury at audition) and the person still has some confidence that they may be able to succeed. But for most people and in most situations, it is an advantage to be confident because the confident person is more likely to try, to exert effort, to focus, and to adhere (e.g., Bandura, 1977; Hays et al., 2007; Hutchinson et al., 2008). Confident dancers are also more likely to set challenging goals and to feel positive about reaching them. Finally, confident persons typically find it easier to stay focused on the task at hand (Hays et al., 2007; see also chapter 6).

Underconfident persons often become distracted by thoughts of their own (perceived) inadequacy and thus are less focused on what they are doing (Maddux, 2002). Take the example of Juliet, a professional dancer. She is certain that she will manage to land the complicated series of jumps that is required for a new choreography, if only she trains well during the coming weeks. Because she is confident, she persists even when the task becomes tiring and frustrating—she is nearly there, after all—and she imagines how fun it would be to get into the first cast for the performance of this role! Her colleague, Janet, has little confidence in her ability to manage the same jump series. She believes she is not fast-footed enough, and fears the artistic director does not like her either. Her low confidence means that she starts to think about how impossible the task is, and how she will probably never make it. Unsurprisingly, she gives up after the first few attempts. Why waste her energy and risk looking silly in front of others if she isn't going to get the role anyway?

> ### THINKING CRITICALLY
>
> - How do you, or your dancers, behave when confident? Not confident? Consider posture and body language.
>   - How might this impact on dance performance?
>   - How might this impact on what an observer might experience?
>   - Is it possible to fake confident behavior? What are the likely consequences?

In sum, overconfidence can exist and can be a problem; however, it also tends to self-regulate relatively quickly. Once dancers experience failure as a result of underpreparation, they rarely continue being underprepared in the future. Instead, underconfident performers are likely to be of far greater concern in the dance world.

How Can Self-Esteem and Self-Confidence Be Strengthened?

Given the many benefits of high, robust levels of self-esteem and self-confidence, it is desirable to strengthen these self-constructs in oneself (for dancers and teachers) and perhaps in others (e.g., teachers helping dancers). Fortunately, the literature is well-developed regarding strategies to strengthen self-efficacy and confidence. This is therefore given a significant amount of space below. First, a more concise presentation of strategies to strengthen self-esteem are provided. Note that persons with very low levels of self-esteem are best referred to a suitably qualified clinical professional, such as a CBT therapist, but evidence-based self-help books may also be beneficial (e.g., Fennell, 2016).

Strengthening Self-Esteem

Self-esteem is a largely stable construct, but we can improve it with conscious, deliberate actions such as those outlined in table 3.2. Many of these are reflective of a task-orientation (chapter 5) and of promoting a task-involving climate (chapter 11).

Strengthening Self-Confidence

Even if dancers consider self-confidence to be important, they may perceive it to be more or less fixed (i.e., something one is born with; Hanrahan, 1996). Indeed, it was reported in an early interview study with high-level dancers from a variety of styles that "Many respondents seemed excited or amazed by the idea of looking at self-confidence as a skill" (Hanrahan, 1996, p. 26). Fortunately, research has provided us with clear advice about how to improve self-confidence. One logical approach is to reverse the sources of self-efficacy identified by Bandura (1977, 1986; also, Maddux, 1995) and supported in subsequent research in sports (e.g., Hays et al., 2007; Thomas et al., 2021). For instance, because mastery experiences are a major source of self-efficacy, it makes sense to try and maximize the number of mastery experiences to enhance self-efficacy or self-confidence, in dancers. Hence, the structure of this section follows the same order as that outlining the sources of self-efficacy. Keep in mind that the psychological skills outlined in Part III of this book are all potentially useful confidence enhancers. Can you see how? In Form 3.1 you can apply your knowledge of self-confidence sources to better understand your own level of self-confidence.

Mastery Experiences (Performance Accomplishments)

To help dancers experience mastery and thereby build confidence, they should regularly feel successful. This involves careful crafting of exercises to pose an appropriate level of challenge while adjusting and individualizing as necessary. This does not mean being the best or being outstanding, nor that easier is better; rather, it means managing most of the set tasks and challenges. Tasks that are too easy will not yield improvements in confidence! Along similar lines, a study with flamenco dance students indicated that accurate feedback on performance is likely to be more helpful than either overly positive (inflated) or overly negative (deflated) feedback (García-Dantas & Quested, 2015). When dancers do not manage, it is imperative that they understand why they did not, and that they are likely to manage with practice, application, and patience. Throughout, it is important to focus on controllable aspects, such as effort level or role interpretation. If focusing on less controllable aspects such as talent or interpersonal comparison, dancers may experience

Table 3.2 **Suggested Strategies for Enhancing Self-Esteem**

	What a dancer can do	What a teacher can do	When to seek professional help

Low, fragile, or contingent self-esteem	• Take pleasure in achievement, with focus on personal progress and aspects within their own control.
	• Focus on constructive action rather than self-critique.
	• Use a training diary in which they evaluate not just what they learned, but also what they did well.
	• Keep exposing themselves to suitable challenges, without avoidance.
	• Stand up for themselves! If the language or behaviors in their studio undermines their self-esteem, then this information should be fed back to them via whatever channels are available. For teachers and professional dancers, this may include saying no to unacceptable demands on employees.
	• If necessary, remove themselves from settings where feedback is repeatedly negative and personal in nature. Changing dance schools is an important message concerning unacceptable teaching methods.
	• Try self-help books*
		• Value dancers as people first and as performers second, for instance by
		  ○ giving equal amounts of attention to dancers of different abilities, and
		  ○ talking positively about things other than performing well, such as being a good friend or being helpful.
		• Structure classes around personal improvement and enjoyment.
		• Focus feedback on
		  ○ constructive action (what to do) rather than critique (what not to do) and
		  ○ actions (what the dancer does) rather than personal characteristics (who the dancer is).
		• Expose dancers to suitable challenges, step-by-step if necessary.
		• Invite and listen to dancer feedback about class structure, feedback styles, and potential improvements.
			• When self-esteem is so low that the dancer feels useless and depressed.
			• When self-esteem is so fragile that challenges in the dance environment cannot be met without avoidance strategies.
			• When self-esteem is so contingent on performance that the dancer feels that they *must* dance well to be good enough as a person.

*For example, Fennell (2016).

mastery for a time, but their sense of confidence will be fragile rather than stable. Following guidelines for effective goal setting (chapter 9) will also help dancers experience mastery.

To feel confident for performance, it is important to have rehearsed in performance-like conditions. Indeed, dancers are less likely to feel confident about an upcoming show if they have not practiced in the correct costume and with lights, sounds, and other performance conditions being in place, even if they have correctly executed the skills in the studio. Therefore, dress rehearsals are crucial. Teachers can also make the studio environment more stagelike by guiding dancers in imagining the stage they will be on, how they will be placed in the wings, and how they will enter and exit the stage. They might play a recording of audience chatter in the background before the actual music plays and applause after. Wearing costumes, not talking, and having curtains drawn will mimic the conditions of performance and thereby boost confidence more than a normal run-through. The same principle underpins the

To build confidence, it is important to design exercises that allow dancers to feel pleased with their accomplishment and effort.

reasons why gradual exposure to challenges and fears is an important self-efficacy enhancing technique (Bandura, 1977). It is a good idea to repeat challenging tasks and expose dancers regularly to challenging situations because this helps reinforce robust self-confidence and leaves less room for self-doubt to creep in. In CBT terms, this is the repeated exposure shown to be so important in clinical settings (see the introduction).

High-level dancers should be helped to understand what makes good preparation so that their confidence ahead of performance grows. This should include more than just rehearsing skills; instead, a balance between technical, artistic, physical, nutritional, and psychological preparation should be emphasized. Dancers need to understand the benefits of rest and recuperation, but it is also a good idea to practice in various states, not just when feeling great. For example, a dancer who practices a difficult solo in the mornings as well as in the evenings, with different partners, and at different energy levels, will likely gain a sense of being able to do it whatever happens; that is, the dancer has a more robust sense of confidence.

Finally, it is important to help dancers who are very self-critical to see and articulate when they have successfully achieved something. Teachers (or perhaps peers) could ask them to describe two or three things they did well in a class and why they think it went well. Writing such reflections in a training diary is a good way for such dancers to start building confidence.

Vicarious Experiences (Modeling)

To help dancers get the most out of vicarious experiences, teachers can demonstrate skills and sequences in several directions or places in the studio by moving either themselves or the dancers around. Teachers can direct learners' attention to the relevant parts of a skill so that they know what aspects to observe (e.g., how to rotate in the hip to facilitate a leg lift, rather than watching the gesture leg). Indeed, research in sports indicates that guiding an observer's attention leads to better learning (e.g., Andrieux & Proteau, 2016). Most likely, it can also avoid learners becoming preoccupied with aspects such as appearance. Encouraging dancers to ask questions about what they see may also help.

Given the importance of model similarity, teachers should keep in mind that they really do not need to present a model of perfection. Being good can really be better than being perfect. Especially when dancers are not confident, it can be useful for peers to demonstrate skills instead of those skills being modeled by the super-competent teacher. However, avoid the trap of always asking the best dancer in class to show the others how things are done, because this is more likely to undermine confidence over time. Instead, use flexible arrangements whereby students perhaps work in pairs to practice their skills of both observation and positive, constructive feedback. Rotate who is demonstrating and specify what dancers should look for. Another approach is to show or describe how now-competent performers struggled to learn something but got there after a process of hard work.

To maximize the likelihood that dancers gain confidence from others, it is important to stay focused on realistic goals (chapter 9) and see others as inspiration rather than a threat (chapter 5). Finally, because of the overwhelming amount of visual material available online, engaging dancers in critical discussion about what they watch might be helpful. What do they watch? How does it make them feel? Are they learning and getting inspired, or are they forever comparing themselves and coming up short?

Persuasion and Social Influences

To make persuasion work, it is important to avoid bombarding dancers with positive feedback at every turn; they may consider it gushing and insincere. But this is far from the same as avoiding positive feedback; research clearly shows the importance of leaders being positive. The important thing is to give thoughtful, personalized, specific, and constructive feedback. So rather than saying "well done, everyone" after an exercise, a teacher can comment to one student about how the exercise became more dynamic after she started working with her feet in a particular way, and to another about how he really shone when he put more energy into an informal studio sharing. Indeed, we should beware of thinking of feedback as either positive or negative; instead, most feedback should be constructive and focused on important actions. This might be either something the dancer has already done (thereby anchoring learning and maximizing the likelihood of them doing it again) or something they can do the next time (thereby focusing their attention on constructive action and conveying positive expectations). Feedback should also be focused on *doing* (what a person does, how a skill worked out) rather than *being* (what a person is like, whether they "have what it takes").

Beyond verbal interaction, consider body language and other nonverbal cues. For instance, what makes the teacher nod and look pleased? Do they ever betray disappointment in someone by the way they stand or gesture? If the way we speak to others matters, it is logical that the way we speak to ourselves matters too. Self-talk should be similarly positive, constructive, and focused on *doing* rather than *being* as interpersonal communications should be (for more on self-talk, see chapter 6).

Imaginal Experiences

Using imagery to boost confidence is outlined properly in chapter 10; however, two key considerations are worth pointing out here. First, dancers who want to improve their self-confidence would do well to undertake vivid, realistic, and regular imagery of their own skills and performances. Second, it is helpful to imagine not only physical and technical skills but also the sense of performing in a confident way (i.e., an emotional aspect of imagery rehearsal).

Physiological States

Physical and mental training are often dealt with separately, but it is perhaps in their integration that we can see the greatest benefits. One example of such integration is that physical conditioning and other health-maintaining strategies (e.g., eating and resting well) help boost your psychological health. Indeed, your confidence in yourself as a dancer or teacher will be greater if you have prepared, fueled, and listened to your body. As an example, dancers who have a continuous conditioning regimen alongside their more technical and artistically oriented dance classes will feel more confident at performance time, because they know they can rely on their strength and stamina. Body confidence will help performance because the dancer is free to focus on the essence of the role.

Most people feel more confident when they are calm than when they are physiologically aroused, such as when experiencing the somatic symptoms of anxiety. Therefore, techniques such as vigorous exercise (so that, e.g., increased heart and breathing rates can be attributed to the exercise rather than to anxiety), relaxation, and massage (to reduce arousal levels) are often used. Dancers can also learn to reinterpret signs of physiological arousal or somatic anxiety as unimportant, or even helpful, to them. Such interpretations will be partly affected by others around us (Bandura, 1977): as such, it is a good idea for instructors to model a positive or neutral attitude to arousal and anxiety and to promote positive talk about anxiety in their classes.

Emotional States

Being aware of our emotional states and how they affect us helps us avoid being victims of our emotions. Dancers may benefit from practicing in a variety of moods and evaluating any effects on performance. Often, bad moods dissipate after a time as we get into the flow of a class or show. Dancers can learn that although listening to their bodies is very important, they do not need to be in an optimal state every time they perform, but that they are capable of doing just fine under a range of emotional states. It is okay to feel vulnerable and downcast; the body is still as capable as on more optimistic and upbeat days, and emotional states do not necessarily have any adverse effect. Indeed, dancers can learn to explore and express their emotional states through their dancing. Dancing is not all about being strong and cheerful!

Mindfulness, which is explored in chapter 8, can be a great aid in dealing with a variety of both physical and emotional states. For instance, dancers can learn to be aware of how they feel and think, without judgment and without trying to suppress negative states. They can learn to see such states as transient and not as something that defines them. Such strategies help dancers avoid getting stuck and help them move on to focusing on the actions that they want to undertake. Indeed, it is perfectly possible to act *as if* one felt confident (e.g., dance with strong bold movements and keep one's head high) even if the "right" emotions are not there. After all, it is the actions that make the dance and invite feedback from others that we then work with.

It has been noted that especially young people may rely on a narrow range of sources of confidence, with mastery experiences being the most central (Thomas et al., 2021; Usher & Pajares, 2008). It would be a great service to young dancers, therefore, if they were helped to utilize a variety of sources of confidence. For instance, helping them feel more prepared via psychological skills training can be constructive, affordable, and realistic (see Part III of this book). In so doing, confidence may fluctuate less over time and situations, because its foundation is broad rather than narrow (Thomas et al., 2011). In Form 3.1, you can apply your knowledge of self-confidence sources to better understand your own level of self-confidence.

Sandra: Case Study of Self-Confidence

Sandra is a college dance student whose teacher expressed concern about her apparent lack of self-confidence. The teacher perceived that Sandra was sometimes disengaged, as if she felt there was no point in trying new things. Sandra confirmed the teacher's worries, saying that she often felt incompetent. As it turned out, Sandra hinged a lot of her confidence on her appearance. This meant that on the rare days that she thought her hair, make-up, and clothes made her look nice, she felt confident; on days that one or more of these aspects were somehow not right, she felt ugly and incompetent. As a result, she often stood at the back of the studio where she was farther from the mirror and less visible to the teacher—and less likely to learn optimally.

On her teacher's recommendation, Sandra was able to access support services where the counsellor asked her two deceptively simple questions:

- What is the process by which you get good at something?
- What would it look like if you were confident?

Over a period of time—and many homework tasks—Sandra began to realize that her confidence had been built on the very rocky foundation of having to look good at all times. But although dance is a visual art and there is constant exposure to mirrors, looking good is hardly the main building block for success. Instead, she must be willing to be challenged, to try and to fail—and sometimes to risk looking silly in doing so. If she has not really put in the work, she cannot expect to be either confident or good at something. With the counselor, Sandra also made a list of confidence-facilitating factors, including things like proper hydration, food, and sleep. She also focused on factors within her own control (e.g., effort). Gradually, Sandra's behavior started to change. Although she certainly did not always feel confident about new tasks, her zest and newfound sense of purpose helped her to act confidently, which created an upward spiral of increasing competence and self-confidence.

Composite case study created on the basis of conversations with Erin Sanchez, MSc, Healthier Dancer Programme manager at OneDanceUK and PhD student in dance psychology at the University of Edinburgh, and with Leigh Skvarla, PhD, licensed professional counselor in Pennsylvania and co-founder of the Center for Grit and Growth.

Form 3.1 — GET PRACTICAL: IDENTIFY THE REASONS YOU ARE CONFIDENT OR NOT CONFIDENT

SOURCE OF SELF-CONFIDENCE	EXAMPLES	IS THIS TRUE FOR ME? (CHECK IF YES)	SUM OF SOURCES (ADD UP CHECKS)	IDEAS FOR HOW TO STRENGTHEN
Mastery experiences "I have done it before."	1. I prepare well, technically, physically, mentally.			
	2. I interpret personal progress as success.			
	3. I set realistic goals.			
	4. I continuously challenge myself to try new things.			
	5. My practicing is similar to how I want to perform.			
Vicarious experiences "I have seen it done."	1. I watch others as a way to learn.			
	2. If I do not understand what is being demonstrated, I ask for clarification.			
	3. I pay close attention to demonstrations.			
	4. I try to watch complex things from different angles.			
	5. I see others as inspiration rather than threat.			
Persuasion "I hear I can do it."	1. Others tell me that I can do it.			
	2. I tell myself that I can do it (positive self-talk).			
	3. I accept positive feedback as true.			
	4. I don't take negative feedback to heart.		___ / 30	
	5. I remind myself of constructive feedback.			
Imaginal experiences "I can imagine myself doing it."	1. I use imagery to practice and plan.			
	2. My imagery is vivid and realistic.			
	3. I include feelings of confidence in my imagery.			
	4. I image things that I do well.			
	5. I image overcoming challenges.			
Physiological states "I feel physically good about it."	1. Physical signs of anxiety are positive or unimportant.			
	2. I feel healthy.			
	3. I feel physically fit.			
	4. I practice in many different physical states.			
	5. I feel that I can rely on my body.			
Emotional states "I feel emotionally good about it."	1. I am generally positive and buoyant.			
	2. My thoughts and emotions do not define what I do.			
	3. I practice in many different emotional states.			
	4. I know that thoughts are not always true.			
	5. I can explore and express emotions through dance.			

Go to HK*Propel* to download this form.

From S. Nordin-Bates, *Essentials of Dance Psychology* (Champaign, IL: Human Kinetics, 2023).

CRITICAL ASPECTS OF RESEARCH INTO SELF-ESTEEM AND SELF-CONFIDENCE

1. Research into self-constructs in dance is lacking. Thorough, in-depth investigations into dancers' self-esteem and self-confidence would be a great addition to the literature and might consider questions such as:
   - *Sources*: What makes dancers feel confident, secure, and valued, and what undermines these same aspects?
   - *Effects*: What happens when dancers do feel confident, secure, and valued? Does it have differential effects on variables typically captured in sport research (e.g., objective performance) and aspects that are more arts-specific (e.g., artistry, role interpretation)? Indeed, many dancers speak of the importance of not just confidence, but also vulnerability and humility.

2. In general life, males typically enjoy higher self-esteem than do females (Orth & Robins, 2014). In sports, there is a gender effect in self-confidence such that males display higher self-confidence than females (e.g., Krane & Williams, 1994; Vargas-Tonsing & Bartholomew, 2006). This is primarily for traditionally male tasks, however, while the reverse effect has been observed in traditionally female tasks (Vealey, 2009). It would be interesting to see whether this applies in dance, which so often is female dominated. Having said this, males in dance/ballet may be treated preferentially to females due to their limited numbers (Clegg et al., 2019). Examining potential gender differences in self-constructs in dance, as well as potential reasons for such differences, would be illuminating.

3. There has been emerging interest in the confidence of sport coaches (e.g., Vealey, 2009). Such research has indicated that more confident coaches are more encouraging toward their athletes, whereas less confident coaches give less encouragement, instead focusing more on instructional and organizational behaviors (Vealey, 2009). Who is more successful? You guessed it—the confident coaches. To date, no studies have examined the confidence of dance teachers. It would be intriguing to determine whether it is primarily previous dance performance success that teachers rely on, or whether education (such as the course you might be reading this book for) can help teachers become more confident. After all, education is a way for teachers to become more prepared for the challenging task of teaching.

KEY POINTS AND RECOMMENDATIONS FOR SELF-ESTEEM AND SELF-CONFIDENCE IN DANCE

1. Self-esteem and self-confidence are not synonymous: self-esteem is foundational and concerns feeling valuable as a person, whereas self-confidence is performance-oriented and concerns feeling able to accomplish tasks. This is an important distinction for anybody wishing to understand what makes dancers feel either valuable and secure (self-esteem), confident, or both.

2. As a personality trait, self-esteem is largely stable over time unless a person experiences major changes in their circumstances or works deliberately to improve it. As a result, dance teachers and schools are unlikely to affect the self-esteem of their dancers in the short term, but they may do so in the long term for those who dance often and intensively and who perceive dance to be important in their lives. Confidence, on the other hand, is more easily affected. Given the wide-ranging benefits of self-confidence and self-esteem, dance teachers and schools would do well to consider how they can support both.

4

Anxiety

"I get nervous when I don't get nervous. If I'm nervous I know I'm going to have a good show."

Beyoncé Knowles, singer

CHAPTER OBJECTIVES

After reading this chapter, you will be able to

1. describe what anxiety is, including its origins as a response to threat;
2. discuss cognitive and somatic symptoms and the importance of control perceptions;
3. outline a range of internal and external sources of anxiety in dance;
4. critically discuss the positive and negative consequences of anxiety on performance and well-being in dance and how they may be affected by a range of factors, including symptom interpretation;
5. apply basic recommendations to manage anxiety, including suggestions from sport psychology, cognitive behavioral therapy, and mindfulness;
6. create an exposure hierarchy to help yourself accomplish tasks that make you nervous; and
7. think critically about the nature and impact of anxiety in dance settings.

Key Terms

anxiety	flight response	state anxiety
anxiety intensity	freeze response	stress
anxiety tolerance	habituation	symptom interpretation
cognitive symptoms	personality traits and states	trait anxiety
exposure	somatic symptoms	
fight response		

The term *anxiety* is from the Latin *anxietās*, which means to be distressed or troubled. Anxiety is an inherent part of being human and can help us function well, yet it causes problems when experienced frequently, at high levels, or when interpreted negatively. An anxious dancer is someone who experiences worry, apprehension, and physiological activation in relation to something that feels uncertain or uncontrollable. This gives us a hint of why anxiety is such a common concern in dance; that is, because many aspects of dance performance are often seen as out of the dancer's control.

What Is Anxiety?

Anxiety is a psychophysiological response to threat that has evolved over millennia. Especially when wild animals were major threats to human survival, anxiety was an adaptive response indeed. Put simply, those who had a developed anxiety response were more likely to be vigilant and careful, and thereby they increased the chances of survival for both themselves and their children. Against this backdrop, the negative press that anxiety has these days may seem surprising. If it helps us survive, is it not positive? The same could be said for the many related responses that essentially refer to the same basic reaction in us that anxiety brings, including somatic arousal and stress.

There are two main reasons why we dislike anxiety. One is that it is fundamentally unpleasant—if being near death in a threatening situation was pleasant, it would not motivate us to save ourselves! As you will have seen in the introduction chapter, we humans are strongly motivated to avoid feeling bad, and we quickly learn to avoid situations, tasks, and people who we perceive to be anxiety-inducing or simply uncomfortable. A second reason is that our ancient response to threat is generic rather than specific to different situations and threats. For instance, the psychophysiological reaction to being chased by a grizzly bear and being judged by a dance jury are quite similar. Our response is simply inherited and may not seem appropriate in our current dance world where few of us have to fend off wild animals or traverse dangerous mountain passes to survive. Instead, our perceived threats are those that seem to challenge our competence, well-being, or sense of self, including not being good enough, looking stupid or incompetent, or not being liked by people. Indeed, the exposure and evaluation inherent in dance competitions and performances account for major changes in bodily homeostasis, including release of the stress hormone cortisol (an internal alarm system; Quested et al., 2011; Rohleder et al., 2007).

Taking a little inspiration from a famous quote by Marie Curie, we might say that anxiety is not to be feared—it is only to be understood. Perhaps we should be grateful to our anxiety response, which has enabled survival across the ages and still now tries to save us in situations that we perceive to be threatening—even if those situations are quite different. In this chapter, we will explore both the positive and negative consequences of anxiety and how they may be accepted, reinterpreted, or managed. Before doing so, however, we first need to clarify the nature of anxiety responses, which rests on the distinction between cognitive and somatic symptoms.

Cognitive and Somatic Symptoms

If you consider what happens to you or to your dancers when anxiety (nerves, fears, stress) strikes, you will quickly be able to list a variety of symptoms. Most likely, you will identify both **somatic** (bodily) and **cognitive** (thought-related) **symptoms**, which demonstrates the psychophysiological nature of anxiety. For instance, you might experience a racing heart, shallow breathing, and butterflies in your stomach as well as a narrowed focus of attention and worried thoughts. Together, these are sometimes referred to as an *acute stress response*, and they are outlined in table 4.1.

Fighting, Fleeing, or Freezing?

How can these symptoms be understood? By going back to the nature of anxiety being a natural human response to threat, the symptoms that we experience can begin to make sense. First, consider what the possible options are when faced with a saber-toothed beast. Is it sufficiently far away for you to run away and thereby save yourself from becoming dinner? This is the **flight response** option. Is it too close for that? Do you believe you may be able to defeat your attacker? Then your natural reaction is typically the **fight response**, because to save yourself, you may have to scare off, harm, or even kill your opponent. And if the threat is already very close and seems clearly superior to you, your anxiety may cause you to freeze like a rabbit in the headlights—the **freeze response**. The freeze response may also happen if various versions of fighting and fleeing have already been attempted without success. Then, we may instead make ourselves as inconspicuous as possible, or even play dead, to make ourselves less eye-catching or attractive prey.

The preceding examples may seem extreme and in no way dance-related, but the three typical reactions to threat (fight, flight, or freeze) can be translated into responses you may experience or see in the dance domain. For instance, some dancers feel so anxious ahead of an upcoming audition that they avoid it altogether—a flight response. A dance teacher who is so stressed about an upcoming premiere that she believes will not go well because the cast seems really underprepared might snap at her colleagues and argue over details in an uncharacteristic way—a fight response. Some dancers might respond to their fears by becoming physically still while remaining hyperattentive to what is going on around them (such as watching very carefully how a person they find scary moves around the room:

Lettering art by Ink & Lise. Used with permission.

Go to HK*Propel* to find a full-sized version of this and other lettering art.

Table 4.1 Cognitive and Somatic Symptoms That Make Up the Acute Stress Response (Anxiety Reaction)

Somatic symptoms	Cognitive symptoms
Raised heart rate	Apprehension
Raised breathing rate (although in a freeze response, you may hold your breath)	Focus on the perceived threat (outward) or on one's own thoughts and somatic symptoms (inward)
Muscle tension or trembling	Self-doubt
Sweating	Catastrophizing (thinking the worst will happen)
Sharpened senses (increased peripheral vision, ears perk up)	Concentration difficulties
Cold, prickly, or clammy hands and feet	Negative images (experiencing in your mind what you do not want to happen)
Stomach complaints ("butterflies," need to go to the toilet frequently)	
Reduced pain perception	
Adrenaline released, causing a rush, restlessness, or fidgeting	

One symptom of cognitive anxiety is a tendency to focus inward, getting lost in thoughts of how things may play out.

Will they stop to look at me?). By blending into the background, they may escape the attention they wish to avoid and can prepare their next move. The following quote from a dancer turned choreographer illustrates this kind of response when she describes how women in her previous company tried to avoid attention and criticism:

> The idea was wear black . . . and don't stand out. Just look like the girl next to you as much as possible, be in line. Then you won't get shouted at. You know, if you don't hear your name, it's good. (Clements & Nordin-Bates, 2022, p. 7).

This kind of freeze response is essentially the body putting fight and flight on hold. All three of the outlined reactions are initiated by the autonomic nervous system with one of its two subsystems being activated: the parasympathetic nervous system accounting for freeze-type responses and the sympathetic nervous system accounting for fight and flight responses. The latter dominate, with freeze-type reactions coming into play if fighting or fleeing for some reason do not seem possible.

In light of these typical inherited responses, our symptoms can be understood. For instance, raises in heart rate and breathing rate help get oxygen around our bodies, which is useful when trying to either flee or fight because both involve physical exertion. Indeed, these are the same responses that the body initiates when you start any cardiovascular exercise. The sharpening of vision and hearing is logical because having our senses operate optimally will help us detect further threats more quickly. Our blood is diverted toward major muscle groups, which facilitates both fighting and fleeing; this is the reason why hands and feet may feel cold, prickly, or clammy. It also explains why we may experience butterflies in the stomach or digestion problems—because blood is diverted away from the nonessential task of digesting food.

Sources of Anxiety

A wealth of reasons may help explain why a dancer or teacher feels anxious. Indeed, if you were to ask 50 dancers why they get nervous, you may well get 50 somewhat different responses (Arnold & Fletcher, 2012). But although the examples that people give are often personal, they are typically underpinned by a feeling of not being in charge or in control in a situation that matters to them. Indeed, Walker and Nordin-Bates (2010) found that a major theme regarding the anxiety experiences of professional ballet dancers was the feeling of being out of control (see also Quested et al., 2011). This is in line with a common definition of **stress**, which states that it is "a substantial imbalance between demand (physical and-or psychological) and response capability, under conditions where failure to meet that demand has important consequences" (McGrath, 1970, p. 20).

We are more likely to become stressed or anxious when something matters greatly to us (e.g., getting into the only dance school that you have aspired to for years) than when it does not (e.g., if you have many other dance schools to choose from). The McGrath definition also highlights that stress and anxiety rise when we feel that demands are greater than what we feel we can deliver (e.g., if parents or teachers require more of us than we feel able to give). Indeed, a recently validated model of anxiety in sports suggests that anxiety is best conceptualized by way of three components: the cognitive and somatic symptoms outlined earlier and perceived control (Cheng & Hardy, 2016; Jones et al., 2019). Thus, if you want to consider whether a situation is likely to cause someone anxiety, you may ask yourself: Is it likely to make them feel out of control (uncertain, incompetent)?

We can make a logical distinction between sources of anxiety located internally and externally. As illustrated in figure 4.1, internal sources would include the following:

> **Personality traits and states** such as high perfectionism, low self-esteem, low self-confidence, or a narrow dancer identity (see chapters 1-3). Because **state anxiety** (i.e., anxiety in a particular moment) occurs in response to a perceived threat, it is logical that personality traits that make a person more prone to perceiving threats often cause state anxiety. Accordingly, research has found that dancers are more likely to be state anxious if they have high levels of **trait anxiety** (i.e., an inherent tendency to perceive situations as threatening), high levels of perfectionism, low levels of self-esteem, feelings of incompetence, and a perceived lack of support (Blevins et al., 2019; Haraldsen et al., 2020; Quested et al., 2011).
>
> As an example, high-level contemporary dance and ballet students with perfectionistic tendencies report higher levels of both somatic and cognitive anxiety than those with no such tendencies (Nordin-Bates et al., 2011). Dancers with high levels of self-esteem and self-confidence are instead going to feel anxious less often or less intensely than those with lower perceptions of their own worth and capabilities (Barrell & Terry, 2003; Neil et al., 2006; Walker & Nordin-Bates, 2010).

> *Psychological characteristics* such as motivation quality (see chapter 5) and attentional focus (see chapter 6) make the anxiety response more or less likely. In particular, dancers driven by extrinsic sources of motivation, such as impressing others, being the best, or other things they cannot fully control, are more likely to be anxious (e.g., Haraldsen et al., 2020; Lacaille et al., 2007). Therefore, dancers will often feel more anxious during tasks or roles focused on demonstrating perfect technique, as compared to roles that emphasize artistry (Walker & Nordin-Bates, 2010).

> *Physical aspects* such as feeling ill or injured (vs. fit and ready) can cause dancers anxiety (e.g., Arnold & Fletcher, 2012; Blevins et al., 2019; Walker & Nordin-Bates, 2010). This is logical, because they then feel less in control of their bodies and their performances and, consequently, also the outcome. Similar reasoning may be applied to the aspect of *preparedness*: When we do not feel prepared, we do not feel in control or on top of things. These latter aspects are closely aligned with the idea of physiological states and mastery experiences being sources of self-efficacy (see chapter 3).

As illustrated in figure 4.1, external sources of anxiety would include the following:

> *Leadership*, including the extent to which leaders (e.g., teachers, choreographers) are perceived to be competent at their jobs (Arnold & Fletcher, 2012). For example, if dancers do not trust that their teacher has prepared them adequately for an upcoming show, they are likely to be more anxious about performing in it. Other sources of anxiety related to leadership are the extent to which dancers perceive their teachers to be placing (overly) high expectations and pressure on them, and if they are perceived to be unsupportive in some way (e.g., Blevins et al., 2019; Walker & Nordin-Bates, 2010). Many of these aspects can be related to the teacher-created motivational climate (e.g., training in a studio where feedback is based on fault-finding or comparing dancers), which is outlined in detail in chapter 11 (see also Nordin-Bates et al., 2012; Quested et al., 2011).

> *Contextual aspects* in the studio or stage can be sources of anxiety, such as when dancers are made to dance in subpar venues with slippery

floors, impractical costumes, or uncomfortable temperatures (e.g., Arnold & Fletcher, 2012; Walker & Nordin-Bates, 2010). Yet again, such aspects are typically perceived to be anxiety-inducing when they make dancers feel threatened or otherwise out of control. Visibility (i.e., being observed or exposed) and social evaluation or perceptions of being judged add to the perception of little control, and thereby anxiety, if these are seen as threats to our sense of being competent and liked by others. The casting decisions of choreographers or scores from judges are therefore logical sources of anxiety for dancers.

› *Cultural and organizational aspects.* At a more overarching level, dancers may become anxious in response to aspects such as insecure positions. For instance, some dancers feel that they have to perform well at all times or else their role, job, or place at a school will be taken away. It is easy see how such insecurity induces anxiety. It is also likely to be common in dance, where jobs and roles have a high rate of turnover and where dancers may not even know the criteria used to cast or appoint someone. Uncertainty is especially likely for independent dancers (Aujla & Farrer, 2015). Other cultural aspects that may lead to anxiety include specific cultural norms (e.g., Arnold & Fletcher, 2012; Blevins et al., 2019; Haraldsen et al., 2020). For instance, if norms related to behavior (e.g., hard work, obedience) and appearance (e.g., being petite) are strict, then more dancers will struggle to feel that they fit in than if norms are more inclusive and wide-ranging. Consequently, more dancers are likely to feel anxious more often.

› *Interpersonal aspects.* Although the relationships between dancers and their teachers and other leaders (e.g., choreographers, managers) are important, dancers may also become anxious in response to other interpersonal relationships (Blevins et al., 2019). These may include dysfunctional relationships with people who are relatively close (peers, colleagues, family) but also with people who are more distant (e.g., audiences, judges, the media). For instance, a dancer in conflict with his dance partner is more likely to become anxious, as is a choreographer who knows that her new work will

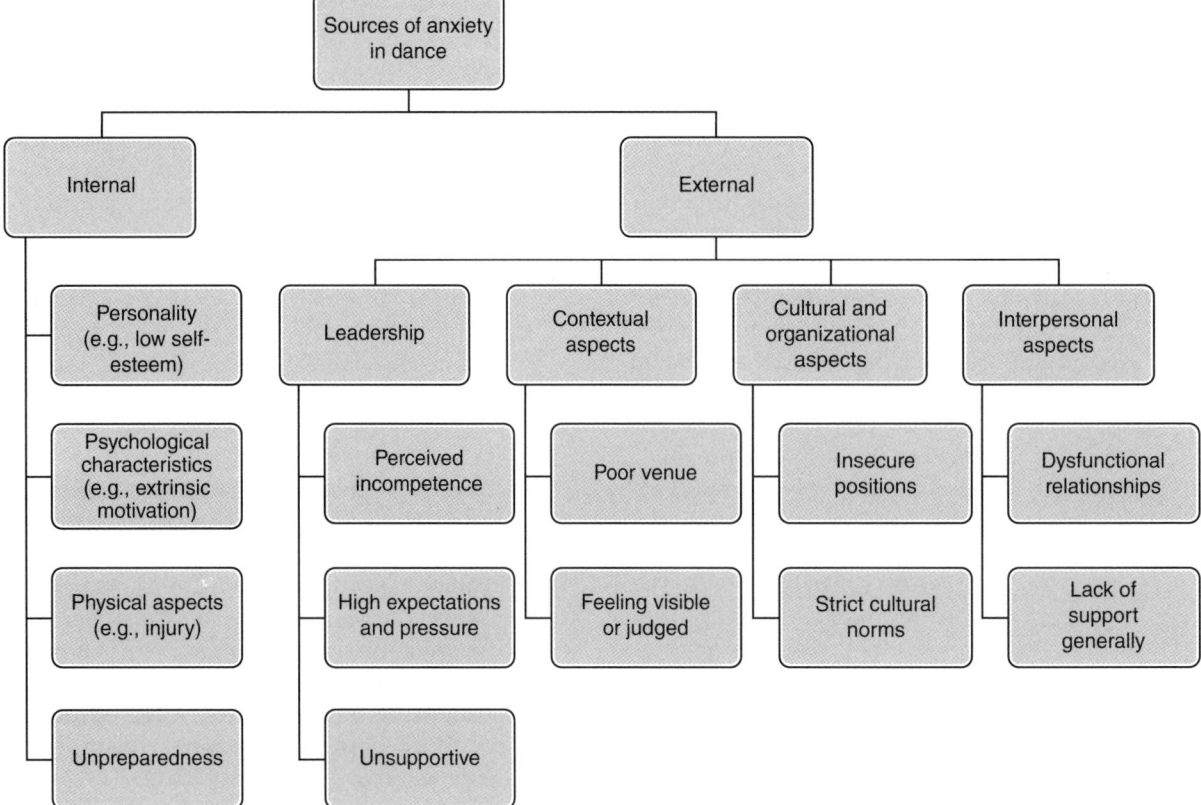

Figure 4.1 Internal and external sources of anxiety in dance.

be evaluated by a newspaper critic who never seems to like her style. Interpersonal aspects may also be sources of anxiety if perceived to be somehow unsupportive. This includes a lack of emotional support (e.g., feeling that one is only loved and appreciated when performing well), informational support (e.g., not having access to good advice), or financial support (e.g., not having enough money to practice as much as one wants or needs to prepare for an audition).

As with many other topics in this book, anxiety is often the result of complex interactions between factors; we therefore need to take an interactionist perspective if we want to get to the heart of anxiety issues in dance. For instance, many dancers will experience anxiety in a dance setting characterized by criticism and low emotional support. Yet the strength of this relationship will be affected by psychological characteristics such as personality (e.g., low self-esteem) and psychological characteristics (e.g., attentional focus on demonstrating flawless technique). Therefore, keep in mind that figure 4.1 is a simplified overview and that the boxes illustrated as separate entities in reality affect each other in multiple ways.

THINKING CRITICALLY

- What sources of anxiety have you experienced?
- Do you and your dance setting have few or many of the sources of anxiety outlined in figure 4.1?
- Have your sources of anxiety changed over time in any way? If so, why?

As an illustration of anxiety sources, consider Jamie who typically gets very nervous. Jamie feels that they have little control over outcomes that are important to them, which include placing in the top three in a regional competition. Jamie is perfectionistic, which means that they set very high goals but are very unsure whether they will be good enough to reach them. Jamie also perceives that their teacher is very critical and focused on mistakes. Being on the competitive circuit, Jamie knows that the opinions of judges will matter greatly in whether their goal of placing in the top three is met, yet Jamie has little idea of how the judges will judge style, choreography, or execution on any given day. Knowing that their parents do not have much money left to support them dancing, Jamie really needs to place well to qualify for a scholarship. To top things off, Jamie obviously cannot control the skill level of other dancers within the competition. Will the other dancers all be better than them? Has the person whom Jamie beat last time trained extra hard for today? With so many aspects seemingly out of control, but still important to them, no wonder Jamie is anxious!

As a contrast, consider Daisy, who has a stable sense of self-esteem and therefore does not feel that her competitive performances define her. Together with her coach, she sets realistic goals that are not based on comparisons with others but rather on accomplishing specific skills. Both her family and her coach are supportive, and the coach gives her feedback focused on specific technical and artistic components—that is, aspects that are within Daisy's control. When she competes, she naturally wants to do well but understands that exact placings will never be controllable; therefore, she prefers to focus on her own goals and how she can communicate the message of her choreography to those watching. Because her attention is mostly on controllable aspects and her sense of self is not based on outperforming others, it is easy to see why Daisy gets less nervous than Jamie.

Consequences of Anxiety

As noted, anxiety can lead to both positive and negative consequences. Which one is more likely depends on several considerations, including **anxiety tolerance**; **anxiety intensity**; dance style, choreography, or role; and **symptom interpretation**.

1. *Anxiety tolerance.* Dancers who are used to experiencing anxiety from time to time—and who exercise their self-awareness—will often learn to tolerate their symptoms. They may, for instance, notice that they can perform regardless of whether they feel restless, have butterflies in their stomachs, or have clammy hands. Moreover, dancers often learn with time that somatic anxiety does not stay elevated for long periods of time; instead, it tends to dissipate after approximately 20 minutes. This is a natural physiological reaction, because the body simply cannot stay on high alert for any length of time. Knowledge of this fact can be of great benefit to dancers. Your anxiety symptoms will change—just hang in there (see also the introduction).

2. *Anxiety intensity.* Many people feel intuitively that mild to moderate anxiety carries fewer negative implications than high or extreme levels: a slightly raised heart rate and a sense of restlessness in the muscles feels okay to many, whereas intense sweating and trembling may lead to actual difficulties, for instance, in partner work (e.g., not getting a good grip in a lift) and in keeping step in time with the music.

3. *Dance style, choreography, or role.* The type of movements that are being performed will also matter (Mellalieu et al., 2004; Walker & Nordin-Bates, 2010). In particular, energetic activities that require mostly gross motor skill execution (e.g., an upbeat, fast jazz sequence incorporating large, bold movements) will be less affected by anxiety than a slow and precise adagio with intricate partnering. In fact, the former type of dancing may benefit from the rush of adrenaline and fighting instinct that the anxiety response can bring.

4. *Interpretation of symptoms.* Young dancers may assume that they are nervous because they are inexperienced and that their symptoms will decrease if and when they become experienced, high-level performers. However, this is not typically the case (e.g., Walker & Nordin-Bates, 2010). Although repeated **exposure** to a situation, activity, or feeling will serve to desensitize us, and thereby lower our anxiety response (see introduction), this is only for very similar situations, activities, and feelings (e.g., Helin, 1989; Walker & Nordin-Bates, 2010). Yet dancers progress in their skills over time, and as they improve, new challenges and, for some, new pressures tend to emerge. For instance, a child may perform only as part of a large group in a small local theater, while a professional dancer may perform solos on large national stages. As a result, the actual symptom intensity of dancers at different levels may not be so different.

What can change is how symptoms are interpreted. Specifically, we may interpret symptoms as either debilitative (unhelpful), facilitative (helpful), or neutral (Hanton et al., 2008; Jones & Swain, 1992). So far, studies in dance are inconclusive, variously indicating that dancers may interpret their symptoms as somewhat debilitative (Nordin & Cumming, 2006), somewhat facilitative (Fish et al., 2004) or both (Walker & Nordin-Bates, 2010). These samples differed in several ways, and it is possible that the lower experience levels of the sample studied by Nordin and Cumming (2006) accounts for their slightly more debilitative interpretation. In this regard, it is interesting to note what research in sports has demonstrated. Specifically, a review into anxiety interpretation research in sports (Hanton et al., 2008) highlighted that performers who interpret their anxiety symptoms as more facilitative

› tend to perform better,
› are more confident,
› are more experienced, and
› use more helpful coping strategies and a wider range of psychological skills.

In contrast, athletes who interpret anxiety as more debilitating typically have more limited coping strategies. Similar findings have been reported in dance (Barrell & Terry, 2003).

Figure 4.2 shows the reciprocal impact of cognitive and somatic symptoms on each other. As you can see, those who interpret their symptoms as debilitative are more likely to experience an escalation of symptoms. By helping dancers to interpret symptoms as facilitative or neutral, however, we can stop this vicious circle. More about how to interpret anxiety in a positive or neutral light is outlined toward the end of this chapter.

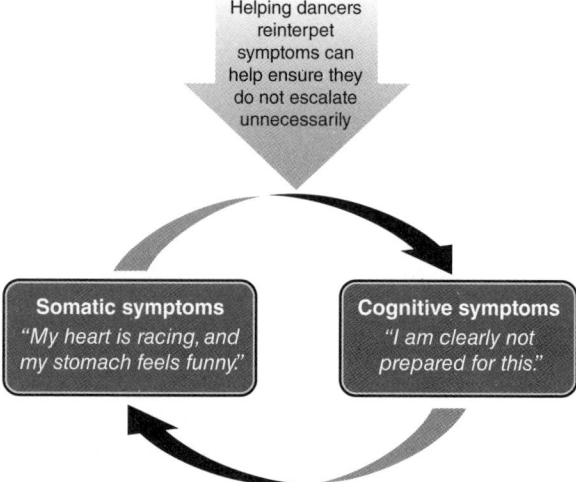

Figure 4.2 The reciprocal impact of somatic and cognitive anxiety symptoms, whereby debilitative interpretation of somatic symptoms may intensify cognitive symptoms of anxiety and vice versa. Reinterpreting somatic symptoms as facilitative or simply neutral (unimportant) can help break this cycle.

Well-Being-Related Consequences of Anxiety

Anxiety is typically associated with ill-being—that is, low levels of well-being. This includes experiences of fear, agitation, distress, and even torment. Anxiety can also keep dancers from sleeping at night, because they cannot let go of thoughts of "what will happen if . . ." Over time, repeated or prolonged exposure to the stress hormone cortisol can cause both psychological and physiological health problems (Marin et al., 2011). Discussion of clinical outcomes is beyond the scope of this book, but it is worth knowing that debilitating anxiety is inherent in a variety of mental disorders, including generalized anxiety disorder, panic disorder, and post-traumatic stress disorder. People with high and generalized levels of anxiety tend to have lower self-esteem and self-confidence and suffer a greater risk of depression.

Anxieties about one's body (e.g., social physique anxiety) also increase the risk of developing an eating disorder, especially when there is comparison and surveillance of bodies, as is typical in dance (Fitzsimmons-Craft et al., 2012; see also chapter 14). Clearly, intense and long-standing anxiety is a source of ill-being for dancers, as it is for people more generally. For example, one study with student dancers found that those reporting higher levels of trait anxiety at the start of the study also reported worsening health over a five-week period (Lench et al., 2010). Importantly, such consequences may only occur when dancers interpret situations as threats rather than as challenges (see Quested et al., 2011).

Performance-Related Consequences of Anxiety

Going back to survival value as the main reason why we all experience anxiety, it is logical that avoidance is a key behavior when we are anxious. Historically, we saved ourselves by avoiding dangerous things such as wild animals and heights and dangerous situations such as being seen as too odd by those we need for protection (i.e., our family and tribe). This avoidance included the fight, flight, and freeze responses mentioned earlier. Fast-forward to the dancers of today. The situations they avoid may include

› standing at the front of the class,
› putting themselves forward (e.g., volunteering to show something to the class),
› taking class with a teacher they find scary (critical, or otherwise unpleasant),
› standing up for themselves and their opinions,
› practicing moves in front of others when they do not feel at least somewhat sure that they will do well, and
› being in evaluative situations such as auditions or competitions.

It is easy to see how avoidance behaviors such as those already listed will affect the training, performance, and growth of dancers. In particular, dancers who are very anxious about what other people think of them will often avoid practicing skills that they really need to practice. One dance teacher gave the following example of how he, as a student, avoided performing badly in front of his class by not doing a task properly at all:

> Since I felt I didn't want to do something bad, the reaction was partly to do something really pitiful. . . . Then there were no comments; it was just so dumb that it couldn't be analyzed . . . it wasn't that anyone said anything mean but just that you felt that the situation was unpleasant. (Nordin-Bates, 2020, p. 30).

Performing artists who endorse goals such as trying to be the best or impress others (i.e., performance approach goals; see chapter 5) to a greater extent also report higher anxiety intensities (Lacaille et al., 2007; Lench et al., 2010). In one of these studies, anxiety intensities were negatively correlated with self-rated performance quality; in other words, those who reported having been more anxious also felt that they had performed worse (Lacaille et al., 2007). Unfortunately, few studies into the anxiety-performance relationship exist as yet, and further research in this area would be welcome.

Anxiety can negatively affect performance, but it can also have positive effects; in addition, performance effects are not as pronounced as many people believe (e.g., Cheng et al., 2011; Woodman & Hardy, 2003). In fact, perceptions of control are a far better predictor of performance than are symptoms of either somatic or cognitive anxiety (Cheng et al., 2011; Jones et al., 2019)! Notably, Cheng and colleagues found that this was mostly true when somatic anxiety was low; when it was high, perceived control seemed to matter less. Another interesting finding from that study was that worst performances were associated with the lowest levels of both somatic anxiety and perceived control. The authors suggested that this might be because performers who feel neither any activation nor any control may be the least likely to mobilize their personal resources to tackle the upcoming performance; that is, they have little impetus for action.

That anxiety can lead to positive consequences is, of course, the reason why it is a natural, inherited response. By removing ourselves from anxiety-inducing situations, for instance, we reinstate homeostasis and a sense of calm and control. Moreover, recall from the early parts of this chapter how anxiety is a broad-based fundamental reaction that does not discriminate well between situations. This lack of specificity is also mirrored in the significant overlap between psychophysiological reactions that we typically have different names for, because we interpret them differently; these include arousal, excitement, and elation. The exhilaration that we get when going on a roller coaster or watching a scary film is, at its roots, the same as the anxiety felt when having to make a speech in front of classmates or colleagues. For dancers, this same reaction underpins the sense of being really alive that they may experience when dancing on stage. Indeed, most dancers freely choose to perform or compete, even when they know that doing so may cause anxiety. In figure 4.3, this spectrum of psychophysiological reactions is illustrated using both negatively (e.g., anxiety) and positively (e.g., excitement) tinted language.

THINKING CRITICALLY

- What symptoms do you experience when you feel anxious in dance?
- What symptoms do you experience when you feel excited in dance?
- Can you detect an overlap between anxiety and excitement?
- In your experience, do symptoms of anxiety mostly help or hinder dancers?

When anxiety is not overly high and when it is interpreted in a more positive light, it helps dancers feel ready to perform. With mild to moderate symptoms, we can feel excited about upcoming events while also reaping the benefits of having a body that is suitably activated. For instance, one principal dancer put it like this:

> I'm always really excited when I'm gonna do a role, and I think about it, dream about it. . . . But it's not nervous like, "oh my God I want to get out of here"; it's like, "my God I'm so nervous but I'm so excited, I can't wait to get out there." (Walker & Nordin-Bates, 2010, p. 137)

Indeed, even dancers who do not typically interpret anxiety as facilitative will recognize that they

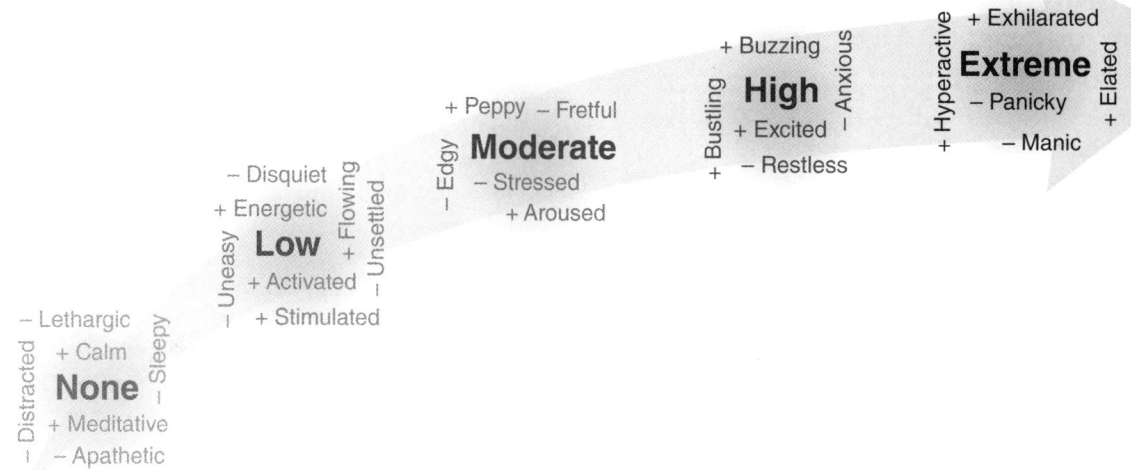

Figure 4.3 Spectrum of psychophysiological reactions ranging from low or no activation to high or extreme activation. The terms associated with these states reflect our interpretation of them as either positive (+) or negative (-).

would not want to go on stage feeling lethargic or sleepy!

How Can Anxiety Be Managed?

Anxiety has been extensively researched in many domains, including sports and mental health. As a result, a vast array of anxiety management strategies has been suggested and investigated (Rumbold et al., 2012). However, the techniques emphasized by different scholars differ with the domain or theoretical underpinnings they use. Three main sets of anxiety management techniques are outlined next. These include a focus on reducing symptoms, as has been common in sport psychology research and practice; a focus on **habituation** or desensitization, as is typical of especially the behavioral part of cognitive behavioral techniques; and last, a focus on symptom acceptance, which is a key part of mindfulness-based approaches.

Reducing Excessive Symptoms: Sport Psychology Perspective

In a systematic review, Rumbold et al. (2012) concluded that a variety of different interventions can help performers to manage stress and anxiety and thereby also enhance performance. They highlighted that several aspects should be considered before settling on a particular intervention, however, including the type of outcome that is intended. Because there are both somatic and cognitive symptoms of anxiety, it makes sense to use techniques that target the symptoms that are specific to an individual. For example, a dancer who is physically over-aroused and therefore breathes in a shallow manner may be well-served by breathing or relaxation techniques. In contrast, a dancer who is mostly troubled by her inability to concentrate because of catastrophizing may be better served by learning to focus constructively (see chapter 6). This is sometimes referred to as the *matching hypothesis* (Maynard et al., 1995a, 1995b). Notably, performers usually experience cognitive symptoms as more debilitative than somatic symptoms (e.g., Jones & Hanton, 2001; Walker & Nordin-Bates, 2010).

Reducing Somatic Symptoms

› *Breathing*. One of the most intuitive things that people say to one another when they detect signs of stress or anxiety is to take a deep breath. There is merit in this suggestion, because deliberately breathing deeply can counteract the shallow breaths that often accompany an anxiety reaction. Because dance is a physical activity, it requires oxygenation, which can be compromised with shallow (or held) breath but supported with deep breaths. To breathe optimally, it is suggested that dancers focus on the breath all the way from its beginning at the nose or mouth, deep into the lungs and with accompanying movement of the diaphragm and stomach, and all the way out again. To avoid hyperventilation with its over-intake of oxygen and subsequent dizziness, care must be taken to exhale fully and slowly. It can be useful to pay particular attention to the little pause that is naturally present between exhalation and inhalation when breathing truly is deep. Taking breaths in this way will typically help slow down the breathing rate, reduce muscle tension, and put focus on something that the dancer can do (rather than on matters outside their control, which often causes anxiety). The breath is also a key component in mindfulness practice (see chapter 8).

› *Relaxation*. Just like breathing exercises, relaxation exercises can help reduce somatic anxiety symptoms such as overly high heart and breathing rates and excessive muscle tension. Sport psychologists have often used classic relaxation exercises such as the progressive relaxation originally devised by Jacobson (1938), and suggestions for how to use such techniques are available in the applied dance psychology book by Taylor and Estanol (2015). Although not strictly focused on achieving relaxation, the body scanning exercises typical of mindfulness practice often have relaxation as a side effect. For more about body scanning, including a sound file that you can try for yourself, see chapter 8.

› *Exercise*. Moving around helps the body handle the adrenaline that is being released when a person is anxious, so a good warm-up or workout can be helpful to anxious dancers. It can also help people see (or attribute) physical movement as the cause for their increased heart and breathing rates rather than as caused by anxiety. Indeed, a well-established behavioral experiment in CBT is to ask an anxious person to exercise and then evaluate their symptoms. How does their heart rate feel? Their breathing? Their overall body? Do these symptoms feel dangerous or problematic? By interpreting the symptoms of anxiety as natural reactions, quite akin to those induced by normal healthy exercise, some of the negativity around anxiety—or the fear of the fear—can be reduced.

› *Music.* Dancers, like athletes, can benefit from using music in a strategic way, including to relax and calm down—or the opposite, to increase arousal and excitement (Karageorghis et al., 2018; Laukka & Quick, 2013). This is because music has the power to activate either our sympathetic nervous system (creating increased arousal) or the parasympathetic nervous system (creating reductions in arousal; for review, see Terry et al., 2020). However, as a recent review points out, the effects of music are typically not large (Terry et al., 2020), so it is perhaps best seen as a complement to other anxiety management strategies.

Reducing Cognitive Symptoms

› *Focus on controllable aspects.* Because anxiety typically arises from a feeling of being out of control, it makes sense that anxiety can be reduced when dancers refocus on factors that are within their control (Cheng & Hardy, 2016; Hanton et al., 2008; Jones et al., 2019; Walker & Nordin-Bates, 2010). Indeed, dancers who focus on uncontrollable aspects (e.g., how good other contestants are in a competition or what teachers and critics think of them) are at greatly increased risk of high anxiety. A useful strategy can be to encourage dancers to make lists of uncontrollable versus controllable factors that are relevant for them and then work to actively increase focus on the latter. Such factors may include, but are not limited to, the factors listed in table 4.2.

› *Reinterpreting symptoms.* As already noted (see also figure 4.2), reinterpreting symptoms as facilitative or unimportant can help reduce cognitive anxiety. This is because we do not "fear the fear" or react unnecessarily to any somatic symptoms that are present. Instead of worrying that butterflies in the stomach are a sign of not being ready or not being good enough, we can simply notice and acknowledge them as a normal sign of activation and of being ready to perform. "Ah, here come the butterflies and the restless legs again! Typical me, around performance time. Now, what was it that I wanted to focus on?"

› *Self-confidence enhancing strategies.* Most of the strategies for enhancing self-confidence (see chapter 3) are suitable also for helping to reduce symptoms of anxiety, especially cognitive anxiety. This is because of the negative correlation (relationship) between self-confidence and anxiety: performers with higher levels of self-confidence typically feel less anxious (e.g., Hanton et al., 2008; Jones et al., 2019). One of the strategies suggested in chapter 3 is to optimize preparation; similarly, dancers can prepare for the unexpected to reduce unwanted anxiety (Taylor & Estanol, 2015). Of course, being prepared and having a backup plan is a good idea generally.

› *Psychological skills.* Several psychological skills can help performers to handle their anxiety (Fletcher & Hanton, 2001; Rumbold et al., 2012; Walker & Nordin-Bates, 2010). Often, applied consultants combine several psychological skills into a package, such as imagery, self-talk, and goal setting. This practice may make it harder to evaluate which specific skill is most helpful (the active ingredient), but it may also maximize the potential helpfulness of the intervention. Dancers can

Table 4.2 **Common Uncontrollable and Controllable Factors in Dance**

Uncontrollable factors	Controllable factors
✓ how competent other dancers are (comparison)	✓ their own goals, especially process goals
✓ what the teacher thinks of them	✓ their own technique
✓ what scores or results judges or juries will award	✓ their own effort level
✓ what the casting will be	✓ interpreting music and rhythm
✓ the size and feel of a studio or stage	✓ what they want to communicate with their movements
✓ weather	✓ processes and the present moment (rather than outcomes)

Note: To learn more about process goals, see chapter 9; for more about nurturing a task orientation, see chapter 5; for more about nurturing a constructive focus, see chapter 6.

also learn several skills that may all be useful, albeit in different situations. For more about psychological skills, see chapters 8-10.

Habituating to Reduce Symptoms: CBT Perspective

As you learned in the introduction, a key component of behavior therapy is gradual systematic exposure aimed at getting a person to habituate to emotions and situations (for a sports example related to anxiety, see Gustafsson et al., 2017). One dancer who was interviewed about her anxiety attributed her very low levels of performance anxiety to her training, which had included regular stage performances from an early age and which she felt "had prepared her for a lifetime of stage appearances" (Walker & Nordin-Bates, 2010, p. 136). One way in which anxiety about upcoming situations can be reduced is therefore to familiarize oneself with that situation as much as possible. For instance, dancers may be able to visit the school, theater, or other venue where they will later compete or perform. If they cannot physically visit, they may benefit from speaking to people who have been in these places before and from seeing pictures or videos that have been recorded there. As you might notice, these preparations are fully in line with the recommendations for strengthening self-confidence outlined in chapter 3.

Once information about the venue or situation has been gathered, the dancer would also do well to incorporate this information into their imagery practice to obtain further familiarization and habituation. They might, for example, imagine going through the dance they will perform on the specific stage they have visited, including its size, lighting, placement of wings, and other key features. For more about rehearsing via imagery, see chapter 10. To practice habituation via exposure for yourself, you can try the exercise outlined in form 4.1. For more inspiration, see Gustafsson et al. (2017). Another way to show how avoidance maintains anxiety over time while exposure can reduce it is via functional analysis (figure 4.4). In this set of two examples, a dancer is due to perform in a new venue, which she knows little about but has heard has a stage with unusual dimensions. In the first example analysis, she prefers not to think about the upcoming show because this causes her anxiety. This avoidance reduces anxiety in the short term but reinforces her belief that performing there is scary. Her anxiety is maintained in the long term, and she performs with less confidence. If she, per the second analysis, is instead encouraged to expose herself to what she fears (e.g., by visiting the venue and imagining performing there on a systematic basis), she will be uncomfortable in the short term yet reduce anxiety and build confidence in the long term.

Accepting Symptoms: Mindfulness Perspective

The idea of interpreting anxiety symptoms as unimportant (neutral) has been mentioned previously in this chapter. Although that literature is based in sports, we can draw parallels to the key component of mindfulness practice known as acceptance. Specifically, mindfulness has been described as "a way of paying attention that entails intentionally being aware of the present moment and accepting things just as they are without judgment" (Kaufman et al., 2018, p. 3). As such, a mindful dancer would observe his symptoms of anxiety, accept them for what they are, and then calmly move on with what he wants to do (e.g., perform a variation). By labeling his symptoms as neither debilitative nor facilitative, he would be less likely to get stuck in thoughts about how such symptoms might affect performance, thereby freeing up valuable cognitive resources for the task at hand—dancing. Of course, avoiding judgment in favor of acceptance may not always come easily, but research shows that it is possible to learn and that it has a range of associated benefits including reduced anxiety and improved performance (Noetel et al., 2019). For a more in-depth consideration of mindfulness for dancers, see chapter 8.

Psyching Up: The Other Side of the Coin

Many dancers are concerned about the effects of high anxiety rather than the opposite: a lack of symptoms. Yet, most dancers do want to feel some level of activation, energy, and excitement. Perhaps most common among dancers who perform the very same show repeatedly (Helin, 1989; Walker & Nordin-Bates, 2010), an absence of symptoms may cause dancers to perform less well because their focus is not on the task at hand. They are also not having as much fun but rather feel blasé or bored. That is, they feel that they are too far down on the spectrum illustrated in figure 4.3.

Little research has explored low arousal and anxiety among dancers or the strategies that may be used to psych up. However, it would seem appropriate that dancers who feel neither anxiety nor excitement can benefit from finding something

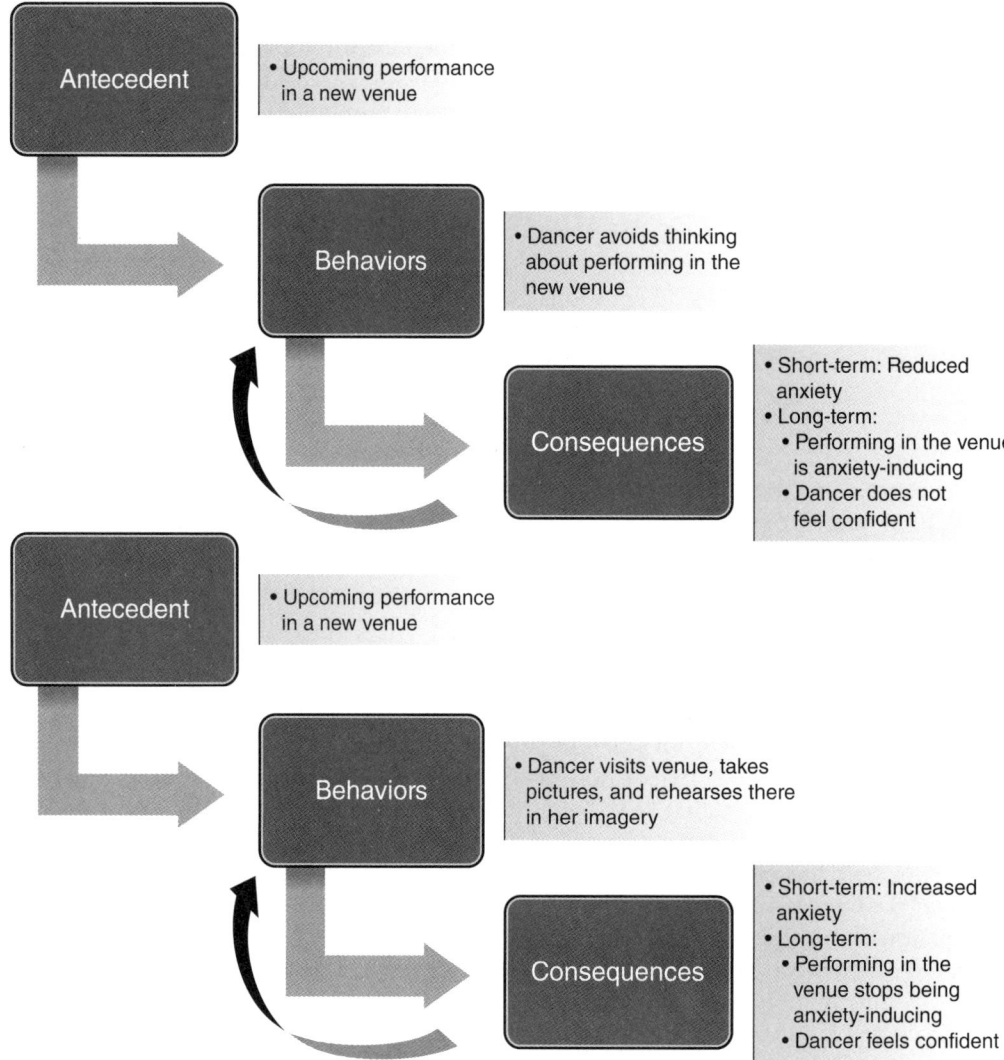

Figure 4.4 Functional analysis examples of how performance anxiety may manifest in dance. The recursive arrows indicate that the consequences make the behavior more likely to reoccur in similar situations in the future (behavior maintenance).

new, however small, to challenge themselves. For instance, a dancer who feels apathetic about a rehearsal that he has done many times before and that he knows will go on for hours could set himself a goal to get a great workout done, regardless of how rehearsal progresses. He might work extra hard with his partner and do extra repetitions or conditioning exercises during waiting times. A musical theater performer who is doing her role for the umpteenth time might challenge herself to bring a new nuance to her role interpretation each night, making it varyingly smooth, strong, or sensuous. Those performing in groups can also help one another in this regard, for instance, by discussing how they can deepen and enhance the messages that they are going to convey. Energizing music and reconnecting with one's long-term goals may also be helpful.

Form 4.1 — GET PRACTICAL: MANAGING ANXIETY BY WORKING WITH AN EXPOSURE HIERARCHY

Think of a task that you would like to accomplish but that makes you nervous or an activity that you avoid doing to escape the feelings of anxiety (stress, fear, discomfort) that they bring. This activity will be at the top of your exposure hierarchy. Write it there and add within the brackets the level of anxiety that you feel it brings on a scale from 0 (no anxiety reaction whatsoever) to 100 (maximal anxiety). Then think about something similar that would still make you nervous but that feels somewhat less daunting. Work your way down until you have a variety of related activities that cause you varying levels of anxiety. The idea is to then work your way up in a systematic and gradual fashion, from the mildly scary and up. Consider a step accomplished when its anxiety rating has decreased to a low/mild level and you feel ready to take on the next step. If these criteria are not fulfilled, keep doing the same (or similar) exposure activity until they are.

EXAMPLES OF EXPOSURE ACTIVITIES

Dancing at the front of the studio; going first; going for something so much that I fall over; dancing after rehabilitating an injury; speaking to people I find intimidating; standing up for myself and my opinions; saying no; saying yes; contributing my opinion in rehearsals; being creative in front of others; improvising; looking at myself in the mirror or on film.

WHAT MAKES A GOOD EXPOSURE ACTIVITY?

1) *It is within your control.* Make sure that you choose activities that are practical, possible, and up to you, rather than dependent on the behavior or goodwill of others (e.g., what a teacher might say or do). This also helps ensure that you can repeat the activity several times, which is typically an important component.
2) *It is specific.* Be precise about what you will do, how you will do it, and for how long.
3) *It is objectively safe.* You need to be prepared to feel discomfort, but you should not be unsafe in any objective sense.

EXAMPLE 1: SPEAKING TO A CHOREOGRAPHER THAT I FIND INTIMIDATING

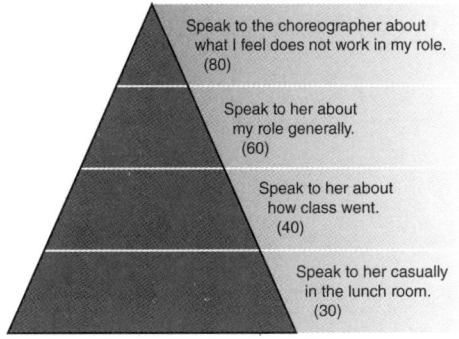

Form 4.1 *(continued)*

EXAMPLE 2: DANCE A COMPLICATED VARIATION, DURING WHICH I PREVIOUSLY INJURED MY FOOT

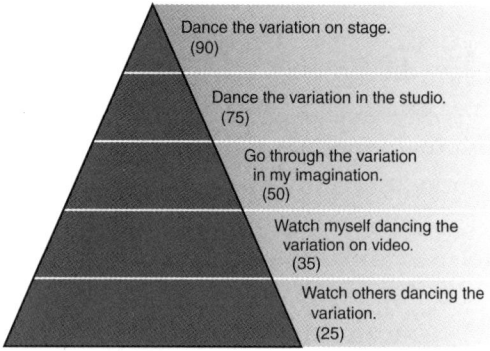 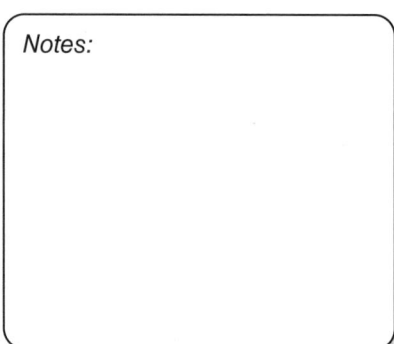

YOUR OWN EXAMPLE: _____

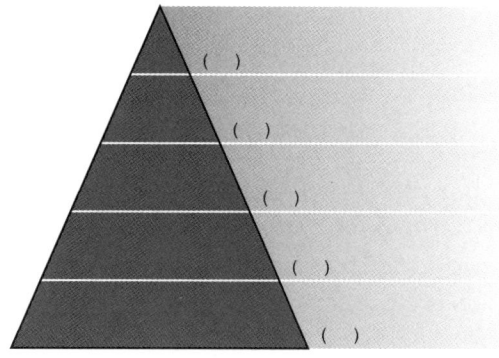 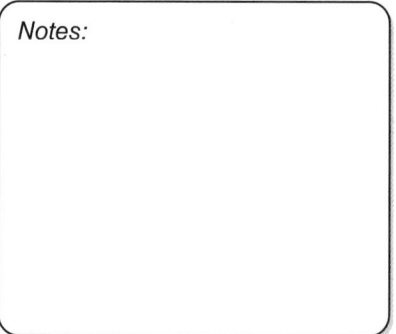

Go to *HKPropel* to download this worksheet.

From S. Nordin-Bates, *Essentials of Dance Psychology* (Champaign, IL: Human Kinetics, 2023).

Anton: Case Study of Anxiety

Anton is a student in his final year. He wants to be a professional dancer but dreads having to audition. Even thinking about auditioning gives him the creeps, so he tries not to think about it at all. When people ask him about his plans, he changes the subject. Eventually, a teacher senses that something is wrong and sets up a meeting with Anton. He is visibly uncomfortable but cannot avoid the topic in a meeting specifically focused on his (lack of) audition plans. Together, they decide that professional help is needed to handle the situation.

The psychologist asks Anton to describe his thoughts, feelings, and behavior around auditions, and together they draw up functional analyses that help Anton realize that his avoidance behaviors have, in fact, perpetuated his anxiety over time. He cautiously agrees to create an exposure hierarchy in which standing at the front while auditioning for his dream company is at the top (most anxiety-inducing). Below that are activities such as setting up a mock audition (scary), doing imagery rehearsals of how auditions might play out (stressful), and finding information about five upcoming auditions (uncomfortable but doable). Although still anxious, Anton understands the psychologist's analogy: to expand your comfort zone, you need to stretch. And just like physical stretching for the splits, results are not instant; only via systematic practice and staying with mild to moderate discomfort for a while will it have an effect. On that basis, Anton agrees that he will try to stay with his anxiety and trust that things will change. The hierarchy had to be updated a couple of times, and sometimes the temptation to give in was overwhelming. But because his ultimate goal of becoming a professional was highly motivating, Anton was gradually able to do what he had decided, however anxious he felt at the start of each new activity on the hierarchy. Once he felt the confidence boost of having accomplished one activity, his motivation grew. With time and practice, auditions felt like they were no longer about survival; instead, they felt like a situation in which Anton would actually be able to demonstrate his technique and his artistry—with or without anxiety symptoms.

Composite case study created on the basis of a conversation with Henrik Gustafsson, PhD, professor in sport science at Karlstad University and sport psychology consultant to the Swedish Olympic Committee.

CRITICAL ASPECTS OF RESEARCH INTO ANXIETY

1. Research into anxiety in dance is limited. What does exist typically studies anxiety as a correlate or outcome of something else, such as motivation or motivational climate perceptions (Haraldsen et al., 2020; Nordin-Bates et al., 2012; Quested et al., 2011); therefore, these studies are referenced in other chapters of this book.

2. The literature (and indeed this chapter) sometimes uses the terms *anxiety* and *stress* interchangeably. Although this is partly legitimate (i.e., because the acute stress response underpins both when considered at the state level), the long-term health effects of stress are highly problematic and thus different from the partly positive approach to anxiety taken in this chapter. To understand when stress and anxiety are likely to lead to positive versus negative outcomes, temporal aspects must be considered.

3. Organizational stressors for dancers and leaders in dance would benefit from research attention in dance, just as it has in sports (Arnold & Fletcher, 2012; Rumbold et al., 2012).

KEY POINTS AND RECOMMENDATIONS FOR ANXIETY IN DANCE

1. Dancers can be greatly helped by understanding that anxiety
   - is a natural, human reaction that is not dangerous,
   - is not necessarily lower among experienced dancers, and
   - is going to dissipate after a short time (around 20 minutes) if the dancer is brave enough to stay in the anxiety-inducing situation without escaping either physically (e.g., leaving the room) or mentally (e.g., by distracting themselves).
2. Performance is more likely to be undermined by feeling out of control or by interpreting anxiety as debilitative than it is by simply having anxiety symptoms. Therefore, helpful strategies are often those that help dancers
   - understand that anxiety is often unimportant and sometimes positive, and
   - feel in control while accepting that not everything can be controlled.

Part II

Dance-Specific Characteristics and Dispositions

5

Motivation

"There was still no likelihood that we could make a living from dance. We were doing it because we loved it . . . We realized how full we felt; we were surrounded by music and dancing and joy."

Alvin Ailey, dancer and choreographer

CHAPTER OBJECTIVES

After reading this chapter, you will be able to

1. describe what motivation is, including how it is conceptualized in achievement goal theory and self-determination theory;
2. outline what task and ego orientations, and self-determined and controlled motivational regulations are;
3. discuss task orientation and basic psychological need satisfaction as sources of healthy motivation in dance;
4. critically discuss the consequences of healthy versus unhealthy motivation in dance;
5. apply basic recommendations to nurture your own healthy motivation; and
6. think critically about the nature and impact of motivation in dance settings.

Key Terms

achievement goals	extrinsic motivation	need satisfaction
amotivation	goal involvement	need thwarting
approach oriented	goal orientation	orthogonality
autonomy	intrinsic motivation	performance orientation
avoidance oriented	mastery orientation	relatedness
basic psychological needs	motivation	self-determination
competence	motivational climate	task orientation
ego orientation	motivational regulations	

The English term *motivation* is from the French *motivation*, and its meaning appears to have been largely constant across time. Specifically, motivation is about the willingness to act or the reasons for doing something. In everyday language, we often speak of motivation only as high versus low or strong versus weak; that is, we focus on the *quantity* of motivation that someone has. As this chapter will delineate, motivation theorists have instead found it more valuable to focus on the *quality* of motivation.

What is Motivation?

Motivation is about the willingness to do something. This can be broad and wide ranging (e.g., motivation to dance, go to school, or go to work) or narrow and specific (e.g., motivation to push a little bit extra in the 10th rehearsal of a challenging variation). It is an important cornerstone in performance psychology, not least because it has been found to affect an assortment of outcomes, including performance and well-being. Indeed, without some sort of motivation there would be no dancing! In psychology, a basic definition of motivation is that it concerns the direction and intensity of effort (Sage, 1977). By *direction*, we mean what it is that the person is motivated to do—for instance, to attend daily class, to audition, or to do conditioning. By *intensity*, we mean the amount of effort that the person puts forth—that is, how hard they work, but also such things as whether they arrive early or late for practice and other more implicit signs of effort and engagement with the activity. This definition is in line with how we usually talk about motivation in everyday language; for instance, we may say we feel really motivated to dance or comment on how unmotivated a student appears to be.

Importantly, the everyday view of motivation only considers it as high (or strong) versus low (or weak)—that is, the quantity of motivation that someone has. Motivation researchers have often found it more valuable to focus on the quality of motivation, because it enables us to answer truly intriguing questions: Why do people dance? Why do two dancers seem equally motivated, but one is more confident and satisfied than another? That is, we may be interested in the well-being-related outcomes of different types (qualities) of motivation. Two main theoretical frameworks have been used extensively to study the motivation of a wide variety of groups such as athletes, students, employees, and dancers: achievement goal theory (AGT; Nicholls, 1984, Roberts, 1993) and self-determination theory (SDT; Deci & Ryan, 1985, 2000; Ryan & Deci, 2000). Because AGT and SDT are both important and complementary, the remainder of this chapter focuses on the nature, sources, consequences, and nurture of motivation as it is conceptualized in these two theories. However, it is worth noting that other theories of motivation also exist.

Achievement Goal Theory Perspective on Motivation

In AGT, a key underpinning principle is that humans strive to experience competence in their pursuits (Nicholls, 1984, 1989). Put differently, we all want to feel able to do things that we value and that are of use to us. In so doing, we have two different conceptions of ability: a **task orientation** and an **ego orientation**.

Task and Ego Orientations

A dancer who is strongly task oriented will feel successful when he improves, works hard, and reaches his own goals. Conversely, a strongly ego-oriented dancer will feel most successful when he is better than others: for instance, when he wins the teacher's approval, learns faster than his peers, or wins a competition. These **goal orientations** also differentiate between the participation motives of different people: strongly task-oriented dancers may give reasons such as fun, learning, and collaboration when asked about why they dance, whereas strongly ego-oriented dancers are more likely to give reasons such as being good at it or that they enjoy winning. In table 5.1, these differences between task and ego orientations are further delineated.

If you are like most people, you will have started to think of your own **achievement goals**, and perhaps those of dancers that you know, when reading the descriptions in table 5.1. Perhaps you found it easy to identify examples of strongly task- and ego-oriented dancers and teachers, or perhaps you found it difficult to make clear categorizations into just two distinct categories. This is because the two achievement goal orientations are not, in fact, something that a person either has or has not; instead, most people are, to some degree, both task and ego oriented (a concept known as **orthogonality**; Roberts et al., 1996). Despite this fact, researchers and practitioners often find it helpful to study and make recommendations for the two goal orientations separately. This helps keep things simple and helps us focus on the goal orientation that dominates at a given time. In the dance research that exists on this topic, dancers in a variety of different styles and levels appear to be more task oriented than ego oriented (Carr & Wyon, 2003; de Bruin et al., 2009; Hanrahan et al., 2009; Lacaille et al., 2007; Nieminen et al., 2001).

Approach and Avoidance Goals

While most theorizing and research into achievement goals in performance domains have focused on the task–ego distinction, some researchers have further delineated these constructs as either **approach oriented** or **avoidance oriented** (Elliot, 1999). In their basic form, approach goals are about moving toward something desirable, and avoidance goals are about moving away from something undesirable. When crossed with the task–ego goal orientations, a 2 × 2 framework emerges (figure 5.1). Unfortunately, AGT researchers use slightly varied terminologies, so to interpret this figure (and the related literature), keep in mind that **mastery orientation** is a synonym for task (orientation, involvement) and **performance orientation** is a synonym for ego (orientation, involvement).

The approach orientations are similar to how task and ego orientations are typically described: Dancers with a strong mastery approach orientation are motivated to learn, improve, and reach their own goals, whereas dancers with a strong performance approach orientation are motivated to be the best

Table 5.1 **Key Distinguishing Features of Task and Ego Orientations**

	Task orientation	Ego orientation
Feels competent or successful when . . .	• Learning • Improving • Reaching own goals • Working hard	• Superior to others • Recognized as good • Not having to put as much effort in as others to achieve the same outcome
Feels incompetent or unsuccessful when . . .	• Failing to reach own goals • Not doing one's best • Reaching a plateau in development	• Losing or feeling inferior to others • Not recognized by others • Having to put more effort in than others to achieve the same outcome
Typical participation motives	• Learning new things • Self-development (e.g., see how far one can get) • Collaboration	• Being good at it • Recognition and prizes • Status
Perceptions of peers	• Collaborators and partners • Inspiring	• Competitors and rivals • Threatening
Acceptable strategies for reaching goals	• More considerate and just (e.g., more likely to collaborate and accept defeat gracefully) • The integrity of the process is more important than the final outcome	• More self-serving (e.g., more likely to be rivalrous or to cheat) • The end justifies the means (superiority/winning is everything)

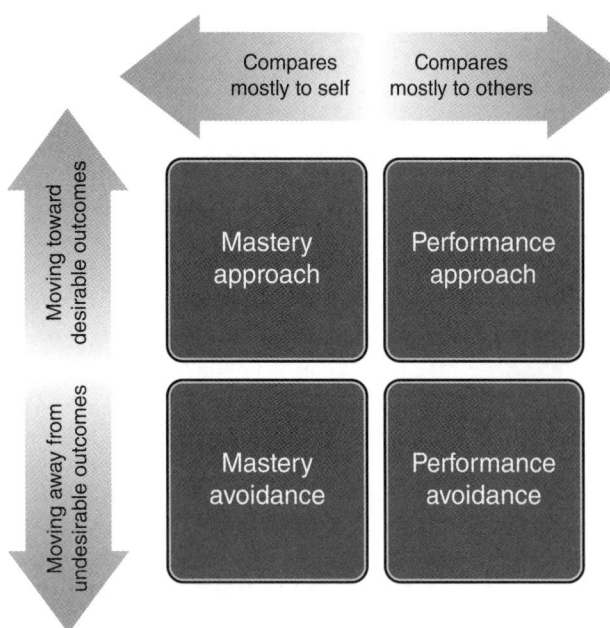

Figure 5.1 The 2 × 2 achievement goal model.
Adapted from Elliot (1999) and Elliot and McGregor (2001).

and demonstrate superiority. Dancers with strong avoidance orientations, in contrast, are primarily motivated to avoid undesirable outcomes. The distinction between performance (ego) approach versus performance avoidance orientations was the first departure from the original dichotomous model of achievement goals, because scholars wanted to distinguish between wanting to be superior and wanting to avoid being inferior to others (Elliot, 1999; Elliot & McGregor, 2001). As such, dancers with strong performance avoidance orientations are motivated to not be the worst dancer in the class, not mess up, and not be seen as inferior. Their behavior is therefore likely to be characterized by avoidance (e.g., standing at the back, not practicing things they are not good at), whereas the behavior of dancers with strong performance approach orientations includes more direct tackling of the tasks they believe are necessary for them to get ahead.

Although little research into this trichotomous approach to goal orientations (i.e., mastery, performance approach, and performance avoidance goals) has been undertaken with dancers, two studies are worth mentioning. Specifically, these investigations demonstrated that both performance approach and performance avoidance goals seemed to be detrimental to performing artists in terms of emotional outcomes and performance quality (Lacaille et al., 2005, 2007). Instead, they seemed to benefit most from so-called *intrinsic goals*, such as enjoying and getting absorbed in the artistic experience. Such intrinsic goals were associated with positive emotional outcomes and with performance quality. Finally, the relationship between performance goals (both approach and avoidance) and performance quality was mediated by anxiety; that is, the goals appeared to be detrimental because they increased anxiety among the performers. The authors noted that their results partly diverged from those obtained in education and sports, where performance approach goals have been shown to be partly beneficial. They further speculated that this might be because performing artists often suffer from high levels of trait anxiety. Unfortunately, it seems that no further investigation of intrinsic goals for artists has been pursued as yet, but it certainly represents a valuable line of inquiry.

In a second stage of model development, scholars also subdivided the mastery (task) orientation into approach versus avoidance (Elliot, 1999; Elliot & McGregor, 2001). As such, dancers with strong mastery avoidance orientations are motivated to not be worse than they were before or fail to meet their own goals. For instance, they may worry about not living up to expectations of how they used to, or even *ought to*, perform—a problem not least for some aging dancers. Again, this may lead to less head-on dealing with important tasks than dancers with a stronger mastery approach orientation would typically display (e.g., being eager to practice difficult new tasks, being comfortable standing at the front of the studio).

A rare study examining the 2 × 2 achievement goal framework with dancers showed that student dancers who endorsed performance approach goals to a greater extent also reported greater trait anxiety (Lench et al., 2010). Both performance approach and performance avoidance goals were associated with lower levels of overall health. Moreover, higher levels of either performance avoidance goals or trait anxiety at the start of term predicted worsened levels of health toward the end of term (when controlling for initial health levels). It has also been argued that among highly perfectionistic dancers, avoidance goals are likely to be common (Nordin-Bates & Abrahamsen, 2016).

Sources of Different Achievement Goals

In AGT, goal orientations are conceptualized as relatively consistent—not as stable as personality traits, but like dispositions that are typical of a person. However, it is recognized that these dispositions are subject to change and can be influenced in various ways. The most common way in which this has been studied is via a construct known as the **motivational climate**, which is fully outlined in chapter 11. The motivational climate is the psychosocial atmosphere, structure, and feel of a particular setting, such as a particular dance class (Ames, 1992). It is heavily influenced by the teacher in charge but also by peers (other students, colleagues) and, especially for younger performers, parents (e.g., Keegan et al., 2009).

The interaction of goal orientations and perceptions of the motivational climate are said to result in something known as **goal involvement**—that is, the extent to which a person is task and/or ego involved at a particular time (Ames, 1992). This is further illustrated in figure 5.2.

Consider Jane, who usually has a strong task orientation and a moderate ego orientation. If she is in a motivational climate where she perceives the teacher to focus on individual progress, praise effort, and encourage collaboration, Jane is likely to become strongly task involved and not particularly ego involved. When taking a different class, however, Jane perceives the teacher to focus only on the best dancers in the company. He talks about how competitive the dance world is and shows clear dislike when Jane makes mistakes. In this class, Jane is more likely to have her normally moderate ego orientation enhanced, such that she becomes more ego involved than in the other class.

Consequences of Holding Different Achievement Goals

Literature examining the correlates and consequences of holding a task versus an ego orientation is plentiful, especially in sports. There are major advantages to being strongly task oriented, whereas a strong ego orientation should be considered a risk factor for a variety of problems. The main reason behind such findings is that the factors that help task-oriented dancers feel competent and successful (e.g., their own effort and learning strategies) are under their own control, whereas the factors that make ego-oriented dancers feel competent and successful are not. For instance, the abilities of other dancers or opinions of teachers and judges are common things to focus on in dance, yet they are largely outside of our control. By focusing on such aspects, and even hinging their own sense of competence on it, ego-oriented individuals are effectively letting other people and circumstance influence their sense of success or failure. By focusing on our own learning and progress, we instead put ourselves in charge and help ourselves feel successful to a far larger extent.

Of course, ego-oriented individuals do feel good when they are superior. But no dancer (or human) is superior to others all of the time, in every regard. Therefore, their sense of competence is at best varied (they sometimes feel superior, and they sometimes feel inferior) and at worst suppressed and highly fragile. An example of the latter is when an ego-oriented individual moves

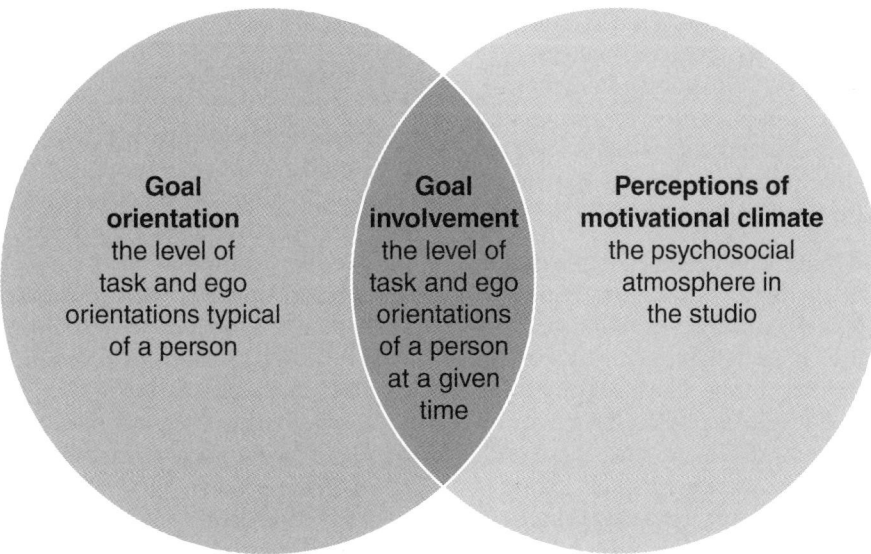

Figure 5.2 The interaction of goal orientations and motivational climate perceptions result in the goal involvement of a dancer at a given time.

up a level and is suddenly surrounded by dancers who are better than they; a phenomenon known as the big-fish-little-pond-effect (Marsh, 1987). It might be valuable for staff in highly selective dance schools to be aware of this potential issue when they welcome a new class of students into their school. In some cases, nearly all those students have been the best in their previous school, but not everyone can be the best in this new class. If the new school does not nurture task involvement, several of the risks associated with ego orientations are likely to emerge. Educators who teach students in or from competitive dance may also need to pay particular attention to the risks inherent in ego involvement (Andrzejewski et al., 2013).

Well-Being-Related Consequences of Achievement Goals

In reviews of achievement goal research in sports and exercise, Lochbaum et al. (2016) and Keegan (2018) summarized the following findings as having consistently emerged in the literature:

> Having a strong task orientation is associated with positive indicators of well-being such as greater perceived competence, self-esteem and positive emotions, lesser negative affect, and with self-determined motivation (a full discussion of self-determination is provided later in this chapter).

> Having a strong ego orientation is associated with some indicators of lesser well-being, such as negative emotions, but also with a range of both more and less self-determined motivational regulations. That is, persons who hold an ego orientation are likely to vary in their sources of motivation, sometimes pursuing activities out of interest and value and sometimes out of a sense of pressure. They are also more likely to suffer from amotivation (losing their motivation entirely).

In the first study into achievement goals in dance, dance students' goal orientations were investigated alongside their perceived purposes of dance (Nieminen et al., 2001). Those with stronger task orientations were more likely to see dance as something that should teach people to be physically active and to reach for high standards. In contrast, those with stronger ego orientations were more likely to report that dance should help people get a good career or high status and teach people to be competitive and not give up. Other studies have found links between dancers' ego orientations and perfectionism (Carr & Wyon, 2003; de Bruin et al., 2009), as well as several aspects of disordered eating (de Bruin et al., 2009). Interviewees in one study reported that interpersonal comparison (an aspect of being ego oriented) might nurture perfectionism, because it induces a striving to be better than others and/or creates a sense of inadequacy (Nordin-Bates, 2020).

Performance-Related Consequences of Achievement Goals

Keegan (2018) and Lochbaum et al. (2016) further summarized the following findings relating to performance as having consistently emerged in the literature:

> A strong task orientation is associated with a variety of attitudes and strategies related to better learning and performance (e.g., believing that effort leads to success, choosing challenging tasks, persistence) and lesser use of maladaptive strategies (e.g., avoidance and cheating). Persons with strong task orientations are also more likely to engage in prosocial moral behaviors.

> A strong ego orientation is associated with a mix of more and less adaptive attitudes and strategies related to learning and performance. For instance, ego-oriented persons engage in both adaptive and maladaptive behaviors (e.g., effort *and* avoidance). They are more likely to believe that talent is the cause of success and to engage in antisocial moral behaviors.

The reason why ego-oriented performers engage in this mixed set of behaviors is probably because they adapt their behaviors to their present situation. For instance, they are likely to put in effort when they are relatively sure that doing so will help them be superior. But if they feel threatened by other seemingly more skilled dancers, they may instead withdraw their efforts. By not even entering comparison, they can avoid the risk of appearing inferior and preserve their volatile sense of competence. As such, teachers (and dancers themselves) would do well to watch for signs of avoidance or for dancers making unexplained excuses (e.g., stating that "My foot is bothering me, so I had better sit this class out" but being seen doing similarly challenging tasks an hour later).

A functional analysis helps to illustrate this phenomenon (figure 5.3). In this set of two examples, a dancer is taking class with several people whom he does not know but who seem to do better than he.

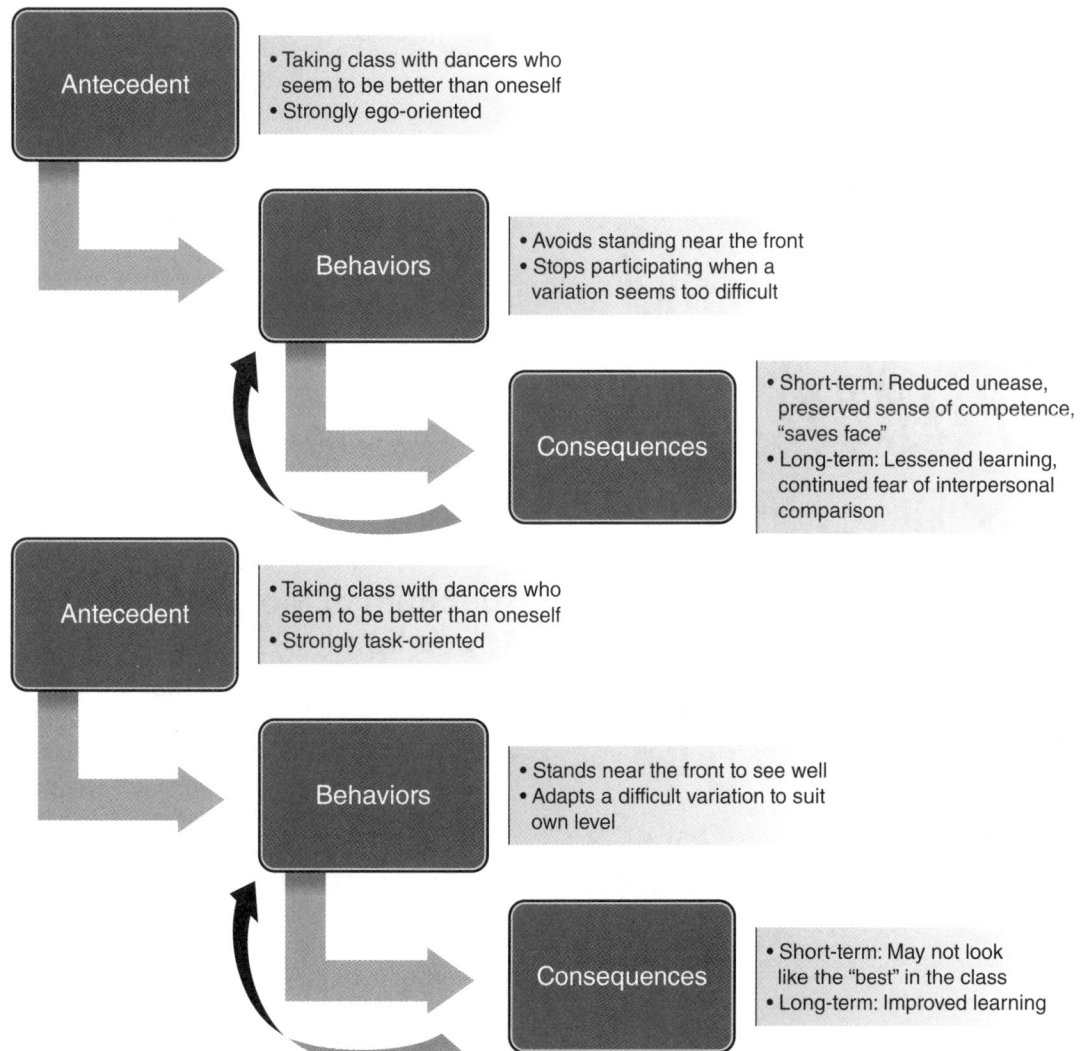

Figure 5.3 Functional analysis examples of how achievement goals may manifest in dance. The recursive arrows indicate that the consequences make the behavior more likely to reoccur in similar situations in the future (behavior maintenance).

In the first analysis, he is also strongly ego oriented, with his sense of competence being hinged upon being superior and looking good. When this does not seem possible, he avoids being seen by standing far from the front and by stepping out altogether when the teacher sets a very challenging variation. By avoiding the situation, the dancer reduces his sense of unease over being inferior, saves face, and preserves (to a degree) a sense of competence. However, this comes with the long-term cost of lesser learning, and his fear of interpersonal comparison will not improve.

If, per the second analysis, our dancer is instead strongly task oriented, then his sense of competence is largely undisturbed by others being supe-rior and he may feel inspired to learn from those who are better. To maximize his learning, he stands near the front and when a variation becomes too difficult, he adapts it by focusing on the legs and simplifying the arms. He may not look the best to the teacher or to others in the class, but he is maximizing his learning.

Another example is when dancers prefer to enter situations (e.g., competitions, classes) where they are guaranteed to win or look superior rather than choose difficult situations where they may learn more. Indeed, we may ask ourselves whether we are trying to *improve* something, or just *prove* something.

Strongly ego-oriented performers are also somewhat more likely to do anything it takes to get

Go to HK*Propel* to find a full-sized version of this and other lettering art.

Lettering art by Ink & Lise. Used with permission.

ahead, including cheating (table 5.1). Such behaviors are more likely than avoidance if the outcome is perceived as so important to the individual that avoiding the situation is not an option. One of the founders of AGT, John Nicholls, summed up the risks of being strongly ego oriented in his famous saying that "when winning is everything, it is worth doing anything to win" (Nicholls, 1989, p. 133). This statement is relevant even to dance contexts that do not comprise actual competitions: For instance, those who want to outperform their peers at any cost may be unhelpful when a classmate is struggling to learn a skill. They may not share advice and information that has the potential to help others; they may continue training and competing while injured; and they may even deliberately stand in front of someone in the studio so that they get the better view of the teacher at others' expense. However, the associations between task orientations and positive outcomes are stronger than those between ego orientations and negative outcomes. Thus, holding a moderate ego orientation may not be problematic as long as it is backed up by a concurrent moderate-to-strong task orientation.

Self-Determination Theory Perspective on Motivation

SDT is a complex metatheory which, in its full form, comprises six minitheories that concern not only the intrapersonal experience of motivation but also the interpersonal styles (e.g., teaching behaviors) that act as antecedents of motivated behavior and a wide range of its outcomes (e.g., Standage et al., 2018). For this introduction to the theory, however, we will stick to the name of the metatheory, SDT, throughout.

Spectrum of Motivational Regulations

In SDT, motivation is conceptualized by way of a spectrum of different types of motivation known as **motivational regulations** (Deci & Ryan, 1985, 2000; Ryan & Deci, 2000). As shown in figure 5.4, these range from **amotivation** (a lack of clear reasons why one would engage in an activity) to **intrinsic motivation**, the holy grail of motivational regulations. Specifically, intrinsic motivation is in evidence when we do something out of inherent interest, joy, or meaningfulness. The quote by Alvin Ailey at the start of this chapter gives a clear example of intrinsic motivation by its use of phrases such as *love*, *joy*, and *fullness*. The quote also hints at an otherwise common source of **extrinsic motivation**—namely, money—by stating that they were *not* driven to dance in order to make a living.

Dancers may be motivated by intrinsic or extrinsic reasons and display varying degrees of **self-determination** versus controlled motivation (figure 5.4). Dancers can also be amotivated. In the latter case, neither intrinsic nor extrinsic sources of motivation are particularly strong, and dancers are likely to doubt why they are there at all. As such, amotivation is clearly a precursor to dropout. In her study of dance in middle schools, Stinson (1997) exemplified amotivation: "[S]ome students found dance to be boring . . . and were not motivated to participate. . . . Lacking both intrinsic and extrinsic motivators, students who experienced dance in this first category had no reason to be engaged" (Stinson, 1997, p. 65, quote abridged).

Extrinsic motivation includes a variety of different motivational regulations, ranging from the most controlled (external regulation) to relatively

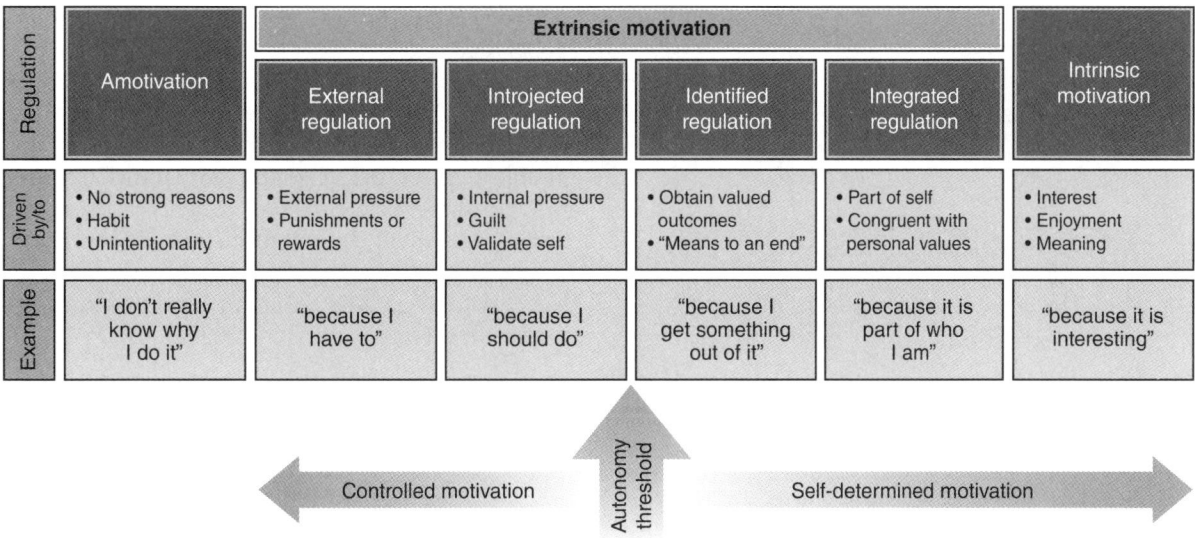

Figure 5.4 The spectrum of motivational regulations in self-determination theory.
Adapted from Deci and Ryan (1985) and Ryan and Deci (2000).

self-determined (integrated regulation). Specifically, external regulation is when a person undertakes a task or behavior because they must. Entirely led by external contingencies, behaviors driven by such motivation are clearly not self-determined, and are therefore not sustainable either. Indeed, such behaviors tend to vanish as soon as the external constraints are removed. For example, consider a young dancer who attends tap dance classes because her father says that it is something she must do. If the father later changes his mind, the dancer is highly likely to quit the tap dance classes in favor of something she is more interested in.

With introjected regulation, the pressure to undertake an activity is not external (as for external regulation) but internal; that is, the dancer performs the task for reasons such as feeling that he *should* do it or because he would feel guilty if he did not. Dancers who are strongly ego involved or perfectionistic, who do something to prove themselves worthy or to validate their self-esteem, typically display introjected regulation. For example, consider a dancer whose heart is in commercial dance but has heard that she will not succeed without a stronger technical foundation. As a result, she feels internal pressure to take ballet classes and feels guilty if she skips them. In sum, both external and introjected regulations are pressured (or controlled) forms of motivation. The next form of motivation on the spectrum, identified regulation, is on the other side of the autonomy threshold and therefore the first that can be considered self-driven (i.e., somewhat self-determined or autonomous in nature).

When dancers willingly do something because they feel it will benefit them, they are displaying identified regulation. This includes those who attend dance classes because their friends do and dancers who take up a conditioning regimen because they know it will help them improve valuable dance skills. While such behaviors are personally important and undertaken voluntarily, they are not truly self-determined because they are not done for their own sake; they are a way to get to something else. The most self-determined form of extrinsic motivation is known as integrated regulation because it represents behaviors that are fully integrated into a person's sense of self. Dancers who dance because it is a way to be themselves or because it represents something they value exemplify this regulation.

Intrinsic motivation is qualitatively different from extrinsic motivation because it is the only regulation that is fully about the activity itself: *it* is interesting, *it* is enjoyable, or *it* is meaningful. Pure expressions of intrinsic motivation in dance therefore include those times when we dance for no other reason than the experience itself—when there is no regard for outcomes, evaluations, or other consequences. We can ask ourselves: Would I do it even if it did not lead to anything in particular? If I did not get paid to do it? If nobody else even cared about whether I did it or not? Although a sense of fun is a valuable form of intrinsic motivation, it is not incompatible with having a serious work ethic (see Bond & Stinson, 2007; Stinson, 1997). Indeed, even hard work can (and perhaps should) be imbued with a deep sense of meaning, absorption, and joy.

> ## THINKING CRITICALLY
>
> - Why do you dance or teach, in general and most recently (e.g., latest class)?
> - What is your most recent experience of dance being truly intrinsically motivating?
> - What examples of motivational regulation can you see in your dance setting?
> - Think of an activity that you have left, stopped doing, or avoided when possible. What was your motivational regulation for that activity?

In dance, research typically reveals higher mean scores for intrinsic motivation (and self-determined forms of extrinsic motivation, such as identified regulation) than for extrinsic motivation (Atienza et al., 2020; Balaguer et al., 2011; Hancox et al., 2015; Nordin-Bates et al., 2017; Norfield & Nordin-Bates, 2012; Quested & Duda, 2011b). Dancers also strive for so-called intrinsic goals (e.g., enjoyment, mastery) to greater extents than they do for extrinsic goals (e.g., appearance, meeting expectations of others; Molnar et al., 2021). Interviews with groups as wide ranging as middle school pupils taking dance as an elective (Stinson, 1997); young students in dance talent centers (Aujla et al., 2014); recreational ballet, modern, competitive, and folk dancers (Nieminen, 1998); and independent contemporary dancers (Aujla & Farrer, 2015) confirm that intrinsic motivation is the major driving force to dance. Participants in these studies have reported their love and passion for their art form and how their enjoyment was derived from several factors, including self-expression, movement sensations, skill development, and excitement around performance time (see also Alter, 1997; Bond & Stinson, 2007). It makes sense that inherent interest and the pursuit of something personally meaningful often underpins the drive shown by dancers, not least because careers are typically unpredictable and not very well paid. The latter is especially pertinent for independent dancers (Aujla & Farrer, 2015).

Some dancers, of course, persevere and even succeed despite suboptimal motivational profiles. For instance, recent interviews with professional performers clearly exemplified the variety of motivational regulations that can be experienced (Haraldsen et al., 2020a; see also Bond & Stinson, 2007). Importantly, these vary both *between* people (e.g., someone being more self-determined than another) and *within* people (e.g., one person being more self-determined in some phases of talent development than in others). Some performers made it to the top of their profession with low levels of self-determination, but this seemed to carry high costs in terms of impaired well-being (Haraldsen et al., 2020a).

Sources of Intrinsic and Extrinsic Motivation

As in AGT, SDT theorists propose that humans strive to experience a sense of competence in their lives (Deci & Ryan, 1985, 2000; Ryan & Deci, 2000). But while AGT focuses rather squarely on the need for competence, SDT proposes the existence of three **basic psychological needs**: **autonomy**, **competence**, and **relatedness** (also known as belonging). As outlined in SDT, autonomy is a sense of volition and of being oneself; constructs such as authenticity and empowerment are closely related to autonomy. We therefore feel autonomous when we are doing things that are in line with our goals and values, when we have a say, and when we feel respected for who we truly are. For example, one interview study indicated that the opportunity to create one's own movements and to have the freedom to express one's true self were major reasons why dance was perceived to be fun for middle school pupils (Stinson, 1997).

We feel competent when we master tasks and challenges, when we feel a sense of control over what happens to us, and when we generally feel good enough. As an illustration, young dancers often describe task mastery and overcoming challenges as enjoyable aspects of dance (Aujla et al., 2014). Conversely, a lack of challenge or a sense of repetitiveness can undermine the passion and motivation of young dancers, thereby contributing to dropout (Walker et al., 2012). Lastly, SDT stipulates that we experience relatedness when we feel welcomed and cared for—that is, when we feel surrounded by warmth and have meaningful friendships and other relationships. Accordingly, the opportunity to interact and cocreate with peers can be a major reason why dance is perceived to be enjoyable (Stinson, 1997).

When the three basic psychological needs are met, humans experience not only **need satisfaction** but also healthy motivation and optimal functioning (Deci & Ryan, 2000; Ryan & Deci, 2000). In other words, dancers who feel autonomous, competent, and related experience a variety of both intrapersonal (e.g., optimized performance and well-being) and interpersonal benefits (e.g., rewarding relationships). In contrast, **need thwarting** is highly problematic (Bartholomew et al., 2011; Deci & Ryan, 2000; Ryan & Deci, 2000). Such thwarting is more than simply not having one's needs met; instead, it refers to the active undermining of needs (table 5.2; for more details, see Deci & Ryan, 2000; Bartholomew et al., 2011; Standage et al., 2018).

In SDT-based studies, dancers report their basic needs to be at least moderately, if not highly, satisfied (Hancox et al., 2017; Nordin-Bates, 2020;

Collaboration and peer learning help nurture task involvement, an aspect of healthy motivation.

Table 5.2 **How Satisfaction, Unsatisfaction, and Thwarting of the Basic Needs for Autonomy, Competence, and Relatedness May Be Experienced**

Need	When this need is satisfied, this can make a dancer feel . . .	When this need is unsatisfied, this can make a dancer feel . . .	When this need is thwarted, this can make a dancer feel . . .
Autonomy	• A sense of meaning • Authentic • Following own path	• Disinterested • Not heard • Pointless	• Controlled, manipulated • Intimidated • Pressured
Competence	• Good enough • In progress • Able to master challenges	• Unclear over what needs to be done • As though skill makes little difference	• Inadequate • Inferior • Unable to affect what happens
Relatedness	• Connected • Close	• Disconnected • As though they do not fit in	• Disrespected • Alienated, bullied

Spending time talking about things both inside and outside of dance helps nurture relatedness, one of three basic psychological needs.

Norfield & Nordin-Bates, 2012; Quested & Duda, 2009, 2010; 2011a; Quested et al., 2011c). Dancers in some of these studies, comprising young students (Nordin-Bates, 2020; Quested & Duda, 2009, 2010) and adult community dancers (Norfield & Nordin-Bates, 2012), rated their relatedness as the most highly satisfied need, while their autonomy experiences were more moderate. This seems to contrast the experiences of independent dancers, whose autonomy is great but their relatedness more limited: because they more often worked alone, they sometimes lacked the friendships and sense of teamwork that dancers in schools and companies may have (Aujla & Farrer, 2015). At the same time, they reported value in creating a social support group for themselves and argued that social skills were an important part in being successful.

As yet, few studies have examined need thwarting in dance. In the studies that have, levels of need thwarting generally appear to be relatively low but also varied (Hancox et al., 2017; Haraldsen et al., 2019, 2020b). In a longitudinal study of junior elite performers, it was found that the need for competence was the most likely to be thwarted (approximately 40% of the performers), while the need for relatedness was the least likely (approximately 10%; Haraldsen et al., 2020b).

Consequences of Need Satisfaction and Self-Determination

SDT is one of the most well-researched topics in sport and exercise psychology; further, it is a vigorously researched topic in several other domains such as health care, education, and business. There are also a growing number of SDT-based publications in dance. As a result, we have a strong evidence base to draw conclusions from regarding the consequences of intrinsic versus extrinsic motivation and of higher versus lower need satisfaction.

Well-Being-Related Consequences of Need Satisfaction and Self-Determination

In their review of consequences associated with different motivational regulations and of different degrees of need satisfaction in sports and exercise, Standage and colleagues (2018) outlined the following:

› Need satisfaction nurtures self-determined types of motivation, and need thwarting nurtures non-self-determined types of motivation.

› Those who have their needs satisfied, and consequently undertake activities for self-determined reasons, enjoy a variety of well-being-related benefits such as greater enjoyment, positive affect (e.g., interest and excitement), vitality, self-esteem, better coping skills, and a higher health-related quality of life. They also experience less anxiety, negative affect, boredom, and unhappiness, and have a lower risk of burnout.

› Those whose needs are unsatisfied and are consequently involved for less self-determined (more controlled) reasons experience the opposite—less enjoyment, more negative affect (e.g., upset and guilty), lower self-esteem, poorer coping skills, and a lower health-related quality of life. They experience more anxiety, boredom, and unhappiness, and have a higher risk of burnout.

› When performers' needs are not only unsatisfied but actively thwarted, outcomes become yet more troublesome: in fact, studies have found relationships between need thwarting and severe psychophysiological problems such as burnout, depression, and disordered eating.

In two of the first studies of SDT in dance, Quested and Duda (2009, 2010) found that dance students with more satisfied basic needs also reported more positive affect. Less satisfied needs were associated with more negative affect. These findings were later confirmed through studies using a more novel methodology, in which dance students completed diaries for one week (Hancox et al., 2017) and one month (Quested et al., 2013). The former study further indicated that when dancers perceived their needs to be thwarted, more negative affect was in evidence. Using diary methods, researchers can focus on within-person variations rather than only on general differences between people (as is typical of traditional cross-sectional questionnaire studies). Intriguingly, one of these studies also indicated differences between different contexts; for instance, the need for competence predicted affect most strongly during performance times, whereas relatedness was the stronger predictor for classes (Quested et al., 2013). The authors reasoned that the need for competence is likely more salient around performances because of dancers being on display to demonstrate their abilities, while daily training affords more focus on social aspects.

The work of Quested and colleagues has given us several other novel contributions. For instance, these authors have demonstrated that dance students with generally higher need satisfaction on performance day experience lower levels of performance anxiety and salivary cortisol (a stress hormone; Quested et al., 2011). These dancers were also more likely to perceive the upcoming performance as a challenge rather than a threat. This makes sense, because need satisfaction is partly about feeling competent and supported, both of which should help dancers feel threatened less readily. In a longitudinal study, vocational school dancers whose needs became less satisfied over a three-month period also experienced increased symptoms of burnout (Quested & Duda, 2011a). For example, those who felt less competent reported increases in the burnout symptom known as *reduced sense of accomplishment*, and those who felt reductions in any need satisfaction were more likely to report the burnout symptom known as *devaluation* (i.e., starting to doubt the value of dance). Another two dance studies indicated that controlled forms of motivation (external regulation, amotivation) are positively associated with burnout symptoms, but the reverse is true for more self-determined forms (Balaguer et al., 2011; Nordin-Bates et al., 2017). Dancers experiencing greater levels of extrinsic motivation also seem to experience greater anxiety regarding their bodies (known as *social physique anxiety*; Quested & Duda, 2011b).

In a more recent SDT-based study, interviews with professional performers gave in-depth real-life accounts of both more and less self-determined motivational processes (Haraldsen et al., 2020a). All interviewees gave examples of both positive (high self-determination, well-being) and negative (low self-determination, ill-being) processes, but it was possible to discern an overall pattern: the higher the level of self-determination, the more likely a performer was to thrive. For instance, those performers (characterized as "thriving") spoke more about helpful personal characteristics (strong self-esteem) and symptoms of well-being (positive affect, flow, self-realization). Performers at the other end of the scale (characterized as "just surviving") spoke more about problematic personal characteristics (low self-esteem, anxiety, perfectionism, obsessiveness) and ill-being (exhaustion, eating disorders).

In a subsequent longitudinal study, it was demonstrated that performers who experienced high and increased thwarting of the needs for autonomy and competence also experienced increases in anxiety over that time period (Haraldsen et al., 2020b). They also evaluated their own performance level as lower. Such maladaptive motivational patterns appeared to be more common among performing artists (dance and music students) than among athletes, which reinforces the need for more research and positive interventions in our domain. The fact that studies using highly varied methodologies yield highly compatible findings lends strong support to the idea that dancers' levels of need satisfaction and thwarting really do matter for their well-being.

Performance-Related Consequences of Need Satisfaction and Self-Determination

The consequences of self-determination extend to performance-related factors in various sport and exercise settings (Standage et al., 2018). In particular, having one's needs satisfied and being involved for self-determined reasons have been associated with adaptive behaviors that are conducive to performance improvement, including the following:

- Putting in greater effort
- Perseverance over time
- Exercising more
- Performing better in a comparative sense

In dance, we do not as yet have any research capturing actual performance (e.g., assessment grades or similar), perhaps because it is notoriously difficult to capture dance performance objectively. However, self-determined motivation is associated with stronger intentions to continue participating in dance (Balaguer et al., 2011). Along similar lines, community dancers with healthier motivational profiles (i.e., those who reported their needs to be more satisfied and who had higher levels of intrinsic motivation) were more likely to report that they put a lot of effort into their dance practice (Norfield & Nordin-Bates, 2012). When interviewing independent dancers about their motivation to stay in a challenging career, its inherent autonomy was one of the main themes that emerged (Aujla & Farrer, 2015). For instance, the dancers spoke of how they really valued the sense of being free to create, work flexibly, and pursue their own vision. Basic needs satisfaction, and especially autonomy, also seems to nurture creativity in dance, but need thwarting may inhibit creativity while nurturing perfectionism (Clements & Nordin-Bates, 2022; Nordin-Bates, 2020; Watson et al., 2012).

How Can Healthy Motivation Be Nurtured? An Intrapersonal Perspective

Because of the variety of benefits associated with healthy motivation, it becomes important to understand how such motivation can be nurtured in dance contexts. In the following sections, healthy motivation is considered to be task involved and self-determined, with separate sections used for each to remain clear about their theoretical homes in AGT and SDT, respectively. That said, these theoretical approaches (and their associated recommendations) are fully compatible; for instance, being strongly task involved allows dancers to have their basic psychological needs satisfied more often and more fully. The following sections focus only on intrapersonal strategies; interpersonal influences (especially how teachers can nurture healthy motivation among their dancers) are considered comprehensively in chapter 11.

Nurturing One's Own Task Involvement

Being task oriented is fundamentally about interpreting personal improvement as success and therefore focusing on self-referenced learning, effort, and collaboration. Because goal orientations are conceptualized as relatively stable, however, it makes more sense to try to nurture one's task *involvement* rather than one's task *orientation.* However, repeated positive experiences with being task involved over time should also nurture a task orientation. Key recommendations in this regard are the following:

- *Set clear goals to work toward*, ensuring that they are personally meaningful and individually referenced; that is, they should represent improvements in your own previous skill level rather than comparisons to the skills of others (for more about goal setting, see chapter 9).
- *Focus on what you need to do during class.* If you get distracted by your fellow dancers' abilities, gently redirect your focus to the task at hand. If this is difficult, try asking the teacher for specific artistic or technical details to work with.
- *Take pride in your individual progress*, regardless of what others in your class may be doing or accomplishing. Progress is key!
- *See others as inspiration* rather than threat. What they are capable of says nothing about what

you can or cannot do, but if you stay curious and positive you may learn something.
> *Be friendly and collaborative.* Helping each other learn is of mutual benefit!

Nurturing One's Own Self-Determined Motivation

Most academic work into how self-determination can be nurtured has been concerned with teachers, coaches, or other authority figures. Yet dancers can, of course, be proactive individuals in their own right and work to support their own basic psychological needs. This is explored in some detail in the Get Practical exercise in form 5.1 but the following are some key suggestions for bolstering one's own basic need satisfaction:

> *Support your own autonomy.* First, ensure that your primary reason for dancing is because *you* want to dance rather than dancing to satisfy someone else. The more self-aware you are, the more able you will be to identify what you truly want (i.e., your own goals and values) and gradually choose or structure your dance training in that direction. Try to make your journey (i.e., long-term goals) and daily tasks (i.e., short-term goals) as personally meaningful and interesting as possible.
> *Support your own competence.* To feel competent, it is helpful to stay focused on your own process and progress (i.e., task involvement). Keep in mind that it is a teacher's job to help you improve, so seek their feedback if it is not forthcoming. But do not rely just on teachers; also trust your own sensations and any other sources of input you can access. Dance at your own level without avoidance (hiding) or trying to prove anything to others. This may involve adapting exercises so that they actually suit your body.
> *Support your own relatedness.* Stay mindful of the fact that everyone you meet in dance is a human first and a dancer/teacher second. Stay open and friendly and support one another. Seek and value collaboration and other interactive experiences; dance is, in many ways, a team sport. Finally, remember to talk to your fellow dancers not just about dance but about life in general.

Form 5.1 GET PRACTICAL: SUPPORTING YOUR OWN BASIC PSYCHOLOGICAL NEEDS

This exercise includes several suggestions for how you may enhance your own basic psychological need satisfaction in dance but also in life. By doing so, you can support your own intrinsic motivation, well-being, and performance success. The suggestions are ordered from more general and fundamental (which may be harder or take longer to affect) to more specific (e.g., things you can do in dance classes). Some may have an immediate effect, and others may take longer. To do this exercise thoroughly, it may help to integrate it into a goal-setting diary or planning app.

BASIC PSYCHOLOGICAL NEED	HOW CAN I SUPPORT THIS NEED?	MY CHOSEN SUGGESTION IS . . .	WHERE, WHEN, AND HOW WILL I DO THIS?	NOTES ON MY PROGRESS
Autonomy	1. Dance because *you* want to.	(e.g., 10)	(e.g., During adagio, I will think about portraying my own story.)	(e.g., This has helped me feel more connected to the movement, I want to try this during allegro next.)
	2. Choose classes and teachers who value you for who you are.			
	3. Set your own long-term goals. What do you really want to do?			
	4. Spend time with people who value your input.			
	5. Stand up for who you are. Respect your individuality.			
	6. Work to develop your own movement signature/personal style.			
	7. Critically engage with material, asking *why* and *how* things may be done. There are many ways to do something right!			
	8. Seek out inspiration that has personal meaning to you.			
	9. Set your own short-term goals. What is important to you, today?			
	10. Within class, explore ways to make the movements your own.			
Competence	1. Choose classes and teachers that provide you with high-quality constructive information.			
	2. Where feedback is not forthcoming, seek it.			

Form 5.1 *(continued)*

	3. Restructure any negative feedback into constructive terms.			
	4. Use multiple sources of feedback: teacher opinions, your own sensations, video, peers, and so forth.			
	5. Focus on individual improvement.			
	6. Focus more on processes than on outcomes.			
	7. Help each other learn for mutual benefit.			
	8. Set yourself suitably challenging goals based on your own competence level (not that of others).			
	9. Adjust exercises so that they suit your actual level and needs.			
	10. Let yourself be immersed in artistic processes, where how "good" you are does not matter.			
Relatedness	1. Choose classes and teachers that make you feel welcome.			
	2. Nurture your relationships with both teachers and peers.			
	3. Spend time with people to talk about non-dance matters.			
	4. Show that you are interested in others as people, not just as dancers.			
	5. Collaborate rather than compete with your peers.			
	6. Talk about shared goals that you have as a group.			
	7. Be friendly and generous before, during, and after classes.			
	8. Smile at others, both dancers and teachers.			
	9. Ask other dancers for help and say thanks for the input you receive.			
	10. Keep an eye out for anyone who looks like they might be struggling.			

Go to HK*Propel* to download this form and the Person First, Dancer Second lettering art.

From S. Nordin-Bates, *Essentials of Dance Psychology* (Champaign, IL: Human Kinetics, 2023).

Mindy: Case Study of Motivation

Mindy is a dance student in her second year of preprofessional training. She trained in several styles before deciding on modern dance and has always loved dance. There were ups and downs over the years, of course, and certainly she preferred some teachers over others. But overall, she just enjoyed it: her best friends were in dance, she was always learning something new, and in her local dance school she could speak up and contribute her views. Because of these positive experiences, it was easy for Mindy to make dance her career choice, and she successfully auditioned for a high-level school.

Unfortunately, problems started almost right away. For a start, some of the other students had pretty sharp elbows—rather than wanting to be friends, they seemed almost threatened by Mindy. Classes were highly structured and technical, and students were expected to follow every instruction and correction made by every teacher, preferably without questioning or adapting anything. Her mind was set on a professional career, so Mindy accepted this fact even though it made her uncomfortable; after all, the teachers should know what it takes to succeed in this industry, right? Yet over time, the technique focus became increasingly frustrating, and Mindy realized she could barely remember when she last felt real joy in movement, as she did when she was younger.

She also began to wonder if some of her fellow students identified so tightly with the old-fashioned dance idea of total commitment that they freely did things that were not good for them, like dancing injured. One classmate admitted that he was grateful for any teacher attention, even if it was all critique. Mindy's doubts escalated. Where was the love of dance in all this? Why could she not stay motivated, despite being in a supposedly great school? Everyone always said that a dance career "is not for everyone," so perhaps she just didn't have what it took? Or was there another way? Did one have to lose the joy in movement just to be a serious dancer?

Composite case study created on the basis of a conversation with Heidi Haraldsen, PhD, associate professor in education/pedagogy at the Oslo National Academy of the Arts, Norway.

CRITICAL ASPECTS OF RESEARCH INTO MOTIVATION

1. Research into achievement goals uses varied terminology, with ego orientation being synonymous with *performance*, *outcome*, and *competitive goal orientation*. *Task orientation* is synonymous with *mastery* and *learning goal orientation*.

2. Several of the minitheories within SDT have great potential to further our understanding of motivational processes in dance. For instance, causality orientations theory (COT; e.g., Deci & Ryan, 2000; Standage et al., 2018) proposes that persons have inherent (trait) orientations toward either autonomy (e.g., they are disposed to orient toward self-determined motivation) or control, or they have an impersonal orientation (a tendency to consider themselves incompetent). Although COT has not received any research attention in either dance or sports as yet, it would be intriguing to discover more about how such trait-expressions of self-determination versus control affect the performance and well-being of dancers.

3. Future dance research is warranted regarding how perceptions of competence are nurtured and how they affect dancers. For instance, those who are very unsure of themselves and perhaps hinge their sense of competence on performing well and impressing others (i.e., contingent self-esteem; see chapter 3) are likely to think they need more positive feedback and easier tasks to feel competent. Conversely, those who are sure of themselves and confident that their competence is not defined by whether they fall over or look silly in front of others are less likely to have their sense of competence threatened in a class where they do not manage

every task. As such, we might hypothesize that the relationship between events (success rate, interpersonal relationships) and competence need satisfaction is moderated by self-esteem.

KEY POINTS AND RECOMMENDATIONS FOR MOTIVATION IN DANCE

1. Although an ego orientation may help dancers perform well and feel good when they are superior, maintaining a strong task orientation is always going to be a more stable path to success. Helping the dancer feel in control facilitates many aspects—from focus and perseverance in tough times to enjoyment and camaraderie.
2. When the basic psychological needs of autonomy, competence, and relatedness are met, dancers display healthier, more sustainable self-determined motivation. In turn, such motivation facilitates both performance and well-being.
3. AGT and SDT are not specific to dance or even performance domains; as such, the recommendations in this chapter are just as applicable in school and work settings.

Attentional Focus

"There are likewise three kinds of dancers: first, those who consider dancing as a sort of gymnastic drill, made up of impersonal and graceful arabesques; second, those who, by concentrating their minds, lead the body into the rhythm of a desired emotion, expressing a remembered feeling or experience. And finally, there are those who convert the body into a luminous fluidity, surrendering it to the inspiration of the soul."

Isadora Duncan, dancer

CHAPTER OBJECTIVES

After reading this chapter, you will be able to

1. outline what attentional focus is;
2. critically discuss the nature of internal and external attentional foci, implicit and explicit forms of skill learning, and the relationships between them;
3. describe the consequences of using different attentional foci in dance;

4. describe flow as an example of optimal attentional focus in dance;
5. apply basic recommendations to nurture optimal attentional focus;
6. use practical exercises to enhance your ability to identify and switch between different attentional foci; and
7. think critically about the nature and impact of attentional focus in dance settings.

Key Terms

attention	external focus of attention	internal focus of attention
concentration	flow	ironic processing
constrained action hypothesis	focus	paralysis by analysis
explicit learning	implicit learning	selective attention

The term *attention* is from the Latin *attendere*, meaning to give heed to or stretch toward. The term *focus* also derives from Latin (*focus*), which originally meant the fireplace or center of the home; later, it was used in mathematics to denote a point of convergence and thereafter the center of activity or energy. Attentional focus in dance, then, might be thought of as the point (or center) toward which we stretch our energy and cognitive resources. As this chapter will outline, the way in which we do so matters greatly for our engagement, learning, and performance under pressure.

What Is Attentional Focus?

We all have an intuitive feel for what attentional focus is and what it feels like to be focusing more or less constructively. In psychology, **attention** is a relatively broad, multidimensional concept that comprises several aspects such as **concentration**, **selective attention**, dividing attention between multiple tasks or stimuli, and refocusing one's attention after being distracted (e.g., Moran et al., 2018). Concentration, or **focus**, is a specific aspect of attention that refers to the deliberate decision to attend fully to some action, such as when a dancer has full focus on a single movement, feeling, or idea. Importantly, that movement, feeling, or idea does not have to be small or narrowly conceived; indeed, we might focus on how a body part moves *in relation to* the rest of the body or on how my movements fit into the overall theme of a production.

In practice, the words *attention*, *focus*, and *concentration* are used interchangeably. And in learning and thinking about attentional focus (e.g., reading this chapter and reflecting on your habits) you are engaging in the metacognitive activity of attending to your attention! More than 130 years ago, psychology legend William James put it this way:

> Everyone knows what attention is. It is taking possession by the mind, in clear and vivid form, of one out of what seems several simultaneously possible objects or trains of thought. Focalization, concentration of consciousness are the essence. It implies withdrawal from some things in order to deal effectively with others. (James, 1890, p. 403-404)

Many believe in the advantages of maintaining focus over time, and this idea does have merit; if your focus constantly skipped about between different thoughts and stimuli, that would quickly become problematic. Indeed, having a very limited attention span is a key ingredient in attention deficit disorders and some learning disabilities. Yet we should also be aware that the human mind typically transitions to a new thought 6.5 times every minute, which leads to a rough estimate of more than 6,000 thoughts per day (Tseng & Poppenk, 2020). Given this intense mental activity, is it realistic to expect dancers to stay focused over the duration of a performance, a class, or even a single exercise? To get to the heart of this issue, we need to consider what optimal attentional focus really is.

First, fewer dancers will be focusing "correctly" at any given time if there is only one thing that is considered "correct" to focus on. If there are instead many things that can be part of optimal focus, then more dancers will be able to keep a flexible yet maintained focus for longer periods of time. For example, a whole variety of different movement ideas, intentions, images, and sensations might all be potentially constructive places for the mind to focus on and to switch between. As a result, dance teachers can help dancers focus constructively by cueing several things (rather than one) to focus on. Perhaps we may then avoid situations such as the one uncovered in an interview study, in which the most commonly reported focus of attention during dance class was on totally unrelated things, such as going home and paying bills (Hanrahan, 1996)!

Telling others (or oneself) to "stop thinking" or "don't think so much" is not recommended. The brain has no off switch, and it is far more helpful to encourage dancers to focus on one or more specifically identified constructive areas. Second, we know from studies of mindfulness that reducing irrelevant thoughts may not matter as much as learning to accept that thoughts will wander. It is more effective to move on by refocusing attention on what is important in the moment. This more realistic view encourages us to consider refocusing as a more important task than maintaining focus. For more information on this topic, see chapter 8.

The notion of focus maintenance being rather utopian is also related to the concept of selective attention. Again, William James introduced this notion particularly well:

> Millions of items of the outward order are present to my senses which never properly enter into my experience. Why? Because they have no *interest* for me. *My experience is what I agree to attend to.* Only those items which I *notice* shape my mind—without selective interest, experience is an utter chaos. (James, 1890, p. 402)

Among other things, James's quote highlights that focusing is not a black-or-white, dichotomous mental activity that you either do or do not do. Instead, we are always focused on something—even if that something changes frequently. It also highlights that the number of things we could potentially attend to is enormous. Indeed, how aware of your left foot were you before you read this sentence? Are you paying attention to the amount of daylight coming in through your window just now? For dance, the issue becomes a matter of identifying what a suitable focus of attention is at any given time and then making it so engaging that it is straightforward to maintain focus on it over time—or to switch between a set of different but task-relevant foci.

An analogy of walking a dog can help underscore the nature of attention. Assume that you are out walking your dog, "Concentration," in a spacious, open area where it does not have to be kept on its leash, such as in a woodland. If Concentration is like most dogs, it will not always walk slavishly next to you; instead, it will run around and explore. We might say that it is distracted by many different stimuli (trees, bushes, other animals) or that it is adept at shifting its focus onto whatever seems most interesting. When something ceases to be interesting, Concentration simply moves on to the next thing. It may run around a lot or be out of sight for periods of time. Yet unless this is highly atypical for your dog (or you are a real worrier), you are unlikely to say that you have "lost Concentration." Instead, you probably trust that it will return to you. At some point, you decide that the walk is over and that you need to retrieve your dog and get home. What do you do? Simply waiting for Concentration to return might be an option, but it may not be especially effective. Instead, you probably have some tricks ready to attract it back to you. For instance, you may tempt it with a game or a treat. By making yourself more interesting than the available alternatives, you get Concentration back more quickly.

The dog-walking analogy helps to illustrate several points: First, we never really lose concentration, but it is simply redirected onto things we may see as less desirable (see Moran et al., 2018). Second, motivation is a key consideration, such that concentrating is far easier when we are interested in and enjoy a task. Finally, it is helpful to have strategies available to redirect concentration as needed. In this chapter, these issues will be explored in depth because attentional focus is of enormous importance in dance. Indeed, much of what a teacher does via verbal instructions, physical demonstrations, and other cues (e.g., rhythmical sounds, body language) to help their dancers learn and perform are really different ways of directing dancers' attention to something considered worth focusing on: artistry, technique, collaboration, musicality—the list is long. Experts in the area have even said that "it is difficult to conceive of any aspect of psychology that may be more central to the enhancement of skill learning and expert performance than attention" (Abernethy et al., 2007, p. 245).

Because of its importance, it is somewhat surprising that so little attention (!) has been given to research and systematic evidence-based practice into this area in dance. This chapter, therefore, relies heavily on research conducted in motor learning and sports, complemented by dance-specific research where possible. It also integrates suggestions from a recent book specifically devoted to the topic: *Attention and Focus in Dance: Enhancing Power, Precision, and Artistry* (Guss-West, 2020). Attentional focus is inherently linked to many other topics in performance psychology and beyond, and there is much to be learned about it also through other topics and domains, which may use different terminologies. For instance, research into embodiment and kinesthesia in dance is closely linked to attention (e.g., Ehrenberg, 2015), and persons with strong task versus ego involvement will typically focus their attention on different things (see chapter 5). Even more overlap is evident between attentional focus and the topics of mindfulness (essentially, a particular way of paying attention; see chapter 8) and imagery (because imagery is often used to direct attention; see chapter 10).

Internal and External Focus of Attention

A rich body of literature in sports and motor learning divides attentional focus styles into two main categories: internal and external (for a review, see Wulf, 2013). An **internal focus of attention** is concerned with consciously adjusting and controlling different parts of the body. In other words, it is a piecemeal, or fragmented, way of attending (paying attention). Dancers who focus on the angle of their foot, the correct placement of their shoulder blades, or the turnout of their hips are using an internal focus of attention. Similarly, instructions such as "point your toes," "lower your shoulders," and "shift your weight over the hip" induce an internal focus. This attentional style relies on dancers to integrate and automatize many different instructions, cues, and corrections over time in order to make complex movements and fast choreography possible. For instance, it would be impossible to attend to ten different technical corrections regarding one's pirouette while actually doing a pirouette in a performance.

An **external focus of attention** is concerned with the patterns, effects, and intentions of movement; as such, it is conducive to a more global way of attending, which is functional in complex movements and fast choreography. Dancers who focus on such things as projecting, pushing the floor away, or the intention of the choreography are using an external focus of attention, and teaching instructions such as "project your arabesque across the entire diagonal," "push the floor away like you are taking off into space," and

Focusing externally helps enhance performance and absorption in the moment.

"let your movements tell us how you feel" induce an external focus. Note that internal and external foci typically have the same goal (learning and performing well), and both can be directed toward small intricate details as well as larger aspects of movement.

Table 6.1 provides an overview of key differences between internal and external foci. Included are examples for complex movement sequences generally and for some key movements more specifically: pliés or other knee bends, pirouettes, jumps, and balances. For a far wider range of examples, see Guss-West (2020). As she points out, dance terminology can be a rich source of external focusing instructions; for instance, terms such as *spiral*, *fondu*, *undercurve*, and *enveloppé* all represent global instructions relating to movement qualities and shapes, provided that the dancers have a good understanding of what they mean.

Keep in mind that designing suitable external foci is much about individualization and personal preference; therefore, variety, creativity, and open communication is advised. To optimize movement, dancers should also be encouraged to create their own ideas for what they can focus on. Doing so also avoids classes becoming overly teacher-centric, instead serving to strengthen the dancers' autonomy which has a range of benefits (see chapter 5).

An internal focus is not about sensory information from one's body, nor is an external focus just about the external environment (Guss-West, 2020). Indeed, focusing on expanding with the breath would be considered external because it is about sensations and intentions. Touch, music, partner work, and even teacher demonstrations are other valuable external focus stimulus cues (Guss-West, 2020; see also Karin, 2016). Finally, it is *attentional* focus rather than *visual* focus that is dealt with; indeed, researchers in this area who wish to compare the effects of external and internal foci typically ask all experimental participants to keep their eyes (visual focus) straight ahead (Wulf, 2013).

In a small-scale survey with current and former professional ballet dancers, participants were asked what they typically focused on during typical movements (Guss-West & Wulf, 2016). Overall, just over one-third (36.1%) used an internal focus,

Table 6.1 **Key Distinguishing Features of External and Internal Attentional Foci**

	Internal focus	External focus
Typical ingredients	• Body parts • Rules	• Movement effects; outcomes; and qualities
Body control and coordination	• Conscious; deliberate; mind organizes body	• Unconscious; body organizes itself
Direction	• Self-focused	• Outwardly focused
EXAMPLES		
General	• Coordinate body parts • Technical precision • Doing it right • Self-adjustment	• Expressivity; storytelling • Audience communication • Musicality; sensations • Props; touch; partnering
Pliés/kneebends	• Bend your knees • Knees over your toes • Don't stick your bum out	• Melt into the floor • Move straight up and down, like an elevator
Pirouettes	• Pull your stomach in • Hold your foot in place • Keep your shoulders down	• Spin like a spiraling whirligig • Feel the vertical axis going right through you • Push the floor away
Jumps	• Push off your feet • Work your thighs • Keep your shape in the air	• Project into the sky • Let your breath power you • Imagine jumping over a water puddle
Balance	• Stay on the second toe • Hold your shape still • Don't move	• Send out roots in all directions under you • Imagine being held by a partner's strong hands

Props can facilitate an external focus.

while just under one-third (27.7%) used an external focus, typically in the form of metaphorical images. The remainder (36.1%) reported using a mixture of both. Interestingly, there seemed to be differences between movements, such that the grand jeté yielded a somewhat greater proportion of external focus responses (e.g., jumping over a lake). In contrast, arabesque yielded a greater proportion of internal focus responses (e.g., elongated arms, straight leg). The authors speculated that the quickness of the grand jeté would leave less time to think (and therefore less risk of conscious control), while the far slower arabesque leaves more time to think, which might explain the predominance of internal focusing.

THINKING CRITICALLY

- What do you typically focus on in dance class? In performance? If there is a difference between the two, why might this be?
- Why do you think you have the attentional focus habits that you have? Are they due to how your teachers have cued you or something else?
- Think of a small number of movements that you do regularly and habitually. What kinds of external foci might you try in order to keep these movements fresh and engaging?

Explicit and Implicit Learning

Skill learning can take many forms but may be considered as primarily **explicit learning** or **implicit learning** (Masters, 1992; Masters et al., 2019). The explicit route is focused on learning through information and rules, promoting conscious control over body parts, and an internal focus (e.g., how to hold one's arms; how to point one's foot), whereas the implicit route is focused on learning without knowing that learning is actually taking place (as we do when acquiring, for instance, our mother tongue or the ability to eat with cutlery in childhood). As such, knowledge that is held explicitly can be verbalized, but those who know something (e.g., a dance skill) implicitly may struggle to explain how they do what they do.

As you can see, there is distinct overlap between the body of literature primarily focused on skill learning, and the literature about attentional focus, which was outlined earlier in this chapter. In the motor learning literature, several ways of inducing implicit learning have been used (Masters et al., 2019), and they are not all easy to translate to real-life dance practice. However, dance-specific literature outlines how implicit learning is encouraged when using an external focus (e.g., analogies, metaphorical images) and when focusing on global aspects such as musicality and sensory information (Karin, 2016). Moreover, making the learning of new skills easy enough that errors are few (but not entirely absent) seems to promote implicit learning by reducing the effortful conscious processing that is associated with error management (Masters et al., 2019).

Traditional theories of skill learning typically outline a series of stages whereby skills are first learned explicitly by way of rules and conscious control (i.e., an internal focus), and gradually transitioned into implicit forms of knowledge through a long period of practice (Masters, 1992). The three steps in figure 6.1 mirror such theories, such as the much-cited *cognitive*, *associative*, and *autonomous* stages of learning (Fitts & Posner, 1967). Learning in this manner does lead to gradual mastery, but it is slow and cumbersome—a bit like walking up a long staircase toward one's goal. In contrast, learning implicitly with the aid of external foci has the advantage of promoting faster and more resilient mastery—a bit like taking the lift to one's goal (Karin, 2016; Lola & Tzetzis, 2021; Masters, 1992; Masters et al., 2019; Wulf, 2013).

It is entirely possible to attend to precise detailed movements and to technical skill learning via external focusing instructions (Guss-West, 2020). For instance, dancers can be helped to understand the complexities of specific movements without naming body parts if instructions are imagery based

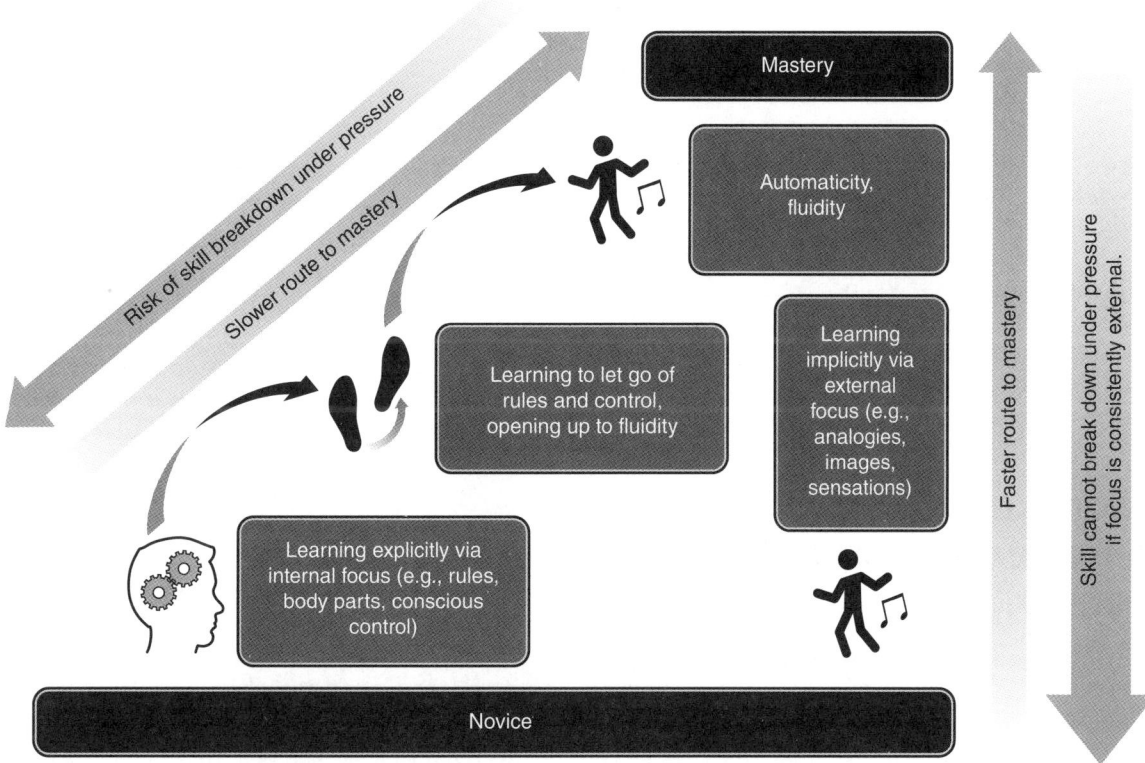

Figure 6.1 The curved arrows indicate that a person may progress from the early (novice) to the late (mastery) stage of skill learning as they learn and improve. The downward diagonal arrow indicates that persons may also move in the opposite direction if they begin to attend to skill mechanics despite skills being automated. This process of refocusing attention on explicit rules, conscious control, and other internal aspects helps explain the breakdown of skills under pressure.

(e.g., spiral the leg outward, form a C-shape, make as large a curve as you can, trace an arc in the air). Given their noted overlaps, Figure 6.1 combines two literatures: one typically reporting that learning is accelerated when using an external focus (e.g., Wulf, 2013) and another typically reporting that explicit and implicit approaches yield similar amounts of learning, but that those who learn explicitly are more susceptible to skill breakdown under pressure (e.g., Masters et al., 2019).

If you are (or were) a dancer, consider how you learned to perform pirouettes. Alternatively, consider another complex yet everyday task such as learning to ride a bicycle. In the early stages of learning these complex movements, there are many things to learn such as the different actions of the arms, the legs, and the head. If you were taught to focus on one body part at a time and given specific, explicit rules of how things should be, your performance was probably inconsistent at first. You were probably only able to attend to one aspect of the skill at a time (e.g., movement of the legs), because you used all your cognitive resources on getting the mechanics just right. Yet if you later became an accomplished dancer (or bicycle rider) you were, over time, able to integrate the various parts of the skill into a whole-body movement (i.e., you master the skill implicitly). With this automation of skills, you no longer needed to use so much of your cognitive resources, leaving them free to be used toward other ends—communication, for instance. Put differently, the previously explicit learning becomes implicit, maximizing fluidity and minimizing energy expenditure (e.g., Beilock & Carr, 2001; Fitts & Posner, 1967). Unfortunately, learning explicitly leads to an internal focus of attention and, as further outlined later, suboptimal learning as well as a greater risk of skill breakdown under pressure.

Performance-Related Consequences of Different Attentional Foci

Literature examining the correlates and consequences of focusing internally versus externally is plentiful in motor learning and sport psychology. Notably, it is entirely focused on consequences related to performance rather than well-being; as such, this section is fully focused on the former. Overall, there are major advantages to focusing externally, whereas focusing internally is problematic in several ways. Wulf (2013) summarized the following findings as having consistently emerged in the literature:

> Using an external focus of attention is associated with faster learning and with better movement effectiveness, such as being accurate and consistent. This has been demonstrated for a variety of fundamental movement tasks such as balance, movement accuracy, and force production. For instance, a study in gymnastics confirmed that focusing externally led to greater jump height and movement form than focusing internally (Abdollahipour et al., 2015). Although not specifically researched in dance, these aspects of movement effectiveness are clearly pertinent to dance.

> Using an external focus of attention has also been shown to relate to better movement efficiency, such as being fluid and not using more effort than is necessary. This too has been demonstrated for an assortment of tasks related to endurance, strength, and speed, which appear highly relevant to dance.

> Complex skills benefit more from an external focus of attention.

> The outcomes of learning with external focusing instructions seem to be enduring, such that effects are retained in studies using follow-up measures some time after the main experiment has ended.

> The external focus effect has been demonstrated with a wide variety of tasks, ages, and skill levels; that is, it seems to be relatively universal. It is stronger even than performer preferences, such that people perform better with an external focus even if they express a preference for focusing internally! However, it may be difficult to improve the performance of very experienced performers by brief or occasional external focusing instructions: if they have performed the task thousands or even millions of times before (e.g., professional ballet dancers doing pliés), their skill may be so automatized that new focusing information simply becomes distracting.

> The inefficiency associated with an internal focus may spread beyond the muscle groups that ought to be involved in a particular movement; that is, focusing on a body part when doing a movement (e.g., focusing on the thigh muscles when doing a jump) can lead

to elevated unnecessary muscle engagement not only in the thighs but also in other muscle groups as a result of poorer coordination between them.

Later research suggests that the benefits of focusing externally extend also to artistic aspects of performing. In a study with musicians, those asked to focus externally (expressiveness, audience communication) were rated as performing significantly better than those asked to focus internally (finger movements, playing correctly) regarding both technical precision and artistic expression (Mornell & Wulf, 2019). In other words, technique did not seem to be compromised by the focus on artistry. Other studies indicate that learning through imagery (analogy, metaphor) uses less working memory than learning explicitly, thus freeing up cognitive resources for other tasks (e.g., Lam et al., 2009a, 2009b; Lola & Tzetzis, 2021), which for dance could involve artistry.

Studies with both athletes and dancers (e.g., Chua et al., 2018; Guss-West & Wulf, 2016; Karin & Nordin-Bates, 2020; Stoate & Wulf, 2011) indicate that the habitual or preferred focus of performers can be highly varied and not always optimal. Indeed, swimmers in the study by Stoate and Wulf (2011) who habitually focused internally (e.g., on hip rotation) swam more slowly than those who reported that their attentional focus was typically external and global (e.g., on overall tempo). As such, there seems to be room for improvement regarding the promotion of an external focus (Guss-West & Wulf, 2016).

Attentional Focus Research in Dance

To date, three studies have set out to determine potential effects of dancers focusing internally versus externally (Andrade et al., 2020; Chua et al., 2018; Teixeira da Silva et al., 2017). All have examined effects on pirouette performance en dehors, yet methods and findings varied. In the first, children learned to pirouette to the right using either an internal or external focus (Teixeira da Silva et al., 2017). The latter group outperformed the former during the main experiment, after a two-day break (retention test), and when asked to perform a pirouette to the left for the first time (transfer test). They also felt more competent. Two other studies invited experienced adult dancers and assessed performance via movement kinematics and blinded expert observations of movement quality (Andrade et al., 2020; Chua et al., 2018). Neither found any significant differences in pirouette performance as a function of internal versus external focusing instructions. It is possible that these dancers, who had presumably done pirouettes many hundreds or thousands of times before, were simply unable to perform well (or better) within the constraints of very short-term interventions that encouraged them to leave their habitual focus. Similar arguments have been used to explain the lack of improvement with external focusing for top-class acrobats (Wulf, 2008).

Interestingly, participants in one of these studies were better able to adhere to internal rather than external focusing instructions, which could indicate that the chosen image was suboptimal (Andrade et al., 2020). Participants in the other study did not always prefer the focus that produced the objectively best performance (Chua et al., 2018). Accordingly, the authors stated that "the findings prompt us to consider the importance of individualizing instructions to meet individual needs rather than prescribing the same type of instruction for all" (p. 156). Other methodological issues may also help explain the varied results. For instance, focusing on alignment is relatively global rather than about conscious control of body parts; as such, it is perhaps not a fully internal focusing instruction (Andrade et al., 2020). Participants in the study by Chua et al. (2018) were instructed to use an X on the wall as a focus for their visual spotting during all focusing conditions—arguably an external focusing cue that might have overridden other instructions. For more information on how study methods affect results in this domain, see Wulf (2013).

Further examples of how different foci affect dancer's learning, including how imagery may be used effectively to promote implicit learning via an external focus, is provided by Karin (2016). She describes how many teachers and, consequently, dancers attempt to improve and overcome movement problems (e.g., problems balancing) via conscious control over movements in a piecemeal fashion and how this is counterproductive to smooth, natural, and expressive movement. In a small-scale study with young ballet students, imagery and sensory information were used to promote implicit engagement (Karin & Nordin-Bates, 2020). After five workshop days, students reported feeling more creative in ballet and experienced fewer perfectionistic thoughts. They also increased their use of implicit evaluation sources (e.g., using sensations as indications of dancing well). One highly perfectionistic participant reported how she had learned to approach class in a more creative and authentic manner: "[N]ot everything is about doing things right, that is the best. But that you dance for real" (p. 7). If studies using more sophisticated designs go on to confirm and extend such findings, the promotion of implicit learning via external focusing seems useful for the promotion of creativity among dancers in general, especially for the most perfectionistic.

For another illustration of how attentional focus may affect dancers, consider the functional analyses in figure 6.2. In this set of two examples, a teacher is concerned about some of her dancers whom she perceives to be working hard and listening well to instructions; yet, they do not progress particularly fast, and they struggle with artistry and self-consciousness in improvisation and performances.

When the teacher realizes that her instructions are primarily about adjusting body parts in isolation (first analysis), she begins to see how the problem is maintained; her instructional style induces an internal focus for students, and their problems are a logical consequence of that. As the teacher begins to experiment with instructions focused on the purpose behind movements, musicality, and rhythm, her students gradually learn to focus more externally (second analysis). Short-term benefits include greater absorption in the exercises as well as heightened enjoyment. In the longer term, consequences should also include improvements in the rate of learning, artistry, and reduced self-consciousness.

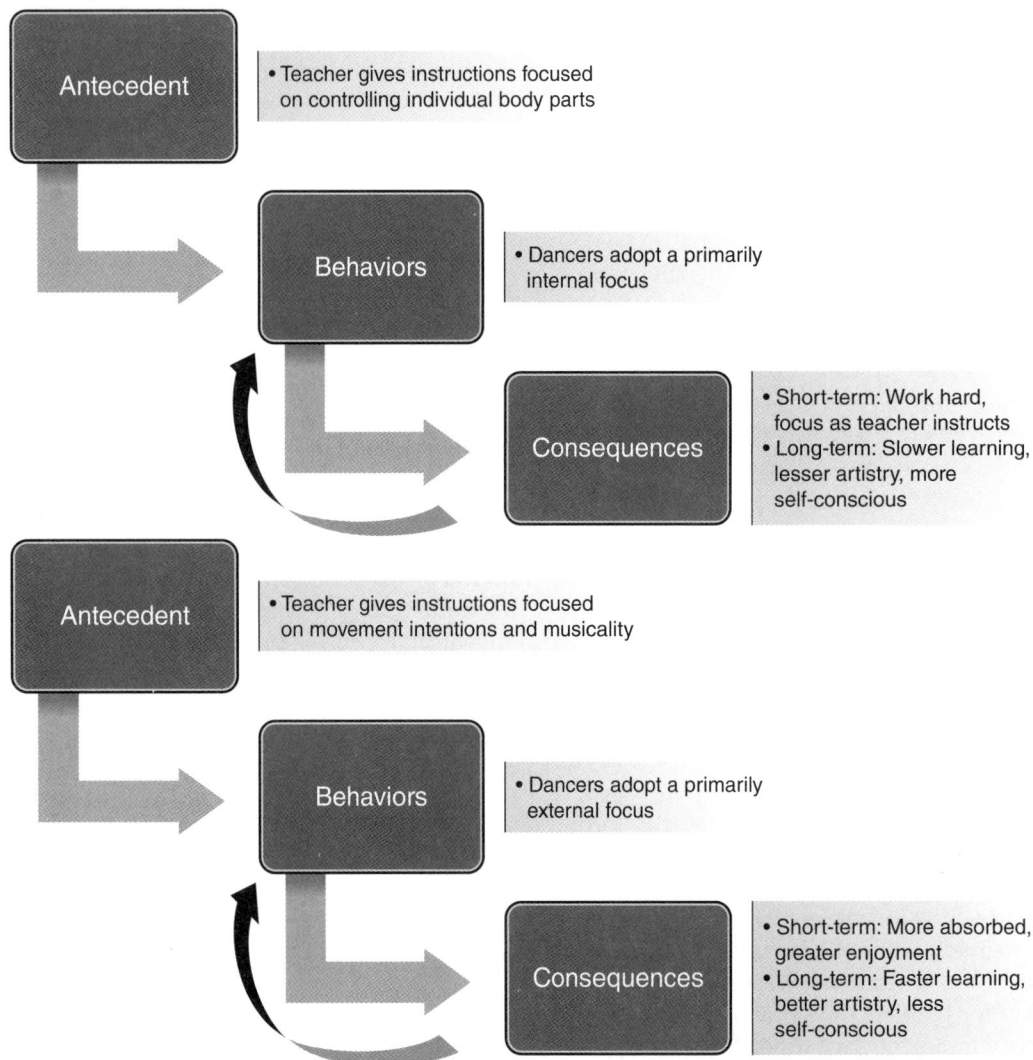

Figure 6.2 Functional analysis examples of how different attentional foci may manifest in dance. The recursive arrows indicate that the consequences make the behavior more likely to reoccur in similar situations in the future (behavior maintenance).

Why Attentional Focus Has an Impact

The reason that focusing externally is superior to focusing internally is outlined in the **constrained action hypothesis** (Wulf et al., 2001), which states that an external focus promotes efficient neuromuscular coordination by using unconscious, fast, and automatic control processes (see also Karin, 2016; Masters, 1992; Masters et al., 2019). In contrast, an internal focus encourages conscious control over movements, which engages a slower cognitive system that constrains the motor system. It is logical that such interference with automatic processes leads to more disjointed movements. Interestingly, several teachers participating in an interview study noted that more perfectionistic dancers tend to move in stiffer, more disjointed ways. For instance, one teacher commented:

> [W]hen you want to do it perfectly you become a bit mechanical, a bit stick-like . . . you can see a fear of doing things wrong that doesn't result in movement. It becomes different aspects stacked on top of one another which in each moment perhaps is perfect, but it still isn't what you want to see. (previously unpublished quote from ballet teacher interviewed in Nordin-Bates, 2020)

The body inherently seems to know the best way to coordinate itself in order to achieve a given movement outcome, feel, or expression, and we do best in staying out of its way without interfering with the mechanics of how to get there. Dancers have also reported that they feel more like they are *dancing* rather than just executing steps when using an external rather than an internal focus (Guss-West, 2020; Karin, 2016; Karin & Nordin-Bates, 2020).

Further theorizing in this area has suggested that focusing instructions make such a difference because an internal focus leads to heightened self-awareness (Wulf & Lewthwaite, 2010). These authors suggested that internal focusing instructions become a self-invoking trigger that make performers more likely to self-evaluate and therefore decrease their performance or even choke. Taking dancers *out of themselves* by promoting an external focus thus becomes important. Examples of this have also been provided via studies into imagery (e.g., Overby, 1990; Vergeer & Hanrahan 1998). In one such study, a dancer gave the following example of a useful image, which can be seen as an explanation for the advantage of external focus:

> Sometimes when you're learning a new skill, you can become bogged down by the physics of the movement. And sometimes it takes someone to say to you "try and just let the air come out of the top of your head." And suddenly you're not so much worried about your foot . . . and that will just allow the leg to do what it needs to do. (dancer interviewed in Nordin & Cumming, 2005, p. 407)

Interestingly, several dancers in that study reported avoiding more technical imagery at times such as before going on stage, because it might make them attend to tasks they felt should be done on autopilot (Nordin & Cumming). An additional consideration is the distance effect whereby the more distal the focus, the greater the performance improvement (Wulf, 2013). In sports, this may involve focusing on jumping as close as possible to a target (a more distal external focus) rather than on jumping as far away as possible from the starting lines (a more proximal external focus; Porter et al., 2012). For dancers, this could translate into instructions being worded as "push into the earth" rather than "push into your shoes," or "project into space" rather than "project into the corner of the room" (for more examples, see Guss-West, 2020).

Attentional Focus and Flow

Although there is a lack of research into well-being-related consequences of different attentional foci, attentional focus is inherently linked to **flow**, a well-researched phenomenon linked to aspects of both performing and feeling well. More specifically, flow is a state of total absorption often perceived to be an optimal experience (Csikszentmihalyi, 1990). Flow is described in terms of nine different facets (Jackson & Csikszentmihalyi, 1999), several of which are directly related to attentional focus: that concentration is fully on the task at hand; that perception of time is transformed; and that there is a so-called *action-awareness merger*, which refers to a sense of being one with one's activity or surroundings. In one study with dancers, action-awareness merging was the most commonly mentioned facet of flow: "Dancers felt as though everything 'came together' through the music, character and movement, and that they were connected to everything and everyone, yet there was a feeling of conscious-unconscious awareness." (Panebianco-Warrens, 2014, p. 64).

Another facet of flow is loss of self-consciousness, which aligns with the idea that external focusing helps avoid a preoccupation with the self (Wulf & Lewthwaite, 2010). Said a dancer in another flow study: "I couldn't say that I am conscious of my thoughts. I am just enjoying the purity of the movement and how it felt for me" (Hefferon & Ollis, 2006, p. 150). In fact, all interviewees in that study reported a loss of self-consciousness when in flow, because the total absorption left no room for irrelevant thoughts or stimuli: "It's totally the music, the steps, myself. It's like being in your own bubble" (p. 150).

As has perhaps become obvious, flow has a number of positive correlates and outcomes; for instance, it is intimately linked to enjoyment and creativity (Csikszentmihalyi, 1990). In dance, flow experiences can, among other things, support creative risk taking and a sense of interpersonal connection (Urmston & Hewison, 2014). Given these positive connotations, it is encouraging that some studies suggest dancers to be experiencing flow relatively often (e.g., Thomson & Jaque, 2012).

Paralysis by Analysis: How Attentional Focus Relates to Skill Breakdown Under Pressure

An attention-related phenomenon that has been the subject of considerable study is that of **paralysis by analysis**, or the breakdown of skilled performance under pressure (Beilock & Carr, 2001; Ehrlenspiel, 2001; Gucciardi & Dimmock, 2008; Lam et al., 2009a, 2009b; Lola & Tzetzis, 2021; Masters, 1992; Mesagno & Beckmann, 2017; Wulf, 2013). In sports, this is also referred to as choking or reinvestment (Masters & Maxwell, 2008). Essentially, it is the problem that occurs when a performer suddenly starts attending to technical bodily details of skills that have become automatized. How do I angle my arms in that partnering sequence? Should the leg be at 80 degrees or 70 degrees? And are we really starting to count on 6? To understand why this is problematic, we need to consider the way in which the skill was originally learned (figure 6.1).

Skills learned via explicit rules, conscious control, and attention to body mechanics (i.e., an internal focus) are more likely to break down under pressure (e.g., Beilock & Carr, 2001; Lam et al., 2009a, 2009b; Lola & Tzetzis, 2021; Masters, 1992; Masters & Maxwell, 2008; Wulf, 2013). This is because performers revert to the mode in which they originally learned, trying to consciously control skills that have been automated (see the downward diagonal arrow in figure 6.1). Doing so interferes with the fast unconscious motor program that has been developed and disrupts the fluid, automatic, and well-coordinated action; in essence, the master reverts to the style of the novice.

In a dance context, the pressures that can lead to skill breakdown can include the following:

> Performance anxiety
> High expectations from a demanding self, teacher, choreographer, or audience
> Tiredness and fatigue
> Stress around injury or illness
> Some other cognitive load (e.g., too many things to think about)

In one study, the performance of trampolinists deteriorated when coaches called out task-relevant instructions (i.e., cues that induced explicit processing) during performances (Hardy et al., 2001). However, the decrement only occurred when performers were anxious (getting the coach cues two hours before competing) and did not occur in a less anxious practice setting. Similar results have been obtained for many other skills, alongside evidence that focusing on a single global process goal or cue word (e.g., *smooth*) can counteract such effects (e.g., Gucciardi & Dimmock, 2008; Mullen et al., 2016).

Unfortunately, it is not unusual for dancers who are anxious before an important performance, for example, to start to think about technical details and small parts of a choreography that should be automated by that stage. Presumably, this happens because they learned via explicit rules and a focus on body parts rather than via imagery or other external focusing instructions (Karin, 2016). Other dancers understand this problem intuitively:

> I find it can almost jinx you if you start thinking about what steps, start second-guessing yourself at that point. Once I put my makeup on, get ready to go, don't ask me about the steps because I'm not going to be able to tell you, or if I take the time to think about it I'm changing my focus in a way, and I don't think I should. (modern dancer interviewed in Vergeer & Hanrahan, 1998, p. 63-64)

In applied terms, this highlights that using an external focus is especially important during times of stress, anxiety, or other pressure, when dancers may start to doubt themselves. Dancers need to trust that the body knows. Even better, of course, is if learning is continuously implicit, with an external focus of attention being used already from the earliest stages (Liao & Masters, 2002; Lola & Tzetzis, 2021). There are no explicit rules to revert to if those were never obvious to begin with; or, put differently, there can be no paralysis if there is no analysis (see the rightmost part of figure 6.1; see also Karin, 2016).

Who Is More Likely to Experience Paralysis by Analysis?

Sport research has provided valuable information regarding the characteristics that make some performers more susceptible to skill breakdown under pressure (Beilock & Gray, 2007; Gucciardi & Dimmock, 2008; Hill et al., 2009, 2010; Hill & Shaw, 2013; Jordet & Hartman, 2008; Mesagno & Beckmann, 2017). Beyond the focus on internal aspects (body mechanics, skill details) that is inherent to the issue, these characteristics include the following:

› *High expectations and pressure*. Performers who place high expectations on themselves, or perceive pressure, demands, and expectations from others, are more likely to suffer paralysis by analysis (see chapter 2).
› *Narrowly defined identity*. Dancers who define themselves exclusively in terms of dance are more at risk because success in dance is so central to who they are (see chapter 1).
› *Self-criticism*. Dancers who have low self-esteem or self-confidence, high levels of perfectionistic concerns, and a fear of failure are more at risk (see chapters 2-3).
› *Anxiety*. When anxious, focus often becomes more narrow and internal, which makes highly anxious dancers more at risk (see chapter 4).
› *Self-consciousness*. When feeling exposed or that we are going to be evaluated (perhaps especially on our bodies), focus tends to become more narrow and internal, which makes self-conscious dancers more at risk.
› *Avoidance motivation*. Dancers driven by a need to not perform poorly or embarrass themselves are at greater risk (see chapter 5).
› *Focus on uncontrollable factors*. Dancers who have a high ego orientation, compare themselves to others, and rely greatly on the opinions of others are more likely to be at risk (see chapter 5).

How Can Optimal Attentional Focus Be Nurtured?

The wide range of benefits associated with focusing externally makes it important to understand how such a focus can be nurtured in dance. Next, a wide range of factors are summarized under two broad headings: setting the stage for optimal attentional focus and promoting the use of psychological skills.

Setting the Stage for Optimal Attentional Focus

Teachers, and to some extent dancers themselves, can implement several different strategies that help set the stage for optimal attention focus. These include promoting an awareness of what attentional focus is and can lead to; identifying what is important; focusing on what to do, rather than what not to do, and on controllable aspects; nurturing healthy motivation; and practicing in performance-like conditions.

Promote Awareness of What Attentional Focus Is and Can Lead To

Our attentional focus is usually not something that we attend to—it just happens. But by paying attention to our attention (i.e., metacognition), we can learn more about our habitual patterns of focusing and what they lead to in terms of performance and well-being. For more about how this may be achieved, see Guss-West (2020).

Identify What Is Important

To focus constructively, dancers need to know what actually is suitable to focus on at any given time. As you now know, a general recommendation emanating from this chapter is that focusing externally is important, but what this actually means for a given movement, variation, or phrase is still up to individual dancers and their teachers. Therefore, teachers would do well to plan their lessons with an eye to what is most important and constructive for each exercise. Planning some instructions, cue words, and other stimuli ahead of time (e.g., I want to work on the lift sequence today; what instructions and images can convey the desired quality?) will help their dancers to focus constructively, and therefore learn, once class is underway. Ideally, this would include several different external foci to make exercises engaging and absorbing for as many dancers as possible. For instance, a single exercise may be constructively focused on through its music, its movement intentions, its tactile components in lifts, and via several images or cue words.

It can be especially important to identify suitable focus points for stressful events such as auditions, competitions, and performances because they typically elevate the anxiety that can predispose some dancers to experience paralysis by analysis. Teachers can, for instance, do their dancers a favor by resisting any temptation to correct technical minutiae in the lead-up to such important events. Instead, they can help dancers lose themselves in the story, the music, and the performing experience. This is particularly pertinent for anxious, perfectionistic dancers.

Focus on What to Do Rather Than What Not To Do

Avoid saying "don't" and "no" because such words provide nothing constructive for dancers to get absorbed into. In fact, studies have shown that instructions to *not* do something can make that very thing more likely to happen, especially when one is somehow under pressure—an effect known as **ironic processing** (for a dance example, see Dugdale & Eklund, 2003). These unwanted effects are particularly likely when a performer has low emotional stability (Barlow et al., 2016). In sum, both teacher instructions and personal self-talk should focus on what *to* do, especially during times of stress and with less emotionally stable individuals.

Focus on Controllable Aspects

Focusing on uncontrollable aspects such as the skill levels of other dancers, the opinions of teachers, and the scoring of juries is problematic, because less attentional capacity is left for doing the actual task at hand and it can leave dancers feeling inferior or even powerless. This is, in part, because focusing on the uncontrollable can undermine our basic need for competence (see chapter 5). Hence, dancers need to direct their focus to aspects that are within their control such as their own movements, the way they use their energy, how they collaborate, and their musical interpretation. As you can see, these recommendations are fully compatible with using an external focus of attention.

Nurture Healthy Motivation

As William James informed us way back in 1890, focusing is a lot easier when one is appropriately motivated. Therefore, recommendations for nurturing healthy motivation (see chapters 5 and 11) are likely to help promote optimal focus. Intrinsic motivation is also an important predictor of flow—in fact, the autotelic nature of flow means that it only really happens when we are doing a task for its own sake (Csikszentmihalyi, 1990).

Practice in Performance-Like Conditions

Gradual exposure to pressure can help performers habituate to distractions as well as to anxiety (Mesagno & Beckmann, 2017). For instance, dance teachers may make rehearsals progressively more like the actual performance by incorporating lights, sounds, correct time intervals, and so on. You may remember from chapter 3 that this kind of simulation practice is also a useful way to enhance self-efficacy.

Promoting the Use of Psychological Skills

Dancers can also implement several different psychological skills to help nurture optimal attentional focus. Teachers can encourage their dancers to use these skills and can also use them for their own benefit (e.g., to promote focus when leading long rehearsals). These psychological skills include imagery; realistic rather than perfectionistic goals; constructive, externally focused self-talk; and mindfulness.

Use Imagery

Research has established that imagery (e.g., metaphors and analogies) can be a particularly useful way of nurturing an external focus of attention to promote learning, high-level performance, and more (Karin, 2016; Lam et al., 2009a, 2009b; Liao & Masters, 2001; Lola & Tzetzis, 2021; Wulf, 2013). Because the associations and effects of images are often personal, it is a good idea for dance teachers to provide several different images and encourage dancers to create their own. For more recommendations for imagery practice, see chapter 10.

Set Realistic Rather Than Perfectionistic Goals

Having personally motivating, suitably challenging, and engaging process goals makes focusing much easier. Process goals are specific controllable actions and tasks such as "moving dynamically through my whole range of motion" or "staying in tune with my dance partner." Dancers should identify suitable process goals ahead of time and use them in practice before they need them in stressful situations (e.g., auditions, competitions). For more about goal setting, see chapter 9.

Use Constructive, Externally Focused Self-Talk

Process goals can be an excellent foundation for creating self-talk statements (also known as cue words). To be optimally helpful, such self-talk should be constructive (relevant to the task at hand and under personal control), global, and externally focused (Mullen et al., 2016). For instance, dancers may benefit from self-talk statements that express an overall movement intention or quality, such as *fluid*, *sinking*, or *powerful*. Teachers are very important in this process—indeed, research indicates that more positive and less negative self-talk is evident for performers who perceive their instructors as more supportive (Zourbanos et al., 2011). Therefore, teachers should consider that what they say (e.g., instructions focused on controlling separate body parts vs. global movement intentions) may over time become the inner voice (self-talk) of their dancers.

Practice Mindfulness

Learning to be fully present in the moment without judgment is an art and a practice that can have great benefits to dancers and to teachers as regards attentional focus and beyond. The Get Practical exercises in form 6.1 can be considered exercises in mindfulness, because they are about focusing fully and nonjudgmentally on different aspects of the present and switching between them. For more information, see chapter 8.

Form 6.1 — GET PRACTICAL: SHIFTING FOCUS

Doing these two exercises can help you increase your awareness of different attentional focus possibilities and learn to switch between them. In essence, they are exercises in selective attention. One is a dance-based exercise for which there are written instructions and reflection prompts. The second is a sound file that you can use in nearly any dance or everyday context.

SHIFTING FOCUS 1: EXPLORING INTERNAL AND EXTERNAL FOCUS IN DANCE

Choose an exercise that you are currently practicing. Start with something that is not too difficult or exhausting. If you do the exercise physically, be somewhere with plenty of space (e.g., a studio). If you prefer, you can do the exercise in your imagination. If you are a teacher, you can lead the exercise with your dancers.

1. During the first run-through, focus fully on body parts and technical corrections. For instance, how are you holding your shoulders? How much tension is appropriate in the arms? How do the muscles in your legs feel? Consider briefly how you felt and how it went.

2. Before doing a second run-through, decide on a particular quality or dynamic that you want to convey with your movements. For instance, you might want to make your exercise smooth and slippery, sharp and pointed, or melancholic and vulnerable. Make a clear decision before you do the exercise again, focusing fully on your desired quality. Consider briefly how you felt and how it went.

3. In a third run-through, put on some music. Then focus fully on the music and what it tells you. Really let the music lead you through the exercise, paying attention to the small details in the musical phrase. Again, consider briefly how you felt and how it went.

4. When you have finished, reflect on what you experienced. What felt more normal/habitual? What felt different with the three different foci? Do you have any recommendations to yourself regarding how to focus or help others focus in the future?

SHIFTING FOCUS 2: EXPLORING ATTENTIONAL FOCUS ANYWHERE

This exercise can be done just about anywhere: while relaxing at home, when riding the bus, standing in a queue, during warmup, or while dancing. Noticing in detail and labeling without judgment is a great way to bring yourself back to the present. To get better at shifting your attentional focus, play the sound file in your headphones many times and in many different contexts.

Go to HK*Propel* to download this form and to access the sound file for the second focusing exercise outlined here.

From S. Nordin-Bates, *Essentials of Dance Psychology* (Champaign, IL: Human Kinetics, 2023).

Fabian: Case Study of Focus

Fabian is a 28-year-old dancer in a neoclassical company where instruction is plentiful, detailed, and body-oriented. For instance, he is often given corrections related to his turnout ("hold your turnout throughout the movement") and the way he holds his shoulders ("down a bit; now rotate the scapula"). He works diligently in trying to coordinate the myriad corrections he is given and tries to check his progress in the mirror. He also frequently compares himself to others in the company. Although he improves, he often feels overwhelmed and inadequate. A couple of times he has frozen up completely and his mind went blank before going on stage: "I have no idea what I am doing!" When asked about his best dance memory, however, he recollects workshops with a choreographer that were truly absorbing. The dancers had been encouraged to work on aspects of a story in collaborative improvisation and got really immersed in the experience. According to Fabian, the absence of mirrors and technical corrections helped. It was a groundbreaking experience that Fabian wanted to take with him into the future. Hence, he took notes about what they had done and started to experiment with using story-led dancing in class. This was hard, not least because the teachers he met daily continued to give corrections based on body parts. Yet over time, Fabian noticed that these teachers also gave some more holistic and imagery-based instructions, even if only occasionally. He noted those in his diary and made more continuous use of them. Eventually, he also created his own images for particular movements, variations, and choreographies. Although he is frustrated about not having been provided with more such experiences throughout his career, he is satisfied about the improvements that he notices in his focus, confidence, and artistry.

Composite case study created on the basis of a conversation with Clare Guss-West, MA, attention and focus specialist in professional dance and dance-based health.

CRITICAL ASPECTS OF RESEARCH INTO ATTENTIONAL FOCUS

1. The "mother discipline" for this chapter is more motor learning and less traditional sport psychology, which helps account for the following differences between the present chapter and other chapters in this book:
    - *The focus on learning and performance effects.* Future research into how attentional focus affects aspects of well-being, including self-confidence and performance anxiety, are warranted. For instance, the self-invoking trigger effect proposed to result from internal focusing instructions (Wulf & Lewthwaite, 2010) may well induce social physique anxiety, or may be more common among those already high in such self-evaluative tendencies.
    - *The predominance of experimental study designs.* A distinct advantage of the many experimental studies underpinning this chapter is that we can be more confident regarding the direction of causality than for many other topics. A potential disadvantage can be the ecological validity/limited generalizability to applied settings.
2. Research into attentional focus in dance is in its infancy, and we know little about potential variations between individuals, teachers, movements, and dance styles. Indeed, all studies into internal versus external focus in dance were undertaken in ballet. Contemporary dance literature and practice has close connections to somatic approaches to attention, for which the discussion is perhaps more about promoting kinesthetic ahead of visual attention (e.g., Ehrenberg, 2015). Yet even if this kind of focus is directed inward (and typically called internal), it can vary in the extent to which it is concerned with specific body parts versus, for instance,

global sensations and movement intentions. Studies into these aspects would help advance the field (see also Toner & Moran, 2015, and Wulf, 2016).

KEY POINTS AND RECOMMENDATIONS FOR ATTENTIONAL FOCUS IN DANCE

1. The human body is an integrated whole rather than a set of bits and pieces; similarly, dancing is often of highest quality when the body works as a seamless whole. Therefore, it makes sense to structure dance training in this manner: focus on wholeness and movement effects (external focus) rather than on individual body parts (internal focus). Trust the body to work out how a movement should be coordinated.

2. Designing instructions and feedback to encourage an external focus requires time and careful consideration by teachers, and it is unlikely that any teacher (or dancer) can focus only externally all the time. However, the time invested will likely pay off in enhanced learning and performance for the dancers—and in a more absorbing, rich experience for dancers and teachers alike.

3. Even when previous learning has been explicit and internally focused, the strategic use of psychological skills can promote improved performance and can help to counteract the risk of skill breakdown under pressure.

7

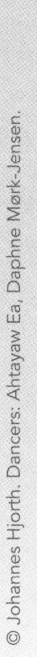

© Johannes Hjorth. Dancers: Ahtayaw Ea, Daphne Mørk-Jensen.

Creativity

"Creativity is allowing oneself to make mistakes.
Art is knowing which ones to keep."

Scott Adams, artist and comic strip author

CHAPTER OBJECTIVES

After reading this chapter, you will be able to

1. describe what creativity is;
2. outline different ways of viewing creativity, including its different aspects (cognitive, social, embodied), process- and product-based views, and creativity at different levels (mini-c, little-c, Pro-c, and Big-C creativity);
3. critically discuss a range of sources of creativity, including relatively stable (personality traits) and more malleable ones (teacher behaviors, particular activities);
4. describe a range of correlates of creativity, including links to well-being, ill-being, and performance;
5. apply basic recommendations to nurture creativity in dance;

6. undertake structured reflection regarding your own creativity or the extent to which you nurture creativity in others; and
7. think critically about the nature and impact of creativity in dance settings.

Key Terms

Big-C creativity	divergent thinking	little-c creativity
convergent thinking	intrinsic motivation principle of creativity	mini-c creativity
creativity		Pro-c creativity

The term *creativity* derives from the Latin word *creō*, meaning to create or make. While this origin appears similar to how we use the term today, its use has varied greatly throughout time and between cultures. For instance, creativity was long considered as something divine that humans were not capable of. Later on, creativity was often considered the prerogative of only the most eminent artists. As you will see in this chapter, the modern view is that *everyone* is capable of being creative but also that activities such as dance are not inherently creative, even if part of the so-called creative arts.

What Is Creativity?

Although descriptions and definitions of **creativity** in dance can vary (Chappell & Hathaway, 2019), a commonly accepted definition in psychology is that it is about the combination of *novelty* (originality, newness) and *usefulness* (appropriateness, practicality; Amabile, 1983/2018; Runco & Jaeger, 2012). The usefulness criterion sometimes baffles people because it may carry connotations of conformism or rule adherence—for some, the antitheses of creativity. It is also not uncommon for dance experts to be uncomfortable with the idea of tying creativity down into a single matter-of-fact definition (Clements & Redding, 2020; Mead, 2012; Weber & Reed, 2020). Yet most would probably agree that if a task is set to create 16 counts of movement material, simply leaving the room to drink coffee instead would not be considered creative. While such an action may be surprising (i.e., meet the novelty criterion), it does not match the task that was set (the usefulness criterion). *Meaningfulness* may be a dance- or arts-specific way of conceiving of usefulness, such that an audience member or teacher may find a dancer's movements creative if they are perceived to be novel and meaningful in the context of the work (Clements & Redding, 2020).

There is extensive research into creativity in dance, much of it interview-based; as such, we have a wealth of descriptions of what it is understood to be. Typical descriptions include words and phrases such as *generating, exploring, experimenting, transforming,* and *manipulating* (Clements & Redding, 2020), *openness to the unusual* (Chappell, 2007), *courage, taking risks,* and *avoiding patterns* (Biasutti & Habe, 2021).

Other recent examples include "*thinking broadly, resisting the fixity of ideas and terms,* and *approaching them from multiple perspectives at once,*" "*breaking out of a comfort zone,*" and "*a unique or individual artistic voice*" (all from Weber & Reed, 2020, p. 4).

Creativity is often highly valued in dance. Indeed, even a quick look around dance school websites or prospectuses tends to reveal statements about how they aim to train creative artists, innovative performers, or similar (see Rowe & Zeitner-Smith, 2011). This is partly because creativity is seen as useful in its own right, with potential transfer to other areas of life (e.g., school, work) and also for those who do not pursue dance as a career (e.g., Henley, 2014; Simonton, 2000; Sowden et al., 2015; Torrents et al., 2013). For those who do wish to become professionals, creativity is important because dancers are frequently called upon to contribute to the creative process of dance making (Butterworth, 2004; Farrer, 2014; Rowe & Zeitner-Smith, 2011; Salosaari, 2001; Whittier, 2017). The ability to make personal role interpretations is also important; in fact, artistic directors of major ballet companies find such creativity critical when promoting dancers to principal rank, alongside openness and imagination (Schwab, 2016). Finally, creativity is an obvious component of several other dance careers, such as choreography (Clements & Nordin-Bates, 2022; Lavender & Predock-Linnell, 2001) and freelance portfolio work (Aujla & Farrer, 2015; Watson et al., 2012).

Given the value placed on creativity in dance, it is unsurprising that it has been studied using several different angles, populations, and methods. Yet given its place in this introductory dance psychology book, the present chapter is not a comprehensive review of the dance creativity literature. Rather, it is an attempt to locate creativity as an important characteristic that can and should be studied from a dance science perspective. The focus is consequently on creativity as a psychological characteristic and how it links to topics such as personality, motivation, and psychological skills. For the interested reader, there are plenty of other writings on dance creativity to explore, including those focused on dance education, artistry, and history (e.g., Chappell & Hathaway, 2019; Press & Warburton, 2007; Smith-Autard, 2002; Whittier, 2017).

Cognitive, Embodied, and Social Aspects of Creativity

In psychology, studies into creativity have often been focused on individual cognitive processes such as **divergent thinking**: the extent to which an individual is able to generate many original responses to a problem. This is considered valuable because such thinking is associated with real-life creative achievements (Jauk et al., 2014). Within this tradition, creativity is typically captured through questionnaires and tests asking participants to generate as many uses as possible for common objects (e.g., a paperclip or a brick) within a given time frame (Guilford, 1963). Responses are considered regarding their number (fluency), the different categories generated (flexibility), and how developed they are (elaboration), as well as how many people generate the same answer (frequency). Dance students may score more highly on some aspects of measures like these when compared to non-dancers (Minton, 2003) and professionals more highly than novice dancers (Fink et al., 2009). In sports, there seems to be a modest though significant correlation between divergent thinking and divergent moving (Richard et al., 2018). However, there may be little crossover between divergent thinking scores like these and creativity ratings made by dance experts (Clements, 2017).

Many point out that divergent thinking tests are somewhat artificial and should probably be seen as tests of *creative potential*, rather than of creativity per se (e.g., Richard & Runco, 2020). For instance, some people may be great divergent thinkers (or movers) yet not necessarily perform creatively (Runco & Acar, 2012). It is encouraging therefore that alternative ways of observing and analyzing divergent dance movements have been developed (e.g., May et al., 2020; Torrents et al., 2010, 2013; Torrents Martín et al., 2015).

Notably, divergence is only one aspect of creativity: In addition to such idea generation (whether cognitive or physical), there must often be some selection of ideas or products with which to move forward after the more free-flowing ideas generation phase or the creative process would not be complete (e.g., Chappell, 2007; Lavender & Predock-Linnell, 2001). In psychology terms, this capacity to identify and select the most promising creative idea is known as **convergent thinking** (Cropley, 2006; see also May et al., 2020). As you can see, this aspect is related to the usefulness criterion in the definition of creativity provided at the start of the chapter. As dancer and choreographer Mikhail Baryshnikov allegedly put it: "The problem is not making up the steps but deciding which ones to keep."

The reliance on cognitive aspects of creativity, such as verbally describing or writing down solutions to a problem, also does not account for the fact that dance is inherently embodied; that is, dance creativity is typically experienced and expressed with the body (e.g., Chappell, 2007; Farrer, 2014; Lussier-Ley & Durand-Bush, 2009; Łucznik, 2015; Press & Warburton, 2007; Weber & Reed, 2020). As a result of this embodied nature, putting one's experiences of creativity into words can be difficult for young dancers (Chappell, 2007) and even for experts in creative dance and choreography (Clements & Redding, 2020). Partly as a result of such dilemmas, arts- and education-based researchers often advocate observation, prolonged engagement, reflective practice, and practice-as-research methods. Still, interviews remain a popular choice among researchers, and learning to verbalize can aid critical engagement and thereby creativity (Chappell, 2007; Johnston, 2006).

Creativity in dance is also inherently social (sometimes known as collaborative or communal; Biasutti, 2013; Chappell, 2007; Giguere, 2011; Łucznik, 2015; Press & Warburton, 2007; Rowe & Zeitner-Smith, 2011; Torrents et al., 2010; Watson et al., 2012). Indeed, authors in the area of creativity encourage dancers to use their bodies to think and interact with others (e.g., Lussier-Ley & Durand-Bush, 2009; Whittier, 2017). Creativity may therefore be seen as resulting from a complex interaction between individuals, surrounding people (dance partners, teachers, choreographers), and also the wider environment (e.g., dance studio climate, political context; Amabile, 1983/2018; Csikszentmihalyi, 1996; Hennessey, 2019; Richard & Runco, 2020; Simonton, 2000). In one study, a group of young dancers, their teachers, and guest choreographers all agreed that collaboration can be challenging, but it provides for greater opportunities to learn and be creative (Watson et al., 2012). Observation studies have shown that dancing in pairs seems to produce more divergent responses than dancing alone (Torrents et al., 2010, 2013). Dance educators may need both experience and highly attuned awareness to group dynamics to balance individual and social creativity, but if this is done sensitively, even conflict can be a source of creativity (Chappell, 2007).

Overall, the research into creativity is varied and disparate. In many ways, this diversity is a strength; for instance, researchers with many kinds of expertise contribute knowledge using varied methods. Yet disparity in how creativity is viewed can also be bewildering. Some have pointed out that unless there is some agreement and transparency about what creativity is and how it may be captured, there is a real risk of bias and unfairness in assessment (Clements & Redding, 2020). If dancers do not fully understand the criteria by which they are being judged and selected ("What do they mean by creative problem-solving?"), it is hard to see how goal setting and training can be optimized and a sense of competence can grow. As discussed in chapter 4, a perceived lack of control typically underpins anxiety.

At the same time, perceptions of creativity are often deeply personal, and any assessment of novelty and usefulness is subjective. Indeed, experts in the area argue that creativity is meaningful only within the norms of the area where it is being considered (Amabile, 1983/2018; Csikszentmihalyi, 1996), stating such things as "[M]ost everything we think we understand about creativity and the creative process is socioculturally dependent" (Hennessey, 2019, p. 386). Dance researchers too have highlighted that what is considered creative may vary across cultures (Chappell & Hathaway, 2019; Mead, 2009).

Creative Products and Creative Processes

Much attention, both in research and real life, has been devoted to creativity as an outcome or product. For instance, we may judge the creativity of products such as movement phrases, choreographies, or costumes. Some dance research includes assessment of creative products (Fink & Woschnjak, 2011; Torrents et al., 2010, 2013; Torrents Martín et al., 2015), and the consensual assessment technique developed by Amabile (1983/2018) for other art forms seems transferable to dance. Yet many artists and dance scholars highlight the importance of the creative process (e.g., Biasutti, 2013; Chappell, 2007; Clements & Redding, 2020; Farrer, 2014; Łucznik, 2015; Lussier-Ley & Durand-Bush, 2009; Press & Warburton, 2007; Rowe & Zeitner-Smith, 2011; Watson et al., 2012; Weber & Reed, 2020). Researchers taking this perspective typically use qualitative methods to understand something about the complexities of a creative process, while also accounting for the subjective, embodied, and social nature of creativity.

A distinct limitation of assessing creativity at a single point in time (e.g., as an end product) is that it often needs time to grow (e.g., Biasutti & Habe, 2021; Clements & Redding, 2020; Watson et al., 2012). Because dance is often about putting on a performance for an audience (i.e., a product), there is value in understanding creativity both as a process and as a product (Chappell, 2007; Clements & Redding, 2020). For instance, the tipping point at which a creative process turns into rehearsals for a polished performance can be very challenging because the open exploration and risk taking typical of the creative process may cease (Chappell, 2007). In the midway model, Smith-Autard (2002) proposed that creativity can ensue when a series of aspects are balanced: This includes a focus on products, knowledge, technique, and objectivity on the one hand, and a focus on processes, imagination, feelings, and subjectivity on the other.

Creativity Is for Everyone: Continuum of Creativity

It is readily obvious, even to non-dance experts, that choreography is a creative practice—at least, it is supposed to be. As such, choreographers (especially famous ones) are often seen as inherently creative individuals. Many have turned against this exclusive, rather elitist, and trait-based focus on creativity, instead arguing that creativity is available to each and every one of us given the right conditions, hard work, and good habits (e.g., Amabile, 1983/2018; Csikszentmihalyi, 1996; Farrer, 2014; Press & Warburton, 2007; Tharp, 2003). To clarify this idea, scholars created the Four C model of creativity (Kaufman & Beghetto, 2009). In this model, **Big-C creativity** (genius-level creativity) and **mini-c creativity** (personally meaningful creativity) are placed at opposite ends, with **little-c creativity** (everyday creativity of those with a reasonable amount of skill in the area) and **Pro-c creativity** (creative excellence of professionals in the area) in between. For an overview, see table 7.1.

Table 7.1 **Four Levels of Creativity**

	mini-c	little-c	Pro-c	Big-C
Description	Experiences, actions, and events that are novel and meaningful at a personal level (e.g., in a learning process)	Everyday creativity of reasonably accomplished individuals	Creative excellence at the professional level	Genius-level creativity recognized by the wider culture as historically important (perhaps only posthumously)
Level of creativity	Personal, small	Moderate	Large	Revolutionizing; a paradigm shift
Dance example	Dancers faced with a movement problem who find solutions that are appropriate for the task and new to them	Dancers who win choreographic awards at school	Professional dancers or choreographers who consistently get reviewed by critics as creative	Dance professionals credited with inventing new styles (e.g., Isadora Duncan)
Dance research example	Studying children's cognitions in a creative dance process[a]	Studying the impact of imagery training on student dancer's creativity[b]	Studying how choreographers perceive that ballet shaped their creativity[c]	Studying the lives of eminent creators such as Martha Graham[d]
Typical research methods	Varied, including questionnaires, tests, interviews, and observations			Biographical research and interviews with renowned individuals; quantitative methods difficult due to very small sample sizes

Time, maturity, and training →

[a]Giguere (2011).
[b]May et al. (2020).
[c]Clements & Nordin-Bates (2022).
[d]Gardner (1993).
Note: Based on Kaufman & Beghetto (2009).

As shown in table 7.1, the Four C model suggests that creativity may be understood to exist at four levels (Kaufman & Beghetto, 2009). It is only the Big-C level that is considered exclusive, with the model authors suggesting that many people can be experiencing mini-c, little-c, and even reach Pro-c in their lives. Moreover, people demonstrating Pro-c and Big-C will have engaged extensively in mini-c and little-c activities, both during development and continuously in their lives (Kaufman & Beghetto, 2009).

The Four C model delineates different levels of creativity and can be used as a foundation when designing new studies or understanding published studies (e.g., which level of creativity is most studied with a particular population). Yet equating creativity with fame and recognition is somewhat problematic, and some argue that we should focus on what the different levels have in common rather than what differentiates them (Runco, 2014). Indeed, underpinning principles and activities may well be the same at all levels, and the levels may best be viewed as a continuum rather than as distinct categories (Amabile, 1983/2018; Runco, 2014).

Dancers are often creative in the production of new dance works but credit for any creative success is typically attributed to the choreographer only (Farrer, 2014). Raising awareness of dancers' input and experiences thus becomes an important act of empowerment in what has historically been a hierarchical domain. Yet the historical lack of recognition for dancers' own creativity alongside its primarily embodied (rather than verbal) nature makes it difficult to study (Farrer, 2014). Therefore, traditional psychological research methods such as questionnaires and interviews may be limited. Researchers interested in advancing dance creativity research are therefore encouraged to try and bridge the gap between such methods and the more hands-on qualitative approaches of arts-based researchers.

> **THINKING CRITICALLY**
>
> - Is creativity valued in your dance settings and styles?
> - When you think of creativity in dance, do you mostly think of
>   a. Cognitive, social, or embodied aspects?
>   b. Processes or products?
>   c. Creativity at lower (mini-c or little-c) or higher levels (Pro-c or Big-C)?

Sources of Creativity

To a degree, creativity is part of one's personality and has therefore been subjected to the standard nature-versus-nurture debate that characterizes the topic of personality generally (see chapter 1). For instance, people may describe creativity in traitlike terms ("She is just so creative!"), and funding may be awarded to artists who are generally considered to be creative. Others emphasize the mini-c or little-c perspective and primarily focus on creativity sources that dancers and teachers can decide to use as tools. Aspects of both nature (personality) and nurture (teacher behaviors, particular activities) are considered next, alongside potential dance style differences.

Personality Traits and Personal Characteristics as Sources of Creativity

Openness to experience is one of the Big Five personality traits (Costa & McCrae, 1992; see chapter 1). Because it comprises curiosity, imagination, originality, and openness to new ideas, it is easy to see its connection to creativity. Indeed, it has been clearly demonstrated across domains that openness predicts creativity (e.g., Jauk et al., 2014; Richard & Runco, 2020). In one such study, creative success in the arts was best predicted by a combination of openness to experience and intelligence (de Manzano & Ullén, 2018). In another recent study, dance teachers identified openness, intelligence, and self-confidence as important for creativity because they were seen to encourage experimentation, risk taking, persistence, and asking questions (Clements & Redding, 2020).

Openness (e.g., as expressed in a curious, inquiring attitude) was similarly recognized as important in a study with young dancers alongside confidence or courage, flexibility, and resilience (Watson et al., 2012). Participants in that study also recognized that while some of these characteristics were stable aspects of their personalities (i.e., traits), others developed and evolved over time because of personal goals and life experiences. The authors also encouraged dancers to view vulnerability and anxiety around creative exploration as natural reactions that can be embraced and explored in their own right; a perspective fully in line with the gradual exposure and acceptance advocated in chapters 4 and 8. Others point out that although confidence may be a characteristic of creative people, it does not necessarily predispose them to more creative ideas; instead, it may be what helps them dare to try and to persist (Clements & Redding, 2020). As such, the creative ideas of more confident people are more likely to be seen and recognized, whereas those of less confident people may be left undeveloped and unseen.

In the study with young dancers, several personality characteristics were shown to be complementary yet partly in opposition; for instance, both confidence and vulnerability, openness and focus, flexibility and resilience were valued personal characteristics for creative processes (Watson et al., 2012). These dance-specific findings resemble the domain-general writing of Mihaly Csikszentmihalyi (1996), an authority on topics such as creativity and flow. It is possible that the combination of several characteristics (e.g., the ability to switch between being open and focused), rather than possessing specific ones in isolation, might be key to creativity (Watson et al., 2012). Figure 7.1 provides a visual (but not exhaustive) illustration of this idea.

Another personal characteristic shown to underpin creativity is intrinsic motivation (Amabile, 1983/2018; Hennessey, 2019; Richard & Runco, 2020). Indeed, creativity researcher Theresa Amabile created the **intrinsic motivation principle of creativity**, which states that people are most likely to be creative when driven by intrinsic aspects such as genuine interest, joy, and personal meaning than by extrinsic aspects such as pressure, guilt, or reward. In line with this principle, a recent review concluded that "Without the right kind of motivation, we are unlikely to play with ideas, take risks, or feel at all comfortable with the possibility of failure. Without the right kind of motivation, creativity is nearly impossible" (Hennessey, 2019, p. 374).

Further reinforcing the link between them, both intrinsic motivation and creativity are undermined by expected rewards, deadlines, and competition,

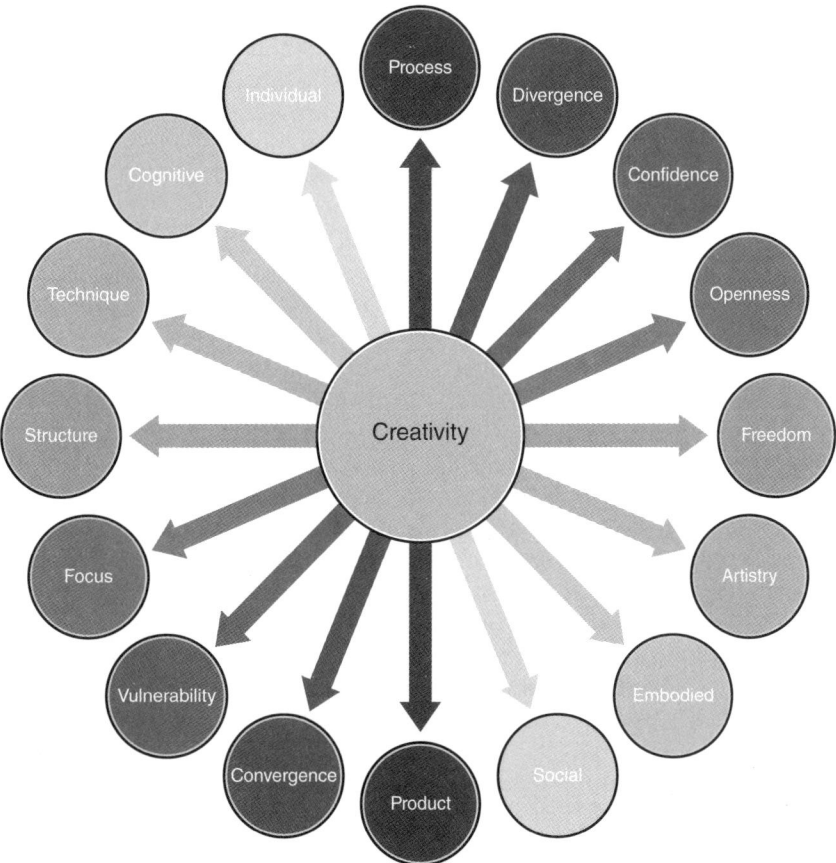

Figure 7.1 Creativity may arise when a number of seemingly opposing aspects are balanced (i.e., both poles are attended to rather than one to the exclusion of its opposite).

although only when perceived to be controlling (Amabile, 1983/2018; Hennessey, 2019; see also chapter 5). In studies with dance educators, many seemed uneasy about assessing dancers because they acknowledged that it could stifle creativity (Clements & Redding, 2020; Weber & Reed, 2020).

Studies in dance largely mirror those in other domains regarding the importance of intrinsic motivation (Biasutti, 2013; Clements & Nordin-Bates, 2022; Giguere, 2011; Nordin-Bates, 2020; Watson et al., 2012). For instance, a study with young children reported that the most common emotional response in the creative process was pleasure (Giguere, 2011), and a key theme emerging from interviews with choreographers concerned their strong intrinsic drive to create (Clements & Nordin-Bates, 2022). Especially the women spoke of the importance of inner drive and persistence as they had to fight expectations and traditions on their way to becoming choreographers.

Teacher Behaviors as a Source of Creativity

Researchers agree that creativity may never emerge if the environment is not supportive (Press & Warburton, 2007; Richard & Runco, 2020). This is explored next primarily via the theoretically grounded construct of healthy motivational climates (see chapter 11), with the value of making specific time for creative dance practice also being noted.

Healthy Motivational Climates

Teachers who create dance climates that are task-involving and supportive of the three basic psychological needs of autonomy, competence, and relatedness are more likely to nurture creativity (Clements & Nordin-Bates, 2022; Nordin-Bates, 2020; Watson et al., 2012; Weber & Reed, 2020). This is, of course, directly related to the importance of intrinsic motivation as a personal characteristic. To nurture creativity, educators need to value dancers as individuals and empower them to use their voices, both autonomy support strategies (Chappell, 2007; Clements & Nordin-Bates, 2022; Giguere, 2011; Karin & Nordin-Bates, 2020; Nordin-Bates, 2020; Salosaari, 2001; Watson et al., 2012; Weber & Reed, 2020; Whittier, 2017). One teacher expressed it as follows: "[Y]ou have to pass on certain knowledge and your skills but then give them the choice to use their skills and that knowledge . . . it is really important to give them a voice" (Watson et al., 2012, p. 163).

Butterworth's (2004) spectrum of five choreographic styles ranges from didactic (choreographer as expert, dancer as instrument) to democratic (choreographer as collaborator, dancer as co-owner). As shown through this spectrum, creative skills such as divergent thinking and moving, interactivity, and critical engagement with material are more likely to be nurtured when choreographic styles are more democratic (i.e., autonomy supportive). Arguably, the spectrum could also be seen as a spectrum of teaching styles. Could it be used as a foundation for research, where observers note the prevalence of different styles within a class, set of classes, or a choreographic process? Might relationships be found between the prevalence of different styles and the dancers' basic psychological needs satisfaction? How might variables such as age, level of competence, and confidence moderate any relationships found?

Although autonomy (e.g., a sense of freedom to explore) is the most easily identified as a source of creativity, support for the other two basic psychological needs also is important. This includes helping dancers to feel competent by maintaining a process focus, making the studio a safe space to explore and make mistakes, individualizing challenges and matching them with fun, and showing that there are many ways of doing something right (Biasutti, 2013; Biasutti & Habe, 2021; Nordin-Bates, 2020; Watson et al., 2012; Whittier, 2017). Literature also supports the need for relatedness (meaningful belonging) by encouraging collaboration, providing warm support, and creating a sense of community or a close-knit atmosphere (Nordin-Bates, 2020; Watson et al., 2012; Whittier, 2017).

On the opposite side of the spectrum, a lack of individualization, flexibility, and variety thwart autonomy and therefore creativity (Clements & Nordin-Bates, 2022). Interestingly, some participants in that study spoke of how they created their own little acts of rebellion to counteract their regimented training, perceiving this to be an autonomy boost. Other creativity thwarters include criticism and dichotomous views on what is right versus wrong (which undermine perceived competence; Clements & Nordin-Bates, 2022; Nordin-Bates, 2020; Watson et al., 2012). Feeling safe and valued is relevant for teachers and choreographers too: When they do not feel safe or valued or are under pressure to deliver, they are likely to limit the extent to which they "try things out whole-heartedly and . . . take risks" (Chappell, 2007, p. 44).

An illustration of how perceptions of teacher attitudes and behaviors may affect dancers' creativity is provided in the functional analyses shown in figure 7.2. In both examples, a dancer is faced with a creative task. In the first example, this task is set within an atmosphere that the dancer feels is judgmental, because she perceives that the teacher has set views on what she wants to see (the "right" way to do the task). As a result, our dancer hides at the back of the studio and only engages half-heartedly. This way, she avoids feeling awkward and escapes negative evaluation. Unfortunately, such experiences lead to her long-term creative development being limited. In the second example, our dancer is faced with a creative task in an atmosphere perceived to be encouraging and nonjudgmental. Therefore, she feels safe to engage fully in the task. While the possibility of feeling awkward may remain (e.g., when going outside her comfort zone), she also has the opportunity to experience full engagement and flow. In the long term, such experiences can contribute to greater creative development.

A key aspect of nurturing creativity is giving freedom, but it is usually not a do-whatever-you-like kind of freedom. Instead, many highlight the importance of freedom within boundaries (Chappell, 2007; Clements & Nordin-Bates, 2022; Farrer, 2014; Mead, 2009, 2012; Nordin-Bates, 2020; see also figure 7.1). This may involve improvising with clear goals (Biasutti, 2013) or varied constraints (Torrents Martín et al., 2015). Boundaries can also be the counts available (create an eight-count phrase to cross the floor), the kind of movement quality desired (move any body part, always in a jagged and angular way), or experimentation with pre-choreographed movement (using the phrase you have just learned, experiment with two different emotions you can express with it).

Making Space for Creativity

Some studies have highlighted the importance of having specific classes for creative dance on the timetable (Rowe & Zeitner-Smith, 2011; Watson et al., 2012). Although more common in contemporary dance, it would be fascinating to see research into what kind of impact such classes might have in formalized, traditional dance forms such as classical ballet (e.g., Biasutti, 2013; Whittier, 2017) or classical Indian dance (Anoop & Malshe, 2011).

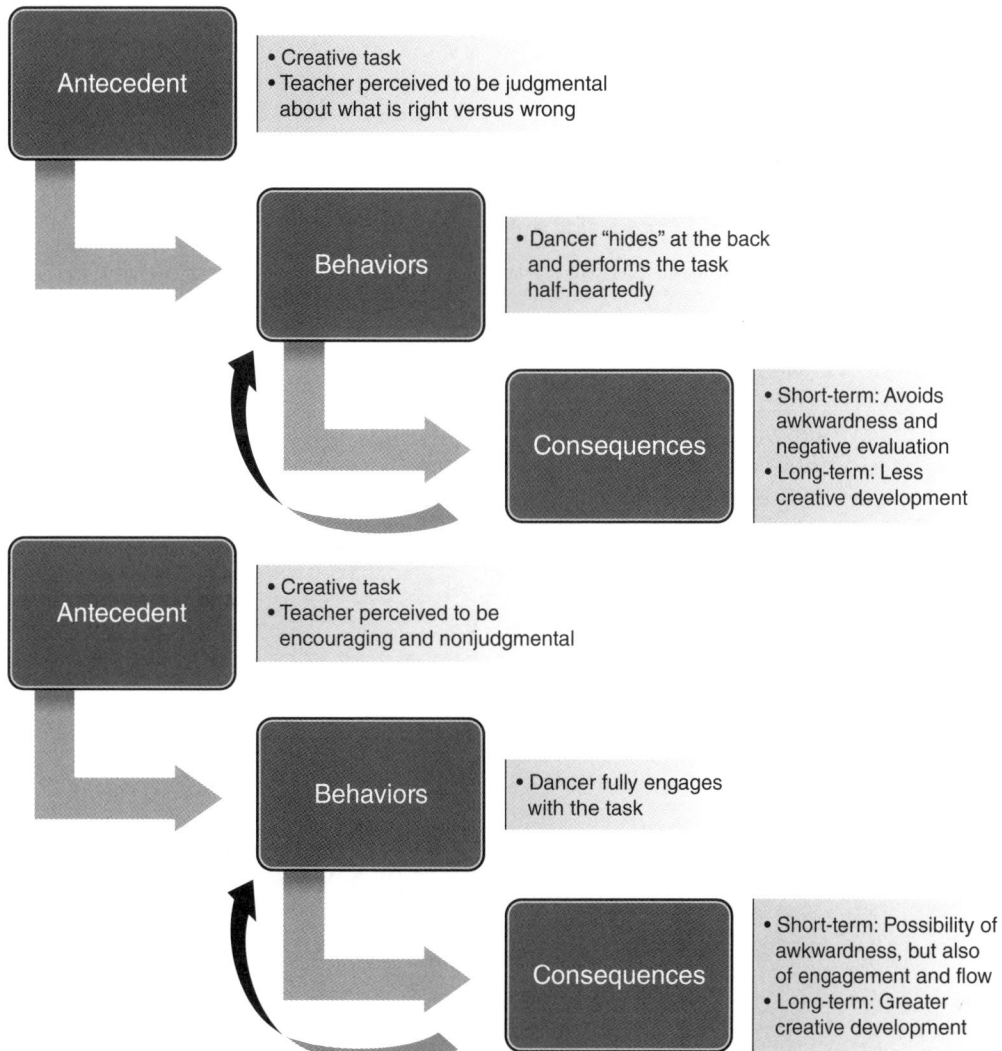

Figure 7.2 Functional analysis examples of how different perceptions of teacher attitudes and behaviors may affect creativity in dance. The recursive arrows indicate that the consequences make the behavior more likely to reoccur in similar situations in the future (behavior maintenance).

Still, having specific creative classes should not be an excuse for other classes to be uncreative: Because of the value of creativity, it should probably suffuse dance teaching overall. Indeed, there is sometimes an assumption that knowledge should come before creativity (Sowden et al., 2015), but creativity development often needs time and gradual growth. We may link this to the Four C model presented earlier (Kaufman & Beghetto, 2009): People will not arrive at Pro-c or Big-C creativity without a long history of mini-c and little-c experiences.

Particular Activities as Sources of Creativity

Dancers, teachers, and choreographers all engage in particular activities to nurture their creativity. Although these can be personal and idiosyncratic, three kinds of activities stand out as particularly important: improvisation, use of psychological skills, and the seeking of inspiration and variety. These can be either teacher-led (e.g., teachers giving varied imagery in class) or self-led (e.g., dancers seeking their own inspiration).

Improvisation

Improvisation, or the creation of something on the spur of the moment, nurtures creativity because it allows dancers to explore movement possibilities and take risks with an open-minded curious mindset. It is often believed to be a highly authentic personal process characterized by freedom and expressivity (Biasutti, 2013). As such, the characteristics of improvisation overlap with the characteristics of creativity itself. Biasutti points out that improvisation is typically a dancer-led activity, with the teacher being more of a facilitator than someone who delivers knowledge; as such, improvisation affords participants a high level of autonomy. In Biasutti's (2013) study with teachers, one participant emphasized the role of autonomy as follows: "Dance improvisation allows you to reclaim what it is yours; it allows you to be not only an interpreter, but also a creator" (p. 135).

Because it involves bodies and minds in synchrony, improvisation is essentially embodied creativity in action (Łucznik, 2015). Of course, dance practitioners have known this for far longer than psychology has been an area of study, and improvisation is frequently used as a creative tool (Biasutti, 2013; Biasutti & Habe, 2021; Chappell, 2007; Giguere, 2011; Kirsh et al., 2020; Łucznik, 2015; Richard & Runco, 2020; Rimmer, 2013; Lavender & Predock-Linnell, 2001; Sowden et al., 2015; Torrents et al., 2010, 2013; Torrents Martín et al., 2015; Watson et al., 2012; Whittier, 2017). Neuroimaging research further confirms the use of improvisation to enhance creativity in dance; specifically, the neural regions associated with creativity are more active when dancers imagine improvisational dance than a standardized dance (the waltz; Fink et al., 2009). Notably, improvisation can be used at all levels and with all ages, at all different stages of a dance class, in developing choreography and on stage (e.g., Biasutti, 2013; Biasutti & Habe, 2021). Nevertheless, the divergence of improvisation may need to be complemented by more convergent activities such as selecting, composing, and critical thinking (Lavender & Predock-Linnell, 2001).

In a recent review of creativity in sports (Richard & Runco, 2020), improvisation was described as a source of creativity because it facilitates immersion in the present moment and nonjudgmental attitudes—a description that suggests similarities with mindfulness (see chapter 8). These authors further highlighted that along with freedom, exposure to discomfort (i.e., going outside one's comfort zone) may be necessary for creativity to ensue, and improvisation can certainly fit this criterion (Richard & Runco, 2020). Improvisation can also have the added benefit of showing teachers what kinds of choices dancers make when free to do so (Whittier, 2017). This might illuminate potential gaps in the dancers' competencies and can therefore inform teaching.

Improvisation is an accessible way to nurture creativity.

Improvisation might be especially useful to those who have become stifled by technique, self-consciousness, and self-criticism, although it may have to proceed slowly so as not to become overwhelming (e.g., from more to less guided; Biasutti & Habe, 2021; Nordin-Bates, 2020). For instance, perfectionistic dancers may find improvisation tasks uncomfortable because they involve uncertainty and the potential for looking silly. As one teacher put it: "really strongly perfectionistic people, they struggle with improvisation. . . . [for them] there is one right and many, many wrongs." (previously unpublished quote from dance teacher interviewed in Nordin-Bates, 2020). At the same time, it may be possible to reduce perfectionistic thinking through engagement in absorbing creative dance practice (Karin & Nordin-Bates, 2020).

Psychological Skills: Imagery and Mindfulness

Imagination is inherent to creativity, with dancers and choreographers using it to create and develop movements as well as solve movement problems (e.g., Biasutti, 2013; Choi & Kim, 2015; Giguere, 2011; Hanrahan & Vergeer, 2001; May et al., 2011, 2020; Nordin & Cumming, 2005; Torrents et al., 2013; Weber & Reed, 2020; Whittier, 2017). It is intimately linked to both improvisation and inspiration. For example, choreographers often ask dancers to improvise based on metaphorical images, then select and combine bits of the emerging material into a gradually emerging creation (e.g., Kirsh et al., 2020). Yet while imagery can enhance creativity in dance (e.g., Karin & Nordin-Bates, 2020), it does not always do so (May et al., 2020); hence, further research into how to optimize this process is warranted. For an in-depth consideration of imagery, see chapter 10.

As part of the mindfulness revolution, research has highlighted that mindfulness can be another way of nurturing creativity (Lebuda et al., 2016). Interestingly, it is not the awareness (i.e., focused attention) aspect of mindfulness that is conducive to creativity; rather, aspects such as open monitoring seem to be more helpful (the ability to pay attention to a range of stimuli without judgment). Alternatively, different aspects of mindfulness may be helpful in different stages of a creative process (Lebuda et al., 2016). In a study with modern dance students, participants described how truly being in the moment, with acceptance and without overthinking or denying thoughts and feelings, was helpful to them and their creative processes (Lussier-Ley & Durand-Bush, 2009). For an in-depth consideration of mindfulness, see chapter 8.

Inspiration and Variety

Accessing a variety of dance styles and being exposed to an array of different art forms are sources of inspiration and creativity for many, as are guest choreographer projects and choreographic workshops (Clements & Nordin-Bates, 2022; Clements & Redding, 2020; Kim et al., 2020; Nordin-Bates, 2020; Rowe & Zeitner-Smith, 2011; Watson et al., 2012). Of course, this is a balancing act; there are only so many hours in the day and exposure to breadth and variety cannot always be added on top of deep engagement in one's main dance style without risk of overload (Rowe & Zeitner-Smith, 2011).

Sport research indicates that although spending a lot of time in deliberate practice can support creativity, participating in many, varied, playful, and informal activities is associated with greater creative potential than simply spending many hours in organized adult-led practice (Richard & Runco, 2020). Recommendations for creative environments consequently include having partly unstructured training sessions with movement variability, elements of randomness, and opportunities for performers to structure their own training activities (Richard & Runco, 2020). Variation within dance may include using different locations, class structures, and music styles (Clements & Nordin-Bates, 2022; Kim et al., 2020; Nordin-Bates, 2020). In an intervention with teenage dancers, one participant reported that the use of varied imagery in class made him more creative; it also made classes more fun (Karin & Nordin-Bates, 2020).

Dance Style as a Source of Creativity

We should be mindful of assumptions that dance is somehow inherently creative simply because it falls under the creative arts (Chappell, 2007; Whittier, 2017). Instead, any dance practice has the potential to be creative or uncreative, depending on the behaviors of its participants. At a general level, however, dance styles do differ in teaching traditions, performance demands, and in other ways. Thus, it is no surprise that dancers in different styles also seem to differ in creativity. In the only study to examine this issue quantitatively, modern/contemporary dancers scored more highly on a test of divergent thinking than did jazz dancers, who in turn scored more highly than ballet dancers (Fink & Woschnjak, 2011). Moreover, the modern/contemporary dancers scored lower than both jazz and ballet dancers on conscientiousness. The findings may suggest that aspects of personality lead

VERSATILITY AND creativity BEGIN WITH VARiETY

WHAT WILL YOU DO DIFFERENTLY TODAY?

Go to *HKPropel* to find a full-sized version of this and other lettering art.

Lettering art by Ink & Lise. Used with permission.

people to take up, and persist with, dance styles that match their inherent disposition (nature); it is also possible that differences are due to teaching styles (nurture). The typically greater emphasis on creativity in contemporary styles than in ballet is likely to affect its participants, especially if they are training intensively over many years (e.g., Alterowitz, 2014; Morris, 2003; Nordin-Bates, 2020; Salosaari, 2001).

In one study, some teachers and students struggled to see how creativity could be nurtured in ballet, whereas other teachers and students were both informed and enthusiastic (Nordin-Bates, 2020). For instance, one teacher argued:

> [Ballet technique] is so often misinterpreted. Both teachers and students can't, aren't allowed to enjoy what this technique has to offer: when it is linked to different bodies, to infinite possibilities. . . . not to try and push everyone into a mold but to try and understand the flow within the technique . . . It is often that people work in a very boring way in ballet classes . . . they grow up with that 'you are brainless when you do ballet. You just obey; there is no creativity.' And it is beautiful to see it change. It is just, you have to open this window. (previously unpublished quote from dance teacher interviewed in Nordin-Bates, 2020)

In a similar vein, choreographers in another study typically felt that their ballet training had provided them with invaluable skills, but that their creativity had been more thwarted than inspired in the process (Clements & Nordin-Bates, 2022). In particular, hierarchy, rigidity, expectations of obedience, and punishment were perceived to thwart creativity. For some, this directly fueled their desire to become choreographers rather than remain employed as dancers. Importantly, poor creativity nurture in ballet appears more likely for females than for males (e.g., Clegg et al., 2019; Clements & Nordin-Bates, 2022). For more about traditional ballet teaching being potentially autonomy (and creativity) suppressive, see chapter 11.

Although the literature focuses mostly on classical ballet and contemporary dance, it is worth considering style differences and the influence of tradition on creativity more widely. Indeed, classical Indian dance has also been criticized for requiring years of unquestioning obedience before "earning the right" to be creative (Anoop & Malshe, 2011), and some critique of modern dance is remarkably similar to that leveled at classical ballet (Lakes, 2005; Lussier-Ley & Durand-Bush, 2009).

THINKING CRITICALLY

- When were you last creative? What did it feel like?
- Can you find examples of teaching practices that you either use or are exposed to and that nurture or thwart creativity?

Correlates of Creativity

Creativity is considered valuable in its own right; indeed, enhanced creativity has been listed as a consequence of several other topics in this book (e.g., of being more intrinsically motivated and of practicing mindfulness; see chapters 5 and 8). Hence, this section focuses more on correlates rather than consequences of creativity, while making use of the same headings as those used in other chapters—that is, well-being and performance-related correlates of creativity. Links between creativity and ill-being are also considered.

Well-Being Related Correlates of Creativity

The following well-being related constructs have been shown to correlate with creativity:

> *Enhanced well-being.* Positive emotions and self-esteem often accompany creativity (Lussier-Ley & Durand-Bush, 2009; Richard & Runco, 2020), which is unsurprising. Many of the things that nurture creativity also nurture well-being, including healthy motivational climates and personal characteristics such as intrinsic motivation and self-confidence. In positive psychology, creativity is considered a form of optimal human functioning (Simonton, 2000).

> *Freedom to be and develop oneself.* Although the dance literature rarely uses these terms, it is evident between the lines that developing personal expression, voice, and movement signature is possible through creative exploration; thus, creativity is a source of self-actualization (e.g., Kim et al., 2020). Indeed, some leave dance because of a lack of creative opportunities (Clements & Nordin-Bates, 2022; Watson et al., 2012).

> *Enhanced psychological characteristics and skills.* Creative behaviors (e.g., improvisation) seem capable of enhancing psychological skills such as mindfulness (Richard & Runco, 2020), concentration, self-confidence, and intrinsic motivation (e.g., Biasutti, 2013; Biasutti & Habe, 2021). In some cases, the relationships between creativity and these skills and characteristics appear to be reciprocal (e.g., self-confidence making a dancer dare to try and be creative, and creative success enhancing self-confidence further).

Ill-Being Related Correlates of Creativity

Many areas of psychology (e.g., performance, social, cognitive, and positive psychology) as well as dance education view creativity in distinctly positive terms. Strong links have also been demonstrated between creativity and other desirable constructs (e.g., intrinsic motivation, well-being). At the same time, there has been debate and research into the links between creativity and mental illness since antiquity (Simonton, 2019). Indeed, the mad genius stereotype is alive and well, and you can probably think of several popular films in which artists are portrayed as both highly creative and severely mentally ill. Research only partly supports this stereotype, with experts concluding that it is exaggerated and overgeneralized, although with some basis in reality (Silvia & Kaufman, 2010).

In fact, there are links between creativity and forms of mental illness such as mood disorders and schizotypy (a personality characteristic that sets people at risk of developing schizophrenia). However, creativity is more often associated with subclinical manifestations of such problems than with full-blown disorders because the latter also bring significant impairments (Silvia & Kaufman, 2010; Simonton, 2019). These authors also point out that persons with subclinical disorders may in some cases be highly creative thinkers (e.g., experience unusual thoughts, generate divergent ideas). Yet they may not actually produce anything creative because doing so also requires other aspects (e.g., motivation, persistence, collaboration). In sum, *some forms* of (milder) mental ill-being may be associated with *some forms* of creativity in *some forms* of art. Moreover, these problems may exist only at the highest levels (i.e., Big-C creativity) and have few if any implications for people in general (e.g., for little-c creativity; Kaufman & Beghetto, 2009).

Performance-Related Consequences of Creativity

While creativity is a performance-related outcome in its own right, it is of course also a precursor to the creation of choreography and of stage performances more generally. This varies from the development of steps and movements early on in the process to the creative interpretation of a role or transmission of a message when actually on stage. Creativity can also support dance performance-related skills and characteristics such as the development of one's own movement signature (e.g., Biasutti & Habe, 2021; Lavender & Predock-Linnell, 2001; Whittier, 2017). Finally, individuals with better motor creativity seem to adapt better to failure (Richard et al., 2018), perhaps because they perceive tasks to be less difficult and they persist for longer. These individuals also report more positive emotions than their less creative counterparts.

Beyond dance-specific outcomes, dance teachers use improvisation as a creative tool to foster physical and perceptual-motor skills such as motor development, balance, perceptual awareness, and coordination (Biasutti, 2013; Biasutti & Habe, 2021). Teachers in these studies further described how improvisation nurtured cognitive skills such as critical thinking and reflection and social skills such as listening and relating to others. Along similar lines, improvisation and group-based choreographing are used in schools to support children's cognitive development (Giguere, 2011; Minton, 2003). In an experimental investigation in this area, children who had taken part in a dance improvisation task as short as 10 minutes scored significantly higher on two creativity tasks than children in a control group (Sowden et al., 2015). Because the tests used were not dance- or even art-specific, the authors suggested that their findings may be used to support the use of creative arts in general education. Some "go even further and claim that improvisation helps children to develop general strategies for coping with life challenges and encourages them to create their own individual flexible mind-set, which is crucial for living in a contemporary society" (Biasutti & Habe, 2021, p. 60).

How Can Creativity Be Nurtured?

Given the high value placed on creativity, its nurture is of central interest to many. However, the extent to which creativity is being stimulated in preprofessional dance training has been criticized (e.g., Butterworth, 2004; Clements & Nordin-Bates, 2022; Morris, 2003; Rowe & Zeitner-Smith, 2011; Salosaari, 2001). In particular, it is argued that many schools focus almost exclusively on technical excellence rather than on the nurture of creative artists. Not only can this limit artistic development (and thereby success), but it may also stifle personal development (e.g., Morris, 2003). Several ways of nurturing creativity are suggested next; many represent the practical use or implementation of the sources of creativity already described, so this section is deliberately kept brief. For readers specifically interested in ballet, Weidmann (2018) and especially Whittier (2017) outline a wealth of strategies for how not only creativity but also technique, awareness, and critical reflection may be nurtured. A key point is that technique and creativity do not have to be at odds with one another but can be mutually reinforcing skills.

> *Value and encourage personal characteristics associated with creativity.* Dancers should be encouraged to be open, curious, and flexible in their approach to tasks and challenges. Similarly, individuality, flexibility, and originality should be valued over homogeneity and rigid rule adherence. For recommendations regarding how self-confidence may be supported, see chapter 3; for recommendations of how to manage self-criticism, see chapter 2.

> *Nurture intrinsic motivation, joy, and interest.* To do so, teachers should create healthy motivational climates—that is, be task-involving and support the three basic psychological needs of autonomy, competence, and relatedness. Supporting autonomy is especially important, including giving dancers a sense of freedom within varied boundaries (Biasutti, 2013; Clements & Nordin-Bates, 2022; Nordin-Bates, 2020). For more specific guidance, see chapter 11. In brief, there are five key ways of supporting creativity via autonomy:

>> 1. *Provide choice.* For instance, teachers can ask students to experiment with different choices and to reflect on how those affect technique, movement quality, and expressivity (Whittier, 2017).
>> 2. *Put dancers in charge of their own development.* For example, teachers can encourage dancers to take responsibility for their own learning (Choi & Kim, 2015) and ask them open-ended questions (rather than the teacher providing all the answers; Torrents et al., 2013). Asking dancers to set their own goals and evaluate their own progress before looking to a teacher for input are other ways to help put dancers in charge. Such autonomy support can encourage problem-solving and problem-finding, both of which are part of creativity (Giguere, 2011; Mead, 2012). The teacher is a guide, not an all-knowing authority who cannot be questioned.
>> 3. *Encourage individuality.* Help dancers to appreciate, explore, and develop their own movement signatures so that not only creativity but also self-confidence is encouraged.
>> 4. *Encourage experimentation.* Allow dancers to take risks and experiment, and then discuss any outcome (success/failure) for its learning potential in a nonjudgmental atmosphere.
>> 5. *Approach rather than avoid.* Sport researchers further suggest that leaders should encourage performers to *approach* open-ended problems with an open mind rather than tell them how to *avoid* problems (Richard & Runco, 2020).

> *Set tasks that include experimentation and risk taking, such as improvisation.* This can be done within any given class, but for dancers at higher levels (e.g., full-time training) it can be

valuable to add sessions that are inherently about creativity.

> *Use psychological skills such as imagery and mindfulness.* For instance, teachers may introduce one new image per class and gradually ask students to share their own and try out the images of their fellow students. They could also try guiding dancers to focus on particular aspects of a movement or variation in a curious nonjudgmental way while staying open-minded and process oriented. For more guidance, see chapters 8 and 10.

> *Seek inspiration and variety.* Inspiration is highly personal, and so a curious openness and a willingness to explore will be valuable characteristics in identifying inspiration sources. It may involve simply trying and experimenting with varied experiences outside of dance (e.g., engaging with a range of art forms, people, and cultures) and inside dance practice (e.g., using varied music; mixing up the order of exercises; trying different dance styles, teachers, and schools). For example, dancers may be given a variety of rhythms or music styles and asked to explore the differential impacts they have on movement. Sport researchers further suggest that leaders make small changes to the practice environment on a regular basis, remove barriers, and allow freedom (Richard & Runco, 2020).

> *Encourage working in flexible groups.* Creativity is typically a social phenomenon, so it stands to reason that group work can be an effective way of nurturing creativity (e.g., Chappell, 2007; Whittier, 2017). For instance, dancers might work in pairs or in small groups not only to create but also to reflect on material, solve problems, and so forth (e.g., Mead, 2012). In this way, even everyday class learning can become a creative process of discovery (Whittier, 2017).

> *Consider somatically informed practices.* Autonomy and individuality are inherent aspects of somatic practices; as such, some dance scholars have highlighted how somatic practices, or somatically informed dance training, are likely to enhance creativity by stimulating fine-tuned awareness, embodiment, and autonomy (e.g., Jackson, 2005; Weber & Reed, 2020; see also Lussier-Ley & Durand-Bush, 2009).

Use forms 7.1 and 7.2 to consider how you nurture creativity.

Nature is often a powerful source of inspiration.

© Johannes Hjorth. Dancer: Felicia Andersson.

Form 7.1   GET PRACTICAL: CONSIDER YOUR CREATIVITY (TEACHER VERSION)

This is an exercise to help you reflect on how you nurture creativity. You can reflect on a single day or on a whole week; on a recurrent basis (e.g., as part of a training diary) and/or as a basis for goal setting. Mark yourself on the scale in accordance with what you did. Last, note whether you felt that your dancers accomplished something creative (novel and suitable), however small or large. What do you notice?

TODAY/THIS WEEK, I ENCOURAGED OR HELPED MY DANCERS TO . . .	HOW OFTEN? WRITE A NUMBER IN THE BOX CORRESPONDING TO THE FOLLOWING: 1 = NEVER 2 = RARELY 3 = OCCASIONALLY 4 = REGULARLY 5 = VERY OFTEN	NOTES (E.G., WHEN, WHAT)
Experiment and take risks		
Expose themselves to variety and/or inspiration		
Take part in improvisation or another creative task		
Collaborate or learn from others		
Use imagery in a creative way		
Exercise their autonomy		
Be open-minded and curious		
Feel intrinsically motivated (e.g., interest, joy)		
Feel safe to explore		
To what extent did your dancers accomplish something creative: both novel (unusual, surprising) and suitable (appropriate, meaningful)?		

Go to HK*Propel* to download this form.

From S. Nordin-Bates, *Essentials of Dance Psychology* (Champaign, IL: Human Kinetics, 2023).

Form 7.2 — GET PRACTICAL: CONSIDER YOUR CREATIVITY (PERSONAL VERSION)

This is an exercise to help you reflect on your own creativity. You can reflect on a single day or on a whole week; on a recurrent basis (e.g., as part of a training diary) and/or as a basis for goal setting. Mark yourself on the scale in accordance with what you did and felt. Last, note whether you felt that you accomplished something creative (novel and suitable), however small or large. What do you notice?

TODAY/THIS WEEK, I . . .	HOW OFTEN? WRITE A NUMBER IN THE BOX CORRESPONDING TO THE FOLLOWING: 1 = NEVER, 2 = RARELY, 3 = OCCASIONALLY, 4 = REGULARLY, 5 = VERY OFTEN	NOTES (E.G., WHEN, WHAT)
Experimented and took risks		
Exposed myself to variety and/or inspiration		
Took part in improvisation or another creative task		
Collaborated or learned from others		
Used imagery in a creative way		
Exercised my autonomy		
Was open-minded and curious		
Felt intrinsically motivated (e.g., interest, joy)		
Felt safe to explore		
Did something creative: both novel (unusual, surprising) and suitable (appropriate, meaningful)		

Go to HK*Propel* to download this form.

From S. Nordin-Bates, *Essentials of Dance Psychology* (Champaign, IL: Human Kinetics, 2023).

Caroline: Case Study of Creativity

Caroline's parents thought that dance training would be an outlet for her imagination and boundless energy, and non-dance friends seemed to believe that dancers were somehow all naturally creative. Yet, as a young dancer, Caroline did not feel creative at all. In fact, she used to say to her friends that "creativity is what people think dance is, yet dance training often isn't." Instead, she felt that training was much more about trying to do everything technically right, with little room to express or to be herself. Even for performances, the required artistry seemed to be about doing exactly as the rehearsal director said. While this felt okay at first, it quickly got boring once a role had been rehearsed and performed for a little while.

After going to see a professional performance one evening, Caroline and her friend were discussing what they had just seen: a really engaging, emotionally laden piece of art. But how did this match up to what they were doing in the dance studio every week? To them, even the most senior students at their school did not seem much like artists. Did their teachers simply expect creativity to develop naturally once technical know-how was in place? Feeling uneasy about the apparent mismatch, Caroline and her friends continued watching varied performances and started taking classes with other teachers. They discovered that when teachers focused more on emotions, sensory input, and storytelling, they felt free to explore. For many of them, this also made classes more varied and enjoyable. Caroline eventually came to view creativity as a tool to enhance her own well-being because when engaged in creative exploration, she was not comparing herself to others or becoming judgmental about her technical abilities. As one of her friends put it: "Creativity is why many of us do dance in the first place—so how can using and developing it *not* be a priority, at all ages?"

Composite case study created on the basis of conversations with Janet Karin, OAM, previously of the Australian Ballet School and an expert in integrating imagery and somatosensory principles into ballet training and rehabilitation, and with Lucie Clements, CPsychol, a consultant dance psychologist and creativity expert in the United Kingdom.

CRITICAL ASPECTS OF RESEARCH INTO CREATIVITY

1. Almost all research into creativity in dance is focused on dance participants or performers at different levels: from children to professionals. There are also studies with choreographers. In moving forward, it would be valuable to study the creativity of dance teachers to a greater extent. For instance, how can teachers be supported to develop creative lesson plans, rehearsals, and other teaching-related outputs?

2. Research into creativity in dance has often been qualitative, which has provided us with a rich source of knowledge about creative experiences and processes. There are also some (often small-scale) quantitative investigations, such as standardized cognitive psychology tests of divergent thinking (for an intriguing exception from cognitive science, see Kirsh et al., 2020). In moving forward, it would be rewarding to see the study of creativity become more firmly integrated into performance psychology, not least to obtain a better understanding of generalizability. For instance, the embodied nature of dance creativity could perhaps be linked to the construct known as motor creativity in sports—that is, the ability to produce new motor patterns either to express an idea or an emotion, or to solve a preset movement problem (e.g., Richard et al., 2018).

3. The inherent diversity of the creativity literature is both its main strength and a source of confusion. Readers would do well to remember that no single study proves anything or can research creativity in its entirety. Rather, each study contributes some piece, be it small or large, to our ever-growing puzzle of understanding of the intriguing human capacity that is creativity.

KEY POINTS AND RECOMMENDATIONS FOR CREATIVITY IN DANCE

1. Creativity is a valuable skill, both in dance and in life generally, because it is part of being successful *and* a source of well-being and self-actualization.
2. Although there are aspects of personality that help make some people more creative, we should focus our energies on how creativity can be nurtured in everyone—that is, focus on facilitating everyday creativity in daily dance practice. In that way, more people can experience the benefits of being creative, and higher levels of creativity will become more likely too.
3. Creating healthy motivational climates (e.g., autonomy support) and nurturing helpful personal characteristics (e.g., openness, confidence) and psychological skills (e.g., imagery, mindfulness) would make for a solid foundation from which creativity can grow; adding improvisation and variety will likely help it flourish.

Part III
Psychological Skills

Mindfulness

"For me, to enter into motion is to enter into meditation."

Maurice Béjart, dancer and choreographer

CHAPTER OBJECTIVES

After reading this chapter, you will be able to

1. describe what mindfulness is;
2. critically discuss four key components of mindfulness;
3. outline techniques or therapeutic approaches that incorporate mindfulness, including acceptance and commitment therapy (ACT) and self-compassion;
4. describe a range of consequences of mindfulness, including effects on well-being and on performance;
5. apply basic recommendations to practice mindfulness both formally (meditation) and informally (in dance and in everyday tasks); and
6. think critically about the nature and impact of mindfulness in dance settings.

Key Terms

acceptance	breathing space	psychological flexibility
acceptance and commitment therapy (ACT)	cognitive defusion	self-compassion
	common humanity	self-kindness
body scanning	mindfulness	

> The term *mindfulness* is a translation of the word *sati* from the ancient Indian language of Pali, meaning approximately awareness, or "memory of the present." The term *mindful*, in contrast, is from the Old English *myndeful*, which originally meant "of good memory"; later, it came to mean attentive, thoughtful, and to bear something in mind. The memory-related aspects of these terms may suggest a thinking back (remembering) that is not commensurate with the present-moment awareness characterizing mindfulness. Indeed, as you will learn in this chapter, the ability to detach past and future from the present is one of the key aspects making mindfulness so valuable.

What Is Mindfulness?

Mindfulness is an open-minded, nonjudgmental way of attending to the present moment (Kabat-Zinn, 2013). It also involves curiosity regarding one's experience (What am I feeling and doing? What is going on just now?) without attaching oneself to a stimulus so much that we become enmeshed with it (e.g., become lost in thought). If we did, we would miss the next moment as it arrives and becomes the new now, which would not be mindfulness in the present! In this sense, mindfulness has an element of detached observation about it, and metaphors about this observer mindset abound in the literature. For instance, authors guide us to observe thoughts and sensations as they come and go like clouds in the sky, cars on the road, or leaves floating past on a bubbling stream. Metaphors like these also aim to nurture a view of stimuli, distractions, and experiences as fleeting—something to note, but also to let go.

The heightened state of present-moment awareness along with a sense of acceptance (nonjudgment) is proposed to result in richer experiences—essentially, living to the full (Kabat-Zinn, 2013; Kaufman et al., 2018). Indeed, the aim of mindfulness practice is not to change experiences or to increase or reduce the levels of particular thoughts or emotions; rather, the aim is to alter our *relationship* to experiences, thoughts, and emotions (Gardner & Moore, 2017, 2020; Kabat-Zinn, 2013; Kaufman et al., 2018). This includes regarding internal experiences such as performance anxiety as normal reactions that come and go and not as threats that should be avoided (Gardner & Moore, 2020).

For dance, mindfulness can mean being fully present in a class or performance with all senses—seeing, hearing, and feeling what is going on in each moment rather than ruminating over past mistakes or worrying about doing the next exercise successfully. Scholars also explain how mindfulness will help us detach or defuse from reacting instinctively (doing things out of habit); instead, mindfulness enables us to make conscious choices about our responses and actions. This includes the feedback a teacher gives to dancers (e.g., the first thing that springs to mind, highly dependent on the current mood, or feedback that is truly useful to the dancer at that time) and the way dancers approach movements they have performed many times before (e.g., going through the motions, or doing them with intent). Especially around performances and similarly pressured times, emotions tend to run high, and dancers and staff alike may react in ways that they later find suboptimal or even damaging. For instance, frayed nerves may underpin irritated words or angry gestures, which rarely help either the upcoming performance or interpersonal relationships.

Mindfulness has become so popular over the last decade or so that many speak of a "mindfulness revolution." Indeed, research and practice in this area has skyrocketed in a wide range of domains such as health care, education, business, and sports. At least three academic books have been published about mindfulness as it applies to sports just in the past handful of years (Baltzell, 2016; Henriksen et al., 2019; Kaufman et al., 2018), and several countries provide mindfulness-based psychological services to their Olympic athletes (see Gardner & Moore, 2017; Henriksen et al., 2019). Research and academic writing about mindfulness in dance has been sparse, although two of the aforementioned books include chapters related to dancers (Kaufman et al., 2018; Moyle, 2016).

Anyone who has read dance magazines or blogs or listened to podcasts over the last few years knows that the *practice* of mindfulness in dance has increased in line with the mindfulness revolution, even if accompanying research has not kept pace. Some university dance programs have also implemented mindfulness into their curricula (Moyle, 2016). Keep in mind that many dancers, teachers, and others (e.g., yoga, Pilates, and other somatic practitioners) have been using mindfulness principles for years, whether or not they label them as such. This includes such aspects as attending to bodily sensations, working with the breath, immersion in the present, and cultivating openness without judgment. Of course, there are also numerous overlaps between mindfulness and other ways of conceptualizing attention (see chapter 6).

Components of Mindfulness

As noted in the preceding descriptions, mindfulness comprises several components that will now be outlined in more detail. Before doing so, however, it can be informative to consider the opposite—namely, mindlessness. We have probably all had experiences such as sitting in a position for a long time, not noticing any discomfort until the body protests violently in the form of pins-and-needles sensations that almost stop us from standing up or from moving at all; chances are you were so distracted by other things (e.g., an engaging TV program) that you were mindless in regard to your bodily signals. Many of us have also eaten a whole bowl or bag of snacks so mindlessly that we look up in surprise when it is suddenly empty and realize that we barely tasted what we ate. Or, perhaps you have traveled to a familiar place such as your school or workplace and arrived not really knowing how you got there (Kabat-Zinn, 2013).

Unlike the highly pleasant sensation of autopilot that characterizes flow (see chapter 6), mindless experiences like these make us realize that we sometimes operate on a kind of autopilot that means we miss out—on bodily signals, opportunities for learning, or enjoyment. In activities such as dance, we may also be doing familiar tasks and movements out of habit while our minds are elsewhere. In reflecting on our own such experiences, or perhaps discussing them with students, we can begin to see how cultivating mindfulness can be helpful in dance practice. To further this understanding, let us consider four key components that characterize mindfulness: present-moment awareness, curiosity, openness, and **acceptance** (nonjudgment; for more details, see Kabat-Zinn, 2013).

Present-Moment Awareness

A key defining feature of mindfulness is that attention, or awareness, is centered on the present moment. As noted in chapter 6, however, most people cannot maintain attention on the present moment over any particularly long period of time. The emphasis in mindfulness practice is therefore on recognizing where one's attention is and then bringing it back to the present. Indeed, it is recognized that the human mind is designed to time-travel—that is, move between thoughts of the past, present, and future. Rather than training for an elusive perfect focus, therefore, mindfulness practice is about noticing when (and where) the mind has wandered, and then gently bringing it back to the present (figure 8.1).

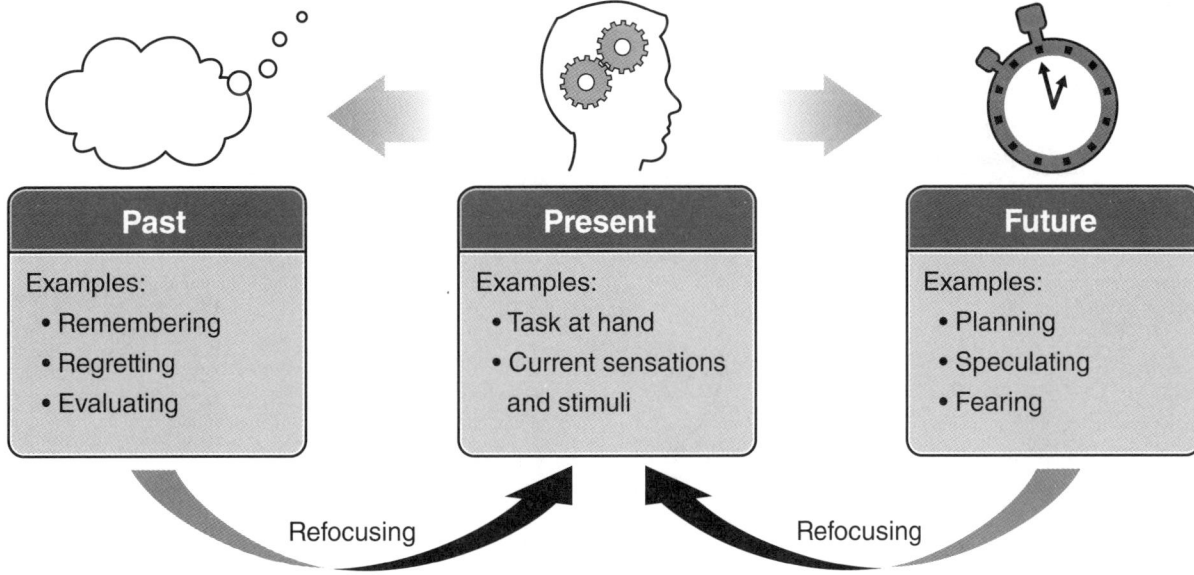

Figure 8.1 The human mind is highly adept at shifting its focus between the past, present, and future.

Although learning from the past and planning for the future are both important and valuable, getting caught up can be problematic if it means the present moment is not fully available for learning and performing dance, or for simply experiencing life. Given the propensity of our minds to time-travel, refocusing will need to occur often. Some liken this repetitive action to the physical repetitions of tasks in activities such as sports and dance—a form of mental weight lifting in which noticing and refocusing are a way of being present rather than a sign of somehow focusing imperfectly (Kaufman et al., 2018). For dancers, it might involve noticing ("here are the butterflies in the belly again") without judgment ("it is normal to worry at a time like this") before refocusing ("now back to the exercise").

The preceding example is similar to the recommendation to focus on constructive aspects under personal control offered in chapter 6. However, mindfulness practice is *not* about exerting control in the form of suppressing or avoiding either internal (e.g., thoughts, feelings) or external (e.g., difficult situations) experiences. Indeed, it is very difficult to control thoughts and feelings (try *not* thinking of a pink elephant!), and they should be allowed to both come and go without us becoming unduly preoccupied with them. Instead, one's own *actions* are more controllable; consequently, changing actions (i.e., behavioral change) rather than changing thoughts and feelings should be the focus. Reductions in rumination and anxiety typically occur as a by-product of such a focus on actions.

In many mindfulness meditations, the breath is used as the present-moment anchor (e.g., Kabat-Zinn, 2013; Kaufman et al., 2018). This has two main benefits: first, it is readily available, because as long as you are alive, it is always present. As such, the breath is something we can always return to regardless of place, activity, mood, or anything else. Second, focusing on the breath often has the benefit of slowing it down, leading to a relaxation response that many find pleasant and beneficial. That said, it is perfectly possible to use other stimuli as anchors; for instance, food is used as the anchor in mindful eating, and repetitive physical actions such as the foot strike against the ground can make useful anchors in walking and running (e.g., Kaufman et al., 2018). For dance, the appropriate anchor is likely to vary with the type of exercise, but examples include music, storytelling, or touch (e.g., in contact improvisation; Urmston & Hewison, 2014). Figure 8.2 shows that there can be many potential stimuli to attend to at any given time, even when focus is on the present rather than on the past or the future. Part of mindfulness practice is becoming aware of them, accepting them,

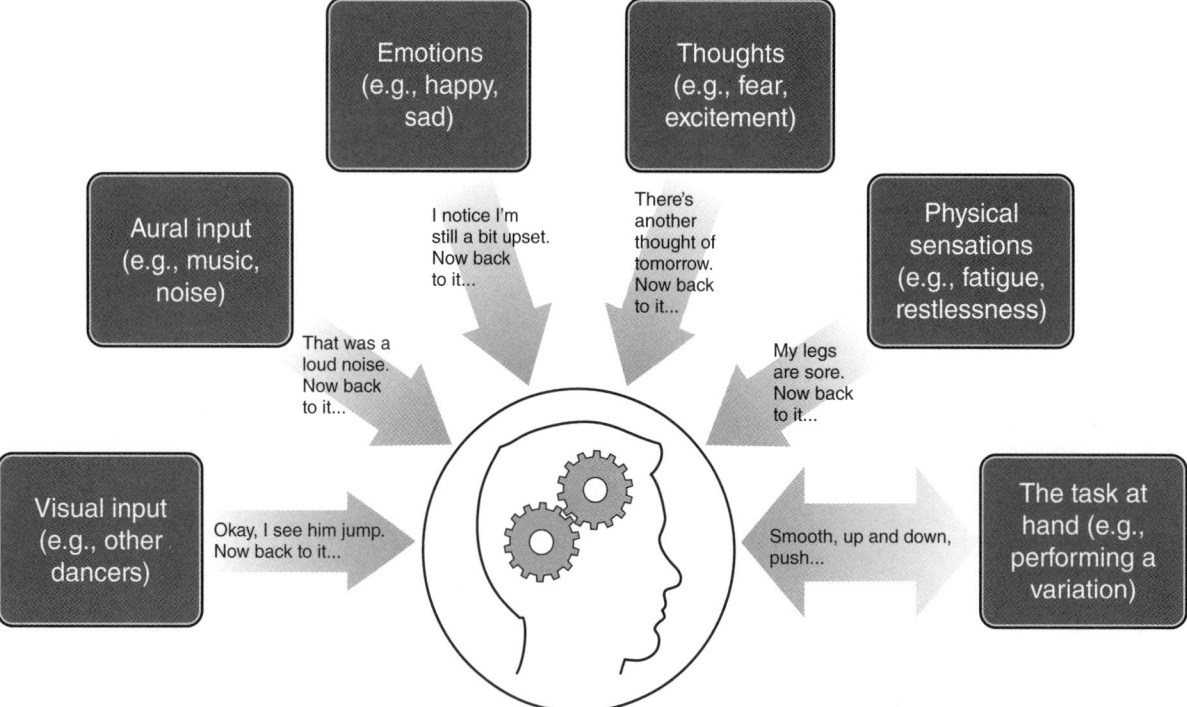

Figure 8.2 Part of mindfulness training is observing the many potential stimuli available even within a single present moment and then redirecting one's focus to a specific stimulus (e.g., the task at hand).

and choosing what to focus on, rather than having the mind simply skip between whatever is most distracting, emotive, or fun at the time.

Curiosity

By cultivating a curious attitude, we are more likely to explore without judgment and avoid preconceived ideas about what an experience will be like. In mindfulness meditations using the breath as an anchor, this may involve a deliberate focus on how the breath feels in various places in the body (e.g., the nostrils, the chest, the belly). By focusing in great detail, we are more easily able to maintain focus because the stimulus is multisensory and rich enough to be engaging. We can even try to approach a situation as if for the first time, which in mindfulness is sometimes known as "beginner's mind" (Kabat-Zinn, 2013). Indeed, it takes curiosity to be willing to really sense what something as mundane and automatic as the breath is like! In a study with modern dance students, one participant illustrated beginner's mind when speaking of how he tuned into his body: "It is as if this new time, is the first time that I am taking a class, and I go, 'Ah! Wow! This is fun!' I rediscover that I love this." (Lussier-Ley & Durand-Bush, 2009, p. 211). What might happen if such a curious attitude was used more often in everyday tasks such as warm-up?

Openness

In mindfulness, being open to whatever is experienced is another important component. This means noticing and being aware of both internal and external stimuli, including distractions, rather than avoiding, ignoring, or suppressing them—which we typically do since we do not like feeling anxious, awkward, or incompetent. In this regard, mindfulness practice is similar to the exposure treatments in classical CBT, in which participants are gradually guided through experiences they find unpleasant or frightening and are encouraged to experience those situations fully and without avoidance; in so doing, they notice that the unpleasantness reduces after a short while (see the introduction and chapter 4). In mindfulness, the openness and acceptance of all kinds of experiences and emotions is considered key to living life to the full—or as Jon Kabat-Zinn (2013) likes to call it, "embracing the full catastrophe"!

Nonjudgment (Acceptance)

To be truly open-minded, it is also important to nurture an accepting attitude toward whatever is being experienced—whether good or bad, pleasant or unpleasant. The word *acceptance* is often misinterpreted as indicating resignation, yet in a mindfulness context it does not mean giving up (e.g., Kaufman et al., 2018); instead, we might see it as closer to *fully acknowledging* the current reality—that is, seeing it for what it is. By accepting that things are the way they are and allowing ourselves to feel what we feel (e.g., not performing as well as hoped; not being selected; being stressed), we can more easily make informed choices and move on than if we get caught up in wishing or expecting things to be different. Part of acceptance is also knowing that everything (e.g., thoughts, emotions, events) is in constant flux; it comes and goes, and we should neither cling to, struggle against, or suppress these experiences (Gardner & Moore, 2017; Kabat-Zinn, 2013).

THINKING CRITICALLY

- When are you mindful in dance and in your everyday life? Consider all four components of mindfulness as you reflect on your experiences.
- Can you find examples of when you have been acting mindlessly?
- What do you normally notice and pay attention to in a dance class? Is there anything you might miss?
- Are there particular aspects of your dance practice that nurture or thwart mindful attention? You might consider such aspects as interpersonal relationships, feedback styles, and expectations.

Acceptance and Commitment Therapy/Training

Acceptance and commitment therapy (ACT) is a therapeutic school within the third wave of CBT in which mindfulness is complemented by value-driven commitment and action (Hayes, 2004). Values are what truly drive a person; as such, they are more fundamental than goals, which are specific targets that can be reached. Because values make an important foundation for optimal goal setting, they are introduced properly in chapter 9. For now, it is sufficient to note that ACT-based approaches encourage performers to identify their values and act in accordance with them regardless of whether thoughts and emotions are perceived as suboptimal (Gardner & Moore, 2017; Hayes, 2004). In so doing, ACT promotes **psychological flexibility**.

A psychologically flexible dancer might, for instance, mindfully observe her churning stomach and restless legs, accept these as a natural part of being nervous, and then refocus and go ahead with her performance because it is important to her.

ACT, then, encourages us to go ahead with what we want to do without waiting for "the right feeling" or letting limiting thoughts or beliefs get in our way (e.g., "Will I be good enough? What will they think of me if I fail?"). As author Pearl S. Buck put it, "You cannot make yourself feel something you do not feel, but you can make yourself do right in spite of your feelings." An important component in this process is **cognitive defusion**, or the detachment of oneself from one's thoughts (Hayes, 2004; Healy et al., 2008). For instance, consider how the following affect you:

> "I am useless."
> "I am having a thought that I am useless."
> "I have noticed that I have a thought that I am useless."

For many people, taking on the defused, detached observer perspective present in the second statement, and even more so in the third, can help question whether thoughts are actually true.

Self-Compassion

Another type of therapy or training that is part of the third wave of CBT is **self-compassion**. Like ACT, it is closely linked with mindfulness; indeed, some mindfulness programs incorporate self-compassion elements (e.g., Baltzell & Akhtar, 2014), and a leading definition of self-compassion incorporates mindfulness as one of its three core elements (Neff, 2003). To be compassionate (whether toward oneself or others), we must first be aware of what is going on in a nonjudgmental way—that is, we must be mindful. With a particular focus on self-care during times of challenge and difficulty, the other two core elements of self-compassion are **self-kindness** and **common humanity** (Neff, 2003). The self-kindness element involves a warm, understanding, and accepting attitude toward oneself and one's failings—for instance, being kind rather than critical toward oneself after making mistakes in a show, just like we typically are toward a best friend or a young child. The common humanity element is about broadening one's perspective, recognizing that all people are imperfect, make mistakes, and suffer. As such, our failings and difficulties are normal and expected rather than something to be avoided or chastised.

No research has explored self-compassion in dance, but a growing number of studies in sport indicate its potential. For instance, a self-compassion intervention with female athletes resulted in reduced self-criticism, concern over mistakes, and rumination (Mosewich et al., 2013; this represents reduced perfectionistic concerns; see chapter 2). Outside of sports, it has also been shown that persons with higher levels of self-compassion are *more* motivated and put more effort into self-improvement after failure than those lower in self-compassion (Breines & Chen, 2012). Studies like these should help debunk any misconceptions about self-compassion being equivalent to laziness or resting on one's laurels, and they offer intriguing possibilities for future research in dance.

Origins of Mindfulness

As a practice, mindfulness has its roots in Eastern—specifically Buddhist—traditions reaching back around 2,500 years. In the West, mindfulness is often secularized, with its religious connotations removed. Two persons often credited with bringing mindfulness to the West are Thich Nhat Hanh, a Vietnamese Buddhist monk, and Jon Kabat-Zinn, a medical professor at the University of Massachusetts Medical School. In particular, Kabat-Zinn and his colleagues created the now well-evidenced eight-week program known as mindfulness-based stress reduction (MBSR; see Kabat-Zinn, 2013). At first used with patients suffering chronic pain, MBSR has since been used and adapted to a wealth of contexts, including sports (Kaufman et al., 2018).

Consequences of Mindfulness

Literature examining the correlates and consequences of mindfulness is plentiful, not least in sports. Key findings from this research are summarized next using the broad headings of well-being and performance-related consequences.

Well-Being-Related Consequences of Mindfulness

In reviews of the literature, the following well-being-related consequences have been shown to correlate with mindfulness (as a trait or disposition) and/or to be an outcome of mindfulness- and acceptance-based interventions (Gardner & Moore, 2017, 2020; Kaufman et al., 2018; Noetel et al., 2019):

> *Improved mindfulness.* Although it may seem obvious that mindfulness practice should make

people more mindful, these effects are important because mindfulness is both a psychological skill (a practice or tool) and a valued psychological characteristic (outcome) in its own right; that is, performers value their increased ability to be present, open, and nonjudgmental.

> *Improved focus and awareness.* Another logical and highly valued consequence of mindfulness practice is an enhanced ability to focus on task-relevant actions and stimuli, including being able to shift attention as required. Studies have also shown that mindfulness practice leads to the maintenance of attention requiring gradually less effort over time.

> *Better emotion regulation and decreased experiential avoidance.* By cultivating the somewhat detached openness and nonjudgmental awareness that are characteristic of mindfulness, our ability to regulate emotions is improved. Put differently, people tend not to overreact, suppress their emotions, or experience steep ups and downs in their moods because they are more calmly observing and accepting things the way they are. Over time, this equanimity may translate into positive emotions becoming more frequent while negative emotions become less frequent. Remember, however, that actual levels (e.g., frequency with which an emotion is experienced) are typically less important than the way in which emotions are interpreted and handled (see chapter 4).

> *Flow.* There is considerable conceptual overlap between mindfulness and flow (a form of optimal experience; see chapter 6); for instance, both involve full concentration in the present moment without self-consciousness. As a result, it makes sense that mindfulness practice can enhance the frequency or duration of flow among performers. In essence, mindfulness practitioners experience truly enjoyable, absorbing moments more often.

> *Relaxation.* The physiological relaxation response is often triggered through exercises such as deep breathing and body scanning (see the Get Practical exercises toward the end of this chapter), and many appreciate relaxation as a readily available benefit of mindfulness practice. Just like for emotion regulation, however, the aim of mindfulness practice is not to become relaxed, which is seen more as a side effect. Accordingly, typical mindfulness meditations do not tell participants to relax, but rather to observe without judgment.

> *Reduced stress, anxiety, rumination, and symptoms of burnout.* Numerous studies indicate benefits related to anxiety and overload, and similar cross-sectional relationships have been found in dance (Blevins et al., 2022). One way in which this can occur is by reducing experiential avoidance (see the introduction). Another is by optimizing attention; that is, not allowing thoughts and emotions relating to the past (e.g., ruminating on mistakes) or the future (e.g., anxiety about upcoming events) spread way beyond their actual duration. Instead, they can be acknowledged and accepted ("Okay, I am nervous; that is pretty usual for me at times like this.") before attention is redirected to the task, or experience, at hand (figure 8.1).

Go to *HKPropel* to download lettering art highlighting the importance of not "fearing one's fear."

> *Increased optimism and self-confidence.* Because there is typically an inverse relationship between anxiety and self-confidence, it makes sense that interventions capable of reducing anxiety can also enhance confidence. By reducing experiential avoidance while enhancing the regulation of attention and emotions, we feel more capable (i.e., confident) and more optimistic that we can reach goals or live a meaningful life.

> *More autonomous motivation.* Studies suggest that mindfulness stimulates healthy (autonomous) motivation (Donald et al., 2020). The openness inherent in mindfulness practice nurtures interest, and by being aware yet not judgmental, we gain the freedom of choosing our responses in situations rather than acting in ways that may be suboptimal (e.g., habitually or impulsively); that is, we become more autonomous (see chapter 5 for an explanation of the importance of autonomy).

> *Improved mental health.* Evidence from the clinical domain indicates that mindfulness can be used in the prevention and treatment of several forms of mental ill health, including depression, clinical anxiety, and disordered eating (Beccia et al., 2018; Blanck et al., 2018). Importantly, there are also contraindications to using mindfulness; in particular, persons with ongoing psychiatric disorders or a history of trauma should consult a psychologist or psychiatrist before participating in a mindfulness intervention (Van Dam et al., 2018).

Performance-Related Consequences of Mindfulness

Beyond improvements in various aspects of well-being, reviews of the literature have also indicated effects of mindfulness- and acceptance-based interventions on performance-related aspects (Gardner & Moore, 2017, 2020; Kaufman et al., 2018; Noetel et al., 2019):

› *Actual (sports) performance.* Many different studies have demonstrated that systematic mindfulness practice can lead to performance enhancement, including coaches rating their athletes as performing better, objective performance measures (e.g., running times, rankings), and improved learning among novices.
› *Injury.* Studies have indicated that mindfulness programs can help prevent injury in sports (Ivarsson et al., 2015; Naderi et al., 2020) and have positive effects on well-being, acceptance, and nonreactivity during injury rehabilitation (Moesch et al., 2020).
› *Practice-related behaviors.* In music, preliminary evidence indicates that a mindfulness intervention can lead to several benefits likely to enhance performance indirectly, such as solo practice becoming more efficient, better communication with one's teacher, and better body awareness (Czajkowski et al., 2020).
› *Creativity and expressivity.* Also in music, studies suggest that mindfulness can lead to improved creativity and expressivity, alongside several well-being-related benefits (Czajkowski et al., 2020; Langer et al., 2009). An innovative study with orchestral musicians is worth highlighting (Langer et al., 2009). In this intervention, professional musicians enjoyed performing well-known pieces more when focusing on offering subtle new nuances than when trying to replicate the finest performance they could remember. Musically educated audiences also preferred the former. The authors argued that the repetition inherent in gaining and maintaining classical music expertise can become mindless, but that simple instructions that encourage active engagement and conveyance of new nuances can enhance mindfulness, and thereby also enjoyment, creativity, and performance quality (Langer et al., 2009).

Although the summarized studies focused on performers, researchers have also examined mindfulness practice with sport coaches with similar effects (e.g., Lundqvist et al., 2018). It is logical that teachers, choreographers, and other dance leaders would also benefit from practices that can enhance their abilities to focus; to remain open-minded, accepting, and flexible; and to interact with others without undue influence from emotions. Of course, benefits to personal health (e.g., reduced stress, improved sleep) are highly positive also.

Mindfulness Research in Dance

Most of the literature connecting dance and mindfulness have taken a therapeutic perspective—for instance, by comparing dance- and mindfulness interventions on outcomes such as depression (Pinniger et al., 2012) or nurturing mindfulness through dance (Marich & Howell, 2015). One small-scale investigation reported that young women who dance regularly might be more mindful in their everyday lives than their sedentary peers (Muro & Artero, 2017).

Most recently, it was found that university dance students who reported being the least mindful also scored more highly for stress and negative affect than their more mindful peers (Blevins et al., 2022). They also rated themselves lower on aspects of dance-specific recovery. It was concluded that dancers with higher levels of dispositional mindfulness likely cope better with stress and achieve a better recovery-stress balance.

The only published evidence to date relating to a mindfulness intervention in dance is in a book chapter outlining the implementation of mindfulness for university dance students (Moyle, 2016). Using ACT as its foundation, the program included a range of exercises, including sitting and walking meditations; yoga nidra; and exercises directing mindful awareness to the breath and the body, sounds, feelings, emotions, and more. Running for two years, dance teaching staff were invited to attend alongside the students and were therefore able to weave aspects of mindfulness into the students' other classes. In each year, questionnaire-based assessments indicated no significant changes in mindfulness among the students (Moyle, 2016), although qualitative (open-ended surveys and diaries) feedback was positive; for instance, students commented on benefits to well-being as well as performance, such as improved focusing abilities. An assessment task later in the term revealed that the majority of students (nearly 80%) referenced mindfulness as a practice that had helped them progress their dance technique. Indeed, the integration of mindfulness with somatic practice and dance technique seemed to be particularly appreciated. Several reasons for the nonsignificant quantitative effects were discussed, including timetabling issues and inconsistent attendance. Those planning to set up their own mindfulness intervention are likely to benefit from considering the in-depth descriptions and candid reflections made by such program facilitators (Moyle, 2016; see also Bernier et al., 2014; Kaufman et al., 2018). For a critical view on research into mindfulness, see also Van Dam et al. (2018).

An example of how different degrees of mindfulness may play out in dance classes is provided in the functional analyses illustrated in figure 8.3. In the first example, a dancer's everyday classes are focused on fault-finding, with much critical evaluation ("not like that!"; "faster!"). As a result, the dancer is not very mindful; for example, he thinks a lot about what will happen if he makes another mistake. Being self-critical makes him feel that he is working hard ("real dancers are never satisfied!"), but he often struggles to focus on the task at hand and to refocus after having made mistakes. In the long term, this is likely to undermine his potential to learn and perform well.

In the second example, the dancer takes classes where feedback is all about the tasks at hand and what makes them engaging; for instance, dancers are encouraged to explore, discover, and dive into the experience. As a result, the dancer is not judgmental and more mindful. One of several likely short-term

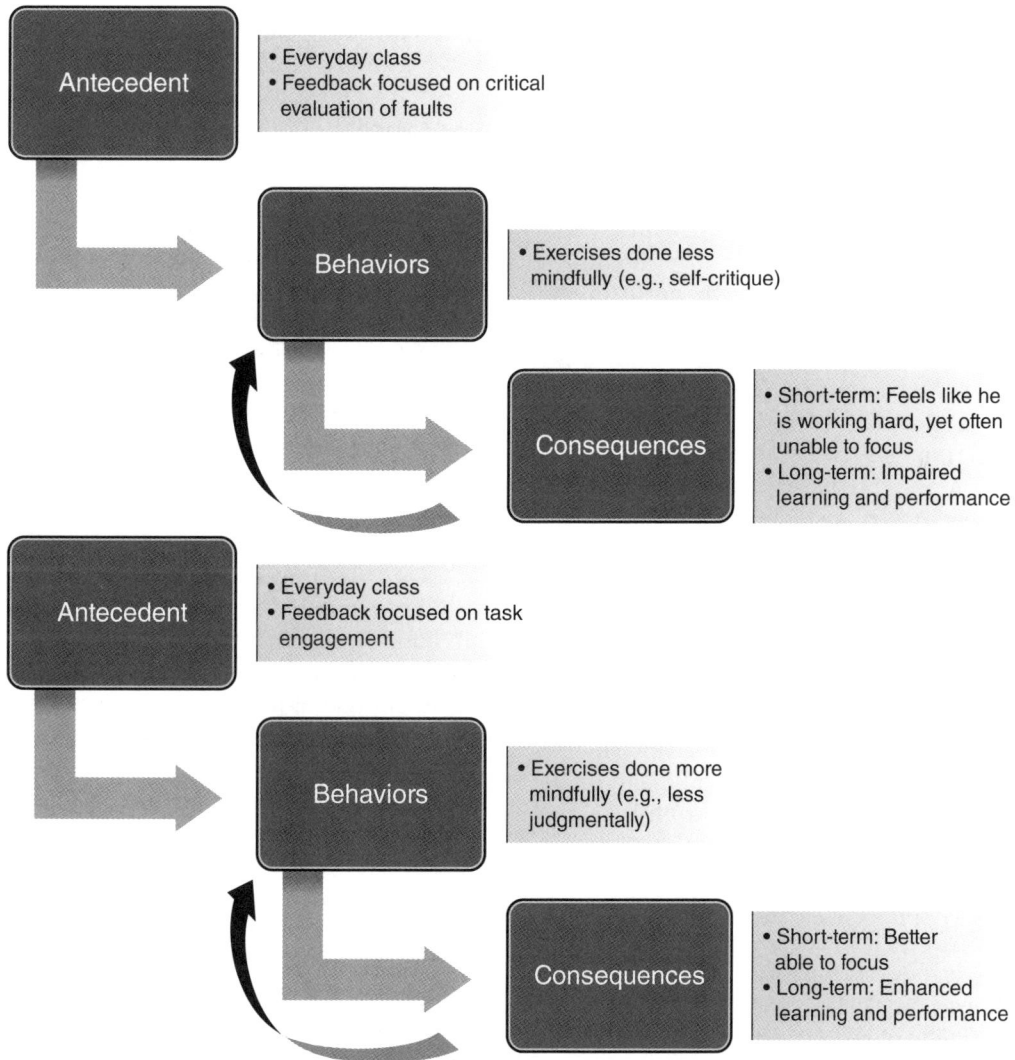

Figure 8.3 Functional analysis examples of how different degrees of mindfulness may manifest in dance. The recursive arrows indicate that the consequences make the behavior more likely to reoccur in similar situations in the future (behavior maintenance).

effects include being able to focus and refocus better, which in the long run will aid learning and performance development.

Why Mindfulness Has an Impact

The reasons (mechanisms) why mindfulness can affect both how we feel and how we perform are multifaceted and perhaps not yet entirely understood (Donald et al., 2020; Gardner & Moore, 2017, 2020; Kaufman et al., 2018; Van Dam et al., 2018). It is also likely that different aspects of mindfulness practice (e.g., observation vs. nonjudgment) have different effects on different outcomes (Birrer et al., 2012). Nevertheless, some key mechanisms are these:

› *Improved attention regulation.* Improved attention regulation has already been listed as a valuable *consequence* of mindfulness. Repeatedly redirecting one's attention to task-relevant stimuli should lead to performance benefits, but it is also a *mechanism* by which mindfulness exerts its effects. For instance, after a mindfulness intervention with young elite figure skaters, one of the performers stated: "Before, I wasn't sure what to think about just before jumping. Now I know exactly." Her coach remarked: "Whatever happens, even if she falls at the beginning of the program, she picks herself right up and keeps on going, whereas before she would have been devastated, and would have performed badly for the rest of the program" (Bernier et al., 2014, p. 310).

› *Improved emotion regulation and acceptance.* Improvements in the regulation of emotion can also be both a valuable consequence and a mechanism of mindfulness. The improved ability to see emotions as nonthreatening internal events that come and go, and that do not need to be changed or avoided, contributes to psychological flexibility and a host of associated benefits. Along similar lines, the greater acceptance fostered by mindfulness practice helps performers to not get stuck in thoughts; as a result, they can make more well-considered decisions. Some have argued that this can also reduce the likelihood of paralysis by analysis, or the breakdown of skilled performance under pressure, that is discussed in chapter 6 (Birrer et al., 2012).

› *Decreased experiential avoidance.* Because mindfulness practice fosters acceptance of situations and stimuli as they are, it can also reduce the extent to which performers try to avoid difficult situations or uncomfortable emotions; in turn, reduced experiential avoidance has logical knock-on benefits for performance and well-being. After a mindfulness intervention, several music student participants reported lessened avoidance when encountering challenges; for instance, one student said, "If I felt that I wasn't in a kind of mental state, or physical state where the practice was working, it also gave me permission to walk away for a bit but not to throw all my toys out the pram and go back maybe 5 minutes later having done a meditation." (Czajkowski et al., 2020, p. 11).

Several other potential avenues by which mindfulness may exert its effects have been proposed (Birrer et al., 2012; Donald et al., 2020; Kaufman et al., 2018). One complication in delineating these is that there is overlap between some constructs (e.g., emotion regulation and experiential avoidance) and between what is considered to be a mechanism versus a consequence. Moreover, there is some conceptual confusion regarding what makes up dispositional mindfulness compared with the components of mindfulness practice versus the outcomes of mindfulness (Birrer et al., 2012; Van Dam et al., 2018). Authors also use different theories and methods in their search for explanations; for instance, while some may use theories of motor control, others pursue neuroscientific explanations (e.g., Gardner & Moore, 2020).

As an example of the latter, Kaufman et al. (2018) reviewed the mindfulness and flow literatures, including some of the evidence indicating neurological changes resulting from mindfulness practice. As a result, they proposed enhanced emotion regulation and attention regulation as the two main pathways between mindfulness practice and flow. In other words, flow is more likely for performers who are more mindful, because they are better able to self-regulate both their attention and their emotions. It was also proposed that a nonjudgmental attitude would be likely to boost these effects (Kaufman et al., 2018). Indeed, it is easier to refocus on the task at hand if challenges (e.g., having made a major mistake in an audition, or dancing after returning from injury) are accepted as they are, rather than if we are caught up in worries, rumination, or emotional ups and downs.

How Can Mindfulness Be Nurtured?

Mindfulness can be practiced both formally and informally, and scholars in the area point out that both are crucially important for the learning and maintaining of mindfulness as a skill and a habit (Kabat-Zinn, 2013). Examples of both are described next.

Formal Mindfulness Practice: Meditation

Formal mindfulness training typically comes in the form of meditations. Two of the most typical are meditations with a focus on the breath (also called **breathing spaces**), and **body scanning**; examples of both are included as sound files in the Get Practical part of this chapter. Although both types can be done in any posture, especially breathing space meditations are typically done sitting down. In so doing, we are encouraged to sit upright with a straight spine, in a combination of comfort and alertness. With closed eyes or an unfocused gaze, we focus on the sensations of the breath: how it feels, and where we can feel it (e.g., at the nose, in the chest, in the belly). When the mind wanders, we simply notice that it has done so (and perhaps to where; e.g., saying "future plan" or "memory" to oneself) before refocusing on the current breath.

As previously mentioned, refocusing is expected to have to occur often, and the nonjudgmental aspect of mindfulness is crucial here—that is, not chastising oneself for not focusing well all the time, but acknowledging or even congratulating oneself for having noticed that the mind wandered. Indeed, noticing means we are present and therefore mindful. Recordings for sitting meditations with a focus on the breath are often around 5 minutes long, although they can be as short as 1 minute and as long as 45-60 minutes. For beginners, a steady voice that guides the practice throughout is often perceived to be helpful; for more experienced meditators, such frequent guidance can feel unnecessary or even disturbing. Accordingly, some mindfulness recordings have long pauses.

Body scanning involves directing focus to specific body parts, one at a time. For instance, the sound file included with this chapter starts with a focus on the right big toe, moves on to the other toes, the foot, the ankle, the lower leg, and so on until the entire body has been scanned. Others prefer to scan down

Body scanning is a form of meditation that can be practiced in groups in a dance studio.

from the top of the head. Because of the many body parts to go through, body scan recordings are typically longer than sitting meditations with a focus on the breath; somewhere around 20-30 minutes appears to be common. However, once the skill of body scanning is learned, a person can accomplish a quick version in a matter of minutes or even seconds; for dancers, this can be useful at the start of a class or before performing. Indeed, body scanning often reveals whether there are areas of unnecessary tension.

In the spirit of mindfulness, meditators are not told to relax (i.e., change); instead, they are encouraged to simply observe and perhaps breathe into specific areas of the body. Yet even without being told to relax, it is common for the body to auto-adjust itself when mindful awareness is brought to different areas in this way (e.g., let tension go; adjust posture). Finally, it is common for body scans to incorporate various other aspects; for instance, many give some attention to the breath and how it is perceived in various parts of the body. In the recording included with this chapter, aspects of gratitude are included because gratitude can have significant benefits (e.g., Howells & Fitzallen, 2020), is highly compatible or even enhanced with mindfulness (Chen et al., 2017; Kaufman et al., 2018), and has been suggested as helpful to dancers (Nordin-Bates & Abrahamsen, 2016).

Ways to Practice Formally: Apps and Programs

Besides the introductory exercises included in this chapter and in chapter 6, readers are encouraged to explore the wide variety of mindfulness resources that are available and find something that suits them. This includes books (e.g., Kabat-Zinn, 2013; Kaufman et al., 2018), smartphone apps, and organizations that offer mindfulness courses.

Importance of Regularity in Formal Mindfulness Practice

Many people experience immediate benefits such as a sense of calm and of being grounded following short mindfulness exercises (e.g., 5-minute breathing space), and there are studies indicating benefits after just a brief mindfulness induction (e.g., Langer et al., 2009; Gardner & Moore, 2020). Presumably, however, such benefits will be short-lived. Mindfulness interventions that obtain significant effects typically use 6- to 8-week programs in which participants meet one or more times weekly but are also asked and reminded to meditate by themselves for anything between a few minutes to 45 minutes per day. Many are based on the 8-week-long MBSR program devised by Kabat-Zinn. Such interventions have important benefits, yet mindfulness experts argue that mindfulness is more of a lifestyle than a tool to pick up when we feel like it and expect it to work (Kabat-Zinn, 2013). Indeed, they point out that athletes do not expect that they can do physical training as and when they feel like it, or suddenly need to be stronger; instead, they work diligently over many months and years to achieve desired physical and technical goals—including when they do not feel like it (Kaufman et al., 2018).

A person's need for formal mindfulness practice is likely to depend on many things, including how mindful they are from the beginning (dispositional/trait mindfulness; Kee et al., 2012). Other aspects that likely matter include personality (e.g., being open-minded vs. judgmental and self-critical) and how much the formal practice affects one's everyday life (e.g., only 5 minutes of meditation, or "ripples on the water" for the rest of the day). As with other psychological skills, the only hard and fast recommendations are perhaps: (1) to take inspiration from the duration and intensity of published studies that have shown significant effects, and (2) to be systematic and deliberate in one's approach. The latter might include keeping track of time spent and of any perceived benefits, drawbacks, and challenges.

Informal Mindfulness Practice: Attitude to Practice Anywhere and Anytime

Many mindfulness exercises direct attention to internal experiences such as the breath and different body parts. As valuable as those exercises can be, it is important to remember that we can be mindful *anywhere*, *anytime*, and in noticing *anything*. Everyday mindfulness practice, then, can be noticing what is around you as you walk to work or school; how it *really* feels to do everyday tasks such as eating, showering, or brushing teeth; and what stimuli there are in any given dance class. Mindful eating might be highly relevant to intensively training dancers, for whom optimal energy intake is so important yet for whom eating can also become fraught with stress and guilt. In eating mindfully, both optimal energy intake and sheer enjoyment in eating should be enhanced because attention to both internal signals and present-moment experiences are enhanced (see Beccia et al., 2018; Lattimore et al., 2017; Stanszus et al., 2019).

Mindful Movement: Integrating Mindfulness with Dance Practice

Many dance teachers and movement professionals encourage mindful awareness in their practices. This is perhaps particularly evident in yoga, some forms of which are deeply intertwined with mindfulness practice (e.g., Hatha yoga; Kabat-Zinn, 2013; Kaufman et al., 2018). Indeed, mindfulness programs often incorporate mindful yoga sequences. Pilates has also been shown to facilitate mindfulness among dance students (Caldwell et al., 2013). Yet *all* movement can be done mindfully—and mindlessly. As such, dance is not inherently mindful even if there is intense concentration and high body awareness; for instance, dancers can be very focused yet also judgmental (e.g., self-critical). For yoga to be mindful practice, those practicing it need to do so with present-moment awareness, curiosity, openness, and acceptance. Similarly, any form of dance (however habitual or regimented) can in theory become mindful practice if those same components are attended to.

Teacher Encouragement to Be Mindful

Mindfulness is typically portrayed as a personal practice, with home practice being a key feature. To integrate mindfulness into dance, however, it would seem important to also consider the influence of teachers. Indeed, it can be a very good thing to include teachers or coaches in mindfulness programs taught to performers (Kaufman et al., 2018; Moyle, 2016). One reason is that the participation of staff sends a clear signal that mindfulness is something to be taken seriously; another reason is that staff are then better able to integrate reminders and prompts into their practice. As yet, no literature exists that discusses how different teaching or coaching styles affect the inclination toward mindfulness among performers, and research in this area would make for a useful contribution to the literature. However, it is reasonable to assume that teachers will encourage mindful dancing if they promote such things as focus on bodily sensations and awareness; individual experience; open-minded, nonjudgmental exploration; external focusing (see chapter 6); and process rather than outcome goals (see chapter 9). If this could be complemented with regular formal mindfulness practice in the studio, perhaps for five minutes at the start and/or end of each class, it might be a helpful springboard for dancers to become more mindful.

The open-minded curiosity encouraged in mindfulness practice is sometimes known as beginner's mind (Kabat-Zinn, 2013). We can compare this to the attitude and demeanor that many of us have on holiday but less so at home. For instance, consider how you behave when walking down a street in an intriguing city for the first time, how attuned you are to your senses when visiting a beautiful forest, or how you take in every aspect of a stunning seaside location. In table 8.1, a set of imaginary scenarios are

Table 8.1 **Sample Scenarios to Imagine in the Studio to Promote Mindfulness and Awareness**

Scenarios	Reflection prompts
1. You are on holiday in a beautiful place that you have never visited before. There is lots to see, hear, and smell. Walk around the space and take it all in.	• How did you move? • How was your posture? • Where did you direct your eyes? • How did you feel? • Did you learn something that you can bring with you into normal studio practices, auditions, or performances?
2. You have forgotten your water bottle in the studio and must now go back to retrieve it. Another class, perhaps with older/highly skilled dancers, has already started. Go into the studio to get your bottle.	
3. You are going to audition for a role that you really want. There are many other dancers there, and they look highly competent. Now enter the studio, noticing where the jury is located. Then take your place, ready to begin the audition.	
4. You are at a party for your best friend's birthday, and everyone you know seems to be there. Great music is playing. Move around the space, seeing and interacting with everyone.	

Sitting meditation with a focus on the breath is an accessible form of mindfulness practice.

provided for teachers to use with young dancers. In essence, it is an exercise in mindfulness that also incorporates imagery. Adjustments to suit specific age groups, preferences, and requirements will be needed, but it is likely that mindful awareness, especially regarding movement habits, can be raised through exercises like this.

Martin: Case Study of Mindfulness

Martin is a university dance student in musical theater. He is making good progress but is intrigued by the different styles of his teachers and how this affects him. For example, his jazz class includes a warm-up that remains the same all term. Because this warm-up has gotten so engrained in his body, Martin often just goes through the motions. One morning, he suddenly realized that they were four exercises into the class, but he could remember little of the first three! This state of autopilot is both comfortable and a bit worrying to him. In one of his modern classes, the teaching style is very teacher driven. But with all choices and decisions made for them, the students don't seem all that mentally engaged with the physical movement—almost like mind and body were separate entities. They do, however, worry about getting things right because the teacher is also quite strict and wants things done properly.

Recently, the dance department started offering an elective course in mindfulness, and Martin signed up along with some of his friends. At first they were a bit bored by the theoretical parts, and focusing in those meditations was certainly not easy. But something about the classes made them all continue, week after week. Toward the end of term, the teacher invited them to reflect on their experiences, and many agreed that the experiential exercises were the best—the ones where you really get to try things out. They also agreed that the mindfulness class made for a welcome space in their days—a place to focus on being, rather than always focus on doing. Martin could now begin to see the reasons why his teachers' different styles affected him the way they did; that is, classes indirectly led them to be more or less judgmental, more or less curious, more or less in the moment. He was also able to become more mindful by deliberately paying attention to bodily sensations when going through exercises, and gradually he found it easier to notice when his attention drifted away and to direct it back onto the task at hand.

Composite case study created on the basis of a conversation with Peta Blevins, PhD, a dance educator, researcher, and coach specializing in psychological skills and safe dance practice in Perth, Australia.

GET PRACTICAL: BREATHING SPACE AND BODY SCAN

In these exercises, you can try out two mindfulness meditations for yourself: one shorter breathing space and one longer body scan. If you are a dancer, you may want to try them out at home first; if you are a teacher, you may want to try them out in the studio with your dancers. Although there may be some instant benefits (e.g., sense of calm), remember that regular practice is typically needed before achieving any lasting result.

Go to HK*Propel* to listen to audio clips Breathing Space and Body Scan.

CRITICAL ASPECTS OF RESEARCH INTO MINDFULNESS

1. While any well-designed study into mindfulness in dance would advance the literature in some sense (given the absence of empirical studies in our domain), we should remember that dancers are just people. Therefore, the research evidence indicating that mindfulness can be beneficial to people in sports, health care, and other domains is highly likely to translate to dance. It would therefore be particularly interesting to see research developments focused not only on *whether* mindfulness helps dancers but also on *how* such benefits can be facilitated in real-life dance contexts and understanding the underlying mechanisms. For instance, is there a minimum "dose" required for mindfulness interventions to have positive lasting effects? How can space be made in the busy schedules of dance companies and schools to facilitate such programs? Does the increased emotional awareness associated with mindfulness practice also enhance artistry?

2. A related issue concerns the populations involved in mindfulness interventions. Because of the time commitment required, it is likely that voluntary participation (a requirement for ethical research) is an important component for a program to have significant impact. However, self-selection of highly motivated individuals may also mean that it is mostly persons who are already interested in mindfulness, and perhaps are relatively mindful already, who sign up—a kind of "preaching to the converted." In real-world dance contexts, those who need mindfulness the most (e.g., the most self-critical and judgmental) may be the hardest to reach because they may well not sign up.

3. If you have read chapter 6, you will recall that a key recommendation from the attentional focus literature is that focusing is best done externally (e.g., movement effects), but focusing internally (e.g., on body parts) can be problematic. It may therefore be confusing that mindfulness includes many exercises that encourage a focus on the body. Importantly, mindfulness is about nonjudgmental awareness and

not about controlling or interfering with body parts. Second, if there is no movement goal beyond simple awareness (such as in a body scan), then the internal–external focus distinction may not apply (Stephens & Hillier, 2020). Some research even suggests that mindfulness interventions can lead to a greater likelihood of focusing externally (Kee et al., 2012). For further discussion of this topic, see Kaufman et al. (2018), Noetel et al. (2019), Toner and Moran (2015), and Wulf (2016).

KEY POINTS AND RECOMMENDATIONS FOR MINDFULNESS IN DANCE

1. Mindfulness can be of great use to dancers and teachers in enhancing dance practice as well as life more broadly. Indeed, studies have shown that mindfulness practice can help people both feel better and perform better. Improvements in the regulation of attention and emotion as well as greater acceptance and lesser avoidance seem to underpin such benefits.

2. Mindfulness can be practiced both formally (through meditation) and informally (by paying attention to whatever is going on at the time in an open, curious, and accepting way). Dance teachers can also encourage mindful movement by attending to those same aspects in their instructions and feedback.

Goal Setting and Self-Regulation

"I set as my goal to be the best dancer I could be.
Not the most famous, or the highest paid dancer,
just the best I could be. Out of this discipline came
great freedom and calm."

Suzanne Farrell, dancer

CHAPTER OBJECTIVES

After reading this chapter, you will be able to

1. describe what goal setting is, including process, learning, performance, and outcome goals;
2. critically discuss how goals may be set in dance, given its often subjective nature;
3. describe consequences of goal setting, including effects on well-being and performance;

4. outline the components of the self-regulation cycle;
5. apply the recommendations summarized under the SMART GOALS acronym to enhance goal setting and self-regulation in dance;
6. identify your values to facilitate meaningful goal setting; and
7. think critically about the nature and impact of goal setting and self-regulation in dance settings.

Key Terms

assigned goals	objective goals	self-regulation
fundamental goal concept	outcome goals	subjective goals
	performance goals	values
learning goals	process goals	

The term *goal* stems from the Middle English *gol*, meaning a barrier or limit of some kind, but has been used since the Middle Ages to refer to the end point of a race or the object (purpose) of one's effort. Our current understanding of goals is that they are about giving purpose to our strivings. As you will learn in this chapter, there are several types of goals, and their inherent differences make them suitable to focus on at different times. Only with a good understanding of goal types and principles can we make goal setting a truly rewarding process so that it does not become the barrier or limit associated with the original meaning of the word.

What Is Goal Setting?

A goal is a reflection of purpose and can refer to either the quantity or quality of some kind of performance or action (Locke & Latham, 2019). In a commonly used definition, goals are described as "what an individual is trying to accomplish; it is the object or aim of an action" (Locke et al., 1981, p. 126). By setting goals, dancers and teachers decide on an aim for what they are doing and can then craft their activities and focus accordingly; this can give a sense of direction and meaning. Of course, it is fundamentally human to set goals for daily tasks and to have aims or dreams for the future, so people set goals all the time: get up at 7 a.m., get into a particular school, master a tricky pirouette, get through all the required material on time, or plan one's class at least one day before it is scheduled. As such, goal setting is rarely unknown to dancers. In this chapter you will learn more about how to make this natural human tendency into a deliberately crafted psychological skill, such that it can become truly effective. This can be valuable, because most people set goals that are too vague or general, which means that they do not significantly affect behavior (Locke & Latham, 2019).

The researchers most famously associated with goal setting are Locke and Latham (1990, 2019; Latham & Locke, 1991), who began their work in the 1970s with the consistent discovery that setting specific and challenging goals for performance (or productivity) enhanced performance beyond that achieved by people who set themselves vague goals such as "do your best." Indeed, those who set vague goals often performed no better than those who set no goals at all. Accordingly, Locke's and Latham's goal-setting theory states that higher performance is obtained when setting specific, high goals, as opposed to easy or vague goals.

Since the 1970s, goal setting has become a cornerstone of applied sport psychology, and it is a technique used frequently by athletes, coaches, and sport psychologists alike (e.g., Burton & Weiss, 2008; Jeong et al., 2021; Roberts & Kristiansen, 2012; Weinberg et al., 2001). This literature also highlights that a defining characteristic of elite performers is setting goals for daily practice, giving a clear aim and plan for each practice session (Roberts & Kristiansen, 2012). Goal setting is also an integral part of exercise and health interventions (McEwan et al., 2016; Swann et al., 2021). Although goal setting has been recommended for dancers (Carattini, 2020; Nordin, 2009; Taylor & Estanol, 2015), there are no published empirical investigations in this area. For this reason, the present chapter is built around evidence from other domains (sport, exercise, industrial psychology), although it is contextualized for dance throughout.

Not everyone benefits from specific difficult goals for performance (Jeong et al., 2021; Latham & Brown, 2006; Locke & Latham, 2019; McEwan et al., 2016; Swann et al., 2021). In particular, there can be negative effects of specific challenging goals if a person

> is a novice and the task is highly complex;
> lacks the requisite ability required to perform the necessary tasks;
> perceives that they lack ability—that is, they have low self-efficacy (see chapter 3);
> there is a lack of control over outcomes (so-called environmental uncertainty); and
> the goals are distal (far away in time), without being broken down into specific more proximal goals.

When one or more of the listed complications are present, setting specific and challenging goals can be problematic (Latham & Locke, 1991; Locke & Latham, 2019). As an example, consider dancers in a company that is staging a new production. It would be unwise for dancers with low levels of self-confidence, high levels of self-doubt, and little say over the casting to set themselves the goal of perfectly performing the lead role on opening night. Given their personality and that casting is not under their control, such goals would be either useless or counterproductive—for example, they may result in anxiety. This does not mean that goal setting is not a useful tool for such dancers, but they may need to learn about how to set goals that are effective for them. In particular, they need to consider the *types* of goals that they set.

Subjective and Objective Goals

Specificity is key to effective goal setting because specific goals tell us clearly what it is that we want to reach and make the planning of goal achievement strategies easier. Specific goals are typically also **objective goals**, so that it is easy to know when they have been achieved. Vague, do-your-best goals are instead inherently **subjective goals**, making it difficult to know when they have been mastered. With subjective goals, evaluations of goal progress become affected by personal opinions, moods, and preferences. Latham and Locke (1991, p. 215) stated that such goals were less effective "because the ambiguity inherent in doing one's best allows people to give themselves the benefit of the doubt in evaluating their performance." It can be argued that for highly self-critical people, the problem is rather the opposite; they never give themselves the benefit of the doubt and rarely if ever consider their performances to be good enough! In either case, specific goals are more helpful because they make the required tasks more obvious and progress evaluations easier. Of course, a dancer may begin a goal-setting process with a loosely formulated goal (or dream) that they can then specify, narrow down, and adjust to make it as specific and as objective as possible.

Dance is a subjective art form that does not always lend itself to the setting of objective, easily measurable goals such as doing 20 press-ups in a specific time, running 3 times per week, or being able to get through an intense variation at a heart rate below 170 beats per minute. Indeed, dancers often want to improve subjective aspects such as artistic qualities, partnerships, or musicality. Such goals are clearly valuable and important even if they are not objective. Therefore, dancers are advised to specify their goals as far as possible, so that they are not vague (e.g., what aspects of artistry do they wish to enhance?). For more suggestions on how to work practically with goal setting in dance, including with subjective goals, see the recommendations toward the end of this chapter.

Outcome, Performance, Learning, and Process Goals

In performance psychology, goals have typically been delineated by distinguishing three goal types (e.g., Jeong et al., 2021; Roberts & Kristiansen, 2012). Known as **outcome goals, performance goals**, and **process goals**, they differ in their relative size, or scope, with outcome goals typically being focused on long-term outcomes. Winning a role, getting a job, being admitted into a particular school or company, and placing in the top three at a competition are all examples of outcome goals. As you can see, these goals are typically objective, specific, and measurable: a dancer either gets the job or she does not; he gets cast for a role or not.

Examples of performance goals include being able to get into the splits, mastering a triple pirouette, or being able to hold a particular balance for four seconds. While these goals can be highly ambitious and challenging, they lack the comparative or exclusive aspect inherent to outcome goals; indeed, everyone in a class can, in principle, learn a difficult variation (a performance goal) but not everyone can get cast in a particular role (an outcome goal). Even when a dancer performs better than ever before, he may be outdone at audition by someone who performs even better. In line with the name, then, performance goals are about performance improvement and are, as such, under greater personal control.

Researchers outside of sports have also investigated a related type of goal known as **learning goals** (e.g., Latham & Brown, 2006; Swann et al., 2021). Such goals focus on learning or finding a specific number of ways in which something can be done or learning the procedures needed to (later) master a particular task. As such, examples of learning goals include finding and trying out two different core strength classes, testing out three ways in which a musical rhythm may be expressed, or generating four alternative endings to a piece. As their name suggests, learning goals focus on specific targets for one's learning, as opposed to the focus on task achievement that is inherent to performance goals. Thus, learning goals are arguably even more controllable than performance goals, because they are more open-ended and not focused on a single specified achievement.

Research suggests that learning goals can be particularly useful in the early stages of a process and facilitate deep-level learning and understanding (Swann et al., 2021). In contrast, performance goals should only be set when an individual has the requisite ability, commitment, feedback, and other resources (e.g., facilities) available (Jeong et al., 2021; Locke & Latham, 2019; Swann et al., 2021). Indeed, pressure to achieve highly challenging performance goals can lead to both anxiety and surface-level learning. From a practical point of view, then, it may be wise to consider goal setting as a process that is only partly about goal achievement ("Did I reach my goal?") and mostly about a process of learning and progress ("How far did I get?").

The example performance goals (e.g., getting into the splits) were described in specific and measurable terms. Yet it may still not be 100% clear when they have been reached. For instance, does a triple pirouette count as having been mastered if the dancer lands it somewhat clumsily? What about if a dancer mostly knows a variation but can only perform it under particular conditions (e.g., with one partner but not another)? Clearly, it is important that performance goals are carefully delineated. What exactly is the goal, and how will the dancer know when it has been mastered and it is time to move on? You probably know some people who set challenging goals and can confidently declare when they have reached them; you probably also know people who seem to work forever on perfecting a task, never seeing that they have mastered it well enough. For this reason, dancers with low self-confidence, who are anxious or perfectionistic, are likely to benefit especially from being really clear in their goal setting process. They may also need more input and support: "Yes, Clara, that really is fine now! Time to move on!"

As for process goals, these have been described in several different ways in the literature: from specific goals to keep in mind during a class (e.g., staying mindfully present in one's body; projecting into the sky; daring to make mistakes) to specific actions or tasks to accomplish (e.g., do yoga three times per week; write in a training diary every day). Whatever the case, process goals can be thought of as stepping-stones: the actions necessary to either enhance an experience in the moment (e.g., have a better class) or reach longer-term learning, performance, and outcome goals (Burton & Weiss, 2008). Process goals can include strategies and be derived from the instructions, images, and corrections that teachers impart during classes and rehearsals ("Stay connected to each other throughout"; "really melt into the plié here"; "sharp!"). Because they are highly specific, dancers may need to have several different process goals for any given class, rehearsal, or performance. A useful way of linking goal setting to self-talk and attentional focus is to use goal progress evaluations from one day to create self-talk statements or cue words for the next day (Nordin, 2009; see also chapter 6).

A goal setting process can usefully start by identifying what a dancer wants to achieve in the longer term. If this is an outcome goal (e.g., get cast for a particular role), then suitable performance or learning goals can be set next (e.g., learn the role; master specific skills) followed by process goals that enable the performance and learning goals and that guide daily practice. Interestingly, sport researchers have demonstrated that setting a combination of outcome, performance, and process goals enhances performance more than just using one goal type (Filby et al., 1999). If what the dancer wants to achieve in the longer term is more of a performance goal, the goal setting process can simply exclude outcome goals altogether; most likely, they are only useful if they are truly motivating to the individual dancer. Process goals, on the other hand, are useful for everyone. In fact, the **fundamental goal concept** refers to the notion that focusing on a combination of process and performance goals is far more likely to improve performance and keep self-confidence stable, even though outcome goals can be highly motivating (Burton & Weiss, 2008).

As illustrated in figure 9.1, outcome goals may be considered the top rung of a ladder; a desirable place to be ("I made it!") but hard if not impossible to reach without lower rungs to gradually climb (performance and process goals). Again, long-term goals can also be performance goals.

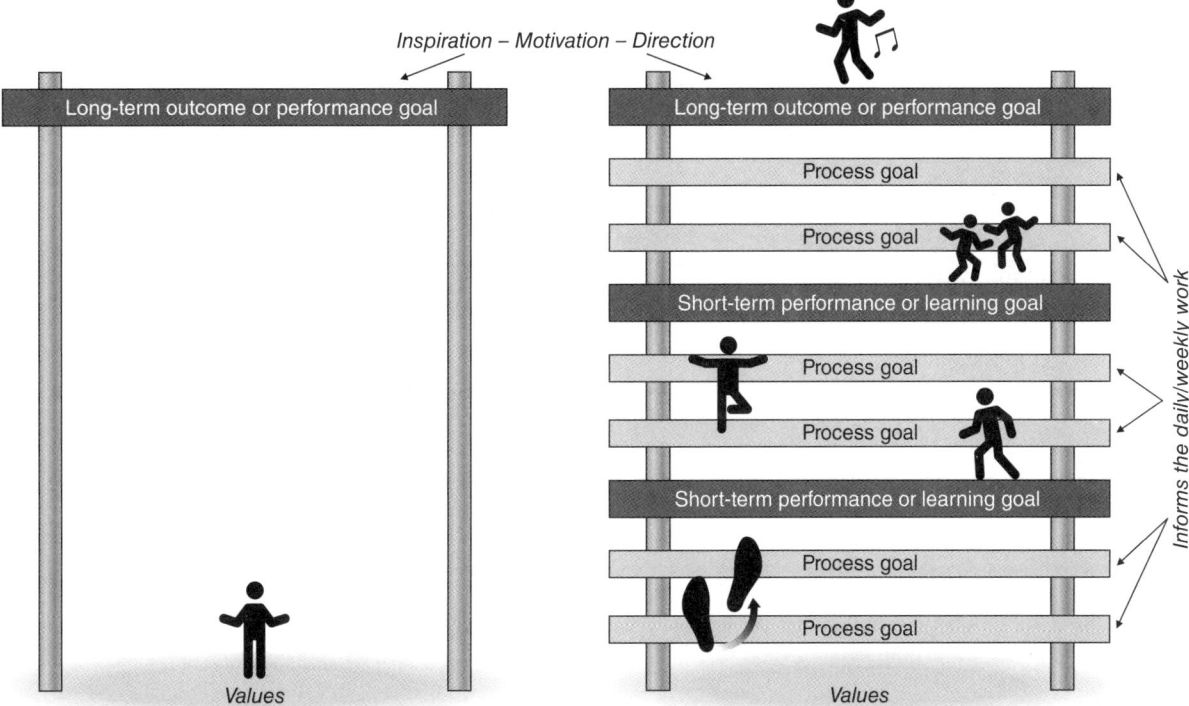

Figure 9.1 Outcome or performance goals represent a desirable top rung; performance, learning, and process goals represent the lower rungs that help to gradually elevate a dancer's learning and skills; and meaningful goals originate in personal values.

THINKING CRITICALLY

- What types of goals do you normally set, and why?
- If there are goal types that you do not use, can you think of any reasons why this might be (e.g., personality, motivational climate in your dance setting)?
- Can you use figure 9.1 to create (write, draw) a specific example of goal setting in dance, including three or four types of goals?

Go to HK*Propel* to download a blank version of figure 9.1 to fill in.

Dancers may find goal setting frightening or off-putting for at least two reasons:

1. *Equating goals with outcome goals only.* This is a common mistake, and because of the partial lack of control that we have over the achievement of outcome goals, any resulting anxiety is logical (see Weinberg et al., 2001).

2. *Being in a hierarchical environment that makes them feel disempowered.* Dancers may have a sense that there is little point in setting their own goals because powerful others are in charge of what is taught, who is cast, and so on. This is the environmental uncertainty (lack of control over outcomes) referred to in the first point.

The different goal types may be illustrated along a continuum of control (figure 9.2). Given the different extents to which they are under personal control as well as their proximity (i.e., typically being concerned with the shorter vs. longer term), it makes sense to focus on them at different times. In particular, outcome goals can be inspiring, motivating, and valuable parts of long-term planning. But when actually dancing (in the studio, on stage), they are likely to be distracting because they are not concerned with the task at hand—that is, *how* to dance. Instead, process goals are most useful while dancing (e.g., Burton & Weiss, 2008; Kingston & Hardy, 1997). For dancers who find goal setting anxiety-inducing, learning to

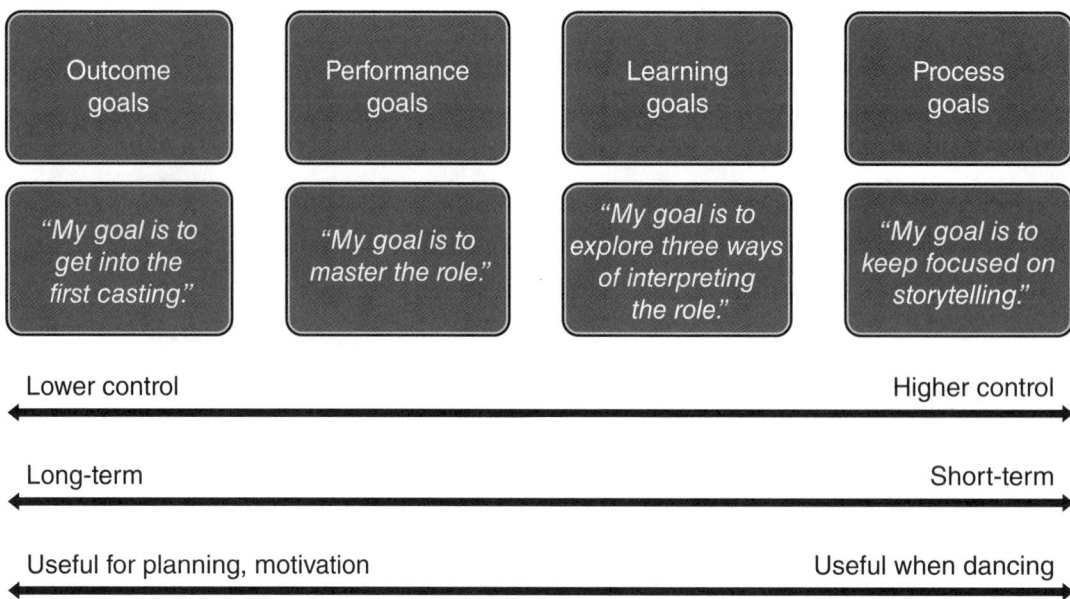

Figure 9.2 Outcome, performance, learning, and process goals may be understood to be on a continuum of personal control.

shift focus toward more personally controllable goals can be a rewarding experience.

Sources of Goals: Assigned Goals Versus Personal Values

The goals that dancers work toward can originate either in themselves or in others. In the broader goal-setting literature, the latter have been studied under the name of **assigned goals**—that is, goals that persons such as teachers, managers, or parents set for performers. While assigned goals can enhance performance, goal setting is often more effective when set in collaboration (Locke & Latham, 2019; Roberts & Kristiansen, 2012). For dance, this means that dancers will perform better when they set specific personally challenging goals participatively *with* their class or teacher; they are likely to perform suboptimally if they only have goals that are set *by* their teacher.

When leaders set goals for their performers, performance can still be enhanced as long as the rationale (logic) behind such a goal is communicated in a friendly way and with good rationale (Latham & Locke, 1991; Locke & Latham, 2019). If you have read chapters 5 or 11, you may recognize this kind of behavior as a form of autonomy support that helps boost intrinsic motivation, performance, and more. In a multifaceted goal-setting process, leaders may set an overall outcome goal for a group or class (e.g., which choreography to perform at the end-of-year show), but personal goals are then set participatively with each individual dancer (see Weinberg et al., 2001). Finally, it appears logical that dancers are more likely to do well with this kind of outside-in goal-setting process if they truly value, like, and identify with the person assigning the goal; research into this issue is warranted.

The most authentic and personally meaningful goals are likely to be those derived from personal **values** (figure 9.1). This kind of inside-out goal setting is a key part of acceptance and commitment therapy (ACT; see the introduction) and the third wave of CBT (Larsen et al., 2019). Specifically, *values* (what is truly important to a person) and *committed action* in a personally valued direction are two of ACT's six core processes (Henriksen et al., 2019). We may consider values as our inner compass: what we want to be, represent, or stand for. Unlike goals, we cannot reach our values; instead, they should act as a consistent guide. Although they can change with maturity, personal growth, and development, values are typically consistent over time. When values influence the types of goals that we set, we are more likely to find them worthwhile, commit to them, work to reach them, and feel deep satisfaction from doing so. Some examples of values and corresponding goals are provided in table 9.1.

Acting in line with one's values (valued direction) is not always easy or pleasant. Indeed, doing so can be both uncomfortable and challenging, such as forgoing junk food in favor of a healthy dinner or

Table 9.1 **Values and Goals Are Distinct Yet Related**

VALUES: WHAT A PERSON WANTS TO STAND FOR		EXAMPLES OF GOALS: WHAT A PERSON DECIDES TO DO
General value examples	Examples of value expressions	
Relationships	I want to have close and fulfilling relationships	I will aim to make two new friends by the end of this term
Fairness	I want to be fair and just	I will speak to every student individually at least once per week
Learning	I want to learn and develop throughout life	I will attend professional development workshops annually
Helping others	I want to bring joy to other people's lives	I will help organize a community dance event next month
Health	I want to put my health first	I will monitor training load, food, and sleep in my diary

speaking up against an unfair management decision. Yet by doing so we can feel more authentic and derive a deeper sense of meaning. In the Get Practical exercise later in the chapter (form 9.1), you can work to identify your own personal values. For now, you may just want to ask yourself: What kind of dancer (or teacher/manager/other role) do I want to be?

Consequences of Goal Setting

The literature investigating the consequences (outcomes) of goal setting is vast, although primarily in domains such as organizational and industrial psychology (e.g., Locke & Latham, 2019). A solid body of literature also exists for goal setting in sports (Burton & Weiss, 2008; Jeong et al., 2021; Kingston & Hardy, 1997; Roberts & Kristiansen, 2012; Weinberg et al., 2001) and exercise (McEwan et al., 2016; Swann et al., 2021), but not a single study into the effects of goal setting in dance has been published. Next, key findings from research syntheses are summarized using the usual broad headings of performance- and well-being-related consequences.

Performance-Related Consequences of Goal Setting

Research into goal setting has primarily focused on its effects on various performance outcomes, with overwhelmingly positive outcomes (Burton & Weiss, 2008; Jeong et al., 2021; Kingston & Hardy, 1997; Locke & Latham, 2019; McEwan et al., 2016; Swann et al., 2021; Weinberg et al., 2001). Indeed, it has been concluded that "goal setting is arguably the most effective performance enhancement technique in the behavioral sciences" (Burton & Weiss, 2008, p. 344). The following are two examples of performance-related consequences of goal setting:

1. *Improved performance.* The most robust finding in the goal-setting literature is that it reliably enhances performance.
   - This effect is consistent for a wide variety of tasks, levels of expertise, populations, countries, and intervention durations.
   - Moderately difficult goals set for the long *and* short term appear to be particularly helpful. Still, what is meant by short (part of a session? one week?) and long (one month? three years?) is highly varied in the literature and, no doubt, in applied practice.
2. *Behavior change.* Goal setting is also an effective way of changing health-related behaviors, such as taking up a new form of exercise or increasing daily physical activity levels.
   - These effects too are robust across a wide range of behaviors (activities), different populations and settings, and intervention durations.

Well-Being-Related Consequences of Goal Setting

Beyond performance benefits, the following well-being-related variables have been demonstrated to be outcomes of, and more generally associated with, goal setting:

1. *Improved motivation.* One of the most central effects of goal setting is its effect on motivation; indeed, goal setting is often described as a primarily motivation-enhancing skill or tool (Jeong et al., 2021; Latham & Locke, 1991; Roberts & Kristiansen, 2012). Even the effects

of goal setting on performance are considered to result in large part from enhanced motivation. For more about the mechanisms by which goal setting exerts its effect, see the "Why Goal Setting Has an Impact" section.

2. *Enhanced focus.* Goals provide specific targets (tasks, actions) onto which dancers can place their focus. For example, a focus on relevant performance and perhaps outcome goals can ensure that dancers stay oriented toward goal achievement (e.g., "I will avoid working too hard in the gym today because muscle soreness would distract from my main goal of focusing on artistry at this time."). When dancing, wisely devised process goals can keep dancers from being distracted and help them focus on the task at hand ("Distracted again! Back to focusing on projecting . . ."). As for motivation, the effects of goal setting on performance are considered to result in part from enhanced focus (see the "Why Goal Setting Has an Impact" section). For more on the use of holistic process goals to enhance attentional focus, see chapter 6.

3. *Improved self-confidence.* Because goal setting is a helpful tool on the way to mastery, it can enhance self-confidence (or its more specific form, self-efficacy; see chapter 3). For example, a clearly stated goal coupled with regular progress monitoring helps dancers see that they are improving. The goal setting/self-confidence relationship also exists in reverse, because more confident dancers are likely to set themselves more challenging goals (e.g., Latham & Locke, 1991).

4. *Enhanced positive affect.* By setting goals that are specific, moderately difficult, and realistic, dancers will increase the likelihood of experiencing several forms of positive affect, such as joy and satisfaction; quite simply, it is fun to strive for (and reach) something that is personally meaningful. Of course, setting goals that are too easy to reach will result in little pride, whereas setting excessively difficult goals will lead to little satisfaction because they are rarely if ever reached. This helps explain why perfectionistic dancers typically experience little if any satisfaction or pride, even when they work hard and progress.

5. *Anxiety management.* In learning to set appropriate goals and focusing on different goals at different times, dancers can be helped in managing anxiety and related constructs (e.g., fear of failure). In particular, process goals are valuable points of focus that limit anxiety because they are proximal, under personal control, and conducive to enhancing a performance or an experience in the moment. Conversely, setting inappropriate goals (e.g., only outcome goals or ambitious performance goals in the face of environmental uncertainty) often *causes* anxiety (see figures 9.1 and 9.2).

Why Goal Setting Has an Impact

Goal setting affects performance to the extent that it affects behavior. Locke and Latham (1990, 2019; Latham & Locke, 1991) clarify that key mechanisms help explain the goal setting/performance relationship (i.e., act as statistical mediators between goal setting and performance): goal setting focuses attention, enhances effort and persistence, and promotes the pursuit and use of goal attainment strategies.

1. *Goal setting focuses attention.* The setting of a suitably challenging and meaningful goal focuses attention on what one is doing. This includes identifying discrepancies between the goal and one's current level and becoming curious and more detailed than usual about the components that make up a skill. For example, a dancer who sets herself a goal to accomplish a challenging jump sequence might notice that her stamina is insufficient or that she holds her breath, which causes tension. She might also ask others for help in identifying where she currently goes wrong. By way of this attentional focusing, work on goal achievement can become targeted and more efficient. It also means that the dancer is more likely to avoid distractions and forgo temptations.

2. *Goal setting increases effort and persistence.* When working toward something that we really want to achieve, we try harder and become active in monitoring our progress. Goal setting can serve to increase effort in this way at single moments in time or over a period of time—in other words, persistence. For instance, instead of stopping as soon as we feel tired during body conditioning, we are more likely to keep going if we can see that we have a good chance of meeting our target time, distance, or repetitions. Especially if we perceive progress to be good, confidence and motivation grow and we continue to work

until the goal is reached ("If I keep going, I will make it!"). If we instead decide that progress is insufficient, we may either give up ("I will never make it anyway!") or persist in order to make goal achievement more likely ("If I try again tomorrow, I might manage it."). Hence, dancers with higher levels of self-confidence are more likely to increase their efforts, but those with poor self-confidence are more likely to give up (see chapter 3); as such, helping dancers believe that they can achieve their goals is an important task for leaders, parents, and peers alike.

3. *Goal setting increases the pursuit and use of goal attainment strategies.* When a goal feels important, our desire to reach it extends to problem-solving and creativity; that is, we become more likely to plan, create strategies, and find new ways of reaching our goal. For instance, we might ask for help, read books, watch film clips online, and devise inventive ways of practicing that we would not otherwise try.

For a specific example of how more versus less efficient goal setting processes may affect dancers, consider the functional analyses in figure 9.3. In this example a dancer, Julia, is in a high-performance setting (e.g., a selective school) where there are expectations of continuous improvement and success. In the first example, Julia responds to this kind

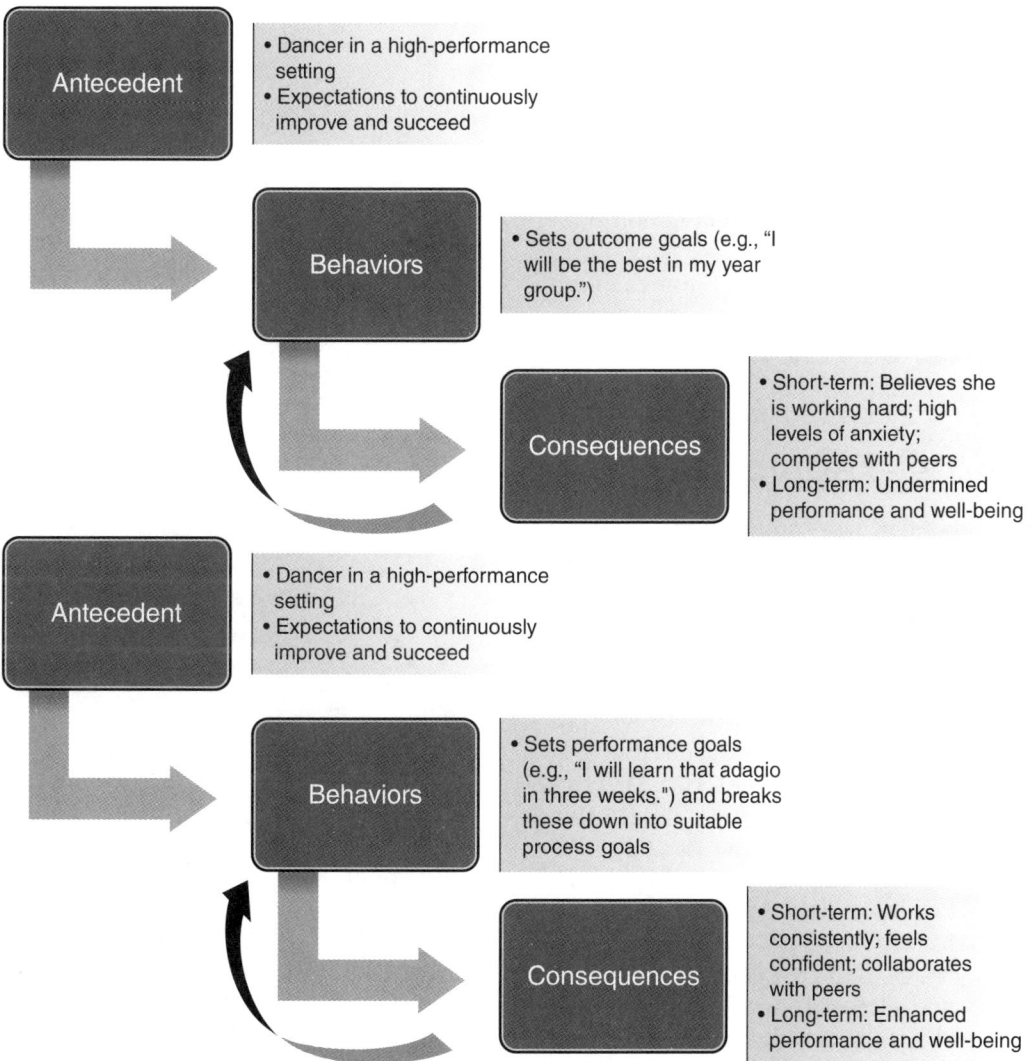

Figure 9.3 Functional analysis examples of how different types of goals may affect dancers. The recursive arrows indicate that the consequences make the behavior more likely to reoccur in similar situations in the future (behavior maintenance).

of atmosphere or expectations to improve (whether internal or external) by setting outcome goals for herself, such as being the best in her year group. These help her feel that she is doing her best to improve. Yet by failing to break this down into suitable performance and process goals, a long-term consequence is that her performance does not improve. Because she is focusing on something that is partly outside of her control, she also experiences anxiety (see chapter 4), and her goal is based on interpersonal comparison, which leads her to compete with her peers (see chapter 5). Overall, her long-term well-being is undermined.

In the second example, Julia instead responds to the high expectations by setting performance goals, such as being able to learn a particular adagio in three weeks. She gets help to break this down into suitable process goals (stepping-stones), so that she knows what aspects of the adagio she mostly needs to work on and what to think about when doing so. This kind of goal setting is under greater personal control, which helps her feel confident and to work consistently. Because it is not in competition with anyone else, Julia collaborates with her peers (e.g., they help one another with tips and filming). These aspects help boost her well-being, and her performance is improved as a result of the specific goals she has set.

What Is Self-Regulation?

Self-regulation refers to systematic efforts to direct thoughts, feelings, and actions toward the attainment of goals (Zimmerman, 2000). Dancers who are effective self-regulators are metacognitively aware; that is, they know what they are thinking, feeling, and doing (McCardle et al., 2019). Through this awareness, they are better able to see the consequences of their decisions and behaviors and better able to make changes as they see fit. Effective self-regulators are typically proactive, reflective individuals who take responsibility for their own learning and development; for instance, they take the initiative, ask their instructors specific questions, and use psychological skills such as goal setting and imagery. In contrast, a poor self-regulator might be someone relatively passive, who practices out of habit or perhaps just does as they are told; poor attendance, lack of forethought, and being unfocused are other signs of limited self-regulation (McCardle et al., 2019; Zimmerman, 1998, 2000).

Although goal setting is a fundamental part of self-regulation (Latham & Locke, 1991; Zimmerman, 2000), the latter can involve a number of other psychological skills (e.g., imagery, mindfulness) as well as behaviors and emotions. As such, self-regulation can be considered a broader process and more of an umbrella concept than is goal setting. Several models illustrate self-regulation as a cyclical process (Kirschenbaum, 1984; Zimmerman, 1998, 2000). For instance, Kirschenbaum (1984) considered the self-regulation process to consist of five related stages: problem identification, commitment, execution, environmental management, and generalization (figure 9.4).

As outlined by Kirschenbaum (1984), the first stage of self-regulation is identifying a problem (e.g., "I am not strong enough to manage these lifts.") and believing that change is possible ("I could get stronger."). Of course, this does not have to be an actual problem but could simply be a goal or aim ("I want to get stronger."). A highly self-regulating dancer takes responsibility for continuously identifying such problems or areas of improvement. This can be through self-awareness, by seeking feedback and inspiration, and by generally pursuing learning in various ways (e.g., reading books, taking courses, watching performances).

In the second stage of self-regulation, the dancer makes the all-important commitment to rectify the identified problem or to work toward the goal she has set. For instance, she may initiate a goal-setting

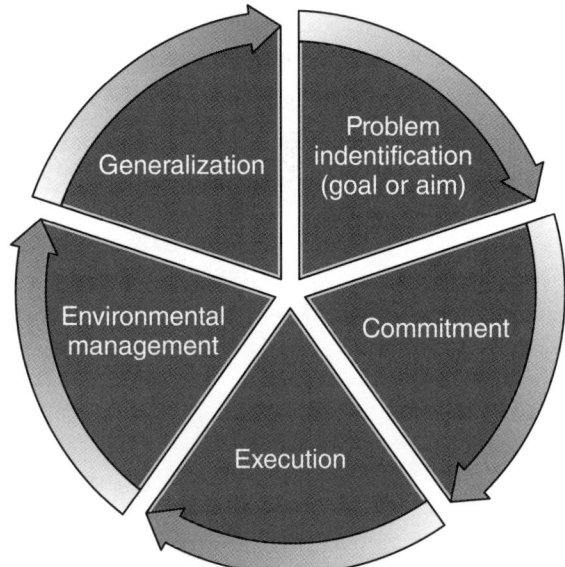

Figure 9.4 The five-stage model of self-regulation.
Based on Kirschenbaum (1984).

process, make plans, and tell people about her new plans. This takes her into the third stage, where actual behavioral changes are made. For example, our dancer might begin to work at her goal of going to the gym three times per week, lifting weights, and so on. Goal monitoring and feedback form inherent parts of the execution stage as the dancer keeps track of her progress or lack of progress. As pointed out by Kirschenbaum (1984), regular note-taking and video feedback can be valuable during this stage. This might include making brief notes after classes or rehearsals about (1) what was focused on, (2) what was learned, and (3) what to focus more on next time. The dancer can then re-read these prior to the next class or rehearsal in order to arrive prepared. Sport research suggests that self-reflection may even be the most crucial self-regulatory mechanism (for a review, see McCardle et al., 2019).

In the fourth stage of the self-regulation cycle, performers need to manage the impact of their environments. For instance, physical issues such as injury or illness may get in the way of progress; changes in teachers or casting may affect the opportunities to practice particular skills; or family commitments may require the dancer to alter plans. Hence, flexibility is key: How else can I reach my goal? What new strategies or time plans do I need to make?

Finally, goals and associated new behaviors typically need to be generalized across many days and perhaps settings for self-regulation to be successful and complete; this represents the fifth and final part of the cycle. For example, our dancer who wanted to become stronger to manage difficult lifts may need to practice strength training not only for a few weeks in one gym with one training program. Instead, she might need to devise plans for how to continue this training when going on tour, when rehearsal timings change, and when she is tired. Put simply, the new behavior needs to be anchored in her life.

Self-regulation is highly demanding, requiring much time and energy; therefore, it is not surprising that many self-regulation attempts are abandoned partway through (Kirschenbaum, 1984; Zimmerman, 2000). In many ways it is easier to do what one has always done, practice on autopilot, or rely on what other people say (i.e., not actively identify performance problems, or areas for potential improvement; stage 1). And even when this is done, it is easier to just express vague intentions rather than truly commit and commence a goal-setting process (i.e., not complete stage 2). Even if goals are committed to, it is common for people to work hard at achieving them for only a short while (i.e., an incomplete stage 3); think of all those resolutions that result in record numbers of new gym memberships in January, followed by a sharp decrease in gym attendance by February. The challenges continue: even for persons self-aware and dedicated enough to complete the first three stages of self-regulation, it is challenging to keep new behaviors going when life throws new challenges their way, when progress is not forthcoming, and so on (i.e., for environmental management and generalization, stages 4-5, to be insufficient).

Because it is so demanding, it is logical that self-regulation is a skill that characterizes top elite performers: most of us are simply not that dedicated or self-aware (for a review, see McCardle et al., 2019). Nevertheless, keep in mind that the preceding descriptions are of idealized self-regulation processes, and that using some of them is still likely to be better than using none at all. Interestingly, research suggests that negative feedback, poor self-efficacy, and critical self-monitoring can predispose people to self-regulatory failure, especially on tasks that are not yet well learned (Kirschenbaum, 1984). Hence, self-monitoring should be positive (e.g., making notes about what went well and why) and instructional (e.g., making notes about technical aspects and not about success/failure with a task).

The self-regulation model is cyclical because once a new behavior has been generalized and anchored in a person's everyday life, it is no longer under the same intense scrutiny; as such, new performance problems or goals can be identified, and a new cycle begun. It is also possible to hop off the cycle during any given stage if self-monitoring or feedback suggests that something is not working. For example, a dancer may notice that his goal was too ambitious, or a teacher finds that her new class structure did not yield the expected results (both "problems"). In such cases, effective self-regulation would mean making a deliberate return to stage 1 rather than continuing to do something that is ineffective.

THINKING CRITICALLY

- To what extent do you self-regulate your dance involvement?
- To what extent is self-regulation encouraged and fostered in your dance setting?
- Can you use figure 9.4 to create (write, draw) two specific examples of self-regulation related to dance: one which

succeeded (i.e., went full circle) and one which failed partway through for some reason?

Go to HK*Propel* to download a fillable version of figure 9.4.

How Can Goal Setting and Self-Regulation Be Optimized?

Because goal setting is a key part of sport psychology, advice on how it can be optimized is relatively abundant and well researched. Advice on self-regulation optimization is less available, although practicing psychological skills such as mindfulness (see chapter 8) should help promote the self-awareness that underpins self-regulation. A technique known as performance profiling was recently shown to enhance dancers' self-awareness (Castillo & Chow, 2020); as such, performance profiling may be a useful tool for promoting self-regulation. Beyond such awareness-promoting strategies, well-executed goal setting is in itself a way of enhancing self-regulation. For all these reasons, the next sections of applied recommendations are primarily focused on goal setting.

Setting SMART GOALS

Even if you have not studied performance psychology before, chances are that you have come across the acronym SMART in relation to goal setting. It is widely used across sport, exercise, education, management, and coaching psychology, and there appears to be agreement that the S stands for *specific*; M stands for *measurable*; and T is usually about goals needing to be *timed*, *time-bound*, or similar. The A and the R variously reflect recommendations for goals to be *achievable*, *agreed-upon*, or *action-oriented*, *realistic*, and *relevant*. To capture these important aspects but also incorporate a slightly more nuanced and in-depth view that accounts for wider and more recent research findings (e.g., Kwasnicka et al., 2021; Larsen et al., 2019; Locke & Latham, 2019; Swann et al., 2021), the acronym SMART GOALS is proposed here. This acro-

Keeping a training diary helps dancers write down, keep track of, and evaluate their goals.

Table 9.2 SMART GOALS for Dancers and Teachers

Component	Recommendation	Dance examples
Specific	Make goals specific enough that you clearly know what you want to achieve.	Be able to perform a complex movement sequence while staying on the beat all the way through.
Measurable	Decide how you will know when the goal has been reached.	When able to do the entire sequence in time with the music according to evaluations by both self and a peer.
Autonomous	Working toward a goal should ideally make a person feel autonomous (like themselves).	The dancer sets the goal themselves but with input from others.
Realistic	Make goals an enticing but realistic challenge, not about unreachable perfection.	After speaking to his teacher and watching online film clips, the dancer is confident that the goal is realistic.
Time-Bound	Set a date or time by which the goal should be reached.	The performance goal is to be reached two weeks prior to a particular competition.
Grounded	Goals should be grounded in the individual (in line with their values).	The dancer likes the sequence and the music; challenging himself to continuously develop is in line with his values.
Organized	Write goals down and evaluate progress regularly.	The dancer registers his goal in a digital training diary. Work (tasks, effort) is registered daily, and interim evaluations take place weekly.
Adjustable	Stay flexible, adjusting goals or tasks as needed.	A cold sets the dancer back; he shifts the final date for goal achievement somewhat and adds more mental practice as a replacement task.
Logical steps	Break long-term goals down into several short-term goals; set more process, performance, and learning goals than outcome goals.	The overall goal is broken down into 1-minute chunks (bits of choreography), with a specific number of days for each chunk. Practice is twice physically after each class, and 10 minutes of imagery every other day. A teacher suggests he focus on relaxing his weight into the floor, which becomes a process goal.
Supported	Share goals with peers and teachers, supporting each other.	The dancer regularly discusses his goal with a teacher and joins up with peers weekly to help each other via film and discussions.

nym comprises recommendations that goals should be *specific, measurable, autonomous, realistic, time-bound* as well as *grounded, organized, adjustable,* set in *logical* steps, and *supported* (table 9.2 provides an overview of these features):

> *Specific, measurable, realistic, time-bound, and in logical steps.* In line with the aforementioned evidence, dancers are recommended to set goals that are as specific and measurable as possible. Goals should also be realistic (not too easy, not too hard) and set in logical steps (e.g., break down long-term goals into several short-term goals; see figure 9.1). By making goals time-bound (i.e., setting a date or time by which to achieve the goal), the frames for the process are further delineated. All these aspects help to guide the daily work and make monitoring and evaluation more objective and rewarding.

> *Autonomous.* In line with the motivation literature (see chapters 5 and 11), dancers are recommended to focus on goals that are their own and that feel personally relevant. Dance is typically taught in groups rather than fully personalized; moreover, no teacher can feel what an individual dancer's body feels like on a particular day or fully know all dancers' personal dreams or sense of purpose. Therefore, dancers (especially those at higher levels) should have their own goals rather than rely solely on the goals and directives of teachers or rehearsal directors. While they cannot typically ignore the tasks or requirements that are set by leaders, dancers can be advised to set personal goals

within existing structures. For instance, the process goal of working with varied dynamics can be integrated into almost any class. Ambitious dancers may also want to keep an eye on the extent to which the structures provided (e.g., types of classes in a school; choreographic style of a company) actually align with their own personal long-term goals and values.

> *Grounded.* In line with the ACT literature, dancers are recommended to set goals in line with their personal values—who they ultimately want to be. For an example of how personal values can be identified, see the Get Practical exercise (form 9.1). For more information and exercises related to personal values, see Larsen et al. (2019).

> *Organized.* To clarify, monitor, evaluate, and remember one's goals, they should be written down and organized in some visible and accessible place. For example, goals can be recorded in a training diary or app or by putting notes or a poster on a notice board or wall. Dancers may also get creative with where they write their process goals, such as on the insole of their dance shoe or on a piece of tape that is then put on their water bottle, to act as reminders.

> *Adjustable.* Goal setting is no exact science, and there are many reasons why goals may not be achieved. It is therefore important to keep a flexible attitude and to individualize all goal-setting processes (e.g., Jeong et al., 2021; Kwasnicka et al., 2021). Indeed, an overemphasis on goal achievement as a black-or-white dichotomy ("Did you succeed or fail?") can undermine the effects of goal setting on progress, learning, and satisfaction. Monitoring, feedback, and evaluations should focus more on what progress was made and what was learned, including learning about strategies that did not work. In so doing, the commitment that is crucial to any goal-setting program will be nurtured. It is also important to stay open to unexpected benefits; for instance, tips from friends may strengthen friendships more than dance ability. With time and practice, dancers will also learn more about what works for them and about the goal-setting process itself.

> *Supported.* Goals are best set in a supportive task-involving climate, with leaders who encourage performers to focus on the task at hand and on their own personal progress (Roberts & Kristiansen, 2012; see also chapter 11).

Further Recommendations for Setting Effective Subjective Goals

Dancers often wish to improve on aspects that are inherently subjective, such as artistry, movement quality, or staying confident in rehearsals. When setting such goals, it is particularly important to carefully delineate what is meant. For example, they can discuss what "sharper movement quality" means with their teacher, or make notes in a diary about what "staying confident" means to them. What kinds of behaviors would indicate that they were confident? Once the goal is specific and clear, dancers can seek feedback from multiple sources to reach "multi-subjectivity": while not objective, getting multiple points of view at least means they rely on the opinions of several people rather than on one person's opinion. For instance, dancers might rate their own subjective perceptions, ask their teacher, and ask a friend to film them.

Dancers can also make subjective experiences measurable by using rating scales. For psychological constructs such as motivation and self-confidence, they might borrow items (questions, statements) from established questionnaires, which are sometimes available online. In other cases, writing one's own items might be best. For example, a dancer who wants to stay confident throughout rehearsals might decide that for her, confidence is expressed in making eye contact with the rehearsal director; in making her movements large and expressive; and in speaking up as soon as she is unsure of a step. She then rates herself on a scale from 1 (did not do this at all) to 5 (did this often) after each rehearsal.

Another scoring system is known as goal attainment scaling (Kiresuk et al., 1994). With this type of scoring approximately five descriptions of probable outcomes are developed, ranging from least favorable to most favorable. The best possible outcome (e.g., behaved confidently throughout rehearsal) is given a score of +2 while the worst possible (e.g., did not behave confidently at all) is given a score of −2. No change from the baseline is given a score of 0. By rating oneself (or teachers rating things like student engagement, perhaps) on a regular basis, it becomes possible to get a good overview of behavior change. Further suggestions on how to use goal setting with dance students alongside journaling and self-talk is found in Carattini (2020).

Form 9.1	GET PRACTICAL: IDENTIFYING VALUES TO SET MEANINGFUL GOALS

In this exercise, you will be asked to reflect on how you want people to perceive you over time. *Take your time*. This exercise will have few, if any, benefits if it is done superficially. Make notes as you reflect. You may want to close your eyes and imagine the scenario as vividly as you can. For a fully imagery-based version of this exercise, see Larsen et al. (2019).

> **Welcome to your retirement party!**
>
> After many years in a successful dance career, it is time to hang up your dancing shoes.
>
> Everyone you have ever met in dance will be at your retirement party.
>
> **What will they say about you?** Consider at least three different people.

Person 1 was: _____ (name/role in your life)
S/he said that I was:
  1.
  2.
  3.

Person 2 was: _____ (name/role in your life)
S/he said that I was:
  1.
  2.
  3.

Person 3 was: _____ (name/role in your life)
S/he said that I was:
  1.
  2.
  3.

Based in your reflections, write down your values. You can do so in the table below or wherever suits you best. Then formulate up to three goals that are in line with your values. What do you want to achieve or learn? Consider this a starting point—you can always update it later. For instance, you could formulate three goals for a single value; adjust to suit yourself.

VALUES: WHAT I WANT TO STAND FOR	GOALS: THINGS I WANT TO DO AND REACH
1.	
2.	
3.	

(continued)

Form 9.1 *(continued)*

Next, consider the SMART GOAL acronym, as described in this chapter to further hone your goals. This will help make them effective. Consider where and how to write down, monitor, and evaluate your goals.

COMPONENT	TO CHECK WITH YOUR GOALS	YOUR NOTES
Specific	Is the goal specific enough that you clearly know what you want to achieve?	
Measurable	How will you know when the goal is reached?	
Autonomous	Does working toward this goal make you feel autonomous (like yourself)?	
Realistic	Does the goal feel like an enticing but realistic challenge?	
Time-bound	Have you set a date/time by which the goal should be reached?	
Grounded	Is the goal grounded in you (in line with your values)?	
Organized	Have you written the goal down? When/how will you evaluate progress?	
Adjustable	Remember to stay flexible, adjusting goals and/or tasks as needed	
Logical steps	Have you broken long-term goals down into several short-term goals, and set more process, performance, and learning goals than outcome goals?	
Supported	Have you shared your goals with peers/teachers?	

Go to HK*Propel* to download this form.

George: Case Study of Goal Setting and Self-Regulation

George is a ballet dancer in his first year as a company member. Although he had set himself the goal of becoming a professional dancer and has achieved it, he really dislikes goal setting. For him, setting some goal, far into the future, about what you *should* achieve by a certain date just adds pressure. Besides, ballet is full of unknowns: Who will get cast for what role? What will this choreographer want to do? So, George only works on the daily tasks that ballet masters, rehearsal directors, and choreographers set for him; the future will simply have to work itself out.

After a while a new dancer, Sam, joins the company and his way of working seems quite different: Far from only doing as he is told, Sam asks for feedback on things that *he* wants to work on. George quietly squirms in the background; how will their normally authoritarian instructors react? To his surprise, they seem quite pleased. George is intrigued and decides to talk to Sam. Fancy being so self-directed!

It turns out that Sam and George view goals quite differently. When George set goals like "get the lead role," he felt a lot of pressure. And when he didn't reach them, he was deflated: all that work, for nothing! Sam, however, sets goals like "pull off a quadruple pirouette," and feels this is something he is in charge of. After all, he says, "Who says I can't do it? Sure, it takes work: for a start, you have to break it down. What are the aspects of doing four turns correctly? Just finding that out can become your first goal. You might find you need to work on one technical and one physical aspect; so you search for information, and you ask other people. And then you have a handful of little things to work on and decide what takes your fancy on a given day. Some days you just want to sweat; some days you want to be an artist, or whatever. But you keep working on things that move you in the right direction. Goals shouldn't make you feel tied down—they should be inspiring!" Hearing Sam speak, George starts to feel motivated to set a goal of his own—for something he is really interested in doing (rather than something he should be doing) and one that puts him in charge. After this chat, he isn't afraid of asking a friend for help along the way.

Composite case study created on the basis of conversations with Professor Gene Moyle, DPsych, Queensland University of Technology, Australia, an ex-dancer and experienced performance psychology practitioner in dance and elite sport, and with Carolyn Carattini, DCI: ballet teacher, ex-dancer and founder of www.propsforballet.com: a resource for dance teachers to learn about psychological skills in ballet.

CRITICAL ASPECTS OF RESEARCH INTO GOAL SETTING AND SELF-REGULATION

1. In this book, the topics of goal setting and motivation (specifically, achievement goal theory [AGT]) are outlined in separate chapters, yet both areas of literature clearly center on the term *goals*, which may cause confusion. The reason for the separation is that goal setting is described as a psychological skill or tool, typically used for a discrete period of time (e.g., a six-month goal-setting process leading up to a major event). In contrast, achievement goals are described as the fundamental outlook of a person, either at a specific time (task- and ego-involvement) or more generally (task and ego orientations; see chapter 5). However, it is logical that strongly task-oriented individuals are likely to set primarily performance, learning, and process goals because they focus on individual progress and learning. Strongly ego-oriented individuals are instead likely to set more outcome goals because they focus on demonstrating superiority. For more in-depth discussions of the links between goal setting and AGT, see Roberts and Kristiansen (2012) or Burton and Weiss (2008).

2. The goal-setting and self-regulation literatures are large and in many ways persuasive, but there are no empirical investigations with dancers. Studying the

goal-setting and self-regulation practices of dancers and their teachers is highly warranted, including explorations of the ways in which these practices may be optimized.

3. Sport research suggests that self-regulation contributes to learning and to success, as well as to the management of motivation and emotion (coping). It would therefore be intriguing to examine what kinds of dance teacher behaviors are more or less likely to nurture self-regulation among dancers. Given the conceptual overlap between self-regulation and autonomy, it might be that autonomy supportive teachers are best at optimizing this important skill (Goffena & Horn, 2021; see chapters 5 and 11 for more about autonomy and autonomy support).

KEY POINTS AND RECOMMENDATIONS FOR GOAL SETTING IN DANCE

1. Dancers, but also teachers and other leaders, are highly recommended to set goals for enhancing performance or aspects of well-being. The literature points to several recommendations for making such goals optimally effective, including making goals specific, measurable, autonomous, realistic, and time-bound, as well as grounded, organized, adjustable, set in logical steps, and supported.

2. Especially when goals are subjective in nature, dancers are encouraged to be as clear and specific as possible so that the goal-setting process does not become vague, nor does it become too difficult to determine when the goal has been reached.

3. For highly ambitious dancers, working on self-regulation through goal setting and associated strategies (e.g., daily diary writing to enhance self-awareness, progress monitoring) can be advised.

10

Imagery

"Dance is bigger than the physical body. Think bigger than that. When you extend your arm, it doesn't stop at the end of your fingers, because you're dancing bigger than that. You're dancing spirit."

Judith Jamison, dancer and choreographer

CHAPTER OBJECTIVES

After reading this chapter, you will be able to

1. describe what imagery is, including movement quality imagery and mental practice imagery;
2. outline the components of the revised applied model of deliberate imagery use;
3. critically discuss the principle of functional equivalence and how the PETTLEP model may be applied in dance;
4. describe a variety of consequences of imagery, including effects on well-being and on performance;

5. apply basic recommendations to enhance imagery use both while dancing (movement quality images) and as a complement to physical practice (mental practice images);
6. write an imagery script for yourself or for others; and
7. think critically about the nature and impact of imagery in dance settings.

Key Terms

controllability	imagery function	PETTLEP model
debilitative imagery	imagery type	revised applied model of deliberate imagery use (RAMDIU)
external perspective	internal perspective	
facilitative imagery	kinesthetic imagery	visual imagery
functional equivalence	mental practice imagery	vividness
imagery	movement quality imagery	

The term *imagery* often refers to actual pictures and other visual depictions such as the photographs in this book. The focus of this chapter, however, is mental imagery. As such, the root term of what we are trying to get at is *imagination*. Imagination stems from the Latin *imāginātiō*, meaning to *represent* or create a *likeness*. Current understanding of mental imagery is similarly that it is about creating likenesses in the form of mental representations. Importantly, the term *imagery* (and its sibling, *visualization*) is not only about the creation of visual representations; in fact, creating multisensory images is a skill that enhances imagery practice and therefore dance itself.

What Is Imagery?

Imagery is an inherent human capacity for creating mental representations (or simulations) of actions and events in the past, present, and future. Imagery is an intrinsic part of dance and has probably been used for as long as humans have danced; indeed, it is difficult to imagine how any dance would have been created without someone using imagery in the creative process. Those learning the dance are likely to have run it through in their minds (i.e., practiced via imagery) and used imagery as they tried to convey some message or emotion. For instance, embodying animal-like characteristics involves immersing in complex sensory imagery. Accordingly, imagery has a rich history in dance technique, choreography, and the somatic practices pioneered by persons such as Mabel Todd and Lulu Sweigard (see Overby & Dunn, 2011).

The present chapter focuses on dance imagery from an integrated dance and sport psychology perspective, with the more established and robust sport literature being used as a foundation. Indeed, imagery as mental practice is one of the most widely researched psychological skills in sports and one of the most widely practiced (Cumming & Williams, 2013; Simonsmeier et al., 2021). For our purposes, however, it may help to begin with a definition created specifically for dance: "Dance imagery is the deliberate use of the senses to rehearse or envision a particular outcome mentally, in the absence of, or in combination with, overt physical movement. The images may be constructed of real or metaphorical movements, objects, events, or processes" (Overby & Dunn, 2011, p. 9). This definition is more useful to us than those typically used in other domains for two main reasons: First, it points out the possibility of using imagery while moving; this differs from the sport literature in which imagery is almost exclusively discussed as occurring in the absence of movement (e.g., Guillot & Collet, 2008; Toth et al., 2020). Second, it accounts for **movement quality images**, such as metaphors, which are also not commonly discussed in sports. It is valuable to keep such differences in mind as you read the imagery literature, including the current chapter and beyond.

Revised Applied Model of Deliberate Imagery Use

To delineate and better understand imagery, researchers developed a framework outlining where, when, what, and why imagery is used (the 4Ws; Munroe et al., 2000). The 4Ws framework was later used as a foundation for qualitative research in dance (Muir et al., 2018; Nordin & Cumming,

2005). Integrating the 4Ws framework with the ever-progressing research into imagery in several domains, researchers extended its utility by developing a model known as the **revised applied model of deliberate imagery use** (RAMDIU) for sports, dance, exercise, and rehabilitation (Cumming & Williams, 2013). The components of this model are outlined in table 10.1 and described next.

What Dancers Image

There are many ways of categorizing **imagery types**, both in dance (e.g., Batson & Sentler, 2017; Franklin, 2014; Hanrahan & Vergeer, 2001) and sports (e.g., Cumming & Williams, 2013; Guillot & Collet, 2008). In this chapter, categories and names used reflect those commonly used in recent dance research, integrated with research in sports (see Pavlik & Nordin-Bates, 2016). In that terminology, the most commonly used type for many dancers is *technique* or *execution imagery*, such as imagining oneself going through steps, routines, corrections, and scenarios (Muir et al., 2018; Nordin & Cumming, 2005, 2006a; Pavlik & Nordin-Bates, 2016). Also known as direct imagery, this is the **mental practice imagery** typically focused on in sport research. Other types of mental practice images include mastery and goal images. The former includes imagining oneself being focused, confident, and in control, or perhaps overcoming challenges, whereas the latter includes imagining oneself working toward or reaching goals. Dancers may be using more technique/execution imagery than athletes, who in turn may be using more mastery imagery than dancers (Pavlik & Nordin-Bates, 2016). Future research into mastery imagery in dance would be beneficial, including how it may be taught and optimized.

In interviews with young dancers, goal images depicted outcome goals (e.g., winning a competition) but also performance goals (e.g., reaching a particular standard) and process goals (e.g., continuing to try; Muir et al., 2018). Dancers also imagine their environment or context, such as audiences, lights, and spacing of a choreography (Muir et al., 2018; Nordin & Cumming, 2005). Finally, dancers may engage in body-related images such as those depicting physical appearance, injuries and healing, or anatomical structures (Hanrahan & Vergeer, 2001; Nordin & Cumming, 2005). The latter are inherent in somatic practices such as ideokinesis (Sweigard, 1978) and the Franklin Method (Franklin, 2014).

Distinct from mental practice images is a category concerned with various forms of **movement quality images** (Hanrahan & Vergeer, 2001; Nordin & Cumming, 2005, 2006a; Pavlik & Nordin-Bates, 2016). This incorporates the metaphorical imagery* so commonly used in dance, and which is sometimes known as indirect imagery (e.g., painting the space with one's toes; moving like seaweed). Specific qualities (e.g., smooth), and actions (e.g., floating) also fall into this category, as do dramatic themes (e.g., grief) and more holistic imagery of characters and stories (e.g., imagining being one's character; embodying a role). Movement quality images differ from mental practice images because they are typically used *while* dancing. This is important not least because many dancers prefer to image while moving rather than while still (Hanrahan et al., 1995; May et al., 2011).

The present chapter describes mental practice images and movement quality images separately because they are usually researched in that way. In practice, they are often integrated. A common example is when dancers mentally rehearse movements they learned in class, including a teacher-provided metaphor. Another is when a teacher plans a class through imagery (e.g., which exercises to include) and plays around with ideas for imagery instructions to try (e.g., "I'll do the enchaînement first using bouncy words; once they know it, I'll ask them to do the steps with anger, and lastly melancholy").

Why Dancers Image

Imagery function (*why*) refers to the reasons for doing imagery (Cumming & Williams, 2013) and comprise cognitive, motivational, artistic, and healing-related reasons (Muir et al., 2018; Pavlik & Nordin-Bates, 2016). Cognitive reasons include learning, memorizing steps, planning, evaluating performances, and reviewing choreography. For instance, dancers may practice through imagery instead of physically, thereby saving energy. In a famous example, Cuban dancer Alicia Alonso described how she learned to dance *Giselle* in complete bedrest while recuperating from eye surgery ("Alicia Alonso," 2021). She accomplished this feat by using her imagination while her husband moved her hands and fingers—that is, marking. Using imagery to enhance body awareness and alignment are other examples of cognitive reasons for imagery use; indeed, teachers of kinesiology, somatics, and conditioning often use imagery as a teaching tool (e.g., Franklin, 2014; Kirk, 2014; Krasnow & Deveau, 2010).

---

*Strictly speaking, images suggesting doing something "as if" are not metaphors but analogies or similes, but we will stick here to the term *metaphorical imagery* as it is so commonly used.

Table 10.1 **Components of the Revised Applied Model of Deliberate Imagery Use Contextualized for Dance**

Model component	Description	Subcategories and considerations	Dance examples

What	Type	• Mental practice images
		  ◦ Technique/execution
		  ◦ Goals
		  ◦ Mastery
		  ◦ Context
		  ◦ Body-related
		• Movement quality images
		  ◦ Metaphorical
		  ◦ Specific qualities or actions
		  ◦ Dramatic themes
		  ◦ Characters and stories
			• Going through in one's mind:
			  ◦ A movement phrase
			  ◦ How to reach a goal
			  ◦ Overcoming a challenge
			  ◦ The stage, with scenery
			  ◦ The femur rotating in its socket
			• Imagining:
			  ◦ Projecting into space
			  ◦ Sharp; rocking
			  ◦ Rebellion
			  ◦ Being Mercutio

Why	Reason	• Cognitive • Motivational • Artistic • Healing	• To learn • To feel confident • To convey a feeling • To accelerate rehabilitation
Where	Location	• In dance • Outside dance	• In the studio • At home
When	Situation	• Before, during, and after dancing • Outside dance	• While waiting one's turn • When stressed
Who	Characteristics of the imager	• Level • Experience with imagery • Age • Disposition or personality • Gender	• Elite imaging more than novices • Dancers creating more sophisticated images over time • Younger dancers might use more play-based imagery • Task-oriented dancers might enjoy movement quality imagery more • Female dancers may be imaging their appearance more than males
How	How imagery is being done	• Speed • Frequency and duration • Valence and deliberation • Visual perspective and viewing angle • Agency • Sensory modalities used	• Imaging variations in real time • Imaging 5 minutes/day • Debilitative images arising spontaneously • Imaging externally from slightly above (as if in a tiered theater) • Imaging others doing a solo • Focusing on kinesthetic and tactile imagery
Imagery ability	Extent to which a dancer can image	• Vividness • Controllability	• Imagery is almost like real experience • Dancer able to adjust imagery speed
Meaning	Imagery will be more effective when perceived to be personally meaningful		• Dance teachers recommending dancers to adapt images for their personal needs
Outcome	Ideally, outcome should match function, but images may be ineffective (no outcome) or yield unexpected outcomes		• Teacher successfully uses imagery to create exercises for a class, additionally gaining confidence for teaching

Note: Adapted from Cumming and Williams (2013).

Motivational reasons concern the use of imagery to change how one thinks or feels, and include imaging to enhance self-confidence, focus, motivation, and imagery for anxiety management. In the words of one professional dancer:

> I was imagining this solo a week and a half before I was actually on stage, every single night because I was that nervous. And I suppose that when I feel that way, the more I do it and the more I imagine myself being confident and believing I can do it . . . then it's almost like I can control them: my nerves, and my anxiety. . . . because it's almost like I've been there, I've done that. (previously unpublished quote from dancer interviewed in Nordin & Cumming, 2005)

As you undoubtedly know, dancers also use imagery for artistic reasons such as enhancing expressivity, for choreographing, enhancing movement qualities, and communicating with audiences (Muir et al., 2018; Nordin & Cumming, 2005; Pavlik & Nordin-Bates, 2016). Indeed, any storytelling, acting, and embodiment of a role involves using imagery for artistic purposes. Doing so is also linked to meaning making, because dancers use imagery to keep movements fresh and alive rather than habitual and static. A fourth and final subcategory is healing reasons, whereby dancers use imagery as a tool for recuperation, pain management, and injury recovery.

Any given image (i.e., *what*) can be used for several reasons (*why*; Cumming & Williams, 2013; Nordin & Cumming, 2005). For example, the metaphor of moving with chewing-gum-like threads sticking to the arms may be used to obtain a particular movement quality one day, and for sheer enjoyment another day. Dancers also interpret content differently. For example, two dancers may both imagine themselves performing on stage: one to rehearse and memorize the steps, and another to improve his self-confidence.

Where and When Dancers Image

Dancers use imagery in a variety of locations and at different times. Some of the most common include imaging before, during, and after dance classes and performances; at home and while traveling; when tired, injured, or when perceiving that physical practice has not been adequate (for a review, see Pavlik & Nordin-Bates, 2016). Most professional dancers in one study reported that imagery could be used anywhere and anytime (Nordin & Cumming, 2005). Yet they also reported that the types of imagery used could vary across the year, with mental practice images being more frequent in rehearsal periods and movement quality images being more frequently used in performance periods. An overlap with attentional focus should be noted here; specifically, imagery focused on body mechanics may induce an internal focus while movement quality images are more likely to induce an external focus, which is typically more helpful, especially for performing (Hanrahan, 1996; Hanrahan & Vergeer, 2001; Nordin & Cumming, 2005; see also chapter 6).

Young dancers image in dance settings, at home, and at school (Muir et al., 2018). For instance, participants in a study by Muir and colleagues spoke about putting on music and dancing around the kitchen while imagining being on stage. They also provided examples of using imagery after mistakes and when encountering difficulties. Dance teachers use imagery too, of course, including before (e.g., to plan) and during classes (e.g., to convey instructions and encourage particular movement qualities). As dancers become more accomplished, the images offered by teachers tend to become more frequent and complex, and teachers also encourage dancers to use imagery outside of practice (Bolles & Chatfield, 2009; Nordin & Cumming, 2006b, 2006c, 2007). Dancers who use more imagery when healthy also seem to do so when injured (Nordin-Bates et al., 2011b); in other words, it seems to be a skill that dancers can transfer into new and challenging situations if they have an established imagery habit.

Who Is the Dancer Doing Imagery?

In the RAMDIU, the characteristics of the imager are considered under the heading of *who*. This is because imagery may be affected by personal characteristics such as level of expertise, imagery experience, and personality or dispositions (Cumming & Williams, 2013). Dancers of all levels and ages use imagery, but higher-level performers do so more frequently than those at lower levels, presumably due to their greater dedication (Pavlik & Nordin-Bates, 2016). Interestingly, differences between levels may not be evident around performances—a sign that these important times trigger imagery for dancers more generally (Nordin & Cumming, 2007). Instead, the greater dedication of higher-level dancers is evident in their more extensive imagery use in training situations (e.g., to plan and review their goals and learning). One study demonstrated that although higher achievement level was related to improvements in imagery, years in dance were not (Nordin & Cumming, 2006c). Thus, age may matter more or less in dance imagery use, depending on how it is captured. Still, the imagery of children is likely to differ at least somewhat from that of adults (Muir et al., 2018), and research helping us to develop age-appropriate imagery guidelines is warranted.

Personal characteristics that can matter include perfectionism and motivation (Cumming & Williams, 2013). For example, more task-oriented performers might engage in more process-focused images, such as rehearsing skills and metaphors, that allow them to become absorbed, whereas more ego-oriented performers might engage in more goal imagery, such as seeing themselves succeed. Research into this issue is needed, however. What has been investigated is the relationship between imagery and perfectionism (Nordin-Bates et al., 2011a). In that study, more perfectionistic dancers reported more debilitative images. They were also more likely to be female than the less perfectionistic dancers. There is only one investigation into potential gender differences in dancers' imagery, which demonstrated no differences in imagery ability between male and female Spanish dancers (Paris-Alemany et al., 2019). In the RAMDIU, gender is included on the basis of research showing that female exercisers reported more appearance- and health-related images than male exercisers, who instead reported more technique-related images (Cumming, 2008).

How Dancers Image

The way in which imagery content is generated and interpreted is known as its characteristics (*how* of imagery). A rather broad construct, it includes such things as the speed of imagery (real time, slower, or faster), frequency (rarely vs. often), duration (short vs. long sessions), valence (facilitative vs. debilitative), deliberation (spontaneous vs. deliberate), visual perspective (internal, external or switching between the two), viewing angle (e.g., "seeing" oneself from the front, side or back), agency (imaging oneself vs. others), and the sensory modalities used (visual, kinesthetic, auditory, tactile, and so on; Cumming & Williams, 2013; Muir et al., 2018; Nordin & Cumming, 2005; Pavlik & Nordin-Bates, 2016). Many of these characteristics are revisited later in this chapter, including in the section on the **PETTLEP model** (Holmes & Collins, 2001) and the section on optimizing imagery use; therefore, they are outlined relatively briefly here.

Most of the imagery characteristics in the RAMDIU have been exemplified in dance. For instance, dancers may use imagery in slow-motion to rehearse a complicated variation, or in fast-forward when quickly running through a long performance (Muir et al., 2018; Nordin & Cumming, 2005). Dancers image from an **internal** (first-person) **perspective** when seeing things as if through their own eyes, and from an **external** (third-person) **perspective** when seeing things as a spectator.*

Although the internal visual perspective is truer to life (as this reflects what we see when physically dancing), the external perspective can sometimes provide additional information. Indeed, we typically see more of our surroundings than of our own bodies when looking through our own eyes! Imagery instructions using the words "see yourself" are therefore likely to induce an external perspective. In reality, many dancers and choreographers use a combination of perspectives to gain a maximal amount of useful information (Hanrahan, 1996; Hanrahan & Vergeer, 2001; Nordin & Cumming, 2005).

Although dancers normally intend to use **facilitative imagery** to help themselves, it is clear that **debilitative imagery** does arise (Muir et al., 2018; Nordin & Cumming, 2005; Nordin-Bates et al., 2011a, 2011b). For example, a dancer might try to rehearse a complex variation in his mind but keeps being disturbed by images of himself being off center. In such cases, the recommendation is to simply acknowledge the image and start over again.

When discussing imagery, many think of **visual imagery**—of seeing something in their mind's eye. But physical dance practice is not only about visual aspects, and so mental dance practice should not be either. In fact, a recent meta-analysis revealed that while imagery generally enhanced sport performance, effects were only significant when **kinesthetic imagery** or mixed modalities were emphasized (Toth et al., 2020). In dance, visual and kinesthetic are the most commonly used imagery modalities (Pavlik & Nordin-Bates, 2016); that is, dancers typically both see and feel their bodies when imaging. Other senses can also be important; for instance, touch can be an important part of mentally rehearsing a piece with a lot of partnering. Some scholars particularly highlight the importance of kinesthetic and tactile imagery in

---

*Note that *imagery perspective* is a term exclusively used to further our understanding of visual imagery; other sensory modalities are inherently internal (e.g., kinesthetic images). It is also a term derived from the mental practice imagery literature; for movement quality imagery what we "see" can be more abstract and not necessarily possible (e.g., seeing our joints from inside our bodies).

making dance a truly embodied experience (Batson & Sentler, 2017). Given the centrality of music in dance, auditory imagery is another way of making imagery vivid and realistic. Auditory imagery can also incorporate self-talk and a teacher's voice ("one-and-two-and-duck-and-rise"). In practice, dancers integrate multiple senses (e.g., Coker et al., 2015; Hanrahan & Vergeer, 2001; Heiland et al., 2012) which, as will be discussed later, is a good idea for enhancing vividness and effectiveness.

Imagery Ability

It stands to reason that the effectiveness of imagery will depend on the extent to which a person can image. Imagery ability has two aspects: the **vividness** of the images generated, and their **controllability** (Cumming & Williams, 2013). Controllability is the extent to which a person can control their images—for instance, by transforming and adapting them to suit their needs. Vividness refers to the lifelikeness of images, ranging from nonexistent (just the idea of an image) to fully realistic (as vivid as real experience). To experience your own ability to image in different modalities, see figure 10.1. You can also design your own version of this exercise by imaging different imagery types (e.g., metaphors, abstract shapes).

In dance, it seems that professional dancers are proficient imagers (Nordin & Cumming, 2005), although there are variations both between individuals (some are more skilled than others) and within individuals (e.g., a person being able to image certain types of images more vividly than others, or imaging more clearly at certain times; Cumming & Williams, 2013; Heiland et al., 2012; Heiland & Rovetti, 2013). It is unclear whether dancers image better visually or kinesthetically (Abraham et al., 2017, 2019; Coker et al., 2015; Paris-Alemany et al., 2019; Pavlik & Nordin-Bates, 2016), although imagery interventions do seem to enhance dancers' imagery abilities (Abraham et al., 2017, 2019). Imagery ability is also positively correlated with imagery frequency (Nordin & Cumming, 2006a).

Age differences are likely in imagery ability. For those teaching children, Muir and Munroe-Chandler (2017) provide an overview of imagery ability development across childhood, with accompanying recommendations. Guidelines are also available for layered stimulus-response training, an evidence-based tool for enhancing imagery ability (Cumming et al., 2017). Engaging in such training can be time well spent because high imagery ability is associated with superior performance and better confidence (Cumming et al., 2017). In the words of one professional dancer: "[I]f you couldn't use it . . . I don't think you could progress as much or express as much. With your movements." (Nordin & Cumming, 2005, p. 405).

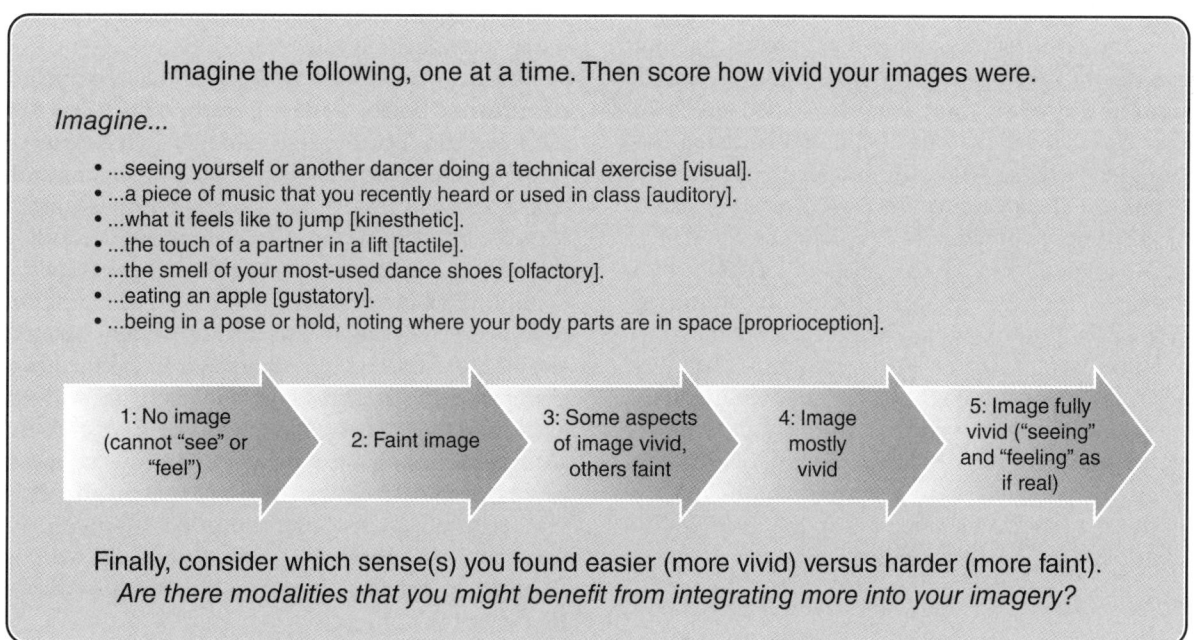

Figure 10.1 Imagining with specific sensory modalities will give you an idea of your ability to generate vivid images.

Personal Meaningfulness of Imagery

In the RAMDIU, it is stipulated that imagery will be more effective when it is personally meaningful (Cumming & Williams, 2013; Wakefield et al., 2013). Dance authors have given similar recommendations, although likely with movement quality images in mind (e.g., Hanrahan & Vergeer, 2001; Heiland et al., 2012; Klockare et al., 2011). To become meaningful, individualization is recommended. For instance, teachers can provide a variety of movement quality images so that dancers can choose one that suits them, and they can encourage dancers to share images with each other. When writing scripts for mental practice imagery, performers should be involved so that the resulting script (and subsequent practice) is meaningful to them; indeed, performer-generated scripts result in better imagery ability for the script and stronger physiological activation (Wilson et al., 2010). Personalization has the added benefit of strengthening dancer autonomy, which in turn has a wide array of benefits (see chapters 5 and 11). To write your own imagery script, see the Get Practical exercise (form 10.1).

Outcomes of Imagery

When imagery works as intended, outcome should match function. For instance, a dancer who wants to soften his movement quality (the *why*) might be successful in doing so (the *outcome*) as a result of the image used (the *what*; e.g., "caress the air"). But if the image does not work for him, outcomes may not be as desired; for instance, he might find the image uninteresting or silly and experience no benefit. In other cases, there may be additional benefits. For example, a dancer who uses imagery to learn does so, but she also becomes more focused as a result. An additional consideration is that the RAMDIU focuses on deliberate imagery use, yet dancers often experience triggered imagery (Nordin & Cumming, 2005, 2007). With triggered imagery, there may not have been any reason to image (e.g., music triggers inspiration for a choreographer who spontaneously starts to imagine movement). In one study, a student dancer responded to the question of why she images with, "Well, why do you breathe? I don't know. It just seems like, you know, that's what you do" (Bolles & Chatfield, 2009, p. 10).

THINKING CRITICALLY

- What types of imagery do you engage in and why?
- Are there any sensory modalities that you find easier or more difficult?
- Can you use the components of the RAMDIU to create a description of your current imagery use and to create suggestions for new imagery habits to try?

Sources of Imagery

Dancers, teachers, and choreographers use various means to stimulate their imagery such as retrieving memories, listening to music, or creating some other trigger (Nordin & Cumming, 2005, 2007). As in the earlier example of Alicia Alonso's imagery while recovering from eye surgery, touch can be another powerful trigger or imagery aid. For more artistic imagery uses, sources are presumably highly idiosyncratic; as noted in chapter 8, inspiration may come from almost any source. Yet for optimal vividness, a certain familiarity seems to help. In a study using brain imaging of an expert break-dancer, familiar (break dancing) music led to greater activity in a brain area involved in movement processing than did dance imagery to unfamiliar (classical ballet) music (Olshansky et al., 2015). As such, the authors argued that the familiar music genre led to more sophisticated imagery.

Other common sources of dance imagery include pictures and books (Batson & Sentler, 2017; Franklin, 2014; Nordin & Cumming, 2005, 2007). In one investigation into imagery sources and types, auditory (metaphorical image described in words), tactile (touch), and visual (anatomical model) stimuli all improved plié arabesque performance (Heiland et al., 2012). Observation is another powerful source of imagery, whether live or through video: Research shows that by watching others, we are better able to generate realistic and vivid images (e.g., Williams et al., 2011). This is good news for dance, which so often relies on visual demonstrations of movements for its instruction. If you have read chapter 3, you may recall that observation is also a valuable source of self-efficacy. Recommendations for how to optimize the use of observation are provided in that chapter.

Form 10.1 GET PRACTICAL: IMAGERY SCRIPT WRITING

An imagery script is a written description of what to include in one's imagery, in the form of a story. Using a script supports focus and means that you do not have to rely on memory when going through an imagery experience. Scripts can be written down and read aloud (e.g., a teacher reading to a group) or recorded digitally to be played through headphones (e.g., for a dancer in their spare time). The script can also be integrated with relevant music. Somewhat older dancers (e.g., mid-teens upward) might write their own scripts. A teacher can write the script for younger dancers, although individual input and discussion is always important.

Following published guidelines (Cumming & Williams, 2013; Williams et al., 2013), it is recommended that those wanting to write a script consider the following aspects:

ASPECT	TO CONSIDER
Who it is for	Consider such things as age, imagery ability, and individual preferences. Beginners may need scripts that are just 1-2 minutes long, while experienced imagers may benefit from 20+ minutes, using more complex images.
Why image	Consider the main 1-2 reasons why imagery is being used. For instance, does the dancer want to memorize a solo, get into character, or handle nerves?
What to image	Once desired outcomes are established, content can be decided. For example, to memorize, focus may be directed to the order and rhythm of the skills in a variation; to get into character, appropriate metaphors might be created. For anxiety management, symptoms can be included ("you feel the usual butterflies in your stomach") but adding acceptance and equanimity ("you know this means you are ready; leave the butterflies alone and focus on the task at hand").
Where and **When** to image	Consider timings and locations that will be effective (e.g., functionally equivalent) but also realistic. For instance, it may be desirable to do imagery on stage, but stage access may be restricted. Therefore, the dancer might do imagery standing in the studio instead, adding context images of the stage as appropriate (e.g., stage dimensions, lights).
How to image	Consider which sensory modalities and emotions are appropriate and include mentions of these (e.g., "you feel that . . . , you see the . . ."). Preferences for visual imagery perspective (internal vs. external) should be considered, although it may be helpful to include aspects of both to enhance imagery skill.

For details about each of the components, please see the relevant sections in this chapter (e.g., table 10.1) and the guidelines from Williams et al. (2013). Remember these points:

1. The more individualized the script, the more personally meaningful it will become; this also results in greater effectiveness.
2. Like any training program, a script is unlikely to be ideal in its first version. Try it out and adjust to suit.
3. However good it is, the script will need to be updated over time in line with learning, choreography changes, and increasing familiarity with imagery.

(continued)

Form 10.1 *(continued)*

4. For advanced imagers, having a set of scripts that deal with the same situation (e.g., competition) yet incorporate different challenges can be useful. For example, one version may depict the ideal (everything going as planned). Another version may incorporate problems with costume, and a third may consider a warm-up that is cut short, and so on. By imagining a range of scenarios (and coping successfully with them), dancers can really build confidence that they are able to deal with whatever is thrown at them.

SAMPLE IMAGERY SCRIPT

It is the morning of the show, and you are on your way to the venue. The familiar symptoms are there: a slightly unsettled stomach, and a restlessness that makes you fidget. You know these are just signs that you are about to do something important that you care about, and you accept the symptoms as they are. There is no need to do anything differently from how you have planned. See yourself arriving at the venue, and what it looks like there. [pause]

Notice any bodily reactions that you have as you pass through the doors and get to the changing room. As you get in, you start going through your planned routine of what needs to be done in terms of clothing changes, hair and make-up, and so on. [pause]

At times, you get uninvited thoughts of how it will be if things don't go according to plan. You accept these too, knowing that thoughts are not facts and that they both come and go. Then you refocus on what you want to do. As your preparations are done, you make your way to the warm-up. See the people who are there and hear the music that has started to play. [pause]

You take your space on the floor and begin to warm up. Feel your body when it moves through the familiar exercises and feel how your heart rate starts to increase. You trust your body and all the practice that you have behind you. Go through the key warm-up exercises one by one, focusing specifically on how your body feels increasingly ready to perform. Thoughts and feelings may come and go; you simply acknowledge them and then refocus on the exercise. [pause]

It is now time for the performance to begin. Perhaps you immerse yourself in the music or in the emotions of the role or story that you will portray. Really sense those emotions, metaphors, musical phrasings, or stories in your body, and notice how they affect your movement quality as you wait for your stage entry. [pause] You are there in the wings, waiting for your cue, and there—you are on.

Notice what you can see and hear once you are on stage: the dimensions of the stage, the lights, and the audience. You take it all in and know that you are ready for this. [pause] Now continue to go through your variation—seeing, feeling, and hearing all the key aspects. Let your body become one with your role, conveying the role or message that is the essence of the piece. [pause]

Example addition for experienced imagers: Partway through the first variation, you notice that the angle of the stage lights makes it hard for you to see properly/your costume restricts you/your partner is out of sync. Notice any reactions to this challenge, and then refocus on what you are doing. Regardless of your reactions you maintain a calm clear focus on what you can control: your steps, your characterization, and your expression.

Go to HK*Propel* to download this form.

From S. Nordin-Bates, *Essentials of Dance Psychology* (Champaign, IL: Human Kinetics, 2023).

Teacher Instructions and Encouragement to Image

Beyond the provision of actual stimuli, such as pictures or music, teachers and choreographers support dancers' imagery by providing encouragement and instructions. Indeed, they often use imagery-laden language that dancers use to inspire and shape movement (e.g., Klockare et al., 2011; May et al., 2011; Nordin & Cumming, 2006c). At times, such language can be far more effective than technical instruction; in one study, students were reportedly confused by instructions to move in the three space planes until a metaphor of a metal sheet cutting their bodies was introduced (Torrents et al., 2013). In another study, a dancer was particularly frustrated by a choreographer who could not provide rich enough imagery to guide her:

> He just wasn't very . . . good at explaining, he'd just show it again and say, "It's got to be . . . like *this*," or something, and you're like, "Yes, but what *is* that?" "Eh, I don't know, you just take your arm up." And he'd be doing it in this amazing way, and you'd be like "Well, but how, what does that mean?" And that's very frustrating, if somebody can't explain what they're doing. (Nordin & Cumming, 2006b, p. 25)

Although teachers both use and encourage imagery, they typically do not do so systematically (Pavlik & Nordin-Bates, 2016). Imagery use might even be taken for granted at higher levels (e.g., to rehearse) but *how* to use it is still assumed rather than taught. Yet dancers appreciate and benefit from input about imagery as a psychological skill (Abraham et al., 2017; Bolles & Chatfield, 2009; Nordin & Cumming, 2006b, 2006c). In one study, higher-level dancers reported having been encouraged to image (i.e., do imagery as mental practice) more frequently than did lower-level dancers and having been given metaphorical images by teachers more often (Nordin & Cumming, 2006c). The dancers reported that this was the case both at the time of the study and when they were children. It would be interesting to discover whether those with imagery-encouraging teachers are actually more likely to reach higher levels or whether high-level dancers perceive and remember teacher behaviors differently.

Imagery Development

Like physical and technical dance skills, imagery use tends to be more advanced at higher levels of dance (for a review, see Pavlik & Nordin-Bates, 2016). This regards both quantity (i.e., more experienced dancers doing imagery more often) and quality (e.g., more experienced dancers generating more complex, detailed, and multisensory images, with greater control). Imagery types may also differ with experienced dancers using more movement quality and anatomical images and less imagery of appearance and basic metaphors (Bolles & Chatfield, 2009; Nordin & Cumming, 2006b). Young dancers have described imaging mostly outcomes when they were little, but that these images gradually deepened to include the process of moving toward that outcome (Muir et al., 2018). The increased time and energy spent on dance probably accounts for much of these effects, along with increased maturity. Dancers also seem to become better at generating facilitative images, with debilitative images becoming less frequent with experience (Muir et al., 2018; Nordin & Cumming, 2006c; Nordin-Bates et al., 2011b)—perhaps an indication of the greater emotional stability that people tend to gain with age (see chapter 1).

© Johannes Hjorth. Dancer: Ahtayaw Ea.

Consequences of Imagery

The literature investigating correlates and consequences of imagery is large. While this is especially true for sports, the dance literature is larger for imagery than for several other topics, and it has grown in recent years. Next, key findings from these two bodies of research are synthesized using the usual broad headings of well-being-related and performance-related consequences.

Well-Being-Related Consequences of Imagery

In reviews of the literature, the following well-being-related variables have been shown to be outcomes of imagery interventions in sports (Simonsmeier et al., 2021), have been identified as correlates of imagery in quantitative dance research, and/or are described as consequences of imagery use in qualitative research with dancers (Pavlik & Nordin-Bates, 2016):

- *Improved self-confidence*. By using imagery, dancers can become more confident about their skills; indeed, imaginal experiences are one of six sources of self-efficacy (situation-specific self-confidence) outlined in Bandura's (1977) theory of self-efficacy (see chapter 3).
- *Anxiety management*. Imagery helps performers deal with anxiety. For instance, dancers can habituate to their anxiety by rehearsing experiences (with accompanying anxiety symptoms) in their minds. This is the imagery equivalent of the exposure treatment typical in cognitive behavioral therapy (see introduction). In becoming accustomed to one's symptoms and by treating them with acceptance and equanimity, they become less anxiety-provoking and thus reinterpreted as less debilitating—or even facilitative. Movement quality images can also provide a helpful point of focus for anxious dancers (see the functional analysis examples later in this chapter).
- *Changed moods and emotions*. Imagery can inspire strong emotions—for instance, when reviving a memory of a joyous or distressing time. As such, images can be used to help dancers feel better in themselves but also to inform the moods and emotions of a choreography. For example, imagery allows performers to experiment with and hone the emotions they wish to experience or express when dancing (e.g., imagining doing steps fluidly, excitedly, tentatively, and so forth).
- *Improved motivation*. Engaging in imagery can help increase intrinsic motivation. For instance, the immersion that is possible through movement quality imagery can help dancers feel that a movement or class is truly meaningful. Images can also add fun and humor, encouraging dancers of all ages to play. Imaging long-term goals may help boost motivation when faced with challenges, because it reminds dancers of their reasons for working hard. Finally, dancers who note improvements from imagery practice are likely to enjoy their growing sense of competence (Abraham et al., 2017).
- *Improved focus*. A valuable link exists between the use of movement quality images and an external focus; this, in turn, is considered a valuable way of focusing because of its wide array of benefits (see chapter 6).

Performance-Related Consequences of Imagery

Beyond improvements in various aspects of well-being, reviews of the literature have also noted effects of imagery interventions on performance-related aspects in sports (Simonsmeier et al., 2021; Toth et al., 2020) and dance (Pavlik & Nordin-Bates, 2016):

- *Improved technical and physical performance*. Sport research clearly shows that imagery can enhance motor learning and performance. In fact, the combination of physical and mental (imagery) practice enhances performance more effectively than physical practice alone. Although physical practice is usually more effective than imagery, the effects can sometimes be comparable. The effects of imagery are robust across many settings, age groups, and levels, and retention tests indicate that these effects appear to last.
- *Improved dance performance*. In stark contrast to the sport literature in which all interventions use mental practice imagery, early intervention studies in dance all used movement quality images (for a review, see Pavlik & Nordin-Bates, 2016). For example, children learned faster with metaphors than with purely technical instructions (e.g., jumping over a puddle; Sacha & Russ, 2006). These children also appeared more engaged and attentive, especially in the early stages of learning. More recently, the impact of movement quality and body-related images from the Franklin Method (e.g., "spine as a rocket") have been examined,

with largely positive results (Abraham et al., 2019; Heiland et al., 2012; Heiland & Rovetti, 2013). For instance, student dancers improved aspects of développé performance after a three-day intervention coupling imagery with anatomical information (Abraham et al., 2019). In another movement quality imagery intervention (e.g., "heels like the prow of a ship leaving the dock"), no performance effects were noted (Couillandre et al., 2008).

> *Mental practice imagery* has also begun to be examined in dance (Abraham et al., 2017; Coker et al., 2015; Ritchie & Brooker, 2018). In the first such study, imagery had no measurable effects on elite dancers' performances of pliés or sautés (Coker et al., 2015). It may be difficult to affect the performance of well-engrained movements in a group of elite dancers with a short-term (one-hour) intervention, and the study design was limited. A more rigorous (randomized controlled trial), longer (six-week) and more theoretically grounded intervention registered significant elevé performance enhancement in a group of young dancers (Abraham et al., 2017). In an imagery intervention within contemporary dance classes, ballet students appeared to dance in a more embodied way, becoming more reliant on feel rather than surface-level thinking (Ritchie & Brooker, 2018).

> *Enhanced artistry and creativity.* Qualitative research and other dance writings clearly outline the importance of imagery as a creative and choreographic tool—from young children in their early dance classes to professional choreographers' practice and on-stage performances (e.g., Batson & Sentler, 2017; Hanrahan & Vergeer, 2001; May et al., 2011; Pavlik & Nordin-Bates, 2016). In one intervention using movement quality imagery, dance students appeared to gain in creativity while decreasing perfectionistic cognitions (Karin & Nordin-Bates, 2020). For more about the use of imagery to enhance creativity, see chapter 7.

> *Enhanced posture and other aspects of body control.* Dance has a rich heritage of somatic practices that utilize imagery as a core component; often, these aim to enhance various aspects of bodily awareness and control, such as posture and alignment (see Overby & Dunn, 2011). Imagery has also been shown to improve aspects of alignment in ballet (Couillandre et al., 2008).

> *Prevention and rehabilitation of injury.* Research in other domains has shown measurable benefits of imagery for injury prevention and rehabilitation. For example, an intervention performed during anterior cruciate ligament rehabilitation yielded both physical improvements (reduced knee laxity) and psychological benefits (reduced stress; Maddison et al., 2012). A combination of images was used, including mental rehearsal of rehab exercises (i.e., technique images), imagining successfully dealing with emotions (mastery), and imagining tissues returning to normal (body-related). In dance, intervention study authors have explained how improvements in alignment, muscle recruitment and technique that can result from imagery will contribute to injury prevention (e.g., Abraham et al., 2019; Couillandre et al., 2008). That some dancers do use imagery to prevent and rehabilitate injury has also been noted in descriptive research (Nordin & Cumming, 2005; Nordin-Bates et al., 2011b). Furthermore, there is some indication that psychological skills training incorporating imagery as one of several components can reduce injuries among dancers (Noh et al., 2007). For more suggestions of how to integrate imagery into injury rehabilitation, see chapter 13.

Why Imagery Has an Impact

The reasons (mechanisms) why imagery can influence how we feel and perform are multifaceted and not yet entirely understood. However, neuroscientific evidence helps us understand something about the way in which mental practice imagery works. These represent direct effects of imagery on performance, but there are also indirect effects via psychological variables such as self-confidence. Finally, the potential reasons for the effectiveness of movement quality imagery will be considered.

Direct Effects of Imagery: Functional Equivalence and the PETTLEP Model

To understand the direct effects of imagery on performance, researchers have been aided by the neuroscientific principle of **functional equivalence** (e.g., Jeannerod, 2001). This principle is founded on the notion that the brain networks activated during mental imagery partially overlap with those activated during actual perception and movement. In the case of visual imagery, this means that partly the same networks in our brains light up (activate) when we actually look at something (visual perception) and when we image that same something. Similarly, the networks that light up during kinesthetic imagery overlap with those activated during actual physical movement. Truly effective imagery, therefore, is functionally equivalent to actual perception (e.g., visual and auditory imagery) and actual movement. In this way, mental and physical practice are, in some sense, one and the same thing. This helps explain why imagery can have similar, although normally weaker, effects to physical practice. For a visual illustration of this notion of overlap, see figure 10.2; keep in mind, however, that the relative sizes of the different areas in the figure are not intended as accurate representations.

Helpfully, the neuroscientific findings have been translated into practical recommendations in the PETTLEP model (Holmes & Collins, 2001). The acronym is simply the gathering of the first letter from each of these components: physical, environmental, task, timing, learning, emotion, and perspective. Each component concerns an aspect of imagery that should be made as functionally equivalent as possible to real action (practice, performance, or perception). It can therefore be used as a checklist of sorts for both research and applied practice. Although the notion of functional equivalence between movement and imagery is now considered to be more complex than originally thought, researchers still conclude that the postulates of the model hold up to scientific scrutiny (Wakefield et al., 2013). Indeed, studies in sports, using many different tasks and populations, have demonstrated that incorporating one, or ideally several, aspects of the PETTLEP model into an intervention helps make it more effective (e.g., Wakefield et al., 2013).

Interestingly, sport research has only recently confirmed that imagery can be enhanced by adding small movements that resemble the movements the imagery is designed to enhance (Guillot et al., 2013); in dance, of course, this practice is commonplace and typically goes by the name of *marking* (Pavlik & Nordin-Bates, 2016). Other ways of enhancing the functional equivalence between imagery and actual practice is to use relevant music and props. The components of the PETTLEP model and associated recommendations for dance imagery are outlined in table 10.2.

Older writings in both sports and dance tended to advocate imagery after a relaxation procedure (see Pavlik & Nordin-Bates, 2016; Wakefield et al., 2013). In light of the evidence supporting the PETTLEP model such practices would seem contraindicated; to lie down with one's eyes closed is hardly equivalent to how most dances are learned or performed! Still, the PETTLEP model is focused on enhancing motor skill performance and other functions of imagery (e.g., using imagery to relax or to get into character for a role) may benefit from different recommendations. It also stands to reason that imagery will only be effective if the dancer is able to focus at least moderately well and doing imagery in a relaxing place may promote focus. Further research is required to address questions such as these.

Indirect Effects of Imagery Through Psychological Constructs

Imagery can also affect performance due to indirect effects through psychological variables such as self-confidence. For example, a dancer can feel more confident about her audition after imaging; this increased confidence enhances performance as she executes her movements more fully. The functional analyses in figure 10.3 illustrate how imagery can affect attentional focus, and thereby performance. In the first example, Jennifer experiences strong pre-performance anxiety for an upcoming performance. Her worries cause her to go over steps in great detail, fussing over skills that have already been automated. Keeping her mind busy in this way, Jennifer feels a bit better—at least she is working hard! Yet the detailed, technical imagery undermines the automaticity by which she is able to do the steps, and she experiences paralysis by analysis during the show (i.e., a major performance decrement; see chapter 6). In the second example, Jennifer's classmate Sarah prepares for the same performance with similar anxiety levels. Her approach to imagery is different, however, and she asks her teacher for an image to enhance her role interpretation. The image enables Sarah to immerse herself in her role, aiding automaticity and reducing

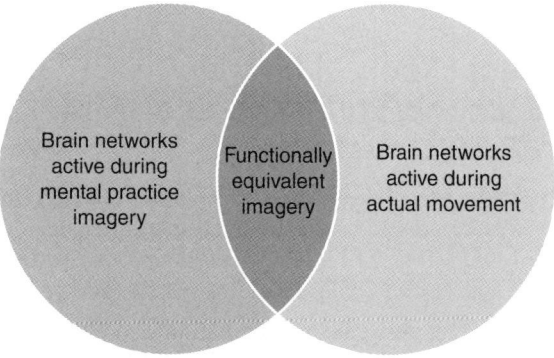

Figure 10.2 Brain networks activated during mental practice imagery and during actual movement partially overlap. This underpins the principle of functional equivalence and the recommendations of the PETTLEP model.

Table 10.2 **Components of the PETTLEP Model With Dance Examples**

Aspect	Description	Dance example
Physical	The performer should adopt appropriate posture and position while imaging	Dancer images standing up, perhaps adding small movements (marking)
Environmental	Imagery should be performed in the same environment as the actual movement will be performed	Dancer images in the studio as part of practice (e.g., while waiting his turn), and on stage before performance season
Task	Tasks imaged should be appropriate for the imager's skill level	Dancer images what is practiced physically in classes and rehearsals
Timing	Imagery should primarily be done in real time	Dancer uses appropriate music to help keep imagery in time and rhythm
Learning	Imagery content should be updated in line with learning	As challenge increases in class and rehearsal, so does the imagery
Emotion	Appropriate emotions should be incorporated into the imagery	Dancer images how he wants to feel (e.g., smooth) and emotions appropriate to particular choreographies
Perspective	Visual imagery should mostly be done from an internal perspective, as this is most functionally equivalent with actual movement	Dancer uses mainly internal visual imagery, with some use of external visual images when additional information can be gained (e.g., spacing)

Note: Adapted from Holmes and Collins (2001).

Imagery practice can be made more functionally equivalent by integrating music and small movements (marking).

the risk of her sharing Jennifer's fate. As an added long-term benefit, Sarah experiences growing abilities to image and to express herself.

Why Movement Quality Imagery Has an Impact

Movement quality images might enhance performance for several reasons, including enhanced understanding of complex movements and concepts (Bolles & Chatfield, 2009; Guss-West, 2020; Heiland & Rovetti, 2013; Karin, 2016; Nordin & Cumming, 2006b; Pavlik & Nordin-Bates, 2016; Torrents et al., 2013). For instance, a good metaphor might communicate a range of technical or anatomical information in a single holistic image. Dancers may also find metaphors more effective than technique images if they are perceived to give more guidance about how to do a movement (Muir et al., 2018). Other potential pathways include facilitation of optimal attention, enhancement of self-awareness and embodiment, refinement of internal motor plans, and promotion of whole-body integration (e.g., Abraham et al., 2019; Guss-West, 2020; Heiland & Rovetti, 2013; Karin, 2016). At this point, however, these potential mechanisms have been suggested rather than investigated systematically, and further research into the mechanisms behind the effects of movement quality imagery is warranted.

How Can Imagery Be Optimized?

Although the theoretical models introduced in this chapter were designed around mental practice imagery, most of their principles are likely to enhance movement quality imagery also. In line with the RAMDIU (Cumming & Williams, 2013), therefore, it is recommended that the function of imagery (*why*) is determined first: What do I want to achieve?

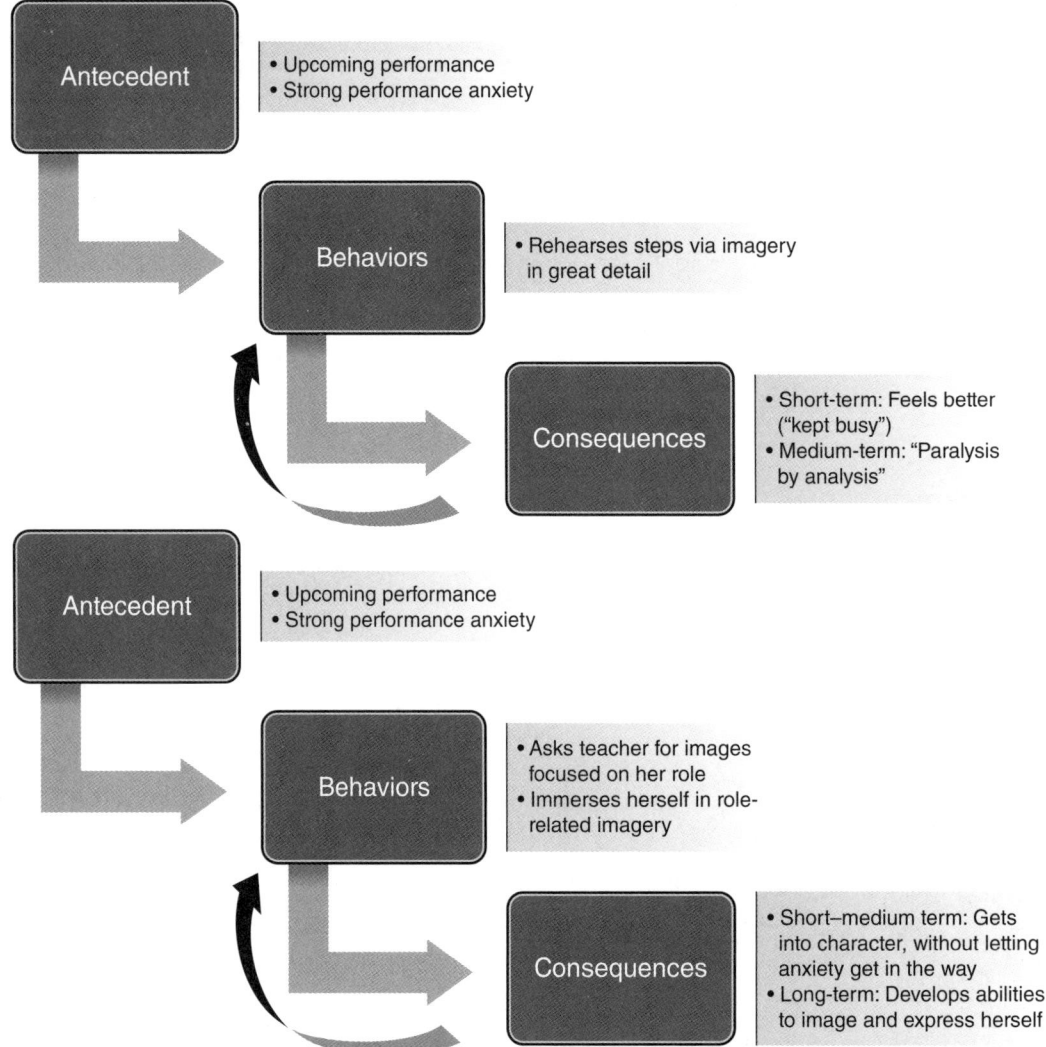

Figure 10.3 Functional analysis examples illustrating how different types of imagery may affect dancers. The recursive arrows indicate that the consequences make the behavior more likely to reoccur in similar situations in the future (behavior maintenance).

Thereafter, imagery types (*what*) likely to obtain the desired outcome can be selected, and the process planned to suit (*how*; e.g., frequency, perspective, and relevant sensory modalities). After considering RAMDIU components, the PETTLEP model can be used to ensure that images are as functionally equivalent to intended behavior as possible.

Optimizing Imagery in Motion: Movement Quality Imagery in Action

Given the many benefits of movement quality images, teachers are recommended to infuse their instructions with imagery. Depending on how naturally this comes to a teacher, images may be created on the spot or be preplanned. In any case, it is probably advantageous to gather new images on a regular basis, for instance, from books (e.g., Franklin, 2014; Guss-West, 2020; Karin et al., 2017), courses, watching other teachers, or otherwise. An image that works for one dancer may not work at all for another, so a rich variety is valuable, as is individualization. Dancers should be encouraged to personalize images that are given to them as well as to create and share their own (e.g., Hanrahan & Vergeer, 2001; Heiland et al., 2012; Nordin & Cumming, 2006b).

Optimizing Imagery During Breaks in the Action: Mental Practice in Class

It is beneficial to make mental practice imagery an integral part of class. For example, teachers may encourage dancers to mentally rehearse their goals for class before it starts or lead a brief imagery review after class has ended. Dancers can then be asked to image what they learned and did well (to anchor and reaffirm learning and boost perceived competence) and what they wish to focus on more in their next class (to aid goal setting). Even if short, such sessions indicate to dancers that imagery is worth taking seriously and can be a reminder to practice outside class.

Optimizing Imagery Outside of Dance: Mental Practice as Extra Training

For committed dancers in search of improving their performance and well-being, imagery practice should be an obvious addition to their schedule. This is especially the case when physical practice is not possible (e.g., when injured or traveling), inadequate (e.g., not enough time available to rehearse on a new stage), or needs to be cut down (e.g., when there is risk of overtraining). Literature suggests that such imagery should be deliberate and regular but does not need to take long. A recent meta-analysis found increased benefits with longer imagery practice times (Simonsmeier et al., 2021), but this does not necessarily mean that more is *more*. In fact, there seems to be an inverted-U relationship between session length and impact, and sessions of about 20 minutes 3 times a week appear to be optimal (Schuster et al., 2011). In some interventions as little as 10 minutes provided significant benefits (Toth et al., 2020), and for beginners just a few minutes can be a good start. Interventions lasting 4-6 weeks were found to be effective, but so were interventions lasting just 1-3 weeks (Toth et al., 2020). Of course, content (e.g., imagining a single movement vs. long variations) will affect the session length required, as will a dancer's age, commitment, and ability to focus.

Dancers can benefit from building up their images in layers (Hanrahan & Vergeer, 2001; Nordin & Cumming, 2005, 2007). For example, beginners might start by visually imaging short, simple variations. Once this has been mastered, they can gradually add content and sensory modalities (e.g., kinesthetic aspects of how the movement feels, the music, and then appropriate emotions). Those who are able to generate and control rich multisensory images may want to add challenges (e.g., costume failures, partnering mistakes) and practice how to handle such problems. For guidance on how to practice layering, see Cumming et al. (2017) and the Get Practical exercise for this chapter (form 10.1).

Isaac: Case Study of Imagery

Isaac, a 14-year-old ballet student, has poor posture. He is sure of this; he gets told all the time. To help him, his teachers variously tell him to lengthen his spine, lower his shoulder blades, and move his chest forward. Although he does try, the instructions seem to have little effect beyond a very short-term straightening up that looks rather tense. At one point, Isaac gets encouraged to go through choreography in his head before a show, and he can actually *see* his own slightly hunched-over posture in his mental image of himself!

Isaac subsequently meets a new teacher at the school, who seems to work differently from the others. For a start, he seems to be a great believer in the use of imagery and storytelling. At first Isaac and his friends find it all a bit weird. Isn't all that stuff more for kids, like when you first start dancing and pretend to be a butterfly or an airplane? Yet after a while, an exercise has such a profound effect on Isaac that he rapidly changes his mind. The exercise began with the teacher asking them to look forward out of their eyes. They did so, quietly wondering to themselves what this was about. Next, the teacher asked them to smell forward out of their noses, smile forward with their mouths, and listen forward with the ears. Then they were asked to do the same things, but in reverse; that is, they imagined having eyes on the backs of their heads and were asked what they could see. Next, what could they smell out of their back-of-the-head noses? How might they listen if someone was whispering behind them? Finally, what did it feel like to smile with a mouth on the back of the head? Even after this rather short exercise, Isaac immediately felt taller and lighter, and his chest was more open. He was surprised to see how much better his posture looked in the mirror.

Composite case study created on the basis of a conversation with Janet Karin, OAM, previously of the Australian Ballet School and an expert in integrating imagery and somatosensory principles into ballet training and rehabilitation.

CRITICAL ASPECTS OF RESEARCH INTO IMAGERY

1. Dance imagery intervention studies often recruit small samples, lack control groups, and combine imagery with other instructional modes (e.g., touch), which make it difficult to come to conclusions about the influence of imagery on dance. Hence, there is a need for researchers to use theoretical models and follow published recommendations to a greater extent than has hitherto been the case, while maintaining methodological diversity.

2. Some studies have found poor correlations between objective results (e.g., biomechanically assessed task performance) and subjective evaluations (dancers believing they have improved; e.g., Heiland et al., 2012). Researchers should therefore carefully consider what measures are best suited to their needs.

3. Dance and sports have much in common, and so the emphasis on mental practice imagery in sports and on movement quality imagery in dance is surprising. It would be valuable if researchers conducted further rigorous interventions with dancers to evaluate mental practice imagery. For instance, could a rehearsal process be enhanced by using consistently implemented imagery, such that dancers who received such training became better prepared for performance?

KEY POINTS AND RECOMMENDATIONS FOR IMAGERY IN DANCE

1. Imagery can be of great value in enhancing dance practice. Because it costs nothing, is 100% portable, and can be varied ad infinitum, it should perhaps be considered *the* supplementary training tool of choice for dancers.

2. Teachers are encouraged to nurture the imagery of their dancers. They can do so by providing rich varied movement quality imagery within classes (to use while dancing), by integrating mental practice (e.g., at the end of class), and by encouraging dancers to use imagery outside of dance (e.g., at home or while traveling).

Part IV
Dance Environments and Challenges

11

Motivational Climates

"I do not teach children. I give them joy."

Isadora Duncan, dancer

CHAPTER OBJECTIVES

After reading this chapter, you will be able to

1. describe what motivational climates are, as conceptualized in achievement goal theory;
2. describe the interpersonal styles studied in self-determination theory and how they contribute to motivational climates;
3. outline research findings regarding the likely consequences of healthy (task-involving, need supportive) and unhealthy (ego-involving, controlling) motivational climates;
4. critically discuss what may underpin the interpersonal style of dance teachers;
5. apply basic recommendations to create healthy motivational climates; and
6. think critically about the nature and impact of motivational climates in dance settings.

Key Terms

- autonomy support
- controlling leadership
- disempowering coaching
- ego-involving climate
- empowering coaching
- rationale
- task-involving climate

The English term *climate* is from the ancient Greek *klima*, and its main use is related to long-term manifestations of weather and atmospheric conditions. However, we have also used the word *climate* in a more figurative sense for several hundred years, typically to describe the "moral atmosphere," or "feel," of a particular context or situation. When paired with the word *motivation*, *climate* becomes focused on the interpersonal actions and structures that affect motivational states. For dance, then, motivational climates concern the social environment, or "feel," of a dance class, studio, or school.

What Is a Motivational Climate?

As you know from chapter 5, motivation researchers typically find it important to consider the quality of motivation rather than just its quantity. You may also recall that motivation quality is often studied via two major theoretical frameworks: achievement goal theory (AGT; Nicholls, 1984, 1989; Roberts, 1993) and self-determination theory (SDT; Deci & Ryan, 1985, 2000; Ryan & Deci, 2000). In the present chapter, we will delve into the interpersonal aspects that affect motivation quality according to both AGT and SDT. Therefore, you need to be familiar with the constructs introduced in chapter 5 before continuing with this chapter.

The term *motivational climate* originates in AGT (Ames, 1992); however, it is used as the title and umbrella concept for this entire chapter because the interpersonal styles that have been studied in SDT-based research as either supporting or thwarting basic psychological needs go hand in hand with those studied in AGT as creating either task- or ego-involving motivational climates. Some theorists have integrated constructs from both theories and thereby developed new phrases such as **empowering** (task-involving, need supportive) and **disempowering** (ego-involving, controlling) **coaching** (Duda, 2013).

Achievement Goal Theory Perspective: Task- and Ego-Involving Climates

Similar to the intrapersonal delineation of achievement goals into task- and ego-oriented goals, AGT theorists proposed that motivational climates can be task- and ego-involving (Ames, 1992). A **task-involving climate** conveys that success is about improvement and learning; such a climate typically involves encouragement to compare oneself to oneself (intrapersonal comparison), a focus on individual effort and improvement, viewing mistakes as part of learning, and collaboration as a valuable activity. An **ego-involving climate**, on the other hand, views success in terms of superiority. As such, these climates typically involve comparisons that are objective (e.g., who is the first to manage a difficult jump) or normative (e.g., who performs a variation with the highest technical competence). They are also more likely to feature rivalry between dancers, and teachers who favor some students over others and punish mistakes. So-called natural talent also becomes of greater interest (Ommundsen, 2001). In table 11.1, key differences between task- and ego-involving climates are summarized.

Research clearly shows that dancers in a wide variety of different styles and levels perceive their motivational climates as more task than ego oriented (Aujla et al., 2015; Carr & Wyon, 2003; de Bruin et al., 2009; Draugelis et al., 2014; Hancox et al., 2015; Nordin-Bates et al., 2012, 2014, 2016; Norfield & Nordin-Bates, 2012; Quested & Duda, 2009, 2010; Stark & Newton, 2014; Walker et al., 2011). Interestingly, one study indicated that teens (in this case, 13-18 years old) perceived their dance climates to be more ego-involving than did their younger peers (10-12 years old; Walker et al., 2011). Another study indicated that dancers perceived their studio climate to become more ego-involving over a six-month period leading into performance season (Nordin-Bates et al., 2012). Similarly, a non-AGT-based study found that dance students perceived their dance classes to become more disciplined and structured over time (van Rossum, 2001).

Table 11.1 **Characteristic Features of Task- and Ego-Involving Motivational Climates**

	Task-involving climates	Ego-involving climates
View on success	Success is improvement	Success is superiority
Assessments	Dancers compared to their own previous level	Dancers compared to others
Encourages and rewards	• Individual progress • Effort	• Objective or normative success • Talent
Interpersonal relations	• Collaboration • All dancers are equally important	• Rivalry • Favoritism
View on mistakes	• Part of the process • A way to learn	• Something to be avoided • May be punished

Some class designs are more likely to encourage interpersonal comparison than others.

In sum, it is possible that increased demands (associated with either aging or performance pressures) may lead teachers to become more ego-involving. Indeed, a study in sports found similar results and argued that high-level training environments are "prone to degrade" (become more ego-involving) as competition increases (Le Bars et al., 2009, p. 283).

Like goal orientations, task- and ego-involving climate features are orthogonal (Roberts et al., 1996); that is, they may coexist to varying degrees. For instance, a dance teacher may be largely focused on individual progress during the term, praising dancers who work in a focused, dedicated way to improve their own skills (i.e., she is task-involving). As the stress of looming examinations increases, however, she starts to compare dancers to one another and praises those who best perform the required skills (i.e., becomes more ego-involving, or "degrades").

Self-Determination Theory Perspective: Need-Supportive Versus Controlling Leadership

As you know from chapter 5, a cornerstone of SDT is that all humans require their basic psychological needs of autonomy, competence, and relatedness to be satisfied in order to experience self-determined motivation, well-being, and optimal functioning (Deci & Ryan, 1985, 2000; Ryan & Deci, 2000). It is therefore valuable to understand how these needs can be supported, as well as the opposite: how they become thwarted. This theme was introduced in chapter 5 from an intrapersonal perspective (i.e., how a person can support their own needs). In this chapter, we move on to the interpersonal perspective that most research in the area has focused on. This typically regards the dance teacher, but may also include other leaders (e.g., choreographers, managers), parents, and peers.

Need-Supportive Leadership

Because autonomy is about feeling volitional, free, and like oneself, it can be supported by seeing dancers as individuals; by giving opportunities for input, choice, and shared decision making; and by encouraging dancers to set their own goals, to experiment, and to express individuality (Deci & Ryan, 1985, 2000; Ryan & Deci, 2000). Another crucial component of **autonomy support** is to provide meaningful **rationale** (Assor et al., 2002)—that is, explaining why particular tasks are set or certain behaviors are required. Through rationale, dancers can better see the point of performing tasks and behaviors and are more likely to find them meaningful. For example, a teacher may explain that "lifting your leg this way helps you move it more freely," thereby helping students to understand that doing so is meaningful and worth learning. As a result, they are likely to feel more autonomous. Providing autonomy support is also likely to make a teacher seem more knowledgeable, because they are open to explaining the background to their actions and decisions and inviting comments and input.

Because our sense of competence is supported when we feel able and in control, it can be supported by ensuring that tasks are challenging but not overwhelming, by giving clear structured input, and by giving positive constructive feedback (Deci & Ryan, 1985, 2000; Ryan & Deci, 2000). Conveying belief in dancers' abilities through nonverbal means (e.g., pat on the back, encouraging nods) will also support perceived competence. For instance, consider dancers who are struggling to learn new material. By clarifying and perhaps adapting the exercise (or encouraging the dancers to do so), the teachers can help students feel more competent and successful. To further support the dancers' growing sense of competence, the teacher can then follow up the new attempts with positive ("This time the phrasing was cleaner; well done!") and/or constructive feedback ("Next time, try to move your arm a little faster.").

Because we feel related when experiencing warmth and rewarding relationships, our need for relatedness may be supported by taking an interest in each dancer as a person first and as a performer second, by encouraging collaboration and friendships among dancers, and by generally being warm and understanding. As an illustration, consider a company in which leaders care equally about their dancers regardless of their performance level and truly want to know how they feel. In such a company, relatedness is likely to be strong, not only for the dancers but for the leaders too, because need support has the distinct advantage of working bidirectionally (Solstad et al., 2015).

Controlling Leadership

Because need thwarting is highly problematic (Bartholomew et al., 2009, 2011; Deci & Ryan, 2000; Ryan & Deci, 2000; see also chapter 5), it is important to consider how leaders sometimes thwart the needs of their dancers. Such behaviors are often considered under the umbrella term of **controlling leadership** (Bartholomew et al., 2009, 2010) because they are concerned with leaders exercising their higher level of power to make dancers conform, obey, or behave in particular ways—that is, to control them. For instance, controlling leaders may manipulate, threaten, intimidate, pressure or punish their dancers, or make them do meaningless repetitions of a task against their best interests. They may say that exercises must be done in a particular way because "I said so," "it is the only way to do it right," or "that is just the way it is." In so doing they thwart autonomy, because dancers feel far from agency and meaningfulness.

Controlling leaders may also make dancers feel inadequate or inferior by being harsh and critical, by pointing out every mistake, by being sarcastic ("Have you not kept up?"), or by shaming them in front of others. Such behaviors thwart competence because dancers do not feel good enough or in control. Finally, controlling leaders may make dancers feel alienated or disrespected by distancing themselves from them, by emphasizing their own superiority ("I am the boss"), by not caring about them as people (only as performers if and when they perform excellently), or by bullying and belittling them. Clearly, such behaviors would thwart dancers' needs for relatedness.

In SDT-based studies, dancers report that they perceive their basic needs to be at least moderately (if not highly) supported by their teachers (Quested & Duda, 2009, 2010, 2011a, 2011b). Similarly, perceived levels of controlling leadership generally appear to be low (Haraldsen et al., 2019). At the same time, the authoritarian behaviors described by numerous authors as characteristic of traditional dance teaching can be seen as examples of controlling dance leadership (e.g., Aalten, 2005; Alterowitz, 2014; Hamilton & Stricker, 1989; Johnston, 2006; Lakes, 2005; Morris, 2003; Pickard, 2015; Smith, 1998). In such texts, examples of teachers and choreographers who belittle, insult, patronize, publicly shame, and even hit dancers abound, with dancers expected to be silent, obedient, and grateful receivers of whatever instructions their leader chooses to deliver.

In a rare qualitative investigation using SDT as a foundation, it was demonstrated that professional performers varied in their climate perceptions: from mostly need supportive to mostly controlled (Haraldsen et al., 2020), with differences across people, time, and contexts. This serves as a useful reminder that motivational climate perceptions (just like need satisfaction and motivational regulations) are complex, multifaceted, and subject to change. For example, all the interviewed dancers described their relatedness as mostly supported by good friendships, but autonomy as increasingly thwarted due to a strong frustration with what they perceived to be a rigid, authoritarian training system.

In a strong backlash against authoritarian practices, numerous scholars have proposed strategies to promote learning, health, and success in dance, and indeed a humanization of the art (e.g., Alterowitz, 2014; Barr & Oliver, 2016; Berg, 2017; Burnidge, 2012; Choi & Kim, 2015; Green, 2003; Ritchie & Brooker, 2020; Rowe & Xiong, 2020; Salosaari, 2001; Shilcutt et al., 2020; Whittier, 2017; Zeller, 2017). For example, Morris (2003) argued that teachers should treat ballet vocabulary as flexible rather than static and invite dancers to shape their own learning (i.e., autonomy support); if not, both technical and creative development are likely to be stymied. The authors seeking progress in this area outline their approaches using highly varied terminologies (e.g., feminist pedagogy, student agency, empowerment, somatic authority, activist approach, intentionality), all of which encompass need-supportive behaviors. SDT should perhaps not be seen as a panacea, but using shared terminology to a greater extent would allow for better synthesis and comparison of individual studies, thereby enhancing understanding and the formulation of clear guidelines for practice.

Origins of Motivational Climates: What Makes Teachers Support or Thwart Healthy Motivation?

A key finding from sports is that when leaders' own basic psychological needs are fulfilled, when they coach for self-determined reasons, or when they generally feel well, they are more likely to support the needs of people in their charge (for a review, see Matosic et al., 2016; Rocchi & Pelletier, 2017). Other antecedents of autonomy support include coaches who perceive their group to be socially united (Solstad et al., 2015) and work environments that provide support, job security, and professional development opportunities (Matosic et al., 2016; Rocchi & Pelletier, 2017). Non-sport research further indicates that cultural norms and relativist versus absolutist beliefs (i.e., knowledge is relative and subjective vs. certain and objective) can influence the extent of need support provided by teachers (Matosic et al., 2016). These findings appear relevant when considering different dance subcultures and how they may embrace need-supportive teaching to varying extents.

On the darker side, studies indicate that sport coaches are more likely to experience need thwarting and controlled motivation when they experience some form of ill-being, stress, pressure, or limitation (e.g., being evaluated, work-life conflict, unsupportive colleagues, few development opportunities; Matosic et al., 2016; Morbée et al., 2020; Rocchi & Pelletier, 2017). Studies in education have found a sense of obligation to comply with a school curriculum to be a source of pressure for teachers, which may be relevant also in dance (Matosic et al., 2016). Dancer and choreographer Murray Louis suggested something similar many years ago: "Many choreographers get the reputation for being bastards. When one is fighting for his life, when one is drowning, he forgets his manners; he hasn't time to cut his nails" (Louis, 1980, p. 122).

Leaders with poor quality motivation experience greater ill-being, support their performers' needs to a lesser extent, and become more controlling toward their performers (Matosic et al., 2016; Morbée et al., 2020; Rocchi & Pelletier, 2017). Leaders are also more likely to be controlling when they are ego-involved, narcissistic, or perceive their performers to be disengaged (Lakes, 2005; Matosic et al., 2016, 2017). In a particularly strong example, Gus Solomons, Jr. (a choreographer, critic and educator, and former dancer for Martha Graham and Merce Cunningham), shared the following in an interview:

> I was very insecure and very unhappy. My self-affirmation was wrapped up in the results I was getting from the students. And if they weren't doing what I wanted, . . . then it made me angry because then I was failing. Because, see, it was all about me. . . . Well, I have spent a lot of time thinking about this. . . . I simply got angry if I was not getting what I needed. . . . My reaction was "Do it! Make me feel good!" Over the course of time, as I became better able to deal with my own issues, I didn't need to get affirmation from the students. . . . So I just became just much more joyful about teaching because then we were all collaborating together. (from Lakes, 2005, p. 10)

Along similar lines, a study in dance and aesthetic sports found that more perfectionistic leaders reported supporting their performers' basic needs to a lesser extent (Nordin-Bates & Jowett, 2022). In sum, it appears that the personal concerns of leaders are passed on to performers—a kind of rubbing off—through impaired need support.

Need-supportive leadership is positive not only for performers: indeed, coaches who *provide* more need support also perceive their *own* needs to be more satisfied (Solstad et al., 2015). In sum, therefore, dance teachers who feel well and who are themselves self-determined are likely to teach better, with benefits both to themselves and others. We may see this as a trickle-down effect; knowing what the basic psychological needs are and how they can be supported is important not only for teachers but also managers and other leaders. Given the prevalence of insecure jobs in the dance industry, this is certainly something to consider. Although leaders may try to bring forth results by controlling behaviors, this is likely to backfire; indeed, supporting basic psychological needs will always be the better way to nurture healthy motivation, performance, adherence, and well-being—even when one is under pressure or when teaching the seemingly unmotivated (Matosic et al., 2016).

Finally, keep in mind that the potential origins of motivational climates outlined in this section are only indicative of the research conducted in performance psychology and with an SDT lens. Many other potential explanations exist, not least from areas such as dance pedagogy and dance history. For instance, Lakes's (2005) account of potential reasons behind authoritarian behaviors in dance includes its historical roots (e.g., emergence of the vocational school system) and the common practice of dancers becoming teachers on the basis of technical and artistic expertise rather than pedagogical and reflective skills. In one interview study, the Confucianist ethos of Korean society was described as the source of hierarchical leadership that could not be questioned but which caused the dancers high levels of stress (Noh et al., 2009).

Consequences of Motivational Climates

A key concern of researchers and practitioners alike is the influence that motivational climates have. The present section focuses on theoretically grounded AGT- and SDT-based research, but other approaches to studying dance leadership and its impacts also exist (e.g., Rafferty & Wyon, 2006; van Rossum, 2004).

An Achievement Goal Theory Perspective: Consequences of Task- and Ego-Involving Motivational Climates

While the research foundation in dance may be relatively small, the correlates and consequences of perceiving one's training and performance climate as either task- or ego-involving have been examined for several decades in domains such as sports (e.g., Harwood et al., 2015; Keegan, 2018). As a result, it has become clear that there are major advantages to perceiving one's climate as task-involving, whereas ego-involving features are problematic in several ways. The reasons behind such findings are the same as for task and ego orientations; that is, task-involving climates help more dancers feel competent and successful more often, whereas ego-involving climates undermine this possibility. Only the best dancers are likely to feel competent and successful in an ego-involving climate, yet even they are likely to struggle, at least over time: partly because nobody is constantly the best, and partly because the rivalry and favoritism that often feature in such a climate does nobody any favors. For instance, being the teacher's pet may alienate an individual from their peers, thus undermining friendship and a sense of equality (i.e., the need for relatedness).

Ego-involving climates also tend to be associated with a view that talent is important (Ommundsen, 2001). Yet talent is often perceived to be out of a dancer's control (see chapter 12). Relying on talent therefore makes a dancer's sense of competence fragile, because who knows exactly what their talent is or allows? If they move up to a more selective competitive group, they may wonder: "What if I don't have what it takes at this new level?" Or as they are aging, "What if I no longer have what it takes?" Clearly, a climate that focuses on aspects within dancers' control (e.g., effort, use of good learning strategies, and collaboration) is far more likely to promote both well-being and performance.

Well-Being-Related Consequences of Task- and Ego-Involving Motivational Climate Perceptions

In reviews of the correlates and outcomes related to motivational climates, Harwood et al. (2015) and Keegan (2018) presented a variety of findings as consistently emerging from the sport and physical activity literature. Overall, they are very similar to those for individual goal orientations (see chapter 5):

> Task-involving climate perceptions are associated with indicators of healthy individual motivation, including task orientation, greater need satisfaction, and self-determined motivational regulations. Indeed, both AGT and SDT stipulate that the influence of motivational climate perceptions on well-being is *mediated by* individual achievement goals (AGT) and need satisfaction/self-determined motivation (SDT). Put simply, motivational climate perceptions affect individual motivation, which in turn leads to particular outcomes (see figure 11.1).

> Task-involving climate perceptions are also associated with well-being indicators such as self-esteem and self-confidence, perceived competence, positive affect, and flow (absorption in optimal experience; Csikszentmihalyi, 1990). They are also associated with lower levels of negative affect and negative cognitions (e.g., worry).

> Ego-involving climate perceptions are associated with indicators of unhealthy individual motivation, including ego orientation, lower need satisfaction, and controlled motivational regulations.

> Ego-involving climate perceptions are also associated with lower levels of self-esteem and self-confidence, and with more frequent negative affect, negative cognitions (e.g., worry), and perfectionism.

Several studies into motivational climates and their correlates have been conducted in dance. In one of the first, it was confirmed that university dance students who perceived a more ego-involving motivational climate were more likely to be ego oriented, but those who felt they were dancing in a more task-involving motivational climate were more likely to be task oriented (Carr & Wyon, 2003). Moreover, ego-involving climate perceptions (in particular, perceiving that teachers punished mistakes) predicted stronger anxiety and perfectionistic concerns. A later study demonstrated that when dancers perceived their training climate to become more ego-involving over time, they also became more anxious (Nordin-Bates et al., 2012). A qualitative case study has further illustrated how anxiety and perfectionism may be nurtured through ego-involving motivational climates (Nordin-Bates & Abrahamsen, 2016). On a more positive note, students who reported that their motivational climate was more task-involving were also more likely to be highly engaged in dance (i.e., confident, vigorous, dedicated, and enthusiastic; Draugelis et al., 2014). In that study, it also appeared that perceptions of the dance climate as highly task-involving could act as a buffer, keeping up the confidence and dedication of anxious dancers.

Dancers who perceive their training climate to be more task-involving are also more likely to report that their basic psychological needs are satisfied, whereas the opposite is true for ego-involving climate perceptions (Norfield & Nordin-Bates, 2012; Quested & Duda, 2009, 2010). In turn, higher levels of need satisfaction are associated with more positive and less negative affect (Quested & Duda, 2009, 2010), and with enjoyment and self-reported effort (Norfield & Nordin-Bates, 2012). Studies like these highlight the compatibility of AGT and SDT and illustrate a sequence whereby motivational climate perceptions influence various outcomes through individual motivation quality. For an illustration of such a sequence, see figure 11.1. AGT-based measures of motivational climates have also been combined with a measure of caring climates (i.e., the extent to which dance students perceived their

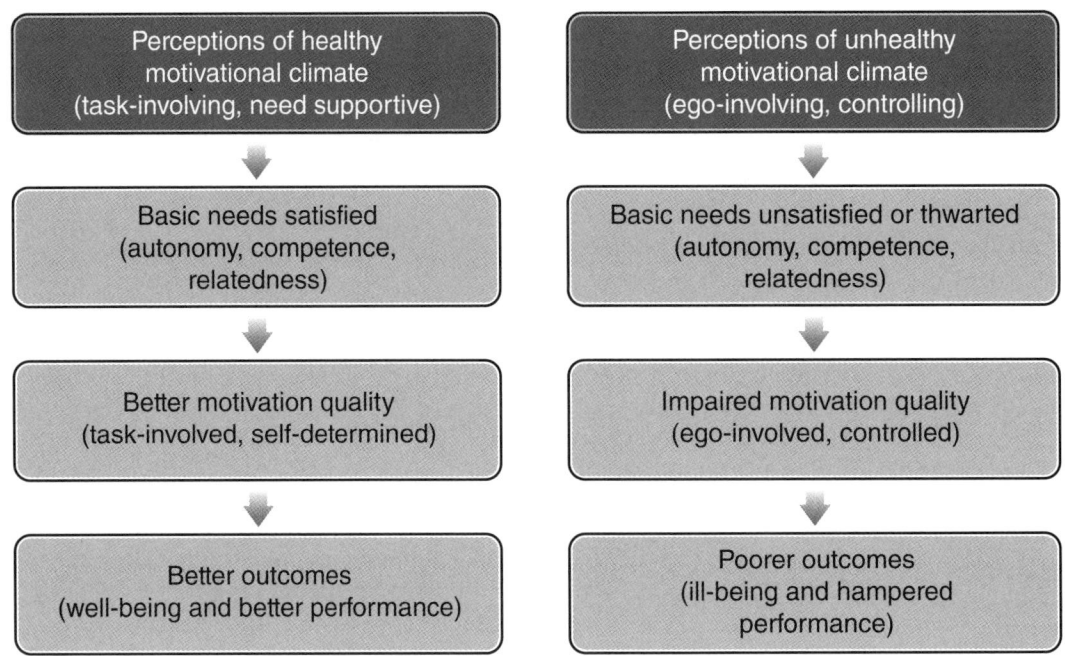

Figure 11.1 The motivational sequences inherent to AGT and SDT, whereby perceptions of the motivational climate/interpersonal styles affect motivation quality and ultimately well-being- and performance-related outcomes. In SDT, this is additionally shown to occur with need satisfaction as an interim step.

studio to be welcoming, supportive, and valuing of individual students; Stark & Newton, 2014). It was found that dancers in climates characterized as high in task-involving and caring features, yet low in ego-involving features, reported better well-being than dancers in climates that were more ego- and less task-involving and caring. For instance, the former group experienced more positive and less negative affect as well as better relationships to both teachers and peers.

A study with dancers and gymnasts found that dieting frequency was best predicted by ego orientation, focus on body mass, and perceptions of the motivational climate as less task-involving (de Bruin et al., 2009). Along similar lines, dancers in more task-involving and caring climates report better body esteem than their peers in more ego-involving climates (Stark & Newton, 2014). Overall, it is possible that task-involving climates exert a protective effect on performers' health (de Bruin et al., 2009). Like most studies in this area, however, these investigations were cross-sectional in nature; as such, we may only draw conclusions about relationships between variables (i.e., correlates of motivational climate perceptions) and not about causality (i.e., consequences, effects).

Most results in this literature are consistent and in line with what might be expected, but some are not. First, Carr and Wyon (2003) noted that dancers who perceived teachers to emphasize effort and learning (a task-involving feature) seemed more likely to exhibit both perfectionistic strivings and concerns. Second, a longitudinal study indicated that dancers who perceived a more task-involving climate increased their perfectionistic strivings over time (Nordin-Bates et al., 2014). Finally, task-involving climate perceptions have predicted increased risk of disordered eating development over time among male dancers (Nordin-Bates et al., 2016).

What can be made of these seemingly contradictory findings? First, even task-involving features can perhaps be taken too far: If dancers feel pressure to work *very* hard and *constantly* improve, it is possible they may develop perfectionistic tendencies or even disordered eating attitudes. Another possibility is that the way in which task-involving motivational climate features are typically measured in these studies (i.e., via the perceived motivational climate in sport questionnaire [PMCSQ-2]; Newton et al., 2000) is not fully in line with the underlying conceptualization or intent of the construct. For instance, an item such as, "The teachers make sure dancers improve on skills or movements they're not good at," is presumably meant to be interpreted as teacher support for individual progress (i.e., task involving).

However, it might also be scored highly by dancers who perceive their teacher to be pressuring them (e.g., "You had better work until you know this solo perfectly!"). For an in-depth discussion on the PMCSQ-2 and its applicability to dance, see Hancox et al. (2015).

Finally, it is possible that when dancers perceive themselves to be in a truly task-involving climate, they are more willing to admit to problems such as disordered eating (Nordin-Bates et al., 2016). As you can see, not all research in the area is fully in line with theory. Nevertheless, the main message remains intact: Task-involving climates are consistently associated with positive correlates and outcomes (Harwood et al., 2015; Keegan, 2018).

Performance-Related Consequences of Task- and Ego-Involving Motivational Climate Perceptions

A summary of established findings regarding motivational climate perceptions and performance-related variables in sport and physical activity (Harwood et al., 2015; Keegan, 2018) is provided next. Again, you will notice that these are similar to the correlates of individual goal orientations outlined in chapter 5.

› Task-involving climate perceptions are associated with attitudes and strategies related to better learning and performance, such as persistence, effort, and help-seeking, with adherence and with prosocial moral functioning (e.g., respect for others, fairness). They are also related to performing better in an objective sense, to a lesser use of maladaptive learning strategies (e.g., avoidance, self-handicapping), and to less antisocial moral functioning (e.g., deception, cheating).

› Ego-involving climate perceptions are associated with greater use of maladaptive learning strategies and with more antisocial moral functioning.

Related literature shows that being in a task-involving climate benefits not only youngsters and performers in development, but also elite athletes (Pensgaard & Roberts 2002). Few studies have explored performance-related correlates or outcomes of motivational climates in dance, but students in a talent center who perceived their climate to be more ego-involving were less likely to adhere (stay in dance) over time (Aujla et al., 2015). Most recently, it was found that children who were told that pirouettes were a skill that can be learned (a more task-involving instruction) performed better than children who were told that pirouettes were about ability (a more ego-involving instruction; Harter et al., 2019).

To further illustrate the potential influence of motivational climate perceptions on dancers, consider the functional analyses in figure 11.2. Different antecedents (i.e., teacher behaviors indicative of ego- vs. task-involving climates) result in different dancer behaviors (i.e., greater ego- vs. task-involvement) and therefore also different consequences. Starting with the first example analysis, consider Angela who is taking class with a teacher who is mostly concerned with the most skilled dancers in the room—those he perceives to be naturally talented. He points out uncontrollable aspects (e.g., leg length) as favorable, and praises those who perform tasks better than their peers. Attempting to enhance learning, he tells those he perceives to be less talented to observe how their supposedly more talented peer does things. Wary of what this climate means in terms of being labeled as successful or not, Angela only practices things she is good at, especially when the teacher might be watching. For instance, she mostly sits in the splits during warm-up because she feels competent at it. This way, Angela maintains her sense of competence in the short term; but because stretching is not an optimal warm-up task, she is less prepared for class and has increased her risk of injury. She has also hampered her learning, because she avoids trying new things that may suit her better.

Now consider Angela in a more task-involving climate (second example analysis; figure 11.2). Here, she feels that the teacher is mostly focused on individual progress, encouraging all dancers to challenge themselves at whatever level they may be. He praises those who are putting in effort and remain focused on the task at hand and suggest that they learn together through collaborative tasks such as pair work. Because this climate makes her feel safe, Angela chooses to practice many things that she wants to learn, whether the teacher is watching or not. For instance, she does a full range of warm-up tasks to prepare for class, including those she is not particularly good at. That this does not make her look good or superior to others is of little concern, and she reduces her risk of injury in the upcoming class. She has also maximized her learning because she tries new things.

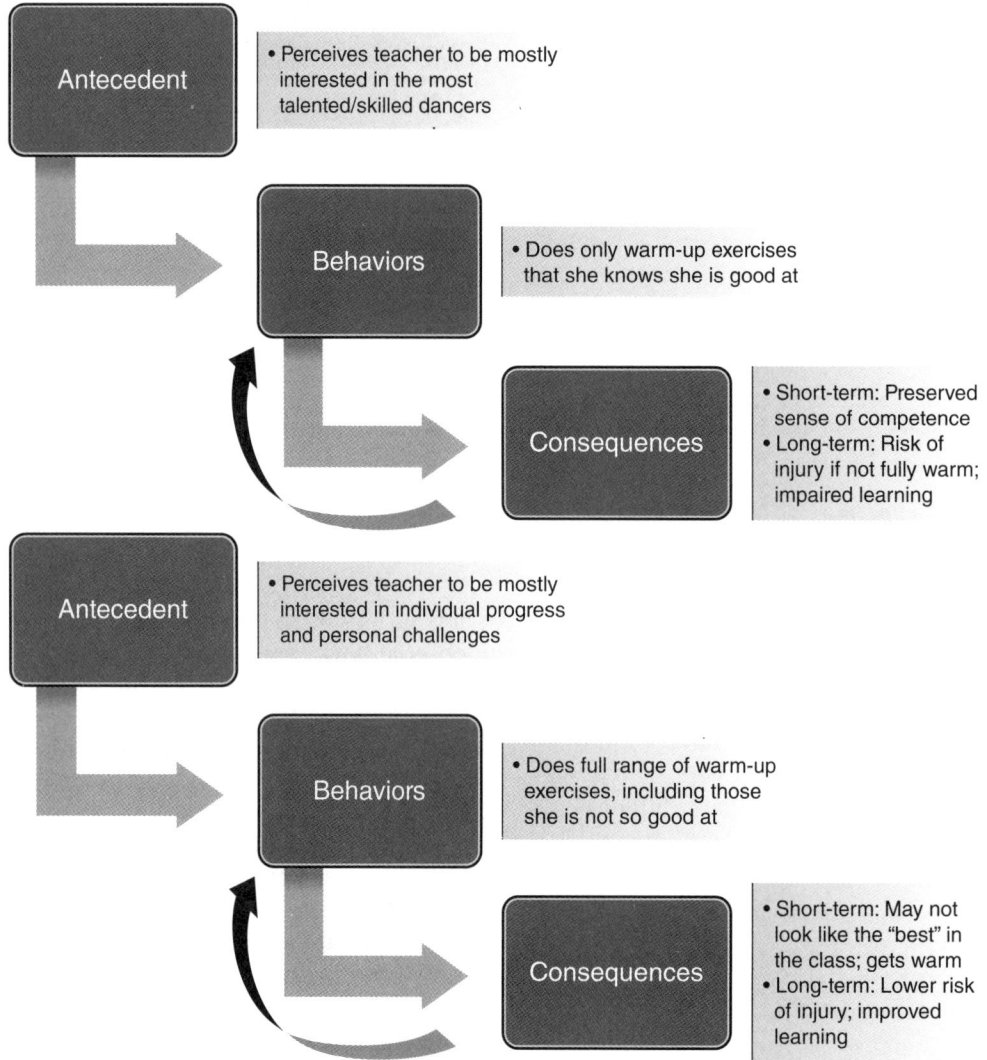

Figure 11.2 Functional analysis examples of how different motivational climate cues may induce different behaviors and outcomes for a dancer. The recursive arrows indicate that the consequences make the behavior more likely to reoccur in similar situations in the future (behavior maintenance).

THINKING CRITICALLY

- What characterizes the motivational climate where you dance or teach? Can you identify task-involving features, ego-involving features, or both?
- Do you have experience of a motivational climate that changed over time? If so, did that have any particular consequences?
- How can even highly selective and competitive dance settings ensure that they remain task-involving?

Consequences of Need-Supportive Versus Controlling Leadership

The extensive evidence base that underpins SDT means that there is ample evidence from sports and exercise regarding the correlates and consequences of experiencing higher versus lower levels of need support. The literature has also grown regarding experiences of controlling coaching in sports, and an increasing number of SDT-based publications have emerged in dance. Overall, this literature suggests that we can be confident in need support being associated with positive consequences, and controlling leadership being associated with negative consequences.

Well-Being-Related Consequences of Need-Supportive Versus Controlling Leadership

In reviewing research into coach interpersonal styles in sports, SDT scholars (Bartholomew et al., 2009; Ntoumanis et al., in press; Standage et al., 2018) have highlighted the following results:

> Perceptions of need support are associated with greater need satisfaction and with having self-determined motivation for an activity, both in the short term and in the long run (even across many years).

> Those who perceive greater need support are more likely to report indices of well-being such as positive affect, vitality, enjoyment, satisfaction, and self-esteem. They are also less likely to report signs of ill-being (e.g., burnout, depression).

> Perceptions of controlling behaviors from leaders are associated with experiencing greater need thwarting and more controlled motivation.

> Those who perceive their coach to be controlling are also more likely to report indices of ill-being such as negative affect, anxiety, shame, guilt, low self-esteem, burnout, depression, and disordered eating.

Several studies have examined perceptions of need-supportive teacher behaviors in dance, their correlates, and their consequences. Two of the first confirmed that perceptions of autonomy support from dance teachers is positively associated with self-determined motivation and negatively associated with controlled motivation and amotivation (Balaguer et al., 2011; Quested & Duda, 2011b). These studies yielded further results in line with the motivational sequence illustrated in figure 11.1: For instance, when autonomy support was not perceived to be forthcoming, amotivation was more pronounced, which in turn predicted lower self-esteem, greater social physique anxiety, and body dissatisfaction (Quested & Duda, 2011b). The authors suggested that amotivated dancers may engage in health-compromising behaviors as a result of their unsatisfied need for autonomy. In another study, vocational dance students perceived a decrease in autonomy support over a period of a school year, a change associated with increased burnout symptoms (Quested & Duda, 2011a).

In a later study with vocational students, perceptions of empowering (task-involving and need supportive) and disempowering (ego-involving and controlling) environments were captured (Hancox et al., 2017). When dancers perceived an empowering climate, positive affect during classes improved, and this change was mediated by heightened need satisfaction. Conversely, dancers who perceived a disempowering climate increased their negative affect during class, a change mediated by heightened need thwarting. Findings from qualitative investigations support these quantitative findings: For instance, when young dance students felt encouraged to take responsibility for their own learning (i.e., autonomy support), this seemed to enhance motivation and commitment (Aujla et al., 2014). In contrast, poor relatedness support (e.g., difficulty making friends) can contribute to dropout (Walker et al., 2012).

Recent literature further indicates that the SDT-derived constructs of controlling leadership and psychological need thwarting can help explain why and when perfectionistic concerns become problematic. Specifically, junior elite performers with higher levels of perfectionistic concerns were more likely to report higher levels of both controlled motivation and performance anxiety, partly because their need for competence was thwarted (i.e., statistical mediation; Haraldsen et al., 2019). The perfectionistic performers were more likely to experience these problems when they perceived their learning climate to be controlling. Put differently, controlling climates seem to exacerbate the risk that performers with perfectionistic concerns will experience problems. The positive converse of such effects was demonstrated in another recent study in which higher levels of autonomy support seemed to buffer perfectionistic dancers from experiencing symptoms of burnout while boosting their engagement (Jowett et al., 2021).

Performance-Related Consequences of Need-Supportive Versus Controlling Leadership

The consequences of need-supportive and controlling leadership extend to performance-related factors (Ntoumanis et al., in press; Standage et al., 2018). These include greater engagement, adherence over time, better exercise intentions and attendance, and better actual performance for performers who perceive higher degrees of need support. The literature regarding performance-related consequences of controlling leadership is small but has been associated with lesser engagement. Of course, leaders who use controlling strategies do this for a reason—because they teach the way they were taught, for example. Moreover, such methods *can* improve performance in the short term as performers do their utmost to please their instructor and avoid negative consequences (e.g., punishment). It is especially in the long run that negative effects on performance-related consequences emerge, but well-being-related consequences can be instant. For example, a dancer whose ballet master shouts at them that they "really should be better at this by now" may try very hard indeed to succeed (potentially leading to a short-term performance improvement), even if they are seething inside (a well-being decrement).

Perceptions of need support positively predict self-determined motivation in dance; this, in turn, predicts intentions to continue dancing (Balaguer et al., 2011). Need support, especially for autonomy, also nurtures creativity in dance (Clements & Nordin-Bates, 2022; Nordin-Bates, 2020; Watson et al., 2012). Conversely, controlling leadership behaviors may inhibit creativity while nurturing perfectionism (Nordin-Bates, 2020). Some teachers are intuitively aware of these kinds of effects: for instance, teachers in one study explained how they deliberately invited student input and valued individuality (i.e., autonomy support) and created a safe, friendly environment (relatedness support) while refraining from being critical and fussing over details (competence thwarting), so as to help students let go of worries and thereby promote learning, development, and creativity (Nordin-Bates, 2020).

How Are Healthy Motivational Climates Created?

Because healthy motivational climates are associated with a wide variety of benefits, it is crucial for leaders to know how to create such climates. As noted, we have considered task-involving and need supportive motivational climates to be healthy climates. Separate sections follow for each to remain clear about their theoretical homes in AGT and SDT, respectively. But these theoretical approaches are fully compatible; for instance, a task-involving climate typically supports the basic psychological needs. The sections that follow focus only on interpersonal strategies, and specifically teacher-led behaviors; for more information about what individual dancers can do to support their own healthy motivation, see chapter 5.

Creating a Task-Involving Climate

As already outlined, task-involving climates promote the belief that success is about improvement, and consequently, they focus on self-referenced learning, effort, and collaboration. Hence, the creation of such a climate involves teachers (or other leaders) implementing such strategies and behaviors. In the education domain, researcher Epstein (1989) created the acronym TARGET to encompass six dimensions of a task-involving climate: task, authority, recognition, grouping, evaluation, and timing (table 11.2). The TARGET-approach became widespread in applied sport psychology, and some have used it in structured interventions. In one such study, it was found that not only did instructors trained in TARGET principles become perceived as more task-involving, but their performers also reaped benefits in terms of healthy motivation and engagement (Cecchini et al., 2014). In dance, Andrzejewski and colleagues (2013) expressed concerns over the preoccupation with outcomes and interpersonal comparison over process and optimal development that they saw in their students, especially among those from highly competitive studio settings. As an antidote, they provided several examples of how TARGET principles may be used in dance.

Go to HK*Propel* to download the lettering art highlighting the importance of focusing on improving, rather than proving, oneself.

Perhaps you have already noticed significant overlap between the principles outlined here and what you already know about support for basic psychological needs; as you move into the following section, see if you can specifically map the six TARGET dimensions to support for each of the needs of autonomy, competence, and relatedness.

Supporting Basic Psychological Needs

Teixeira et al. (2020) involved a large team of SDT experts in an unprecedented attempt to compile need-supportive behaviors used successfully in research interventions, resulting in a total of 21 well-evidenced techniques. Based in such evidence, table 11.3 presents a list of behaviors specifically geared to dance.

We should be mindful that the need-supportive strategies outlined in table 11.3 are not necessarily better the more often they are used. Just like motivation itself, need support is as much about quality as it is about quantity. Taking choice as an example, every exercise in a class should probably not be open to choice because structure and timekeeping are then likely to suffer. The important thing is that dancers do get opportunities to choose things that

Table 11.2 **TARGET: Six Dimensions to Create a Task-Involving Motivational Climate**

	Underpinning principles
Task	- Create meaningful and varied tasks - Focus on learning and improvement - Downplay competitive aspects and rivalry - Use tasks/setups that make interpersonal comparison difficult - Focus on process over product (outcome) - Adapt tasks to individual needs (or let participants do so for themselves)
Authority	- Allow performers input in decision making - Let performers take on leadership roles - Use peer-to-peer feedback - Provide choices - Encourage dialogue
Recognition	- Reward individual progress, not objective success - Treat everyone with equal respect
Grouping	- Use varied, heterogeneous groupings - Avoid grouping by ability - Encourage collaboration
Evaluation	- Evaluate progress toward individual goals, not just success - Evaluate privately, not in front of others - Positively evaluate the learning inherent in mistakes
Timing	- Give enough time to master tasks (avoid time pressure) - Let performers have an input regarding time required

One way to nurture a healthy motivational climate is to encourage interactive peer learning.

Table 11.3 **Strategies to Support the Basic Psychological Needs of Dancers**

Need	Support technique	Example
Autonomy	1. Give opportunities for choice and input	"How are the legs today? Do you need to do jumps or choreography first?"
Autonomy	2. Give rationale for requested tasks and behaviors	"Let's do some more conditioning to get the strength we need to perform and avoid injury later in performance season."
Autonomy	3. Encourage dancers to identify their own values and goals and link tasks to these	"What is your goal for today's class, John? What can I do to help you reach it?"
Autonomy	4. Use inviting nonjudgmental language	"Let's try this," "We could consider" (rather than "You must," "We ought to")
Autonomy	5. Encourage experimentation, individuality, and creativity	"Try several ways to do it, and then pick one that you want to work with."
Competence	1. Provide a clear and fair structure	"This year we will work on part X of the syllabus. You can look at it here anytime to see what we have done and what we have left."
Competence	2. Individualize tasks	"Decide if you want to do this exercise as set, with an extra pirouette, or perhaps without arms. Challenge yourselves at your own level."
Competence	3. Provide clear, constructive feedback	"You worked well with the technical aspects that time. See if you can now emphasize the different rhythms too."
Competence	4. Encourage dancers to use multiple sources of feedback (not just teacher input)	"Try this a few times and see if you can sense internally how the weight transfers in the tilt. Then use the mirror if you find it helpful. Ask me if you are unsure."
Competence	5. Help dancers identify and overcome challenges	"If you want to audition for that production, what steps do you need to take? Perhaps you can make a list of goals and what you need help with."
Relatedness	1. Take an interest in dancers' perspectives	"It seems you are having a tricky time with that step. So did I when I was a student! Do you want to talk about it?"
Relatedness	2. Be positive and supportive regardless of skill/level/success rate	"All you can do is try, and I can tell you are giving it your all. Either you get there with practice, or we change the solo slightly."
Relatedness	3. Put people first and performances second by taking an interest in individuals	"How is school going? Are you enjoying your new class?"
Relatedness	4. Listen empathically, without interrupting	"Injury rehab can be frustrating. How are you feeling, really?"
Relatedness	5. Encourage collaboration	"Work on this task in pairs, taking turns to give constructive feedback."

matter to them (i.e., meaningful choice). Similarly, positive and constructive feedback are very important, but drowning dancers in gushy feedback is likely to be unhelpful. Some strategies can be offered very frequently (e.g., clear, constructive feedback), but others are perhaps only possible to do occasionally (e.g., helping dancers to identify challenges). In summary, use common sense and let the exercise enhance self-awareness and critical thinking rather than become a check-the-box exercise. The proactive teacher can of course monitor the effects of providing more or less of a particular strategy; What happens when more versus less rationale is used? Having dancers complete anonymous end-of-term evaluations can also be a good way of understanding more about how various strategies are perceived.

The exercise provided in form 11.1 is the practical application of the strategies teachers can use to support dancers' basic psychological needs

Form 11.1 GET PRACTICAL: CREATING A HEALTHY MOTIVATIONAL CLIMATE

Below are several strategies for supporting the basic psychological needs of dancers. You can use the worksheet to (a) monitor and enhance your teaching practice, (b) identify which need support strategies you as a dancer are offered, or (c) identify the need support strategies that you observe in someone else's class, and whether they seem to have any particular impact.

NEED	SUPPORT TECHNIQUE	I DID/ EXPERIENCED THIS (CHECKMARK)	HOW WAS IT DONE?	REFLECTION ON EXPERIENCE AND POTENTIAL IMPROVEMENTS
AUTONOMY	1. Give opportunities for choice and input			
	2. Give rationale for requested tasks and behaviors			
	3. Encourage dancers to identify their own values and goals and link tasks to these			
	4. Use inviting nonjudgmental language			
	5. Encourage experimentation, individuality, and creativity			
COMPETENCE	1. Provide a clear and fair structure			
	2. Individualize tasks			
	3. Provide clear, constructive feedback			
	4. Encourage dancers to use multiple sources of feedback (not just teacher input)			
	5. Help dancers identify and overcome challenges			
RELATEDNESS	1. Take an interest in dancers' perspectives			
	2. Be positive and supportive regardless of skill/level/success rate			
	3. Put people first and performances second by taking an interest in individuals			
	4. Listen empathically, without interrupting			
	5. Encourage collaboration			

Go to HK*Propel* to download this form.

From S. Nordin-Bates, *Essentials of Dance Psychology* (Champaign, IL: Human Kinetics, 2023).

(table 11.3). Table 11.3 lists strategies and provides brief examples, and form 11.1 includes space to check what strategies are used, make notes about how this was done, and record personal reflections on the experience and any potential improvements. Dance teachers can use the worksheet to become aware of strategies they already use, which strategies they do not use, and what they may therefore want to try in the future. Alternatively, dancers can use the worksheet to identify which of the need-supportive strategies they receive in various classes and evaluate whether these behaviors seem to relate to how they feel and perform. It can be illuminating to discover what seems to be most meaningful and important to oneself; in the long run it may help dancers select classes, styles, or studios in which they can develop optimally while also thriving emotionally and socially. A third option is to use the worksheet as an observation tool—for instance, in a team-teaching context or as a student observation project. What strategies are observed? Do they seem to have any particular consequences?

Mary: Case Study of Motivational Climate Change

Mary is a contemporary technique teacher who is increasingly frustrated by her second-year students. They just seem so—lazy! When she speaks to them they say almost nothing in response, and their physical engagement in her classes is just as lackluster. Venting her frustrations in the staff room to the dance health teacher one day, Mary got an unexpected answer. Rather than the agreement she typically got from colleagues, this teacher suggested a possible reason behind the passivity of the group—specifically, that they might be low in confidence. The teacher explained that when the students are asked to try something new and just stand there, this might be a sign of uncertainty and fear rather than laziness. They simply might not want to fail in front of their teacher or their classmates. Although she hadn't considered this before, something about what her colleague said rang true for Mary, and their conversation became focused on what they could do as a team to help the student group. In a meeting with all the teachers, it was agreed that they would try to encourage these students as much as possible and avoid exercises that made comparisons likely. Some suggested designing more exercises to face away from the mirrors, and to encourage collaboration in small groups. One teacher even put a poster on the main studio wall, saying "It's not failing—it is problem-solving" in big capital letters.

It took time, and it was no miracle cure. However, by the end of term the teachers recognized a change in the group: The students took more chances, and they cheered each other on more. When they fell, they didn't seem to think it was quite such a big deal anymore but could pick themselves up and carry on without looking embarrassed. In an end-of-year tutorial, one student said that what made the biggest difference for her was when one teacher made a big mistake and "didn't go all funny about it." It was the first time that a teacher didn't seem like unreachable perfection, and it surprised her how this had made her admire her teacher more, rather than less, because it helped her feel "okay to be human, too."

Composite case study created on the basis of a conversation with Imogen Aujla, PhD, dance psychology lecturer, researcher, and life coach, Dance in Mind (www.danceinmind.org).

CRITICAL ASPECTS OF RESEARCH INTO MOTIVATIONAL CLIMATES

1. Nearly all research in this area relies on questionnaire-based ratings of how performers *perceive* teachers to be and behave. But perceptions can be affected by an assortment of factors and are not objective facts about teacher behavior. To date, dance research has revealed two aspects related to teacher perceptions:
   - Teachers typically rate themselves as better leaders (e.g., more democratic, more supportive) than how their dancers see them (Rafferty & Wyon, 2006; van Rossum, 2004). This is probably a reflection of the self-serving bias to

which most of us are prone: Put simply, most people see themselves as more competent than the average.
- Dancers with high levels of perfectionistic concerns may perceive motivational climates as more ego and less task-involving (Nordin-Bates et al., 2014). This is probably because perfectionistic individuals are highly sensitive to any indications that they are not competent, making it difficult for them to let go of, for instance, critique. Less perfectionistic dancers of the same teacher may rate them differently.

2. Other social influences in addition to teachers affect dancers, their motivational quality, and associated outcomes. Unfortunately, there is no research into either peer- or parent-initiated motivational climates in dance, and only a little in sports (Harwood et al., 2015). In other words, it is an area ripe for investigation.

3. Providing need support likely requires teachers to have a good level of knowledge and understanding; indeed, we may speculate that teachers who lack confidence or who feel out of their depth stick rigorously to their plans without adaptations (poor competence support), are not open to questions (poor autonomy support), and remain distant from dancers (poor relatedness support). Further research into potential differences in need support between teachers with different amounts of pedagogical training or different confidence levels would be illuminating.

4. Task-involving climate perceptions are "more good than ego-involving climate perceptions are bad" (Harwood et al., 2015; Keegan, 2018). This is likely because task-involving climates are consistently helpful, whereas the effects of ego-involving climates vary depending on the performers' perceived competence: Those with low or unstable competence perceptions are likely to feel and perform poorly in such climates, whereas those with high and stable competence perceptions may do well. Still, this is likely to be true only in the short term. Who feels superior in every task every day?

KEY POINTS AND RECOMMENDATIONS FOR MOTIVATIONAL CLIMATES IN DANCE

1. Some may assume that ego-involving motivational climates are useful in promoting skill development or elite performance, but they are actually more likely to inhibit learning and development. This is because key features of ego-involving climates (e.g., focus on being the best, interpersonal comparison) can lead to dancers adopting maladaptive strategies such as only putting in effort when they believe they will be superior, and hiding when they do not. Teachers would do well to create task-involving climates regardless of the level they teach at.

2. Supporting the basic psychological needs of both dancers and teachers should be a key concern for dance schools. Whether the primary aim is to promote enjoyment, health, or top performance, it is best done through need satisfaction for all involved.

12

Talent

> "Some people seem to think that good dancers are born, but all the good dancers I have known are taught or trained."
>
> Fred Astaire, dancer

CHAPTER OBJECTIVES

After reading this chapter, you will be able to

1. describe what talent, talent identification, and talent development are;
2. critically discuss the multifaceted and dynamic nature of talent;
3. describe aspects of both nature and nurture as they pertain to dance talent, with particular emphasis on the difficulties of identifying talent in young people;
4. outline how deliberate practice, deliberate play, and early specialization might affect dancers;
5. apply basic recommendations to optimize talent identification and development in dance;

6. undertake structured reflection regarding the extent to which typical features of successful talent development environments are present in your own setting; and
7. think critically about the nature and impact of talent identification and development in dance.

Key Terms

deliberate play	growth mindset	talent
deliberate practice	holistic ecological approach	talent development
diversification	Matthew effect	talent identification
early specialization	relative age effect	
fixed mindset	self-fulfilling prophecy	

The term *talent* has a long and varied history. For instance, it has meant *balance* or a *sum of money* in classical Latin and Greek and *will* or *desire* in Old French. Since the Middle Ages, it has come to denote *natural aptitude*, *innate gift*, or *extraordinary skill*. As you will learn in this chapter talent is highly complex, which makes it extremely difficult to specify, identify, and predict. For instance, anybody's skill or aptitude is often tightly bound to one of the old meanings of the term talent—namely, a person's will or desire (i.e., their motivation).

What Is Talent?

Many in the dance world, including performers, teachers, managers, critics, and audiences, are obsessed with talent. We applaud it in theaters, we praise it in students, and we make highly influential judgments about children's futures on the basis of its assessment: If you are seen to be talented, you are more deserving. No wonder that demonstrating talent becomes top priority for so many! But what is talent, really, and what contributes to its emergence? Questions like these have kept scholars busy for decades and are likely to keep doing so; as such, this book chapter is far from conclusive and will not provide all the answers. Yet it is hoped that in integrating dance research with critical reflections on the far more extensively researched area of sport talent, important questions about the nature, identification, and nurture of dance talent can be brought to light.

As you go through this chapter, the following definitions may be helpful to keep in mind (all from Baker et al. (2017, pp. 1-2, but with the word *sport* removed from "high performance sport setting"):

› **Talent** is "innate, identifiable factors that affect our long-term development."
› **Talent identification** "refers to the process of identifying and/or selecting individuals who possess a quality (or qualities) that predicts some form of future attainment."
› **Talent development** "reflects the range of influences on the process of skill acquisition in the high performance setting."

Talent is Multifaceted

What do you think about when you hear the word *talent*? Write down at least three things. Ask a friend or two to do the same and compare your notes. Did you write down the same or different things?

A simple exercise like this can be a good way of reminding ourselves of the multifaceted nature of talent. Yet dance practice, much like sport, has often relied on a narrow range of assessments, such as the presence of specific anatomical or physiological features (e.g., long legs, flexibility). Ballet, in particular, has traditionally focused on anatomical features, with selections favoring females with petite, linear, prepubescent physiques (i.e., late maturers; Hamilton et al., 1997; Mitchell et al., 2016, 2022; Oreck et al., 2004; Pickard, 2013). For some, retaining such a physique is so important that puberty becomes a real threat (Mitchell et al., 2016). Although these aspects are focused on dancers' bodies, they are not only about identifying physical capacities that can better perform the requisite skills; they also reflect aesthetic preferences (e.g., Walker et al., 2010). There has been strong critique of such criteria, especially when narrowly defined and culturally biased (Chua, 2014b; Oreck et al., 2004; Warburton, 2002). Although critique has often been leveled specifically at ballet, dance scholar Edward Warburton (2002, p. 104) critiqued the practice of holding one-off auditions focused on few and subjectively judged talent characteristics in dance more generally:

> In dance auditions, whether implicitly or explicitly, examiners typically profile students first by physical attributes. As the audition moves into full swing, examiners rate dancers according to a series of tasks that require a wide range of skills, such as physical control and recall, coordination and agility, spatial awareness, rhythm and musical phrasing. People who do well in these high-stakes auditions, which assess exclusively kinaesthetic and musical abilities, are escorted into the rarefied world of dance. . . . Are they really the measures that should be used?

The role of psychological factors is often overlooked when talent is discussed or assessed, yet research strongly indicates their importance (e.g., Abbott & Collins, 2004; Blijlevens et al., 2018; Chua, 2014b; Dohme et al., 2019; Olszewski-Kubilius et al., 2019; Ross & Shapiro, 2017; Walker et al., 2010). To some extent, the role of psychological factors in expertise and talent has been interwoven throughout this book. Numerous chapters describe differences between elite and sub-elite performers in psychological traits and characteristics (e.g., personality, self-confidence, attentional focus) and in psychological skills (e.g., goal setting, self-regulation, imagery). Other chapters clarify that psychological characteristics facilitate learning and dance performance (e.g., healthy motivation and motivational climates, mindfulness, creativity). Similarly, reviews of the literature make it clear that

> [I]ndividuals who become outstanding performers and producers have more than just raw talent in the domain or opportunities to develop their talent—they have the will, drive, and focus to take advantage of the opportunities with which they are presented, and the capacity to persist through failures even as the bar for success gets higher. (Olszewski-Kubilius et al., 2019, p. 161)

In table 12.1, a comprehensive list of psychosocial skills associated with talent development are presented. They are derived from an extensive investigation that included literature reviews and feedback from international experts from a variety of domains, including the arts (Olszewski-Kubilius et al., 2019).

Although these skills may vary in their importance at different stages of talent development (Bailey & MacMahon, 2018; Blijlevens et al., 2018; Olszewski-Kubilius et al., 2019), the evidence for this is inconclusive in other domains and has not yet been studied in dance. Therefore, table 12.1 is presented as food for thought and as an impetus for future research. What skills are valued in your dance context? Which might be most important at different stages of expertise, and how could they be nurtured?

Overall, there is clear evidence that talent is a multidimensional construct, with numerous components having been associated with talent in dance (Aujla & Redding, 2014; Baum et al., 1996; Chua, 2014a, 2014b; Oreck et al., 2004; Redding et al., 2011; Walker et al., 2010; Warburton, 2002) just like in circus (Bailey & MacMahon, 2018), music (Haroutounian, 1995), and sport (Abbott & Collins, 2004; Baker & Horton, 2004; Baker et al., 2018, 2019; Vaeyens et al., 2008; Weissensteiner, 2017). For instance, the talent assessment process (TAP) developed for dance is based on 10 criteria falling into three interrelated categories: skills (e.g., physical, spatial, rhythm), creativity (including movement quality and expressiveness), and motivation (perseverance, ability to focus; Oreck et al., 2004; see also Baum et al., 1996). Clearly, some of the psychological characteristics said to be associated with talent development in table 12.1 are assessed as part of the TAP; in other words, it is not always clear to what extent different characteristics are targets for talent *identification*, talent *development*, or both.

In addition to features inherent to a person, such as anatomy, physiology, and psychology, many other features are seen as crucial components of (or related to) talent. In figure 12.1 a wide range of constructs are synthesized into 12 broad components that make people more or less likely to be viewed as talented. They include seven components that are inherent in a person and thus have an element of heritability (genetic influence). However, even genetically influenced components are affected by one's environment, can be trained, and can take time to emerge; as such, they are not static indicators of talent (Baker et al., 2019). In figure 12.1, they are summarized into the following:

1. musicality and artistry (e.g., being rhythmical and expressive),
2. anatomy (e.g., limb length, external hip rotation for some dance styles),
3. physiology (e.g., balance, flexibility),
4. cognition (e.g., ability to learn and memorize movement material),

Table 12.1 **Psychosocial Skills Associated With Talent Development**

Overall category	Subcategories of important psychosocial skills	Example from dance literature
1. Creative risk-taking	Accepting ambiguity; open to experience; working within constraints; elegant problem finding and formulation; developing a personal style/niche; transformational ideas	". . . as a dancer it's up to you to colour it—the choreographer gives you the movement and then as a dancer, you're there to give it the light, the dark, the shade, the colour, the dynamics, and that's your job and that's what you, as an artist, are required to do. I think what makes a good artist is somebody who's able to find all these different qualities. And that's when you start putting your soul into it and your personality and life experience." (Professional dancer in Critien & Ollis, 2006, p. 191)
2. Social skills	Eliciting and showing respect; empathy and compassion; collegiality; reliability; conscientiousness; ability to work in teams or be a leader as appropriate; professionalism; charisma	"I think I am a good people person, that is one of my. . . . I'm very sociable and I like people. . . . I think being sociable and open is a really important thing." (Professional dancer in Aujla & Farrer, 2015, p. 8)
3. Metacognitive self-regulation	Time management, organizational skills; knowing strengths and weaknesses; work-life balance; making talent area a priority; capitalizing on strengths and compensating for weakness	"You need to be independent. . . . You need to say, 'Stop, I can do this by myself, so that I know how to do it by myself when I'm living in other places.' Especially as a dancer, I think you need to be really independent." (Young dancer in Sanchez et al., 2013, p. 15)
4. Motivational self-regulation	Goal setting; commitment, perseverance, persistence; self-efficacy, self-confidence; "rage to master" (particularly strong drive)	"You have to believe in yourself, be determined, want it and have the right frame of mind 'cos if you're thinking 'this is bad, this time is going to be even worse,' it will be. You are your best teacher. You have to help yourself think positive stuff and start again. If you keep trying you will get better. Just don't give up." (Young dancer in Pickard & Bailey, 2009, p. 167)
5. Emotional self-regulation	Regulation of arousal/relaxation; coping with challenge; coping with failure/resiliency; anxiety management	"[Y]ou [need to] shift from emotion to emotion and you really wear that emotion with your whole body to communicate." (Professional circus artist in Ross & Shapiro, 2017, p. 118)
6. Cognitive self-regulation	Focusing attention/distraction and concentration control; use of appropriate learning/practice strategies; teachability	"[I]t's a certain focus, a certain concentration, a certain use of flow . . . you know . . . you can see it. The ones that just go deeper in what they do, within those situations, within their understanding." (Program leader for dance talent development center in Watson et al., 2012, p. 7)
7. Insider knowledge	Presentation skills; tasteful self-promotion; networking; reputation management; knowing the "game" and how to play it	"You have to go to the theater and say 'hello' and smile. This is all-important—how we react, how we act." (Dance teacher in Chua, 2015, p. 187)

Note: Categories and descriptions from Olszewski-Kubilius et al. (2019), with examples added from dance literature.

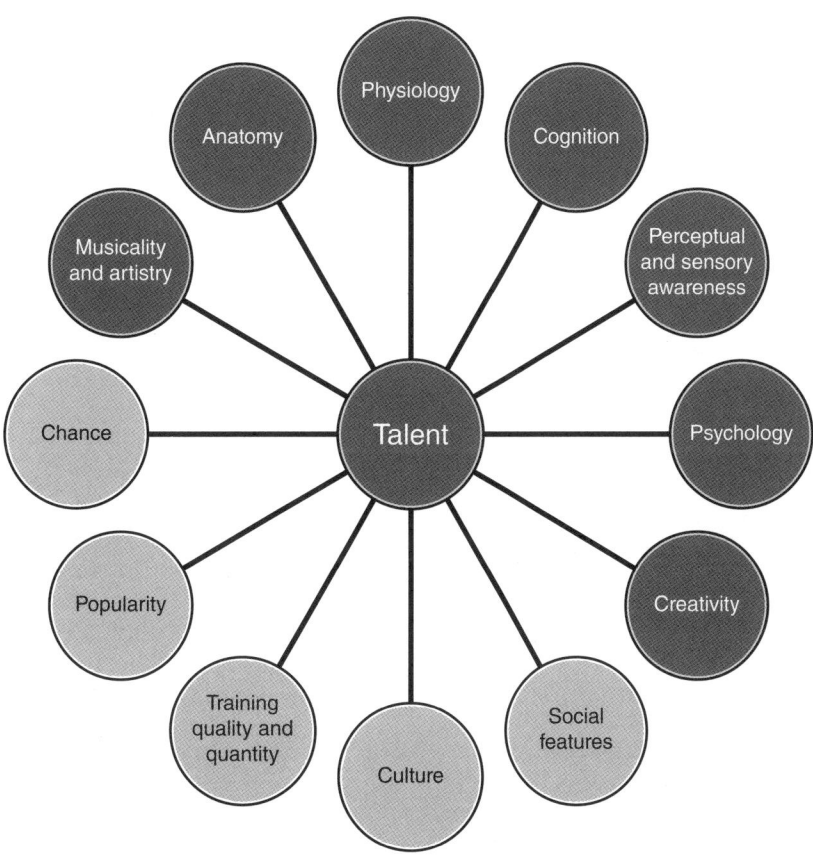

Figure 12.1 Talent is a multifaceted construct.

5. perceptual and sensory awareness (e.g., fine-tuned awareness of sensory information),
6. psychology (e.g., conscientiousness, ability to maintain motivation over time), and
7. creativity (e.g., ability to generate novel and useful ideas).

Five additional components contribute to the expression, identification, and development of talent:

8. social features (e.g., support from teachers, parents and peers, and the social skills to make the most of such relationships),
9. culture (e.g., living in a place that promotes dance as a valuable activity),
10. training quality and quantity (e.g., being able to regularly access high-quality training; this is also affected by socioeconomic status),
11. popularity (it is harder to be identified as talented in very popular dance forms),
12. chance (e.g., being in the right place at the right time).

You may, of course, think of additional components or choose to group and describe the talent components differently. Still, the key point is that talent is inherently multifaceted and complex. As such, it can be interpreted differently: for instance, some find artistry most important while others focus more on technical ability. Its inherent complexity also means that talent is notoriously slippery, or hard to measure. This may seem obvious, but it has a direct influence on such things as who gets selected for a role, school, or company position.

Finally, a weakness in one area may be compensated for by a strength in another (Abbott & Collins, 2004; Oreck et al., 2004; Vaeyens et al., 2008; Weissensteiner, 2017). For example, dancers with lower technical abilities may compensate with their artistry and passion. Such compensation is especially likely in complex activities like dance, which does not rely heavily on a single component for success (in the way that, for example, 100-meter sprinting relies on speed). Examples of such compensation are plentiful in the dance world: for example, ballet icon Margot Fonteyn has been described as an example of mind over matter. Her torso was inflexible, and her by no means perfect legs were limited in their range of movement: but she thought herself into becoming a great dancer. . . . The sad eyes and the inclinations of her head lent such expression to the gestures of her lovely arms, that her torso and legs were overlooked. (Richard Buckle in Pickard, 2012, p. 39)

Further research in other dance styles is highly warranted, not least because compensation seems even more likely in styles such as contemporary dance, where the definition of success is likely to be highly variable.

Talent Is Dynamic

In addition to being multifaceted, talent is dynamic and changes across time—or at least it seems to, depending on how we define and measure it (Abbott & Collins, 2004; Baker & Horton, 2004; Baker et al., 2018, 2019; Redding et al., 2011; Vaeyens et al., 2008). Next we will consider four aspects of the dynamic nature of talent, including maturity, short-term variations in the skills that a dancer displays, changes in success criteria over time, and the ever-changing nature of dance. As if these were not enough, different components of talent interact with one another (Baker et al., 2019): For example, environmental aspects such as teacher-dancer relationships affect psychological aspects (e.g., a dancer's motivation).

Maturity

Age and maturity affect physiological talent components, with aspects such as coordination generally improving over time but dipping during the adolescent growth spurt. The (temporary) loss of such a valued characteristic can have important implications, as pointed out by this young dancer: "You could have a growth spurt like a week before your audition and you're like, 'Oh, my goodness, what do I do?'" (Mitchell et al., 2022, p. 275). More generally, maturity and training will both affect the kinds of abilities that a dancer displays and thus whether she is likely to be labeled as talented or not. Indeed, we typically consider early and fast learning to be signs of talent, even though we know that children mature at different rates. Late maturers may not develop appropriate attentional focusing abilities or self-regulation until later in their teens or early adulthood. Such late bloomers will not make the cut if talent selection occurs early and may therefore never realize their potential. As Abbott & Collins (2004, p. 401) put it:

[T]he desired behaviour can emerge quite suddenly when (or if) all the components reach critical functioning and the context is appropriate. Due to this late emergence of components, as age increases the number (and accuracy) of identified "potentially talented" individuals will increase. Clearly, therefore, the earlier a talent identification procedure is employed, the more potentially talented individuals will be eliminated.

Maturity considerations are, of course, mostly relevant to dance forms in which selections are made before puberty. Training is typically also intensified during puberty—a time of large-scale physiological, psychological, and social changes. It seems to make little sense to conduct selections at a time when so many things are in flux (e.g., Mitchell et al., 2016, 2022). Unless success is conceived of as something that only occurs in adolescence, even late maturers will develop eventually! If selecting early, the effects of maturation will then be unknown, making talent selection more of a gamble (Walker et al., 2010). Of course, not all dance styles or schools have restrictive attitudes regarding body types, and they delay selections until much after puberty.

Short-Term Variations in Displayed Talent

Psychological constructs such as self-confidence and performance anxiety can affect dancers' audition performances and consequently their likelihood of being identified as talented (e.g., Baum et al., 1996; Oreck et al., 2004). One young dancer recollected her first audition experience as follows:

I was at my audition for vocational school. I'd dreamed about it and talked about the day for weeks. I really, really wanted it. . . . Then everything went wrong. I just couldn't make my body do what I wanted. My brain wouldn't work. I felt so nervous. I was so worried and the more I worried the worse it got. Everyone was watching and I knew that they were judging me as a bad dancer. I felt so bad, so low, so unhappy. When it was over I cried for days. (Pickard & Bailey, 2009, p. 176).

The dancer behind this quote fortunately returned to dance with increased determination, thus showing the importance of resilience. Still, such identification by performance level, especially when done with young people, may undermine rather than serve talent identification and development in the long term (Baker et al., 2018).

Changing Success Criteria

The characteristics that help a dancer succeed at an early age are not always the same as those required for successful adult performance. For instance, the hypermobility that helps a youngster impress judges with her flexibility may become a risk factor for injury during later intensive, full-time training (e.g., Walker et al., 2010). Another dancer may be seen as talented due to his above-average technical abilities during teenage years yet struggle as an adult performer when required to perform expressive roles. Some have argued that it is ironic how some dancers commit to becoming professionals while they are still children, considering that the expressivity often required in professional performances is enhanced by the rich and varied life experiences possessed only by adults (Pickard, 2012).

A talent development project with young dancers in a mixture of styles found that those who later got selected into vocational training (an indicator of success) were fitter in several ways than those who did not; for example, they were stronger, more flexible, jumped higher, and balanced better (Redding et al., 2011). Yet all these variables improved significantly over the two-year duration of the project, making them dubious targets for talent identification, especially at young ages.

The Ever-Changing Nature of Dance

Finally, an important aspect of the dynamic nature of talent concerns dance as an ever-changing art. Today is not tomorrow, and nobody knows what will be considered good, skilled, or creative in the future (Bailey & MacMahon, 2018; Daprati et al., 2009). Yet if we select dancers based on what was considered successful yesterday, we *create* a truth—at least if only those who fit into the predetermined mold are given the chance to develop their talents.

In addition to the noted short- and long-term variations in how talent manifests itself, it is worth remembering that some aspects of talent are more malleable than others. For instance, some of the components illustrated in figure 12.1 are not under an individual's control, including anatomy, culture, and—of course—chance. In contrast, the quality of a training environment is highly malleable and controllable. As such, honing the talent development environment is the most constructive focus for those interested in talent optimization (e.g., Critien & Ollis, 2006; Walker et al., 2010).

Relative Age Effect: When Maturation Is Taken for Talent

In education (e.g., Vestheim et al., 2019) and sports (Baker et al., 2014, 2018) a **relative age effect** (RAE) exists. The RAE concerns performance advantages for children born early in any given selection year (e.g., January-March) when compared with children born late in the same year (e.g., October-December). For activities that divide children by birth year, it leads to an overrepresentation of children born early, and an underrepresentation of children born late in each year group. The RAE emerges because those born earlier are often stronger and generally more mature than those born later; these developmental advantages make them more likely to be selected as talents. Essentially what has occurred is that early maturation is taken for talent. That the RAE persists across many activities and across time indicates that leaders have strong and pervasive beliefs in physical parameters as stable indicators of future success, despite there being well-established negative effects (Wattie & Baker, 2017).

The RAE has mostly been researched in sports where basic capacities such as strength and speed are strong performance indicators, such as in football. Studies into RAE in technical aesthetic activities such as dance (van Rossum, 2006) and aesthetic sports (Baker et al., 2014; Hancock et al., 2015; Langham-Walsh et al., 2021) are far fewer in number, and some found no evidence for RAE. In one such study, however, splitting the sample by age led to a "normal" RAE being found for gymnasts under 15 years of age, whereas an inverse RAE was evident for those over 15 years (Hancock et al., 2015). That is, it was far more common for older teen gymnasts to be born *later* in the year. A likely reason is that women's gymnastics has traditionally favored petite, immature bodies.

It would be interesting to see nuanced research into potential RAEs in dance. For instance, are dancers more likely to be identified as talented if they are psychologically and socially mature yet somewhat physically immature (see Hancock et al., 2015; Mitchell et al., 2016)? Differences between dance styles and genders are likely in this regard because different qualities may be sought. Indeed, one study found an inverse RAE for some of the apparatuses used in women's artistic gymnastics but not for others (Langham-Walsh et al., 2021). The authors argued that these effects may be due to **self-fulfilling prophecies**, whereby leaders expect performers of a particular stature to succeed in particular events; as a result, coaches invest more time and effort into such person-apparatus matches. The progress resulting from these special attentions is then attributed to the accurate talent predictions of the leader rather than to the increased resources they were given (Horn et al., 2001).

Matthew Effect: When Better Provision is Taken for Talent

Consider an example of a dance school which, at first glance, appears to be successful: they select dancers by audition at early ages, and some of these dancers (but rarely others) proceed into professional careers. But what if this school is the only one to provide quality dance training, and "side-entries" from other dance schools are not made possible? This may well be the case in small countries or regions where there is only one high-level school. In such cases rejected and deselected dancers may never have a realistic chance of reentering the system. This way, only students from the one school will graduate into professional careers, and it appears as though their procedures are valid: "Only our dancers get jobs, so we must clearly be doing something right!" Yet it will never be known to what extent this was the result of who was selected or a result of the better resources that they were given. This phenomenon is sometimes known as the **Matthew effect**, after the Bible verse Matthew 13:12: "For to the one who has, more will be given, and he will have an abundance, but from the one who has not, even what he has will be taken away" (English Standard Version).

Figure 12.2 illustrates an example of the Matthew effect. This hypothetical setting has three selection points, at which dancers are either selected (upper arrow) or not (lower arrow). The selected dancers are given superior resources, such as highly qualified teachers, good studio spaces, and various forms of support (e.g., physiotherapy, individualized conditioning). Because these resources help the selected advance faster, they are more likely to be selected again in the future and to eventually be successful in dance (e.g., reach their potential, obtain professional status). The disadvantages of being rejected instead mean access to inferior resources, such that it becomes increasingly difficult to catch up.

Who is encouraged to audition for selection in the first place, and what happens to dancers who

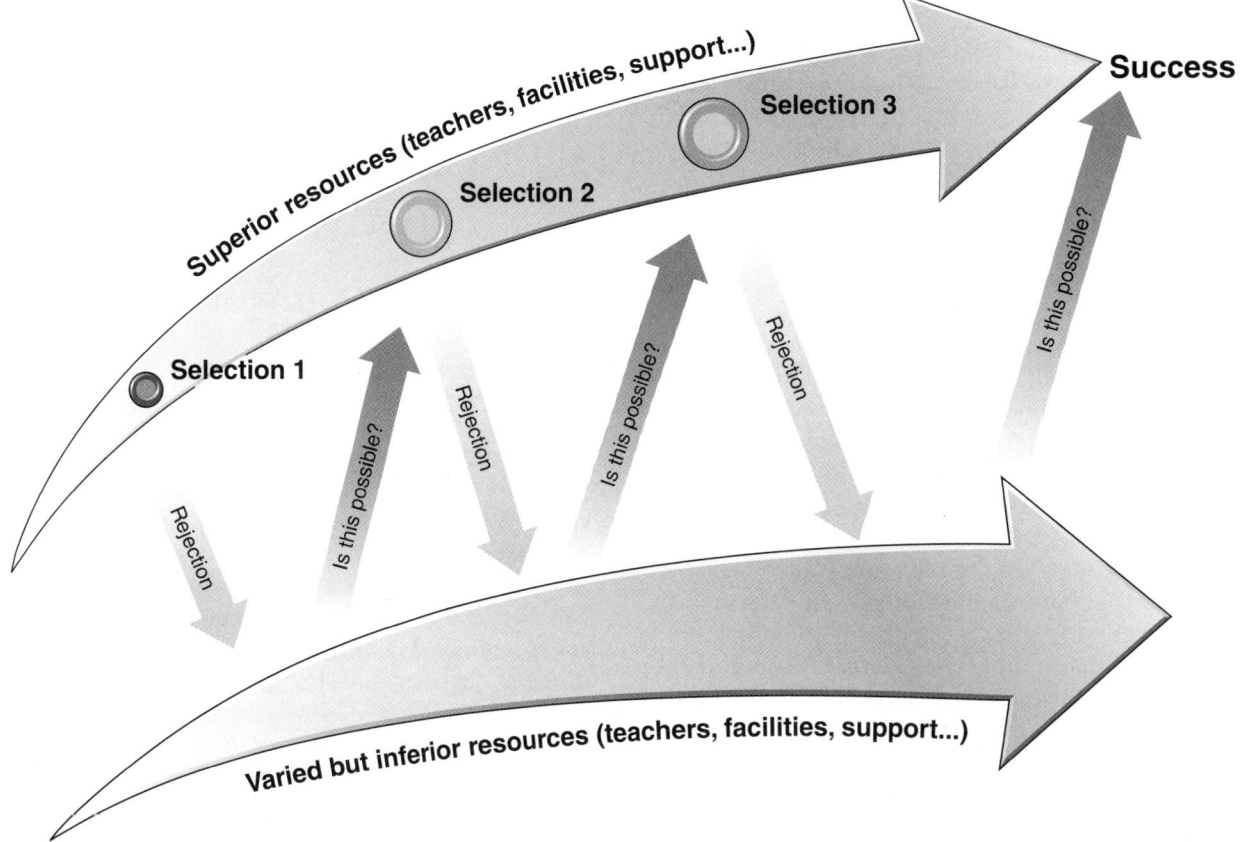

Figure 12.2 Talent selection processes may lead to a Matthew effect, or widening gap between dancers, because the resources given to the selected tend to differ considerably from those available to the rejected.

are unsuccessful at audition? Indeed, a key question is the extent to which rejected dancers are given opportunities for reselection (Baker et al., 2018; Güllich & Cobley, 2017). Where this is possible (e.g., in a city with multiple high-quality schools and regular open auditions), dancers from a variety of schools and backgrounds are likely to become professionals. In a rare published example, a young male from an underprivileged background is offered the chance to take up ballet at the age of 18, quickly discovers that he loves it, and goes on to pursue a professional career (Chua, 2014b).

Overall, systems and schools should aim to be as permeable as possible, with multiple points for reentry, so as to optimize the development of many. In new, diverse, and fluid styles or activities such permeability is typical, such as in the recruitment of skilled dancers, gymnasts, and trampolinists into the circus (Bailey & MacMahon, 2018; Ross & Shapiro, 2017). Within dance, it will help if there are many different places where dancers can train, get support, and so on. Naturally, the latter is a matter of resources and the popularity of dance in any given place. Finally, the notion of success will matter; there are certainly many other views of success beyond becoming a professional dancer.

THINKING CRITICALLY

- What physical, psychological, or other attributes do you see as talent indicators in your dance style?
- Given the assessment procedures currently used in your dance setting, is there a risk of talented dancers being missed?
- Might self-fulfilling prophecies, RAEs, or Matthew effects exist in your dance setting?

Talent Identification Is Inherently Difficult

Because talent is multifaceted and dynamic and maturation can affect how talent is expressed and perceived (e.g., via RAEs), we can conclude that talent identification is very difficult. This is especially the case when done before puberty (Baker et al., 2018; Güllich & Cobley, 2017; Vaeyens et al., 2008). Early identification rests on the assumption that there are early signs that are at least somewhat valid and reliable indicators of performance later in life (Baker et al., 2018). This, in turn, assumes that talent is also at least partly fixed and unchangeable; a notion we already considered to be problematic.

Performing arts scholars have emphasized the challenges inherent in identifying talent when faced with student groups that may range from novices to those with many years of training (e.g., Baum et al., 1996; Oreck et al., 2004). It is easy to say that one is looking for "raw talent," but what this means in practice warrants further investigation. Even in top schools, which typically have experienced professionals performing the talent identification, the high dropout rates put the validity and reliability of selections into question (Güllich & Cobley, 2017). For example, an early study at the School of American Ballet (Hamilton et al., 1997) reported a dropout rate of 55% over a four-year period. In a study of young dancers in UK talent centers representing a mixture of styles, those who dropped out were in many ways similar to those who graduated (Walker et al., 2012).

Clearly, numerous factors affect the validity and reliability of talent identification processes, not least because young people leave dance for a wide range of reasons beyond insufficient talent (Walker et al., 2012). Some argue that talent can both appear (e.g., when reaching a particular level of maturity) and disappear (e.g., when becoming seriously injured; Abbott & Collins, 2004), despite its partly innate nature. In table 12.2, the problems associated with talent identification are summarized.

Sources of Talent

Where does talent come from? Are good dancers born, made, or a bit of both? Does intensive, focused training help, and does it help more when it starts early in life? Next, we will consider these issues in some depth and introduce the concept of talent development environments.

Nature Versus Nurture

The classic nature-nurture debate is highly relevant in relation to dance talent; that is, are talented dancers born (nature) or made (nurture)? Those who advocate a nurture position might endorse the opening quote for this chapter by Fred Astaire, who famously claimed that "all the good dancers I have known are taught or trained." Those advocating a nature position might instead agree with artistic director and choreographer George Balanchine, who is cited as saying:

Table 12.2 **Problems Associated With the Predictive Accuracy of Talent Identification Procedures, Especially When Done Early**

Components		Description/example
1	Task demands	Top-level performance relies on the interaction of several skills, and strengths in some may compensate for weaknesses in others.
2		Different skills may vary in their relative importance over time.
3		Dance is ever changing, and the skills required of future performers are not fully knowable today.
4	Performer characteristics	Physical and psychological maturation occur at somewhat varied ages and affect dancers in different ways.
5		Psychological factors affect how skills are expressed and developed yet are difficult to capture.
6		Dancers may not retain the skills that they display early on, and they may also develop other skills later.
7	Environmental factors	Prior dance training will affect the skill exhibited by dancers at selection and their scope for improvement.
8		Background factors such as socioeconomic conditions and family support influence talent development yet are rarely suitable as selection criteria.
9		It is not possible to ascertain which dancers will develop and thrive in (vs. stagnate, drop out from) the talent development environment provided to selected dancers.
10	Test quality	The validity and reliability of the assessments used in selection are often unknown but are unlikely to be high because a) they typically assess only a limited range of skills or characteristics, and b) talent is complex and often subjectively perceived.

Note: Adapted from Güllich and Cobley (2017).

"One is born to be a dancer. No teacher can work miracles, nor will years of training make a good dancer of an untalented pupil. One may be able to acquire a certain technical facility, but no one can ever 'acquire an exceptional talent.'"

Of course, there is some truth to these words: Reviews of the literature clarify that genetic heritability affects "the vast majority of variables on which people can vary" (Simonton, 2017, p. 13). Some examples include flexibility, general intelligence, and personality traits such as conscientiousness—all factors that may help a dancer learn and develop faster than their peers, or develop a particular physical skill. Yet genetic (nature) factors typically explain less than half of the variance, leaving much to be explained by environmental factors (nurture; Simonton, 2017).

The truth, then, is found somewhere in between: Both innate components and learning experiences play important roles in dance talent (Baker & Horton, 2004; Simonton, 2017; Vaeyens et al., 2008; Ward et al., 2017). Of course, any dance style with strict requirements regarding largely unchangeable anatomical features is likely to lean more toward the nature position than styles with more open and fluid conceptions of what makes a person talented. Yet others sidestep the issue altogether by focusing on dance as an inherently human activity that is, or at least should be, for everyone.

THINKING CRITICALLY

- Do you primarily think of talent as something innate (nature) or something developed in particular circumstances (nurture)?
- Is nature or nurture more emphasized in your dance setting? What consequences might this have?
- Does the existence of particular innate features mean that certain people should be selected ahead of others? In other words, do we have an obligation to support the realization of natural gifts, or should other factors (such as a child's own interests) decide?

Deliberate Practice

Since the 1990s, a somewhat extreme nurture position has proliferated, especially in the popular press. For instance, books such as *Outliers: The story of success* (Gladwell, 2008) and *Talent is overrated: What really separates world-class performers from everybody else* (Colvin, 2008) argue that talent is largely illusory, and expertise acquisition is entirely down to hard work. Though extreme, these arguments are not unfounded but are based in **deliberate practice** theory and its most widespread (and, arguably, misinterpreted) tenet: that it takes 10,000 hours, or 10 years, to become an expert (Ericsson et al., 1993).

Deliberate practice is doing highly structured and individualized activities in order to enhance performance of specific skills. As such, deliberate practice is effortful (physically and/or mentally), is not associated with immediate rewards, and is not inherently enjoyable (Ericsson et al., 1993). Instead, it is rigorous, slow, and focused work that over time leads to success. In some ways, research has supported this proposition; for instance, there is typically a significant, positive relationship between practice hours and a person's level of expertise (Baker & Horton, 2004; Baker & Young, 2014; Hutchinson et al., 2013; Ward et al., 2017). In a study with figure skaters, elite performers spent more time practicing challenging technical tasks than did their non-elite counterparts (Deakin & Cobley, 2003). There has also been support for the notion that it takes 10,000 hours, or 10 years, to become an expert in domains including music, chess, sports (Baker & Young 2014), and dance (van Rossum, 2001). Evidence like this became the foundation for arguments that expertise (or talent) is more about nurture (i.e., training) than nature (e.g., Colvin, 2008; Gladwell, 2008).

Several caveats of the deliberate practice concept and associated literature should be noted. For example, athletes often enjoy their deliberate practice (Baker & Young, 2014). In fact, higher levels of intrinsic motivation help athletes engage in more deliberate practice over time, and more deliberate practice leads to increased intrinsic motivation (i.e., a reciprocal relationship; Vink et al., 2015). Although no corresponding studies exist in dance, similar findings are likely because dancers are typically more intrinsically than extrinsically motivated (see chapter 5). When dance students described features of their classes at different stages, discipline and a focus on improvement via hard work were key descriptors of the second, more intense stage (van Rossum, 2001). However, both the first (more cozy and playful) stage and the second (more intense) stage were described as motivating.

Two main reasons may help explain why the low-enjoyment dimension of deliberate practice does not always hold true. One is that the deliberate practice framework originated in classical music and chess, activities in which large amounts of solitary practice is the norm (Ericsson et al., 1993; Baker & Young, 2014). Most dance forms, however, share with sports the feature of practicing with others—a social aspect that can satisfy our basic need for relatedness (see chapter 5). Such differences between activities may help explain why athletes—and perhaps also dancers—enjoy their deliberate practice. Another possible reason is that terms such as *fun*, *enjoyment*, and *meaning* have sometimes been used interchangeably: Not all practice is fun, but hard work can be meaningful and therefore still intrinsically motivating. Thus, being clear about what is measured or discussed is important.

A second shortcoming of the deliberate practice framework is that the so-called 10-year rule or 10,000 hours of deliberate practice to reach expertise are overgeneralizations—as overly tidy round numbers typically are. Indeed, the time required to reach expertise is around 10,000 hours or 10 years when reporting on population averages; when looking at spread, it is apparent that the amounts vary enormously (Baker & Young, 2014). In one study, ballet dancers were said to have accumulated 10,301 hours of practice by age 20, but the standard deviation was 4,609 hours (Hutchinson et al., 2013), and we do not know to what extent those hours comprised deliberate practice. Moreover, these numbers appear to be overestimates: ballet dancers typically become professionals (i.e., expert level) before age 20, and calculations were made on the basis of estimates of weekly hours multiplied by 52—that is, allowing for no holidays during their entire lives! Nevertheless, the data suggest that it does not always take 10,000 hours to become an expert.

Finally, it is relatively hard to know what qualifies as deliberate practice. For example, most teachers are surely oriented toward skill improvement and design exercises to help move classes forward at a suitable pace; as such, normal dance classes should count as deliberate practice (Hutchinson et al., 2013). Yet this may only be true at the group level: for some dancers the exercises may be too difficult, too easy, or they are distracted rather than focused on improvement. If so, it would not truly be deliberate practice for them. Thus, it is difficult to conduct research into deliberate practice, especially because studies typically require participants to think back several years to the training they did at different ages. Do *you* know to what extent the hours you danced at age 10 were effortful and deliberately focused on skill improvement? If we do not know, we risk relying on simple number counting (estimated hours of practice; a quantity focus) rather than truly understanding the idea behind the deliberate practice framework: that the *quality* of practice matters (e.g., that it is structured and focused; Ericsson et al., 1993). In fact, dancers who are better at self-regulation (see chapter 9) likely get more learning from each hour of practice (Baker & Young, 2014).

In sum, the deliberate practice framework has had enormous uptake in several domains. Although it has considerable limitations, its main message that quality practice matters more than inherent, natural gifts may help performers feel a sense of control and help their teachers to stay open to development rather than pursue inherently unpredictable talent. That is, a belief in the importance of deliberate practice may help promote a **growth mindset** (Dweck, 2006/2017), as outlined later in this chapter. Importantly, the idea that experts have typically undertaken more training than nonexperts should not be interpreted as a message that "more is always better"; indeed, there are also likely to be expert-novice differences in smartly planned rest and recovery (Baker & Young, 2014; Ericsson et al., 1993).

Deliberate Play and Diversification

Developmental models of talent and skill acquisition often emphasize the role of deliberate practice as an important component for skill development (e.g., Côté et al., 2007; Ward et al., 2017). For instance, the widely used developmental model of sport participation (DMSP; Côté et al., 2007) outlines a pathway toward elite performance as comprising gradual increases in the amount of deliberate practice undertaken from the *sampling years* (first starting out in organized leisure activities in childhood) through the *specialization years* (mid-teens) and into the *investment years* (late teens). Yet such models typically also reflect the important role of play and diversity, especially in childhood.

For instance, the DMSP highlights that children in the sampling years in particular should be active in several different activities, and that practice should comprise a large amount of **deliberate play** (Côté et al., 2007). The key characteristics of deliberate play are outlined and contrasted with deliberate practice in table 12.3.

Because deliberate play is child-led and often creative, it may help develop fundamental motor skills alongside psychological skills such as self-regulation (see chapter 9). That it is done for its own sake should help nurture intrinsic motivation (see chapter 5). Deliberate play should also help mitigate the risks of excessive deliberate practice, such as overtraining and burnout (Côté et al., 2007). Interestingly, one study found that those most likely to progress into a junior national football team were players reporting above-average amounts of club training (i.e., structured practice) in combination with the highest amounts of deliberate play (Sieghartsleitner et al., 2018). It would be intriguing to examine the potential effects of deliberate play in dance, such as when children dance spontaneously at home and set up impromptu performances with siblings or friends.

In the performing arts, the role of a related construct known as **diversification** has rarely been studied, although there is recognition that "the wider the range of artistic experiences to which students are exposed, the more likely it is that their potential talent can be realized" (Oreck et al., 2004, p. 81-82; see also Clements & Nordin-Bates, 2022). Thus, it may be worth reflecting on the nature of dance training, such as it is done in your style, area, or your own life. Is it mainly composed of deliberate practice, deliberate play, or both? Is there diversity within specialized training programs and schools, such as classes in different styles and exposure to multiple art forms and activities? There are likely to be dance style differences, of course; for instance, urban dance

Table 12.3 **Key Characteristics of Deliberate Play and Deliberate Practice**

Deliberate play	Deliberate practice
Child-led	Teacher-led
Intrinsic: done for its own sake	Extrinsic: done to reach a goal later
Done to maximize enjoyment	Done to maximize development
Often has pretend qualities	Typically considered serious
Flexible setup and rules	Explicit setup and rules
Takes place in a variety of settings	Takes place in specific settings (e.g., studios)

Note: Adapted from Côté, Baker, and Abernethy (2007).

forms such as hip-hop and breaking have grown out of less structured subcultures where peer teaching is the norm and training is more playlike. Given the advantages attributed to deliberate play, perhaps more structured dance forms can learn from these street styles. Indeed, many of us could benefit from introducing variety in our lives to facilitate important outcomes such as versatility and creativity.

> Go to HK*Propel* to download lettering art highlighting the value of variety.

Early Specialization

Several scholars and practitioners warn against the costs that may follow from engaging in high amounts of deliberate practice and low amounts of deliberate play already in childhood—that is, from **early specialization** (e.g., Côté et al., 2007; LaPrade et al., 2016). A useful definition of early specialization is that it involves prepubertal (age 12 and younger) children undertaking intense training in a single activity for more than 8 months of the year (LaPrade et al., 2016).

Numerous studies have indicated that those who become senior elite performers often start later; rather than staying behind colleagues who have accumulated practice hours since childhood, late starters typically intensify their training faster as teenagers (Güllich & Cobley, 2017; Hutchinson et al., 2013). Extensive research into participation histories further reveals that many top elite athletes are not exclusively involved in a single sport from a young age; rather, they tend to have participated in a variety of activities across childhood and adolescence (Güllich & Cobley, 2017; Güllich et al., 2021; Kliethermes et al., 2021). Such research further indicates that elite performers' progress in their later-chosen sport is not necessarily linear, and they often train *less* in sport-specific coach-led practice as children. Moreover, early specialization seems to be related to an increased risk of injury (Kliethermes et al., 2021). Partly as a result of such findings, scholars in this area typically recommend that early selection and specialization should be forgone in favor of a "mass and plurality" of young people practicing in many diverse ways (Güllich & Cobley, 2017; LaPrade et al., 2016).

Aesthetic sports and dance are often considered "early specialization activities," presumably due to the widespread availability of such activities to young children, and the possibility to make strong commitments early (e.g., starting children's dance at age 3; going to dance boarding school at age 11). It is surprising, therefore, that almost no research exists into early specialization in dance. But dance is also difficult to characterize in terms of early specialization; for instance, the intense training taking place in vocational schools suggests a high degree of specialization, yet dancers in such schools typically train in several different styles (Downing et al., 2020, 2021); as such, they do not necessarily conform to the definition of early specialization that is centered on single activity participation. As noted in chapter 7, dancers of today are typically required to be versatile, and professional companies often perform varied choreographies. For this reason, it may be worth viewing diversification versus specialization on a continuum from extremely diversified (varied) to extremely specialized (figure 12.3).

Psychosocial risks (e.g., for motivation, burnout, dropout, and identity development) have often been suggested as possible outcomes of early specialization, or from large amounts of deliberate practice in childhood (e.g., Côté et al., 2007). Unfortunately, empirical investigations in this area are few, and the results are highly inconsistent (Kliethermes et al., 2021; Waldron et al., 2020). In the only early specialization study to date to include dancers, degree of early specialization was largely unrelated to performer motivation (Downing et al., 2021). In fact, aesthetic performers scoring more highly for early specialization reported somewhat *lower* degrees of controlled motivation (i.e., they were less likely to

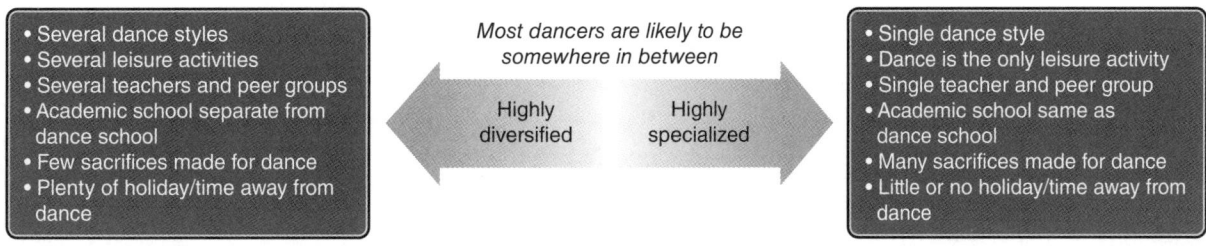

Figure 12.3 Diversification and specialization may be viewed as a continuum, with most dancers likely to fall somewhere between two extremes.

participate out of a sense of pressure; see chapter 5). Of course, such findings are based on reports from participants who have persevered; the voices of those who have dropped out (and may have done so for reasons linked to early specialization) are notably absent. Clearly, there is a need for more research into early specialization in dance so that we may better understand its nature and possible consequences. It will also be important to determine whether any negative outcomes are a result of particular aspects of early specialization, such as high intensity (e.g., risks associated with overtraining) or the exclusive focus on a single activity (e.g., risk of developing a narrow identity; see chapter 1).

The mixed state of research into early specialization has also led to recommendations that research attention should perhaps be directed not only toward the "what" (whether specializing early or not) but also toward the "how" (how specialization is organized and experienced by performers). For instance, are sacrifices such as giving up competing leisure activities made willingly or reluctantly by the specializing dancers? Are diversity and rich experiences provided within the chosen dance style? An important part of understanding the "how" of early specialization, and of talent development more generally, is also to focus on the talent development environment (Downing et al., 2021; Waldron et al., 2020).

Talent Development Environments

It is obvious to most people, and not least to dancers who typically spend many years honing their craft, that the environment in which one is training is of crucial importance. Indeed, it may be of greater importance in dance than in many other activities because dance is often highly teacher led. The most obvious aspect of the talent development environment is the availability of competent teachers, and much talent research (like performance psychology overall) has focused on individual performers and their leaders. Marking a shift from this somewhat narrow focus, a group of researchers studying particularly successful (and in a few cases, unsuccessful) talent development environments have created a **holistic ecological approach** (HEA) to talent development (Henriksen & Stambulova, 2017).

Although the HEA has not been systematically applied to dance, many have recognized the impact of the surrounding environment on dance talent development. In particular, the role of support from parents and peers has been emphasized, including *instrumental* (e.g., paying for and taking a young dancer to classes), *informational* (e.g., giving advice), and *emotional* support (e.g., encouragement, care; Aujla & Redding, 2014; Aujla et al., 2014; Chua, 2014a, 2014b, 2015; Redding et al., 2011; Sanchez et al., 2013; van Rossum, 2001; Walker et al., 2010). The importance of culture has also been recognized (e.g., Hutchinson et al., 2013; Oreck et al., 2004; Pickard, 2013; Sanchez et al., 2013).

An important part of the HEA is a working model of talent development environments (Henriksen & Stambulova, 2017). In this model, the developmental context for any given environment is considered by way of several layers. These layers have been summarized and contextualized for dance in figure 12.4:

› *The individual.* The potential elite performer (e.g., dancer who wants to become a professional) is at the center of the model.

› *The immediate dance environment.* The dancer is surrounded by their immediate environment—that is, people with whom they regularly interact. These include main teachers, peers in the same classes, and perhaps support staff such as physiotherapists and managers. Research with young dancers shows that task-involving motivational climates are associated with adherence to talent development (Aujla et al., 2015; see chapter 11). Interestingly, several highly successful talent development environments in sports have been characterized by the presence of current elite athletes alongside younger peers in the immediate environment (Henriksen & Stambulova, 2017). These mixed and dynamic groupings appear to provide inspiration and role models as well as to support peer learning. It would be interesting to examine what the impact of such environments might be in dance, which is rarely characterized by mixed-ability groupings. The value of role models who are similar to the students has, however, been emphasized in writings about talent development for disabled dancers (Aujla & Redding, 2014).

› *The microenvironment.* The next layer comprises nonperformance agents such as family, school, and non-dance peers as well as agents from the performance domain (e.g., other dance schools). Of course, those who attend boarding school would likely experience the impact of their academic school differently from those attending separate schools for dance and academic study. In one study with

Having a role model can be an important source of motivation and learning.

young talented dancers, the impact of microenvironmental variables including family support, economic means, and religious considerations on talent development were illustrated (Sanchez et al., 2013).

› *The macroenvironment.* In the outermost layer, we again find aspects from both the performance domain (e.g., dance culture, major dance organizations) and nonperformance aspects (e.g., national and general youth cultures). The media and educational system of a country also feature here. The age at which a country makes it possible for youngsters to attend specialist schools is one example of how the macroenvironment affects talent development; clearly, this also varies by dance style. Another example is how dance cultures shape young dancers' perceptions of what kinds of bodies are considered desirable (Pickard, 2013).

› *Time.* A final aspect of the model is its recognition of time; as such, *past*, *present*, and *future* remind us of the dynamic nature of talent.

A major contribution of the HEA is that it recognizes the complex interactions between many aspects (agents) in the lives of performers and on

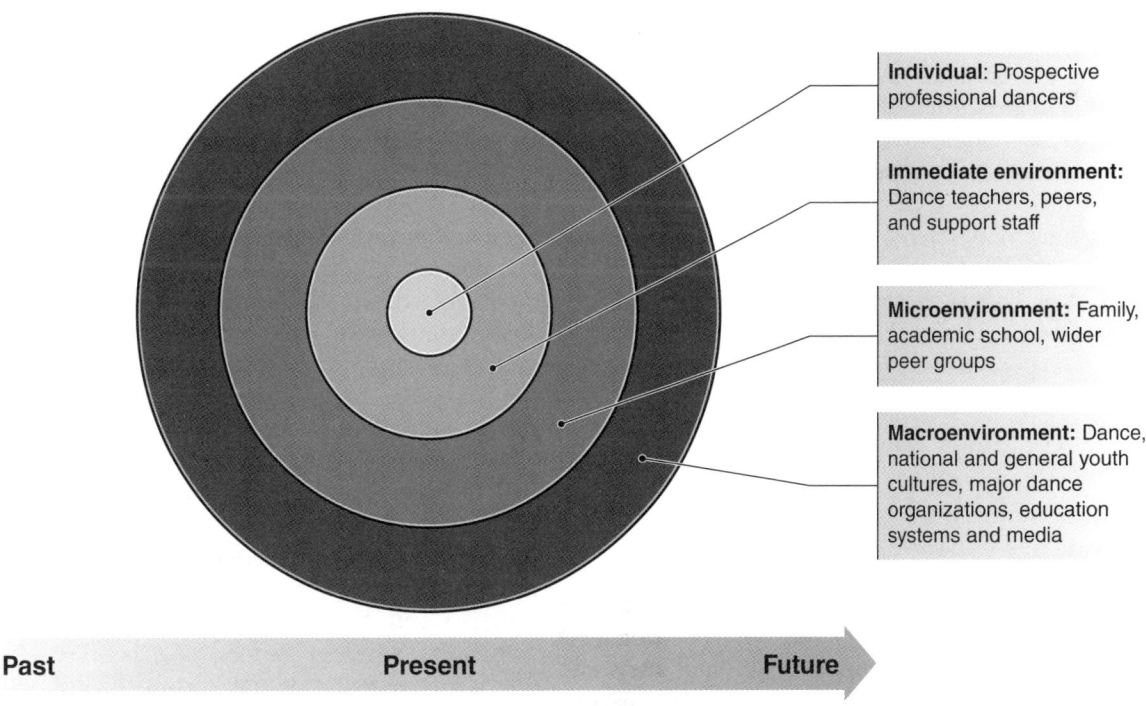

Figure 12.4 A simplified version of the athletic talent development environment working model contextualized for dance.
Adapted from Henriksen and Stambulova (2017).

their subsequent likelihood of success. Given this complexity, it is perhaps no surprise that each environment studied has, to some extent, been unique (Henriksen & Stambulova, 2017). At the same time, several features common to these successful environments have been identified. In the Get Practical exercise (form 12.1), you can learn more about these features and use them as inspiration for your own dance environment.

Consequences of Talent Beliefs and Talent Identification

In this section, literature examining the consequences of being identified as talented on both well-being and on performance-related aspects will be outlined. These are not necessarily as positive as one might first expect but rather comprise a combination of positive and negative potential outcomes. First, however, a different but related area of research will be introduced that focuses on the consequences of holding different beliefs about what talent is.

Consequences of Holding Different Beliefs About Talent

Research has shown that beliefs about the nature of talent can affect a variety of important outcomes, including performance and well-being. In particular, having a growth mindset is important (Dweck, 2006/2017; also Chua, 2014b, 2015; Harter et al., 2019; Wattie & Baker, 2017). When a person has a growth mindset (also known as an incremental theory of ability), they view talent and ability as something dynamic that can be changed and is partly under their control. That is, they align with a nurture view of talent (Wattie & Baker, 2017). As a result, they have adaptive responses to challenge and to failure, such as these:

> Determination, wanting to try again and putting in more effort
> Task-involvement (an aspect of healthy motivation; see chapter 5)
> Attributing failure to controllable factors such as a lack of effort or insufficient preparation

Conversely, there are persons who view talent and ability as largely innate and fixed (also known as an entity theory of ability): "You either have it or you don't." In other words, they align more with a nature view of talent (Wattie & Baker, 2017). Because talent is perceived as uncontrollable, they exhibit less adaptive responses to challenge and to failure, such as these:

> Avoidance, including self-handicapping (giving excuses) or giving up
> Self-judgment and a sense of helplessness
> Ego-involvement (an aspect of unhealthy motivation; see chapter 5)

Unsurprisingly, those with a growth mindset learn and progress more over time and enjoy their participation more (Harter et al., 2019; Ward et al., 2017; Wattie & Baker, 2017). Of course, not everything is changeable or under personal control, and suggesting that every challenge can be solved with effort might lead to problems such as overtraining (Baker et al., 2018; Wattie & Baker, 2017).

The mindset of leaders (e.g., dance teachers, juries) also matters, because leaders with a growth mindset are likely to take a more inclusive view of talent and thus be less selective with young people; they typically also give more feedback (Baker et al., 2018; Ward et al., 2017). Because our mindsets are influenced by significant others, leaders such as educators, juries, and parents should be careful when they use words like *talent*, or expressions like "you have such a gift," because their intended praise might inadvertently promote a fixed mindset (Wattie & Baker, 2017).

An illustration of how different types of teacher praise may affect dancers' mindsets is provided in the functional analyses in figure 12.5. Note that the teacher is positive and complimentary in both examples. In the first example, the teacher praises a student for his talent. But talent is often seen as something fixed and outside one's personal control; therefore, frequent praise of this nature may nurture an entity theory of ability (**fixed mindset**) in the student. Although this may have positive short-term effects such as feeling flattered, the long-term consequences can be problematic, especially if the dancer's ability is later called into question ("Perhaps I don't have what it takes, after all.").

In the second example, praise is given for effort and strategy (e.g., working well). Because such things are controllable, frequent praise of this nature may nurture an incremental theory of ability (growth mindset) in the student. This, in turn, has positive consequences both in the short and the long term, because it helps the dancer feel competent and in control, which stimulates ongoing effort and engagement.

Form 12.1 GET PRACTICAL: SUCCESSFUL TALENT DEVELOPMENT ENVIRONMENTS

In the table are seven features characteristic of successful talent development environments (Henriksen & Stambulova, 2017). You can use the table to better understand such environments and to identify which features are present or absent in your own environment. The table is based on research in sports; as such, exercise critical thinking regarding the applicability of these features to dance, and feel free to suggest your own!

FEATURES	DESCRIPTIONS	PRESENT IN MY DANCE ENVIRONMENT (1 = NOT AT ALL, 5 = VERY MUCH)	PERSONAL REFLECTIONS
1. Supportive relationships	• Inclusivity and support within classes and the school, regardless of level • Good communication	1 2 3 4 5	
2. Proximal role models	• Different levels train together • Higher-level dancers help lower-level dancers learn	1 2 3 4 5	
3. Wider environment supports dancers' goals	• Family, school, friends, and others support the dancers' pursuit of excellence • Different agents communicate and coordinate demands on the dancers' time	1 2 3 4 5	
4. Support for psychosocial skill development	• Dancers are seen as rounded human beings • Psychosocial skills useful to both dance and life are taught and encouraged (e.g., autonomy, commitment, responsibility)	1 2 3 4 5	
5. Diversified training	• Training in multiple dance styles • Versatility is valued	1 2 3 4 5	
6. Focus on long-term development	• Long-term development is seen as more important than early success • Training is age-appropriate	1 2 3 4 5	
7. Strong, coherent organizational culture	• Culture supports the learning environment • Everyday actions are in line with stated overall values	1 2 3 4 5	

Go to HKPropel to download this form.

From S. Nordin-Bates, *Essentials of Dance Psychology* (Champaign, IL: Human Kinetics, 2023).

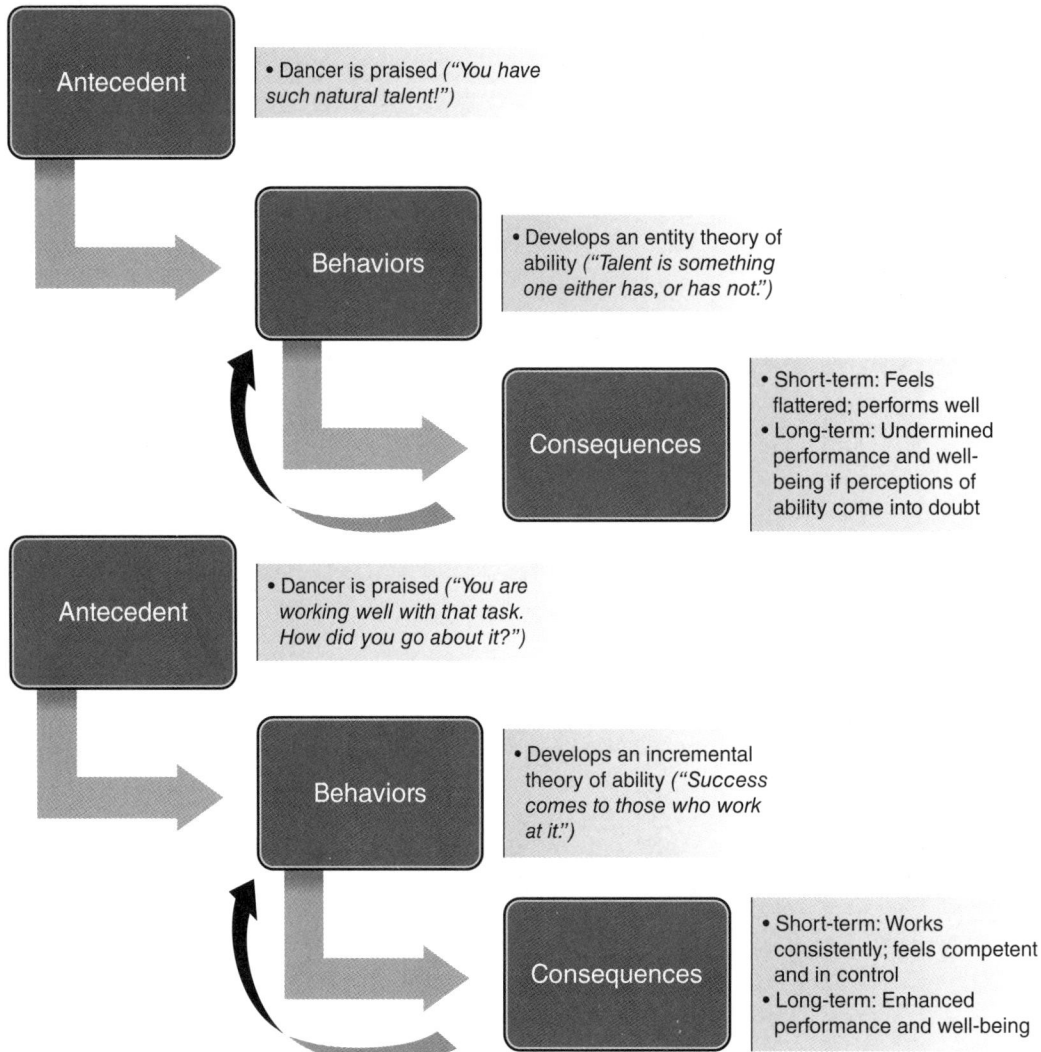

Figure 12.5 Functional analysis examples of how different mindsets (theories of ability) may affect dancers. The recursive arrows indicate that the consequences make the behavior more likely to reoccur in similar situations in the future (behavior maintenance).

Well-Being-Related Consequences of Talent Identification

Research with high-level dancers indicates that many get told that they possess some form of talent for dance, often by a teacher (Aujla et al., 2014; van Rossum, 2001). Some researchers have also addressed what impact such talent identification, or labeling, can have on performers' well-being (Aujla et al., 2014; Baker et al., 2018; Speirs Neumeister et al., 2009; Wattie & Baker, 2017):

› *Improved self-confidence and positive affect.* In many cases, telling a dancer that they are talented has the presumably intended effect of making them feel good; for instance, it can enhance mood and make dancers feel more confident in their abilities. Such positive effects are more likely if the performer is doing well (not failing at the time) and has high perceived competence (Aujla et al., 2014; Wattie & Baker, 2017).

› *Improved motivation.* As a logical consequence of enhanced positive affect and self-confidence, dancers who are told they are talented can also get a motivation boost: "If *they* think I can do it, I really want to go for it!"

› *Increased sense of pressure.* In some cases, the labeling of someone as talented backfires and negatively influences how that person is thinking and feeling about themselves and their abilities. For instance, dancers may feel pressure to consistently deliver top quality performances, progress rapidly, or be the best.

Performance-Related Consequences of Talent Identification

Research has also addressed what impact the identification of someone as talented has on performance-related variables, including:

> *Improved access to resources and possible vulnerability.* An obvious advantage to being selected into a talent program is that such places typically aim to provide better facilities, training times, and teachers. Interestingly, some have argued that such preferential treatment may lead to a situation whereby performers feel controlled by their school, to the point of becoming more susceptible to abuse (e.g., "After all we have done for you . . ."; Malina et al., 2017).

> *Uncertain future performance level.* Research in a variety of sports shows that the factors that predict success early in life are not the same as those predicting success later on (Baker et al., 2018). Accordingly, talent identification models and procedures have rather low predictive validity (Güllich & Cobley, 2017; Vaeyens et al., 2008; Wattie & Baker, 2017). Talent scholar Joe Baker and his colleagues even concluded that "the relationship between current performance and future potential is, at best, imperfect and, at worst, meaningless" (Baker et al., 2019, p. 28). In one review of the literature, it was found that several longitudinal studies identified a predictive power of talent identification procedures of approximately zero. The most successful such procedures (i.e., those that were multifaceted) correctly predicted around 70% of young athletes to higher versus lower performing subsamples over multiple years (Güllich & Cobley, 2017). Yet this meant that the probability of a selected athlete actually reaching world-class level was still only about 0.2% (Güllich & Cobley, 2017). Other key messages from this literature are that earlier selection seems to be associated with greater junior success but lower chances of senior success, and that those who enter talent systems earlier also leave earlier (Güllich & Cobley, 2017).

The findings about talent prediction from sports are especially interesting in light of the talent identification processes illustrated in a study of circus recruiters (Bailey & MacMahon, 2018). Several participants were adamant that their experience and intuition were accurate, using statements such as "Not everybody does it; I can" and "I'm always right" (Bailey & MacMahon, 2018, p. 231, 233). The authors even concluded that "The familiarity achieved through experience over time appears to enable a talent identifier to more or less automatically and immediately assess and recognize a person's capacity, ability, or potential injury." (p. 233). It remains to be examined what the nature, predictive power, and influence of talent identification processes used in dance are. However, the small and somewhat dated literature in this area reports increases in adherence to a 3-year talent program from 30% to 70% when moving from one-off tests led by artists only to multifaceted longitudinal process-based assessments (Oreck et al., 2004).

How Can Talent Identification and Development Be Optimized?

Throughout this chapter you have been introduced to a number of considerations that affect talent identification and development processes. Next, you will find recommendations for how these processes can be optimized in dance contexts.

Retain as Many Dancers as Possible for as Long as Possible

Talent identification is fraught with difficulties. Therefore, avoid selections if possible and create a more open talent development environment (e.g., Vaeyens et al., 2008). In striving to retain "as many as possible for as long as possible" (Erikstad et al., 2021), we not only increase the number of skilled dancers overall but also (and arguably more importantly) provide the benefits of a talent development environment to more young people. Indeed, many have argued that dance talent development should be prioritized over identification (e.g., Critien & Ollis, 2006; Walker et al., 2010).

Make Selections Multidimensional, Longitudinal, and Transparent

When selections must be made, such as when spaces are limited, use a variety of evaluation tools to reflect the multifaceted nature of talent as far as possible. Research suggests that multidimensional approaches that account for maturation are superior to those that are unidimensional (e.g., assessing only anatomical or physiological features; Güllich & Cobley, 2017; Oreck et al., 2004; Weissensteiner, 2017). Moreover, selections should consider the potential for compensatory abilities and not rely overly on the assessment of one or a few skills.

By participating in a longer program over weeks (or even months) in an authentic dance context before rate of progress is assessed by multiple people, many of the problems inherent in cross-sectional tests are avoided (Aujla & Redding, 2014; Baum et al., 1996; Haroutounian, 1995; Oreck et al., 2004; Redding et al., 2011; Vaeyens et al., 2008; Warburton, 2002). Such procedures also have the advantage of giving the dancer a chance to evaluate the school that they are considering, rather than it only being the other way around. Naturally, using single assessments by a small jury is cheap and convenient, but that does not make it good; schools and companies should be aware that better assessment is more costly (Warburton, 2002).

Finally, it is recommended that assessors are clear—both in their own minds and in communication with dancers and parents—that talent identification is imperfect and impermanent. They should be transparent about criteria and procedures used and aim to provide feedback to everyone regardless of outcome.

Carefully Consider the Role of Psychological Factors in Selection

Although the importance of psychological factors in talent identification and development is indisputable (e.g., Abbott & Collins, 2004; Chua, 2014b; Dohme et al., 2019; Olszewski-Kubilius et al., 2019; Walker et al., 2010), assessing psychological characteristics and skills as part of talent identification procedures is usually not a good idea. This is because performers are likely to answer in ways they believe show them in the most favorable light if they suspect that their answers will be used for selection (i.e., social desirability; Weissensteiner, 2017).

Psychological skills and characteristics are also possible to nurture and to train. It is therefore at best difficult and at worst unethical to try to select dancers based on psychological attributes. Indicators of healthy motivation are possible exceptions; dancers who exhibit strong intrinsic motivation and a healthy passion for dance should perhaps be preferentially admitted into talent development schemes (Abbott & Collins, 2004; Aujla & Redding, 2014; Walker et al., 2010). Motivation can certainly be nurtured, but there is a certain logic to admitting those who are most interested and passionate about dance but not extrinsically or obsessively so.

Make Talent Systems Permeable

As you have learned (or already knew), the talent development journeys of dancers are idiosyncratic and unpredictable. For this reason, it is critically important that talent identification and development systems are permeable—that is, open for reentry at multiple time points (figure 12.2; Güllich & Cobley, 2017; Weissensteiner, 2017).

Make Talent Development a Rich, Varied Experience

To avoid talent development becoming an overly narrow, rigid, and repetitive experience, it is recommended that dancers engage in a variety of styles with several teachers and peer groups. They can also be recommended to partake in non-dance activities and be exposed to other forms of art—both for variety and for nurturing themselves as rounded, creative dance artists and human beings. Experiencing rich diversity within dance should also help young people find dance styles and activities (e.g., performing, choreographing) that they are truly intrinsically motivated for. For more information and recommendations relating to the development of a broad identity, see chapter 1.

Go to HKPropel to download lettering art highlighting the value of variety.

Embrace Challenges in the Talent Development Process

Support in the talent development process is imperative, but research suggests that talent is best developed when challenges are embraced rather than avoided (Collins & MacNamara, 2017). In fact, these authors suggest that the talent development journey should not be overly smooth; for instance, if a young dancer has abundant "natural talent," he might not develop the experience or coping skills required to succeed at higher levels. By encountering progressively larger challenges, performers can instead gradually learn to cope—and in so doing, grow their self-confidence. Post-challenge debriefings are crucial for challenges to lead to growth, however: What did they experience? How can they use that experience to learn and progress?

To Optimize Talent Development, Nurture Psychological Skills

To ensure that challenges (which may include injury, deselection, and performance slumps) lead to growth and learning rather than disillusionment or dropout, performers should be taught psychological skills—and this should not wait until the late teens or when performers are already identified as talented (see also Abbott & Collins, 2004; Blijlevens et al., 2018; Olszewski-Kubilius et al., 2019). Such skills can include those outlined in chapters 8-10 in this book, but the ability to seek social support from peers, family, and dance school staff (teachers, physiotherapists, among others) is also valuable.

To Sustain Talent Development Over Time, Nurture Healthy Motivation

Research specifically focused on talented dancers indicates the importance of teachers who are knowledgeable and structured but also warm and approachable (e.g., Chua, 2014b, 2015; Pickard, 2012; van Rossum, 2001). Such need-supportive teaching is imperative for talent development because the journey from novice to high-level or even professional dancer is long and challenging. Sustaining intrinsic interest and love for dance is therefore of vital importance; without it, talent development will either not happen at all or be an unrewarding or even meaningless slog. In fact, suboptimal forms of motivation are known to predict dropout over time (e.g., external regulation, amotivation, obsessive passion; see chapter 5), whereas a healthy, harmonious passion has been shown to predict adherence to dance talent development over time (Aujla et al., 2015). As noted by these authors, such findings confront the traditional stereotype of dancers having to sacrifice everything for their art. For more information about the importance of nurturing healthy motivation for dancers in general, see chapter 11.

Tim: Case Study of Talent Development

Tim started ballet at age five and increased the number of weekly lessons every year. With several family members involved in dance, this was just the normal thing to do. Already at eight he'd made his decision: He wanted to be a professional dancer! Two years later, he was admitted to a prestigious vocational school where he stayed until graduating at age 18. Since then, he's had a successful career in an esteemed company. At first glance, then, this looks like a story of early specialization. But what is specialization, really, and how does it affect dancers? After all, Tim has also seen some classmates struggle with narrow identities and mental health issues after seemingly similar journeys to his own. In talking to some of them, Tim discovered some differences between those with more and less positive experiences. For instance, his friend Victoria was talent spotted and sent to a top school by her well-meaning parents who felt her gift mustn't be wasted. Victoria described having a sense of obligation throughout her schooling. Although she was buoyed up by frequent positive feedback ("She's such a natural talent!"), she didn't really enjoy the process itself and she resented the exclusive focus on ballet at the expense of seemingly everything else. As she got older and the competition increased, anxiety issues started to surface. She left dance after just two years as a professional.

Tim also worked diligently from an early age, but he also had a strong interest in art and played some tennis. His parents encouraged him to focus on academic subjects in parallel with dancing, because dance is a difficult career at best. They also reminded him that the world is a big place and that there are always options, both outside and inside of dance. Yet with every offer and at every juncture, Tim chose ballet; it was always the most enticing option. Although it is difficult to know what exactly contributes to the different experiences that dancers have, it certainly seems important to feel that the journey is one's own.

Composite case study created on the basis of conversations with Kit Holder, MA, a soloist with Birmingham Royal Ballet, England, and a performance psychology student.

CRITICAL ASPECTS OF RESEARCH INTO TALENT

1. Numerous definitions of talent exist, so it remains difficult to conceptualize and measure unambiguously. Some argue that models of talent development should perhaps be referred to as models of skill development, because talent is an antecedent of skill-based outcomes (Baker et al., 2019).

2. A large proportion of research into talent, deliberate practice, and related topics relies on retrospective recall of activities that have happened years (sometimes decades) ago. Naturally, such research is subject to memory biases.

3. This chapter has loosely considered success as the progression of a dancer to professional status, in line with most of the research in the area. However, success can be defined in many other ways, and people may display dance talent not only in terms of performance ability but also for choreography, teaching, and more (Haroutounian, 1995; Walker et al., 2010). Along with the dominant focus on ballet in dance talent literature, this means that research into different forms of talent in different forms of dance is warranted.

4. When there are more applicants than roles or spaces available, it is probably easiest to select those with the highest levels of physical, psychological, technical, and expressive skill even if these are partly trainable; at the same time, most people would balk if a school selected only dancers with specific body proportions and high emotional stability from affluent families. Even if these aspects indicate talent or enhance talent development, such selections strike us as unfair. Those involved in talent identification should carefully consider the motivation, knowledge, and evidence base underpinning their practices. They can then consider what can realistically be achieved within the boundaries of expertise, time, and budget, as well as potential ethical implications.

KEY POINTS AND RECOMMENDATIONS AROUND TALENT IN DANCE

1. In any talent identification process, or even discussion about talent, exercise caution. Talent is multifaceted, dynamic, and subjective, and nobody has a crystal ball that can accurately predict the future of either individual dancers or of dance as an ever-evolving art form.

2. The risk of missing talent is greater when we select early, when we select stringently (very few individuals), and when there are poor opportunities for the deselected in comparison to the selected. Therefore, talent systems should be as inclusive and permeable as possible.

3. To optimize development is good for everyone, whether identified as talented or not. Hence, focus less on talent identification and more on development, including the development of growth mindsets. In so doing, more people will have the potential to excel—and to surprise us.

Injury

"There are three steps you have to complete to become a professional dancer: learn to dance, learn to perform and learn how to cope with injuries."

David Gere, arts professor, activist, and critic

CHAPTER OBJECTIVES

After reading this chapter, you will be able to

1. describe psychological aspects of dance injury, including psychological risk factors for injury, reactions to injury, and psychological aspects of rehabilitation;
2. describe the stress-injury model and its applicability to dance;
3. critically discuss the role of personality factors and cultural factors in overuse injuries;
4. outline typical reactions to dance injury and how they may change from negative to positive as the injury gets closer to healing;
5. apply basic recommendations to manage psychological risk factors for injury in dance and for enhancing recovery;

6. use an observation and imagery worksheet when injured or encourage others to do so; and
7. think critically about the nature and impact of psychology in relation to injury in dance.

Key Terms

avoidance coping	emotion-focused coping	problem-focused coping
cognitive appraisal	harmonious passion	stress-related growth
coping	history of stressors	stress response
coping skills	obsessive passion	

The term *injury* stems from the Latin word *iniūria*, meaning harm, damage, and something being wrong. Although it can be used to denote non-physical aspects (e.g., injuring someone's character), dance conversations are often firmly focused on injury as a physical phenomenon. Therefore, you may wonder what a chapter on injury is doing in a psychology book! Yet, psychological aspects affect the risk, experiences, and rehabilitation of dance injuries. Therefore, knowledge of injury psychology is valuable to dancers, teachers, and health care practitioners alike.

What Are the Key Psychological Aspects of Injury in Dance?

Injury is a truly multifaceted challenge, with several physical, psychological, and social aspects interacting. It is also a common challenge, with research from varied samples in many countries often identifying injury rates around 80% per year (Hincapié et al., 2008; Laws, 2005; Mainwaring et al., 2001; van Winden et al., 2020; Vassallo et al., 2019). Against this backdrop, it becomes important to consider the factors that contribute to injury and what helps dancers to overcome them. Within the scope of this book, this includes providing an overview of psychological risk factors for injury, dancers' experiences of injury, and psychological aspects of dance injury rehabilitation. These represent some of the more well-researched topics in dance psychology, and so the present chapter cites a larger number of dance-specific investigations than many others in this book. For an overview and examples of these three aspects, see figure 13.1.

Before delving into the psychological aspects of injury, we need to define injury itself. One relevant definition is that "injuries involve bodily tissue damage and/or functional impairments that occur as consequences of engagement in physical activities such as competitive or recreational sport, exercise, dance, or outdoor recreation." (Wiese-Bjornstal et al., 2020, p. 712). Taking a more restrictive approach, the International Association for Dance Medicine and Science (IADMS) define injury as an

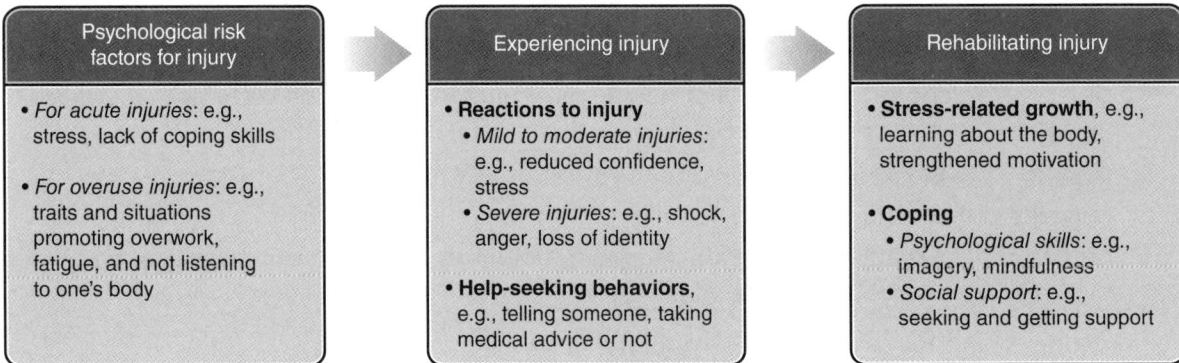

Figure 13.1 An overview of psychological aspects of dance injuries.

"anatomic tissue-level impairment diagnosed by a licensed healthcare practitioner that results in full time loss of activity for one or more days beyond the day of onset. 'Activity' for the sake of this definition means participation in a class, rehearsal, or performance. . . . For those events that fall short of this strict definition of injury the term 'musculoskeletal complaint' should apply." (Liederbach et al., 2012, p. 144)

Because self-report can be an unreliable source of data, focusing on injuries that are diagnosed by appropriate professionals helps to ensure more reliable injury reporting and thereby make studies in this area more comparable. At the same time, the injury definition used will affect the rate of injuries detected. As such, definitions such as the one provided by IADMS likely lead to an underestimation of the number of injuries that dancers actually sustain (Kenny et al., 2018). This is especially the case for overuse injuries, which develop gradually and thus do not allow for an easy yes or no answer to the question of whether a dancer is injured or not. Indeed, you are probably familiar with dancers answering "kind of" or "a bit" to that question. The slow emergence and sometimes intermittent nature of pain and other problems also mean that it is often possible to continue dancing on an overuse injury, even if it is not advisable.

Within the generally high rates of injury in dance, most injuries (60% to 75%) are not acute but rather are overuse or chronic injuries (e.g., Air, 2009; Hincapié et al., 2008; Kenny et al., 2018). From a physiological standpoint, this reflects the large amount of training and meticulous repetition that characterizes the higher levels of many dance styles; indeed, fatigue has been noted as a major cause of injury (Liederbach & Compagno, 2001; Mainwaring & Finney, 2017). For instance, a pioneering study of 500 dance injury reports revealed that most injuries arose when dancers were feeling tired (90%), had danced more than 5 hours that day (79%), and were doing familiar repertoire (79%; Liederbach & Compagno, 2001).

From a psychological standpoint, the large proportion of overuse injuries may be related to the inherent difficulties in identifying the early signs of slowly emerging overuse injuries; indeed, such signs appear to be what dancers are socialized into ignoring, only stopping dance activity in response to more severe, acute injuries (Aalten, 2007; Alexias & Dimitropoulou, 2011; Blevins et al., 2019; Hanrahan, 1996; Kaufmann et al., 2021; Krasnow et al., 1994; Mainwaring et al., 2001, 2003; McEwen & Young, 2011; Tarr & Thomas, 2021; Wainwright & Turner, 2004). For example, a dancer in an early interview study stated: "I tend to push myself too much sometimes. If I'm sick I do go to class. The only way it really stops me sometimes is if I'm just about half dead." (Hanrahan, 1996, p. 22).

Although most of these investigations have focused on classical ballet, studies focused on contemporary dancers at a variety of levels have provided similar findings (Blevins et al., 2019; Markula, 2015; Thomas & Tarr, 2009). Even amateur dancers have been reported to fully accept dancing in pain (Markula, 2015). Further research into a variety of styles and cultures is highly warranted, because a wide array of attitudes toward pain and injury are likely to exist. For those in well-resourced companies and schools, the increased knowledge of dance science and health care provision over time has hopefully increased awareness and use of injury prevention and rehabilitation strategies. The increased use of somatic techniques in dance training may also have affected the extent to which dancers listen to their own bodies. In one study, contemporary dancers valued the body awareness that can result from somatic practices very highly, not least because they felt that it could prevent injuries (Markula, 2015).

Psychological Risk Factors for Acute Injury: Stress-Injury Model

A commonly used model to illustrate how psychological factors may contribute to the risk of sustaining an acute injury centers on stress and is consequently known as the stress and injury model (Williams & Andersen, 1998). Originally developed for sports, it has also been used in several dance investigations (Noh et al., 2003, 2005, 2007; Pollitt & Hutt, 2021; Skvarla & Clement, 2019; van Winden et al., 2020, 2021). For an overview of the components of the stress-injury model using dance-specific language, see table 13.1. In the sections that follow, the different model components will be introduced.

The Stressful Situation

At the heart of the stress-injury model is a potentially stressful situation (e.g., audition or competition), which leads to a **stress response** within an individual; an elevated stress response, in turn, makes a person more likely to become injured (Williams & Andersen, 1998). Research in sports has confirmed the existence of such stress-injury relationships (for reviews, see Ivarsson et al., 2017a; Wiese-Bjornstal et al., 2020). Similarly, a recent systematic review of musculoskeletal injury risk factors among preprofessional

Table 13.1 **Components of the Stress-Injury Model, with Dance Examples**

Stress-injury model component	Dance-relevant examples	Role in the stress-injury process
Potentially stressful situation	- Assessments - Auditions - Performances - Competitions	Trigger
Stress Response		
- Cognitive appraisal	- Interpreting the situation as highly threatening	Mechanisms
- Physiological and attentional changes	- Muscle tension - Narrow, internal focus	
Injury	- Going over on the ankle - Tearing a muscle	Outcome
History of stressors	- Negative life stress - Daily hassles - Previous injuries	Risk and preventive factors
Coping resources	- Social support - Psychological skills	
Personality	- Trait anxiety - Perfectionism - Obsessive passion for dance	

Adapted from Williams and Andersen (1998).

dance students found that several types of stress were associated with elevated injury risk (Kenny et al., 2016; also, Mainwaring et al., 2001; van Winden et al., 2021). It is notable that stress can be related not only to injury frequency but also duration: for instance, dancers reporting higher levels of worry and lower self-confidence and motivation may be injured more often; dancers with higher levels of worry and negative stress in the dance environment may be injured for longer (Noh et al., 2005).

The stress response is thought to convey increased injury risk as a result of two considerations: the **cognitive appraisals** that take place (e.g., interpreting an event as pressuring, threatening, and important), and the accompanying physiological and attentional changes (Williams & Andersen, 1998). These form the central components of the stress response (table 13.1). Physiological changes include overly tense muscles, whereas attentional changes include one or more of the following:

> Distractibility
> Attention disruption (e.g., because of worries or concerns)
> Narrowed attentional focus (e.g., experiencing tunnel vision)

What Makes Dancers Likely to Perceive Situations as Stressful?

The stress-injury model outlines three psychological variables that affect the stress response, including one's **history of stressors**, coping resources, and personality. Relatively extensive research has been conducted into them all, including in dance (Kenny et al., 2016; Mainwaring et al., 2001; Mainwaring & Finney, 2017; Pollitt & Hutt, 2021; also, Blevins et al., 2019), and the following sections introduce them in turn.

History of Stressors

The stress-injury model indicates that performers with high levels of negative life stress, daily hassles (small, accumulating stressors), and previous injuries are at greater risk of an elevated stress response (Williams & Andersen, 1998). Of all the stress-injury model components, having a history of stressors is the most prominent predictor of injury among athletes after elevated stress responses (Ivarsson et al., 2017a). Daily hassles include small irritations and frustrations that gradually accumulate into a heightened stress response. For example, being delayed in traffic might be a minor irritation, but if combined

Research consistently shows that around 80% of high-level dancers sustain at least one injury per year.

with exams at school and an argument at home, there can be significant effects on an individual's level of stress and subsequent injury risk. Negative life stress, in contrast, refers to more major events that often cause heightened stress responses. Examples include relationship issues (e.g., divorce) or major financial insecurity. Dancers leaving home at a young age to pursue vocational training in an unfamiliar city and graduates trying to cope with the demands of life as freelance artists, may therefore be at higher injury risk due to increased life stress (Pollitt & Hutt, 2021).

Coping Resources

Coping is defined as "constantly changing cognitive and behavioral efforts to manage specific external and/or internal demands that are appraised as taxing or exceeding the resources of the person" (Lazarus & Folkman, 1984, p. 141), and those without adequate coping resources typically experience an elevated stress response. In a recent study with contemporary dance students, poor coping skills were a predictor of more serious injuries over a one-year period (van Winden et al., 2020). Other studies have shown that the stress-injury relationship may only exist for those with low coping resources (Ivarsson et al., 2017a; Noh et al., 2003). This is because well-developed **coping skills** help buffer the effects of stress, which means there may be no elevated stress response. Such skills include social support (or ability to ask for help) as well as psychological skills such as imagery, goal setting, self-regulation, mindfulness, self-talk, and relaxation (e.g., Barrell & Terry, 2003; Mainwaring & Finney, 2017; Noh et al., 2009).

In general, **problem-focused coping** is preferable because it is about tackling problems head-on, such as finding root causes of a problem, planning, getting information (e.g., professional injury diagnosis), and mental or physical practice (Nicholls & Polman, 2007). **Emotion-focused coping**, in contrast, aims to reduce the stress resulting from a problem and includes talking to friends and family, crying, using humor, and using stress-reducing practices such as mindfulness. Although these do not address the root cause of a problem, they may be cathartic and can help the dancer gain perspective before using more problem-focused strategies. They can also be useful when a problem is out of one's control, such as when living with chronic pain (Nicholls & Polman, 2007).

One unhelpful set of coping strategies is known as **avoidance coping** and may be considered a subset of emotion-focused coping, because they both focus on alleviating the stress from a problem rather than on addressing the problem itself. Avoidance coping includes strategies such as ignoring pain, avoiding help-seeking, disengaging, or using substances or food (e.g., drinking alcohol, over- or undereating). Although such strategies may help dancers feel better in the moment, they typically increase stress in the long run (Noh et al., 2009). In sum, avoidance coping is problematic, whereas emotion-focused coping can be both more and less helpful, depending on the person and the situation.

If you have read chapter 1, you may recall that personality is likely to influence the types of coping strategies used, even though they are also quite possible to learn.

Personality

The stress-injury model further suggests that personality aspects can increase injury risk if they predispose a person to elevated stress responses (Williams & Andersen, 1998). Although literature in this area is not as established as that for history of stressors or for coping, it appears that performers with higher levels of personality traits such as trait anxiety, perfectionism, or **obsessive passion** are at greater risk of injury. In one interview study, a dancer described her perceptions of how personality might cause stress in this way (Noh et al., 2009, p. 128):

> I think that I have a problem with my personality. When something happened, I couldn't ignore it, even if it is a trivial matter. When I got home, I always thought again and again and again. Some people paid no attention to what was going on, but I couldn't ignore these things. It made me tired and stressed out.

This type of rumination is typical of people with high levels of perfectionistic concerns (see chapter 2). Correspondingly, two early and small-scale studies found correlations between perfectionism and injury in dance (Krasnow et al., 1999; Liederbach & Compagno, 2001; also, Nordin-Bates & Abrahamsen, 2016); a more recent investigation did not (van Winden et al., 2020). Small, varied populations and measurement differences may account for the varied results. In sports, a methodologically stronger investigation has supported the existence of a perfectionism-injury relationship (Madigan et al., 2018). Specifically, youth athletes with higher levels of perfectionistic concerns were more likely to sustain an injury over a 10-month period.

Obsessive passion is another personality disposition that may heighten injury susceptibility. It is defined as an uncompromising drive to engage in an activity (e.g., dance) that is associated with internal pressure and struggling to detach oneself from that activity, even in the face of adverse consequences (Vallerand et al., 2003). Obsessive passion is contrasted with **harmonious passion**, a flexible form of engagement associated with healthy persistence that still allows a person to engage in other activities without guilt or distress. In one study, more harmoniously passionate dance students from a mixture of styles reported shorter acute injury durations than their peers (Rip et al., 2006). The associated finding that obsessively passionate students reported longer durations for their chronic injuries is an example of how aspects of the stress-injury model can be useful in understanding not only acute but also overuse injuries.

Intervening to Weaken the Stress-Injury Relationship

The authors of the stress-injury model originally suggested that interventions should target the stress response to reduce injury risk; it was suggested that imagery, relaxation, and social support would be helpful in this regard (Williams & Andersen, 1998). More recently, mindfulness has been added to the list of potentially useful interventions for injury prevention (Ivarsson et al., 2015; Naderi et al., 2020). This makes sense, because mindfulness practice improves our ability to identify when focus has wandered and bring it back to the present in a nonjudgmental way (see chapter 8). Thus, mindfulness addresses the core of the stress-injury model by helping to reduce the attentional narrowing and disrupted attention thought to underpin elevated injury risk. Research has also made clear that interventions may target one or more of the psychological antecedents of the stress response. Therefore, interventions may address any one of the central components of the model, whereas the original model included mention of interventions only in regard to the stress response itself.

Several interventions have been conducted to try and reduce the risk of injury through psychological means, and many have been successful (for reviews, see Ivarsson et al., 2017a; Wiese-Bjornstal et al., 2020). To date, two such interventions have been conducted in dance. In the first, Noh et al. (2007) recruited ballet students with somewhat poor coping skills for a 12-week intervention. Three groups were created: an autogenic training (a form of relaxation training) group, a broad-based coping skills (including imagery, self-talk, and autogenic training) group, and a no-intervention control group. Dancers in the broad-based intervention improved their coping skills to a greater extent than dancers in the other two groups, and improvements were also found for psychological characteristics such as concentration. Participants also reported their injuries for 48 weeks post-intervention, with the broad-based intervention dancers reporting shorter injury durations than control group dancers. Finally, there was some indication that injury frequency differed between the groups, although it did not reach statistical significance (Noh et al., 2007).

A subsequent intervention with college dance students comprised a shorter time frame (four weeks) and yielded no significant effects on coping skills (Skvarla & Clement, 2019). Unfortunately, injury incidence became difficult to measure in a small sample over a short time frame. A key difference between the studies is that Noh et al. (2007) specifically recruited dancers with limited coping skills, whereas Skvarla and Clement (2019) did not; in fact, the latter cohort was already somewhat knowledgeable about psychological skills. Although this meant that they likely had less potential for improvement, they did wish for psychological skills training more often and for longer. It is an important task for future researchers to identify optimal populations, intervention durations, and session content, with the ultimate aim of developing interventions that are effective not only in terms of outcomes but are also time and cost efficient.

Beyond the Stress-Injury Model: Other Psychological Risk Factors for Dance Injury

Although the stress-injury model is the most widely used model of its kind, researchers keep identifying additional variables that can affect injury risk (e.g., Ivarsson et al., 2017a). These have not yet made it into any published model modification attempts, but the following additional risk factors for injury are worth noting, not least to increase awareness of warning signs (Adam et al., 2004; Kenny et al., 2016; Liederbach & Compagno, 2001; Mainwaring et al., 2001; Mainwaring & Finney, 2017; Martin et al., 2021; Pollitt & Hutt, 2021; Shrier & Hallé, 2011; Wiese-Bjornstal et al., 2020):

› Perceptions of fatigue and poor sleep
› Negative moods, low self-confidence, and general psychological distress
› Narrow dancer identity (see chapter 1)
› Disordered eating (see chapter 14)
› Various forms of pressure and lack of support (e.g., having to learn quickly and always perform at one's peak)
› Poor self-care and not seeking help as appropriate

A recent international investigation asked high-level ballet dancers to retrospectively score their injuries and motivational climate perceptions over the past two years (Kaufmann et al., 2021). Those who recalled their main teacher/ballet master as being more disempowering (i.e., ego involving and need thwarting; see chapter 11) were more likely to sustain both acute and overuse injuries during that time. The relationship was stronger for overuse injuries, probably because they occur over a period of time (rather than as accidents); therefore, they are more likely to be affected by the motivational climate.

Sociological literature has emphasized dance subculture as an inherent risk factor for dance injuries. Primarily focused on ballet, such literature goes as far as labeling ballet as a "culture of risk," in which hierarchical structures, a constant striving for perfection, competitiveness, and unquestioning obedience combine to enhance injury risk (e.g., Aalten, 2007; McEwen & Young, 2011; Pickard, 2012; Turner & Wainwright, 2003; Wainwright & Turner, 2004). This is thought to occur if and when dancers come to internalize messages such as "no pain, no gain," that more training is always better, or that pain is to be ignored and danced through rather than talked about or taken as a warning. Although this literature has often not specified whether the increased risk is for acute or chronic injuries, both could be true. For instance, the stress inherent in a culture of risk would likely contribute to a generally elevated stress response among dancers; according to the stress-injury model (Williams & Andersen, 1998), this should make them more susceptible to acute injuries.

The noted cultural risk factors likely also predispose dancers to overwork and to ignoring early warning signs of injury—both precursors of fatigue and overuse injuries (Kenny et al., 2016; Liederbach & Compagno, 2001; Mainwaring & Finney, 2017). Along similar lines, personality dispositions such as narrow identity, obsessive passion, and perfectionism can make a dancer more likely to return from a previous injury too quickly, thereby increasing the risk for reinjury. This is because dancers with such characteristics have strong internal pressures to constantly work and improve, making any time off a stressful experience.

Figure 13.2 provides an example of how functional analysis may be used to understand the potential role of cultural risk factors in predisposing dancers to overuse injuries. In the first example, Jason is dancing in a company with a strong no pain, no gain culture, in which dancing with pain is seen as a sign of commitment to the company and to dance itself. As a result of his immersion in this culture, Jason is more likely to ignore his body when it is sending pain signals, even though he knows that they may indicate the first signs of an injury. By ignoring his pain and continuing to dance, Jason experiences the short-term benefits of feeling committed and that he is doing the right thing. Because he does not stop dancing or seek help, he is also less likely to get medical attention for his pain. Yet in the long term, he increases his risk of overuse injury; he may also experience longer injury durations when he eventually does have to stop dancing (e.g., when pain becomes unbearable).

In the second example, Jason has started dancing in another company where the culture is quite

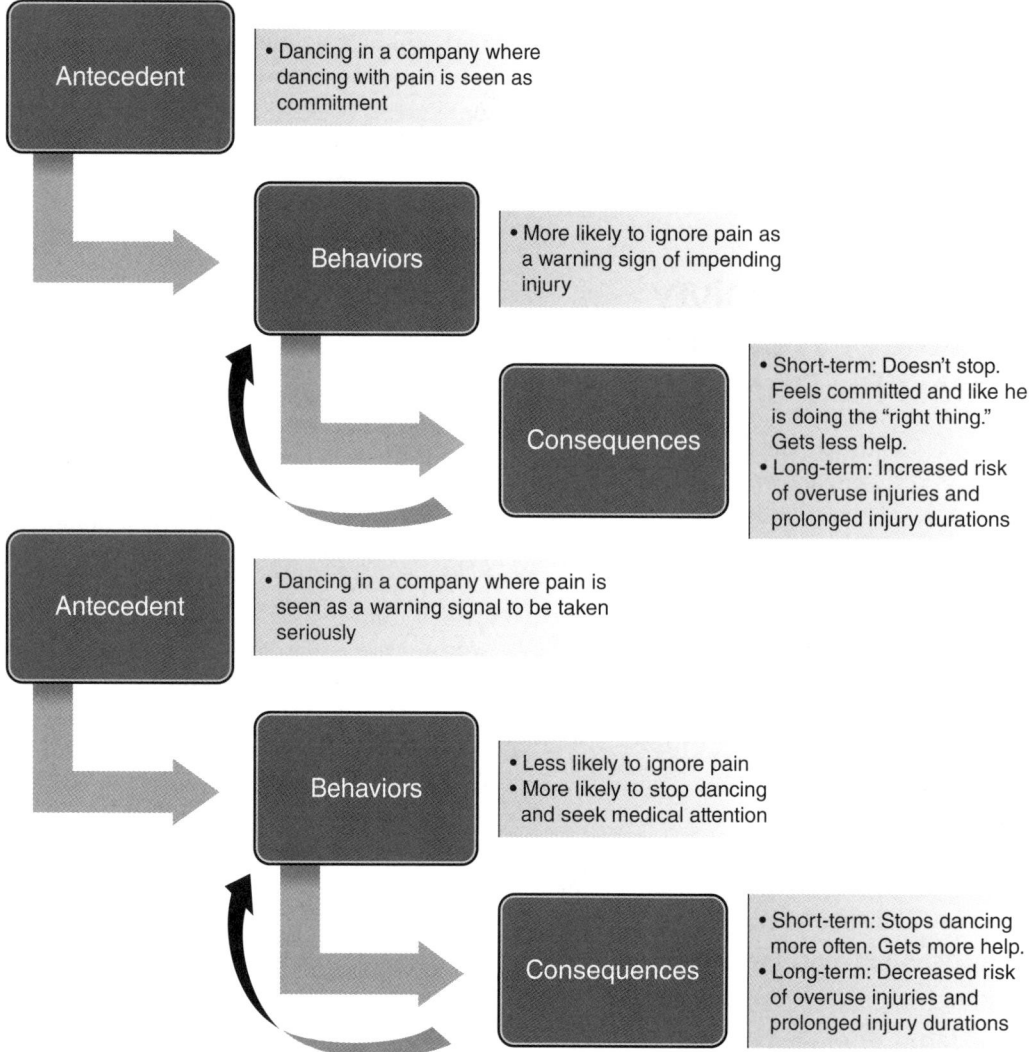

Figure 13.2 Functional analysis examples of how different cultures may lead to different injury-related behaviors and how these can affect a dancer's risk of overuse injuries. The recursive arrows indicate that the consequences make the behavior more likely to reoccur in similar situations in the future (behavior maintenance).

different: Here, there is education of dancers and staff on matters of anatomy, physiology and injury, and dancing in pain is discouraged. Indeed, dancers are told to interpret pain as an important warning signal. After being in this environment for a time, Jason becomes more likely to stop dancing when experiencing pain and seeks help more quickly. Although this has the short-term cost of having to stop dancing more often, he gets more help and understands that he is reducing the likelihood of both overuse injuries emerging and of injuries becoming prolonged in duration.

Stress is highly relevant also to overuse injuries. A recent study in sports is illuminative: adult athletes from a variety of sports were grouped on the basis of their scores for stress, several personality variables, and perceptions of their coach-athlete relationship (Martin et al., 2021). It emerged that athletes with strong athletic identity and perfectionistic concerns, moderate levels of perfectionistic strivings, poor coach-athlete relationships, and very high levels of negative life stress were more likely to suffer from overuse injuries. Notably, it was the combination of these variables that appeared to convey increased risk rather than any one of them in isolation.

> **THINKING CRITICALLY**
>
> - Can you identify any psychological risk factors for injury in yourself or in your dancers?
> - Have you noticed yourself or your dancers experiencing physiological or attentional changes as a result of stress?
> - Is your dance environment a culture of risk or a context within which pain is seen as a warning sign and injuries are openly discussed without stigma?

It can be difficult to discern the order of causality in relating psychological variables to injury, especially because the literature includes studies with cross-sectional study designs. For example, one study found significant correlations between dance injury and several psychological variables including stress, negative moods, sleep quality, and social support (Adam et al., 2004). Yet it was not possible to determine whether psychological distress led to prolonged injury durations or whether the experience of being injured for longer led dancers to feel distressed. As the authors stated, it is also possible (even likely) that there are reciprocal relationships between these variables. This leads us into the next section, which focuses on dancers' experiences of injury.

Dancers' Injury Experiences

It is self-evident that injury has psychological sequelae, and literature reviews describe how injured performers typically experience mild to moderate negative consequences such as reduced confidence, stress, and anxiety (Mainwaring & Finney, 2017; Wiese-Bjornstal et al., 2020). After more severe injuries, dancers may experience shock, disbelief, anger, confusion, grief, depression, a loss of identity, or all of these (Mainwaring et al., 2001, 2003; Markula, 2015; McEwen & Young, 2011; Turner & Wainwright, 2003; Vassallo et al., 2019; Wainwright & Turner, 2004). For instance, a case description of a student who had to stop dancing after a hip injury cited her as saying:

> I was no longer the person I wanted to be—a dancer. I felt like an intruder in a world of which I was no longer a part. The question I asked myself everyday was "Who am I when I am no longer a dancer?" (Mainwaring et al., 2003, p. 59)

Some dancers even feel guilty about being injured, for instance if they perceive injuries to be their own fault because they were not enough in tune with their bodies (Markula, 2015). At other points in their interviews, dancers in that study confessed to dancing in pain and through injury—for example, not to let others down. Ignoring the warning signs and either delaying or putting off seeking help until it is absolutely necessary have often been reported in the dance literature (Aalten, 2007; Alexias & Dimitropoulou, 2011; Blevins et al., 2019; Krasnow et al., 1994; Mainwaring et al., 2001, 2003; McEwen & Young, 2011; Wainwright & Turner, 2004). Krasnow and colleagues (1994, p. 8) wrote: "By not seeking help, the dancer can pretend that the injury is simply an annoyance and that he or she can continue to rehearse." In essence, this is avoidant coping: a failure to see and accept reality as it is. Although this literature paints a rather bleak picture, a recent investigation with professional dancers indicated that although 57% of full-time dancers and 72% of part-time dancers feared the repercussions that an injury might have (Vassallo et al., 2019), very few reported hiding or ignoring injuries.

High levels of obsessive passion may help explain why dancers do not reduce activity while injured or why they might avoid seeking help for their injuries. Indeed, obsessively passionate dancers are more likely to ignore injury-related pain, report that pride prevents them from seeking treatment, and are less likely to stop dancing when injured (Rip et al., 2006; see also Markula, 2015). In the study by Rip et al. (2006), dancers reporting higher levels of harmonious passion were instead *less* likely to ignore or hide their injuries and more likely to engage in self-initiated injury prevention strategies. Although using different theoretical frameworks, findings from other studies are similar. For example, a participant in an interview study explained her experiences of struggling to take time off from injury:

> I find that ballet and dancing is something that I need to do. . . . I've been off for injuries, I've almost got a little bit depressed because I miss it so much. So for me it's something I just have to do. (McEwen & Young, 2011, p. 169.)

To date, no studies have examined potential differences between dance subcultures or motivational climates regarding the likelihood of dancers ignoring their injuries or avoiding help-seeking. However, it appears likely that such behaviors would be more common in subcultures where extreme levels of commitment to dance, mental toughness, silence, and obedience are valued (Blevins et al.,

2019; Mainwaring et al., 2001; McEwen & Young, 2011; Noh et al., 2009). Dancers appear to sustain more injuries in motivational climates characterized by controlling leadership and favoritism (i.e., disempowering climates; Kaufmann et al., 2021).

Sociological studies have found that even when dancers acknowledge pain, this does not necessarily stop them from dancing; in one way or another, they perceive that it is worth it (Aalten, 2007; McEwen & Young, 2011; Tarr & Thomas, 2021; Turner & Wainwright, 2003; Wainwright & Turner, 2004). Sports research has shown that having a strong, narrowly defined identity can make performers more vulnerable at such times (see Wiese-Bjornstal et al., 2020). This is logical, of course: the narrower the identity, the more one stands to lose from not being able to perform (see chapter 1).

Several studies, all involving dancers from a mixture of styles, have focused on injured dancers' help-seeking behaviors. In one study, most (68.5%) told someone about their injuries, although the same proportion continued dancing on their injury (Nordin-Bates et al., 2011; also, Laws, 2005). In a more recent investigation, around 75% of professional dancers reported that they would seek a professional opinion, whereas a slightly smaller proportion (40% to 51%) would continue to dance while injured, albeit carefully (Vassallo et al., 2019). Employment status seemed to make a difference in that study; although 60% of the full-time professionals would tell someone within their company, only 35% of part-timers would do the same.

Age might also affect the help-seeking behaviors of injured dancers, although the evidence in this regard is limited and mixed. For instance, one study found that older dancers were more likely to continue dancing on an injury and to delay seeking treatment than were younger dancers (Air, 2009). In another investigation, older dancers reported listening to their bodies to a greater extent, perhaps a result of having learned that not doing so can cause injuries to become unnecessarily severe (Tarr & Thomas, 2021). Further research is required to understand which groups of dancers are more likely to suffer in silence and the reasons behind such behaviors.

There can be significant anxiety about what other people will think and say when a dancer becomes injured and associated fears about one's career or progression possibilities (Alexias & Dimitropoulou, 2011; Krasnow et al., 1994; Mainwaring et al., 2001, 2003; Macchi & Crossman, 1996; McEwen & Young, 2011; Vassallo et al., 2019). As one dancer put it: "Only if it is a very serious injury would I consider saying something. In all cases, it would be a sign of weakness and soon he will be in search of my replacement." (Alexias & Dimitropoulou, 2011, p. 97). Several authors in this area point out that such experiences are sometimes compounded by actual negative reactions from significant others, such as teachers not believing a dancer is injured or expecting them to dance in pain (e.g., Macchi & Crossman, 1996).

In some cases, anger and frustration are expressed at medical practitioners, for instance if they are perceived not to understand the particular needs of dancers (Blevins et al., 2019; McEwen & Young, 2011). Such mistrust may also underpin findings that dancers sometimes put off seeking advice, feel misunderstood by medical practitioners, and do not necessarily follow the advice that is given (Blevins et al., 2019; Krasnow, 1994; Mainwaring et al., 2001, 2003; Markula, 2015). However, findings indicating mistrust of medical practitioners may be varied or specific to certain groups or cultures. Indeed, other studies, partly from other countries, have found that injured dancers generally do follow medical advice (Lai et al., 2008; Nordin-Bates et al., 2011), and that there are high levels of satisfaction with existing provision (Air, 2009).

Structural differences in health care and insurance between countries are likely to affect dancers' use of and attitudes toward health professionals, as are individual differences regarding finances and what is considered affordable (Air, 2009; Laws, 2005; Markula, 2015). Unsurprisingly, dancers access medical care to a greater extent when it is freely available (Air, 2013). The growth of dance medicine and science should have increased the proportion of dancers with access to appropriate medical support, although even recent studies indicate that there is still a stigma surrounding dance injuries (Vassallo et al., 2019). Of those reporting that stigma existed, around 50% reported that it made them delay seeking help.

Psychological Aspects of Injury Rehabilitation

A variety of psychological aspects characterize and affect injury rehabilitation (Brewer, 2010; Ivarsson et al., 2017b; Mainwaring & Finney, 2017; Pollitt & Hutt, 2021; Wiese-Bjornstal et al., 2020). For instance, negative thoughts and emotions (e.g., stress, loneliness, negative moods, frustration, jealousy, and fear of reinjury) may follow a dancer from the time of injury and through at least parts of rehabilitation; as such, there is overlap between the second and third parts of this chapter (i.e., injury experiences and psychological aspects of rehabilitation; see also figure 13.1).

The second part illustrated how this is significant in and of itself—that is, because such reactions can be intense, distressing, and difficult to navigate. In this third part, we home in on the rehabilitation phase and how it may be optimized to facilitate recovery and return to full activity. To do so, the nature and impact of positive and negative reactions to rehabilitation are considered, and the role of psychological skills during rehabilitation is introduced.

Nature and Impact of Psychological Reactions on Injury Rehabilitation

Positive responses (e.g., feeling confident, intrinsically motivated, and ready) can facilitate a return to activity, but negative responses (e.g., negative moods, fear of reinjury) can prolong the time it takes for performers to return (Brewer, 2010; Ivarsson et al., 2017b; Wiese-Bjornstal et al., 2020). In dance, this has been shown by studies finding that longer injury durations can be predicted by greater levels of stress, worry, and obsessive passion, and lower levels of self-confidence (Mainwaring & Finney, 2017; Noh et al., 2005; Rip et al., 2006). Negative reactions are typical and expected, but positive reactions also emerge, especially as an injury gets closer to healing. Such positive responses are sometimes referred to as **stress-related growth** (see Wiese-Bjornstal et al., 2020) and can include the following (Aalten, 2007; Forsdyke et al., 2016; Mainwaring et al., 2001; Macchi & Crossman, 1996; Tarr & Thomas, 2021; Wainwright & Turner, 2004; Wiese-Bjornstal et al., 2020):

› Motivation being revitalized by realizing what one truly values ("Yes, I really do want this!")
› Optimism and joy (e.g., when making progress in rehabilitation)
› Realizing that injuries do not take as long as feared
› Gaining perspective, gratitude, and insight
› Learning more about oneself as a person
› Learning about anatomy, physiology, conditioning, and the value of rest and recovery
› Starting to appreciate the importance of health and of taking pain and other warning signs seriously

As an example, a dancer in Aalten's (2007, p. 120) ethnography of ballet culture and the dancing body stated:

> I used to be that dancer who could almost die of pain and still go on smiling. . . . I have had to learn how to discover my own boundaries. I really needed my injury to teach me that. Now I know what I can do and this is so much better, because now I can prevent myself from getting injured.

Ideally, of course, dancers should learn to listen to their bodies *before* they incur severe injuries. An advantage of the increased knowledge production in dance medicine and science ought to be that dancers, teachers, and other leaders learn not only from their own mistakes but also from those of others and from systematic research. Desirable outcomes may occur serendipitously, but structured psychological skills training can be helpful and leaves the process less to chance (e.g., Brewer, 2010).

Working through an injury can result in stress-related growth, and it can also represent one of the challenges thought to be important in talent development (see chapter 12). However, for it to become advantageous, performers may need to be appropriately debriefed (e.g., by discussing what is learned; Collins & MacNamara, 2017). Ideally, they should also be well prepared (e.g., by having learned coping skills), unlike in the preceding quote. After an intense yet ultimately rewarding process of working through a challenge like injury, performers are likely to feel more confident about tackling other challenges in the future. Indeed, we are typically more distressed by our first injury than we are about subsequent injuries (Forsdyke et al., 2016).

The balance of negative versus positive reactions is likely to depend on several factors, including personality (e.g., tendency to view injury as a challenge or threat) and rehabilitation progress (e.g., Mainwaring et al., 2001; Macchi & Crossman, 1996). Having a chronic or recurring injury may be associated with lower perceived control and therefore may be experienced as more concerning and stressful. Still, having a mindset that it *can be* fulfilling and a chance to grow is associated with more successful rehabilitation (Forsdyke et al., 2016). Dancers who sustain career-ending injuries are likely to experience particularly strong and challenging reactions; in such cases, clinical support is warranted.

Ivarsson and colleagues (2017b) argued that the prolonged time before return to activity as a result of negative psychological responses may be due to impaired confidence in the injured body part, but also because negative affective responses can lead to a prolonged stress response in the body, which is known to impair healing. Their literature review also indicated that return to activity was quicker for those adhering better to their rehabilitation protocols. Fortunately, adherence did not seem to be adversely affected by negative affective reactions. Overall, the authors recommended that performers use psychological skills to manage stress and other negative reactions to injury (Ivarsson et al., 2017b).

Consequences of Using Coping Skills During Injury Rehabilitation

Literature in both sports (Brewer, 2010; Gennarelli et al., 2020; Ivarsson et al., 2017a; Wiese-Bjornstal et al., 2020) and dance (Mainwaring et al., 2003; Pollitt & Hutt, 2021) shows that psychological skills can enhance rehabilitation. Such skills include goal setting, self-regulation, imagery, mindfulness, self-talk, and relaxation, which are introduced in other parts of this book (i.e., chapters 8 through 10). Another valuable coping skill is seeking and making use of social support (Blevins et al., 2019; Macchi & Crossman, 1996; Mainwaring et al., 2003; Wiese-Bjornstal et al., 2020). Indeed, social support helps performers feel more confident, supported, and motivated and is therefore an important predictor of rehabilitation adherence (Forsdyke et al., 2016; Gennarelli et al., 2020; Wiese-Bjornstal et al., 2020). Table 13.2 provides example uses of key coping skills both in everyday training situations (i.e., pre-injury) and in rehabilitation (post-injury).

The skills outlined in table 13.2 form part of problem-focused coping, which we have already described as providing valuable stress-buffering effects (and is therefore injury preventive). Literature similarly indicates that problem-focused coping is associated with more successful injury rehabilitation (Forsdyke et al., 2016). These authors concluded that "restoring the self" was an important rehabilitation target and recommended that injured performers, and the team around them, build self-confidence (see chapter 3); work to handle stress and anxiety (see chapter 4); and strive to satisfy the three basic psychological needs of autonomy, competence, and relatedness (see chapter 5). When these are fulfilled, rehabilitation is likely to be both more tolerable and shorter in duration (Forsdyke et al., 2016). Regarding anxiety, it was recommended that successful rehabilitation protocols address the common dual fears of reinjury and of returning to full activity. In the next two sections, more specific consequences for both well-being and performance of using psychological skills during injury rehabilitation will be considered.

Well-Being-Related Consequences

Literature indicates an array of benefits to the well-being of performers by using psychological skills

Table 13.2 **Coping Skills for Everyday Training and Rehabilitation**

Coping strategy	Examples of use pre-injury (in everyday training)	Examples of use post-injury (in rehabilitation)
Goal setting	• To improve technique • To improve self-confidence	• To motivate rehabilitation exercises • To build confidence in an injured body part
Self-regulation	• To identify areas for development • To monitor and reflect on progress	• To seek information about injury • To monitor and reflect on rehabilitation progress
Imagery	• To hone technique • To memorize	• To keep up with technique • To promote tissue healing
Mindfulness	• To increase body awareness • To hone attentional focusing ability	• To accept difficult emotions • To reduce stress
Self-talk	• To direct focus to performance-appropriate aspects • To become more positive about oneself	• To direct focus to rehabilitation-appropriate aspects • To become more positive about one's injury
Relaxation	• To reduce muscle aches • To promote sleep	• To reduce excessive tension • To promote rest
Social support seeking	• To get advice and support for dance • To maintain a rounded identity	• To get advice and support about injury • To get help with logistical issues (e.g., getting around)

Note: This list is intended to be illustrative but not exhaustive.

during rehabilitation (Brewer, 2010; Gennarelli et al., 2020; Ivarsson et al., 2017a; Noh et al., 2007; Pollitt & Hutt, 2021: Wiese-Bjornstal et al., 2020):

› *Improved mood.* When performers engage in psychological skills training programs during rehabilitation, they report feeling more positive and less depressed.
› *Improved self-confidence.* For example, dancers using systematic imagery can become more confident in their bodies ahead of returning to full activity.
› *Reduced tension, stress, anxiety, and pain.* The deliberate use of skills such as imagery and relaxation can help rehabilitating performers to experience lower muscular tension, reinjury anxiety, daily stress, and pain (e.g., Maddison et al., 2012).
› *Enhanced motivation.* By using skills such as setting appropriately challenging yet realistic goals, rehabilitation motivation can be enhanced. Long-term goal setting can also help build autonomous motivation for a return to dance activity ("Doing these exercises now will help me return stronger, and I really look forward to being able to take part in the end of year show").
› *Stress-related growth.* As noted, some performers are able to grow psychologically during what is otherwise a stressful time. Such stress-related growth is more likely for those who use psychological skills. Mindfulness might be especially useful in this regard, given that it is helpful in promoting balance, gratitude, and perspective.

Performance-Related Consequences

The literature further indicates that several performance-related benefits may be experienced as a result of using psychological skills during rehabilitation (Brewer, 2010; Gennarelli et al., 2020; Ivarsson et al., 2017a; Noh et al., 2007; Pollitt & Hutt, 2021: Wiese-Bjornstal et al., 2020):

› *Better adherence to rehabilitation.* When using psychological skills such as goal setting and positive self-talk, performers stick to their rehabilitation programs to a greater extent. For example, dancers may be tempted to skip long, tedious, and painful rehabilitation exercises after a while. With a good goal setting program, it is easier to see how the daily work relates to overall progress and to the ultimate goal of returning to full activity.
› *Physiological improvements.* Psychological skills training can improve many physiological components that are important in rehabilitation and when returning to activity, such as strength, balance, range of motion, and muscular endurance. For example, a combination of relaxation and guided imagery has been shown to improve knee function among athletes who have undergone knee reconstruction (see Gennarelli et al., 2020; also, Maddison et al., 2012).
› *Faster return to activity.* The aforementioned positive outcomes (i.e., better rehabilitation adherence, physiological improvements, and enhanced well-being) combine to help performers return to full dance activity more quickly.

Using Psychology to Reduce Injury Risk and Optimize Rehabilitation

Based on the research evidence introduced previously, a number of recommendations may be made, including building an open culture and listening to the body; nurturing healthy motivation and self-esteem; encouraging help-seeking from appropriate health professionals; using or encouraging psychological skills; seeing injury as an opportunity to grow; seeking or providing social support; observing and sharing good examples; and considering professional psychological help. Each will now be introduced in turn.

Build an Open Culture and Listen to the Body

Pain and injury are inherently complex constructs. Although the pains associated with slight overwork may be harmless, the distinction between "good pain" and "bad pain" is difficult to establish. To have any chance of minimizing injury risk in this regard, leaders should do their best to encourage a culture of working smart (rather than just hard), avoiding any tired clichés such as "go hard or go home" or "what doesn't kill you makes you stronger." Dancers as well as teachers should be encouraged to listen to their bodies; openly discuss perceptions of fatigue, pain, and injury; and be supported in any decisions to skip certain exercises or classes. More generally, we must avoid creating a culture in which dancing through injury is hailed as commitment, and mental toughness while deciding to heed one's pain signals is seen as laziness.

Nurture Healthy Motivation and Self-Esteem

Dancers who dance because they find it intrinsically meaningful and enjoyable, who have a flexible form of passion for dance, and who generally feel that they are worthwhile (regardless of their performance level at a given time) are more likely to be able to limit or stop their engagement when their bodies say no. In so doing, many overuse injuries are likely to be prevented. Therefore, the recommendations for nurturing healthy motivation (see chapters 5 and 11) and self-esteem (see chapter 3) are relevant also for injury prevention and for improving rehabilitation outcomes.

Encourage Help-Seeking From Appropriate Health Professionals

The sooner a dancer gets help with an injury, the better rehabilitation is likely to be. Thus, schools and companies should encourage dancers to visit health professionals as appropriate. For well-resourced full-time establishments, such support should be available on-site; when this is not possible, they can provide an up-to-date list of suitable providers in their area. Beyond the obvious advantages to individual dancers, such support can also save resources (e.g., having fewer company dancers unable to perform at any given time). Dancers should be encouraged to adhere to rehabilitation programs but not overdo things; doing more than advised is likely to prolong rather than accelerate rehabilitation. Similarly, dancers should never be pressured into returning before they are ready.

Use or Encourage Psychological Skills

Psychological skills can be useful to dancers both in preventing and rehabilitating injuries. Their use should therefore be generally encouraged. Because other chapters in this book include detailed recommendations for psychological skills use generally (i.e., pre-injury; see chapters 8 through 10), the suggestions that follow focus on rehabilitation.

› *Goal setting*. Some dancers are skilled goal setters, and performance psychology professionals can certainly help. Still, health professionals such as physiotherapists, medical doctors, and conditioning coaches may be the most important sources of information for goal setting during rehabilitation. Indeed, physiotherapists typically provide injured dancers with an estimate of the time required to return to dance (i.e., a performance goal) and specific exercises to do to get there (i.e., process goals/goal achievement strategies). To help dancers benefit from such goals, health professionals should be well-versed in goal-setting principles (see chapter 9) and able to communicate clearly and compassionately so that dancers feel understood and well-informed.

› *Imagery*. Dancers often use imagery for mental rehearsal in everyday practice, and this skill should be applied (or intensified) during rehabilitation. For example, dancers can use imagery to mentally rehearse technique and choreography while resting at home. They can also do imagery in class, intermixed with watching or doing the exercises that they can still physically practice. For example, someone with a shoulder injury might be able to do certain exercises with her legs while imagining the movement of the arms. Healing imagery can also be helpful, such as imagining the restoration of an injured body part and how it gradually becomes able to move as before. In the Get Practical exercise (form 13.1), you will find a worksheet that can be used by injured dancers to optimize the use of imagery while observing class. Because dancers are more likely to use imagery during injury rehabilitation periods if they are already familiar with it from their normal practice (Nordin-Bates et al., 2011), imagery should be well integrated into dancers' and dance schools' normal routines.

› *Mindfulness*. The negative emotions typically experienced as a result of injury can become easier to handle with mindfulness practice. In so doing, performers can learn to accept reality such as it is, even if it is undesirable; this helps prevent undue accumulation of stress. Mindfulness also helps people gain a sense of perspective that can be of benefit far beyond a specific injury. Moreover, mindfulness meditation often has the side effect of inducing relaxation.

› *Self-talk*. During challenging times such as injury, self-talk can become negative (e.g., "Why me? I will never catch up now!"). To facilitate recovery, therefore, dancers can try to monitor the self-talk that they spontaneously engage in. If the identified self-talk seems counterproductive, they can design new self-talk statements that help direct their attention

Form 13.1 GET PRACTICAL: OBSERVATION AND IMAGERY WORKSHEET FOR INJURED DANCERS

Use this sheet to help yourself learn and stay active and positive during classes in which you cannot fully physically take part. With imagery you can rehearse/dance in your mind, and it is recommended that you use several senses (e.g., imagine how movements feel and look). You may want to first listen to the teacher, then watch the exercise, and then rehearse it in your imagination. You can also combine physical (dancing with uninjured body parts) with mental practice. For example, you might dance with the arms while imagining the legs.

Dancer name: _____

Class (type/style): _____ **Date:** _____

What Can You Do? Planning Before Class

First, plan what you can do in the next class. Ask your teacher or therapist if you are unsure.

What I can do physically:
1. _____
2. _____

What I can do through imagery:
1. _____
2. _____

Ideas for how to integrate imagery into exercises that I can only partly do physically:
1. _____
2. _____

What Did You Learn? Making Notes During and After Class

During and after class, make notes below to support your learning.

My general level of functioning today (ability to dance as normal):

0%   25%   50%   75%   100%

_____

Today, I learned:
1. _____
2. _____
3. _____

In my imagery practice after class, I want to continue practicing the following:
1. _____
2. _____
3. _____

Other notes (e.g., information, corrections, musical timings):
_____
_____

_____
Go to HK*Propel* to download this worksheet.

From S. Nordin-Bates, *Essentials of Dance Psychology* (Champaign, IL: Human Kinetics, 2023).

to constructive, positive things such as the progress they are making with rehabilitation exercises or the good support they are getting.

For dancers who sustain career-ending injuries, psychological skills such as goal setting and mindfulness are likely to be especially helpful, alongside work on identity (see chapter 1) and career transitions (Ivarsson et al., 2015; Wiese-Bjornstal et al., 2020; Willard & Lavallee, 2016).

See Injury as an Opportunity to Grow

Although difficult, seeing injuries as challenges rather than threats, and as a chance to grow as a person, is associated with better recovery (Forsdyke et al., 2016). Thus, helping dancers toward such a mindset is an important task. Friends, family, teachers, and health practitioners can all help in this endeavor, for example, by sharing good examples of such growth from themselves or from people they have met and worked with. Practitioners such as physiotherapists may take this one step further by putting examples of successful injury rehabilitation outcomes on their noticeboards, websites, or similar places. Injured dancers can take the time off from dance as an opportunity to revisit their motivation for dance ("Is this truly what I want?"), to consider other options ("Is this a good time to start that course I heard about?"), to work on things they normally do not make time for (e.g., technical limitations, core instability, immersion in other artistic activities), and—not least—to spend quality time on self-care (e.g., sleep, massage, meditation) and with family and friends.

Seek or Provide Social Support

Social support can include family, teachers, and friends both inside and outside of dance. For example, dancers may need home visits from friends in the early stages of a severe injury but can later seek out friends by themselves as they become more mobile. Several types of social support exist, and it may be worth considering which types are most important to you (if you are injured) or to an injured dancer you know (e.g., a student of yours, a friend):

› *Emotional support.* This includes listening, showing understanding, and generally being empathetic.
› *Instrumental/logistic support.* Parents and peers can play an important role in helping the injured dancer get around, especially so that they do not feel stuck at home. Parents might also provide financial support for services such as physiotherapy and counseling, if possible and if required.
› *Informational support.* Health practitioners and other suitably qualified individuals can support the injured dancer by giving advice about injury and rehabilitation, and friends can help by taking notes or filming parts of class and share these with the injured dancer. Similarly, teachers can keep the injured dancer informed about what is going on in classes and rehearsals, thereby helping the dancer keep up. Teachers should, however, refrain from giving advice outside their expertise, such as telling dancers to undertake a particular treatment because "it worked for me." More specific guidance about how dance teachers can be supportive have been provided by Mainwaring et al. (2003), including recommendations for modification of dance activities, alternative activities during dance practice, activities outside the studio, and encouragement of psychosocial strategies for recovery.

Observe and Share Good Examples

If you have read chapter 2, you know that modeling (aka observation) can be a valuable tool for enhancing self-efficacy. Literature further supports the use of observation during rehabilitation, whereby learning from others can help injured performers feel better and adhere better to rehabilitation (Wiese-Bjornstal et al., 2020). As regards watching class, effects can range from an increased sense of competence and relatedness with classmates to intense frustration and jealousy (Hanrahan, 1996; Macchi & Crossman, 1996; Mainwaring et al., 2001, 2003). It is therefore important to ascertain how dancers are feeling before telling them to watch classes, weighing up the pros and cons of doing so. By giving dancers specific tasks to do in the studio (i.e., not just watch passively), their reactions are also likely to be more positive and their learning will be greater. For example, injured dancers may be involved as teaching assistants (Mainwaring et al., 2001) or be asked to engage in an active combination of watching and imagery rehearsal (see the Get Practical exercise form 13.1).

Consider Professional Psychological Help

Thus far, recommendations have highlighted skills and behaviors that dancers themselves can do (e.g., goal setting) or that significant others can facilitate (e.g., social support). Yet the reactions to injury and the process of rehabilitation can be truly challenging, and the option of seeking professional psychological support should be considered. For example, a dancer who is experiencing grief and loss of identity following a career-terminating injury should be referred to a clinical specialist (e.g., psychologist, psychotherapist). In one study conducted with visitors to a dance medicine clinic, 60% of dancers scored above cutoff for one or more forms of psychopathology, meaning that they met requirements for clinical referral (Air, 2013). Most of these injured dancers reported levels of psychological distress higher than those of the general population. Although gender and dance style appeared unrelated to distress levels, higher-level dancers were more likely to be affected. Importantly, these problems did not necessarily recede after medical treatment, suggesting that psychological support is essential.

Qualified psychological support is imperative at high levels of distress, but professional support need not be limited to problem-solving: instead, it can and should be used proactively, such as when a dancer seeks out a performance psychologist to work on goal setting and imagery. Not only is this likely to enhance performance and well-being for the dancer generally, but it may help reduce their injury risk and equip them with valuable coping skills for injury rehabilitation, if and when that becomes necessary.

Ida: Case Study of Injury

Ida is a 20-year-old dancer who had recently started to audition for professional contracts. She more or less grew up in dance, having taken dance classes since age three and with a father who was a dance teacher. For many years, Ida seemed to have it all—a strong yet flexible body, a strong drive to succeed, and lots of insider know-how about the dance industry. These factors combined to see Ida through full-time dance education, eventually graduating top of her class. She had just begun to audition for full-time dance work, eager to make a good impression and to make her father proud. Then disaster struck in the form of a severe injury to her left foot. Her narrow identity meant that the injury was a huge blow; beyond the normal sadness and frustration, there was also an intense sense of injustice and an unfamiliar lack of trust in her own body, which did not abate during the weeks of physiotherapy that followed.

Realizing that something had to be done, Ida asked for ideas from friends. A psychologist with experience of working with dancers was recommended to her. After seeing the psychologist for a few sessions, Ida could finally begin to see her injury not as a disaster but as a challenge from which she could gain valuable lessons. Under the psychologist's qualified guidance, they worked through such things as the memory of the injury (that horrible sound of bone breaking), they set up goals for what to work on during the rehab period, they engaged in systematic imagery practice of the injured foot working smoothly at full capacity, and addressed performance blocks related to reinjury anxiety. Ida is now an advocate for the role of psychology in dance, helping to dispel myths of what psychology is and can do. Indeed, injury can be a good way in to discovering psychology, because high-level dancers do get injured. A lot.

Composite case study created on the basis of a conversation with Britt Tajet-Foxell, CPsychol, consultant psychologist to the Royal Ballet, London, England, the Norwegian National Ballet, and to several other schools, companies, and national sports teams.

CRITICAL ASPECTS OF RESEARCH INTO PSYCHOLOGICAL ASPECTS OF INJURY

1. The dance injury literature can be difficult to draw conclusions from because injury is often defined in different ways (Kenny et al., 2016; Mainwaring & Finney, 2017; Wiese-Bjornstal et al., 2020). A common definition would yield more comparable findings, but every definition has advantages and disadvantages. Many dance injuries are never reported to a health practitioner but can still affect dancer's health and performance.

2. Although research suggests that psychological interventions can help prevent injury as well as facilitate injury recovery, research into the mechanisms underlying such effects is warranted (Brewer, 2010). For instance,
   - Does improved self-efficacy mediate between an imagery training program and time to recovery?
   - Is the effect of a goal-setting program on return to full strength mediated by improved adherence to home exercise programs?

KEY POINTS AND RECOMMENDATIONS AROUND PSYCHOLOGICAL ASPECTS OF INJURY IN DANCE

1. Dancers are more likely to become injured if they experience high levels of stress; being stressed, in turn, is more likely when dancers experience challenging life circumstances, lack coping skills, and possess particular personality traits. These same factors are likely to make dancers struggle with rehabilitation. It is worth being aware of the cumulative nature of stress and avoiding new challenges (e.g., auditions) at times that are already stressful for other reasons (e.g., problems at home or at school/work).

2. Injuries are typically considered to be about physiology and technique, and treatment consequently focuses on physical therapy, rest, and perhaps adjustments of dance technique. Yet as the literature summarized in this chapter has shown, injuries are also inherently about psychological factors. In some cases this means referring injured dancers for professional, psychological care; in other cases, and for prevention, teachers and staff such as physiotherapists can support an injured dancer psychologically (Pollitt & Hutt, 2021). For example, they can be generally supportive (e.g., by being a good listener and by providing information) and can encourage or help a dancer to use psychological skills (e.g., goal setting for rehabilitation, imagery to maintain technique, mindfulness for self-care).

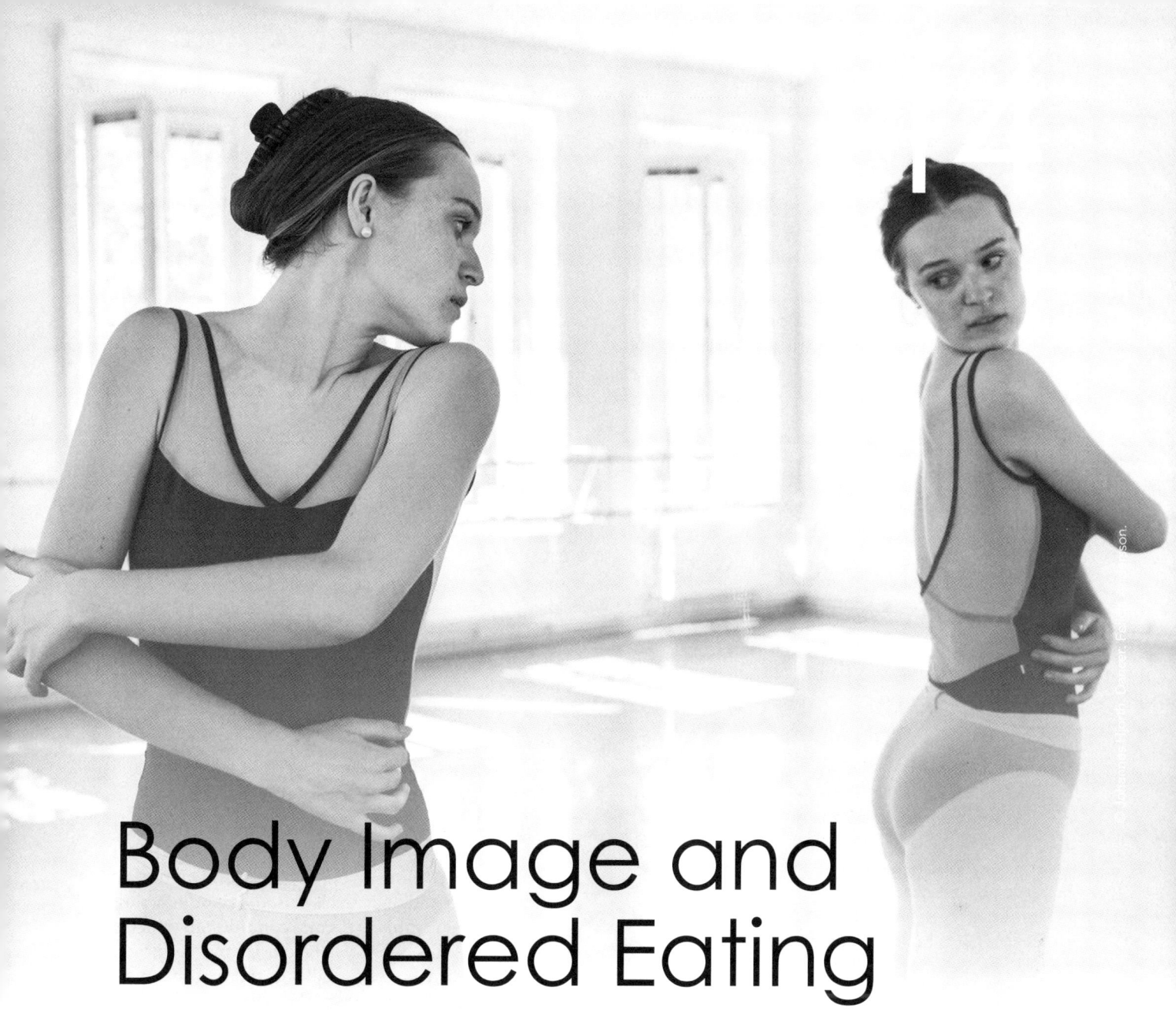

Body Image and Disordered Eating

"So many dancers feel that what they look like is more important than who they are. This is a real danger for dancers who focus for years on appearances and think of themselves as merely a body. The choreographer can't work with them in the realm of ideas. It's a huge problem if they haven't been connecting internally. If they've decided that what's inside is of little value, they can only try to approximate some kind of look."

Alonzo King, choreographer

CHAPTER OBJECTIVES

After reading this chapter, you will be able to

1. describe what body image is, including positive and negative aspects;

2. describe the spectrum between optimal nutrition and eating disorders through disordered eating;
3. critically discuss a range of sources (risk factors) for the development of negative body image and disordered eating in dance;
4. outline research findings regarding the consequences of negative body image and eating disorders;
5. apply basic recommendations to prevent, identify, and manage negative body image and disordered eating in dance; and
6. think critically about the nature and impact of body image and disordered eating in dance settings.

Key Terms

anorexia nervosa	eating disorder not otherwise specified (EDNOS)	positive body image
binge eating disorder		self-objectification
body appreciation	eating disorders	self-surveillance
body dissatisfaction	functional body orientation	thin-ideal internalization
body image	functional body satisfaction	thinness and restriction expectancies
body image flexibility	negative body image	
bulimia nervosa	other specified feeding or eating disorder (OSFED)	thinness-related learning
disordered eating		

The clinical term *anorexia nervosa* originates in the Greek *anorexia*, meaning "without appetite," and the Latin *nervosa*, meaning "nervous." Anorexia nervosa is the best-known eating disorder, and it has been studied extensively in dance research. However, as you will learn in this chapter, it is not the most common—in fact, many studies find that it is the *least* common eating disorder. Therefore, increasing awareness of what constitutes an eating disorder is an important goal of dance psychology. To do so, we also need to introduce various subclinical expressions (together known as disordered eating) and its key risk factor: negative body image.

What Is Body Image?

Body image refers to the perceptions, thoughts, and feelings that we have about our bodies (Grogan, 2008). It is multifaceted, with a main distinction being made between **positive** and **negative body image**; each of these will be introduced using a foundation of literature from clinical psychology and examples from dance research.

Negative Body Image

Negative body image is a multifaceted construct that may comprise one or both of the following (Allen & Walter, 2016): low levels of body appreciation or body esteem, and high levels of **body dissatisfaction** or body dysmorphia (a mental condition in which a person obsesses over perceived appearance flaws).

Body dissatisfaction is the most thoroughly investigated of these constructs, at least in dance. It represents how people feel about their appearance and is considered to exist when a person's image of their body does not match the body that they see as ideal; for instance, they may desire a different weight or shape (e.g., Petrie, 2020). But although negative body image in dance is often discussed in terms of thinness, body weight, and shape (Tiggemann et al., 2014), it can also be a drive for muscularity or a dissatisfaction with some perceived flaw (e.g., body type, lack of turnout, foot structure) or specific body area (for examples, see Radell et al., 2020; Ravaldi et al., 2006; Toro et al., 2009).

Negative body image is common among people of all ages, although more so for females (Allen & Walter, 2016). It tends to escalate during adolescence. In one study, nearly 500 young women (from average age 13.5 years) were followed for eight years; there were linear increases in body dissatisfaction as well as in perceived pressure to be thin and in **thin-**

ideal internalization (i.e., when a person has made thinness into an ideal for themselves; Rohde et al., 2015). Given these results for society generally, it is unsurprising that there are a large number of reports of negative body image in dance (Alexias & Dimitropoulou, 2011; Benn & Walters, 2001; Bettle et al., 2001; Dryburgh & Fortin, 2010; Heiland et al., 2008; McEwen & Young, 2011; Nerini, 2015; Oliver, 2008; Pickard, 2013; Price & Pettijohn, 2006; Ravaldi et al., 2006; Reel et al., 2005; Robbeson et al., 2015; Swami & Harris, 2012; Tiggemann & Slater, 2001; Van Zelst et al., 2004). Body image for female dancers especially can be a difficult balancing act. On one hand, there are the largely aesthetic demands for thinness, and on the other hand are the requirements for strength and endurance necessary to perform and sustain intense training (e.g., Chin & Clements, 2021).

The sheer number of investigations into negative body image in dance (and their sobering results) indicate that body image pressures and problems are perceived to be particularly prevalent in this domain. Accordingly, dancers typically report greater levels of body dissatisfaction and drive for thinness than do non-dancers (e.g., Ackard et al., 2004; Bettle et al., 2001; Kulshreshtha et al., 2021; Nerini, 2015; Robbeson et al., 2015; Silverii et al., 2022). Even young recreational ballet students have reported greater body dissatisfaction than same-aged peers who are not physically active (Nerini, 2015).

Numerous authors have described the ideal body for dancers as thin, linear, flat-chested, and long-legged—an ideal so pervasive and so difficult to attain that negative body image is considered a logical consequence (e.g., Aalten, 2007; Benn & Walters, 2001; Dryburgh & Fortin, 2010; Green, 1999; Neumärker et al., 1998; Pickard, 2013). It appears, however, that this literature has sometimes equated "dancer" with "female ballet dancer," which may have led to a skewed or limited picture—not all dancers have the same body image or body image problems. Indeed, it can differ across dance settings or contexts, and dancers may have more positive attitudes toward their bodies in performances and in social situations than in dance classes, where pressures relating to the body are often intensified (Francisco et al., 2012b; Toro et al., 2009; Van Zelst et al., 2004).

In popular discourse, it is often argued that the drive for thinness so common especially among female ballet dancers can be at least partly attributed to the selection and promotion of particularly thin, long-limbed, androgynous-looking ballerinas by New York City Ballet director George Balanchine (e.g., Oliver, 2008). Although this began nearly 100 years ago, the legacy of the "Balanchine body" is still very much alive today (e.g., Aalten, 2007; Barr & Oliver, 2016; Gvion, 2008; Pickard, 2013). For example, the authors of a qualitative study reported the following:

> The interviewees seemed to agree that the ballet body could be described as "Tall, thin, no boobs, no hips. No womanly features at all. A stick basically with long legs, lots of legs and arms." The modern ideal was reportedly more forgiving, but being "overweight" was clearly unacceptable. (Reel et al., 2005, p. 46)

Classical ballet is associated with the most extreme body ideal, and ballet dancers have been found to report higher body weight discrepancies (i.e., body weight dissatisfaction) than, for instance, contemporary dancers (e.g., Swami & Harris, 2012). Still, ballet is certainly not the only style associated with pressures to look a particular way, and body image pressures have also been reported in modern dance, Kathak, jazz, and commercial styles (Chin & Clements, 2021; Green, 1999; Heiland et al., 2008; Kulshreshtha et al., 2021; Reel et al., 2005; Van Zelst et al., 2004). For example, modern dance students in the study cited above perceived numerous weight-related pressures and were highly conscious of their weights and appearances (Reel et al., 2005). Most of them perceived that lightness and thinness conveyed performance advantages and that the thinnest dancers got chosen for the best roles. Of course, modern and contemporary dance styles are varied and constantly in flux (e.g., Barr & Oliver, 2016), making it difficult to draw generalizable conclusions about body image in such styles. Cruise ship dancers, who perform in multiple styles, have given examples of both negative and positive body image, the latter being associated with an increasing focus on being "strong rather than skinny" as they became professionals (Chin & Clements, 2021).

Positive Body Image

Just like its negative counterpart, positive body image is a multifaceted construct and may include one or more of the following facets (Tylka & Wood-Barcalow, 2015):

› **Body appreciation**: appreciating one's health, bodily features, and functionality
› **Functional body orientation**: focusing on how one's body feels and functions more than on how it looks
› **Functional body satisfaction**: satisfaction with what one's body can do and experience

> **Body image flexibility**: willingness to experience and accept perceptions, thoughts, and feelings about one's body without trying to change them, while acting in line with personal values (essentially mindfulness, acceptance, and commitment related to the body; see chapter 8)

Importantly, positive body image is not just the opposite of negative body image, because it is possible to experience both to some degree (Tylka & Wood-Barcalow, 2015). These authors emphasize that although it is difficult to be immune to all body-image-related messages, persons with positive body image seem to actively protect it. For example, they might avoid negative talk about bodies (e.g., "fat talk"), seek out others with positive body image, actively question body images portrayed in the media, and engage in positive self-care (e.g., yoga, but also certain forms of sport and dance; for a review, see Tylka & Wood-Barcalow, 2015). Unfortunately, some have suggested that fat talk is common among dancers (Dantas et al., 2018).

In the first study into body appreciation in dance, street dancers reported higher levels of this construct than did matched non-dancer controls (Swami & Tovée, 2009). There were also no differences in actual–ideal weight discrepancies between these two groups. In comparison to non-dancers, modern dance students (Langdon & Petracca, 2010) and recreational belly dancers (Tiggemann et al., 2014) have reported more positive and less negative body image. The authors explained that their results may reflect the emphasis on strength and power inherent in street dance and the embodiment inherent in belly dance. Both styles may also be seen as inclusive, allowing people with many different shapes to take part and excel. In a subsequent study, contemporary dancers reported higher body appreciation and body awareness than ballet dancers (Swami & Harris, 2012). Body image also varied by level, with body awareness and body responsiveness being higher for dancers at higher than at lower levels. Beginner ballet students reported higher levels of body appreciation than advanced ballet students did, whereas the opposite was true for contemporary dance students at different levels. The Get Practical exercise "Promoting Positive Body Image" (form 14.1) is inspired by research into positive image (e.g., Piran, 2005; Tylka & Wood-Barcalow, 2015). You can use it for yourself or for dancers that you teach.

Eating Disorders Versus Disordered Eating

Eating disorders are extreme disturbances in an individual's thoughts, emotions, and behaviors regarding food, weight, and body perceptions. However, they are rarely due to problems with only these areas; instead, they are mental illnesses that reflect underlying psychopathology. Along with body image, eating disorders was one of the first topics of study in dance psychology, and it is the most extensively researched. As such, we know quite a bit about its nature, prevalence, and risk factors.

Eating attitudes and behaviors can be said to exist on a spectrum from healthy eating (with no/little eating disorder risk) to a clinically diagnosed eating disorder (figure 14.1). According to experts in this area, the healthy eating (optimal nutrition; Wells et al., 2020) end of the spectrum is characterized by

> sufficient nutritional intake for both physical and mental health,
> an ability to adapt food intake to changing circumstances (e.g., altered training intensity),
> flexible reasoning about food,
> an ability to eat socially,
> freedom from strongly limiting restrictions and rigidities (e.g., avoiding whole food groups, always counting calories, or eating in a particular way), and
> a healthy body image.

As shown in figure 14.1, **disordered eating** is the subclinical "gray zone" in which some dysfunctional attitudes and/or behaviors are present, although not enough to warrant a clinical diagnosis (Petrie, 2020). Although less severe, disordered eating should be taken seriously for at least two reasons: First, it can still cause major problems to a dancer. Second, it is the major precursor, or springboard, from which a clinical eating disorder can develop (Chamay-Weber et al., 2005). Because it is less severe, more dancers will experience disordered eating than an eating disorder (Petrie, 2020). It is also possible (or even likely) that individuals move back and forth along the spectrum (Wells et al., 2020). For example, a dancer may exhibit more disordered eating during a highly competitive summer school where dancers dance and eat together than at home with their family on holiday.

Form 14.1 GET PRACTICAL: PROMOTING POSITIVE BODY IMAGE

This exercise is inspired by research into positive image (e.g., Piran, 2005; Tylka & Wood-Barcalow, 2015). You can use it for yourself or for dancers that you teach, using one or more strategies. Choose whether you want to focus on a single class, a day, or a week.

ASPECT	EXAMPLE STRATEGIES	YOUR CHOICE OF WHAT TO DO AND HOW
Functional body orientation Focusing on how the body feels and functions more than on how it looks	• Exploring bodily sensations and capacities • Using the mirror judiciously	
Body appreciation and functional body satisfaction Appreciation for and satisfaction with what the body is, can do, and can experience	• Being impressed with the ever-developing capacities of the body • Expressing gratitude for what the body can do • Engaging in self-care (e.g., massage)	
Body image flexibility Willingness to experience and accept thoughts and feelings about the body without trying to change them while acting in line with values	• Actively questioning what kinds of body images are portrayed in the media/dance and how this makes dancers feel and act • Mindfulness meditation focused on acceptance and commitment	

Go to HK*Propel* to download this worksheet.

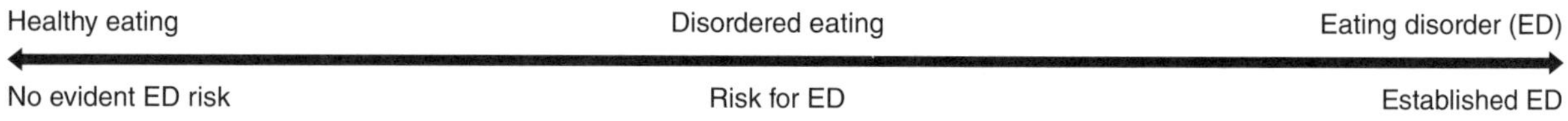

Healthy eating	Disordered eating	Eating disorder (ED)
No evident ED risk	Risk for ED	Established ED

Figure 14.1 Disordered eating exists on a spectrum.

Adapted from American Psychiatric Association (2013) and Wells, Jeacocke, Appaneal, et al. (2020).

The Clinical Nature of Eating Disorders Makes This Chapter Different

Eating disorders are clinical problems that need clinical diagnoses and treatment. Most readers of this book will therefore not work with it in the same way as with other topics in the book. For instance, you are highly encouraged to use the guidelines for implementing goal setting in your own practice (chapter 9) or for creating healthy motivational climates (chapter 11). For eating disorders and disordered eating, your role is likely to be different in at least two ways:

1. Teachers, dancers, dance scientists, and dance psychology consultants do *not* give advice about or treatment for eating disorders, nor about nutrition planning, unless they have specialist training that authorizes them to do so.
2. Having basic knowledge about what disordered eating and eating disorders are should improve the chances that problems can be
   - *Prevented* as far as possible (e.g., by detecting and limiting risk factors in the dance environment)
   - *Detected*, ideally sensitively and at an early stage
   - *Acted upon* in a suitable manner (e.g., appropriate clinical referrals made)

Preventive work, early detection, and appropriate referrals are incredibly important because of the regrettably low recovery rates for clinical eating disorders. Indeed, eating disorders are among the deadliest of all mental disorders (Arcelus et al., 2011). For these reasons, including a chapter about this clinical topic in an otherwise nonclinical book is warranted.

Clinical Eating Disorders: Diagnostic Criteria

A common way to diagnose and describe clinical eating disorders is by using criteria set out in the *Diagnostic and Statistical Manual of Mental Disorders* (DSM), published by the American Psychiatric Association (APA). The latest edition is the fifth of its kind; accordingly, it is known as the DSM-V (APA, 2013). The eating disorders most relevant to dance include **binge eating disorder, bulimia nervosa, anorexia nervosa**, and **other specified feeding or eating disorder** (OSFED), and they are outlined in table 14.1.

The previous edition of the DSM (DSM-IV) included a relatively broad category known as **eating disorder not otherwise specified (EDNOS)**. This diagnosis has typically been the most common (and anorexia the least common) in research with dancers, athletes, and general populations alike (Arcelus et al., 2014; Liu et al., 2016; Petrie, 2020; Ravaldi et al., 2006; Ringham et al., 2006; Rohde et al., 2015). Due to concerns over EDNOS becoming a catch-all category, it was replaced with OSFED in DSM-V (APA, 2013).

Each DSM revision naturally aims to improve in validity and reliability, but it also makes research undertaken with different editions more difficult to compare; for instance, binge eating disorder was not a diagnostic category prior to 2013, and there appears to be no published data on this disorder in dance as yet. Because most studies cited here rely on earlier editions of the DSM (especially DSM-IV), prevalence rates may be lower than if DSM-V criteria had been used (Petrie, 2020). Similarly, Arcelus et al. (2014) reported that some dancers with an EDNOS diagnosis in the studies included in their meta-analysis may have been diagnosed with anorexia or bulimia nervosa with the updated DSM-V criteria.

Signs and Symptoms of Disordered Eating

Because disordered eating is diverse and multifaceted, its manifestations are highly varied. It is important to be aware of an array of more and less visible signs to identify disordered eating in practice (table 14.2). Because only qualified clinicians can diagnose eating disorders, the signs and symptoms included in the table are not specified as belonging to a specific diagnosis; nor are they specific to clinical eating disorders but apply to disordered eating more widely.

Table 14.1 **Defining Features of Clinical Eating Disorders: Binge Eating Disorder, Bulimia Nervosa, Anorexia Nervosa, and OSFED**

Eating disorder	Summary	Key characteristics
Binge eating disorder	Periods of uncontrollable binge eating at least once/week for 3 months	Repeated episodes of binge eating associated with three or more of the following: the person • eats much faster than normal; • eats until uncomfortably full; • eats large amounts without feeling physical hunger; • eats alone due to shame over the large amounts; and • feels very guilty, depressed, or disgusted by themselves afterward. The person is clearly pained by the binge eating, feels out of control, and does not regularly use compensatory behaviors.
Bulimia nervosa	Periods of uncontrollable binge eating and compensatory behavior(s) at least once/week for 3 months	Binge episodes characterized by a person who • eats during a limited specific time period (e.g., 2 hours) considerably larger amounts of food than they normally would during a corresponding time and circumstances; • perceives having lost control over the eating; • repeats compensatory behavior(s) so as not to gain weight (e.g., vomiting, fasting, exercise); and • has a self-image overly affected by weight and shape.
Anorexia nervosa	Drastic weight reduction as a result of self-imposed food limitations	Characterized by • inadequate energy intake in relation to needs; • overly low weight in relation to age, gender, growth curve, and health; • intensive fear of gaining weight/becoming fat, or persistent behavior(s) that prevent weight gain, despite being underweight; and • disturbed body image regarding weight/shape, self-image overly impacted on by weight/shape, or persistent denial of the seriousness of the low body weight.
Other specified feeding or eating disorder (OSFED)	Eating disorders that cause clinically significant distress and impairment but do not fulfill all criteria for another eating disorder	Characteristics of OSFED vary widely, but examples include • Atypical anorexia nervosa (e.g., retained menstruation or weight in normal range despite significant weight loss), and • Compensatory disturbance (e.g., repeated compensatory behaviors to affect weight/shape without preceding binge eating).

Note: Adapted from American Psychiatric Association (2013).

Prevalence of Eating Disorders in Dance

The literature into eating disorders in dance has reported vastly different prevalence rates and types of data in different studies. For example, one study with ballet dancers reported a lifetime eating disorder prevalence of 83% and many similarities between dancers and clinical eating disorder patients (Ringham et al., 2006). The sample consisted of only 29 female high-level professional and student ballet dancers in the United States, aged 19.66 years on average. Dancers self-selected into the study and partook in an individual clinical screening interview focused on lifetime prevalence ("Have you ever . . ."). As such, the generalizability of this study is likely to be low.

In a contrasting example, Tseng and colleagues (2007) studied 655 female student dancers in Taiwan and yielded an overall prevalence for eating disorders of 8%. These students partook in several styles and were aged, on average, 15.8 years. Recruitment took place through their schools, and time to complete questionnaires was provided during school

Table 14.2 **Warning Signs for Disordered Eating in Dance**

Psychological warning signs	Physiological warning signs	Behavioral warning signs
Body-related	**Dance-related**	**Dance-related**
• Body dissatisfaction; fear of weight gain	• Drastic weight change	• Isolates from others
• Sensitive regarding own body, clothes, etc.	• Reduced strength, focus, and coordination	• Hides (e.g., wears loose clothes or several layers; stands at the back)
• Distress around food and when exercising is not possible	• Recurrent injuries (especially stress fractures) or illness; slow healing	• Increased dedication and excessive training (especially cardiovascular exercise)
• Overvalues importance of weight/shape	• Dizziness, extreme tiredness, or fainting	• Restlessness, hyperactivity
Other	**Other**	**Food-related**
• Self-esteem low and/or contingent on weight	• Dry, brittle, and lifeless hair, skin, and nails	• Avoids eating situations; denies hunger
• High perfectionism	• Discolored or swollen hands or feet	• Preoccupied with and/or sensitive around food
• Mood swings, irritability, or flat mood	• Raw knuckles and tooth enamel decay	• Refuses to accept there is a food/weight problem
• Unsociable, introverted	• Menstrual dysfunction (missing or having irregular periods, or not having started periods by age 15)	• Excessive use of chewing gum or water
• Sleep problems	• Often feeling cold	• Visits toilet after meals
• Comorbid diagnoses such as anxiety or depression	• Frequent headaches and stomach problems	• Sudden changes in food preferences, developing allergies or rituals
• Rigidity ("must" do things in certain ways)	• Sore throat, cold sores, bad breath	• Cooks for others but does not eat

Note: Based on information from the National Eating Disorders Association (NEDA; 2021a, 2021b), the DSM-V (APA, 2013), the Australian Institute of Sport and National Eating Disorders Collaboration position statement on disordered eating in high-performance sport (Wells et al., 2020), and dance research reviewed in this chapter.

hours (a subsample later completed diagnostic interviews). Questionnaires were focused on prevalence of problems in the past year. Clearly, studies vary greatly regarding design and, consequently, their results. It is therefore important not to rely on results from a single investigation when discussing the prevalence of eating disorders in dance in general, especially from studies with small homogeneous samples. Percentages are also not especially helpful for sample sizes under 100 persons.

Against the backdrop of inconsistent findings, it is helpful that there are now two meta-analyses into eating disorders in dance. In the first, 33 papers published between 1985 and 2012 were included (Arcelus et al., 2014). Overall, it was found that dancers should be considered an at-risk group for eating disorder development, because prevalence in this group (12%) was three times higher than for general populations used as comparisons. When examining specific diagnoses, dancers were more likely to suffer from anorexia and from EDNOS than the general population (Arcelus et al., 2014). Ballet dancers ran an even greater risk, with rates of 16.4% for eating disorders (vs. the overall dancer rate of 12%). This comprised 14.9% of ballet dancers reporting EDNOS (vs. 9.5% for dancers generally), 4% reporting anorexia (vs. 2%), and 2% reporting bulimia (vs. 4.4%).

A second meta-analysis focused exclusively on ballet dancers, confirming that this group experiences higher rates of disordered eating and also more negative body image than comparison groups (Silverii et al., 2022). For example, ballet dancers reported higher drive for thinness, greater body dissatisfaction, and more bulimic symptoms. Because most of

Signs of body dissatisfaction include dancers trying to hide their bodies, wearing unusually baggy clothes, and avoiding looking in the mirror.

the papers included in the two meta-analyses studied female ballet dancers, the conclusions that may be drawn regarding eating disorder prevalence for other dance styles and genders are limited.

Prevalence of Disordered Eating and Eating Disorders: General Patterns

Beyond studies examining the prevalence of clinical eating disorders in a particular group, numerous comparative studies in dance and sport have examined differences in prevalence between different groups of people (for reviews, see Arcelus et al., 2014; Kong & Harris, 2015; Petrie, 2020; Wells et al., 2020). Overall, such studies have provided us with evidence that disordered eating and eating disorders are more common

> *Among females than males.* This is the case in the general population, sports and dance alike.

> *Among dancers and athletes than the general population.* Note, however, that rates in general populations can also be high: for example, recent reviews have noted prevalence rates of between 7.5% and 15% for young people (Kong & Harris, 2015; Rohde et al., 2015).

> *In weight-related, judged, and aesthetic activities.* Dance fits into this category alongside sports such as gymnastics, figure skating, and artistic swimming.

> *Among performers at higher rather than lower levels.* Most likely, this is because higher-level performers are more invested in their activity, participate more intensely, and are subjected to greater pressures (Annus & Smith, 2009). For instance, older ballet students and those in higher-level schools have reported greater weight dissatisfaction and more disordered eating symptoms than younger students or those from less prestigious schools (Dotti et al., 2002; Thomas et al., 2005).

> *In styles, schools, and companies that promote a thinness ideal.* As already noted, this has commonly been associated with classical ballet.

For a visual overview of these prevalence patterns, see figure 14.2.

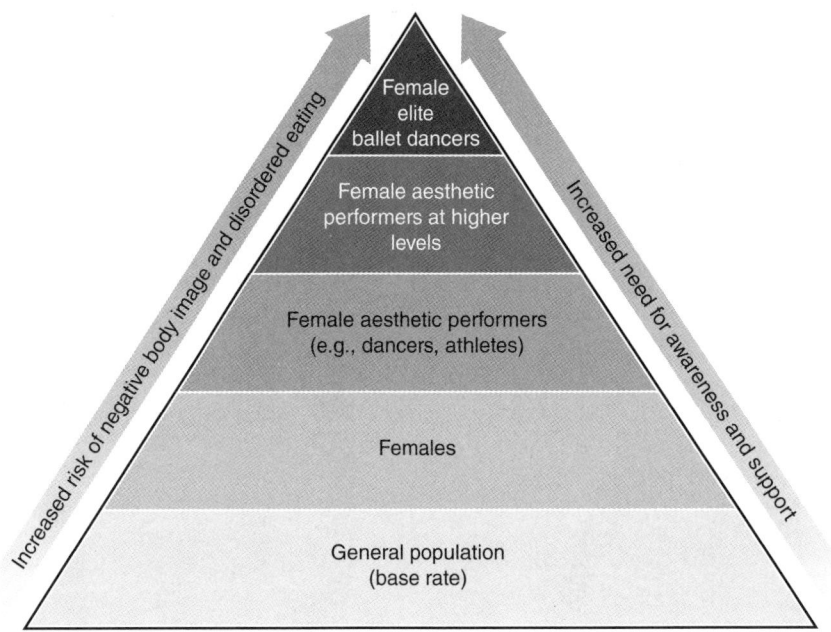

Figure 14.2 The prevalence of disordered eating is higher in certain groups, including females, aesthetic performers, higher-level performers, and in styles that promote a thinness ideal. As such, female elite ballet dancers are at highest risk because they are members of each of the groups associated with increased risk.

Even those who no longer participate in recreational ballet report higher levels of **self-surveillance**, **self-objectification**, and disordered eating than those who have never danced (Tiggemann & Slater, 2001). The authors reasoned that the self-objectification of training in front of mirrors and performing for others had become engrained, such that they continued monitoring their appearances. Similarly, women who had participated in dance as children reported a higher drive for thinness, more bulimic symptoms, and poorer impulse control than a comparison group who had never danced (Ackard et al., 2004). They were also somewhat more perfectionistic and tended to prefer a lower body mass index (BMI). Again, the authors attributed their findings to a lasting impact of dance training on mental health.

It is possible that some, or all, of the problems investigated by Tiggemann and Slater (2001) and by Ackard et al. (2004) are related to underlying vulnerabilities that made some women more likely to choose dance in the first place. The authors also did not assess dance style, intensity, or length of participation, which makes it difficult to assess the true long-term impact of dance training. However, qualitative research indicates that issues around weight, body shape, and self-surveillance can continue long after a dancing career is over (Dryburgh & Fortin, 2010). One study even found that girls who participate in dance or aesthetic sports report higher weight concerns than their peers in nonaesthetic sports, or no sports, already when five years old (Davison et al., 2002). Those who continued until age seven were also more weight-concerned than those who had stopped before that age.

Prevalence of Eating Disorders: Measurement Considerations

As noted, more dancers experience subclinical disordered eating than clinical eating disorders, because the latter is more extreme. Thus, it is important to consider whether a study has examined disordered eating or eating disorders when interpreting its results. Another measurement consideration is that some studies ask about current behavior (e.g., eating behaviors in the past 28 days), whereas others ask about a lifetime prevalence. Clearly, such differences in method may yield differences in results.

Many studies rely on self-report questionnaires, which cost less time and money and whose anonymity can be preferable to some. However, self-report questionnaires may yield higher prevalence rates than expert-led clinical interviews (Petrie, 2020). The former are also not diagnostic per se. For example, researchers often use questionnaires such as the eating attitudes test-26 (EAT-26; Garner et al., 1982), for which there is a clinical cutoff score of 20. While persons scoring above this cutoff are considered to be high risk, likely to have an eating disorder, and warranting follow-up, they are not actually diagnosed. Clinical interviews can be diagnostic and are considered more reliable (Torstveit et al., 2008), but they are far more costly in terms of both time and money, especially for larger samples and for the repeated measurements required in longitudinal studies.

Finally, there is reason to believe that self-report studies underestimate the true prevalence of eating disorders in at-risk populations, of which dance is one (Torstveit et al., 2008). Certainly, it is not unusual for dancers to opt out of studies when they hear that they will be asked questions about their attitudes and behaviors toward food, weight, and shape. Denial is typical of persons suffering from anorexia nervosa, which means that there might well be underreporting of that disorder in studies using self-report questionnaires (at least if questions are obviously about the aspects that the person is in denial about).

Disordered Eating Among Male Dancers

Research consistently shows that females run a greater risk of developing disordered eating, both generally and in activities such as dance. Yet males also experience body- and weight-related pressures, body dissatisfaction, disordered eating, and eating disorders (e.g., Pickard, 2013). In a study with young talented dancers from a variety of styles, cross-sectional data indicated equal prevalence of disordered eating attitudes for young males (7.6%) and females (7.3%; Nordin-Bates et al., 2011). However, when this cohort was followed over a two-year period it became clear that females ran a greater risk of developing disordered eating over that time (Nordin-Bates et al., 2016). This reinforces the importance of not putting too much trust in prevalence rates from single studies, especially if they are cross-sectional and based on self-report. These studies also indicated that the risk factors for disordered eating may differ somewhat for male and female dancers (Nordin-Bates et al., 2011, 2016; see also Kong & Harris, 2015). Unfortunately, the evidence in this regard is as yet limited and difficult to draw conclusions from. Research outside of dance indicates that sexuality is a risk factor for men but not for women; thus, gay and bisexual male dancers may have a higher risk of developing disordered eating (Feldman & Meyer, 2007).

The male body has become more objectified over time, with increased attention being paid to muscularity and extreme levels of fitness (e.g., in the media; Oliver, 2008; Petrie, 2020). In the general population, it has become clear that rates of disordered eating among males have not only increased but are also higher than previously recognized because of the dominant focus on females and thinness ideals (Lavender et al., 2017). Similarly, most disordered eating research in dance has focused on the drive for thinness, with the drive for muscularity or fitness being overlooked. Further research into disordered eating among male dancers is therefore warranted, including in-depth investigations into specific risk factors.

Origins of Negative Body Image and Disordered Eating in Dance

The origins of, or risk factors for, negative body image and disordered eating development among dancers are presented together in this section for two main reasons. The first is that they share so many similarities that keeping them separate would mean much repetition. The second reason is that negative body image is both a risk factor for and a key component of disordered eating (Allen & Walter, 2016; Arcelus et al., 2015; Arthur-Cameselle et al., 2017; Chamay-Weber et al., 2005; Francisco et al., 2012a, 2012b; Kulshreshtha et al., 2021; Liu et al., 2016; Rohde et al., 2015; Tseng et al., 2007; Tylka & Wood-Barcalow, 2015). As such, factors that elevate the risk of a dancer developing a negative body image will also be risk factors for disordered eating. And because disordered eating is a precursor of eating disorders, any risk factor for the former is also a risk factor for the latter.

The sections that follow describe many different risk factors, including some inherent in a person's demographic and biological makeup, risk factors in dancers' personalities and behaviors, in general life, and in the dance environment (see figure 14.3). In line with most research into these topics in dance and sport, and the overall focus of this book, there is an emphasis on psychosocial factors.

The risk factors are grouped into distinct sections in an attempt to provide clarity in an extensive literature. However, real life does not lend itself to being neatly divided into boxes, and many of the risk factors overlap and interact. Put differently, variations in life circumstances, dance-specific pressures, and individual characteristics combine to increase or decrease a person's susceptibility. In figure 14.3, the curved arrows are there to suggest such interactivity.

Some researchers have specifically investigated what might *trigger* disordered eating in a vulnerable person; for dance, it is particularly noteworthy that stress can bring out an otherwise absent association

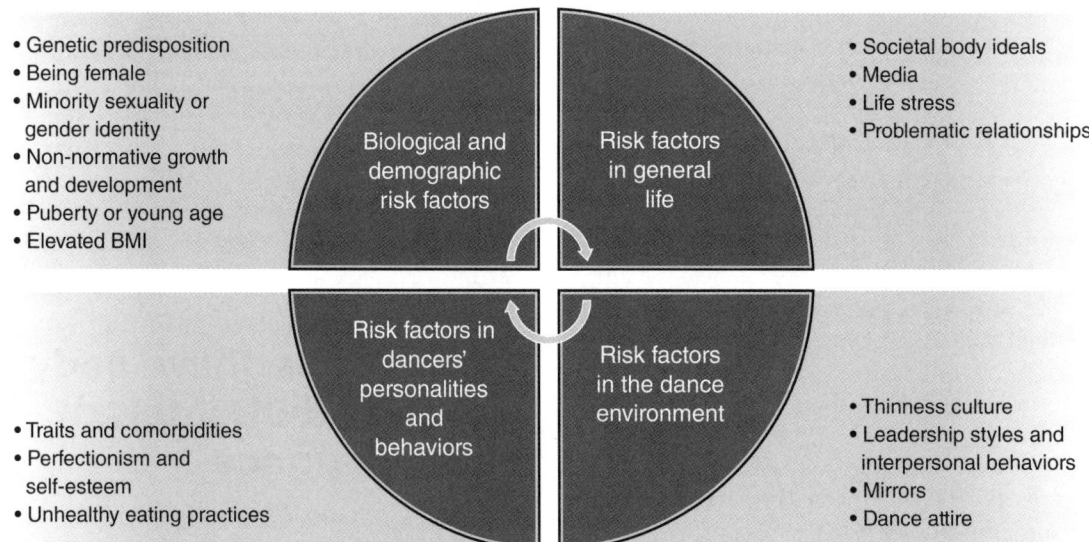

Figure 14.3 Risk factors for negative body image, disordered eating, and eating disorders.

between predisposing factors (e.g., perfectionism, low self-esteem) and disordered eating (Sassaroli & Ruggiero, 2005). Finally, the categories described concern *general* risk factors that increase the likelihood of disordered eating; it remains possible for dancers of any age, gender, dance style or level, or body composition to develop it (Wells et al., 2020).

Biological and Demographic Risk Factors

Many biological and demographic factors make negative body image and disordered eating more likely, including genetic predisposition, being female, having a minority sexuality or gender identity (LGBTQI+), experiencing growth and development patterns that differ from the norm (e.g., girls who go through sexual maturation particularly early), and going through puberty (or just young age; Chamay-Weber et al., 2005; Petrie, 2020; Wells et al., 2020). For example, a dislike or sense of lack of control over bodily changes (e.g., breast development, or being the last boy in the class to go through the adolescent growth spurt) are risk factors for young dancers, not least when these coincide with increased demands in dance training in the early teens.

Several studies have indicated that dancers with higher BMI are more likely to report disordered eating (de Bruin et al., 2009; Francisco et al., 2012b, 2013; Tseng et al., 2007), presumably because they are more dissatisfied. Yet this is not always the case; indeed, dancers are frequently underweight but still report body dissatisfaction and disordered eating (e.g., Toro et al., 2009). The label "elevated BMI" in figure 14.3 denotes a BMI higher than a dancer might like or that is the norm in their dance setting; it does not indicate objectively high BMI. In one study, there was no relationship between BMI and disordered eating; however, having a BMI higher than 18 was significantly associated with intense weight dissatisfaction for artistic reasons, but not for personal reasons (Toro et al., 2009).

Risk Factors in General Life

Because disordered eating exists outside of dance settings, researchers have identified risk factors in everyday living (for reviews, see Chamay-Weber et al., 2005; Wells et al., 2020). These include societal body ideals, media, life stress, and problematic relationships.

Many, if not most, societies endorse a body ideal that is fit, thin (especially for females), and muscular (especially for males), and pressures to be thin increase strongly during the teenage years (Rohde et al., 2015). An important way in which such body ideals are promoted is through media such as advertising, magazines, films, and—not least—social media. It is well-established that social media content that idealizes thinness, muscularity, and/or fitness are detrimental to body image (e.g., Vandenbosch et al., 2021).

Another set of risk factors for body dissatisfaction and disordered eating is being exposed to major life stressors or feeling out of control regarding important aspects of life (e.g., Arthur-Cameselle et al., 2017; Francisco et al., 2012a; Froreich et al., 2017; Gvion,

2008). This can occur during or after events such as life transitions (e.g., changing schools, pubertal development), abuse, trauma (including dance injury), death, or divorce in the family. Developing disordered eating in response to such life stress occurs because the person tries to exercise control over "whatever they can" (in this case, eating and weight) when other things seem chaotic and uncontrollable. For example, dancers may attempt excessive control over their food intake as a (misguided) coping mechanism when dancing/exercising is not possible after an injury (Aalten, 2007; Reel et al., 2018). This is likely to be exacerbated if the person has a narrow dancer identity and feels replaceable in their role or company.

Having one's basic psychological needs (i.e., autonomy, competence, and relatedness) thwarted or chronically unsatisfied is another risk factor for disordered eating (Froreich et al., 2017). This also speaks to a lack of control as people do not feel in charge of their lives (autonomy), feel unable to control what happens to them (competence), or feel alienated from others (relatedness). For more about psychological need fulfillment and thwarting, see chapters 5 and 11. Finally, disordered eating can become more likely when a person experiences problematic relationships in their life (e.g., being bullied, family dysfunction; Arthur-Cameselle et al., 2017). In dance, disordered eating has been associated with a lack of family support, with having close relatives engaged in weight reduction practices (Tseng et al., 2007), and with having received comments from parents about weight, eating, and/or losing weight (Francisco et al., 2013).

Risk Factors in Dancers' Personalities and Behaviors

Several personality traits and characteristics have been shown to increase the risk for developing negative body image and disordered eating, as have specific eating behaviors (Chamay-Weber et al., 2005; Petrie, 2020; Wells et al., 2020). The most commonly studied and best-established personality risk factors are self-esteem and perfectionism, which are further outlined later alongside general personality traits and comorbidities, and unhealthy eating practices. Beyond these factors, another personality characteristic that might predispose dancers to problems with body image and disordered eating is having a narrow dancer identity (Langdon & Petracca, 2010). As these authors stated, "simply identifying as a dancer is related to agreement with dancer norms, including that of poorer body image" (p. 362).

In another study, the authors speculated that the seemingly lower degree of competitiveness they had found among young gymnasts than among dancers might be related to the former group attending "normal" schools each day prior to gymnastics training, unlike the dancers whose integrated schooling meant they were with a single peer group all day, every day (Francisco et al., 2012a). There is as yet little research into the role of a narrowly defined identity in disordered eating, but it stands to reason that total immersion in the dance environment from a young age may influence identity development as well as body image. For more about identity, see chapter 1.

It has further been argued that disembodiment, or detaching oneself from one's body, might predispose dancers to negative body image; for instance, authors have suggested that treating the body as a tool or machine rather than listening to it and respecting it is deeply problematic (e.g., Aalten, 2007; Alexias & Dimitropoulou, 2011; Gvion, 2008; Piran, 2005). For example, one dancer in an interview study stated: "My body was nothing but raw material preventing me from achieving a goal. It was as if my body couldn't stop me from achieving my aims" (Gvion, 2008, p. 81).

Before moving on to specific personality aspects, a striking comparison made between "good athletes" (i.e., characteristics that many athletes strive to possess, and coaches encourage) and anorexia nervosa patients made many years ago is worth considering (Thompson & Sherman, 1999). Specifically, these experts outlined how traits such as mental toughness, dedication to training, a striving for perfection, being coachable and unselfish, and training in spite of pain were often seen as characteristic of good athletes. They also noted how similar or somewhat exaggerated versions of those same characteristics were typical of patients diagnosed with anorexia nervosa, including being ascetic; engaging in excessive training; being perfectionistic, obedient, and self-sacrificing; and denying discomfort and pain. Although you may or may not agree that all the former characteristics signify a good dancer, the similarities are remarkable. A more recent study proposed that characteristics like these indicate an "overconformity to the sport [or dance] ethic" (Coker-Cranney & Reel, 2015). The authors speculated that because it includes uncritical acceptance of norms and a willingness to do whatever it takes, overconforming performers may see disordered eating behaviors as necessary and even required to succeed.

> **THINKING CRITICALLY**
>
> - Are the "good athlete" traits noted by Thompson and Sherman (1999) seen as desirable in your dance setting?
> - Which, if any, of the "good athlete" traits are sought, encouraged, and rewarded in your dance setting? (This may be done more or less explicitly)
> - Are there alternative traits, characteristics, or behaviors that you believe should be promoted and that would not be as similar to a mental illness?

General Personality Traits and Comorbidities

If you have read chapter 1 then you will know that our personalities affect a very wide assortment of outcomes, and disordered eating is no exception. For example, studies have shown that low emotional stability, low extroversion and, at times, low conscientiousness (Allen & Walter, 2016) as well as negative affectivity (i.e., an increased tendency to experience unpleasant emotional states like fear, sadness, and frustration; Rohde et al., 2015) can all elevate risk. In a study with dance students, those with an eating disorder reported higher levels of neuroticism (i.e., low emotional stability) than their non-eating disordered peers (Liu et al., 2016).

Comorbidities are concurrent mental health issues such as anxiety or depression, and they too increase the risk of disordered eating (Arcelus et al., 2015; Arthur-Cameselle et al., 2017; Estanol et al., 2013; Liu et al., 2016; Tseng et al., 2007). In a welcome departure from the norm of examining risk factors, Estanol et al. (2013) investigated both risk factors and potential protective factors for disordered eating among student dancers. Like other studies, they found that weight pressures predicted disordered eating; additionally, this risk was partially mediated by negative affect (anxiety and depression; see also Arcelus et al., 2015). Moreover, dancers who reported having better coping skills (and more favorable psychological characteristics, such as confidence) reported lower levels of disordered eating (Estanol et al., 2013).

Perfectionism and Self-Esteem

Perfectionism (and related characteristics such as competitiveness and interpersonal comparison) is one of the most thoroughly established risk factors for disordered eating in dance and in sport (Arthur-Cameselle et al., 2017; Chin & Clements, 2021; de Bruin et al., 2009; Dryburgh & Fortin, 2010; Goodwin et al., 2014a; Heiland et al., 2008; Nordin-Bates et al., 2011, 2016; Penniment & Egan, 2012; Reel et al., 2005; Silverii et al., 2022; Thomas et al., 2005; Toro et al., 2009). For instance, a participant in an interview study shared how she felt her eating disorder was a result of "Always having to be perfect and super type A . . . and needing control over every single part of my life, especially my body" (Arthur-Cameselle et al., 2017, p. 205).

Research indicates that perfectionistic concerns (i.e., being highly self-critical, worrying about mistakes and personal adequacy) are typically a stronger predictor of disordered eating than are perfectionistic strivings (i.e., desiring flawlessness and having particularly high goals; Arcelus et al., 2015; Goodwin et al., 2014a; Nordin-Bates et al., 2011, 2016). Still, these studies also indicate that having high or increasing perfectionistic strivings should still be considered a vulnerability (see chapter 2). For instance, a study with young dancers found that disordered eating increased over a two-year period not only for those exhibiting stronger perfectionistic concerns than their peers, but also for female dancers whose levels of either perfectionistic strivings or perfectionistic concerns increased over time in relation to themselves (Nordin-Bates et al., 2016). This suggests that educators may need to be watchful for signs of increased perfectionism among their dancers, even if they are not necessarily the most perfectionistic ones in the studio.

Low or contingent self-esteem is another well-established risk factor for disordered eating (Arthur-Cameselle et al., 2017; Dryburgh & Fortin, 2010; Goodwin et al., 2014b; Liu et al., 2016; Nordin-Bates et al., 2016; Petrie, 2020) and includes feeling inadequate or punishing oneself by food restriction for somehow being unworthy (see chapter 3). An ethnographic study that included interviews with a principal ballet dancer who had recovered from an eating disorder provided the following account of such problems:

> I always thought that my main problem was my weight and that I would be chosen more if only I would be thinner. But this is not how it works. You have to be yourself. Dancers have to work with their own bodies, not with some idealized image of it. You have to know what you are worth and accept that maybe you will not be chosen for every ballet. (Esther Protzman in Aalten, 2007, p. 118)

Unhealthy Eating Practices

Dieting, rigid or restrictive eating, and misinformation about nutrition may predispose a dancer to disordered eating (Arthur-Cameselle et al., 2017; Rohde et al., 2015). Indeed, many eating disorders begin with dieting. A related problem is when disordered eating behaviors are modeled by others (Aalten, 2007; Benn & Walters, 2001; Dryburgh & Fortin, 2010; Petrie, 2020) This is especially likely if it is a high-performance environment in which a young and impressionable person spends a lot of time. For instance, a dancer may imitate peers who eat salad rather than carbohydrate-rich options at lunchtime, or teachers and other role models who skip meals. Such behaviors may represent a way of demonstrating commitment to dance, trying to fit in, or avoiding critical comments.

Risk Factors in the Dance Environment

Although problems with negative body image and disordered eating exist in society generally and thus can be unrelated to dance participation, research clearly shows that particular features in a performance environment can contribute to their development (Petrie, 2020). In some cases, it is a major reason or cause; in other cases, it is a trigger for an already vulnerable individual. As Petrie (2020) has pointed out, high-level performers spend much of their time in environments that involve almost constant exposure to bodies: one's own, those of others, and body-related talk. As such, dance organizations may either increase or decrease the risk of dancers developing disordered eating depending on how they are organized and perceived (Dantas et al., 2018; Piran, 2005).

Many have asked whether dancers are already vulnerable to disordered eating development before entering dance or whether the dance environment puts them at greater risk (e.g., Arcelus et al., 2014). Although it is a difficult question to research and to answer conclusively, the answer is likely to be "a bit of both." In particular, research clearly indicates that the origins (or risk factors) for disordered eating are both personal (e.g., genetics, personality) *and* related to non-dance environmental factors (e.g., family, general societal pressures), as outlined above, as well as dance-specific factors (e.g., pressure to be thin). For example, high levels of perfectionism may facilitate dance participation as it may, to some extent, lead to short-term performance success (see chapter 2). Yet perfectionism is also an underlying vulnerability, which might become activated (or acted upon) in dance environments that promote thinness, unrealistic body ideals, and restricted eating (e.g., Penniment & Egan, 2012; Thomas et al., 2005).

In line with this reasoning, a study with young adult women found that past dance participation was unrelated to disordered eating in adulthood (Annus & Smith, 2009). However, elevated disordered eating symptoms were reported by those who had experienced more **thinness-related learning** in dance classes (i.e., their dance experiences included weighing, weight- and shape-related comments, other pressure from teachers, and/or disordered eating behaviors among dance peers). This finding was later confirmed in a study of high-level dancers from ballet and jazz (Penniment & Egan, 2012). In both investigations, the relationship was mediated by **thinness and restriction expectancies**; that is, those who had experienced more thinness-related learning in dance classes reported more disordered eating partly because they believed that their lives would be better if they dieted and were thinner.

In the second of these investigations, those with higher levels of perfectionism reported experiencing more thinness-related learning in their dance classes (Penniment & Egan, 2012). It may be that perfectionists pick up and recall more such cues in their environments; it may also be that dancers become more perfectionistic in environments where there is a lot of thinness-related learning. Third, it is possible that perfectionistic dancers are more likely to select into or stay in such environments. A study that found no differences in disordered eating prevalence between female dance students and non-dancers concluded that dance should not be considered a risk factor per se, but that critical environments are the more likely culprit (Toro et al., 2009). Similarly, Dryburgh and Fortin (2010, p. 106) concluded after an interview study with ballet and contemporary dancers that "It is not the art of dance that is at fault as much as an outdated modality of teaching and working that places too much emphasis on an unattainable ideal body type."

Four sets of interrelated risk factors that may be present in the dance environment are outlined next, including thinness culture, leadership styles and other interpersonal behaviors, mirrors, and dance attire.

Thinness Culture

There are numerous indications of how the dance world, and especially classical ballet, promotes thinness as an ideal. Indeed, many dancers seem to interpret dance culture as simply requiring thinness (Dantas et al., 2018). Dancers, teachers, and scholars have often described the risks inherent in these environments, where there is constant scrutiny of dancers' bodies and surveillance through mirrors and teachers' gazes (e.g., Benn & Walters, 2001; Dryburgh & Fortin, 2010; Green, 1999; Pickard, 2013). The importance of aspiring toward an idealized body weight and shape is clearly conveyed from early ages and into professional life. For example, a 15-year-old dancer in vocational ballet school spoke of the importance of "looking nice" (i.e., slim) as follows:

> I'm not fat but I'm not skinny . . . got to try and keep quite nice and slim, so you look nice in a leotard and your tights and everything. That's the main thing really. It's the most important thing here. (Pickard, 2013, p. 11)

More specific aspects of thinness culture that may increase the likelihood of dancers suffering from negative body image and/or disordered eating include the following:

> *Weight-related pressures*, such as particularly thin dancers being favored for roles and jobs, or dancers being weighed often, by teachers, or in front of others (Annus & Smith, 2009; Arthur-Cameselle et al., 2017; Benn & Walters, 2001; Chin & Clements, 2021; Estanol et al., 2013; Francisco et al., 2012a, 2012b; Kong & Harris, 2015; Penniment & Egan, 2012; Reel et al., 2005, 2018; Rohde et al., 2015; Toro et al., 2009). It can also be simply the perception that one's director or other gatekeeper knows and cares about what weight one is, notices weight gains, and so on (Coker-Cranney & Reel, 2015). Unfortunately, research suggests that a high proportion of dancers perceive such weight-related pressures (e.g., Annus & Smith, 2009; Reel et al., 2005).

> *Exposure to thin, idealized bodies through dance-related media* (Arthur-Cameselle et al., 2017; Benn & Walters, 2001; Heiland et al., 2008; Nerini, 2015; Oliver, 2008; Swami & Tovée, 2009). For example, a study with young dancers found that those who reported greater perceptions of media pressures to be thin and had internalized the thin ideal to a greater extent also experienced greater body dissatisfaction (Nerini, 2015). It is likely that the 24/7 access to dance content on social media, which often portrays highly idealized bodies, has increased the sense of pressure put on especially young dancers to conform to the thinness aesthetic.

> *Thinness and restriction expectancies* (i.e., a belief that thinness will enhance performance). This is especially likely in dance styles or roles for which lower weight actually does help performance to some extent but also when it is simply believed to do so; for example, dancers may believe that it will become easier to jump or be lifted if they weigh less even when this is only partly true (Arthur-Cameselle et al., 2017; Benn & Walters, 2001; Gvion, 2008; Reel et al., 2005).

Leadership Styles and Interpersonal Behaviors

In addition to the covert pressures inherent in thinness culture, several more overt interpersonal behaviors and leadership styles also predispose dancers toward negative body image and disordered eating:

> *Critical comments, body shaming, or weight-related teasing* from teachers, directors, judges, critics, peers, or parents (Aalten, 2007; Alexias & Dimitropoulou, 2011; Annus & Smith, 2009; Benn & Walters, 2001; Chin & Clements, 2021; Dantas et al., 2018; Dryburgh & Fortin, 2010; Francisco et al., 2012a; Green, 1999; Gvion, 2008; Heiland et al., 2008; Penniment & Egan, 2012; Toro et al., 2009). This includes teachers disparaging a student's weight, speaking about the thinnest dancers as role models, or telling dancers they will get cast for a particular role if they lose a specific amount of weight within a certain time. In an often-cited example, dancer Gelsey Kirkland described the following encounter with George Balanchine, her company director:

> [H]e halted class and approached me for a kind of physical inspection. With his knuckles, he thumped on my sternum and down my rib cage, clucking his tongue and remarking, "must see the bones." I was less than a hundred pounds even then. . . . He did not merely say, "Eat less." He said repeatedly, "Eat nothing." (Kirkland & Lawrence, 1986, pp. 55-56)

Although such extreme examples are hopefully rare today, a majority (73%) of vocational dance students had received critical comments about their bodies in a study undertaken not so long ago (Goodwin et al., 2014b). This was most commonly from a dance teacher (63%) and was typically perceived to have quite a bit of impact (38%) or a lot of impact (20%). The vast majority (> 80%) also remembered the incident clearly. When comparing dancers who recalled having received a critical comment about their body with those who had not, the former group reported more disordered eating (Goodwin et al., 2014b).

Liu et al. (2016) found that dance students with an eating disorder were more likely to recall having been teased for being overweight than their non-eating-disordered peers. Although a variety of other variables were also associated with disordered eating symptoms (including comorbid psychiatric diagnoses, body dissatisfaction, low self-esteem, and neuroticism), the strongest predictors were overweight-related teasing alongside body dissatisfaction.

› *Positive reinforcement (e.g., praise from a teacher) on weight loss or other disordered eating behavior* (Aalten, 2007; Gvion, 2008; Petrie, 2020). Praise from significant others in our lives represents potent positive reinforcement, which makes behavior maintenance likely. Similarly, unintentional weight loss as a result of illness may trigger disordered eating if the weight loss gave some sense of satisfaction (Arthur-Cameselle et al., 2017; Dryburgh & Fortin, 2010). For these reasons, leader approval of weight loss, disordered eating behaviors, or risk factors such as restrictive eating or excessive exercise are dangerous. This is the case even if done unintentionally or in a misguided attempt to be kind or helpful. A particularly disconcerting passage from a qualitative study illustrates this point:

Limor remembers how high she felt when people mentioned she has lost too much weight: I'll never forget that day. The day my over-thinness was acknowledged, I felt in heaven. It was as if I accomplished the major mission of my life. (From Gvion, 2008, p. 82)

› *Unhealthy motivational climates and controlling leadership,* such as that characterized by power imbalances, interpersonal comparisons, favoritism, punishment, and control (Bartholomew et al., 2011; Dryburgh & Fortin, 2010; Francisco et al., 2012a). In an interview study with young dancers about disordered eating risks, teachers seemed to be the major source of influence, with problems noted when teachers were feared, hostile, not accessible, or had favorites (Francisco et al., 2012a). Other literature has suggested that healthy motivational climates may help protect dancers from body dissatisfaction and disordered eating (de Bruin et al., 2009; Stark & Newton, 2014). Unfortunately, the evidence in this regard is purely cross-sectional; in a longitudinal study with a larger sample of dancers, motivational climate perceptions were unrelated to disordered eating for females and both unclear and contradictory for males (Nordin-Bates et al., 2016). Thus, further research into this issue is necessary.

› *Subjective judgments and individual preferences of artistic directors and other leaders.* In some dance styles, companies, and schools, there are teachers and artistic directors who act as powerful gatekeepers; for example, they may control who gets to compete, who gets cast for roles, and who gets promoted. The subjective nature of dance may exaggerate the power that such people hold, because it makes the criteria vague: Who will he pick? What does she see in *that* guy? What do they *really* think about me? Such uncertainties, in combination with power, can make dancers dependent, anxious, and obedient, which in turn makes them more vulnerable to other influences regarding body image and eating behaviors. As Benn and Walters (2001, p. 147) put it:

The power of management, of school entrance selectors, company directors, teachers and choreographers, cannot be underestimated in the search for external influences on a dancer's body image. These are the gatekeepers of the profession who hold the key to others' life-chances and their view of the "preferred look" for the female dancer mattered.

Mirrors

A large number of studies have been conducted into the use of mirrors and how they may affect dancers' body image, as well as other related outcomes (Benn & Walters, 2001; Dantas et al., 2018; Dryburgh & Fortin, 2010; Ehrenberg, 2010; Green, 1999; Gvion, 2008; Oliver, 2008; Pickard, 2013; Reel et al., 2005; Radell et al., 2002, 2003, 2004, 2011, 2014, 2017, 2020, 2021). In particular, Sally Radell and her colleagues have explored the impact of the mirror in dance classrooms for more than two decades. Often using a quasi-experimental approach, they have compared groups of young adult student dancers who take the same dance class with the same teacher, but with or without mirrors (Radell et al., 2002-2021). As these studies have made clear, the mirror can be a source of negative body image.

Research by other authors has confirmed that mirrors contribute to problems such as self-surveillance and body dissatisfaction (Benn & Walters, 2001; Dryburgh & Fortin, 2010; McEwen & Young, 2011; Reel et al., 2005). Indeed, high-level dancers often have preferences for where to stand and where (not) to look (Benn & Walters, 2001). Along similar lines, Petrie (2020) explained how performers compare and judge their appearances and behaviors against internalized mental representations of some ideal by engaging in activities such as interpersonal comparison ("Am I fitter than they?"), checking one's body in the mirror, and self-weighing. Petrie goes on to explain how these activities cause performers to become "hyper-self-focused," which almost inevitably results in the discovery of various discrepancies between the real and the ideal self.

An important finding in this area is that dancers taught with mirrors sometimes feel worse about their bodies at the end of a semester than at its beginning (Radell et al., 2011, 2017, 2020). In contrast, dancers taught without mirrors may *increase* their body satisfaction (Radell et al., 2002, 2004). Even adagio performance appears to improve more for students taught in nonmirrored studios (Radell et al., 2003, 2004). These benefits are not universal, however; for example, body satisfaction decrements when taught with a mirror seem more pronounced in ballet than in modern dance (Radell et al., 2020) and more for higher-level than for lower-level dance students (Radell et al., 2011). It would be interesting to examine whether psychological traits such as self-esteem moderate the impact of mirrors on body image and other outcomes, such that the negative impact is greater for dancers with lower self-esteem.

A major problem with mirror use is that it can become distracting (Ehrenberg, 2010; Radell et al., 2003, 2004, 2011). Indeed, dancers sometimes report self-consciousness, self-critique, and stress when dancing with mirrors, whereas dancing without a mirror enables them to tune into internal sensations (Ehrenberg, 2010; Green, 1999; Oliver, 2008; Radell et al., 2011, 2014). Mirrors may also encourage dancers to focus more on poses than on movement (Ehrenberg, 2010; Radell et al., 2014). As the authors explained, "Relying on one's reflection in the mirror can become a 'crutch' which prevents dancers from fully developing their kinaesthetic sensibilities and thus inhibits their full potential" (Radell et al., 2014, p. 171). More advanced students may even devise ways of avoiding the mirror to enable a focus on kinesthesia (Radell et al., 2017). Yet despite the negative effects, many value the mirror as a learning tool—for instance, when trying to improve alignment (Ehrenberg, 2010; Radell et al., 2014, 2020, 2021). As such, authors in this area often advise a judicious use of mirrors rather than simply removing them.

Dance Attire

Having to wear tight-fitting or revealing dance clothing can be another risk factor for negative body image and disordered eating development (Benn & Walters; 2001; Chin & Clements, 2021; McEwen & Young, 2011; Petrie, 2020; Price & Pettijohn, 2006; Reel et al., 2005). In an experimental study, students took their standard ballet class wearing regulation uniform one day (black leotard, pink tights) and whatever they wanted on another day (Price & Pettijohn, 2006). Dancers reported more positive perceptions of their bodies when they chose their own clothing; they also felt more comfortable and enjoyed their dancing more. Importantly, none chose tight-fitting or revealing clothing when they were able to choose. College student dancers in another study identified the mirror as their number one source of pressure, although dance uniforms came a close second (Reel et al., 2005). Interviewees explained how this was because their uniform (leotard and tights) made them more aware of their weight and appearance; it was particularly the case for female dancers with somewhat larger breasts. A participant in another study stated:

> We would have fitting sessions where we had to rehearse in costumes and I was like: "Oh the show is next week. Now I'm going on the carrot diet." We actually saw ourselves as being fatter than we were although I think I had a healthy way of seeing myself despite my weight problems. Mind you, I had a period where I showered in the dark. (Dryburgh & Fortin, 2010, p. 100)

Consequences of Body Image and Disordered Eating

Dance researchers have typically considered aspects of body image and disordered eating (including eating disorders) to be outcomes in and of themselves; as such, research into their consequences is scarce. The current section is therefore largely based on non-dance literature and is kept relatively concise. You will notice quite a bit of overlap with the earlier sections on symptoms and risk factors because some consequences are symptoms to watch out for in dance settings (e.g., concentration difficulties, recurrent injuries). Other consequences are less visible but nonetheless valuable to be aware of (e.g., impaired growth and development, reduced bone mineral density).

Consequences of Negative Body Image

Research into negative body image has found it to be associated with an array of problematic correlates and consequences, including the following:

› *Self-objectification.* This refers to seeing one's body, or even one's person, as a product or commodity to be marketed and displayed (Chin & Clements, 2021; Radell et al., 2017; Tiggemann & Slater, 2001).

› *Negative affect.* The negative thoughts and feelings about one's body that form an inherent part of negative body image logically comprise, or produce, anxiety, guilt, and shame.

› *Concentration difficulties.* The self-objectification associated with negative body image and frequent exposure to one's own appearance in mirrors leaves fewer attentional resources available for other more productive and positive activities, such as focus on the act of dancing, inner experiences, or the propensity to become truly immersed in an activity (i.e., achieve a flow state; Tiggemann & Slater, 2001; see chapter 6).

› *Avoidance behaviors.* Dancers with negative body image may avoid standing near a mirror, or performing in front of (some) others, to avoid having to put their body on display (Dryburgh & Fortin, 2010; Toro et al., 2009).

› *Disordered eating.* Negative body image is a major predictor of disordered eating because having negative thoughts and feelings about one's body can result in behavioral responses such as restrained eating (i.e., an attempt to fix the "problem"). If they persist, such reactions can become disordered eating (Petrie, 2020).

For an illustration of how negative body image might result in disordered eating, consider figure 14.4. In this functional analysis, Annie, a dancer with strong body dissatisfaction, is feeling stressed because she has an important rehearsal coming up. She does not feel entirely prepared and is worried about how the rehearsal director will examine her body in the new revealing costume. As a response to this stress, Annie comforts herself with food; however, her eating gets out of control, and she does not stop until uncomfortably full. While she binges, the negative thoughts and feelings are pushed to one side (the immediate consequence); however, this is quickly followed by intense guilt: "How could I do this to myself?"

Annie's guilt becomes the antecedent in the second functional analysis. To cope with her guilt, Annie decides to get rid of the excess calories: She makes herself vomit and then goes for a long hard run. The immediate consequence is that she feels better: "I'm back in control!" In the longer term, of course, the consequences of both bingeing and purging are impaired health and performance. But the short-term consequences associated with bingeing (e.g., suppressing unwanted emotions) and purging (e.g., reducing guilt) are powerful, which means that they tend to recur, following one another in cycles. This is especially the case if purging leads to highly restricted eating and intense exercise because the resulting low energy-state makes new binges more likely.

Correlates and Consequences of Positive Body Image

Both physical health and psychological well-being are likely to be supported by positive body image (Tylka & Wood-Barcalow, 2015). For example, persons with positive body image engage in more self-care and experience less psychological distress alongside better health. Similarly, promoting positive body image seems to make health-enhancing behaviors such as regular exercise more likely, while making unhealthy dieting and disordered eating less likely (Tylka & Wood-Barcalow, 2015).

Health-Related Consequences of Disordered Eating

Key results of the research into the health-related impact of disordered eating are highlighted in this section (APA, 2013; NEDA, 2021a, 2021b; Wells et al., 2020). Although these results are more likely to occur and to become severe for clinical eating disorders, they can also accompany subclinical disordered eating (Chamay-Weber et al., 2005).

1. *Major physical health problems for all bodily systems*
   - Dehydration, energy and nutritional deficiencies, and electrolyte imbalances
   - Fatigue and frequent headaches
   - Menstrual dysfunction
   - Impaired growth and development
   - Suppressed immune responses and frequent illness

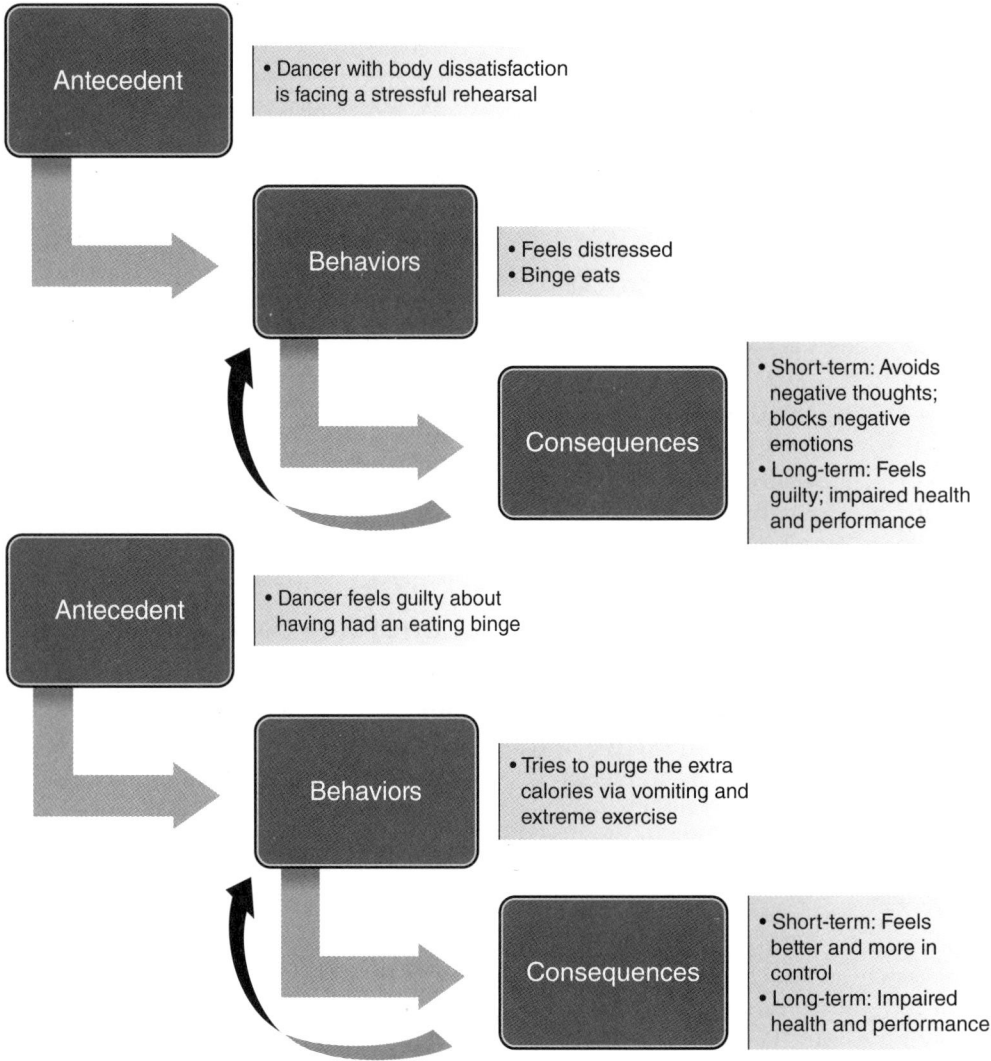

Figure 14.4 Functional analysis examples of how two disordered eating behaviors, bingeing and purging, may manifest. The recursive arrows indicate that the short-term consequences make the behavior more likely to reoccur in similar situations in the future (behavior maintenance).

- Gastrointestinal issues (e.g., dyspepsia, chronic constipation, stomach pains)
- Cardiovascular changes (e.g., hypotension, irregular heartbeat)
- Reduced bone mineral density, leading to greater risk of fractures and osteoporosis

2. *Major mental health problems*
   - Depression and anxiety
   - Personality disorders
   - Substance abuse and self-harm
   - Suicidal ideation and death

Performance-Related Consequences of Disordered Eating

Although the aforementioned health-related consequences of disordered eating should be of greatest concern, it is also worth knowing that disordered eating carries an assortment of performance-related consequences (APA, 2013; Chamay-Weber et al., 2005; Wells et al., 2020). Because these may appear relatively early (i.e., while eating problems are still subclinical), they serve as valuable warning signs.

› Difficulties with concentration and coordination
› Reduced energy, strength, and stamina

> Taking longer to recover and gain training adaptations (e.g., get stronger from body conditioning)
> Dizziness or fainting
> Recurrent injuries and slow healing

How Can Healthy Body Image Be Nurtured?

For dancers to feel and perform at their peak, they need to be at ease with their bodies. Because the body is very much in focus in dance contexts, it is therefore important that all talk about bodies is constructive and positive. Importantly, this is *not* done by appearance-based compliments (e.g., "You have such a good body for dance" or "You look great"). In fact, delivering such compliments frequently may have the opposite effect, because they suggest that appearance is important and promote self-surveillance (see Tylka & Wood-Barcalow, 2015). Instead, educators do well to promote a culture in which bodily capacities are seen to be ever-developing, impressive, and something to be grateful for.

Practices that emphasize somatic agency and embodiment may help build such a culture, further helping dancers to become aware of their bodies from the inside and staying attuned to its messages (e.g., Aalten, 2007; Barr & Oliver, 2016; Green, 1999; Oliver, 2008; Piran, 2005; Tiggemann et al., 2014; Van Zelst et al., 2004). Knowledge of dance history and feminist pedagogy may assist in this endeavor; as dance scholars Barr and Oliver (2016, p. 99) wrote:

> The idealized perfect body is not monolithic. Its form is elusive; it is a reflection of the era and its cultural values, and at times a response to the unspoken hierarchies within the art form itself. Highlighting particular moments in dance history and how the "perfect body" influences teaching-learning paradigms of the time also plays a role in this inquiry. . . . these writings are reminders that multiple perfect bodies exist within any era and that much of the time, discourse on the idealized body focuses on the female dancer.

Positive body culture may also be sustained by focusing on body functionality over appearances (Petrie, 2020), by emphasizing strength and fitness over weight and thinness, and by nurturing growth mindsets (see chapter 12). An aspect of positive body culture pertaining to female dancer health relates to menstruation; specifically, regular periods can be talked about as a valuable sign that the body is in good working order. Dancers with menstrual dysfunctions should be referred to a specialist for disordered eating assessment, as should dancers with stress fractures (Wells et al., 2020). Doing so in time can help prevent a multitude of problems, not least impaired bone health and osteoporosis.

The use of tight-fitting clothing and costumes that cannot be altered to suit individual bodies should be discussed openly rather than simply done "because it is what we have always done" (Oliver, 2008). In fact, dancers should be allowed free choice of clothing when possible (i.e., when there is not a particular reason for specific uniforms). When it is not possible, dancers should be told the reasons and allowed to give input regarding clothing. Mirrors should be used judiciously rather than habitually. Most of us are strongly drawn to visual stimuli, which means that focusing on internal or other sensory feedback can be difficult if there is a mirror in front of us; it simply takes over (e.g., Radell et al., 2021).

How Can Disordered Eating Be Prevented, Identified, and Managed?

Research in dance (Bar et al., 2017; Piran, 1999; Torres-McGehee et al., 2011; Yannakoulia et al., 2002) and in the more well-established domain of sports psychology (Petrie, 2020) both indicate that systematic intervention programs can have positive effects on a variety of risk factors for, and symptoms of, disordered eating. Experts have recommended that such programs should

> be theory- and evidence-based (e.g., cognitive behavioral therapy, mindfulness, self-compassion; e.g., Rohde et al., 2015; Turk & Waller, 2020; Voelker et al., 2019);
> target established risk factors such as negative body image, self-esteem, and perfectionism (Petrie, 2020);
> use a whole-school approach (i.e., not just involve students or staff, but rather both; Piran, 1999, 2005);
> be relevant, interactive, and engaging to its audience (e.g., by having the intended population help design the content); and

> encourage reflection and action outside of scheduled sessions (e.g., homework tasks, things to try in practice).

Next, further practical recommendations emerging from research in this area have been summarized. Not all interventions yield positive effects; it can be truly difficult to obtain significant behavior change and perhaps especially culture change.

How Disordered Eating Can Be Prevented

Prevention efforts for something as complex as disordered eating can (and often should) be as multifaceted as the problem itself. For instance, it is appropriate to teach individual dancers or groups of dancers about skills and strategies that they can use to enhance self-awareness, set healthy goals based in their personal values, and cope with stress in productive ways (e.g., Estanol et al., 2013). However, it is inappropriate to direct all prevention efforts at individuals because disordered eating is typically also interpersonal and cultural in nature. As such, working with dance schools, companies, and families is more likely to be effective than only working with individuals; it is also more fair and less likely to "blame the victim." Especially dance settings that provide intense training, attract dancers with underlying vulnerabilities (e.g., young, highly perfectionistic, narrow identities), and promote a thinness ideal have a moral obligation to work preventively. This is because the already existing risk factors in such settings make it more likely that even occasional or otherwise minor triggers (e.g., a passing comment about body shapes) yield unfortunate results. Put differently, those who work in an environment full of tinder simply cannot afford to light a single match.

Build Positive Body Image

Because negative body image is a major predictor of disordered eating and positive body image may prevent it, nurturing the latter is imperative; for suggestions of how this may be achieved, please refer to the previous section, "Positive Body Image."

Reduce the Emphasis on Weight and Thinness

There should be zero tolerance for critical comments about body shapes and weight, for body shaming, weight-related teasing, and similar weight-related pressures. Weighing of dancers has few purposes in dance and should be kept to a minimum (e.g., school nurses weighing students to ensure they are developing in line with recommendations for their age). Teachers should not be involved in weighing or even discuss dancers' weights. Moreover, employment and casting practices should be monitored to ensure that the thinnest dancers are not being favored for roles or jobs.

Depending on one's role in dance, it may be important to keep an eye on what is being portrayed in dance-related media and other outlets, such as the pictures displayed on school walls and the promotional materials produced by a company. Is it thinness, muscularity, artistry, or something else that is being portrayed, and to what extents? Are these messages in line with the organization's values?

Provide Ongoing Education for Staff and Dancers

Dancers and dance organization personnel should all have up-to-date information about what disordered eating is, its key risk factors, and what can be done. For instance, they need to understand that thinness will not always enhance performance and that underfueled dancers are not only going to feel worse but also learn, develop, and perform far below their potential. In short, nutrition education is paramount, as is information and positive attitudes toward growth and development. Evidence-based education can also contribute to the promotion of positive body culture, per the previous section, by conveying a message that food is fuel (as well as a platform for positive social interaction and pleasure) rather than a source of shame (e.g., Lunde & Holmqvist Gattario, 2017).

Consider What Is Being Reinforced Around Food, Weight, and Shape

Because disordered eating behaviors are elicited, maintained, and intensified in line with the reinforcements that they incur (or are expected to incur), removing such reinforcements can reduce the unhealthy behaviors (see the introduction for more about extinguishing behaviors). Educators especially, but also dancers, should therefore not praise or give specific attention to dancers who have lost weight, who eat restrictively, or who exercise incessantly. Avoid commenting on dancers' meal choices, snacking habits or similar, and refer any concerns to an appropriately qualified professional (e.g., dietitian, nutritionist). Teachers and other leaders should instead aim to be positive role models regarding food and weight, for instance, by eating healthy meals together with dancers and not complaining about their own bodies. Of course, this can be difficult; teachers carry their own weight- and body-related experiences with them and may benefit from critically considering those influences before they can be role models (Piran, 2005). Last but not least, there should be adequate time set aside for lunch and other breaks, to send a clear message that eating and recovery are important.

Create Healthy Motivational Climates and Nurture Autonomy

Disordered eating is more likely to emerge in climates characterized by imbalances of power, interpersonal comparisons, punishment, and control. Therefore, it is important to create healthy motivational climates in which dancers are treated respectfully and basic psychological needs are more likely to be satisfied (see chapters 5 and 11). For example, dancers whose needs are satisfied should be more likely to feel safe, speak up for themselves, respect their bodies, and be proud of their individuality.

Look Out for the Vulnerable Dancers

Dancers with low emotional stability, low or contingent self-esteem, high levels of perfectionism, or a narrow dancer identity should be considered more vulnerable to disordered eating development. These dancers may be more attentive to weight-related stimuli and interpret events differently (Annus & Smith, 2009). For instance, they may perceive their learning environment as more comparative and problematic and remember teacher behaviors as more critical than their less perfectionistic peers do (Nordin-Bates et al., 2014). Although the existence of these personal vulnerabilities might suggest that disordered eating is not the dance environments' "fault," such vulnerabilities are prevalent in dance. As such, there should be increased awareness, attentiveness, and support available for such dancers. For more information about narrow identities, perfectionism, and self-esteem, see chapters 1, 2, and 3, respectively.

Educators should also keep in mind that dancers with unusual growth and development (e.g., early maturing females), high BMI, high levels of stress and pressure in life, or with health issues (injury or illness, including mental illness) may be more at risk and should refer them for support as appropriate.

Let Professionals Do What They Are Qualified to Do

Teachers, choreographers, ballet masters, and other artistic staff are presumably hired on the basis of their expertise in dance technique and artistry. It is therefore unfair, as has sometimes been the case in the past, that such leaders take on roles outside of their expertise, such as giving nutrition advice. Instead, let teachers teach, let choreographers choreograph, let nutritionists or dietitians give advice about food and energy, and let psychologists or psychiatrists provide psychological support.

Practice Mindfulness and Self-Compassion

Several effective intervention programs have been conducted to indicate that mindfulness and self-compassion practices can help reduce the extent to which performers endorse thinness as an ideal, build positive body image, and prevent disordered eating development (Turk & Waller, 2020; Voelker et al., 2019). Mindfulness helps people tune in to their internal reactions (e.g., self-critical thoughts about one's body), for instance, when faced with pressure to look a particular way and handle such reactions nonjudgmentally. In learning to be mindful and treating ourselves with compassion, we can avoid acting impulsively to stressful experiences (Tylka & Wood-Barcalow, 2015). This can be useful in many situations, one of which is when faced with discrepancies between idealized images of dancers' bodies and our own, imperfect one (see chapter 8). Put differently, mindfulness and self-compassion practices teach us to acknowledge negative emotions rather than deny or push them away; this, in turn, can help reduce over- or undereating as ways of suppressing negative thoughts and emotions (e.g., Turk & Waller, 2020).

How Eating Disorders Can Be Identified and Managed

Although diagnoses and treatment for eating disorders can only be undertaken by clinicians, dance organizations can and should facilitate this work in three main ways: by having (and using) an eating disorders policy, by having established referral pathways, and by addressing concerns directly and supportively.

Create a Useful Eating Disorders Policy

Many organizations have policies because they know they "should," but these same policies may not be truly integrated into daily practices. For a matter as important as disordered eating, this is not a feasible approach. Instead, staff in dance organizations should create such a policy together, perhaps in collaboration with invited experts, and actively discuss how it can

Avoiding eating situations is a warning sign for disordered eating. Peer support can be crucial in supporting such dancers.

be used. Coauthorship should help promote knowledge, ownership, and actual use, and somewhat regular updates also act as reminders. For advice on how to create a policy like this, see One Dance UK (n.d.). The policy should comprise basic information about the warning signs (e.g., red flags) to watch for and clear guidance on what will be done in case of concern.

Establish a Referral Pathway

In high-level sports, organizations are recommended to maintain a "core multidisciplinary team" consisting of, at least, a doctor, a sports dietitian, and a psychologist (Wells et al., 2020). Although such teams may be unusual in dance as yet, it is something to aspire to. When there is no in-house expertise, there should still be established referral pathways such as a list of appropriately qualified local clinicians who have agreed to be the first point of contact for school or company management when concerns about a dancer have been identified. It is also highly encouraged that dance organizations display some kind of poster or contact information for an eating disorder organization on their noticeboard, website, and/or handbook. This may include a link to a chat, a help line, or something similar.

Address Concerns Directly and Supportively

Humans are strongly motivated to avoid uncomfortable situations. Unfortunately, "sticking our heads in the sand" may well happen when we become concerned that someone struggles with disordered eating. As this chapter has hopefully made clear, however, the seriousness of the issue means that the temporary awkwardness in approaching a dancer must be overcome in favor of long-term health considerations. Thus, use kindly phrased expressions of concern when concerns have arisen, such as "I've noticed that you haven't been eating lunch lately. Let's talk about it," or "You seem to be having a tough time, and I'd like to help you if I can." Of course, the dancer in question may well say no and not want to talk; the disordered eating policy should provide guidance about what to do in such situations. Even when discussion seems difficult, there should be ongoing support, kindness, and patience, not least because unsociability, irritability, and social withdrawal are in themselves symptoms of disordered eating.

Derian: Case Study of Disordered Eating

Derian was a student in a vocational school focused on neoclassical training. He was considered a real talent, and one of the teachers took a particular interest in Derian: "With a bit more work, you really stand a chance for a job in one of the top companies!" Derian was flattered, of course, and started to work harder. The teacher began investing more time in him, and the feedback got more specific and critical; for instance, he suggested that Derian's jumps would surely improve with daily strength training; it might also be good to cut down on calories, to look his best. After all, male dancers often perform shirtless. Derian followed the advice, because the teacher seemed to know what he was talking about—and he invested so much time in Derian. The increased training and reduced energy intake soon took effect, but not as intended; instead, Derian felt tired all the time, and his jumps certainly got no higher. Perhaps he was eating too much fat? He decreased his intake further.

When Derian had been persuaded by his family to enter eating disorders treatment he was distressed, fatigued, and experienced an irregular heartbeat. He also struggled with a minor shoulder injury, which never seemed to improve. During treatment, he finally got to rest and rehabilitate; he slept better and noticed how much easier it was to focus. He learned about the mechanisms that trigger and maintain eating disorders and realized that the short-term reinforcements associated with teacher attention and promises of success had taken precedence over all health concerns, with disastrous consequences. After much deliberating, he realized that he still did want to dance; however, it had to be on his terms, and in an environment focused more on dance itself and less on body weight and shape. He therefore visited several schools before joining one where he felt both safe and excited about the future.

Composite case study created on the basis of a conversation with Klara Edlund, Ph.D., clinical psychologist and licensed psychotherapist, specialized in eating disorders in aesthetic activities.

CRITICAL ASPECTS OF RESEARCH INTO BODY IMAGE AND DISORDERED EATING

1. Body image and disordered eating are the most well-researched topics in dance psychology; as such, this chapter comprises far more dance-specific literature than other chapters in this book. Positively, this includes research with a wider variety of styles and from scholars in more countries. It is also the only chapter for which numerous studies (especially those with small samples and/or nonvalidated measures from the 1980s and 1990s) have been excluded, primarily for reasons of chapter length.

2. Most studies in this area are cross-sectional in nature, which inevitably limits the conclusions that may be drawn. For example, it is conceivable that dancers who receive critical comments about their weight develop lower self-esteem and/or disordered eating; it is also possible that dancers with lower self-esteem and/or disordered eating are more sensitive to comments about their weight, and thereby remember them more readily (Annus & Smith, 2009; Coker-Cranney & Reel, 2015; Dantas et al., 2018; Goodwin et al., 2014b; Liu et al., 2016; Nordin-Bates et al., 2014).

3. There is little research into gender roles, sexuality, or ethnicity in relation to dancers' body image or disordered eating, and it has therefore not been discussed here. However, these constructs may well affect how dancers feel and act in relationship to their bodies (Feldman & Meyer, 2007; Green, 1999; Langdon & Petracca, 2010; Ravaldi et al., 2006), making further research in this area highly warranted.

4. Future interventions should be theory- and evidence-based and target not only dancers; instead, targeting organizations may well have a greater effect because they create the subculture in which dancers receive their training—an impact far

greater than occasionally visiting intervention staff can ever hope for. Interventions should also target young dancers, around the brink of adolescence, because risk factors are present already at this young age (Nerini, 2015; Rohde et al., 2015).

KEY POINTS AND RECOMMENDATIONS FOR BODY IMAGE AND DISORDERED EATING IN DANCE

1. Dancers and their educators cannot work directly with clinical issues like eating disorders, but it is imperative that they possess knowledge of basic features and risk factors for disordered eating, so that they may contribute to its prevention and identification and make clinical referrals.
2. There are many risk factors for disordered eating, and some of them are outside the control of both dancers and their educators. However, negative body image and the dance environment can and should be addressed. In particular, leaders should embrace supportive leadership styles that do not focus on weight, instead promoting a functional and appreciative view of dancers' bodies.

Glossary

2 × 2 model of perfectionism—A model created by Gaudreau and Thompson in 2010 (see chapter 2 references) that illustrates four proposed intrapersonal combinations of perfectionistic strivings (PS) and perfectionistic concerns (PC): pure perfectionistic strivings (high PS, low PC), mixed perfectionism (high PS, high PC), pure evaluative concerns perfectionism (low PS, high PC), and non-perfectionism (low PS, low PC).

acceptance—A key component of mindfulness, acceptance (or nonjudgment) is about seeing things as they truly are rather than fighting or suppressing them. Importantly, it is more closely related to *fully acknowledging* than to passive resignation; indeed, it is easier to move on with committed action after one has accepted current reality for what it is.

acceptance and commitment therapy (ACT)—A therapeutic approach that complements mindfulness with value-driven commitment and action. Part of the third wave of CBT.

achievement goals—A key concept in achievement goal theory concerned with how success and competence may be determined in task- and ego-oriented ways.

agreeableness—A personality trait that manifests itself via positive interpersonal qualities such as friendliness, cooperation, consideration, and helpfulness. One of the Big Five personality traits.

amotivation—A motivational regulation outlined in self-determination theory that is about lack of intentionality. A person who is amotivated has no strong reasons to do what they do.

anorexia nervosa—Drastic weight reduction as a result of self-imposed food limitations.

anxiety—A psychophysiological response to threat comprising somatic (bodily) and cognitive symptoms.

anxiety intensity—The level of anxiety symptoms, ranging from none (e.g., feeling calm or lethargic) to extreme (e.g., hyperactivity or panic).

anxiety tolerance—The extent to which a person can tolerate the symptoms of anxiety.

approach oriented—Being motivated to move toward something desirable, such as learning or being the best dancer in the studio.

assigned goals—Goals that are set for a person by someone else, such as when a teacher sets a goal for a dancer.

athletic identity—Defined as "the degree to which an individual identifies with the athlete role" (chapter 1: Brewer et al., 1993, p. 237).

attention—A broad concept comprising concentration, selective attention, divided attention, and the refocusing of attention after distraction.

autonomy—One of three basic psychological needs outlined in self-determination theory that is about feeling a sense of volition and feeling like one's true self.

autonomy support—Providing support for the basic psychological need of autonomy, for instance through rationale, by providing opportunities for input and choice, and by valuing individuality.

avoidance coping—Tools and strategies used by an individual to reduce the stress resulting from a problem, such as ignoring, avoiding, and disengaging. It is a subset of emotion-focused coping that is distinctly maladaptive.

avoidance oriented—Being motivated to avoid something undesirable, such as being the least skilled dancer in the studio or not improving.

basic psychological needs—According to self-determination theory, the three basic psychological needs are autonomy, competence, and relatedness. These predict motivational regulations as well as a wide array of outcomes.

Big Five—The most established set of personality traits to concisely and consistently describe human personality (chapter 1: Costa & McCrae, 1992). Includes agreeableness, conscientiousness, emotional stability, extroversion, and openness to experience.

Big-C creativity—Creativity at the highest level; that of geniuses and paradigm-shifters such as Isadora Duncan or Martha Graham.

binge eating disorder—Periods of uncontrollable binge eating at least once/week for 3 months.

black-and-white thinking—A thinking style or cognitive distortion characteristic of perfectionists and persons with low self-esteem that manifests in viewing experiences as extremes: good or bad, winning or losing, being perfect or being a failure.

body appreciation—Appreciating one's body in terms of health, bodily features, and functionality (chapter 14: Tylka & Wood-Barcalow, 2015).

body dissatisfaction—When a person's image of their body does not match the body that they see as ideal.

body image—How we perceive, think, and feel about our bodies (chapter 14: Grogan, 2008).

body image flexibility—Being willing to experience and accept perceptions, thoughts, and feelings about one's body without trying to change them, while acting in line with personal values (chapter 14: Tylka & Wood-Barcalow, 2015).

body scanning—A common category of meditations in which attention is moved between different body parts. It is one way to practice mindfulness formally that is often found in apps and other programs.

breathing space—A common category of meditations done while sitting, with a focus on the breath. It is one way to practice mindfulness formally that is often found in apps and other programs.

bulimia nervosa—Periods of uncontrollable binge eating and compensatory behaviors at least once/week for 3 months.

classical conditioning—A form of learning (and subsequent behaving) that is steered by making associations between emotions and situations (e.g., auditioning becoming associated with strong anxiety). Also known as respondent conditioning.

cognitive appraisal—An interpretation of an event or situation. A central part of the stress-injury model (chapter 13: Williams & Andersen, 1998), it typically refers to interpretations as being more or less pressuring, threatening, or important.

cognitive behavioral therapy (CBT)—A large umbrella of theories and techniques aiming to understand and modify cognitions, behaviors, and emotions.

cognitive defusion—The detachment of oneself from one's thoughts; that is, the knowledge that thoughts are just thoughts rather than facts. With cognitive defusion, we can observe and acknowledge our thoughts without becoming enmeshed or caught up in them.

cognitive distortions—A set of unhelpful thinking styles or irrational thought patterns. They include black-and-white thinking, catastrophizing, and many more.

cognitive symptoms—Mental signs of anxiety such as apprehension and a narrowed focus of attention.

common humanity—Recognizing that all people are imperfect, make mistakes, and suffer. One of three key component of self-compassion.

competence—One of three basic psychological needs outlined in self-determination theory that is about feeling adequate and able.

concentration—The deliberate decision to fully pay attention to some action or stimulus. Concentration is a specific aspect of attention.

conditional regard—When a caregiver, teacher, or other important person only gives their approval, time, and attention if certain conditions are fulfilled. For instance, a teacher who is only friendly to her dancers when they perform well is giving conditional regard.

conscientiousness—A personality trait that manifests itself via positive task-related qualities such as being disciplined, well-organized, hard-working, and reliable. One of the Big Five personality traits.

constrained action hypothesis—An evidence-based hypothesis stating that the use of an internal focus constrains the motor system because it encourages conscious control, which engages a slower cognitive system (chapter 6: Wulf et al., 2001). Conversely, using an external focus results in unconscious, fast, and automatic control processes that "free up" the motor system.

contingent self-esteem—When a person's evaluation of their self is hinged on something, such as their performance in dance. A dancer with her self-esteem contingent on dance performance evaluates herself positively when performing well and negatively when performing poorly.

controllability—The extent to which a person can control their mental images, for example, by transforming and adapting them to suit their needs.

controlling leadership—Leaders controlling their performers by exercising their higher level of power. For instance, they may try to make dancers conform, obey, or behave in particular ways by pressuring, intimidating, or manipulating. Controlling leadership typically thwarts basic psychological needs.

convergent thinking—Generally, convergent thinking is the ability to give a correct answer to a question, or to do a movement correctly (e.g., as taught). In creativity research, however, convergent thinking is also about being able to identify and select the most promising creative idea after several have been generated.

coping—"Constantly changing cognitive and behavioral efforts to manage specific external and/or internal demands that are appraised as taxing or exceeding the resources of the person" (chapter 13: Lazarus & Folkman, 1984, p. 141).

coping model—Someone who is used to demonstrate a skill or otherwise act as an example for others, and who themselves is learning or struggling at first, but then overcomes the challenge. For instance, a dancer who is observed while gradually learning a variation may act as a coping model to others by showing them that the challenge can be overcome. Can be more effective than mastery models.

coping skills—An umbrella term for tools and strategies that help a person handle challenges. Defined somewhat differently by different authors but may include social support (or ability to ask for help) and psychological skills (e.g., imagery, goal setting, self-regulation, mindfulness, self-talk, relaxation).

creativity—Often described as the production of something novel (new, unique, surprising) and useful (appropriate, meaningful; chapter 7: Amabile, 1983/2018; Runco & Jaeger, 2012). However, researchers and practitioners vary in their take on creativity, and this basic definition may not encompass all that creativity is.

debilitative imagery—Imagery that has negative/hurtful effects.

deliberate play—A form of play that is focused on or related to an activity (e.g., dance, sport). It is child-led, uses flexible rules, and can take place in a variety of locations (e.g., at home, in the school yard). Done to maximize enjoyment and immediate satisfaction but also helps with skill development.

deliberate practice—Working to enhance performance on specific skills by doing highly structured activities. It is typically teacher-led, happens in a specific venue (e.g., studio), is physically and/or mentally effortful, and is done for future progress rather than immediate rewards.

disempowering coaching—Leadership that is both ego involving and controlling.

disordered eating—Subclinical issues around food, weight, and body perceptions; a "gray zone" between healthy eating and clinical eating disorders.

divergent thinking—The extent to which an individual is able to generate many original responses to a problem.

diversification—Including a variety of activities in a person's development or in a school's schedule. Conceptualized as the opposite of specialization.

early specialization—Intense training in a single activity for eight or more months of the year, typically referring to prepubertal children (age 12 and younger; chapter 12: LaPrade et al., 2016). Conceptualized as the opposite of diversification.

eating disorder not otherwise specified (EDNOS)—An earlier broad eating disorder diagnosis category that has been replaced by other specified feeding or eating disorder (OSFED), which is narrower.

eating disorders—Extreme disturbances in an individual's thoughts, emotions, and behaviors regarding food, weight, and body perceptions. Eating disorders are mental illnesses and, as such, clinical issues.

ego-involving climate—A motivational climate characterized by a belief that success is about being superior to others. Such climates typically involve interpersonal comparisons and favoritism, reward objective or normative success, and discourage mistakes.

ego orientation—One of the two main achievement goals outlined in the basic formulation of achievement goal theory. Ego-oriented individuals judge success primarily in terms of superiority.

emotional stability—A personality trait that manifests itself via positive intrapersonal qualities such as being calm, resilient, and stress-tolerant. One of the Big Five personality traits.

emotional states—One of six sources of efficacy information outlined by Bandura (1977; see chapter 3 references) in his theory of self-efficacy. Refers to the idea that if we feel as though our emotional states (e.g., good mood, optimism) are favorable, we will feel more efficacious (confident) about performing a particular skill.

emotion-focused coping—Tools and strategies used by an individual to reduce the stress resulting from a problem, such as talking to friends and family, crying, using humor, and mindfulness. Can be both adaptive and maladaptive.

empowering coaching—Leadership that is both task involving and need supportive.

eudaimonic well-being—Feeling a sense of purpose, growth, and fulfillment. The pursuit of a meaningful life is about eudaimonic well-being.

explicit learning—Learning through verbal instructions about how to perform movements, rules, and conscious control (e.g., "lift your leg to the right, then move the arms above your head").

exposure—A technique from cognitive behavioral therapy based in the principle that by gradually exposing ourselves to that which we fear, we habituate (become accustomed) to symptoms and situations. This way, previously anxiety-inducing stimuli (e.g., a situation) lose their hold over the person.

external focus of attention—Paying attention to effects, qualities, and intentions of movement. It is an outwardly focused way of paying attention that is unconscious of movement mechanics.

external perspective—Visual images experienced from a third-person perspective. In using the external perspective, dancers would "see" themselves in their mind's eye, whether from the front, back, or side. In this way, they would often "see" more of their own bodies than they normally would in the real setting (unless using mirrors there).

extinction—The process by which a behavior reduces and disappears when no reinforcement is forthcoming.

extrinsic motivation—A motivational regulation outlined in self-determination theory that is about undertaking an activity due to external pressure, to seek rewards, or to avoid punishments. It is the most controlled motivational regulation.

extroversion—A personality trait that manifests itself via positive interpersonal qualities such as being sociable, assertive, enthusiastic, and action-oriented. One of the Big Five personality traits.

facilitative imagery—Imagery that has positive/helpful effects.

fight response—A behavioral reaction to anxiety or stress that aims to reduce the perceived threat. May include aggression, hostility, and irritation.

fixed mindset—The belief that ability or talent is innate, static, and thus not under one's personal control (chapter 12: Dweck 2006/2017). Also known as an entity theory of ability and conceptualized as the opposite of a growth mindset.

flight response—A behavioral reaction to anxiety or stress that aims to avoid or get away from the threat altogether. May include leaving a situation or other forms of avoidance (e.g., standing at the back to not be seen).

flow—An optimal experience characterized by total absorption in a task (chapter 6: Csikszentmihalyi, 1990).

focus—A synonym for concentration.

freeze response—A behavioral reaction to anxiety or stress that aims to make ourselves inconspicuous or nonthreatening. May include passivity (e.g., standing still, not talking).

functional analysis—A way of analyzing behavior and its maintenance by listing specific behaviors (B) along with their antecedents (triggers, precursors; A) and consequences (C).

functional body orientation—Focusing more on how the body feels and functions than on how it looks (chapter 14: Tylka & Wood-Barcalow, 2015).

functional body satisfaction—Being satisfied with what the body can do and experience (chapter 14: Tylka & Wood-Barcalow, 2015).

functional equivalence—A neuroscientific principle stating that imagery shares neural substrates with actual perception and movement. Hence, areas of the brain that are active when perceiving something (e.g., hearing music) or doing something (e.g., a step) partially overlap with the areas that are active when imagining (e.g., imagining the same song or step).

fundamental goal concept—Focusing on process and performance goals is far more likely to improve performance and keep self-confidence stable, even though outcome goals can be highly motivating (chapter 9: Burton & Weiss, 2008).

goal involvement—The extent to which a person is task and/or ego-involved at a particular time (chapter 5: Ames, 1992). Said to be the result of the interaction of goal orientations and perceptions of the prevailing motivational climate.

goal orientation—A synonym to achievement goals that is specifically concerned with the trait level (i.e., goal orientations are relatively stable across time and situations).

growth mindset—The belief that ability or talent is malleable and under one's personal control (chapter 12: Dweck 2006/2017). Also known as an incremental theory of ability and conceptualized as the opposite of a fixed mindset.

habituation—The process of becoming accustomed to symptoms and situations. Through repeated prolonged exposure we become habituated, and the previously anxiety-inducing stimulus (e.g., a situation) loses its hold over the person.

harmonious passion—A flexible form of engagement in an activity such as dance that is associated with healthy persistence. Its flexible nature allows a person to engage in other activities without guilt or distress.

hedonic well-being—Feeling happy, well, and satisfied. The pursuit of a pleasurable life is about hedonic well-being.

heritability—The extent to which differences in traits is accounted for by differences in people's genes. It is a concept that applies to populations (groups) rather than to individuals.

history of stressors—A person is said to have a history of stressors if they experience negative life stress, daily hassles (small, accumulating stressors), or have had previous injuries. History of stressors is a component of the stress-injury model (chapter 13: Williams & Andersen, 1998) found to convey an increased risk of an elevated stress response.

holistic ecological approach (HEA)—An approach to talent development that acknowledges the impact of several layers of a prospective elite performer's surroundings, including their immediate environment (e.g., main teacher), the microenvironment (e.g., family), and the macroenvironment e.g., culture), as well as the impact of time (chapter 12: Henriksen & Stambulova, 2017).

imagery—An inherent human capacity for creating mental representations (or simulations) of actions and events, both past and present. It involves one or more of the senses and can be done with or without accompanying movement. A main distinction may be made between mental practice imagery and movement quality imagery.

imagery function—The *why* of imagery; reasons for imaging.

imagery type—The *what* of imagery; imagery content.

imaginal experiences—One of six sources of efficacy information outlined by Bandura (1977; see chapter 3 references) in his theory of self-efficacy. Refers to the idea that if we can imagine doing something successfully, we will feel more efficacious (confident) about doing it for real.

implicit learning—Learning in a way that prevents conscious control or verbal declarative knowledge about movements to be formed. In practice, it is probably most readily achieved by instructing and learning through imagery (analogy, metaphor).

instrumental conditioning—A form of learning (and subsequent behaving) that is steered by the consequences of our actions (e.g., doing more of something because it is fun). Also known as operant conditioning.

interactionist perspective—The view that both nature (e.g., personality, including genetics) and nurture (environment, including teachers, peers, and parents) are important and should be considered in tandem.

intermittent reinforcement—when reinforcement is not constant (after every time a behavior is performed) but occasional. Advantageous for long-term behavior maintenance.

internal focus of attention—Attending to, adjusting, and controlling different body parts. It is a self-focused way of paying attention that is highly conscious of movement mechanics.

internal perspective—Visual images experienced as if through one's own eyes (first-person perspective). In using the internal perspective, dancers would "see" in their mind's eye what they would normally see in the real setting (typically more of others and of the room than of themselves, unless imagining seeing themselves in a mirror).

interpersonal—To do with interactions between people. Interpersonal concepts of high relevance to dance psychology include personality traits such as extroversion and agreeableness, motivational climates, and leadership behaviors.

intrapersonal—To do with oneself. Intrapersonal concepts of high relevance to dance psychology include personality traits (openness to experience, conscientiousness, emotional stability), psychological characteristics (self-confidence, performance anxiety, motivation, attentional focus), and psychological skills (self-regulation, goal setting, imagery, mindfulness).

intrinsic motivation—A motivational regulation outlined in self-determination theory that is about undertaking an activity due to interest, joy, and meaning. It is the most self-determined motivational regulation.

intrinsic motivation principle of creativity—A principle stating that people are most likely to be creative when driven by intrinsic aspects such as genuine interest, joy, and personal meaning (chapter 7: Amabile, 1983/2018).

introversion—The polar opposite of extroversion. As such, it is a personality trait that manifests itself in a person being quiet, preferring time alone or in small groups, and being more focused on their inner life than on outer events.

ironic processing—A phenomenon whereby a performer becomes more likely to do something, simply by being instructed not to do it.

kinesthetic imagery—Imagery using the kinesthetic sense; "feeling" bodily movements and sensations in one's imagery.

learning goals—Goals that focus on finding, developing, or trying a specific number of ways in which something can be done, or procedures needed for later mastery of a task. Examples include finding three companies whose style aligns with one's own, experimenting with two different ways of expressing a rhythm with one's feet, and trying out whether imagery practice is best done in the morning or in the evening.

little-c creativity—Everyday creativity of those with a reasonable amount of skill in the area (e.g., high-level dance students).

mastery experiences—Also known as *performance accomplishments*, one of six sources of efficacy information outlined by Bandura (1977; see chapter 3 references) in his theory of self-efficacy. Refers to the idea that if we feel as though we have done something before, we will feel more efficacious (confident) about doing it again.

mastery model—Someone who is used to demonstrate a skill or otherwise act as an example for others, and who demonstrates competence throughout. For instance, a dancer who is observed while dancing a variation excellently may act as a mastery model to others by showing them that it can be done. Can be less effective than coping models.

mastery orientation—A synonym for task orientation.

Matthew effect—Based on the Bible verse Matthew 13:12 and sometimes summarized as "the rich get richer while the poor get poorer." In performance contexts it refers to a widening of a gap between groups of performers over time—for example, as a result of some being selected and others rejected. Because the selected are typically offered better resources, the gap between performers widen over time as it becomes increasingly difficult for the rejected to catch up.

mental practice imagery—A main type of imagery that incorporates images of technique/execution, goals, mastery, context, and body-related images. Also known as mental rehearsal. Often discussed as something to do when still but may be enhanced by small movements (marking).

mindfulness—An open-minded, nonjudgmental way of paying attention to the present moment (chapter 8: Kabat-Zinn, 2013).

mini-c creativity—Personally meaningful creativity, such as finding a satisfactory solution to a movement problem that is also novel for the individual.

mixed perfectionism—The combination of high perfectionistic strivings (PS) and high perfectionistic concerns (PC). One of the four intrapersonal combinations of PS and PC outlined in the 2 × 2 model of perfectionism. Considered to be problematic.

modeling—A form of learning by watching others do something. A synonym for observational learning and vicarious experiences.

motivation—The direction and intensity of effort (chapter 5: Sage, 1977).

motivational climate—The psychosocial atmosphere, structure, and feel of a specific setting, such as a particular dance class (chapter 5: Ames, 1992). In achievement goal theory, motivational climates are conceptualized as being task involving and ego involving to varying degrees.

motivational regulations—Types or qualities of motivation, as outlined in self-determination theory. Motivational regulations vary in their degree of self-determination and include several types of intrinsic and extrinsic motivation as well as amotivation.

movement quality imagery—A main type of imagery that incorporates images of metaphors, specific qualities or actions, dramatic themes, characters, and stories. Often discussed as something dancers do while moving.

multidimensional—Involving several dimensions. Perfectionism and motivational climates are examples of multidimensional constructs studied in dance psychology. We cannot talk about, or measure, a multidimensional construct as *a single thing* (e.g., yield one score for perfectionism via a questionnaire) because its dimensions must be considered separately.

narrow identity—When a person's identity or self-definition is primarily, even exclusively, taken up by a specific activity such as dance.

need satisfaction—The degree to which the basic psychological needs for autonomy, competence, and relatedness are satisfied.

need thwarting—The degree to which the basic psychological needs for autonomy, competence, and relatedness are thwarted (actively undermined).

negative body image—Negative perceptions, thoughts, and feelings about the body, including high levels of body dissatisfaction or body dysmorphia and/or low levels of body appreciation or body esteem.

negative reinforcement—Removing something and thereby increasing the likelihood of a behavior being performed again, such as avoiding unpleasant or undesirable feelings or situations.

neuroticism—The polar opposite of emotional stability. As such, it is a personality trait that manifests itself via problematic intrapersonal qualities such as being prone to strong emotional reactions (ups and downs), finding it hard to cope with challenges, and a greater risk of anxiety and depression.

non-perfectionism—The combination of low perfectionistic strivings (PS) and low perfectionistic concerns (PC). One of the four intrapersonal combinations of PS and PC outlined in the 2 × 2 model of perfectionism. Typically associated with few problems.

normal distribution—A statistical term describing the fact that data near the mean (e.g., people being moderately conscientious) are more common than data far from the mean (e.g., people being extremely low or high in conscientiousness). In relation to personality, this means that all people tend to exhibit all traits to a lower or higher extent, with the majority falling somewhere in the middle.

objective goals—Goals whose accomplishment is not affected by moods, feelings, or preferences. Can often be answered in yes/no terms that are not disputed (e.g., whether or not a dancer attended a class).

observational learning—Synonymous with vicarious experiences in Bandura's (1977; see chapter 3 references) theory of self-efficacy but is also a more general concept concerned with how we use demonstration and observation to enhance learning and associated cognitions.

obsessive passion—An uncompromising and overwhelming drive to engage in an activity such as dance. Associated with internal pressure and struggling to detach from the activity even in the face of adverse consequences (e.g., take time off when injured).

openness to experience—A personality trait that manifests itself via positive intrapersonal qualities such as being curious, imaginative, open to new ideas, and original. One of the Big Five personality traits.

orthogonality—The notion that constructs are independent and can therefore coexist to varying degrees rather than be either–or. Task and ego orientations are orthogonal, as are need satisfaction and need thwarting.

other specified feeding or eating disorder (OSFED)—Eating disorders that cause clinically significant distress and impairment but do not fulfill all criteria for another eating disorder. Replaced the earlier diagnosis category known as eating disorder not otherwise specified (EDNOS), which was broader.

outcome goals—Goals with a comparative or exclusive aspect to them, which means that they cannot be achieved by everybody. Examples include winning, getting a job, and being cast for a role.

paralysis by analysis—A colloquialism for the breaking down of skilled movement when a performer is under pressure. Also known as choking or reinvestment, this problem can occur when performers start to pay attention to the technical details and body mechanics (i.e., engaging explicitly) of skills that have become automated (i.e., implicit).

perceptions motivational climate—The social environment in a particular setting or context, including aspects of the setup, instructional style and "feel" of a particular dance teacher's classes. In achievement goal theory, motivational climates are conceptualized as being task- and ego-involving to varying extents.

perfectionism—A personality trait comprising perfectionistic strivings and perfectionistic concerns.

perfectionistic cognitions—Automatic thoughts and images concerned with perfection, such as wanting and wishing to be perfect, thinking one has to work hard at all times, and being unable to stand making mistakes. Conceptualized as the state-expression of perfectionism (which is otherwise conceptualized to be trait-like).

perfectionistic concerns (PC)—The tendency to evaluate oneself and one's efforts critically; to be concerned over mistakes, failures, and the opinions of other people; and to feel inadequate.

perfectionistic strivings (PS)—The tendency to seek perfection, set high or even unrealistic goals for oneself, and work very hard to reach them. Some scholars consider high levels of organization and planning to be additional components of PS.

performance goals—Goals that focus on achieving a particular performance standard. Examples include managing to run 5 km, mastering a particular partnering sequence, and being able to lift one's leg above 100 degrees.

performance orientation—A synonym for ego orientation.

personality—Defined as "psychological qualities that contribute to an individual's enduring and distinctive patterns of feeling, thinking, and behaving" (chapter 1: Pervin & Cervone, 2010, p. 8).

personality states—The expression or experience of personality at a given time, such as being anxious at a particular performance.

personality traits—Deep-seated aspects of personality that are largely stable over time and situations, such as generally being prone to experiencing situations as threatening (trait anxiety).

person–environment fit—The extent to which a person's attributes, such as personality traits, are perceived to fit with the environment that they are in. For instance, a dancer with high levels of perfectionistic strivings may be seen to fit into a dance environment focused on high achievement, strict rules, and error elimination.

persuasion—One of six sources of efficacy information outlined by Bandura (1977; see chapter 3 references) in his theory of self-efficacy. Refers to the idea that if we are told (or otherwise persuaded) that we can do something, we will feel more efficacious (confident) about doing it.

PETTLEP model—A model outlining seven aspects to consider when trying to make imagery effective (functionally equivalent to real action), including physical, environmental, task, timing, learning, emotion, and perspective aspects (Holmes & Collins, 2001).

physiological states—One of six sources of efficacy information outlined by Bandura (1977; see chapter 3 references) in his theory of self-efficacy. Refers to the idea that if we feel as though our bodily states (e.g., fitness, health) are favorable, we will feel more efficacious (confident) about performing a particular skill.

positive body image—Positive perceptions, thoughts, and feelings about the body, including body appreciation, functional body orientation, functional body satisfaction, and body image flexibility (chapter 14: Tylka & Wood-Barcalow, 2015).

positive reinforcement—adding something that increases the likelihood of a behavior being performed again, such as a good feeling, positive social interaction, or a reward.

problem-focused coping—Tools and strategies used by an individual to tackle problems head-on, such as finding causes of a problem, planning, practicing, and getting information. Generally considered an adaptive way of coping.

Pro-c creativity—Creative excellence of professionals in an area (e.g., professional dancers and choreographers).

process goals—Specific things to keep in mind while dancing or specific things to do. Typically act as goal achievement strategies (stepping-stones) for learning, performance, or outcome goals. Examples include staying focused on rhythm, doing foot strengthening exercises daily, and exhaling at particular points in a choreography.

psychological flexibility—Being able to stay mindful and choose behaviors aligned with personal values, even if unpleasant thoughts and feelings are present.

punishment—Adding something that decreases the likelihood of a behavior being performed again, such as when a movement is painful or an authority figure yells. Is associated with a range of problems and not recommended.

pure evaluative concerns perfectionism (pure ECP)—The combination of low perfectionistic strivings (PS) and high perfectionistic concerns (PC). One of the four intrapersonal combinations of PS and PC outlined in the 2 × 2 model of perfectionism. Considered to be problematic.

pure personal strivings perfectionism (pure PSP)—The combination of high perfectionistic strivings (PS) and low perfectionistic concerns (PC). One of the four intrapersonal combinations of PS and PC outlined in the 2 × 2 model of perfectionism. Considered to be both beneficial and problematic.

rationale—Explaining why particular tasks are set or certain behaviors are required.

relatedness—One of three basic psychological needs outlined in self-determination theory that is about experiencing a meaningful sense of belonging to others.

relative age effect (RAE)—Essentially, the mistaking of maturity for talent. Children born early in a selection year (e.g., January-March for activities which divide children by birth year) are generally more mature than those born late in that same year (October-December). This greater maturity often conveys performance advantages that make them more likely to be identified as talented.

respondent behaviors—inborn reactions to stimuli that have evolved to support human survival, such as sweating when warm and the stress/anxiety reaction that is evoked in response to threats.

revised applied model of deliberate imagery use (RAMDIU)—A model outlining nine components of imagery including *what*, *why*, *where*, *when*, and *how* imagery is used as well as *who* the imager is, *imagery ability*, *meaning*, and *outcomes* of imagery (chapter 10: Cumming & Williams, 2013).

role-related behaviors—Behaviors that we learn and use to feel effective and fit into specific contexts. They are superficial aspects of personality that are fluid, are easy to observe, and may or may not be representative of our psychological core (who we really are). As such, they are more akin to *states* than *traits*.

safety behaviors—Tricks used to help oneself cope with (avoid) unpleasant sensations, such as distractions, seeking reassurance, or not looking a person in the eye.

selective attention—The cognitive activity of focusing fully on some action or stimulus to the detriment of other actions and stimuli.

self-compassion—Treating oneself with compassion. Self-compassion approaches form part of the third wave of CBT and comprise three components: mindfulness, self-kindness, and common humanity.

self-confidence—Our evaluation of our ability to perform a task successfully.

self-constructs—An umbrella term for a range of constructs related to the self, including self-esteem, self-confidence, self-efficacy, self-worth, and many more.

self-determination—The foundation concept in self-determination theory. We are self-determined when our basic psychological needs are satisfied. Identified regulation, integrated regulation, and intrinsic motivation are increasingly self-determined motivational regulations.

self-efficacy—A person's belief in their ability to successfully complete a task; essentially situation-specific self-confidence.

self-esteem—Our evaluation of our own self, including our overall value as a person.

self-fulfilling prophecy—The process whereby a leader (a) creates expectations about a performer's potential, (b) these expectations translate into differential treatment, (c) that treatment affects the dancer's rate of improvement, and (d) their accelerated or decelerated rate of progress makes the leader conclude that their original prediction was correct.

self-kindness—A warm, understanding, and accepting attitude toward oneself and one's failings. One of three key component of self-compassion.

self-objectification—Seeing one's body (or even person) as an object or product.

self-regulation—Systematic efforts to direct thoughts, feelings, and actions toward the attainment of goals (chapter 9: Zimmerman, 2000). Related to self-awareness, metacognition, and taking responsibility for one's own progress.

self-reinforcing—Doing a behavior or an activity because it feels rewarding (positively reinforcing) in itself rather than doing it because it brings some extraneous benefit.

self-surveillance—Monitoring one's own appearance and behavior.

social desirability—When a person tries to portray themselves in a way that is perceived to be advantageous. Also known as *faking good*.

somatic symptoms—Bodily signs of anxiety such as increased heart rate, breathing rate, and butterflies in the stomach.

state anxiety—The level of anxiety in a particular moment. It is created by the interaction of trait anxiety and environmental/situational factors such as leadership, relationships, and more.

states—Aspects of a person that are superficial, variable, and subject to change. Capturing states is often done by asking a person what they are feeling or doing at that particular moment in time (e.g., asking a dancer how confident he is just before going on stage).

stress—"[A] substantial imbalance between demand (physical and-or psychological) and response capability, under conditions where failure to meet that demand has important consequences" (chapter 4: McGrath, 1970, p. 20).

stress-related growth—Positive responses to challenging situations such as injury. For example, injured dancers may find that they learn about their bodies, develop emotionally, or grow as a person while rehabilitating.

stress response—A psychophysiological response to a stressful situation. A central part of the stress-injury model (chapter 13: Williams & Andersen, 1998), it comprises cognitive appraisal and physiological (e.g., muscle tension) as well as attentional changes (e.g., narrow, internal focus of attention).

subjective goals—Goals whose accomplishment is affected by moods, feelings, or preferences. Can often not be answered in yes/no terms and so are open to dispute (e.g., whether or not a dancer performed well).

symptom interpretation—The way in which symptoms of anxiety (cognitive and somatic) are interpreted by a person as either debilitative (negative, damaging), neutral (unimportant), or facilitative (positive, helpful).

talent—"Innate, identifiable factors that affect our long-term development" (chapter 12: Baker et al., 2017, p. 1).

talent development—"The range of influences on the process of skill acquisition in the high performance setting" (chapter 12: Baker et al., 2017, p. 2, with the word "sport" removed for generalizability).

talent identification—"The process of identifying and/or selecting individuals who possess a quality (or qualities) that predicts some form of future attainment" (chapter 12: Baker et al., 2017, p. 2).

task-involving climate—A motivational climate characterized by a belief that success is about individual improvement. Such climates typically involve intrapersonal comparisons, collaboration, reward effort and progress, and see mistakes as part of learning.

task orientation—One of the two main achievement goals outlined in the basic formulation of achievement goal theory. Task-oriented individuals judge success primarily in terms of self-improvement.

thin-ideal internalization—When a person has internalized thinness as an ideal so that it is a pressure from within rather than from the outside.

thinness and restriction expectancies—Believing that life will be better in some way if one diets and gets thinner.

thinness-related learning—Implicit or explicit messages (e.g., weighing, weight- and shape-related comments from teachers, and disordered eating behaviors among peers) in the dance environment that suggest to a dancer that thinness is valued and important.

trait anxiety—An inherent tendency to perceive situations as threatening. A facet of personality (low emotional stability) and therefore relatively stable over time and situations.

traitlikeness—The extent to which something is like a trait (i.e., deep-seated, stable, and not overly susceptible to outside influences).

traits—Aspects of a person that are deep-seated, relatively stable, and less susceptible to change. Capturing traits is often done by asking a person what they generally feel or do (e.g., asking a dancer how confident he generally is before going on stage).

values—What is truly important to a person; what they want to stand for and be remembered for. Examples include health (e.g., prioritizing health over performance), relationships (e.g., having mutually fulfilling relationships both at home and at work/in dance) justice, and fairness (e.g., promoting equality in dance).

vicarious experiences—Also known as *modeling* or *observational learning*, one of six sources of efficacy information outlined by Bandura (1977) in his theory of self-efficacy. Refers to the idea that if we have seen and understood how other people complete a task, we will feel more efficacious (confident) about completing that same task.

visual imagery—Imagery using the visual sense; "seeing with the mind's eye."

vividness—The lifelikeness of images, ranging from nonexistent (just the idea of an image) to fully realistic (as vivid as real experience).

References

Introduction

Anoop, M., & Malshe, M. (2011). Creativity and the code: Training in Mohiniāṭṭam. *Theatre, Dance and Performance Training*, 2(2), 138-150.

Bandura, A. (1986). *Social foundations of thought and action*. Prentice-Hall.

Bläsing, B., Puttke, M., & Schack, T. (2018). *The neurocognition of dance: Mind, movement and motor skills* (2nd ed.). Routledge.

Chappell, K., Redding, E., Crickmay, U., Stancliffe, R., Jobbins, V., & Smith, S. (2021). The aesthetic, artistic and creative contributions of dance for health and wellbeing across the lifecourse: A systematic review. *International Journal of Qualitative Studies on Health and Well-being*, 16(1), 1950891.

David, D., Cristea, I., & Hofmann, S.G. (2018). Why cognitive behavioral therapy is the current gold standard of psychotherapy. *Frontiers in Psychiatry*, 9, 4.

Draugelis, S., Martin, J., & Garn, A. (2014). Psychosocial predictors of well-being in collegiate dancers. *The Sport Psychologist*, 28(1), 1-9.

Gustafsson, H., & Lundqvist, C. (2016). Working with perfectionism in elite sport: A cognitive behavioral therapy perspective. In A.P. Hill (Ed.), *The Psychology of Perfectionism in Sport, Dance and Exercise* (pp. 203-221). Routledge.

Gustafsson, H., & Lundqvist, C. (2020). Cognitive behavioural therapy in performance enhancement: Using exposure and behavioural experiments with elite athletes. In D. Tod & M. Eubank (Eds.), *Applied Sport, Exercise, and Performance Psychology: Current Approaches to Helping Clients* (pp. 113-128). Routledge.

Gustafsson, H., Lundqvist, C., & Tod, D. (2017). Cognitive behavioral intervention in sport psychology: A case illustration of the exposure method with an elite athlete. *Journal of Sport Psychology in Action*, 8(3), 152-162.

Hays, K.F., & Brown, C.H. Jr. (2004). *You're on! Consulting for peak performance*. American Psychological Association.

Henrich, J., Heine, S.J., & Norenzayan, A. (2010). The weirdest people in the world? *Behavioral and Brain Sciences*, 33(2-3), 61-83.

Juslin, P.N. (2013). From everyday emotions to aesthetic emotions: Towards a unified theory of musical emotions. *Physics of Life Reviews*, 10(3), 235-266.

Kaczkurkin, A.N., & Foa, E.B. (2015). Cognitive-behavioral therapy for anxiety disorders: An update on the empirical evidence. *Dialogues in Clinical Neuroscience*, 17(3), 337-346.

Kluckhohn, C.E., Murray, H.A., & Schneider, D.M. (1953). *Personality in nature, society, and culture* (2nd ed.). Knopf.

Lacaille, N., Koestner, R., & Gaudreau, P. (2007). On the value of intrinsic rather than traditional achievement goals for performing artists: A short-term prospective study. *International Journal of Music Education*, 25(3), 245-257.

Lacaille, N., Whipple, N., & Koestner, R. (2005). Reevaluating the benefits of performance goals. *Medical Problems of Performing Artists*, 20, 11-16.

Lovatt, P. (2019). *Dance Psychology: The Science of Dance and Dancers*. Dr Dance Presents.

Lundqvist, C. (2011). Well-being in competitive sports—The feel-good factor? A review of conceptual considerations of well-being. *International Review of Sport and Exercise Psychology*, 4(2), 109-127.

Mountjoy, M., Brackenridge, C., Arrington, M., Blauwet, C., Carska-Sheppard, A., Fasting, K., Kirby, S., Leahy, T., Marks, S., Martin, K., Starr, K., Tiivas, A. & Budgett, R. (2016). International Olympic Committee consensus statement: Harassment and abuse (non-accidental violence) in sport. *British Journal of Sports Medicine*, 50(17), 1019-1029.

Nordin-Bates, S.M. (2012). Performance psychology in the performing arts. In S.M. Murphy (Ed.), *The Oxford Handbook of Sport and Performance Psychology* (pp. 81-114). Oxford University Press.

Portenga, S.T., Aoyagi, M.W., & Cohen, A.B. (2017). Helping to build a profession: A working definition of sport and performance psychology. *Journal of Sport Psychology in Action*, 8(1), 47-59.

Reinebo, G., Henriksen, K., & Lundgren, T. (2020). Helping athletes make good decisions through the sport lifeline and functional analysis. In K. Henriksen, J. Hansen & C.H. Larsen (Eds.), *Mindfulness and Acceptance in Sport: How to help athletes perform and thrive under pressure* (pp. 19-34). Routledge.

Richard, V., & Runco, M.A. (2020). Creativity: The emergence of a new dimension of sport expertise. In G. Tenenbaum & R.C. Eklund (Eds.), *Handbook of Sport Psychology*, Vol I (4th Ed., pp. 632-649), Wiley.

Ryan, R.M., & Deci, E.L. (2001). On happiness and human potentials: A review of research on hedonic and eudaimonic well-being. *Annual Review of Psychology, 52,* 141-166.

Stark, A., & Newton, M. (2014). A dancer's well-being: The influence of the social psychological climate during adolescence. *Psychology of Sport and Exercise, 15*(4), 356-363.

Wadström, O., & Ekvall, D. (2013). *Idrottsglädje, prestation, utveckling: Kognitiv beteendeterapi för tränare, idrottare och föräldrar [Enjoyment in sports, performance, development: Cognitive behavioural therapy for coaches, athletes and parents.].* Psykologinsats.

Yan, A.F., Cobley, S., Chan, C., Pappas, E., Nicholson, L.L., Ward, R.E., Murdoch, R.E., Gu, Y., Trevor, B.L., Vassallo, A.J., Wewege, M.A., & Hiller, C.E. (2018). The effectiveness of dance interventions on physical health outcomes compared to other forms of physical activity: A systematic review and meta-analysis. *Sports Medicine, 48*(4), 933-951.

Chapter 1

Allen, M.S., Greenlees, I., & Jones, M.V. (2011). An investigation of the five-factor model of personality and coping behaviour in sport. *Journal of Sports Sciences, 29,* 841-850.

Allen, M.S., Greenlees, I., & Jones, M.V. (2013). Personality in sport: A comprehensive review. *International Review of Sport and Exercise Psychology, 6,* 184-208.

Allen, M.S., & Laborde, S. (2014). The role of personality in sport and physical activity. *Current Directions in Psychological Science, 23*(6), 460-465.

Allen, M.S., Vella, S.A., & Laborde, S. (2015). Sport participation, screen time, and personality trait development during childhood. *British Journal of Developmental Psychology, 33*(3), 375-390.

Allen, M.S., & Walter, E.E. (2016). Personality and body image: A systematic review. *Body Image, 19,* 79-88.

Allport, G.W., & Odbert, H.S. (1936). Trait-names: A psycho-lexical study. *Psychological Monographs, 47*(1), 1-178.

Bakker, F.C. (1988). Personality differences between young dancers and non-dancers. *Personality and Individual Differences, 9*(1), 121-131.

Bakker, F.C. (1991). Development of personality in dancers: A longitudinal study. *Personality and Individual Differences, 12*(7), 671-681.

Brewer, B.W., Van Raalte, J.L., & Linder, D.E. (1993). Athletic identity: Hercules' muscles or Achilles heel? *International Journal of Sport Psychology, 24,* 237-254.

Caspi, A., Harrington, H., Milne, B., Amell, J.W., Theodore, R.F., & Moffitt, T.E. (2003). Children's behavioral styles at age 3 are linked to their adult personality traits at age 26. *Journal of Personality, 71*(4), 495-514.

Cattell, H.E.P., & Mead, A.D. (2008). The sixteen personality factor questionnaire (16PF). In G.J. Boyle, G. Matthews, & D.H. Saklofske (Eds.), *The SAGE handbook of personality theory and assessment* (Vol. 2, pp. 135-159). SAGE.

Costa, P.T. Jr., & McCrae, R.R. (1992). *Revised NEO personality inventory (NEO-PI-R) and NEO five-factor inventory (NEO-FFI): Professional manual.* Psychological Assessment Resources.

Coulter, T.J., Mallett, C.J., Singer, J.A., & Gucciardi, D.F. (2016). Personality in sport and exercise psychology: Integrating a whole person perspective. *International Journal of Sport and Exercise Psychology, 14*(1), 23-41.

Crawford, J.J., Gayman, A.M., & Tracey, J. (2014). An examination of post-traumatic growth in Canadian and American ParaSport athletes with acquired spinal cord injury. *Psychology of Sport and Exercise, 15*(4), 399-406.

Daniels, E., Sincharoen, S., & Leaper, C. (2005). The relationship between sport orientation and athletic identity among adolescent girl and boy athletes. *Journal of Sport Behavior, 28,* 315-332.

de Manzano, Ö., & Ullén, F. (2018). Genetic and environmental influences on the phenotypic associations between intelligence, personality, and creative achievement in the arts and sciences. *Intelligence, 69,* 123-133.

De Raad, B., Barelds, D.P., Levert, E., Ostendorf, F., Mlačić, B., Blas, L.D., Hrebíčková, M., Szirmák, Z., Szarota, P., Perugini, M., Church, A.T., & Katigbak, M.S. (2010). Only three factors of personality description are fully replicable across languages: A comparison of 14 trait taxonomies. *Journal of Personality and Social Psychology, 98*(1), 160.

Donachie, T.C., & Hill, A.P. (2020). Helping soccer players help themselves: Effectiveness of a psychoeducational book in reducing perfectionism. *Journal of Applied Sport Psychology,* 1-21. https://doi.org/10.1080/10413200.2020.1819472

Fennell, M. (2016). *Overcoming low self-esteem: A self-help guide using cognitive behavioural techniques* (2nd ed.). Hachette UK.

Ghaderi, A., & Scott, B. (2000). The Big Five and eating disorders: A prospective study in the general population. *European Journal of Personality 14*(4), 311-323.

Hamilton, L.H., Hamilton, W.G., Meltzer, J.D., Marshall, P., & Molnar, M. (1989). Personality, stress, and injuries in professional ballet dancers. *The American Journal of Sports Medicine, 17*(2), 263-267.

Hills, P., & Argyle, M. (2001). Emotional stability as a major dimension of happiness. *Personality and Individual Differences, 31*(8), 1357-1364.

Hollander, E.P. (1967). Principles and methods of social psychology. Holt, Rinehart & Winston.

Jankovic, M., & Bogaerts, S. (2021). Predicting success in the performing arts: Ballet and music. *Psychology of Music, 49*(4) 945-957.

Kerr, G., & Dacyshyn, A. (2000). The retirement experiences of elite, female gymnasts. *Journal of Applied Sport Psychology, 12*(2), 115-133.

Kim, H., Tasker, S.L., & Shen, Y. (2020). How to persevere in a ballet performance career: exploring personal wisdom of retired professional ballet dancers. *Research in Dance Education*, 1-26. https://doi.org/10.1080/14647893.2020.1837765

Kuperman, S., Schlosser, S.S., Lidral, J., & Reich, W. (1999). Relationship of child psychopathology to parental alcoholism and antisocial personality disorder. *Journal of the American Academy of Child & Adolescent Psychiatry, 38*(6), 686-692.

Langdon, S.W., & Petracca, G. (2010). Tiny dancer: Body image and dancer identity in female modern dancers. *Body Image, 7*(4), 360-363.

Levine, M.N. (2004). *Beyond performance: Building a better future for dancers and the art of dance.* The aDvANCE project. https://thedcd.org.uk/wp-content/uploads/2018/03/Beyond-Performance-1.pdf

Marchant-Haycox, S.E., & Wilson, G.D. (1992). Personality and stress in performing artists. *Personality and Individual Differences, 13*(10), 1061-1068.

McAdams, D.P. (2013). The psychological self as actor, agent, and author. *Perspectives on Psychological Science, 8*, 272-295.

Mitchell, S.B., Haase, A.M., Malina, R.M., & Cumming, S.P. (2016). The role of puberty in the making and breaking of young ballet dancers: Perspectives of dance teachers. *Journal of Adolescence, 47*, 81-89.

Orth, U., & Robins, R.W. (2014). The development of self-esteem. *Current Directions in Psychological Science, 23*(5), 381-387.

Pervin, L.A., & Cervone, D. (2010). *Personality: Theory and Research* (11th ed.). Wiley.

Petfield, L., Startup, H., Droscher, H., & Cartwright-Hatton, S. (2015). Parenting in mothers with borderline personality disorder and impact on child outcomes. *Evidence-Based Mental Health, 18*(3), 67-75.

Pickard, A. (2015). *Ballet body narratives: Pain, pleasure and perfection in embodied identity.* Peter Lang.

Roberts, B.W., Luo, J., Briley, D.A., Chow, P.I., Su, R., & Hill, P.L. (2017). A systematic review of personality trait change through intervention. *Psychological Bulletin, 143*(2), 117.

Ronkainen, N.J., Kavoura, A., & Ryba, T.V. (2016). A meta-study of athletic identity research in sport psychology: Current status and future directions. *International Review of Sport and Exercise Psychology, 9*(1), 45-64.

Sabiston, C.M., Gilchrist, J.D., & Brunet, J. (2018). Self-perception in sport and exercise. In T. S. Horn & A. L. Smith (Eds.), *Advances in Sport and Exercise Psychology* (pp. 57-76). Human Kinetics.

Scoffier-Mériaux, S., Falzon, C., Lewton-Brain, P., Filaire, E., & d'Arripe-Longueville, F. (2015). Big Five personality traits and eating attitudes in intensively training dancers: The mediating role of internalized thinness norms. *Journal of Sports Science & Medicine, 14*(3), 627-633.

Specht, J., Egloff, B., & Schmukle, S.C. (2011). Stability and change of personality across the life course: The impact of age and major life events on mean-level and rank-order stability of the Big Five. *Journal of Personality and Social Psychology, 101*(4), 862-882.

Steca, P., Baretta, D., Greco, A., D'Addario, M., & Monzani, D. (2018). Associations between personality, sports participation and athletic success. A comparison of Big Five in sporting and non-sporting adults. *Personality and Individual Differences, 121*, 176-183.

Stephan, Y., Sutin, A.R., & Terracciano, A. (2014). Physical activity and personality development across adulthood and old age: Evidence from two longitudinal studies. *Journal of Research in Personality, 49*, 1-7.

Taylor, L.D. (1997). MMPI-2 and ballet majors. *Personality and Individual Differences, 22*, 521-526.

Turner, B.S., & Wainwright, S.P. (2003). Corps de ballet: The case of the injured ballet dancer. *Sociology of Health & Illness, 25*(4), 269-288.

Voelker, D.K., Gould, D., & Reel, J.J. (2014). Prevalence and correlates of disordered eating in female figure skaters. *Psychology of Sport and Exercise, 15*(6), 696-704.

Wainwright, S.P., & Turner, B.S. (2004). Epiphanies of embodiment: Injury, identity and the balletic body. *Qualitative Research, 4*(3), 311-337.

Willard, V.C., & Lavallee, D. (2016). Retirement experiences of elite ballet dancers: Impact of self-identity and social support. *Sport, Exercise, and Performance Psychology, 5*(3), 266-279.

Chapter 2

Amiot, C.E., Vallerand, R.J., & Blanchard, C.M. (2006). Passion and psychological adjustment: A test of the person-environment fit hypothesis. *Personality and Social Psychology Bulletin, 32*(2), 220-229.

Anshel, M.H., & Mansouri, H. (2005). Influences of perfectionism on motor performance, affect, and causal attributions in response to critical information feedback. *Journal of Sport Behavior, 28*(2), 99-124.

Antony, M.M., & Swinson, R.P. (2009). *When perfect isn't good enough: Strategies for coping with perfectionism.* New Harbinger.

Appleton, P.R., & Curran, T. (2016). The origins of perfectionism in sport, dance, and exercise. In A.P. Hill (Ed.), *The Psychology of Perfectionism in Sport, Dance and Exercise* (pp. 57-82). Routledge.

Atienza, F.L., Castillo, I., Appleton, P.R., & Balaguer, I. (2020). Examining the mediating role of motivation in the relationship between multidimensional perfectionism and well- and ill-being in vocational dancers. *International Journal of Environmental Research and Public Health, 17*(14), 4945.

Barcza-Renner, K., Eklund, R.C., Morin, A.J., & Habeeb, C.M. (2016). Controlling coaching behaviors and athlete burnout: Investigating the mediating roles of perfectionism and motivation. *Journal of Sport and Exercise Psychology, 38*(1), 30-44.

Carr, S., & Wyon, M. (2003). The impact of motivational climate on dance students' achievement goals, trait anxiety, and perfectionism. *Journal of Dance Medicine & Science, 7*(4), 105-114.

Cumming, J., & Duda, J.L. (2012). Profiles of perfectionism, body-related concerns, and indicators of psychological health in vocational dance students: An investigation of the 2 × 2 model of perfectionism. *Psychology of Sport and Exercise, 13*(6), 729-738.

Donachie, T.C., & Hill, A.P. (2020). Helping soccer players help themselves: Effectiveness of a psychoeducational book in reducing perfectionism. *Journal of Applied Sport Psychology.* https://doi.org/10.1080/10413200.2020.1819472

Dunn, J.G., Gotwals, J.K., & Dunn, J.C. (2005). An examination of the domain specificity of perfectionism among intercollegiate student-athletes. *Personality and Individual Differences, 38*(6), 1439-1448.

Eusanio, J., Thomson, P., & Jaque, S. (2014). Perfectionism, shame, and self-concept in dancers: A mediation analysis. *Journal of Dance Medicine and Science, 18*(3), 106-114.

Flett, G., Hewitt, P., Oliver, J., & Macdonald, S. (2002). Perfectionism in children and their parents: A developmental analysis. In G. Flett & P. Flett (Eds.), *Perfectionism: Theory, Research, and Treatment* (pp. 89-132). American Psychological Association.

Gaudreau, P., & Thompson, A. (2010). Testing a 2 × 2 model of dispositional perfectionism. *Personality and Individual Differences, 48*(5), 532-537.

Gotwals, J.K., Dunn, J.G., Dunn, J.C., & Gamache, V. (2010). Establishing validity evidence for the Sport Multidimensional Perfectionism Scale-2 in intercollegiate sport. *Psychology of Sport and Exercise, 11*(6), 423-432.

Gustafsson, H., & Lundqvist, C. (2016). Working with perfectionism in elite sport. In A.P. Hill (Ed.), *The Psychology of Perfectionism in Sport, Dance and Exercise* (pp. 203-221). Routledge.

Haraldsen, H.M., Halvari, H., Solstad, B.E., Abrahamsen, F.E., & Nordin-Bates, S.M. (2019). The role of perfectionism and controlling conditions in Norwegian elite junior performers' motivational processes. *Frontiers in Psychology, 10*, 1366.

Haraldsen, H.M., Ivarsson, A., Solstad, B.E., Abrahamsen, F.E., & Halvari, H. (2021). Composites of perfectionism and inauthenticity in relation to controlled motivation, performance anxiety and exhaustion among elite junior performers. *European Journal of Sport Science, 21*(3), 428-438.

Hill, A.P. (2016). Conceptualizing perfectionism: An overview and unresolved issues. In A.P. Hill (Ed.), *The Psychology of Perfectionism in Sport, Dance and Exercise* (pp. 3-30). Routledge.

Hill, A.P., & Appleton, P.R. (2011). The predictive ability of the frequency of perfectionistic cognitions, self-oriented perfectionism, and socially prescribed perfectionism in relation to symptoms of burnout in youth rugby players. *Journal of Sports Sciences, 29*(7), 695-703.

Hill, A.P., Hall, H.K., Duda, J.L., & Appleton, P.R. (2011). The cognitive, affective and behavioural responses of self-oriented perfectionists following successive failure on a muscular endurance task. *International Journal of Sport and Exercise Psychology, 9*(2), 189-207.

Hill, A.P., Mallinson-Howard, S.H., & Jowett, G.E. (2018). Multidimensional perfectionism in sport: A meta-analytical review. *Sport, Exercise, and Performance Psychology, 7*(3), 235-270.

Hill, A.P., Mallinson-Howard, S.H., Madigan, D.J., & Jowett, G.E. (2020). Perfectionism in sport, dance, and exercise: An extended review and reanalysis. In G. Tenenbaum, & R.C. Eklund (Eds.), *Handbook of Sport Psychology* (4th ed, pp. 121-157). Wiley.

Hill, A.P., Witcher, C.S., Gotwals, J.K., & Leyland, A.F. (2015). A qualitative study of perfectionism among self-identified perfectionists in sport and the performing arts. *Sport, Exercise, and Performance Psychology, 4*(4), 237-253.

Jowett, G.E., Hill, A.P., Curran, T., Hall, H.K., & Clements, L. (2021). Perfectionism, burnout, and engagement in dance: The moderating role of autonomy support. *Sport, Exercise, and Performance Psychology, 10*(1), 133-148.

Jowett, G.E., Mallinson, S.H., & Hill, A.P. (2016). An independent effects approach to perfectionism in sport, dance, and exercise. In A.P. Hill (Ed.), *The Psychology of Perfectionism in Sport, Dance and Exercise* (pp. 85-149). Routledge.

Kain, K., Doob, P.R., & Godfrey, S. (1994). *Karen Kain: Movement Never Lies: An Autobiography.* McClelland & Stewart.

Karin, J. & Nordin-Bates, S.M. (2020). Enhancing creativity and managing perfectionism in dancers through implicit learning and sensori-kinetic imagery. *Journal of Dance Education*, 20(1), 1-11.

Lee-Baggley, D., Nealis, L., & Sherry, S.B. (2016). Working with perfectionists in a clinical context: A practitioner's perspective. In A.P. Hill (Ed.), *The Psychology of Perfectionism in Sport, Dance and Exercise* (pp. 245-271). Routledge.

Madigan, D.J., Curran, T., Stoeber, J., Hill, A.P., Smith, M.M., & Passfield, L. (2019). Development of perfectionism in junior athletes: A three-sample study of coach and parental pressure. *Journal of Sport and Exercise Psychology*, 41(3), 167-175.

Madigan, D.J., Stoeber, J., Forsdyke, D., Dayson, M., & Passfield, L. (2018). Perfectionism predicts injury in junior athletes: Preliminary evidence from a prospective study. *Journal of Sports Sciences*, 36(5), 545-550.

Molnar, D.S., Blackburn, M., Zinga, D., Spadafora, N., Methot-Jones, T., & Connolly, M. (2021). Trait perfectionism and dance goals among young female dancers: An application of the 2 × 2 model of perfectionism. *Journal of Sport and Exercise Psychology*, 43(3), 234-247.

Mosewich, A.D., Crocker, P.R., Kowalski, K.C., & DeLongis, A. (2013). Applying self-compassion in sport: An intervention with women athletes. *Journal of Sport and Exercise Psychology*, 35(5), 514-524.

Nordin-Bates, S.M. (2020). Striving for perfection or for creativity: A dancer's dilemma? *Journal of Dance Education*, 20(1), 23-34.

Nordin-Bates, S.M. & Abrahamsen, F. (2016). Perfectionism in dance: Applied considerations and a case example. In A.P. Hill (Ed.), *The Psychology of Perfectionism in Sport, Dance and Exercise* (pp. 222-244). Routledge.

Nordin-Bates, S.M., Cumming, J., Aways, D., & Sharp, L. (2011). Imagining yourself dancing to perfection? Correlates of perfectionism among ballet and contemporary dancers. *Journal of Clinical Sport Psychology*, 5(1), 58-76.

Nordin-Bates, S.M., & Jowett, G. (2022). Relationships between perfectionism, stress and basic need support provision in aesthetic activity leaders. *Journal of Dance Medicine and Science*, 26(1), 25-33.

Nordin-Bates, S.M., & Kuylser, S. (2020). High striving, high costs? A qualitative examination of perfectionism in high-level dance. *Journal of Dance Education*, 21(4), 212-223.

Nordin-Bates, S.M., Raedeke, T., & Madigan, D. (2017). Perfectionism, burnout, and motivation in dance: A replication and test of the 2 × 2 model of perfectionism. *Journal of Dance Medicine and Science*, 21(3), 115-122.

Nordin-Bates, S.M., Schwarz, J.F.A., Quested, E., Cumming, J., Aujla, I.J., & Redding, E. (2016). Within- and between-person predictors of disordered eating attitudes in dance: Findings from the UK Centres for Advanced Training. *Psychology of Sport and Exercise*, 27, 101-111.

Penniment, K.J., & Egan, S.J. (2012). Perfectionism and learning experiences in dance class as risk factors for eating disorders in dancers. *European Eating Disorders Review*, 20(1), 13-22.

Pickard, A. (2015). *Ballet body narratives: Pain, pleasure and perfection in embodied identity*. Peter Lang.

Quested, E., Cumming, J., & Duda, J. (2014). Profiles of perfectionism, motivation, and self-evaluations among dancers: An extended analysis of Cumming and Duda (2012). *International Journal of Sport Psychology*, 45(4), 349-368.

Rasquinha, A., Dunn, J.G., & Dunn, J.C. (2014). Relationships between perfectionistic strivings, perfectionistic concerns, and competitive sport level. *Psychology of Sport and Exercise*, 15(6), 659-667.

Shafran, R., Wade, T.D., Egan, S.J., Kothari, R., Allcott-Watson, H., Carlbring, P., Rozental, A., & Andersson, G. (2017). Is the devil in the detail? A randomised controlled trial of guided internet-based CBT for perfectionism. *Behaviour Research and Therapy*, 95, 99-106.

Speirs Neumeister, K.L., Williams, K.K., & Cross, T.L. (2009). Gifted high-school students' perspectives on the development of perfectionism. *Roeper Review*, 31(4), 198-206.

Stoeber, J., & Eismann, U. (2007). Perfectionism in young musicians: Relations with motivation, effort, achievement, and distress. *Personality and Individual Differences*, 43(8), 2182-2192.

Stoeber, J., & Otto, K. (2006). Positive conceptions of perfectionism: Approaches, evidence, challenges. *Personality and Social Psychology Review* 10(4), 295-319.

Stoeber, J., & Stoeber, F.S. (2009). Domains of perfectionism: Prevalence and relationships with perfectionism, gender, age, and satisfaction with life. *Personality and Individual Differences*, 46(4), 530-535.

Stoeber, J., Uphill, M.A., & Hotham, S. (2009). Predicting race performance in triathlon: The role of perfectionism, achievement goals, and personal goal setting. *Journal of Sport and Exercise Psychology*, 31(2), 211-245.

Chapter 3

Andrieux, M., & Proteau, L. (2016). Observational learning: Tell beginners what they are about to watch and they will learn better. *Frontiers in Psychology*, 7, 51.

Aujla, I., & Farrer, R. (2015). The role of psychological factors in the career of the independent dancer. *Frontiers in Psychology*, 6, 1688.

Bakker, F.C. (1988). Personality differences between young dancers and non-dancers. *Personality and Individual Differences*, 9(1), 121-131.

Bakker, F.C. (1991). Development of personality in dancers: A longitudinal study. *Personality and Individual Differences, 12*(7), 671-681.

Bandura, A. (1977). Self-efficacy: Toward a unifying theory of behaviour change. *Psychological Review, 84*, 191-215.

Bandura, A. (1986). *Social foundations of thought and action*. Prentice-Hall.

Bandura, A. (1997). *Self-efficacy: The exercise of control*. Freeman.

Baumeister, R.F., Campbell, J.D., Krueger, J.I., & Vohs, K.D. (2003). Does high self-esteem cause better performance, interpersonal success, happiness, or healthier lifestyles? *Psychological Science in the Public Interest, 4*(1), 1-44.

Bettle, N., Bettle, O., Neumärker, U., & Neumärker, K.J. (2001). Body image and self-esteem in adolescent ballet dancers. *Perceptual and Motor Skills, 93*(1), 297-309.

Cerny Minton, S. (2001). Assessment of high school dance students' self-esteem. *Journal of Dance Education, 1*(2), 63-73.

Clegg, H., Owton, H., & Allen-Collinson, J. (2019). Attracting and retaining boys in ballet: A qualitative study of female dance teachers. *Journal of Dance Education, 19*(4), 158-167.

Crocker, J., & Knight, K.M. (2005). Contingencies of self-worth. *Current Directions in Psychological Science, 14*(4), 200-203.

Curran, T. (2018). Parental conditional regard and the development of perfectionism in adolescent athletes: The mediating role of competence contingent self-worth. *Sport, Exercise, and Performance Psychology, 7*(3), 284-296.

Ede, A., Sullivan, P.J., & Feltz, D.L. (2017). Self-doubt: Uncertainty as a motivating factor on effort in an exercise endurance task. *Psychology of Sport and Exercise, 28*, 31-36.

Eklund, M., & Bäckström, M. (2006). The role of perceived control for the perception of health by patients with persistent mental illness. *Scandinavian Journal of Occupational Therapy, 13*(4), 249-256.

Feltz, D.L. (2007). Self-confidence and sports performance. In D. Smith & M. Bar-Eli (Eds.), *Essential readings in sport and exercise psychology* (pp. 278-294). Human Kinetics.

Fennell, M. (2016). *Overcoming low self-esteem: A self-help guide using cognitive behavioural techniques* (2nd ed.). Hachette UK.

García-Dantas, A., & Quested, E. (2015). The effect of manipulated and accurate assessment feedback on the self-efficacy of dance students. *Journal of Dance Medicine and Science, 19*(1), 22-30.

Gould, D., & Maynard, I. (2009). Psychological preparation for the Olympic Games. *Journal of Sports Sciences, 27*(13), 1393-1408.

Gustafsson, H., Martinent, G., Isoard-Gautheur, S., Hassmén, P., & Guillet-Descas, E. (2018). Performance based self-esteem and athlete-identity in athlete burnout: A person-centered approach. *Psychology of Sport and Exercise, 38*, 56-60.

Hagger, M., & Chatzisarantis, N. (2005). *Social Psychology of Exercise and Sport*. McGraw-Hill Education.

Hanrahan, S.J. (1996). Dancers' perceptions of psychological skills. *Revista de psicologia del deporte, 5*(2), 19-27.

Hays, K., Maynard, I., Thomas, O., & Bawden, M. (2007). Sources and types of confidence identified by world class sport performers. *Journal of Applied Sport Psychology, 19*(4), 434-456.

Hays, K., Thomas, O., Maynard, I., & Bawden, M. (2009). The role of confidence in world-class sport performance. *Journal of Sports Sciences, 27*(11), 1185-1199.

Hutchinson, J.C., Sherman, T., Martinovic, N., & Tenenbaum, G. (2008). The effect of manipulated self-efficacy on perceived and sustained effort. *Journal of Applied Sport Psychology, 20*(4), 457-472.

Kitsantas, A., Zimmerman, B.J., & Cleary, T. (2000). The role of observation and emulation in the development of athletic self-regulation. *Journal of Educational Psychology, 92*(4), 811.

Krane, V., & Williams, J. (1994). Cognitive anxiety, somatic anxiety, and confidence in track and field athletes: The impact of gender, competitive level and task characteristics. *International Journal of Sport Psychology, 25*, 203-217.

Maddux, J.E. (1995). *Self-efficacy, adaptation, and adjustment: Theory, research, and application*. Plenum.

Maddux, J.E. (2002). Self-efficacy: The power of believing you can. In C.R. Snyder & S.J. Lopez (Eds.), *Handbook of positive psychology* (p. 277-287). Oxford University Press.

Marchant-Haycox, S.E., & Wilson, G.D. (1992). Personality and stress in performing artists. *Personality and Individual Differences, 13*(10), 1061-1068.

McCullagh, P., & Weiss, M.R. (2002). Observational learning: The forgotten psychological method in sport psychology. In J.L. Van Raalte & B.W. Brewer (Eds.), *Exploring sport and exercise psychology* (pp. 131-149). American Psychological Association.

Moritz, S.E., Feltz, D.L., Fahrbach, K.R., & Mack, D.E. (2000). The relation of self-efficacy measures to sport performance: A meta-analytic review. *Research Quarterly for Exercise and Sport, 71*(3), 280-294.

Neiss, M.B., Sedikides, C., & Stevenson, J. (2002). Self-esteem: A behavioural genetic perspective. *European Journal of Personality, 16*(5), 351-367.

Nordin, S.M., & Cumming, J. (2005). Professional dancers describe their imagery: Where, when, what, why, and how. *The Sport Psychologist, 19*(4), 395-416.

Nordin, S.M., & Cumming, J. (2008). Exploring common ground: Comparing the imagery of dancers and aesthetic sport performers. *Journal of Applied Sport Psychology, 20*(4), 375-391.

Nordin-Bates, S.M., Cumming, J., Aways, D., & Sharp, L. (2011a). Imagining yourself dancing to perfection? Correlates of perfectionism among ballet and contemporary dancers. *Journal of Clinical Sport Psychology, 5*(1), 58-76.

Nordin-Bates, S.M., Walker, I.J., Baker, J., Garner, J., Hardy, C., Irvine, S., Jola, C., Laws, H., & Blevins, P. (2011b). Injury, imagery, and self-esteem in dance healthy minds in injured bodies?. *Journal of Dance Medicine and Science, 15*(2), 76-85.

Nordin-Bates, S.M., Schwarz, J.F., Quested, E., Cumming, J., Aujla, I.J., & Redding, E. (2016). Within- and between-person predictors of disordered eating attitudes among male and female dancers: Findings from the UK Centres for Advanced Training. *Psychology of Sport and Exercise, 27*, 101-111.

Orth, U., & Robins, R.W. (2014). The development of self-esteem. *Current Directions in Psychological Science, 23*(5), 381-387.

Quested, E., & Duda, J.L. (2011). Perceived autonomy support, motivation regulations and the self-evaluative tendencies of student dancers. *Journal of Dance Medicine & Science, 15*(1), 3-14.

Petrie, T.A., Greenleaf, C., Reel, J., & Carter, J. (2009). Personality and psychological factors as predictors of disordered eating among female collegiate athletes. *Eating Disorders, 17*(4), 302-321.

Sabiston, C.M., Gilchrist, J.D., & Brunet, J. (2018). Self-perception in sport and exercise. In T.S. Horn & A.L. Smith (Eds.), *Advances in Sport and Exercise Psychology* (pp. 57-76). Human Kinetics.

Samson, A., & Solmon, M. (2011). Examining the sources of self-efficacy for physical activity within the sport and exercise domains. *International Review of Sport and Exercise Psychology, 4*(1), 70-89.

Schwender, T.M., Spengler, S., Oedl, C., & Mess, F. (2018). Effects of dance interventions on aspects of the participants' self: A systematic review. *Frontiers in Psychology, 9*, 1130.

Shavelson, R.J., Hubner, J.J., & Stanton, G.C. (1976). Self-concept: Validation of construct interpretations. *Review of Educational Research, 46*(3), 407-441.

Thomas, O., Lane, A., & Kingston, K. (2011). Defining and contextualizing robust sport-confidence. *Journal of Applied Sport Psychology, 23*, 189-208.

Thomas, O., Thrower, S.N., Lane, A., & Thomas, J. (2021). Types, sources, and debilitating factors of sport confidence in elite early adolescent academy soccer players. *Journal of Applied Sport Psychology, 33*(2), 192-217.

Usher, E.L., & Pajares, F. (2008). Sources of self-efficacy in school: Critical review of the literature and future directions. *Review of Educational Research, 78*(4), 751-796.

Vargas-Tonsing, T.M., & Bartholomew, J.B. (2006). An exploratory study of the effects of pregame speeches on team efficacy beliefs. *Journal of Applied Sport Psychology, 36*(4), 918-933.

Vealey, R.S. (1986). Conceptualization of sport-confidence and competitive orientation: Preliminary investigation and instrument development. *Journal of Sport Psychology, 8*, 221-246.

Vealey, R.S. (2001). Understanding and enhancing self-confidence in athletes. In R.N. Singer, H.A. Hausenblas, & C.M. Janelle (Eds.), *Handbook of Sport Psychology* (pp. 550-565). Wiley.

Vealey, R.S. (2009). Confidence in sport. In B.W. Brewer (Ed.), *Handbook of Sports Medicine and Science: Sport Psychology* (pp. 43-52). Wiley-Blackwell.

Walker, I.J., & Nordin-Bates, S.M. (2010). Performance anxiety experiences of professional ballet dancers the importance of control. *Journal of Dance Medicine and Science, 14*(4), 133-145.

Walker, I.J., Nordin-Bates, S.M., & Redding, E. (2011). Characteristics of talented dancers and age group differences: Findings from the UK Centres for Advanced Training. *High Ability Studies, 22*(1), 43-60.

Weinberg, R.S., & Gould, D. (2018). *Foundations of Sport and Exercise Psychology* (7th ed.). Human Kinetics.

Woodman, T., Akehurst, S., Hardy, L., & Beattie, S. (2010). Self-confidence and performance: A little self-doubt helps. *Psychology of Sport and Exercise, 11*(6), 467-470.

Chapter 4

Arnold, R., & Fletcher, D. (2012). A research synthesis and taxonomic classification of the organizational stressors encountered by sport performers. *Journal of Sport and Exercise Psychology, 34*(3), 397-429.

Aujla, I., & Farrer, R. (2015). The role of psychological factors in the career of the independent dancer. *Frontiers in Psychology, 6*, 1688.

Barrell, G.M., & Terry, P.C. (2003). Trait anxiety and coping strategies among ballet dancers. *Medical Problems of Performing Artists, 18*(2), 59-64.

Blevins, P., Erskine, S., Hopper, L., & Moyle, G. (2019). Finding your balance: An investigation of recovery-stress balance in vocational dance training. *Journal of Dance Education, 20*(2), 1-11.

Cheng, W.N.K., Hardy, L., & Woodman, T. (2011). Predictive validity of a three-dimensional model of performance anxiety in the context of tae-kwon-do. *Journal of Sport and Exercise Psychology, 33*(1), 40-53.

Cheng, W.N.K., & Hardy, L. (2016). Three-dimensional model of performance anxiety: Tests of the adaptive potential of the regulatory dimension of anxiety. *Psychology of Sport and Exercise, 22*, 255-263.

Clements, L., & Nordin-Bates, S.M. (2022). Inspired or inhibited? Choreographers' views on how classical ballet training shaped their creativity. *Journal of Dance Education*, 22(1), 1-12.

Fish, L., Hall, C., & Cumming, J. (2004). Investigating the use of imagery by elite ballet dancers. *Avante*, 10(3).

Fitzsimmons-Craft, E.E., Harney, M.B., Brownstone, L.M., Higgins, M.K., & Bardone-Cone, A.M. (2012). Examining social physique anxiety and disordered eating in college women. The roles of social comparison and body surveillance. *Appetite*, 59(3), 796-805.

Fletcher, D., & Hanton, S. (2001). The relationship between psychological skills usage and competitive anxiety responses. *Psychology of Sport and Exercise*, 2(2), 89-101.

Gustafsson, H., Lundqvist, C., & Tod, D. (2017). Cognitive behavioral intervention in sport psychology: A case illustration of the exposure method with an elite athlete. *Journal of Sport Psychology in Action*, 8(3), 152-162.

Hanton, S., Neil, R., & Mellalieu, S.D. (2008). Recent developments in competitive anxiety direction and competition stress research. *International Review of Sport and Exercise Psychology*, 1(1), 45-57.

Haraldsen, H.M., Nordin-Bates, S.M., Abrahamsen, F.E., & Halvari, H. (2020). Thriving, striving, or just surviving? TD learning conditions, motivational processes and well-being among Norwegian elite performers in music, ballet, and sport. *Roeper Review*, 42(2), 109-125.

Helin, P. (1989). Mental and psychophysiological tension at professional ballet dancers' performances and rehearsals. *Dance Research Journal*, 21(1), 7-14.

Jacobson, E. (1938). Progressive muscle relaxation. *Journal of Abnormal Psychology*, 75(1), 18.

Jones, G., & Hanton, S. (2001). Pre-competitive feeling states and directional anxiety interpretations. *Journal of Sports Sciences*, 19(6), 385-395.

Jones, E.S., Mullen, R., & Hardy, L. (2019). Measurement and validation of a three factor hierarchical model of competitive anxiety. *Psychology of Sport and Exercise*, 43, 34-44.

Jones, G., & Swain, A. (1992). Intensity and direction as dimensions of competitive state anxiety and relationships with competitiveness. *Perceptual and Motor Skills*, 74(2), 467-472.

Karageorghis, C.I., Bigliassi, M., Tayara, K., Priest, D.-L., & Bird, J.M. (2018). A grounded theory of music use in the psychological preparation of academy soccer players. *Sport, Exercise, and Performance Psychology*, 7, 109-127.

Kaufman, K.A., Glass, C.R., & Pineau, T.R. (2018). *Mindful sport performance enhancement: Mental training for athletes and coaches*. American Psychological Association.

Lacaille, N., Koestner, R., & Gaudreau, P. (2007). On the value of intrinsic rather than traditional achievement goals for performing artists: A short-term prospective study. *International Journal of Music Education*, 25(3), 245-257.

Laukka, P., & Quick, L. (2013). Emotional and motivational uses of music in sports and exercise: A questionnaire study among athletes. *Psychology of Music*, 41, 198-215.

Lench, H.C., Levine, L.J., & Roe, E. (2010). Trait anxiety and achievement goals as predictors of self-reported health in dancers. *Journal of Dance Medicine & Science*, 14(4), 163-170.

McGrath, J.E. (1970). A conceptual formulation for research on stress. In J.E. McGrath (Ed.), *Social and psychological factors in stress* (pp. 10-21). Holt, Rinehart & Winston.

Marin, M.F., Lord, C., Andrews, J., Juster, R.P., Sindi, S., Arsenault-Lapierre, G., Fiocco, A.J., & Lupien, S.J. (2011). Chronic stress, cognitive functioning and mental health. *Neurobiology of Learning and Memory*, 96(4), 583-595.

Maynard, I.W., Hemmings, B., & Warwick-Evans, L. (1995a). The effects of a somatic intervention strategy on competitive state anxiety and performance in semiprofessional soccer players. *The Sport Psychologist*, 9(1), 51-64.

Maynard, I.W., Smith, M.J., & Warwick-Evans, L. (1995b). The effects of a cognitive intervention strategy on competitive state anxiety and performance in semiprofessional soccer players. *Journal of Sport and Exercise Psychology*, 17(4), 428-446.

Mellalieu, S.D., Hanton, S., & O'Brien, M. (2004). Intensity and direction of competitive anxiety as a function of sport type and experience. *Scandinavian Journal of Medicine & Science in Sports*, 14(5), 326-334.

Neil, R., Mellalieu, S.D., & Hanton, S. (2006). Psychological skills usage and the competitive anxiety response as a function of skill level in rugby union. *Journal of Sports Science & Medicine*, 5(3), 415-423.

Noetel, M., Ciarrochi, J., Van Zanden, B., & Lonsdale, C. (2019). Mindfulness and acceptance approaches to sporting performance enhancement: A systematic review. *International Review of Sport and Exercise Psychology*, 12(1), 139-175.

Nordin, S.M., & Cumming, J. (2006). Measuring the content of dancers' images development of the dance imagery questionnaire (DIQ). *Journal of Dance Medicine and Science*, 10(3-4), 85-98.

Nordin-Bates, S.M. (2020). Striving for perfection or for creativity? A dancer's dilemma. *Journal of Dance Education*, 20(1), 23-34.

Nordin-Bates, S.M., Cumming, J., Aways, D., & Sharp, L. (2011). Imagining yourself dancing to perfection? Correlates of perfectionism among ballet and contemporary dancers. *Journal of Clinical Sport Psychology*, 5(1), 58-76.

Nordin-Bates, S.M., Quested, E., Walker, I.J., & Redding, E. (2012). Climate change in the dance studio: Findings from the UK Centres for Advanced Training. *Sport, Exercise, and Performance Psychology*, 1(1), 3-16.

Quested, E., Bosch, J.A., Burns, V.E., Cumming, J., Ntoumanis, N., & Duda, J.L. (2011). Basic psychological need satisfaction, stress-related appraisals, and dancers' cortisol and anxiety responses. *Journal of Sport and Exercise Psychology*, 33(6), 828-846.

Rohleder, N., Beulen, S.E., Chen, E., Wolf, J.M., & Kirschbaum, C. (2007). Stress on the dance floor: The cortisol stress response to social-evaluative threat in competitive ballroom dancers. *Personality and Social Psychology Bulletin*, 33(1), 69-84.

Rumbold, J.L., Fletcher, D., & Daniels, K. (2012). A systematic review of stress management interventions with sport performers. *Sport, Exercise, and Performance Psychology*, 1(3), 173-193.

Taylor, J., & Estanol, E. (2015). *Dance psychology for artistic and performance excellence*. Human Kinetics.

Terry, P.C., Karageorghis, C.I., Curran, M.L., Martin, O.V., & Parsons-Smith, R.L. (2020). Effects of music in exercise and sport: A meta-analytic review. *Psychological Bulletin*, 146(2), 91-117.

Walker, I.J., & Nordin-Bates, S.M. (2010). Performance anxiety experiences of professional ballet dancers: The importance of control. *Journal of Dance Medicine & Science*, 14(4), 133-145.

Woodman, T., & Hardy, L. (2003). The relative impact of cognitive anxiety and self-confidence upon sport performance: A meta-analysis. *Journal of Sports Sciences*, 21, 443-457.

Chapter 5

Alter, J.B. (1997). Why dance students pursue dance: Studies of dance students from 1953 to 1993. *Dance Research Journal*, 29(2), 70-89.

Ames, C. (1992). Achievement goals and the classroom motivational climate. In J. Meece & D. Schunk (Eds.), *Students' perceptions in the classroom: Causes and consequences* (pp. 327-48). Erlbaum.

Andrzejewski, C.E., Wilson, A.M., & Henry, D.J. (2013). Considering motivation, goals, and mastery orientation in dance technique. *Research in Dance Education*, 14(2), 162-175.

Atienza, F.L., Castillo, I., Appleton, P.R., & Balaguer, I. (2020). Examining the mediating role of motivation in the relationship between multidimensional perfectionism and well- and ill-being in vocational dancers. *International Journal of Environmental Research and Public Health*, 17(14), 4945.

Aujla, I., & Farrer, R. (2015). The role of psychological factors in the career of the independent dancer. *Frontiers in Psychology*, 6, 1688.

Aujla, I.J., Nordin-Bates, S.M., & Redding, E. (2014). A qualitative investigation of commitment to dance: Findings from the UK Centres for Advanced Training. *Research in Dance Education*, 15(2), 138-160.

Balaguer, I., Castillo, I., Duda, J.L., Quested, E., & Morales, V. (2011). Predictores socio-contextuales y motivacionales de la intención de continuar participando: Un análisis desde la SDT en danza [Social-contextual and motivational predictors of intentions to continue participation: A test of SDT in dance]. *RICYDE. Revista Internacional de ciencias del deporte*, 7(25), 305-319.

Bartholomew, K.J., Ntoumanis, N., Ryan, R.M., & Thøgersen-Ntoumani, C. (2011). Psychological need thwarting in the sport context: Assessing the darker side of athletic experience. *Journal of Sport and Exercise Psychology*, 33(1), 75-102.

Bond, K.E., & Stinson, S.W. (2007). "It's work, work, work, work": Young people's experiences of effort and engagement in dance. *Research in Dance Education*, 8(2), 155-183.

Carr, S., & Wyon, M. (2003). The impact of motivational climate on dance students' achievement goals, trait anxiety, and perfectionism. *Journal of Dance Medicine & Science*, 7(4), 105-114.

Clements, L., & Nordin-Bates, S.M. (2022). Inspired or inhibited? Choreographers' views on how classical ballet training shaped their creativity. *Journal of Dance Education*, 22(1), 1-12.

de Bruin, A.K., Bakker, F.C., & Oudejans, R.R. (2009). Achievement goal theory and disordered eating: Relationships of disordered eating with goal orientations and motivational climate in female gymnasts and dancers. *Psychology of Sport and Exercise*, 10(1), 72-79.

Deci, E.L., & Ryan, R.M. (1985). *Intrinsic motivation and self-determination in human behavior*. Plenum.

Deci, E.L., & Ryan, R.M. (2000). The "what" and "why" of goal pursuits: Human needs and the self-determination of behavior. *Psychological Inquiry*, 11(4), 227-268.

Elliot, A.J. (1999). Approach and avoidance motivation and achievement goals. *Educational Psychologist*, 34(3), 169-189.

Elliot, A.J., & McGregor, H.A. (2001). A 2 × 2 achievement goal framework. *Journal of Personality and Social Psychology*, 80(3), 501.

Hancox, J.E., Quested, E., Ntoumanis, N., & Duda, J.L. (2017). Teacher-created social environment, basic psychological needs, and dancers' affective states during class: A diary study. *Personality and Individual Differences*, 115, 137-143.

Hancox, J.E., Quested, E., Viladrich, C., & Duda, J.L. (2015). Examination of the internal structure of the behavioural regulation in sport questionnaire among dancers. *International Journal of Sport and Exercise Psychology*, 13(4), 382-397.

Hanrahan, S.J., Pedro, R., & Cerin, E. (2009). Structured self-reflection as a tool to enhance perceived performance and maintain effort in adult recreational salsa dancers. *The Sport Psychologist*, 23(2), 151-169.

Haraldsen, H.M., Halvari, H., Solstad, B.E., Abrahamsen, F.E., & Nordin-Bates, S.M. (2019). The role of perfectionism and controlling conditions in Norwegian elite junior performers' motivational processes. *Frontiers in Psychology*, 10, 1366.

Haraldsen, H.M., Nordin-Bates, S.M., Abrahamsen, F.E., & Halvari, H. (2020a). Thriving, striving, or just surviving? TD learning conditions, motivational processes and well-being among Norwegian elite performers in music, ballet, and sport. *Roeper Review*, 42(2), 109-125.

Haraldsen, H.M., Solstad, B.E., Ivarsson, A., Halvari, H., & Abrahamsen, F.E. (2020b). Change in basic need frustration in relation to perfectionism, anxiety, and performance in elite junior performers. *Scandinavian Journal of Medicine & Science in Sports*, 30(4), 754-765.

Keegan, R.J. (2018). Achievement goals in sport and physical activity. In T.S. Horn and A.L. Smith (Eds.), *Advances in Sport and Exercise Psychology* (4th ed., pp. 265-287). Human Kinetics.

Keegan, R.J., Harwood, C.G., Spray, C.M., & Lavallee, D.E. (2009). A qualitative investigation exploring the motivational climate in early career sports participants: Coach, parent and peer influences on sport motivation. *Psychology of Sport and Exercise*, 10(3), 361-372.

Lacaille, N., Koestner, R., & Gaudreau, P. (2007). On the value of intrinsic rather than traditional achievement goals for performing artists: A short-term prospective study. *International Journal of Music Education*, 25(3), 245-257.

Lacaille, N., Whipple, N., & Koestner, R. (2005). Reevaluating the benefits of performance goals. *Medical Problems of Performing Artists*, 20(1), 11-16.

Lench, H.C., Levine, L.J., & Roe, E. (2010). Trait anxiety and achievement goals as predictors of self-reported health in dancers. *Journal of Dance Medicine & Science*, 14(4), 163-170.

Lochbaum, M., Zazo, R., Kazak Çetinkalp, Z., Wright, T., Graham, K., & Konttinen, N. (2016). A meta-analytic review of achievement goal orientation correlates in competitive sport: A follow-up to Lochbaum et al. (2016). *Kinesiology*, 48(2), 159-173.

Marsh, H.W. (1987). The big-fish-little-pond effect on academic self-concept. *Journal of Educational Psychology* 79(3), 280-295.

Molnar, D.S., Blackburn, M., Zinga, D., Spadafora, N., Methot-Jones, T., & Connolly, M. (2021). Trait perfectionism and dance goals among young female dancers: An application of the 2 × 2 model of perfectionism. *Journal of Sport and Exercise Psychology*, 43(3), 234-247.

Nicholls, J.G. (1984). Achievement motivation: Conceptions of ability, subjective experience, task choice, and performance. *Psychological Review*, 91(3), 328-346. https://doi.org/10.1037/0033-295X.91.3.328

Nicholls, J.G. (1989). *The competitive ethos and democratic education*. Harvard University Press.

Nieminen, P. (1998). Motives for dancing among Finnish folk dancers, competitive ballroom dancers, ballet dancers and modern dancers. *European Journal of Physical Education*, 3(1), 22-34.

Nieminen, P., Varstala, V., & Manninen, M. (2001). Goal orientation and perceived purposes of dance among Finnish dance students: A pilot study. *Research in Dance Education*, 2(2), 175-193.

Nordin-Bates, S.M. (2020). Striving for perfection or for creativity: A dancer's dilemma? *Journal of Dance Education*, 20(1), 23-34.

Nordin-Bates, S.M. & Abrahamsen, F. (2016). Perfectionism in dance: Applied considerations and a case example. In A.P. Hill (Ed.), *The Psychology of Perfectionism in Sport, Dance and Exercise* (pp. 222-244). Routledge.

Nordin-Bates, S.M., Raedeke, T.D., & Madigan, D.J. (2017). Perfectionism, burnout, and motivation in dance: A replication and test of the 2 × 2 model of perfectionism. *Journal of Dance Medicine & Science*, 21(3), 115-122.

Norfield, J. & Nordin-Bates, S. (2012). How community dance leads to positive outcomes: A self-determination theory perspective. *Journal of Applied Arts and Health*, 2(3), 257-272.

Quested, E., Bosch, J.A., Burns, V.E., Cumming, J., Ntoumanis, N., & Duda, J.L. (2011c). Basic psychological need satisfaction, stress-related appraisals, and dancers' cortisol and anxiety responses. *Journal of Sport and Exercise Psychology*, 33(6), 828-846.

Quested, E., & Duda, J.L. (2009). Perceptions of the motivational climate, need satisfaction, and indices of well- and ill-being among hip hop dancers. *Journal of Dance Medicine & Science*, 13(1), 10-19.

Quested, E., & Duda, J.L. (2010). Exploring the social-environmental determinants of well- and ill-being in dancers: A test of basic needs theory. *Journal of Sport and Exercise Psychology*, 32(1), 39-60.

Quested, E., & Duda, J.L. (2011a). Antecedents of burnout among elite dancers: A longitudinal test of basic needs theory. *Psychology of Sport and Exercise*, 12(2), 159-167.

Quested, E., & Duda, J.L. (2011b). Perceived autonomy support, motivation regulations and the self-evaluative tendencies of student dancers. *Journal of Dance Medicine & Science*, 15(1), 3-14.

Quested, E., Duda, J.L., Ntoumanis, N., & Maxwell, J.P. (2013). Daily fluctuations in the affective states of dancers: A cross-situational test of basic needs theory. *Psychology of Sport and Exercise*, *14*(4), 586-595.

Roberts, G.C. (1993). Motivation in sport: Understanding and enhancing the motivation and achievement of children. In R.N. Singer, M. Murphey, & L.K. Tennant (Eds.), *Handbook of Research on Sport Psychology* (pp. 405-420). Macmillan.

Roberts, G.C., Treasure, D.C., & Kavussanu, M. (1996). Orthogonality of achievement goals and its relationship to beliefs about success and satisfaction in sport. *The Sport Psychologist*, *10*(4), 398-408.

Ryan, R.M., & Deci, E.L. (2000). Self-determination theory and the facilitation of intrinsic motivation, social development, and well-being. *American Psychologist*, *55*(1), 68-78.

Sage, G. (1977). *Introduction to motor behavior: A neuropsychological approach* (2nd ed.). Addison-Wesley.

Standage, M., Curran, T., & Rouse, P.C. (2018). Self-determination-based theories of sport, exercise, and physical activity motivation. In T.S. Horn & A.L. Smith (Eds.), *Advances in Sport and Exercise Psychology* (pp. 289-312). Human Kinetics.

Stinson, S.W. (1997). A question of fun: Adolescent engagement in dance education. *Dance Research Journal*, *29*(2), 49-69.

Walker, I.J., Nordin-Bates, S.M., & Redding, E. (2012). A mixed methods investigation of dropout among talented young dancers: Findings from the UK Centres for Advanced Training. *Journal of Dance Medicine & Science*, *16*(2), 65-73.

Watson, D.E., Nordin-Bates, S.M., & Chappell, K.A. (2012). Facilitating and nurturing creativity in pre-vocational dancers: Findings from the UK Centres for Advanced Training. *Research in Dance Education*, *13*(2), 153-173.

Chapter 6

Abdollahipour, R., Wulf, G., Psotta, R., & Palomo Nieto, M. (2015). Performance of gymnastics skill benefits from an external focus of attention. *Journal of Sports Sciences*, *33*(17), 1807-1813.

Abernethy, B., Maxwell, J.P., Masters, R.S., Van Der Kamp, J., & Jackson, R.C. (2007). Attentional processes in skill learning and expert performance. In G. Tenenbaum & R.C. Eklund (Eds.), *Handbook of Sport Psychology* (3rd ed., pp. 245-263). Wiley.

Andrade, C.M., Souza, T.R.D., Mazoni, A.F., Andrade, A.G.D., & Vaz, D.V. (2020). Internal and imagined external foci of attention do not influence pirouette performance in ballet dancers. *Research Quarterly for Exercise and Sport*, *91*(4), 682-691.

Barlow, M., Woodman, T., Gorgulu, R., & Voyzey, R. (2016). Ironic effects of performance are worse for neurotics. *Psychology of Sport and Exercise*, *24*, 27-37.

Beilock, S.L., & Carr, T.H. (2001). On the fragility of skilled performance: What governs choking under pressure? *Journal of Experimental Psychology: General*, *130*(4), 701-725.

Beilock, S.L., & Gray, R. (2007). Why do athletes choke under pressure? In G. Tenenbaum & R.C. Eklund (Eds.), *Handbook of Sport Psychology* (3rd ed., pp. 425-444). Wiley.

Chua, T.X., Sproule, J., & Timmons, W. (2018). Effect of skilled dancers' focus of attention on pirouette performance. *Journal of Dance Medicine & Science*, *22*(3), 148-159.

Csikszentmihalyi, M. (1990) *Flow: The psychology of optimal experience*. Harper & Row.

Dugdale, J.R., & Eklund, R.C. (2003). Ironic processing and static balance performance in high-expertise performers. *Research Quarterly for Exercise and Sport*, *74*(3), 348-352.

Ehrenberg, S. (2015). A kinesthetic mode of attention in contemporary dance practice. *Dance Research Journal*, *47*(2), 43-62.

Ehrlenspiel, F. (2001). Paralysis by analysis? A functional framework for the effects of attentional focus on the control of motor skills. *European Journal of Sport Science*, *1*(5), 1-11.

Fitts, P.M., & Posner, M.I. (1967). *Human Performance*. Brooke/Cole.

Gucciardi, D.F., & Dimmock, J.A. (2008). Choking under pressure in sensorimotor skills: Conscious processing or depleted attentional resources? *Psychology of Sport and Exercise*, *9*(1), 45-59.

Guss-West, C. (2020). *Attention and Focus in Dance: Enhancing Power, Precision, and Artistry*. Human Kinetics.

Guss-West, C., & Wulf, G. (2016). Attentional focus in classical ballet: A survey of professional dancers. *Journal of Dance Medicine & Science*, *20*(1), 23-29.

Hanrahan, S.J. (1996). Dancers' perceptions of psychological skills. *Revista de psicologia del deporte*, *5*(2), 19-27.

Hardy, L., Mullen, R., & Martin, N. (2001). Effect of task-relevant cues and state anxiety on motor performance. *Perceptual and Motor Skills*, *92*(3), 943-946.

Hefferon, K.M., & Ollis, S. (2006). 'Just clicks': An interpretive phenomenological analysis of professional dancers' experience of flow. *Research in Dance Education*, *7*(2), 141-159.

Hill, D.M., Hanton, S., Fleming, S., & Matthews, N. (2009). A re-examination of choking in sport. *European Journal of Sport Science*, *9*(4), 203-212.

Hill, D.M., Hanton, S., Matthews, N., & Fleming, S. (2010). A qualitative exploration of choking in elite golf. *Journal of Clinical Sport Psychology, 4*(3), 221-240.

Hill, D.M., & Shaw, G. (2013). A qualitative examination of choking under pressure in team sport. *Psychology of Sport and Exercise, 14*(1), 103-110.

Jackson, S.A., & Csikszentmihalyi, M. (1999). *Flow in Sports*. Human Kinetics.

James, W. (1890). *The Principles of Psychology*. Vol. 1. Henry Holt.

Jordet, G., & Hartman, E. (2008). Avoidance motivation and choking under pressure in soccer penalty shootouts. *Journal of Sport and Exercise Psychology, 30*(4), 450-457.

Karin, J. (2016). Recontextualizing dance skills: Overcoming impediments to motor learning and expressivity in ballet dancers. *Frontiers in Psychology, 7*, 431.

Karin, J., & Nordin-Bates, S.M. (2020). Enhancing creativity and managing perfectionism in dancers through implicit learning and sensori-kinetic imagery. *Journal of Dance Education, 20*(1), 1-11.

Lam, W.K., Maxwell, J.P., & Masters, R.S.W. (2009a). Analogy learning and the performance of motor skills under pressure. *Journal of Sport and Exercise Psychology, 31*(3), 337-357.

Lam, W.K., Maxwell, J.P., & Masters, R.S.W. (2009b). Analogy versus explicit learning of a modified basketball shooting task: Performance and kinematic outcomes. *Journal of Sports Sciences, 27*(2), 179-191.

Liao, C.M., & Masters, R.S. (2001). Analogy learning: A means to implicit motor learning. *Journal of Sports Sciences, 19*(5), 307-319.

Liao, C.M., & Masters, R.S. (2002). Self-focused attention and performance failure under psychological stress. *Journal of Sport and Exercise Psychology, 24*(3), 289-305.

Lola, A.C., & Tzetzis, G.C. (2021). The effect of explicit, implicit and analogy instruction on decision making skill for novices, under stress. *International Journal of Sport and Exercise Psychology*. https://doi.org/10.1080/1612197X.2021.1877325

Masters, R., & Maxwell, J. (2008). The theory of reinvestment. *International Review of Sport and Exercise Psychology, 1*(2), 160-183.

Masters, R.S. (1992). Knowledge, knerves and know-how: The role of explicit versus implicit knowledge in the breakdown of a complex motor skill under pressure. *British Journal of Psychology, 83*(3), 343-358.

Masters, R.S.W., van Duijn, T., & Uiga, L. (2019). Advances in implicit motor learning. In N.J. Hodges & M.A. Williams (Eds.), *Skill Acquisition in Sport* (3rd ed.). Routledge. https://doi.org/10.4324/9781351189750

Mesagno, C., & Beckmann, J. (2017). Choking under pressure: Theoretical models and interventions. *Current Opinion in Psychology, 16*, 170-175.

Moran, A., Toner, J., & Campbell, M. (2018). Attention and concentration. In A. Mugford & J. G. Cremades (Eds.), *Sport, Exercise, and Performance Psychology: Theories and Applications* (1st ed., pp. 233-250). Routledge.

Mornell, A., & Wulf, G. (2019). Adopting an external focus of attention enhances musical performance. *Journal of Research in Music Education, 66*(4), 375-391.

Mullen, R., Jones, E.S., Oliver, S., & Hardy, L. (2016). Anxiety and motor performance: More evidence for the effectiveness of holistic process goals as a solution to the process goal paradox. *Psychology of Sport and Exercise, 27*, 142-149.

Nordin, S.M., & Cumming, J. (2005). Professional dancers describe their imagery: Where, when, what, why, and how. *The Sport Psychologist, 19*(4), 395-416.

Nordin-Bates, S.M. (2020). Striving for perfection or for creativity? A dancer's dilemma. *Journal of Dance Education, 20*(1), 23-34.

Overby, L.Y. (1990). The use of imagery by dance teachers—Development and implementation of two research instruments. *Journal of Physical Education, Recreation and Dance, 61*(2), 24-27.

Panebianco-Warrens, C. (2014). Exploring the dimensions of flow and the role of music in professional ballet dancers. *Muziki, 11*(2), 58-78.

Porter, J.M., Anton, P.M., & Wu, W.F. (2012). Increasing the distance of an external focus of attention enhances standing long jump performance. *The Journal of Strength and Conditioning Research, 26*(9), 2389-2393.

Stoate, I., & Wulf, G. (2011). Does the attentional focus adopted by swimmers affect their performance? *International Journal of Sports Science & Coaching, 6*(1), 99-108.

Teixeira da Silva, M., Thofehrn Lessa, H., & Chiviacowsky, S. (2017). External focus of attention enhances children's learning of a classical ballet pirouette. *Journal of Dance Medicine & Science, 21*(4), 179-184.

Thomson, P., & Jaque, S.V. (2012). Dancing with the muses: Dissociation and flow. *Journal of Trauma & Dissociation, 13*(4), 478-489.

Toner, J., & Moran, A. (2015). Enhancing performance proficiency at the expert level: Considering the role of 'somaesthetic awareness'. *Psychology of Sport and Exercise, 16*(Part 1), 110-117.

Tseng, J., & Poppenk, J. (2020). Brain meta-state transitions demarcate thoughts across task contexts exposing the mental noise of trait neuroticism. *Nature Communications, 11*(1), 1-12.

Urmston, E., & Hewison, J. (2014). Risk and flow in contact improvisation: Pleasure, play and presence. *Journal of Dance & Somatic Practices, 6*(2), 219-232.

Vergeer, I. & Hanrahan, C. (1998). What modern dancers do to prepare: Content and objectives of preperformance routines. *AVANTE, 4*, 49-71.

Wulf, G. (2008). Attentional focus effects in balance acrobats. *Research Quarterly for Exercise and Sport, 79*(3), 319-325. https://doi.org/10.1080/02701367.2008.10599495

Wulf, G. (2013). Attentional focus and motor learning: A review of 15 years. *International Review of Sport and Exercise Psychology, 6*(1), 77-104.

Wulf, G. (2016). Why did Tiger Woods shoot 82? A commentary on Toner and Moran (2015). *Psychology of Sport and Exercise, 22*, 337-338.

Wulf, G., & Lewthwaite, R. (2010). Effortless motor learning? An external focus of attention enhances movement effectiveness and efficiency. In B. Bruya (Ed.), *Effortless attention: A new perspective in the cognitive science of attention and action* (pp. 75-101). MIT Press.

Wulf, G., McNevin, N.H., & Shea, C.H. (2001). The automaticity of complex motor skill learning as a function of attentional focus. *Quarterly Journal of Experimental Psychology, 54*(4), 1143-1154.

Zourbanos, N., Hatzigeorgiadis, A., Goudas, M., Papaioannou, A., Chroni, S., & Theodorakis, Y. (2011). The social side of self-talk: Relationships between perceptions of support received from the coach and athletes' self-talk. *Psychology of Sport and Exercise, 12*(4), 407-414.

Chapter 7

Alterowitz, G. (2014). Toward a feminist ballet pedagogy: Teaching strategies for ballet technique classes in the twenty-first century. *Journal of Dance Education, 14*(1), 8-17.

Amabile, T.M. (2018). *Creativity in context: Update to the social psychology of creativity*. Routledge. (Original work published 1983).

Anoop, M., & Malshe, M. (2011). Creativity and the code: Training in Mohinīāṭṭam. *Theatre, Dance and Performance Training, 2*(2), 138-150.

Aujla, I., & Farrer, R. (2015). The role of psychological factors in the career of the independent dancer. *Frontiers in Psychology, 6*, 1688.

Biasutti, M. (2013). Improvisation in dance education: Teacher views. *Research in Dance Education, 14*(2), 120-140.

Biasutti, M., & Habe, K. (2021). Dance improvisation and motor creativity in children: Teachers' conceptions. *Creativity Research Journal, 33*(1), 47-62.

Butterworth, J. (2004). Teaching choreography in higher education: A process continuum model. *Research in Dance Education, 5*(1), 45-67.

Chappell, K. (2007). Creativity in primary level dance education: Moving beyond assumption. *Research in Dance Education, 8*(1), 27-52.

Chappell, K., & Hathaway, C. (2019). Creativity and dance education research. In P. Thomson (Ed.), *Oxford Research Encyclopaedia of Education*. Oxford University Press.

Choi, E., & Kim, N.Y. (2015). Whole ballet education: Exploring direct and indirect teaching methods. *Research in Dance Education, 16*(2), 142-160.

Clegg, H., Owton, H., & Allen-Collinson, J. (2019). Attracting and retaining boys in ballet: A qualitative study of female dance teachers. *Journal of Dance Education, 19*(4), 158-167.

Clements, L. (2017). *The psychology of creativity in contemporary dance*. [Unpublished doctoral dissertation]. Trinity Laban Conservatoire of Music and Dance, London, England

Clements, L., & Nordin-Bates, S.M. (2022). Inspired or inhibited? Choreographers' views on how classical ballet training shaped their creativity. *Journal of Dance Education, 22*(1), 1-12.

Clements, L., & Redding, E. (2020). Creativity in higher education contemporary dance: An interpretative phenomenological analysis. *Journal of Dance Education, 20*(2), 88-98.

Costa, P.T., Jr., & McCrae, R.R. (1992). *Revised NEO personality inventory (NEO-PI-R) and NEO five-factor inventory (NEO-FFI): Professional manual*. Psychological Assessment Resources.

Cropley, A. (2006). In praise of convergent thinking. *Creativity Research Journal, 18*(3), 391-404.

Csikszentmihalyi, M. (1996). *Creativity*. Harper Collins.

de Manzano, Ö., & Ullén, F. (2018). Genetic and environmental influences on the phenotypic associations between intelligence, personality, and creative achievement in the arts and sciences. *Intelligence, 69*, 123-133.

Farrer, R. (2014). The creative dancer. *Research in Dance Education, 15*(1), 95-104.

Fink, A., Graif, B., & Neubauer, A.C. (2009). Brain correlates underlying creative thinking: EEG alpha activity in professional vs. novice dancers. *Neuroimage, 46*(3), 854-862.

Fink, A., & Woschnjak, S. (2011). Creativity and personality in professional dancers. *Personality and Individual Differences, 51*(6), 754-758.

Gardner, H. (1993). *Creating Minds*. BasicBooks.

Giguere, M. (2011). Dancing thoughts: An examination of children's cognition and creative process in dance. *Research in Dance Education, 12*(1), 5-28.

Guilford, J.P. (1963). Intellectual resources and their values as seen by scientists. In C.W. Taylor & F. Barron (Eds.), *Scientific Creativity: Its Recognition and Development* (pp. 101-118). Wiley.

Hanrahan, C., & Vergeer, I. (2001). Multiple uses of mental imagery by professional modern dancers. *Imagination, Cognition and Personality, 20*(3), 231-255.

Henley, M. (2014). Sensation, perception, and choice in the dance classroom. *Journal of Dance Education, 14*(3), 95-100.

Hennessey, B.A. (2019). Motivation and creativity. In J.C. Kaufman & R.J. Sternberg (Eds.), *The Cambridge Handbook of Creativity* (2nd ed., pp. 374-395). Cambridge University Press.

Jackson, J. (2005). My dance and the ideal body: Looking at ballet practice from the inside out. *Research in Dance Education*, 6(1-2), 25-40.

Jauk, E., Benedek, M., & Neubauer, A.C. (2014). The road to creative achievement: A latent variable model of ability and personality predictors. *European Journal of Personality*, 28(1), 95-105.

Johnston, D. (2006). Private speech in ballet. *Research in Dance Education*, 7(1), 3-14.

Karin, J., & Nordin-Bates, S.M. (2020). Enhancing creativity and managing perfectionism in dancers through implicit learning and sensori-kinetic imagery. *Journal of Dance Education*, 20(1), 1-11.

Kaufman, J.C., & Beghetto, R.A. (2009). Beyond big and little: The four c model of creativity. *Review of General Psychology*, 13(1), 1-12.

Kim, H., Tasker, S.L., & Shen, Y. (2020). How to persevere in a ballet performance career: Exploring personal wisdom of retired professional ballet dancers. *Research in Dance Education*. https://doi.org/10.1080/14647893.2020.1837765

Kirsh, D., Stevens, C.J., & Piepers, D.W. (2020). Time course of creativity in dance. *Frontiers in Psychology*, 11. https://doi.org/10.3389/fpsyg.2020.518248

Lakes, R. (2005). The messages behind the methods: The authoritarian pedagogical legacy in Western concert dance technique training and rehearsals. *Arts Education Policy Review*, 106(5), 3-20.

Lavender, L., & Predock-Linnell, J. (2001). From improvisation to choreography: The critical bridge. *Research in Dance Education* 2(2), 195-209.

Lebuda, I., Zabelina, D.L., & Karwowski, M. (2016). Mind full of ideas: A meta-analysis of the mindfulness-creativity link. *Personality and Individual Differences*, 93, 22-26.

Lussier-Ley, C., & Durand-Bush, N. (2009). Exploring the role of feel in the creative experiences of modern dancers: A realist tale. *Research in Dance Education*, 10(3), 199-217.

Łucznik, K. (2015). Between minds and bodies: Some insights about creativity from dance improvisation. *Technoetic Arts*, 13(3), 301-308.

May, J., Calvo-Merino, B., Delahunta, S., McGregor, W., Cusack, R., Owen, A.M., Veldsman, M., Ramponi, C., & Barnard, P. (2011). Points in mental space: An interdisciplinary study of imagery in movement creation. *Dance Research*, 29 (supplement), 404-432.

May, J., Redding, E., Whatley, S., Łucznik, K., Clements, L., Weber, R., Sikorski, J., & Reed, S. (2020). Enhancing creativity by training metacognitive skills in mental imagery. *Thinking Skills and Creativity*, 38, 100739.

Mead, D. (2009). A creative ethos: Teaching and learning at the Cloud Gate dance school in Taiwan. *Global Perspectives on Dance Pedagogy: Research and Practice, Conference Proceedings of the Congress on Research in Dance*, 41(S1), 278-283.

Mead, D. (2012). Developing the expressive artist: Constructive creativity in the technique class. *Dance, Young People and Change: Proceedings of the daCi and WDA Global Dance Summit*, 7, 1-7.

Minton, S. (2003). Assessment of high school students' creative thinking skills: A comparison of dance and nondance classes. *Research in Dance Education*, 4(1), 31-49.

Morris, G. (2003). Problems with ballet: Steps, style and training. *Research in Dance Education*, 4(1), 17-30.

Nordin, S.M., & Cumming, J. (2005). Professional dancers describe their imagery: Where, when, what, why, and how. *The Sport Psychologist*, 19(4), 395-416.

Nordin-Bates, S.M. (2020). Striving for perfection or for creativity? A dancer's dilemma. *Journal of Dance Education*, 20(1), 23-34.

Press, C.M., & Warburton, E.C. (2007). Creativity research in dance. In L. Bresler (Ed.), *International Handbook of Research in Arts Education* (pp. 1273-1290). Springer.

Richard, V., Lebeau, J.-C., Becker, F., Inglis, E.R., & Tenenbaum, G. (2018). Do more creative people adapt better? An investigation into the association between creativity and adaptation. *Psychology of Sport and Exercise*, 38, 80-89.

Richard, V., & Runco, M.A. (2020). Creativity: The emergence of a new dimension of sport expertise. In G. Tenenbaum & R.C. Eklund (Eds.), *Handbook of Sport Psychology*, Vol I. (4th ed.), Wiley.

Rimmer, R. (2013). Improvising with material in the higher education dance technique class: Exploration and ownership. *Journal of Dance Education*, 13, 143-146.

Rowe, N., & Zeitner-Smith, D. (2011). Teaching creative dexterity to dancers: Critical reflections on conservatory dance education in the UK, Denmark and New Zealand. *Research in Dance Education*, 12(1), 41-52.

Runco, M.A. (2014). "Big C, Little c" creativity as a false dichotomy: Reality is not categorical. *Creativity Research Journal*, 26(1), 131-132.

Runco, M.A., & Acar, S. (2012). Divergent thinking as an indicator of creative potential. *Creativity Research Journal*, 24, 66-75.

Runco, M.A., & Jaeger, G. (2012). The standard definition of creativity. *Creativity Research Journal*, 24, 92-96.

Salosaari, P. (2001). *Multiple embodiment in classical ballet: educating the dancer as an agent of change in the cultural evolution of ballet*. Theatre Academy.

Schwab, K. (2016). What makes a principal? *Dance Magazine*, September. http://dancemagazine.com/insidedm/magazine/what-makes-aprincipal

Silvia, P.J., & Kaufman, J.C. (2010). Creativity and mental illness. In J.C. Kaufman & R.J. Sternberg (Eds.), *The Cambridge Handbook of Creativity* (pp. 381-394). Cambridge University Press.

Simonton, D.K. (2019). Creativity and psychopathology: The tenacious mad-genius controversy updated. *Current Opinion in Behavioral Sciences, 27*, 17-21.

Simonton, D.K. (2000). Creativity: Cognitive, personal, developmental, and social aspects. *American Psychologist, 55*(1), 151-158.

Smith-Autard, J.M. (2002). *The art of dance in education.* A&C Black.

Sowden, P.T., Clements, L., Redlich, C., & Lewis, C. (2015). Improvisation facilitates divergent thinking and creativity: Realizing a benefit of primary school arts education. *Psychology of Aesthetics, Creativity, and the Arts, 9*(2), 128-138.

Tharp, T. (2003). *The creative habit: Learn it and use it for life.* Simon & Schuster.

Torrents, C., Castañer, M., Dinušová, M., & Anguera, M.T. (2010). Discovering new ways of moving: Observational analysis of motor creativity while dancing contact improvisation and the influence of the partner. *The Journal of Creative Behavior, 44*(1), 53-69.

Torrents, C., Castañer, M., Dinušová, M., & Anguera, M.T. (2013). Dance divergently in physical education: Teaching using open-ended questions, metaphors and models. *Research in Dance Education, 14*(2), 104-119.

Torrents Martín, C., Ric, Á., & Hristovski, R. (2015). Creativity and emergence of specific dance movements using instructional constraints. *Psychology of Aesthetics, Creativity, and the Arts, 9*(1), 65-74.

Watson, D.E., Nordin-Bates, S.M., & Chappell, K.A. (2012). Facilitating and nurturing creativity in pre-vocational dancers: Findings from the UK Centres for Advanced Training. *Research in Dance Education, 13*(2), 153-173.

Weber, R., & Reed, S. (2020). Pedagogical perspectives on developing creativity in dance students. *Journal of Dance Education.* https://doi.org/10.1080/15290824.2020.1827147

Weidmann, C. (2018). A new dialogue in ballet pedagogy: Improving learner self-sufficiency through reflective methodology. *Journal of Dance Education, 18*(2), 55-61.

Whittier, C.J. (2017). *Creative ballet teaching: Technique and artistry for the 21st century ballet dancer.* Routledge.

Chapter 8

Baltzell, A.L. (2016). *Mindfulness and performance.* Cambridge University Press.

Baltzell, A., & Akhtar, V.L. (2014). Mindfulness meditation training for sport (MMTS) intervention: Impact of MMTS with division I female athletes. *The Journal of Happiness and Well-Being, 2*(2), 160-173.

Beccia, A.L., Dunlap, C., Hanes, D.A., Courneene, B.J., & Zwickey, H.L. (2018). Mindfulness-based eating disorder prevention programs: A systematic review and meta-analysis. *Mental Health & Prevention, 9*, 1-12.

Bernier, M., Thienot, E., Pelosse, E., & Fournier, J.F. (2014). Effects and underlying processes of a mindfulness-based intervention with young elite figure skaters: Two case studies. *The Sport Psychologist, 28*(3), 302-315.

Birrer, D., Röthlin, P., & Morgan, G. (2012). Mindfulness to enhance athletic performance: Theoretical considerations and possible impact mechanisms. *Mindfulness, 3*(3), 235-246.

Blanck, P., Perleth, S., Heidenreich, T., Kröger, P., Ditzen, B., Bents, H., & Mander, J. (2018). Effects of mindfulness exercises as stand-alone intervention on symptoms of anxiety and depression: Systematic review and meta-analysis. *Behaviour Research and Therapy, 102*, 25-35.

Blevins, P., Moyle, G., Erskine, S., & Hopper, L. (2022). Mindfulness, recovery-stress balance, and well-being among university dance students. *Research in Dance Education, 23*(1), 142-155.

Breines, J.G., & Chen, S. (2012). Self-compassion increases self-improvement motivation. *Personality and Social Psychology Bulletin, 38*(9), 1133-1143.

Caldwell, K., Adams, M., Quin, R., Harrison, M., & Greeson, J. (2013). Pilates, mindfulness and somatic education. *Journal of Dance & Somatic Practices, 5*(2), 141-153.

Chen, L.H., Wu, C.H., & Chang, J.H. (2017). Gratitude and athletes' life satisfaction: The moderating role of mindfulness. *Journal of Happiness Studies, 18*(4), 1147-1159.

Czajkowski, A.M.L., Greasley, A.E., & Allis, M. (2020). Mindfulness for musicians: A mixed methods study investigating the effects of 8-week mindfulness courses on music students at a leading conservatoire. *Musicae Scientiae.* https://doi.org/10.1177/1029864920941570

Donald, J.N., Bradshaw, E.L., Ryan, R.M., Basarkod, G., Ciarrochi, J., Duineveld, J.J., Guo, J., & Sahdra, B.K. (2020). Mindfulness and its association with varied types of motivation: A systematic review and meta-analysis using self-determination theory. *Personality and Social Psychology Bulletin, 46*(7), 1121-1138.

Gardner, F.L., & Moore, Z.E. (2017). Mindfulness-based and acceptance-based interventions in sport and performance contexts. *Current Opinion in Psychology, 16*, 180-184.

Gardner, F.L., & Moore, Z.E. (2020). Mindfulness in sport contexts. In G. Tenenbaum & R.C. Eklund (Eds.), *Handbook of Sport Psychology* Vol I. (4th ed., pp. 738-750). Wiley.

Hayes, S.C. (2004). Acceptance and commitment therapy, relational frame theory, and the third wave of behavioral and cognitive therapies. *Behavior Therapy*, 35, 639-665.

Healy, H.A., Barnes-Holmes, Y., Barnes-Holmes, D., Keogh, C., Luciano, C., & Wilson, K. (2008). An experimental test of a cognitive defusion exercise: Coping with negative and positive self-statements. *The Psychological Record*, 58(4), 623-640.

Henriksen, K., Hansen, J., & Larsen, C.H., Eds. (2019). *Mindfulness and acceptance in sport: How to help athletes perform and thrive under pressure*. Routledge.

Howells, K., & Fitzallen, N. (2020). Enhancement of gratitude in the context of elite athletes: Outcomes and challenges. *Qualitative Research in Sport, Exercise and Health*, 12(5), 781-798.

Ivarsson, A., Johnson, U., Andersen, M.B., Fallby, J., & Altemyr, M. (2015). It pays to pay attention: A mindfulness-based program for injury prevention with soccer players. *Journal of Applied Sport Psychology*, 27(3), 319-334.

Kabat-Zinn, J. (2013). *Full catastrophe living: Using the wisdom of your body and mind to face stress, pain, and illness* (revised ed.). Bantam Books.

Kaufman, K.A., Glass, C.R., & Pineau, T.R. (2018). *Mindful sport performance enhancement: Mental training for athletes and coaches*. American Psychological Association.

Kee, Y.H., Chatzisarantis, N.N., Kong, P.W., Chow, J.Y., & Chen, L.H. (2012). Mindfulness, movement control, and attentional focus strategies: Effects of mindfulness on a postural balance task. *Journal of Sport and Exercise Psychology*, 34(5), 561-579.

Langer, E., Russel, T., & Eisenkraft, N. (2009). Orchestral performance and the footprint of mindfulness. *Psychology of Music*, 37(2), 125-136.

Lattimore, P., Mead, B.R., Irwin, L., Grice, L., Carson, R., & Malinowski, P. (2017). "I can't accept that feeling": Relationships between interoceptive awareness, mindfulness and eating disorder symptoms in females with, and at-risk of an eating disorder. *Psychiatry Research*, 247, 163-171.

Lundqvist, C., Ståhl, L., Kenttä, G., & Thulin, U. (2018). Evaluation of a mindfulness intervention for Paralympic leaders prior to the Paralympic Games. *International Journal of Sports Science & Coaching*, 13(1), 62-71.

Lussier-Ley, C., & Durand-Bush, N. (2009). Exploring the role of feel in the creative experiences of modern dancers: A realist tale. *Research in Dance Education*, 10(3), 199-217.

Marich, J., & Howell, T. (2015). Dancing mindfulness: A phenomenological investigation of the emerging practice. *Explore*, 11(5), 346-356.

Moesch, K., Ivarsson, A., & Johnson, U. (2020). "Be mindful even though it hurts": A single-case study testing the effects of a mindfulness-and acceptance-based intervention on injured athletes' mental health. *Journal of Clinical Sport Psychology*, 14(4), 399-421.

Mosewich, A.D., Crocker, P.R., Kowalski, K.C., & DeLongis, A. (2013). Applying self-compassion in sport: An intervention with women athletes. *Journal of Sport and Exercise Psychology*, 35(5), 514-524.

Moyle, G.M. (2016). Mindfulness and dancers. In A.L. Baltzell (Ed.), *Mindfulness and Performance* (pp. 367-388). Cambridge University Press.

Muro, A., & Artero, N. (2017). Dance practice and well-being correlates in young women. *Women & Health*, 57(10), 1193-1203.

Naderi, A., Shaabani, F., Zandi, H.G., Calmeiro, L., & Brewer, B.W. (2020). The effects of a mindfulness-based program on the incidence of injuries in young male soccer players. *Journal of Sport and Exercise Psychology*, 42(2), 161-171.

Neff, K. (2003). Self-compassion: An alternative conceptualization of a healthy attitude toward oneself. *Self and Identity*, 2(2), 85-101.

Noetel, M., Ciarrochi, J., Van Zanden, B., & Lonsdale, C. (2019). Mindfulness and acceptance approaches to sporting performance enhancement: A systematic review. *International Review of Sport and Exercise Psychology*, 12(1), 139-175.

Nordin-Bates, S.M. & Abrahamsen, F. (2016). Perfectionism in dance: Applied considerations and a case example. In A. P. Hill (Ed.), *The Psychology of Perfectionism in Sport, Dance and Exercise* (pp. 222-244). Routledge.

Pinniger, R., Brown, R.F., Thorsteinsson, E.B., & McKinley, P. (2012). Argentine tango dance compared to mindfulness meditation and a waiting-list control: A randomised trial for treating depression. *Complementary Therapies in Medicine*, 20(6), 377-384.

Stanszus, L.S., Frank, P., & Geiger, S.M. (2019). Healthy eating and sustainable nutrition through mindfulness? Mixed method results of a controlled intervention study. *Appetite*, 141, 104325.

Stephens, J., & Hillier, S. (2020). Evidence for the effectiveness of the Feldenkrais Method. *Kinesiology Review*, 9(3), 228-235.

Toner, J., & Moran, A. (2015). Enhancing performance proficiency at the expert level: Considering the role of "somaesthetic awareness." *Psychology of Sport & Exercise*, 16, 110-117.

Urmston, E., & Hewison, J. (2014). Risk and flow in contact improvisation: Pleasure, play and presence. *Journal of Dance & Somatic Practices*, 6(2), 219-232.

Van Dam, N.T., van Vugt, M.K., Vago, D.R., Schmalzl, L., Saron, C.D., Olendzki, A., Meissner, T., Lazar, S.W., Kerr, C.E., Gorchov, J., Fox, K.C.R., Field, B.A., Britton, W.B., Brefczynski-Lewis, J.A., & Meyer, D.E. (2018). Mind the hype: A critical evaluation and prescriptive agenda for research on mindfulness and meditation. *Perspectives on Psychological Science, 13*(1), 36-61.

Wulf, G. (2016). Why did Tiger Woods shoot 82? A commentary on Toner and Moran (2015). *Psychology of Sport and Exercise, 22*, 337-338.

Chapter 9

Burton, D., & Weiss, C. (2008). The fundamental goal concept: The path to process and performance success. In T.S. Horn (Ed.), *Advances in Sport Psychology* (pp. 339-375, 470-474). Human Kinetics.

Carattini, C.M. (2020). *Psychological skills in ballet training: An approach to pedagogy for the fulfilment of student potential*. Professional doctoral thesis, Queensland University of Technology. Available at https://eprints.qut.edu.au/207087/

Castillo, E.A., & Chow, G.M. (2020). Implementation and evaluation of a performance-profile intervention with college dancers. *The Sport Psychologist, 34*(1), 1-10.

Filby, W.C., Maynard, I.W., & Graydon, J.K. (1999). The effect of multiple-goal strategies on performance outcomes in training and competition. *Journal of Applied Sport Psychology, 11*(2), 230-246.

Goffena, J.D., & Horn, T.S. (2021). The relationship between coach behavior and athlete self-regulated learning. *International Journal of Sports Science & Coaching, 16*(1), 3-15.

Henriksen, K., Haberl, P., Baltzell, A., Hansen, J., Birrer, D., & Larsen, C.H. (2019). Mindfulness and acceptance approaches: Do they have a place in elite sport? In K. Henriksen, J. Hansen & C.H. Larsen (Eds.), *Mindfulness and Acceptance in Sport* (pp. 1-16). Routledge.

Jeong, Y.H., Healy, L.C., & McEwan, D. (2021). The application of Goal Setting Theory to goal setting interventions in sport: A systematic review. *International Review of Sport and Exercise Psychology*. https://doi.org/10.1080/1750984X.2021.1901298

Kingston, K.M., & Hardy, L. (1997). Effects of different types of goals on processes that support performance. *The Sport Psychologist, 11*(3), 277-293.

Kiresuk, T.J., Smith, A., & Cardillo, J.E. (1994). *Goal Attainment Scaling: Applications, theory, and measurement*. Lawrence Erlbaum.

Kirschenbaum, D.S. (1984). Self-regulation and sport psychology: Nurturing an emerging symbiosis. *Journal of Sport Psychology, 6*(2), 159-183.

Kwasnicka, D., Ntoumanis, N., & Sniehotta, F.F. (2021). Setting performance and learning goals is useful for active and inactive individuals, if goals are personalized and flexible: Commentary on Swann et al. (2020). *Health Psychology Review, 15*(1), 51-55.

Larsen, C.H., Reinebo, G., & Lundgren, T. (2019). Helping athletes clarify their values and become grounded in their sport venture. In K. Henriksen, J. Hansen & C.H. Larsen (Eds.), *Mindfulness and Acceptance in Sport* (pp. 35-46). Routledge.

Latham, G.P., & Brown, T.C. (2006). The effect of learning vs. outcome goals on self-efficacy, satisfaction and performance in an MBA program. *Applied Psychology, 55*(4), 606-623.

Latham, G.P., & Locke, E.A. (1991). Self-regulation through goal setting. *Organizational Behavior and Human Decision Processes, 50*(2), 212-247.

Locke, E.A., & Latham, G.P. (1990). *A theory of goal setting and task performance*. Prentice Hall.

Locke, E.A., & Latham, G.P. (2019). The development of goal setting theory: A half century retrospective. *Motivation Science, 5*(2), 93-105.

Locke, E.A., Shaw, K.N., Saari, L.M., & Latham, G.P. (1981). Goal setting and task performance: 1969-1980. *Psychological Bulletin, 90*(1), 125-152.

McCardle, L., Young, B.W., & Baker, J. (2019). Self-regulated learning and expertise development in sport: Current status, challenges, and future opportunities. *International Review of Sport and Exercise Psychology, 12*(1), 112-138.

McEwan, D., Harden, S.M., Zumbo, B.D., Sylvester, B.D., Kaulius, M., Ruissen, G.R., Dowd, A.J., & Beauchamp, M.R. (2016). The effectiveness of multi-component goal setting interventions for changing physical activity behaviour: a systematic review and meta-analysis. *Health Psychology Review, 10*(1), 67-88.

Nordin, S. (2009). Setting precise aims in an imprecise world: Reflections on goal setting in dance. *Swedish Yearbook of Sport Psychology*, 61-73.

Roberts, G.C., & Kristiansen, E. (2012). Goal setting to enhance motivation in sport. In G.C. Roberts & D.C. Treasure (Eds.), *Advances in Motivation in Sport and Exercise* (3rd ed., pp. 207-228). Human Kinetics.

Swann, C., Rosenbaum, S., Lawrence, A., Vella, S.A., McEwan, D., & Ekkekakis, P. (2021). Updating goal-setting theory in physical activity promotion: A critical conceptual review. *Health Psychology Review, 15*(1), 34-50.

Taylor, J., & Estanol, E. (2015). *Dance psychology for artistic and performance excellence*. Human Kinetics.

Weinberg, R., Butt, J., Knight, B., & Perritt, N. (2001). Collegiate coaches' perceptions of their goal-setting practices: A qualitative investigation. *Journal of Applied Sport Psychology, 13*(4), 374-398.

Zimmerman, B.J. (1998). Academic studying and the development of personal skill: A self-regulatory perspective. *Educational Psychologist, 33*, 73-86.

Zimmerman, B.J. (2000). Attaining self-regulation: A social cognitive perspective. In M. Boekaerts, & P.R. Pintrich (Eds.), *Handbook of Self-Regulation* (pp. 13-39). Academic Press.

Chapter 10

Abraham, A., Dunsky, A., & Dickstein, R. (2017). The effect of motor imagery practice on elevé performance in adolescent female dance students: A randomized controlled trial. *Journal of Imagery Research in Sport and Physical Activity*, 12(1).

Abraham, A., Gose, R., Schindler, R., Nelson, B.H., & Hackney, M.E. (2019). Dynamic neuro-cognitive imagery (DNI™) improves developpé performance, kinematics, and mental imagery ability in university-level dance students. *Frontiers in Psychology*, 10, 382.

Alicia Alonso. (2021, May 25). In *Wikipedia*. Retrieved May 25, 2021, from https://en.wikipedia.org/wiki/Alicia_Alonso#cite_note-:1-4

Bandura, A. (1977). Self-efficacy: Toward a unifying theory of behaviour change. *Psychological Review*, 84, 191-215.

Batson, G., & Sentler, S. (2017). How visual and kinaesthetic imagery shape movement improvisation: A pilot study. *Journal of Dance & Somatic Practices*, 9(2), 195-212.

Bolles, G., & Chatfield, S.J. (2009). The intersection of imagery ability, imagery use, and learning style: An exploratory study. *Journal of Dance Education*, 9(1), 6-16.

Coker, E., McIsaac, T.L., & Nilsen, D. (2015). Motor imagery modality in expert dancers: An investigation of hip and pelvis kinematics in demi-plié and sauté. *Journal of Dance Medicine & Science*, 19(2), 63-69.

Couillandre, A., Lewton-Brain, P., & Portero, P. (2008). Exploring the effects of kinesiological awareness and mental imagery on movement intention in the performance of demi-plié. *Journal of Dance Medicine & Science*, 12(3), 91-98.

Cumming, J. (2008). Investigating the relationship between exercise imagery, leisure time exercise behaviour, and exercise self-efficacy. *Journal of Applied Sport Psychology*, 20, 184-198.

Cumming, J., & Williams, S.E. (2013). Introducing the revised applied model of deliberate imagery use for sport, dance, exercise, and rehabilitation. *Movement & Sport Sciences-Science & Motricité*, 82, 69-81.

Cumming, J., Cooley, S.J., Anuar, N., Kosteli, M., Quinton, M.L., Weibull, F., & Williams, S.E. (2017). Developing imagery ability effectively: A guide to layered stimulus response training. *Journal of Sport Psychology in Action*, 8, 23-33.

Franklin, E. (2014). *Dance imagery for technique and performance* (2nd ed.). Human Kinetics.

Guillot, A., & Collet, C. (2008). Construction of the motor imagery integrative model in sport: A review and theoretical investigation of motor imagery use. *International Review of Sport and Exercise Psychology*, 1(1), 31-44.

Guillot, A., Moschberger, K., & Collet, C. (2013). Coupling movement with imagery as a new perspective for motor imagery practice. *Behavioral and Brain Functions*, 9(1), 1-8.

Guss-West, C. (2020). *Attention and focus in dance: Enhancing power, precision, and artistry*. Human Kinetics.

Hanrahan, C., Tétreau, B., & Sarrazin, C. (1995). Use of imagery while performing dance movement. *International Journal of Sport Psychology*, 26(3), 413-430.

Hanrahan, C., & Vergeer, I. (2001). Multiple uses of mental imagery by professional modern dancers. *Imagination, Cognition and Personality*, 20(3), 231-255.

Hanrahan, S.J. (1996). Dancers' perceptions of psychological skills. *Revista de psicología del deporte*, 5(2), 19-27.

Heiland, T., & Rovetti, R. (2013). Examining effects of Franklin Method metaphorical and anatomical mental images on college dancers' jumping height. *Research in Dance Education*, 14(2), 141-161.

Heiland, T.L., Rovetti, R., & Dunn, J. (2012). Effects of visual, auditory, and kinesthetic imagery interventions on dancers' plié arabesques. *Journal of Imagery Research in Sport and Physical Activity*, 7(1).

Holmes, P.S., & Collins, D.J. (2001). The PETTLEP approach to motor imagery: A functional equivalence model for sport psychologists. *Journal of Applied Sport Psychology*, 13(1), 60-83.

Jeannerod, M. (2001). Neural simulation of action: A unifying mechanism for motor cognition. *NeuroImage*, 14, 103-109.

Karin, J. (2016). Recontextualizing dance skills: Overcoming impediments to motor learning and expressivity in ballet dancers. *Frontiers in Psychology*, 7, 431.

Karin, J., Haggard, P., & Christensen, J.F. (2017). Mental training. In M.V. Wilmerding & D. Krasnow (Eds.), *Dancer Wellness* (pp. 57-70). Human Kinetics.

Karin, J., & Nordin-Bates, S.M. (2020). Enhancing creativity and managing perfectionism in dancers through implicit learning and sensori-kinetic imagery. *Journal of Dance Education*, 20(1), 1-11.

Kirk, J. (2014). Experiencing our anatomy: Incorporating human biology into dance class via imagery, imagination, and somatics. *Journal of Dance Education*, 14(2), 59-66.

Klockare, E., Gustafsson, H., & Nordin-Bates, S.M. (2011). An interpretative phenomenological analysis of how professional dance teachers implement psychological skills training in practice. *Research in Dance Education*, 12(3), 277-293.

Krasnow, D., & Deveau, J. (2010). *Conditioning with imagery for dancers*. Thompson Educational.

Maddison, R., Prapavessis, H., Clatworthy, M., Hall, C., Folet, L., Harper, T., Cupal, D., & Brewer, B. (2012). Guided imagery to improve functional outcomes post-anterior cruciate ligament repair: Randomized-controlled pilot trial. *Scandinavian Journal of Medicine & Science in Sports, 22*(6), 816-821.

May, J., Calvo-Merino, B., Delahunta, S., McGregor, W., Cusack, R., Owen, A.M., Veldsman, M., Ramponi, C., & Barnard, P. (2011). Points in mental space: An interdisciplinary study of imagery in movement creation. *Dance Research, 29* (supplement), 404-432.

Muir, I.L., & Munroe-Chandler, K.J. (2017). Imagery exercises for young Highland dancers. *Journal of Dance Education, 17*(1), 21-26.

Muir, I., Munroe-Chandler, K.J., & Loughead, T. (2018). A qualitative investigation of young female dancers' use of imagery. *The Sport Psychologist, 32*(4), 263-274.

Munroe, K.J., Giacobbi, P.R., Hall, C., & Weinberg, R. (2000). The four Ws of imagery use: Where, when, why, and what. *The Sport Psychologist, 14*(2), 119-137.

Noh, Y.E., Morris, T., & Andersen, M.B. (2007). Psychological intervention programs for reduction of injury in ballet dancers. *Research in Sports Medicine, 15*(1), 13-32.

Nordin, S.M., & Cumming, J. (2005). Professional dancers describe their imagery: Where, when, what, why, and how. *The Sport Psychologist, 19*(4), 395-416.

Nordin, S.M., & Cumming, J. (2006a). Measuring the content of dancers' images development of the dance imagery questionnaire (DIQ). *Journal of Dance Medicine & Science, 10*(3-4), 85-98.

Nordin, S.M., & Cumming, J. (2006b). The development of imagery in dance: Part I. Qualitative findings from professional dancers. *Journal of Dance Medicine & Science, 10*(1-2), 21-27.

Nordin, S.M., & Cumming, J. (2006c). The development of imagery in dance: Part II. Quantitative findings from a mixed sample of dancers. *Journal of Dance Medicine & Science, 10*(1-2), 28-34.

Nordin, S.M., & Cumming, J. (2007). Where, when, and how: A quantitative account of dance imagery. *Research Quarterly for Exercise and Sport, 78*(4), 390-395.

Nordin-Bates, S.M., Cumming, J., Aways, D., & Sharp, L. (2011a). Imagining yourself dancing to perfection? Correlates of perfectionism among ballet and contemporary dancers. *Journal of Clinical Sport Psychology, 5*(1), 58-76.

Nordin-Bates, S.M., Walker, I.J., Baker, J., Garner, J., Hardy, C., Irvine, S., Jola, C., Laws, H., & Blevins, P. (2011b). Injury, imagery, and self-esteem in dance: Healthy minds in injured bodies? *Journal of Dance Medicine & Science, 15*(2), 76-85.

Olshansky, M.P., Bar, R.J., Fogarty, M., & DeSouza, J.F. (2015). Supplementary motor area and primary auditory cortex activation in an expert break-dancer during the kinesthetic motor imagery of dance to music. *Neurocase, 21*(5), 607-617.

Overby, L.Y., & Dunn, J. (2011). The history and research of dance imagery: Implications for teachers. *The IADMS Bulletin for Teachers, 3*(2), 9-11.

Paris-Alemany, A., La Touche, R., Agudo-Carmona, D., Fernández-Carnero, J., Gadea-Mateos, L., Suso-Martí, L., & Cuenca-Martínez, F. (2019). Visual motor imagery predominance in professional Spanish dancers. *Somatosensory & Motor Research, 36*(3), 179-188.

Pavlik, K., & Nordin-Bates, S. (2016). Imagery in dance: A literature review. *Journal of Dance Medicine & Science, 20*(2), 51-63.

Ritchie, A., & Brooker, F. (2018). Imaging the future: An autoethnographic journey of using a guided and cognitive-specific imagery intervention in undergraduate release-based contemporary dance technique. *Research in Dance Education, 19*(2), 167-182.

Sacha, T.J., & Russ, S.W. (2006). Effects of pretend imagery on learning dance in preschool children. *Early Childhood Education Journal, 33*(5), 341-345.

Schuster, C., Hilfiker, R., Amft, O., Scheidhauer, A., Andrews, B., Butler, J., Kischka, U., & Ettlin, T. (2011). Best practice for motor imagery: A systematic literature review on motor imagery training elements in five different disciplines. *BMC medicine, 9*(1), 1-35.

Simonsmeier, B.A., Androniea, M., Buecker, S., & Frank, C. (2021). The effects of imagery interventions in sports: A meta-analysis. *International Review of Sport and Exercise Psychology, 14*(1), 186-207.

Sweigard, L. (1978). *Human movement potential: Its ideokinetic facilitation.* Dodd Mead.

Torrents, C., Castañer, M., Dinušová, M., & Anguera, M.T. (2013). Dance divergently in physical education: Teaching using open-ended questions, metaphors and models. *Research in Dance Education, 14*, 104-119.

Toth, A.J., McNeill, E., Hayes, K., Moran, A.P., & Campbell, M. (2020). Does mental practice still enhance performance? A 24 year follow-up and meta-analytic replication and extension. *Psychology of Sport and Exercise, 48*, 101672.

Wakefield, C., Smith, D., Moran, A.P., & Holmes, P. (2013). Functional equivalence or behavioural matching? A critical reflection on 15 years of research using the PETTLEP model of motor imagery. *International Review of Sport and Exercise Psychology, 6*(1), 105-121.

Williams, S.E., Cooley, S.J., Newell, E., Weibull, F., & Cumming, J. (2013). Seeing the difference: Developing effective imagery scripts for athletes. *Journal of Sport Psychology in Action, 4*(2), 109-121.

Williams, S.E., Cumming, J., & Edwards, M.G. (2011). The functional equivalence between movement imagery, observation, and execution influences imagery ability. *Research Quarterly for Exercise and Sport, 82*, 555-564.

Wilson, C., Smith, D., Burden, A., & Holmes, P. (2010). Participant-generated imagery scripts produce greater EMG activity and imagery ability. *European Journal of Sport Science, 10*(6), 417-425.

Chapter 11

Aalten, A. (2005). "We dance, we don't live." Biographical research in dance studies. *Discourses in Dance, 3*(1), 5-19.

Ames, C. (1992). Achievement goals and the classroom motivational climate. In J. Meece & D. Schunk (Eds.), *Students' perceptions in the classroom: Causes and consequences* (pp. 327-48). Erlbaum.

Alterowitz, G. (2014). Toward a feminist ballet pedagogy: Teaching strategies for ballet technique classes in the twenty-first century. *Journal of Dance Education, 14*(1), 8-17.

Andrzejewski, C.E., Wilson, A.M., & Henry, D.J. (2013). Considering motivation, goals, and mastery orientation in dance technique. *Research in Dance Education, 14*(2), 162-175.

Assor, A., Kaplan, H., & Roth, G. (2002). Choice is good, but relevance is excellent: Autonomy-enhancing and suppressing teacher behaviours predicting students' engagement in schoolwork. *British Journal of Educational Psychology, 72*(2), 261-278.

Aujla, I.J., Nordin-Bates, S.M., & Redding, E. (2014). A qualitative investigation of commitment to dance: Findings from the UK Centres for Advanced Training. *Research in Dance Education, 15*(2), 138-160.

Aujla, I.J., Nordin-Bates, S.M., & Redding, E. (2015). Multidisciplinary predictors of adherence to contemporary dance training: Findings from the UK Centres for Advanced Training. *Journal of Sports Sciences, 33*(15), 1564-1573.

Balaguer, I., Castillo, I., Duda, J.L., Quested, E., & Morales, V. (2011). Predictores socio-contextuales y motivacionales de la intención de continuar participando: Un análisis desde la SDT en danza. [Social-contextual and motivational predictors of intentions to continue participation: A test of SDT in dance]. *RICYDE. Revista internacional de ciencias del deporte, 7*(25), 305-319.

Barr, S., & Oliver, W. (2016). Feminist pedagogy, body image, and the dance technique class. *Research in Dance Education, 17*(2), 97-112.

Bartholomew, K.J., Ntoumanis, N., & Thøgersen-Ntoumani, C. (2009). A review of controlling motivational strategies from a self-determination theory perspective: Implications for sports coaches. *International Review of Sport and Exercise Psychology, 2*(2), 215-233.

Bartholomew, K.J., Ntoumanis, N., & Thøgersen-Ntoumani, C. (2010). The controlling interpersonal style in a coaching context: Development and initial validation of a psychometric scale. *Journal of Sport and Exercise Psychology, 32*(2), 193-216.

Bartholomew, K.J., Ntoumanis, N., Ryan, R.M., & Thøgersen-Ntoumani, C. (2011). Psychological need thwarting in the sport context: Assessing the darker side of athletic experience. *Journal of Sport and Exercise Psychology, 33*(1), 75-102.

Berg, T. (2017). Ballet as somatic practice: A case study exploring the integration of somatic practices in ballet pedagogy. *Journal of Dance Education, 17*(4), 147-157.

Burnidge, A. (2012). Somatics in the dance studio: Embodying feminist/democratic pedagogy. *Journal of Dance Education, 12*(2), 37-47.

Carr, S., & Wyon, M. (2003). The impact of motivational climate on dance students' achievement goals, trait anxiety, and perfectionism. *Journal of Dance Medicine & Science, 7*(4), 105-114.

Cecchini, J.A., Fernandez-Rio, J., Mendez-Gimenez, A., Cecchini, C., & Martins, L. (2014). Epstein's TARGET framework and motivational climate in sport: Effects of a field-based, long-term intervention program. *International Journal of Sports Science & Coaching, 9*(6), 1325-1340.

Choi, E., & Kim, N.Y. (2015). Whole ballet education: Exploring direct and indirect teaching methods. *Research in Dance Education, 16*(2), 142-160.

Clements, L., & Nordin-Bates, S.M. (2022). Inspired or inhibited? Choreographers' views on how classical ballet training shaped their creativity. *Journal of Dance Education, 22*(1), 1-12.

Csikszentmihalyi, M. (1990). *Flow: The psychology of optimal experience* (Vol. 1990). Harper & Row.

de Bruin, A.K., Bakker, F.C., & Oudejans, R.R. (2009). Achievement goal theory and disordered eating: Relationships of disordered eating with goal orientations and motivational climate in female gymnasts and dancers. *Psychology of Sport and Exercise, 10*(1), 72-79.

Deci, E.L., & Ryan, R.M. (1985). *Intrinsic motivation and self-determination in human behavior*. Plenum.

Deci, E.L., & Ryan, R.M. (2000). The "what" and "why" of goal pursuits: Human needs and the self-determination of behavior. *Psychological Inquiry, 11*(4), 227-268.

Draugelis, S., Martin, J., & Garn, A. (2014). Psychosocial predictors of well-being in collegiate dancers. *The Sport Psychologist, 28*(1), 1-9.

Duda, J.L. (2013). The conceptual and empirical foundations of Empowering Coaching™: Setting the stage for the PAPA project. *International Journal of Sport and Exercise Psychology, 11*(4), 311-318.

Epstein, J. (1989). Family structures and student motivation: A developmental perspective. *Research on Motivation in Education, 3*, 259-295.

Green, J. (2003). Foucault and the training of docile bodies in dance education. *Arts and Learning Research Journal*, 19(1), 99-125.

Hamilton, L.H., & Stricker, G. (1989). Balanchine's children. *Medical Problems of Performing Artists*, 4(4), 143.

Hancox, J.E., Quested, E., & Duda, J.L. (2015). Suitability of the Perceived Motivational Climate in Sport Questionnaire-2 for dance research: A think aloud approach. *Journal of Dance Medicine & Science*, 19(4), 149-162.

Hancox, J.E., Quested, E., Ntoumanis, N., & Duda, J.L. (2017). Teacher-created social environment, basic psychological needs, and dancers' affective states during class: A diary study. *Personality and Individual Differences*, 115, 137-143.

Haraldsen, H.M., Halvari, H., Solstad, B.E., Abrahamsen, F.E., & Nordin-Bates, S.M. (2019). The role of perfectionism and controlling conditions in Norwegian elite junior performers' motivational processes. *Frontiers in Psychology*, 10, 1366.

Haraldsen, H.M., Nordin-Bates, S.M., Abrahamsen, F.E., & Halvari, H. (2020). Thriving, striving, or just surviving? TD learning conditions, motivational processes and well-being among Norwegian elite performers in music, ballet, and sport. *Roeper Review*, 42(2), 109-125.

Harter, N.M., Cardozo, P.L., & Chiviacowsky, S. (2019). Conceptions of ability influence the learning of a dance pirouette in children. *Journal of Dance Medicine & Science*, 23(4), 167-172.

Harwood, C.G., Keegan, R.J., Smith, J.M., & Raine, A.S. (2015). A systematic review of the intrapersonal correlates of motivational climate perceptions in sport and physical activity. *Psychology of Sport and Exercise*, 18, 9-25.

Johnston, D. (2006). Private speech in ballet. *Research in Dance Education*, 7(1), 3-14.

Jowett, G.E., Hill, A.P., Curran, T., Hall, H.K., & Clements, L. (2021). Perfectionism, burnout, and engagement in dance: The moderating role of autonomy support. *Sport, Exercise, and Performance Psychology*, 10(1), 133-148.

Keegan, R.J. (2018). Achievement goals in sport and physical activity. In T.S. Horn and A.L. Smith (Eds.), *Advances in sport and exercise psychology* (4th ed., pp. 265-287). Human Kinetics.

Lakes, R. (2005). The messages behind the methods: The authoritarian pedagogical legacy in Western concert dance technique training and rehearsals. *Arts Education Policy Review*, 106(5), 3-20.

Le Bars, H., Gernigon, C., & Ninot, G. (2009). Personal and contextual determinants of elite young athletes' persistence or dropping out over time. *Scandinavian Journal of Medicine & Science in Sports*, 19(2), 274-285.

Louis, M. (1980). *Inside Dance*. St. Martin's.

Matosic, D., Ntoumanis, N., & Quested, E. (2016). Antecedents of need supportive and controlling interpersonal styles from a self-determination theory perspective: A review and implications for sport psychology research. *Sport and Exercise Psychology Research*, 145-180.

Matosic, D., Ntoumanis, N., Boardley, I.D., Sedikides, C., Stewart, B.D., & Chatzisarantis, N. (2017). Narcissism and coach interpersonal style: A self-determination theory perspective. *Scandinavian Journal of Medicine & Science in Sports*, 27(2), 254-261.

Morbée, S., Vansteenkiste, M., Aelterman, N., & Haerens, L. (2020). Why do sport coaches adopt a controlling coaching style? The role of an evaluative context and psychological need frustration. *The Sport Psychologist*, 34(2), 89-98.

Morris, G. (2003). Problems with ballet: Steps, style and training. *Research in Dance Education*, 4(1), 17-30.

Newton, M., Duda, J.L., & Yin, Z. (2000). Examination of the psychometric properties of the Perceived Motivational Climate in Sport Questionnaire-2 in a sample of female athletes. *Journal of Sport Sciences*, 18, 275-290.

Nicholls, J.G. (1984). Achievement motivation: Conceptions of ability, subjective experience, task choice, and performance. *Psychological Review*, 91(3), 328-346.

Nicholls, J.G. (1989). *The competitive ethos and democratic education*. Harvard University Press.

Noh, Y.E., Morris, T., & Andersen, M.B. (2009). Occupational stress and coping strategies of professional ballet dancers in Korea. *Medical Problems of Performing Artists*, 24(3), 124-134.

Nordin-Bates, S.M. (2020). Striving for perfection or for creativity? A dancer's dilemma. *Journal of Dance Education*, 20(1), 23-34.

Nordin-Bates, S.M. & Abrahamsen, F. (2016). Perfectionism in dance: Applied considerations and a case example. In A.P. Hill (Ed.), *The Psychology of Perfectionism in Sport, Dance and Exercise* (pp. 222-244). Routledge.

Nordin-Bates, S.M., & Jowett, G. (2022). Relationships between perfectionism, stress, and basic need support provision in dance teachers and aesthetic sport coaches. *Journal of Dance Medicine and Science*, 26(1), 25-33.

Nordin-Bates, S.M., Hill, A.P., Cumming, J., Aujla, I.J., & Redding, E. (2014). A longitudinal examination of the relationship between perfectionism and motivational climate in dance. *Journal of Sport and Exercise Psychology*, 36, 382-391.

Nordin-Bates, S.M., Quested, E., Walker, I.J., & Redding, E. (2012). Climate change in the dance studio: Findings from the UK Centres for Advanced Training. *Sport, Exercise, and Performance Psychology*, 1(1), 3-16.

Nordin-Bates, S.M., Schwarz, J.F.A., Quested, E., Cumming, J., Aujla, I.J., & Redding, E. (2016). Within- and between-person predictors of disordered eating attitudes in dance: Findings from the UK Centres for Advanced Training. *Psychology of Sport and Exercise, 27*, 101-111.

Norfield, J. & Nordin-Bates, S. (2012). How community dance leads to positive outcomes: A self-determination theory perspective. *Journal of Applied Arts & Health, 2*(3), 257-272.

Ntoumanis, N., Quested, E., & Sivaramakrishnan, H. (in press). Need supportive, thwarting and indifferent interpersonal styles: A 3 × 3 conceptual framework based on self-determination theory. In L. Davis, R. Keegan, & S. Jowett, (Eds.), *Social psychology in sport* (2nd ed). Human Kinetics.

Ommundsen, Y. (2001). Students' implicit theories of ability in physical education classes: The influence of motivational aspects of the learning environment. *Learning Environments Research, 4*(2), 139-158.

Pensgaard, A.M., & Roberts, G.C. (2002). Elite athletes' experiences of the motivational climate: The coach matters. *Scandinavian Journal of Medicine & Science in Sports, 12*(1), 54-59.

Pickard, A. (2015). *Ballet body narratives: Pain, pleasure and perfection in embodied identity*. Peter Lang.

Quested, E., & Duda, J.L. (2009). Perceptions of the motivational climate, need satisfaction, and indices of well -and ill-being among hip hop dancers. *Journal of Dance Medicine & Science, 13*(1), 10-19.

Quested, E., & Duda, J.L. (2010). Exploring the social-environmental determinants of well -and ill-being in dancers: A test of basic needs theory. *Journal of Sport and Exercise Psychology, 32*(1), 39-60.

Quested, E., & Duda, J.L. (2011a). Antecedents of burnout among elite dancers: A longitudinal test of basic needs theory. *Psychology of Sport and Exercise, 12*(2), 159-167.

Quested, E., & Duda, J.L. (2011b). Perceived autonomy support, motivation regulations and the self-evaluative tendencies of student dancers. *Journal of Dance Medicine & Science, 15*(1), 3-14.

Rafferty, S., & Wyon, M. (2006). Leadership behavior in dance application of the leadership scale for sports to dance technique teaching. *Journal of Dance Medicine & Science, 10*(1-2), 6-13.

Ritchie, A., & Brooker, F. (2020). Democratic and feminist pedagogy in the ballet technique class: Using a somatic imagery tool to support learning and teaching of ballet in higher education. *Journal of Dance Education, 20*(4), 197-204.

Roberts, G.C. (1993). Motivation in sport: Understanding and enhancing the motivation and achievement of children. In R.N. Singer, M. Murphey, & L.K. Tennant (Eds.), *Handbook of research on sport psychology* (pp. 405-420). Macmillan.

Roberts, G.C., Treasure, D.C., & Kavussanu, M. (1996). Orthogonality of achievement goals and its relationship to beliefs about success and satisfaction in sport. *The Sport Psychologist, 10*(4), 398-408.

Rocchi, M., & Pelletier, L.G. (2017). The antecedents of coaches' interpersonal behaviors: The role of the coaching context, coaches' psychological needs, and coaches' motivation. *Journal of Sport and Exercise Psychology, 39*(5), 366-378.

Rowe, N., & Xiong, X. (2020). Cut-paste-repeat? The maintenance of authoritarian pedagogies through tertiary dance education in China. *Theatre, Dance and Performance Training*, 1-17.

Ryan, R.M., & Deci, E.L. (2000). Self-determination theory and the facilitation of intrinsic motivation, social development, and well-being. *American Psychologist, 55*(1), 68.

Salosaari, P. (2001). *Multiple embodiment in classical ballet: Educating the dancer as an agent of change in the cultural evolution of ballet*. Theatre Academy.

Shilcutt, J.B., Oliver, K.L., & Aranda, R. (2020). "I Wish Dance Class NEVER Ended": An activist approach to teaching dance. *Journal of Dance Education*. https://doi.org/10.1080/15290824.2020.1791337

Smith, C. (1998). On authoritarianism in the dance classroom. In S. Shapiro (Ed.), *Dance, power and difference* (pp. 123-148). Human Kinetics.

Solstad, B.E., van Hoye, A., & Ommundsen, Y. (2015). Social-contextual and intrapersonal antecedents of coaches' basic need satisfaction: The intervening variable effect of providing autonomy-supportive coaching. *Psychology of Sport and Exercise, 20*, 84-93.

Standage, M., Curran, T., & Rouse, P.C. (2018). Self-determination-based theories of sport, exercise, and physical activity motivation. In T.S. Horn & A.L. Smith (Eds.), *Advances in sport and exercise psychology* (pp. 289-312). Human Kinetics.

Stark, A., & Newton, M. (2014). A dancer's well-being: The influence of the social psychological climate during adolescence. *Psychology of Sport and Exercise, 15*(4), 356-363.

Teixeira, P.J., Marques, M.M., Silva, M.N., Brunet, J., Duda, J.L., Haerens, L., La Guardia, J., Lindwall, M., Lonsdale, C., Markland, D., Michie, S., Moller, A.C., Ntoumanis, N., Patrick, H., Reeve, J., Ryan, R.M., Sebire, S.J., Standage, M., Vansteenkiste, M., . . . & Hagger, M.S. (2020). A classification of motivation and behavior change techniques used in self-determination theory-based interventions in health contexts. *Motivation Science, 6*(4), 438.

van Rossum, J.H. (2001). Talented in dance: The Bloom stage model revisited in the personal histories of dance students. *High Ability Studies, 12*(2), 181-197.

van Rossum, J.H. (2004). The dance teacher: The ideal case and daily reality. *Journal for the Education of the Gifted*, 28(1), 36-55.

Walker, I.J., Nordin-Bates, S.M., & Redding, E. (2011). Characteristics of talented dancers and age group differences: Findings from the UK Centres for Advanced Training. *High Ability Studies*, 22(1), 43-60.

Walker, I.J., Nordin-Bates, S.M., & Redding, E. (2012). A mixed methods investigation of dropout among talented young dancers: Findings from the UK Centres for Advanced Training. *Journal of Dance Medicine & Science*, 16(2), 65-73.

Watson, D.E., Nordin-Bates, S.M., & Chappell, K.A. (2012). Facilitating and nurturing creativity in pre-vocational dancers: Findings from the UK Centres for Advanced Training. *Research in Dance Education*, 13(2), 153-173.

Whittier, C. (2017). *Creative ballet teaching: Technique and artistry for the 21st century ballet dancer*. Routledge.

Zeller, J. (2017). Reflective practice in the ballet class: Bringing progressive pedagogy to the classical tradition. *Journal of Dance Education*, 17(3), 99-105.

Chapter 12

Abbott, A., & Collins, D. (2004). Eliminating the dichotomy between theory and practice in talent identification and development: Considering the role of psychology. *Journal of Sports Sciences*, 22(5), 395-408.

Aujla, I., & Farrer, R. (2015). The role of psychological factors in the career of the independent dancer. *Frontiers in Psychology*, 6, 1688.

Aujla, I.J., Nordin-Bates, S., & Redding, E. (2014). A qualitative investigation of commitment to dance: Findings from the UK Centres for Advanced Training. *Research in Dance Education*, 15(2), 138-160.

Aujla, I.J., Nordin-Bates, S.M., & Redding, E. (2015). Multidisciplinary predictors of adherence to contemporary dance training: Findings from the UK Centres for Advanced Training. *Journal of Sports Sciences*, 33(15), 1564-1573.

Aujla, I.J., & Redding, E. (2014). The identification and development of talented young dancers with disabilities. *Research in Dance Education*, 15(1), 54-70.

Bailey, A., & MacMahon, C. (2018). Exploring talent identification and recruitment at circus arts training and performance organizations. *High Ability Studies*, 29(2), 213-240.

Baker, J., Cobley, S., Schorer, J., & Wattie, N. (2017). Talent identification and development in sport: An introduction. In J. Baker, S. Cobley, J. Schorer, & N. Wattie (Eds.), *Routledge handbook of talent identification and development in sport* (pp. 1-8). Routledge.

Baker, J., & Horton, S. (2004). A review of primary and secondary influences on sport expertise. *High Ability Studies*, 15(2), 211-228.

Baker, J., Janning, C., Wong, H., Cobley, S., & Schorer, J. (2014). Variations in relative age effects in individual sports: Skiing, figure skating and gymnastics. *European Journal of Sport Science*, 14(sup1), S183-S190.

Baker, J., Schorer, J., & Wattie, N. (2018). Compromising talent: Issues in identifying and selecting talent in sport. *Quest*, 70(1), 48-63.

Baker, J., Wattie, N., & Schorer, J. (2019). A proposed conceptualization of talent in sport: The first step in a long and winding road. *Psychology of Sport and Exercise*, 43, 27-33.

Baker, J., & Young, B. (2014). 20 years later: Deliberate practice and the development of expertise in sport. *International Review of Sport and Exercise Psychology*, 7(1), 135-157.

Baum, S.M., Owen, S.V., & Oreck, B.A. (1996). Talent beyond words: Identification of potential talent in dance and music in elementary students. *Gifted Child Quarterly*, 40(2), 93-101.

Blijlevens, S.J., Elferink-Gemser, M.T., Wylleman, P., Bool, K., & Visscher, C. (2018). Psychological characteristics and skills of top-level Dutch gymnasts in the initiation, development and mastery stages of the athletic career. *Psychology of Sport and Exercise*, 38, 202-210.

Chua, J. (2014a). Dance talent development across the lifespan: A review of current research. *Research in Dance Education*, 15(1), 23-53.

Chua, J. (2014b). Dance talent development: Case studies of successful dancers in Finland and Singapore. *Roeper Review*, 36(4), 249-263.

Chua, J. (2015). The role of social support in dance talent development. *Journal for the Education of the Gifted*, 38(2), 169-195.

Clements, L., & Nordin-Bates, S.M. (2022). Inspired or inhibited? Choreographers' views on how classical ballet training shaped their creativity. *Journal of Dance Education*, 22(1), 1-12.

Collins, D., & MacNamara, Á. (2017). A smooth sea never made a skilful sailor: Optimizing and exploiting the rocky road in talent development. In J. Baker, S. Cobley, J. Schorer, & N. Wattie (Eds.), *Routledge handbook of talent identification and development in sport* (pp. 336-346). Routledge.

Colvin, G. (2008). *Talent is overrated: What really separates world-class performers from everybody else*. Portfolio.

Côté, J., Baker, J., & Abernethy, B. (2007). Practice and play in the development of sport expertise. In G. Tenenbaum & R.C. Eklund (Eds.), *Handbook of sport psychology* (3rd ed., pp. 184-202). Wiley.

Critien, N., & Ollis, S. (2006). Multiple engagement of self in the development of talent in professional dancers. *Research in Dance Education*, 7(2), 179-200.

Daprati, E., Iosa, M., & Haggard, P. (2009). A dance to the music of time: Aesthetically-relevant changes in body posture in performing art. *PLoS One, 4*(3), e5023.

Deakin, J.M., & Cobley, S. (2003). An examination of the practice environments in figure skating and volleyball: A search for deliberate practice. In J. Starkes & K.A. Ericsson (Eds.), *Expert performance in sports: Advances in research on sport expertise* (pp. 90-113). Human Kinetics.

Dohme, L.C., Piggott, D., Backhouse, S., & Morgan, G. (2019). Psychological skills and characteristics facilitative of youth athletes' development: A systematic review. *The Sport Psychologist, 33*(4), 261-275.

Downing, C., Redelius, K., & Nordin-Bates, S.M. (2020). An index approach to early specialization measurement: An exploratory study. *Frontiers in Psychology.* https://doi.org/10.3389/fpsyg.2020.00999

Downing, C., Redelius, K., & Nordin-Bates, S. (2021). Early specialisation among Swedish aesthetic performers: Exploring motivation and perceptions of parental influence. *International Journal of Sport and Exercise Psychology.* https://doi.org/10.1080/1612197X.2021.1940239

Dweck, C. (2017). *Mindset-updated edition: Changing the way you think to fulfil your potential.* Hachette UK. (Original work published 2006).

Ericsson, K.A., Krampe, R.T., & Tesch-Römer, C. (1993). The role of deliberate practice in the acquisition of expert performance. *Psychological Review, 100,* 363-406.

Erikstad, M.K., Johansen, B.T., Johnsen, M., Haugen, T., & Côté, J. (2021). "As many as possible for as long as possible"—A case study of a soccer team that fosters multiple outcomes. *The Sport Psychologist, 35*(2), 131-141.

Gladwell, M. (2008). *Outliers: The story of success.* Little, Brown & Company.

Güllich, A., & Cobley, S. (2017). On the efficacy of talent identification and talent development programmes. In J. Baker, S. Cobley, J. Schorer, & N. Wattie (Eds.), *Routledge handbook of talent identification and development in sport* (pp. 80-98). Routledge.

Güllich, A., Macnamara, B.N., & Hambrick, D.Z. (2021). What makes a champion? Early multidisciplinary practice, not early specialization, predicts world-class performance. *Perspectives on Psychological Science.* https://doi.org/10.1177/1745691620974772

Hamilton, L.H., Hamilton, W.G., Warren, M.P., Keller, K., & Molnar, M. (1997). Factors contributing to the attrition rate in elite ballet students. *Journal of Dance Medicine & Science, 1*(4), 131-138.

Hancock, D.J., Starkes, J.L., & Ste-Marie, D.M. (2015). The relative age effect in female gymnastics: A flip-flop phenomenon. *International Journal of Sport Psychology, 46*(6), 714-725.

Haroutounian, J. (1995). Talent identification and development in the arts: An artistic/ educational dialogue. *Roeper Review, 18*(2), 112-117.

Harter, N.M., Cardozo, P.L., & Chiviacowsky, S. (2019). Conceptions of ability influence the learning of a dance pirouette in children. *Journal of Dance Medicine & Science, 23*(4), 167-172

Henriksen, K., & Stambulova, N. (2017). Creating optimal environments for talent development: A holistic ecological approach. In J. Baker, S. Cobley, J. Schorer, & N. Wattie (Eds.), *Routledge handbook of talent identification and development in sport* (pp. 270-284). Routledge.

Horn, T.S., Lox, C.L., & Labrador, F. (2001). The self-fulfilling prophecy theory: When coaches' expectations become reality. In J.M. Williams (Ed.), *Applied sport psychology: Personal growth to peak performance* (4th ed., pp. 63-81). McGraw-Hill.

Hutchinson, C.U., Sachs-Ericsson, N., & Ericsson, K.A. (2013). Generalizable aspects of the development of expertise in ballet across countries and cultures: A perspective from the expert performance approach. *High Ability Studies, 24,* 21-47.

Kliethermes, S.A., Marshall, S.W., LaBella, C.R., Watson, A.M., Brenner, J.S., Nagle, K.B., Jayanthi, N., Brooks, M.A., Tenforde, A.S., Herman, D.C., DiFiori, J.P., & Beutler, A.I. (2021). Defining a research agenda for youth sport specialisation in the USA: The AMSSM Youth Early Sport Specialization Summit. *British Journal of Sports Medicine, 55*(3), 135-143.

LaPrade, R.F., Agel, J., Baker, J., Brenner, J.S., Cordasco, F.A., Côté, J., Engebretsen, L., Feeley, B.T., Gould, D., Hainline, B., Hewett, T., Jayanthi, N., Kocher, M.S., Myer, G.D., Nissen, C.W., Philippon, M.J., & Provencher, M.T. (2016). AOSSM early sport specialization consensus statement. *Orthopaedic Journal of Sports Medicine, 4*(4). https://doi.org/10.1177/2325967116644241

Langham-Walsh, E., Gottwald, V., & Hardy, J. (2021). Relative age effect? No "flipping" way! Apparatus dependent inverse relative age effects in elite, women's artistic gymnastics. *PloS One, 16*(6), e0253656.

Malina, R.M., Cumming, S.P., Coelho-e-Silva, M.J., & Figueiredo, A.J. (2017). Talent identification and development in the context of "growing up." In J. Baker, S. Cobley, J. Schorer, & N. Wattie (Eds.), *Routledge handbook of talent identification and development in sport* (pp. 150-168). Routledge.

Mitchell, S.B., Haase, A.M., Malina, R.M., & Cumming, S.P. (2016). The role of puberty in the making and breaking of young ballet dancers: Perspectives of dance teachers. *Journal of Adolescence, 47,* 81-89.

Mitchell, S.B., Haase, A.M., & Cumming, S.P. (2022). On-time maturation in female adolescent ballet dancers: Learning from lived experiences. *The Journal of Early Adolescence, 42*(2), 262-290.

Olszewski-Kubilius, P., Subotnik, R.F., Davis, L.C., & Worrell, F.C. (2019). Benchmarking psychosocial skills important for talent development. *New Directions for Child and Adolescent Development, 2019*(168), 161-176.

Oreck, B., Owen, S., & Baum, S. (2004). Validity, reliability and equity issues in an observational talent assessment process in the performing arts. *Journal for the Education of the Gifted*, *27*(2), 62-94.

Pickard, A. (2012). Schooling the dancer: The evolution of an identity as a ballet dancer. *Research in Dance Education*, *13*(1), 25-46.

Pickard, A. (2013). Ballet body belief: Perceptions of an ideal ballet body from young ballet dancers. *Research in Dance Education*, *14*(1), 3-19.

Pickard, A., & Bailey, R. (2009). Crystallising experiences among young elite dancers. *Sport, Education and Society*, *14*(2), 165-181.

Redding, E., Nordin-Bates, S., & Aujla, I. (2011). *Passion, pathways and potential in dance: An interdisciplinary study into dance talent development*. Trinity Laban Conservatoire of Music and Dance. Available at https://www.trinitylaban.ac.uk/study/dance/dance-science/dance-science-research/talent-development-the-cat-project/

Ross, A., & Shapiro, J. (2017). Under the big top: An exploratory analysis of psychological factors influencing circus performers. *Performance Enhancement & Health*, *5*(3), 115-121.

Sanchez, E.N., Aujla, I.J., & Nordin-Bates, S. (2013). Cultural background variables in dance talent development: Findings from the UK Centres for Advanced Training. *Research in Dance Education*, *14*(3), 260-278.

Sieghartsleitner, R., Zuber, C., Zibung, M., & Conzelmann, A. (2018). "The early specialised bird catches the worm!"—A specialised sampling model in the development of football talents. *Frontiers in Psychology*, *9*, 188.

Speirs Neumeister, K.L., Williams, K.K., & Cross, T.L. (2009). Gifted high-school students' perspectives on the development of perfectionism. *Roeper Review*, *31*(4), 198-206.

Simonton, D.K. (2017). Does talent exist? Yes! In J. Baker, S. Cobley, J. Schorer, & N. Wattie (Eds.), *Routledge handbook of talent identification and development in sport* (pp. 10-18). Routledge.

Vaeyens, R., Lenoir, M., Williams, A.M., & Philippaerts, R.M. (2008). Talent identification and development programmes in sport. *Sports Medicine*, *38*(9), 703-714.

van Rossum, J.H. (2001). Talented in dance: The Bloom stage model revisited in the personal histories of dance students. *High Ability Studies*, *12*(2), 181-197.

van Rossum, J.H. (2006). Relative age effect revisited: Findings from the dance domain. *Perceptual and Motor Skills*, *102*(2), 302-308.

Vink, K., Raudsepp, L., & Kais, K. (2015). Intrinsic motivation and individual deliberate practice are reciprocally related: Evidence from a longitudinal study of adolescent team sport athletes. *Psychology of Sport and Exercise*, *16*, 1-6.

Vestheim, O.P., Husby, M., Aune, T.K., Bjerkeset, O., & Dalen, T. (2019). A population study of relative age effects on national tests in reading literacy. *Frontiers in Psychology*, *10*, 1761.

Waldron, S., DeFreese, J.D., Register-Mihalik, J., Pietrosimone, B., & Barczak, N. (2020). The costs and benefits of early sport specialization: A critical review of literature. *Quest*, *72*(1), 1-18.

Walker, I.J., Nordin-Bates, S.M., & Redding, E. (2010). Talent identification and development in dance: A review of the literature. *Research in Dance Education*, *11*(3), 167-191.

Walker, I.J., Nordin-Bates, S.M., & Redding, E. (2012). A mixed methods investigation of dropout among talented young dancers: Findings from the UK Centres for Advanced Training. *Journal of Dance Medicine & Science*, *16*(2), 65-73.

Warburton, E.C. (2002). From talent identification to multidimensional assessment: Toward new models of evaluation in dance education. *Research in Dance Education*, *3*(2), 103-121.

Ward, P., Belling, P., Petushek, E., & Ehrlinger, J. (2017). Does talent exist? A re-evaluation of the nature-nurture debate. In J. Baker, S. Cobley, J. Schorer, & N. Wattie (Eds.), *Routledge handbook of talent identification and development in sport* (pp. 19-34). Routledge.

Watson, D.E., Nordin-Bates, S.M., & Chappell, K.A. (2012). Facilitating and nurturing creativity in pre-vocational dancers: Findings from the UK Centres for Advanced Training. *Research in Dance Education*, *13*(2), 153-173.

Wattie, N., & Baker, J. (2017). Why conceptualizations of talent matter: Implications for skill acquisition and talent identification and development. In J. Baker, S. Cobley, J. Schorer, & N. Wattie (Eds.), *Routledge handbook of talent identification and development in sport* (pp. 69-79). Routledge.

Weissensteiner, J.R. (2017). How contemporary international perspectives have consolidated a best-practice approach for identifying and developing sporting talent. In J. Baker, S. Cobley, J. Schorer, & N. Wattie (Eds.), *Routledge handbook of talent identification and development in sport* (pp. 51-68). Routledge.

Chapter 13

Aalten, A. (2007). Listening to the dancer's body. *Sociological Review Monograph*, *55*(1), 109-125.

Adam, M.U., Brassington, G.S., Steiner, H., & Matheson, G.O. (2004). Psychological factors associated with performance-limiting injuries in professional ballet dancers. *Journal of Dance Medicine & Science*, *8*(2), 43-46.

Air, M. (2009). Health care seeking behavior and perceptions of the medical profession among pre-and post-retirement age Dutch dancers. *Journal of Dance Medicine & Science, 13*(2), 42-50.

Air, M.E. (2013). Psychological distress among dancers seeking outpatient treatment for musculoskeletal injury. *Journal of Dance Medicine & Science, 17*(3), 115-125.

Alexias, G., & Dimitropoulou, E. (2011). The body as a tool: Professional classical ballet dancers' embodiment. *Research in Dance Education, 12*(2), 87-104.

Barrell, G.M., & Terry, P.C. (2003). Trait anxiety and coping strategies among ballet dancers. *Medical Problems of Performing Artists, 18*(2), 59-64.

Blevins, P., Erskine, S., Hopper, L., & Moyle, G. (2019). Finding your balance: An investigation of recovery-stress balance in vocational dance training. *Journal of Dance Education, 20*(2), 1-11.

Brewer, B.W. (2010). The role of psychological factors in sport injury rehabilitation outcomes. *International Review of Sport and Exercise Psychology, 3*(1), 40-61.

Collins, D., & MacNamara, Á. (2017). A smooth sea never made a skilful sailor: Optimizing and exploiting the rocky road in talent development. In J. Baker, S. Cobley, J. Schorer, & N. Wattie (Eds.), *Routledge handbook of talent identification and development in sport* (pp. 336-346). Routledge.

Forsdyke, D., Smith, A., Jones, M., & Gledhill, A. (2016). Psychosocial factors associated with outcomes of sports injury rehabilitation in competitive athletes: A mixed studies systematic review. *British Journal of Sports Medicine, 50*(9), 537-544.

Gennarelli, S.M., Brown, S.M., & Mulcahey, M.K. (2020). Psychosocial interventions help facilitate recovery following musculoskeletal sports injuries: A systematic review. *The Physician and Sportsmedicine, 48*(4), 370-377.

Hanrahan, S.J. (1996). Dancers' perceptions of psychological skills. *Revista de Psicología del Deporte, 5*(2), 19-27.

Hincapié, C.A., Morton, E.J., & Cassidy, J.D. (2008). Musculoskeletal injuries and pain in dancers: A systematic review. *Archives of Physical Medicine and Rehabilitation, 89*(9), 1819-1829.

Ivarsson, A., Johnson, U., Andersen, M.B., Fallby, J., & Altemyr, M. (2015). It pays to pay attention: A mindfulness-based program for injury prevention with soccer players. *Journal of Applied Sport Psychology, 27*(3), 319-334.

Ivarsson, A., Johnson, U., Andersen, M.B., Tranaeus, U., Stenling, A., & Lindwall, M. (2017a). Psychosocial factors and sport injuries: Meta-analyses for prediction and prevention. *Sports Medicine, 47*(2), 353-365.

Ivarsson, A., Tranaeus, U., Johnson, U., & Stenling, A. (2017b). Negative psychological responses of injury and rehabilitation adherence effects on return to play in competitive athletes: A systematic review and meta-analysis. *Open Access Journal of Sports Medicine, 8*, 27-32.

Kaufmann, J.E., Nelissen, R.G., Appleton, P.R., & Gademan, M.G. (2021). Perceptions of motivational climate and association with musculoskeletal injuries in ballet dancers. *Medical Problems of Performing Artists, 36*(3), 187-198.

Kenny, S.J., Palacios-Derflingher, L., Whittaker, J.L., & Emery, C.A. (2018). The influence of injury definition on injury burden in preprofessional ballet and contemporary dancers. *Journal of Orthopaedic & Sports Physical Therapy, 48*(3), 185-193.

Kenny, S.J., Whittaker, J.L., & Emery, C.A. (2016). Risk factors for musculoskeletal injury in preprofessional dancers: A systematic review. *British Journal of Sports Medicine, 50*(16), 997-1003.

Krasnow, D., Kerr, G., & Mainwaring, L. (1994). Psychology of dealing with the injured dancer. *Medical Problems of Performing Artists, 9*(1), 7-9.

Krasnow, D., Mainwaring, L., & Kerr, G. (1999). Injury, stress, and perfectionism in young dancers and gymnasts. *Journal of Dance Medicine & Science, 3*(2), 51-58.

Lai, R.Y., Krasnow, D., & Thomas, M. (2008). Communication between medical practitioners and dancers. *Journal of Dance Medicine & Science, 12*(2), 47-53.

Laws, H. (2005). *Fit to dance 2.* Report of the second national inquiry into dancers' health and injury in the UK. Dance UK.

Lazarus, R.S., & Folkman, S. (1984). *Stress, Appraisal, and Coping.* Springer.

Liederbach, M., & Compagno, J.M. (2001). Psychological aspects of fatigue-related injuries in dancers. *Journal of Dance Medicine & Science, 5*(4), 116-120.

Liederbach, M., Hagins, M., Gamboa, J.M., & Welsh, T.M. (2012). Assessing and reporting dancer capacities, risk factors, and injuries: Recommendations from the IADMS standard measures consensus initiative. *Journal of Dance Medicine & Science, 16*(4), 139-153.

Macchi, R., & Crossman, J. (1996). After the fall: Reflections of injured classical ballet dancers. *Journal of Sport Behavior, 19*(3), 221.

Maddison, R., Prapavessis, H., Clatworthy, M., Hall, C., Folet, L., Harper, T., Cupal, D., & Brewer, B. (2012). Guided imagery to improve functional outcomes post-anterior cruciate ligament repair: Randomized-controlled pilot trial. *Scandinavian Journal of Medicine & Science in Sports, 22*(6), 816-821.

Madigan, D.J., Stoeber, J., Forsdyke, D., Dayson, M., & Passfield, L. (2018). Perfectionism predicts injury in junior athletes: Preliminary evidence from a prospective study. *Journal of Sports Sciences, 36*(5), 545-550.

Mainwaring, L.M., & Finney, C. (2017). Psychological risk factors and outcomes of dance injury: A systematic review. *Journal of Dance Medicine & Science, 21*(3), 87-96.

Mainwaring, L.M., Krasnow, D., & Kerr, G. (2001). And the dance goes on—Psychological impact of injury. *Journal of Dance Medicine & Science, 5*(4), 105-115.

Mainwaring, L., Krasnow, D., & Young, L. (2003). A teacher's guide to helping young dancers cope with psychological aspects of hip injuries. *Journal of Dance Education, 3*(2), 57-64.

Markula, P. (2015). (Im)Mobile bodies: Contemporary semi-professional dancers' experiences with injuries. *International Review for the Sociology of Sport, 50*(7), 840-864.

Martin, S., Johnson, U., McCall, A., & Ivarsson, A. (2021). Psychological risk profile for overuse injuries in sport: An exploratory study. *Journal of Sports Sciences, 39*(17), 1926-1935.

McEwen, K., & Young, K. (2011). Ballet and pain: Reflections on a risk-dance culture. *Qualitative Research in Sport, Exercise and Health, 3*(2), 152-173.

Naderi, A., Shaabani, F., Zandi, H.G., Calmeiro, L., & Brewer, B.W. (2020). The effects of a mindfulness-based program on the incidence of injuries in young male soccer players. *Journal of Sport and Exercise Psychology, 42*(2), 161-171.

Nicholls, A.R., & Polman, R.C. (2007). Coping in sport: A systematic review. *Journal of Sports Sciences, 25*(1), 11-31.

Noh, Y.E., Morris, T., & Andersen, M.B. (2003). Psychosocial stress and injury in dance. *Journal of Physical Education, Recreation & Dance, 74*(4), 36-40.

Noh, Y.E., Morris, T., & Andersen, M.B. (2005). Psychosocial factors and ballet injuries. *International Journal of Sport and Exercise Psychology, 3*(1), 79-90.

Noh, Y.E., Morris, T., & Andersen, M.B. (2007). Psychological intervention programs for reduction of injury in ballet dancers. *Research in Sports Medicine, 15*(1), 13-32.

Noh, Y.E., Morris, T., & Andersen, M.B. (2009). Occupational stress and coping strategies of professional ballet dancers in Korea. *Medical Problems of Performing Artists, 24*(3), 124-134.

Nordin-Bates, S.M. & Abrahamsen, F. (2016). Perfectionism in dance: Applied considerations and a case example. In A.P. Hill (Ed.), *The Psychology of Perfectionism in Sport, Dance and Exercise* (pp. 222-244). Routledge.

Nordin-Bates, S.M., Walker, I.J., Baker, J., Garner, J., Hardy, C., Irvine, S., Jola, C., Laws, H., & Blevins, P. (2011). Injury, imagery, and self-esteem in dance: Healthy minds in injured bodies? *Journal of Dance Medicine & Science, 15*(2), 76-85.

Pickard, A. (2012). Schooling the dancer: The evolution of an identity as a ballet dancer. *Research in Dance Education, 13*(1), 25-46.

Pollitt, E.E., & Hutt, K. (2021). Viewing injury in dancers from a psychological perspective—A literature review. *Journal of Dance Medicine & Science, 25*(2), 75-79.

Rip, B., Fortin, S., & Vallerand, R.J. (2006). The relationship between passion and injury in dance students. *Journal of Dance Medicine & Science, 10*(1-2), 14-20.

Shrier, I., & Hallé, M. (2011). Psychological predictors of injuries in circus artists: An exploratory study. *British Journal of Sports Medicine, 45*(5), 433-436.

Skvarla, L.A., & Clement, D. (2019). The delivery of a short-term psychological skills training program to college dance students: A pilot study examining coping skills and injuries. *Journal of Dance Medicine & Science, 23*(4), 159-166.

Tarr, J., & Thomas, H. (2021). Good pain, bad pain: Dancers, injury, and listening to the body. *Dance Research, 39*(1), 53-71.

Thomas, H., & Tarr, J. (2009). Dancers' perceptions of pain and injury: Positive and negative effects. *Journal of Dance Medicine & Science, 13*(2), 51-59.

Turner, B.S., & Wainwright, S.P. (2003). Corps de ballet: The case of the injured ballet dancer. *Sociology of Health & Illness, 25*(4), 269-288.

Vallerand, R.J., Blanchard, C., Mageau, G.A., Koestner, R., Ratelle, C., Léonard, M., Gagne, M., & Marsolais, J. (2003). Les passions de l'ame: On obsessive and harmonious passion. *Journal of Personality and Social Psychology, 85*(4), 756-767.

van Winden, D., van Rijn, R.M., Savelsbergh, G.J.P., Oudejans, R.R.D., & Stubbe, J.H. (2020). Limited coping skills, young age, and high BMI are risk factors for injuries in contemporary dance: A 1-year prospective study. *Frontiers in Psychology, 11*, 1452.

van Winden, D., van Rijn, R. M., Savelsbergh, G., Oudejans, R., & Stubbe, J. (2021). The association between stress and injury: A prospective cohort study among 186 first-year contemporary dance students. *Frontiers in Psychology* 12. https://doi.org/10.3389/fpsyg.2021.770494

Vassallo, A.J., Pappas, E., Stamatakis, E., & Hiller, C.E. (2019). Injury fear, stigma, and reporting in professional dancers. *Safety and Health at Work, 10*(3), 260-264.

Wainwright, S.P., & Turner, B.S. (2004). Epiphanies of embodiment: Injury, identity and the balletic body. *Qualitative Research, 4*(3), 311-337.

Wiese-Bjornstal, D.M., Wood, K.N., & Kronzer, J.R. (2020). Sport injuries and psychological sequelae. In G. Tenenbaum, & R.C. Eklund (Eds.) *Handbook of sport psychology* (4th ed, pp. 711-737). Wiley.

Willard, V.C., & Lavallee, D. (2016). Retirement experiences of elite ballet dancers: Impact of self-identity and social support. *Sport, Exercise, and Performance Psychology, 5*(3), 266-279.

Williams, J.M., & Andersen, M.B. (1998). Psychosocial antecedents of sport injury: Review and critique of the stress and injury model. *Journal of Applied Sport Psychology, 10*(1), 5-25.

Chapter 14

Aalten, A. (2007). Listening to the dancer's body. *Sociological Review Monograph*, 55(1), 109-125.

Ackard, D.M., Henderson, J.B., & Wonderlich, A.L. (2004). The associations between childhood dance participation and adult disordered eating and related psychopathology. *Journal of Psychosomatic Research*, 57(5), 485-490.

Alexias, G., & Dimitropoulou, E. (2011). The body as a tool: Professional classical ballet dancers' embodiment. *Research in Dance Education*, 12(2), 87-104.

Allen, M.S., & Walter, E.E. (2016). Personality and body image: A systematic review. *Body Image*, 19, 79-88.

American Psychiatric Association (APA). (2013). *Diagnostic and statistical manual of mental disorders* (5th ed.). APA.

Annus, A., & Smith, G.T. (2009). Learning experiences in dance class predict adult eating disturbance. *European Eating Disorders Review: The Professional Journal of the Eating Disorders Association*, 17(1), 50-60.

Arcelus, J., García Dantas, A., Sánchez Martín, M., & Río Sánchez, C.D. (2015). Influence of perfectionism on variables associated to eating disorders in dance students. *Revista de Psicología del Deporte*, 24(2), 297-303.

Arcelus, J., Mitchell, A.J., Wales, J., & Nielsen, S. (2011). Mortality rates in patients with anorexia nervosa and other eating disorders: A meta-analysis of 36 studies. *Archives of General Psychiatry*, 68(7), 724-731.

Arcelus, J., Witcomb, G.L., & Mitchell, A. (2014). Prevalence of eating disorders amongst dancers: A systemic review and meta-analysis. *European Eating Disorders Review*, 22, 92-101.

Arthur-Cameselle, J., Sossin, K., & Quatromoni, P. (2017). A qualitative analysis of factors related to eating disorder onset in female collegiate athletes and non-athletes. *Eating Disorders*, 25(3), 199-215.

Bar, R.J., Cassin, S.E., & Dionne, M.M. (2017). The long-term impact of an eating disorder prevention program for professional ballet school students: A 15-year follow-up study. *Eating Disorders*, 25(5), 375-387.

Barr, S., & Oliver, W. (2016). Feminist pedagogy, body image, and the dance technique class. *Research in Dance Education*, 17(2), 97-112.

Bartholomew, K.J., Ntoumanis, N., Ryan, R.M., Bosch, J.A., & Thøgersen-Ntoumani, C. (2011). Self-determination theory and diminished functioning: The role of interpersonal control and psychological need thwarting. *Personality and Social Psychology Bulletin*, 37, 1459-1473.

Benn, T., & Walters, D. (2001). Between Scylla and Charybdis. Nutritional education versus body culture and the ballet aesthetic: The effects on the lives of female dancers. *Research in Dance Education*, 2(2), 139-154.

Bettle, N., Bettle, O., Neumärker, U., & Neumärker, K.J. (2001). Body image and self-esteem in adolescent ballet dancers. *Perceptual and Motor Skills*, 93(1), 297-309.

Chamay-Weber, C., Narring, F., & Michaud, P.A. (2005). Partial eating disorders among adolescents: A review. *Journal of Adolescent Health*, 37(5), 416-426.

Chin, J., & Clements, L. (2021). Body image and "ship life" in female cruise ship performers: An interpretative phenomenological analysis. *Journal of Emerging Dance Scholarship*, 9.

Coker-Cranney, A., & Reel, J.J. (2015). Coach pressure and disordered eating in female collegiate athletes: Is the coach-athlete relationship a mediating factor? *Journal of Clinical Sport Psychology*, 9(3), 213-231.

Dantas, A.G., Alonso, D.A., Sánchez-Miguel, P.A., & del Río Sánchez, C. (2018). Factors dancers associate with their body dissatisfaction. *Body Image*, 25, 40-47.

Davison, K.K., Earnest, M.B., & Birch, L.L. (2002). Participation in aesthetic sports and girls' weight concerns at ages 5 and 7 years. *International Journal of Eating Disorders*, 31(3), 312-317.

de Bruin, A.P., Bakker, F.C., & Oudejans, R.R.D. (2009). Achievement goal theory and disordered eating: Relationships of disordered eating with goal orientations and motivational climate in female gymnasts and dancers. *Psychology of Sport and Exercise*, 10, 72-79.

Dotti, A., Fioravanti, M., Balotta, M., Tozzi, F., Cannella, C., & Lazzari, R. (2002). Eating behavior of ballet dancers. *Eating and Weight Disorders: Studies on Anorexia, Bulimia and Obesity*, 7(1), 60-67.

Dryburgh, A., & Fortin, S. (2010). Weighing in on surveillance: Perception of the impact of surveillance on female ballet dancers' health. *Research in Dance Education*, 11(2), 95-108.

Ehrenberg, S. (2010). Reflections on reflections: Mirror use in a university dance training environment. *Theatre, Dance and Performance Training*, 1(2), 172-184.

Estanol, E., Shepherd, C., & MacDonald, T. (2013). Mental skills as protective attributes against eating disorder risk in dancers. *Journal of Applied Sport Psychology*, 25(2), 209-222.

Feldman, M.B., & Meyer, I.H. (2007). Eating disorders in diverse lesbian, gay, and bisexual populations. *International Journal of Eating Disorders*, 40(3), 218-226.

Francisco, R., Alarcão, M., & Narciso, I. (2012a). Aesthetic sport as high-risk contexts for eating disorders: Young elite dancers and gymnasts perspectives. *The Spanish Journal of Psychology*, 15, 265-274.

Francisco, R., Narciso, I., & Alarcão, M. (2012b). Specific predictors of disordered eating among elite and non-elite gymnast and ballet dancers. *International Journal of Sport Psychology*, 43, 479-502.

Francisco, R., Narciso, I., & Alarcão, M. (2013). Parental influences on elite aesthetic athletes' body image dissatisfaction and disordered eating. *Journal of Child and Family Studies, 22*(8), 1082-1091.

Froreich, F.V., Vartanian, L.R., Zawadzki, M.J., Grisham, J.R., & Touyz, S.W. (2017). Psychological need satisfaction, control, and disordered eating. *British Journal of Clinical Psychology, 56*(1), 53-68.

Garner, D.M., Olmsted, M.P., Bohr, Y., & Garfinkel, P.E. (1982). The eating attitudes test: Psychometric features and clinical correlates. *Psychological Medicine, 12*, 871-878.

Goodwin, H., Arcelus, J., Geach, N., & Meyer, C. (2014a). Perfectionism and eating psychopathology among dancers: The role of high standards and self-criticism. *European Eating Disorders Review, 22*(5), 346-351.

Goodwin, H., Arcelus, J., Marshall, S., Wicks, S., & Meyer, C. (2014b). Critical comments concerning shape and weight: Associations with eating psychopathology among full-time dance students. *Eating and Weight Disorders: Studies on Anorexia, Bulimia and Obesity, 19*(1), 115-118.

Green, J. (1999). Somatic authority and the myth of the ideal body in dance education. *Dance Research Journal, 31*(2), 80-100.

Grogan, S. (2008). *Body image: Understanding body dissatisfaction in men, women and children.* Routledge.

Gvion, L. (2008). Dancing bodies, decaying bodies: The interpretation of anorexia among Israeli dancers. *Young, 16*, 67-87.

Heiland, T.L., Murray, D.S., & Edley, P.P. (2008). Body image of dancers in Los Angeles: The cult of slenderness and media influence among dance students. *Research in Dance Education, 9*(3), 257-275.

Kirkland, G., & Lawrence, G. (1986). *Dancing on my grave: An account of a descent into anorexia, drugs and personal torment in an obsessive search for perfection.* Jove Books.

Kong, P., & Harris, L.M. (2015). The sporting body: Body image and eating disorder symptomatology among female athletes from leanness focused and nonleanness focused sports. *The Journal of Psychology, 149*(2), 141-160.

Kulshreshtha, M., Babu, N., Goel, N.J., & Chandel, S. (2021). Disordered eating attitudes and body shape concerns among North Indian Kathak dancers. *International Journal of Eating Disorders, 54*(2), 148-154.

Langdon, S.W., & Petracca, G. (2010). Tiny dancer: Body image and dancer identity in female modern dancers. *Body Image, 7*(4), 360-363.

Lavender, J.M., Brown, T.A., & Murray, S.B. (2017). Men, muscles, and eating disorders: An overview of traditional and muscularity-oriented disordered eating. *Current Psychiatry Reports, 19*(6), 1-7.

Liu, C.Y., Tseng, M.C.M., Chang, C.H., Fang, D., & Lee, M.B. (2016). Comorbid psychiatric diagnosis and psychological correlates of eating disorders in dance students. *Journal of the Formosan Medical Association, 115*(2), 113-120.

Lunde, C., & Holmqvist Gattario, K. (2017). Performance or appearance? Young female sport participants' body negotiations. *Body Image, 21*, 81-89.

McEwen, K., & Young, K. (2011). Ballet and pain: Reflections on a risk-dance culture. *Qualitative Research in Sport, Exercise and Health, 3*(2), 152-173.

National Eating Disorders Association (NEDA) (2021a). *Emotional and behavioral signs of an eating disorder.* https://www.nationaleatingdisorders.org/toolkit/parent-toolkit/emotional-behavioral-signs

National Eating Disorders Association (2021b). *Physical signs and symptoms of an eating disorder.* https://www.nationaleatingdisorders.org/toolkit/parent-toolkit/physical-signs

Nerini, A. (2015). Media influence and body dissatisfaction in preadolescent ballet dancers and non-physically active girls. *Psychology of Sport and Exercise, 20*, 76-83.

Neumärker, K.J., Bettle, N., Bettle, O., Dudeck, U., & Neumärker, U. (1998). The Eating Attitudes Test: Comparative analysis of female and male students at the public ballet school of Berlin. *European Child and Adolescent Psychiatry, 7*, 19-23.

Nordin-Bates, S.M., Hill, A.P., Cumming, J., Aujla, I.J., & Redding, E. (2014). A longitudinal examination of the relationship between perfectionism and motivational climate in dance. *Journal of Sport and Exercise Psychology, 36*(4), 382-391.

Nordin-Bates, S.M., Schwarz, J.F., Quested, E., Cumming, J., Aujla, I.J., & Redding, E. (2016). Within-and between-person predictors of disordered eating attitudes among male and female dancers: Findings from the UK Centres for Advanced Training. *Psychology of Sport and Exercise, 27*, 101-111.

Nordin-Bates, S.M., Walker, I.J., & Redding, E. (2011). Correlates of disordered eating attitudes among male and female young talented dancers: Findings from the UK Centres for Advanced Training. *Eating Disorders, 19*(3), 211-233.

Oliver, W. (2008). Body image in the dance class. *Journal of Physical Education, Recreation & Dance, 79*(5), 18-41.

One Dance UK (n.d.). *Eating Disorder Policy Advice.* Retrieved January 17, 2022, from https://www.onedanceuk.org/resource/eating-disorder-policy-recommendations/

Penniment, K.J., & Egan, S.J. (2012). Perfectionism and learning experiences in dance class as risk factors for eating disorders in dancers. *European Eating Disorders Review, 20*(1), 13-22.

Petrie, T.A. (2020). Eating disorders in sport: From etiology to prevention. In G. Tenenbaum (Ed.), *Handbook of sport psychology* (4th ed., pp. 694-710). Wiley.

Pickard, A. (2013). Ballet body belief: Perceptions of an ideal ballet body from young ballet dancers. *Research in Dance Education*, *14*(1), 3-19.

Piran, N. (1999). Eating disorders: A trial of prevention in a high risk school setting. *Journal of Primary Prevention*, *20*(1), 75-90.

Piran, N. (2005). The role of dance teachers in the prevention of eating disorders. In R. Solomon, J. Solomon, & S.C. Minton (Eds.), *Preventing dance injuries* (2nd ed., pp. 201-210). Human Kinetics.

Price, B.R., & Pettijohn, T.F. (2006). The effect of ballet dance attire on body and self-perceptions of female dancers. *Social Behavior and Personality: An International Journal*, *34*(8), 991-998.

Radell, S.A., Adame, D.D., & Cole, S.P. (2002). Effect of teaching with mirrors on body image and locus of control in women college ballet dancers. *Perceptual and Motor Skills*, *95*(3_suppl), 1239-1247.

Radell, S.A., Adame, D.D., & Cole, S.P. (2003). Effect of teaching with mirrors on ballet dance performance. *Perceptual and Motor Skills*, *97*(3), 960-964.

Radell, S.A., Adame, D.D., & Cole, S.P. (2004). The impact of mirrors on body image and classroom performance in female college ballet dancers. *Journal of Dance Medicine & Science*, *8*(2), 47-52.

Radell, S.A., Adame, D.D., Cole, S.P., & Blumenkehl, N.J. (2011). The impact of mirrors on body image and performance in high and low performing female ballet students. *Journal of Dance Medicine & Science*, *15*(3), 108-115.

Radell, S.A., Keneman, M.L., Adame, D.D., & Cole, S.P. (2014). My body and its reflection: A case study of eight dance students and the mirror in the ballet classroom. *Research in Dance Education*, *15*(2), 161-178.

Radell, S.A., Keneman, M.L., Mandradjieff, M.P., Adame, D.D., & Cole, S.P. (2017). Comparison study of body image satisfaction between beginning- and advanced-level female ballet students. *Journal of Dance Medicine & Science*, *21*(4), 135-143.

Radell, S.A., Mandradjieff, M.P., Adame, D.D., & Cole, S.P. (2020). Impact of mirrors on body image of beginning modern and ballet students. *Journal of Dance Medicine & Science*, *24*(3), 126-134.

Radell, S.A., Mandradjieff, M.P., Ramachandran, S.R., Adame, D.D., & Cole, S.P. (2021). Body image and mirror exposure: The impact of partial versus full mirror use on beginner-level ballet students. *Journal of Dance Education*. https://doi.org/10.1080/15290824.2021.1939035

Ravaldi, C., Vannacci, A., Bolognesi, E., Mancini, S., Faravelli, C., & Ricca, V. (2006). Gender role, eating disorder symptoms, and body image concern in ballet dancers. *Journal of Psychosomatic Research*, *61*(4), 529-535.

Reel, J.J., Podlog, L., Hamilton, L., Greviskes, L., Voelker, D.K., & Gray, C. (2018). Injury and disordered eating behaviors: What is the connection for female professional dancers? *Journal of Clinical Sport Psychology*, *12*(3), 365-381.

Reel, J.J., SooHoo, S., Jamieson, K.M., & Gill, D.L. (2005). Femininity to the extreme: Body image concerns among college female dancers. *Women in Sport & Physical Activity Journal*, *14*(1), 39-51.

Ringham, R., Klump, K., Kaye, W., Stone, D., Libman, S., Stowe, S., & Marcus, M. (2006). Eating disorder symptomatology among ballet dancers. *International Journal of Eating Disorders*, *39*(6), 503-508.

Robbeson, J.G., Kruger, H.S., & Wright, H.H. (2015). Disordered eating behaviour, body image, and energy status of female student dancers. *International Journal of Sport Nutrition and Exercise Metabolism*, *25*(4), 344-352.

Rohde, P., Stice, E., & Marti, C.N. (2015). Development and predictive effects of eating disorder risk factors during adolescence: Implications for prevention efforts. *International Journal of Eating Disorders*, *48*(2), 187-198.

Sassaroli, S., & Ruggiero, G.M. (2005). The role of stress in the association between low self-esteem, perfectionism, and worry, and eating disorders. *International Journal of Eating Disorders*, *37*(2), 135-141.

Silverii, G.A., Benvenuti, F., Morandin, G., Ricca, V., Monami, M., Mannucci, E., & Rotella, F. (2022). Eating psychopathology in ballet dancers: A meta-analysis of observational studies. *Eating and Weight Disorders: Studies on Anorexia, Bulimia and Obesity*, *27*(2), 405-414.

Stark, A., & Newton, M. (2014). A dancer's well-being: The influence of the social psychological climate during adolescence. *Psychology of Sport and Exercise*, *15*(4), 356-363.

Swami, V., & Harris, A.S. (2012). Dancing toward positive body image? Examining body-related constructs with ballet and contemporary dancers at different levels. *American Journal of Dance Therapy*, *34*(1), 39-52.

Swami, V., & Tovée, M.J. (2009). A comparison of body dissatisfaction, body appreciation, and media influences between street-dancers and non-dancers. *Body Image*, *6*(4), 304-307.

Thomas, J.J., Keel, P.K., & Heatherton, T.F. (2005). Disordered eating attitudes and behaviors in ballet students: Examination of environmental and individual risk factors. *International Journal of Eating Disorders*, *38*(3), 263-268.

Thompson, R.A., & Sherman, R.T. (1999). "Good athlete" traits and characteristics of anorexia nervosa: Are they similar? *Eating Disorders*, *7*, 181-190.

Tiggemann, M., Coutts, E., & Clark, L. (2014). Belly dance as an embodying activity?: A test of the embodiment model of positive body image. *Sex Roles*, *71*(5-8), 197-207.

Tiggemann, M., & Slater, A. (2001). A test of objectification theory in former dancers and non-dancers. *Psychology of Women Quarterly*, 25(1), 57-64.

Toro, J., Guerrero, M., Sentis, J., Castro, J., & Puertolas, C. (2009). Eating disorders in ballet dancing students: Problems and risk factors. *European Eating Disorders Review*, 17(1), 40-49.

Torres-McGehee, T.M., Green, J.M., Leaver-Dunn, D., Leeper, J.D., Bishop, P.A., & Richardson, M.T. (2011). Attitude and knowledge changes in collegiate dancers following a short-term, team-centered prevention program on eating disorders. *Perceptual and Motor Skills*, 112(3), 711-725.

Torstveit, M.K., Rosenvinge, J.H., & Sundgot-Borgen, J. (2008). Prevalence of eating disorders and the predictive power of risk models in female elite athletes: A controlled study. *Scandinavian Journal of Medicine and Science in Sports*, 18(1), 108-118.

Tseng, M.M.C., Fang, D., Lee, M.B., Chie, W.C., Liu, J.P., & Chen, W.J. (2007). Two-phase survey of eating disorders in gifted dance and non-dance high-school students in Taiwan. *Psychological Medicine*, 37(8), 1085-1096.

Turk, F., & Waller, G. (2020). Is self-compassion relevant to the pathology and treatment of eating and body image concerns? A systematic review and meta-analysis. *Clinical Psychology Review*, 79, 101856.

Tylka, T.L., & Wood-Barcalow, N.L. (2015). What is and what is not positive body image? Conceptual foundations and construct definition. *Body Image*, 14, 118-129.

Vandenbosch, L., Fardouly, J., & Tiggemann, M. (2021). Social media and body image: Recent trends and future directions. *Current Opinion in Psychology*, 45, 101289.

Van Zelst, L., Clabaugh, A., & Morling, B. (2004). Dancers' body esteem, fitness esteem, and self-esteem in three contexts. *Journal of Dance Education*, 4(2), 48-57.

Voelker, D., Petrie, T., Huang, Q., & Chandran, A. (2019). Bodies in motion: An empirical evaluation of a program to support positive body image in female collegiate athletes. *Body Image*, 28, 149-158.

Wells, K.R., Jeacocke, N.A., Appaneal, R., Smith, H.D., Vlahovich, N., Burke, L.M., & Hughes, D. (2020). The Australian Institute of Sport (AIS) and National Eating Disorders Collaboration (NEDC) position statement on disordered eating in high performance sport. *British Journal of Sports Medicine*, 54(21), 1247-1258.

Yannakoulia, M., Sitara, M., & Matalas, A.L. (2002). Reported eating behavior and attitudes improvement after a nutrition intervention program in a group of young female dancers. *International Journal of Sport Nutrition and Exercise Metabolism*, 12(1), 24-32.

Index

Note: The italicized *f* and *t* following page numbers refer to figures and tables, respectively.

A

acceptance
 anxiety management 81
 body image 264, 265, 281, 282, 283
 in mindfulness 150, 152-153, 155, 158, 283
acceptance and commitment therapy/training 153-154, 156-157, 170
achievement goal theory
 for motivation 90-96, 91*t*, 181
 and motivational climates 204-205, 205*t*, 208-211, 210*f*, 214
action-awareness merging 119-120, 122
acute stress response 70, 71*t*
agreeableness (personality trait) 22, 23*t*, 27, 28
Alonso, Alicia 185, 190
amotivation 9-10, 94, 96, 97*t*
analysis paralysis/skill breakdown 115*f*, 120-121, 124, 196
anorexia nervosa 266, 267*t*, 268, 273
anxiety
 attentional focus and 120-121, 122
 consequences 75-79, 76*f*, 82*f*, 86, 92, 120
 defining and describing 70
 vs. low arousal 81, 84
 management 11-13, 14*t*, 79-84, 85, 86, 120-121, 122, 154, 155, 156, 172, 187, 194, 196-197
 motivation orientations and 92, 101
 from perfectionistic concerns 42-43, 43*f*, 45, 73
 physiological states/symptoms 60, 65-66, 70-72, 71*t*, 75-76, 76*f*, 77, 78-79, 78*f*, 79-80, 81, 86, 192
 self-confidence and 60-61, 65-66, 80, 120-121
 sources 11-12, 70, 72-75, 74*f*, 82*f*, 86

approach orientation and goals 91-92, 92*f*, 140
assigned goals 170-171
association learning 5, 11-13, 115
athletic identity 29
attentional focus
 analysis paralysis/skill breakdown 115*f*, 116, 120-121, 125
 defining and describing 110-112, 119, 126
 explicit and implicit learning 114-116, 117-118, 121
 flow and 119-120
 goal setting and 122-123, 168, 172
 internal and external 112-114, 113*t*, 116-118, 119, 125, 163-164
 mindfulness and 123, 151-153, 151*f*, 152*f*, 155, 158, 163-164
 optimal, and nurturing 110-111, 121-123, 197
 performance-related consequences 116-117, 118, 120-121
 practical activities 124
auditory imagery 189, 190. *See also* imagery
automatic control processes
 flow states 119-120, 122
 use, vs. analysis paralysis 115*f*, 120-121, 196-197
automatic thoughts 24
autonomous learning 115, 115*f*, 116, 119
autonomy
 class focus and creativity 113, 117-118, 119, 136
 motivational regulations 97, 97*f*, 170
 needs and satisfaction 98-100, 99*t*, 101-102, 103, 104, 206-207, 213
 nurturing healthy motivation 103, 104, 133-134, 140, 155, 206, 216*t*, 283
 perfectionism development and outcomes 41

self-regulation and goal setting 174, 179-180, 182
avoidance behaviors 11-12, 13
 from anxiety, and management 11, 12, 13, 14*t*, 71, 77, 81, 82*f*, 85
 coping 247, 251
 decreasing, via mindfulness 155, 158
 from low self-esteem 12, 55, 61
 orientation and goals (motivation) 91-92, 92*f*, 94-96, 95*f*, 140
 from perfectionistic concerns 42-43, 44, 94
 self-efficacy theory 56-57, 61

B

Balanchine, George 229-230, 263, 276
ballet
 bodies and aesthetics 27, 222, 225-226, 263, 264, 269-270, 275-276
 creativity nurturing 138
 dance terms and attentional foci 113-114
 eating disorders within 267-269, 270*f*, 274, 285
 injury risks and experiences 245, 248, 249-250, 250*f*, 251-252, 253
 perfectionism 38, 40, 41
 personality factors 27, 28-29
 talent identification and development 222-223, 225-226, 229, 231, 241
Bandura, Albert, and self-efficacy theory 4, 55-56, 56-57, 59, 61, 62, 64
beginner's mind 153, 161-162
behavior therapy
 anxiety management 11-12, 13, 14*t*, 79-80, 81, 83, 85
 CBT in dance psychology 3, 4-5, 13, 15
 mindfulness 153-154, 156-157

329

belonging. *See* relatedness
Big-C creativity 130-131, 131*t*
"Big Five" personality traits 22-23
   creativity manifestations 132
   dance manifestations 23*t*, 24-25, 27, 34
   establishing conditions 25, 35
   performance-related consequences 27-28
binge eating disorder 266, 267*t*
biological factors, body image and disordered eating 271, 272, 272*f*
black-and-white thinking 49
bodies and aesthetics
   ballet and dance culture 27, 222, 225-226, 261, 263, 264, 269-270, 270*f*, 271, 275-276, 281, 282
   talent considerations 222-223, 225-226, 227
   thinness culture 275-276, 282
body awareness and control
   imagery use 185, 195, 199
   injury prevention and recognition 245, 252, 253, 254*t*, 255-256
   mindfulness 156, 161
   mirrors use 278
   nurturing healthy body image 281
body dissatisfaction and dysmorphia 262, 263, 268-270, 268*t*, 271, 272-273, 276-278, 279
body image. *See also* disordered eating
   acceptance/nurturing healthy 264, 265, 281, 282, 283
   anxieties 77
   consequences 279
   dancer identities and 29, 273
   defining and describing 262
   flexibility 264, 265
   negative 262-263, 264, 268-270, 271-278, 279
   positive 262, 263-264, 265, 279, 281, 282, 283
   well-being-related consequences of personality 28
body scanning 155, 159-160, 163
brain activity. *See* mental activity
breathing exercises
   anxiety management 79
   mindfulness 152, 153, 155, 159-160, 163
   practical activities 163
bulimia nervosa 266, 267*t*, 268, 279, 280*f*

C

case studies
   anxiety 85
   creativity 144

disordered eating 285
focus 125
functional analyses 8
goal setting and self-regulation 181
imagery 199
injury 259
mindfulness 162-163
motivation 106
motivational climates 218
perfectionism 40, 41, 50
personality 31
self-confidence 66
talent development 241
catastrophizing 49
causality orientations theory 106
CBT. *See* cognitive behavioral therapy (CBT)
choreography and choreographers
   anxiety responses 76
   attentional focus examples 112-113, 120, 125
   collaboration 129-130
   creativity aspects 129-130, 134, 137, 138, 187
   creativity levels 131, 131*t*
   imagery use 184, 185, 187, 190, 193
   motivational climates 207-208
   styles spectra 134
classical conditioning 5, 11-13
clinical interventions and therapies
   for anxiety 13, 77, 85
   for eating disorders and disordered eating 266, 281-282, 283-284
   for injured dancers 258-259
   for low self-esteem 62, 63*f*, 64
   mindfulness use 153-154, 155, 156-157, 163
   for perfectionism 46, 47*t*
clothing 278, 281
coach-athlete relations. *See also* teacher-student relations
   analysis paralysis 120
   confidence and success 68
   injury risk factors 250
   motivational climates and leadership 41, 204, 207-208, 212-213
   talent identification and development 227-228
cognitive behavioral therapy (CBT) 3, 4-5, 15, 81, 153-154
cognitive defusion 150, 154
cognitive distortions 49
   in low self-esteem 55
   in perfectionism 48-49
cognitive symptoms of anxiety 70-72, 71*t*, 76, 77, 79, 80-81

collaboration
   on choreography 129-130
   for creativity 129-130, 141
   task-involving climates 91, 93, 102-103, 204, 211, 214, 218
competence. *See also* talent
   needs and satisfaction 98-101, 99*t*, 101-102, 103, 104-105, 106-107, 206-207, 213
   nurturing healthy motivation 103, 104-105, 206, 216*t*
   task- and ego-involving climates 208-209, 211
concentration. *See* attentional focus
conditioning (learning theory) 4-11
confidence. *See* self-esteem and self-confidence
conscientiousness (personality trait) 22
   consequences 23*t*, 27, 28, 34
   perfectionistic strivings of 34, 38, 39
consensual assessment technique 130
constrained action hypothesis 119
contingent self-esteem 29, 31, 52-53, 75
controllable and uncontrollable factors. *See also* environmental factors
   anxiety reduction focus 80, 86
   attentional focus tips 122-123
   in dance 73-74, 80*t*, 167, 227, 277
   disordered eating risk factors 273, 277, 279, 283
   exposure activities 83
   in goal setting 122-123, 167, 168, 169-170, 170*f*, 174, 181
   imagery 189, 190
   injury and rehabilitation 247, 253
   motivational climates 41, 206-207, 207-208, 209, 211
   talent 58, 63, 229-230, 231-232, 236
   thinking, and mindfulness 152
controlling leadership 41, 206-207, 207-208, 212-214
convergent thinking 129
coping models 59
coping skills 247, 248, 254
   injury rehabilitation 244*f*, 252, 254-255, 254*t*
   injury risk factors 247, 248, 251
   well-being-related consequences of personality 28
core beliefs 24, 25, 55
creative potential 129
creative process 129, 130

creativity
    aspects 129-130, 133*f*
    continuum/levels 130-131, 131*t*, 135
    correlates and consequences 138-140, 156
    dancers' attentional foci and 113, 117-118, 120
    in dance styles 134-135, 137-138, 141
    defining and describing 128-129, 145
    flow and 120, 132
    nurturing 133-134, 139-141, 142-143, 144, 145
    products and processes 130, 134, 139
    research and assessment 128-130, 131*t*, 132-133, 136, 137-138, 140, 144
    sources and activities 132-138, 142-143, 156, 187, 195
    as talent criteria 223, 224*t*
cultural aspects. *See also* dance cultures
    anxiety sources 74
    of creativity 130, 141
    health care 252
    injury risk factors 249
curiosity. *See* creativity; mindfulness; openness to experience (personality trait)

D
dance attire 278, 281
dance cultures
    bodies and aesthetics 222, 261, 263, 264, 269-270, 270*f*, 271, 275-276, 281, 282
    gender issues 54, 68
    injury risk factors 249-250, 250*f*, 251-252, 253, 255
    insider knowledge as talent 224*t*, 225
    motivational climates 14, 44, 93, 106, 133-134, 140, 204-205, 206-207, 207-208
    power and control 169, 181, 206-208, 276
    subjectivity 167, 227, 277
dance imagery. *See* imagery
dance psychology
    avoidance and exposure 11-13, 14*t*
    CBT in 3, 4-5, 13, 15
    conditioning 5-11, 15
    defining and describing 2-3, 14
    purposes 3-4
dancer identity. *See* identity

dance styles
    anxiety responses 76
    bodies and aesthetics 27, 263, 270, 276
    creativity within 134-135, 137-138, 141
    reinforcement and choice 7, 9-10
    research inclusion 15
    specialization 233*f*
    talent considerations 222-223, 226, 227, 230, 240
dance terms 113-114, 113*t*
debilitative imagery 188
debilitative symptoms of anxiety 76, 77, 81
deliberate play 232-233, 232*t*
deliberate practice
    creativity 137
    talent 231-232, 232*t*
detachment, in mindfulness 150, 154, 155
developmental factors
    anxiety 11, 70, 77
    dance talent 229-230
    personality origins 26*f*
    self-esteem building 53-54
developmental model of sport participation 232
disembodiment 273
disordered eating. *See also* body image; eating disorders
    anxiety/depression and 77, 274
    consequences 279-281, 282
    dancer identities and 29, 273, 283
    defining and describing 264, 266, 275, 280*f*
    origins and risk factors 210, 271-278, 272*f*, 279, 280*f*, 282-283, 286
    perfectionism and 41, 44, 272, 273, 274, 275, 283
    prevalence 269-271, 270*f*, 271
    prevention, identification, and management 281-284
    spectrum 266*f*
    warning signs 268*t*, 280-281
divergent thinking 129
diversification, in talent development 232-233, 233*f*, 240

E
early and intense dance training
    narrow identities and outcomes 29, 30, 31
    self-esteem issues 54
    and specialization 233-234, 233*f*, 241
eating disorders. *See also* disordered eating
    consequences 279-280

    defining and diagnosing 264, 266, 270-271
    features 267*t*
    identification and management 283-284
    origins and risk factors 271-278, 279, 280*f*
    prevalence 267-271, 270*f*
eating practices 268*t*, 275, 282-283. *See also* disordered eating
ego and task orientations. *See* task and ego orientations
emotional reasoning. *See* cognitive distortions
emotional stability (personality trait) 22, 23*t*, 25, 38
    consequences 27-28, 155
    disordered eating risk factors 274
emotional states
    anxiety 78*f*, 81, 84
    classical conditioning and 11
    imagery consequences 194
    self-efficacy and self-esteem 52, 60, 66, 67
    self-regulation 155, 158, 174, 224*t*, 247
environmental factors. *See also* controllable and uncontrollable factors
    goal setting and self-regulation 174, 175
    imagery for 185
    negative body image and disordered eating risk factors 272-273, 272*f*, 275-278, 282-283
    personality origins 26*f*
    talent identification and development 226, 227, 228-230, 230*t*, 234-236, 235*f*, 238*t*
exercise therapies 79-80
explicit learning 114-116, 120
exposure and exposure therapy 13
    anxiety responses and management 12-13, 14*t*, 75, 76, 79, 81, 83-84, 85, 194
    challenging situations 12-13, 64, 81, 83-84, 85
    practical activities 83-84
external focus of attention
    descriptions and usage 112-114, 113*t*, 117, 118, 119-121, 122, 125, 185, 187
    mindfulness and attention 163-164
    performance-related consequences 116, 117, 118
    practical exercises 124
    research on 117-118, 125-126
    self-talk 122, 123

external visual perspective, imagery 188
extinction (behavior) 9
extrinsic motivation
   self-determination theory 96-97, 97f, 98-100, 101, 102
   sources 98-100
extroversion and introversion (personality traits) 22-23, 23t, 24-25, 27, 28

F

facilitative imagery 188
facilitative symptoms of anxiety 76, 78-79, 81
feedback and persuasion. *See also* self-talk
   conditioning and reinforcement 5-11, 10t
   criticism vs. mindfulness 157-158, 162-163
   goal setting and self-regulation 174-175, 180
   motivational climates 206, 216, 217
   self-efficacy theory 59-60
   self-esteem strengthening 65, 67
   talent-related 236, 238f
fight, flee, and freeze responses 12, 70-72, 77
fixed mindset 236
flow 119-120, 122
   creativity and 120, 132
   mindfulness and 155, 158
focus. *See* attentional focus
food. *See* eating practices
Four C model of creativity 130-131, 131t, 135
4W framework of imagery 184-185
functional analysis 6-7, 6f, 8, 25
   anxiety in dance 81, 82f
   attentional focus in dance 118, 118f
   creativity in dance 135f
   goal setting in dance 173-174, 173f
   imagery in dance 196-197, 198f
   injury risk factors 249-250, 250f
   within instrumental conditioning 4-5, 5-8, 6f, 7f, 11, 15
   mindfulness in dance 157, 157f
   motivational climates 211, 212f
   motivation in dance 94-96
   negative body image and disordered eating examples 279, 280f
   perfectionism in dance 43, 43f
   personality in dance 26f
   self-confidence in dance 57, 58f
   talent in dance 236, 238f
functional body orientation/satisfaction 263, 265
functional equivalence 195-196
fundamental goal concepts 168

G

gender issues
   body image 262-263
   in dance culture 54, 68
   dancers' imagery 188
   disordered eating and eating disorders 269, 270f, 271, 272, 285
   self-esteem 54, 68
genetics and personality 25-26, 26f, 35
goal attainment
   scaling 180
   strategies 172-174
goal involvement 93
goal orientations (motivation theory) 90-96, 91t, 92f, 93f, 95f, 204-205, 205t
goal setting. *See also* motivation
   anxiety management 80, 172
   attentional focus and 122-123, 168, 172
   consequences 171, 172-174
   defining and describing 166-167
   goal sources 170-171, 171t
   goal types 167-170, 169f, 170f, 173f, 180
   imagery use for 185
   for injury prevention/rehabilitation 247, 254, 255, 256, 259
   nurturing task involvement 102
   optimization 175-178
   practical exercises 172-173
   realistic vs. perfectionistic 122-123
   research 181-182
   within self-regulation 174-175, 178, 182
   SMART GOALS 175-178, 177t
growth mindset. *See also* stress-related growth
   deliberate practice 232
   described 236
   for healthy body image 281
   talent beliefs and consequences 236, 238f, 242

H

habituation. *See* exposure and exposure therapy
harmonious passion 241, 248, 251
health care providers 252, 256, 258, 283, 284
hierarchy of exposure 13, 14t, 83-84, 85
hierarchy of self-constructs 56, 56f
holistic ecological approach to talent development 234-236, 235f

I

identity
   broadening and expanding 30, 30t, 35, 240
   discovery activities 32-33
   disordered eating risk factors 29, 273, 283
   genetic factors in dance 27
   identified motivational regulation 97
   injury experience effects 29, 31, 249, 251, 252, 259
   narrow identity within dance 28-30, 31, 34-35, 44, 121, 249, 251, 252
   research and studies 29-30
   self-esteem and self-confidence elements 52, 53-55, 53t, 56
imagery
   consequences 190, 194-197
   for creativity 137, 141, 187, 195
   defining and describing 184, 185, 186t, 187-190, 188-189, 189f, 193
   efficacy 195-197
   external attentional focus use 113t, 119, 122, 124, 185, 187, 197
   imaginal experiences 60, 65, 67, 194
   mindfulness scenarios 161-162
   PETTLEP model 188, 195-196, 197t, 198
   practical exercises 191-192
   revised applied model of deliberate use 184-185, 186t, 187, 188, 190, 197-198
   sources and instruction 185, 187, 190, 193, 198-199, 200
   types 185, 186t, 193, 194, 195, 197-198, 199
immediate beliefs 24
implicit learning 114-116, 117-118, 121
improvisation
   as creativity source 134, 135-137, 139-140, 140-141
   skill development 139-140
injuries
   defining and describing 244-245
   early specialization 233

experiences 245, 251-252, 253, 257
exposure therapy activities 83
identity struggles 29, 31, 249, 251, 252, 259
imagery use for 185, 187, 195, 256, 257
mindfulness, and prevention/rehabilitation 156, 195, 245, 248, 256
overpreparation and -training risks 43, 44, 244f, 245, 249-250
practical activities 257
psychological aspects 244-256, 244f, 246t, 254t, 258-260
rates 244, 245, 248
stress-injury model 245-249, 246t, 260
inspiration
 creativity nurturing 137, 141
 imagery sources 190
instrumental conditioning 4-5, 5-11, 15
intelligence
 and creativity 132
 performance-related consequences 28
intermittent reinforcement 10-11
internal focus of attention
 descriptions and usage 112-114, 113t, 116-117, 118, 125
 mindfulness and attention 163-164
 practical exercises 124
 research on 125-126
internal visual perspective, imagery 188
interpersonal relations. *See also* coach-athlete relations; parent-child relations; teacher-student relations
 anxiety sources 74-75
 negative body image and disordered eating risk factors 275, 276-277, 282-283
 self-determination motivation theory 96, 99, 206-207
 well-being-related consequences of personality 28
intrapersonal relations
 motivation theory 96, 99, 102-103, 206
 well-being-related consequences of personality 28
intrinsic goals 92, 98. *See also* task and ego orientations
 nurturing healthy motivation 104-105
 nurturing task involvement 102-103

intrinsic motivation
 creativity principle 132-133, 140
 deliberate practice and play 231, 232
 flow conditions 122
 goal setting 170
 imagery consequences 194
 injury prevention 256
 self-determination theory 96, 97-98, 98-101, 102, 104
 self-reinforcement 7, 9
introversion. *See* extroversion and introversion (personality traits)
ironic processing 122

K
kinesthetic imagery 188-189, 190, 196, 199. *See also* imagery
Klimentová, Daria 40, 41

L
leadership
 anxiety sources 73
 motivational climates and self-determination theory 206-208, 212-214, 216t, 217-218
 styles, and negative body image 276-277
learning goals 167, 168, 169f, 170f
learning theory and processes
 conditioning 4-5, 5-13
 explicit and implicit 114-116, 117-118, 121, 125
 improvisation 139-140
 modeling 4, 58-59, 64-65
 stages 115
 task-oriented 94-95, 95f, 204, 211, 214, 215t
little-c creativity 130-131, 131t
low self-esteem. *See* self-esteem and self-confidence

M
mastery
 approach orientation 91, 92
 experiences 57-58, 60, 62-64, 67
 goal setting for 166-168
 imagery use for 185
 models 59
 skill learning processes and rates 115-116, 115f
Matthew effect 228-229, 228f
maturation and maturity
 early specialization 233
 genetics and dance 27
 negative body image risk factors 272
 talent identification and development 222, 226

meaningfulness
 creativity 128, 130
 goal setting importance 102, 103, 170-171, 172-173, 174
 in imagery 186t, 190, 191
 in motivation 96, 97-98, 206, 231
media influences and social media
 body image and 272, 275
 dance identity and 30t
medical practitioners 252, 256, 258, 283, 284
meditations 152, 156, 159-160
mental activity
 attentional focus 110-111, 119, 158
 imagery 195-196, 196f, 256
 mindfulness and 151-153, 152f, 158, 159
 self-regulation 174
mental filtering 49
mental health issues
 clinical interventions and therapies 13, 46, 47t, 77, 85, 258-259, 266, 283-284
 eating disorders and disordered eating 264, 266, 274, 280, 284
 ill-being and creativity 139
 improvement via mindfulness 155, 156
 self-esteem and self-confidence elements 52, 55, 60-61
mental practice imagery 185, 186t, 187, 190, 195, 199
metaphorical imagery 184, 185, 188, 193, 197
mindfulness
 anxiety management 81, 154, 155, 156
 attentional focus and 123, 151-153, 151f, 152f, 155, 158, 163-164
 case studies and scenarios 161-162, 161t, 162-163
 components 151-153
 consequences 154-156, 164
 for creativity 137, 141, 156
 with dance practice 161-162
 defining and describing 150-151
 efficacy 158
 formal and informal practices 159-161, 164
 injury prevention/rehabilitation 156, 195, 245, 248, 256
 research 154-155, 156-158, 163-164
 self-esteem strengthening 66, 155
 therapeutics 153-154
mindlessness 151
mini-c creativity 130-131, 131t
mirrors 277-278, 281

mixed perfectionism 45-46
modeling 4, 58-59, 64-65, 67
motivation. *See also* extrinsic motivation; goal setting; intrinsic motivation; motivational climates
    achievement goal theory perspective 90-96, 91*t*, 181, 204-205, 208-211, 214
    as behavior 4, 90
    ego-involving motivational climates 14, 44, 91*t*, 106
    goal setting effects 168, 169*f*, 170, 170*f*, 171, 172
    injury and rehab responses 253, 254, 255, 256
    nurturing of healthy 98-99, 102-103, 122, 133-134, 140, 206, 241, 256, 283
    for perfectionism 37, 38, 41, 42, 44, 45, 94, 97, 209, 210-211, 213
    reinforcement theory 7, 9-10
    self-determination theory perspective 94, 96-102, 97*f*, 99*t*, 106, 204, 206-207, 208, 210*f*
    talent identification and development 223, 224*t*, 238, 240, 241
motivational climates. *See also* motivation
    consequences 208-214
    creating healthy 214, 217
    defining and describing 93, 204
    ego-involving 204-205, 205*t*, 208-211, 210*f*, 212*f*, 219
    injury risk factors 249-250, 250*f*, 251-252
    negative body image risk factors 277
    origins 207-208
    research and studies 204-205, 207-208, 209-211, 212-214, 218-219
    self-determination theory and 204, 206-207, 208, 212-214, 216*t*
    task-involving 204-205, 205*t*, 208-211, 210*f*, 212*f*, 214, 219
motivational regulations 96-98, 97*f*
movement quality imagery 184, 185, 186*t*, 187, 190, 194-195, 197
music
    for anxiety management 80
    deliberate practice 231
    external attentional focus 113, 117, 118, 122, 124
    imagery (auditory) 189, 190
    mindfulness exercises 156, 162

N

narrow identity 28-30, 31, 34-35, 44, 249, 251, 252
nature vs. nurture debates
    creativity 132
    talent 229-230, 231-232, 236
need satisfaction 98-102, 99*t*
need-supporting leadership 206, 208, 212-214, 216*t*, 217-218
need thwarting 99, 99*t*, 101-102, 206-207, 207-208, 213
negative body image 262-263, 264, 268-270, 271-278, 272*f*, 279
negative reinforcement 9, 10, 10*t*, 15
negative vs. positive cueing 122
neuroticism
    perfectionism and 38
    well-being-related consequences of personality 28
nonjudgment 150, 151, 153, 155, 157-158, 159
non-perfectionism 45, 46
novelty (creativity element) 128, 130

O

objective goals 167. *See also* SMART GOALS
observational learning 58-59, 64-65
obsessive passion, as injury factor 248, 249, 251
openness to experience (personality trait) 22
    and creativity 132
    dance manifestations 23*t*, 24-25, 28, 30
    and mindfulness 153, 161-162
operant conditioning 4-5, 5-11, 15
optimal attentional focus 110-111, 121-123, 197
outcome goals
    goal setting 167, 168, 169, 169*f*, 170, 170*f*, 173-174, 173*f*, 181
    imagery use for 185, 188
overconfidence 61-62
overgeneralizing 49

P

paralysis by analysis. *See* analysis paralysis/skill breakdown
parent-child relations
    injury rehabilitation support 258
    perfectionism development 40-41
    self-esteem development 53-54
    talent development 234
passion
    dancer self-esteem and identity 54
    harmonious 241, 248, 251
    as injury risk factor 248, 249, 251

perfectionism
    case studies 40, 41, 48
    cognitive distortions 48-50, 49
    consequences 38, 42-46, 43*f*, 50, 73
    in dance culture 38, 40, 41, 43-44
    defining and describing 38, 39, 40*t*
    discovery activities 48-50
    disordered eating risk factors 41, 44, 272, 273, 274, 275, 283
    ego orientation (motivation theory) 94, 97
    goal setting tips 122-123
    injury risk factors 248, 249, 250
    management 46, 47*t*, 137
    models 44-46, 45*f*
    research and studies 38-39, 40-41, 42, 43-46, 48, 50
    structure (strivings and concerns) 39, 40*t*, 42-46, 50, 274
    trait development 25, 34, 38, 39
performance accomplishments
    mastery experiences 57-58, 60, 62-64, 67
    as products of creativity 130
performance-based self-esteem 29, 31, 52-53, 75
performance conditions
    anxiety management 81, 122
    anxiety sources 73-74, 82*f*, 120
    imagery script writing for 191-192
    use for mastery experiences 63-64
performance goals 167, 168, 169*f*, 170, 170*f*, 173*f*, 174
performance-oriented identity 29, 31
performance profiling 178
performance psychology 2-3, 4, 15
personal control. *See* controllable and uncontrollable factors
personality. *See also* identity; perfectionism
    aspects and elements 20, 23-24, 27
    biases 27
    consequences 20, 27-28, 34
    creativity within 132, 140, 144
    defining 20, 22
    injury risk factors 247-248, 249, 250
    negative body image/disordered eating risk factors 272*f*, 273-274
    origins 25-26, 35
    recommendations 34-35
    research and studies 20-22, 27-28, 34

stability and change 23-25, 34
structure 20-21, 24-25, 24*f*
traits and states 20-23, 21*t*, 23*t*, 24-25, 27, 34, 35, 132
personal values. *See* values
person-environment fit 41
persuasion. *See* feedback and persuasion
PETTLEP model 188, 195-196, 197*t*, 198
physiological states
   anxiety 12-13, 65-66, 70-71, 71*t*, 72, 73, 75-76, 76*f*, 77, 78-79, 78*f*, 79-80, 81, 192
   dance styles and roles 76
   disordered eating 268*t*, 279-281
   self-efficacy and 60
   self-esteem strengthening 65-66, 67
play, deliberate 232-233, 232*t*
positive body image 262, 263-264, 265, 279, 281, 282, 283
positive reinforcement 7, 9-10, 10*t*, 15
positive vs. negative cueing 122
practical activities and investigations
   creativity activities 142-143
   exposure activities 83-84
   functional analysis 8
   goal setting activities 172-173
   identity discovery activities 32-33
   imagery script writing 191-192
   injury activities 257
   mindfulness activities 163
   nurturing healthy motivation 102-103, 104-105, 217
   of perfectionism distortions 48-50
   positive body image promotion 265
   self-confidence activities 67
   shifting focus 124
   talent development 238*t*
practice, talent elements of 225, 228-229, 231-236, 232*t*. *See also* preparedness
preparedness
   anxiety and management 73, 77, 80, 81, 122
   deliberate practice 231-232
   imagery script writing for 191-192
   need satisfaction and self-determination (motivation) 101, 102
   overpreparation and injury 43, 44, 244*f*, 245, 249-250

overpreparation as safety behavior 13, 14*t*
present-moment awareness 150, 151-152
problem-focused coping 247, 254
Pro-c creativity 130-131, 131*t*
process aspects of creativity 130
process focus/goals
   creativity 130, 134
   goal setting 167, 168, 169, 169*f*, 170*f*, 173*f*, 174, 181
   imagery use for 185, 188
   setting realistic goals 122-123
   task-oriented goal theory 93, 94, 204, 205*t*, 210-211
psyching up 81, 84
psychological flexibility 153-154, 158
psychological help. *See* clinical interventions and therapies
psychological needs
   disordered eating risk factors 273
   in healthy motivational climates 93, 133-134, 206, 207, 208, 210*f*, 214-216, 215*t*, 216*t*
   self-determination theory 98-101, 104-105, 107, 206-207, 212-216, 216*t*
   well-being 3
psychological skills. *See also* coping skills; imagery; mindfulness; psychology and injury; self-regulation
   anxiety management 80-81
   for creativity 137, 139, 141
   goal setting as 166
   for injury prevention and rehabilitation 254-255, 256, 258, 259
   for optional attentional focus 110-111, 122-123, 126
   as talent criteria 223, 224*t*, 240, 241
   via mindfulness 154-155
psychology. *See* dance psychology
psychology and injury
   aspects, in dance 244-245
   injury factors and variables 244*f*, 245-248, 246*t*, 249-252
   injury risk reduction 248-249, 255-256, 258-259
   rehabilitation and optimization 252-255, 254*t*, 256, 258-259
   stress-injury model 245-249
punishment 9, 10*t*
pure evaluative concerns perfectionism 45-46
pure personal strivings perfectionism 45

R

rehabilitation, injury
   help-seeking behavior for 252, 256
   psychological aspects 252-255, 254*t*
reinforcement 7, 9-11, 10*t*, 15
relatedness
   needs and satisfaction 98-101, 99*t*, 101, 103, 105, 206-207, 231
   nurturing healthy motivation 103, 105*f*, 134, 206, 216*t*
relative age effect 227-228
relaxation exercises
   anxiety management 79
   and imagery 196
   for injury rehabilitation 248, 254, 255, 256
   mindfulness 155, 159-160, 256
resilience 56
respondent conditioning 5, 11-13
retirement 29, 31
revised applied model of deliberate imagery use 184-185, 186*t*, 187, 188, 190, 197-198

S

selective attention 111
self-awareness
   attentional focus 119-120
   confidence and 61-62
   and creativity 139
   within stable personality 20
self-compassion and -care
   injury risks and 249, 252, 258
   mindfulness 154, 283
   for positive body image 264, 279, 283
self-consciousness
   loss, via external focus 118*f*, 120
   loss, via mindfulness 155
self-definition and self-identity. *See* identity
self-determination theory
   for motivation 94, 96-102, 204, 206-207, 210*f*
   motivational regulations 96-98, 97*t*
   need-supporting and controlling leadership 206-207, 208, 212-214
   nurturing healthy motivation 102-103, 104-105, 206, 207, 208, 214, 216*t*, 217

self-efficacy
  in goal setting and self-regulation 167, 172, 174
  theory, self-esteem, and self-confidence 4, 55-57, 56-57, 56f, 59-61, 62, 194
self-esteem and self-confidence. *See also* body image
  conceptual distinctions between 53t, 68
  consequences 54-55, 60-62, 120-121
  contingent/performance-based 29, 31, 52-53, 75
  and creativity 132, 139
  defining and describing 52-53, 56f
  excesses and overconfidence 61-62
  goal setting and 167, 172-173, 174, 180
  imagery use and outcomes 185, 187, 189, 191-192, 194, 196-197
  improvement via mindfulness 66, 155
  injury and rehabilitation 246, 251, 253-255, 256
  negative body image and disordered eating risk factors 272, 273, 274, 278, 285
  origins 53-54, 55-60, 62
  practical investigations 67
  strengthening 56, 59, 62-66, 63t, 80
  talent identification consequences 238
  well-being-related consequences of 28, 60-61
self-regulation
  defining and describing 174-175, 174f
  goal setting within 174-175, 178, 182
  optimization 175-178
  research 181-182
  as talent criteria 223, 224t
self-surveillance and -objectification 269-270, 277-278, 279
self-talk
  anxiety management 80
  attentional focus tips 122, 123
  for injury rehabilitation 247, 254, 255, 256, 258
  self-efficacy theory and self-esteem 57, 59, 64, 65
sensory imagery 184, 188-189, 189f, 190, 199
"should" thinking 49

16PF personality model 22
skill breakdown under pressure. *See* analysis paralysis/skill breakdown
SMART GOALS 176-180, 177t
social desirability 50, 240
social influences
  self-efficacy theory 59-60
  strengthening self-esteem 65
social media
  body image and 272, 275
  dancer identity and 30t
social skills
  improvisation development 139-140
  as talent criteria 223, 224t
social support
  injury rehabilitation 247, 254, 258, 259
  skills 100, 241, 247
specialization, early 233-234, 233f, 241
sport participation, developmental model 232
sport psychology and research
  anxiety management 79-80, 81
  dance psychology and 2-3, 15
  disordered eating 281-282, 284
  goal setting 166-167, 171, 172-174, 178-179, 182
  imagery use 184, 185, 188, 194, 196, 200
  mindfulness 150, 156
  motivational climates 210-211
  self-compassion 154
  stress and injury 245-246, 250
stability. *See also* emotional stability (personality trait)
  goal orientations 92-93
  of personality 20, 21t, 23-25
  self-esteem and self-confidence 53, 56f, 68
statelikeness
  anxiety 73
  self-constructs 53, 56f
states, emotional. *See* emotional states
states, personality. *See under* personality
states, physiological. *See* physiological states
stress 72-73, 85, 246-247. *See also* anxiety
stress-injury model 245-249, 246t, 260
stress-related growth 244f, 253, 255, 258, 259
subjective goals 167, 180, 182

subjectivity, in dance 167, 227, 277
success
  coach confidence and 68
  goal orientations, and motivation theories 90-91, 91t, 94-96, 101, 204-205, 205t, 211
  types, and defining 28, 242

T
talent. *See also* competence
  assessment and measurement 222-223, 226, 227, 229, 230t, 239-240
  beliefs about 222, 229-230, 236, 238f
  consequences 236-238, 239
  defining and describing 222, 242
  development 222, 223, 227, 231-236, 238t, 239, 240-241, 242
  dynamic nature of 226-227, 240
  elements of 222-226, 224t, 225f
  identification 222, 226-227, 229, 230t, 238, 239-240, 242
  Matthew effect 228-229, 228f
  relative age effect 227-228
  sources 229-236
  task- and ego-involving climates 204, 208-209
task and ego orientations
  motivational climates 95f, 204-205, 205t, 208-211, 212f, 213, 214, 219
  motivation theory 90-96, 91t, 93f, 214
  nurturing task involvement 102-103, 107, 210-211, 214
teacher-student relations. *See also* coach-athlete relations
  anxiety sources 73, 74, 75, 77
  assigned goals 170
  attentional focus and creativity 113, 117-118, 119, 121-122, 123, 124, 125
  creativity nurturing 133-134, 135-136, 135f, 139-141, 142, 144
  imagery and instruction 185, 186t, 187, 190, 193, 198-199, 200, 206
  injury risk factors 249, 251-252
  instrumental conditioning 5, 6-7, 7f, 8, 9, 11
  mindfulness encouragement 150-151, 161-162, 162-163
  motivational theory and climates 93, 96, 133-134, 135f, 140, 170, 204-205, 206-208, 208-209, 210-211, 212f, 213-214, 215t, 216-219, 216t, 277

negative body image and disordered eating risk factors 12, 276-277, 282-283
talent and development 209, 234-235, 236, 238f, 241
thin-ideal internalization 262-263, 276
thinness culture 275-276, 282
thinness-related learning 275
tolerance, anxiety 75
traitlikeness
  anxiety 73
  causality orientations theory (motivation) 106
  creativity 132, 144
  perfectionism 38-39
  self-constructs 53, 56f, 57, 62, 68
traits, personality. *See* "Big Five" personality traits; perfectionism; personality; self-esteem and self-confidence

2 × 2 achievement goal model 91, 92, 92f
2 × 2 model of perfectionism 44-46, 45f

U
usefulness (creativity element) 128, 130

V
values
  goals and goal setting 169f, 170-171, 171t, 172-173
  mindfulness training use 153-154
variability and variety 137, 141, 144
Vealey, Robin, and sport confidence theory 55, 59
verbal persuasion 59-60, 65, 67
vicarious experiences 4, 58-59, 63-65, 67
visual imagery 188, 195-196. *See also* imagery
vividness, imagery 189, 189f, 190

W
weight issues. *See* bodies and aesthetics; body image; disordered eating; eating disorders
worry. *See* anxiety

Y
youth. *See also* early and intense dance training
  body image and disordered eating 262-263, 270, 272
  imagery use and ability 188, 189, 191, 193, 194-195, 199
  talent identification and development 226-229, 228f, 230t, 231-234, 241

About the Author

Sanna Nordin-Bates is an associate professor at the Swedish School of Sport and Health Sciences in Stockholm. She has taught dance and sport psychology courses for more than 15 years and has authored or coauthored over 40 journal articles in the area. Nordin-Bates has a PhD in sport and exercise sciences, with a focus on dance psychology, from the University of Birmingham. She is a chartered member of the British Psychological Society. She also has further education in cognitive behavioral therapy for elite sport and is a certified mindfulness instructor. Nordin-Bates has served as an applied dance psychology consultant for English National Ballet, the Royal Ballet Upper School in London, and the Royal Swedish Ballet School. She is a fellow of the International Association for Dance Medicine & Science and is a regularly invited speaker and guest teacher at a number of universities and organizations.